An Introduction to Moral and Social Philosophy

Basic Readings in Theory and Practice

An Introduction to Moral and Social Philosophy

Basic Readings in Theory and Practice

Edited by

Jeffrie G. Murphy

The University of Arizona

Wadsworth Publishing Company, Inc.
Belmont, California

ISBN: 0–534–00240–4

L. C. Cat. Card No.:   72–91356

Printed in the United States of America

1 2 3 4 5 6 7 8 9 10—77 76 75 74 73

To Nancy, Sean, and Brendan

Jeffrie G. Murphy is Professor and Head of the Department of Philosophy at the University of Arizona. He received a B.A. degree from the Johns Hopkins University and a Ph.D. from the University of Rochester. During the academic year 1968–69 he was awarded a fellowship from the National Endowment for the Humanities for a year of study at the School of Law, University of California, Los Angeles. He has taught at the University of Minnesota, the University of Michigan, and the University of California, Los Angeles. In 1972 he received an Excellence in Teaching award at the University of Arizona. The author of several articles in moral, legal, and political philosophy, he has also edited two other anthologies for Wadsworth (Civil Disobedience and Violence, *1971; and* Punishment and the Rehabilitative Ideal, *forthcoming) and is the author of* Kant: The Philosophy of Right *(1970). He has served on the Board of Directors of the Arizona Civil Liberties Union and until recently served as Chairman of the Arizona Civil Liberties Union Committee on Psychiatric Justice.*

Preface

The purpose of this anthology is to provide a sourcebook of basic readings for an introductory undergraduate course in moral and social (including political and legal) philosophy. It grows out of several years of teaching such a course at the University of Arizona and elsewhere and the conviction, based on this experience, that it is desirable to combine these two subjects into one course at the introductory level. Students naturally and quite rightly want to trace out the social and political consequences of various moral positions; and it is, in my judgment, impossible to come to terms with social and political philosophy without a basic background in moral thinking.

I have divided the anthology into three parts: Moral Philosophy, Social Philosophy, and Practical Applications. In the first two parts I have presented lengthy selections (complete wherever possible) from classical moral and social philosophers and some contemporary articles which elaborate or criticize these classical positions in a current idiom. No attempt has been made to represent every conceivable moral and political position. My plan has instead been to have certain basic and influential types of moral and social theory presented at sufficient length to allow the student to study the arguments for each position in depth. (Unless otherwise noted, all selections are reprinted in their entirety.) For it is the study of *arguments,* and not the mere survey of conclusions, which constitutes the study of philosophy and which distinguishes that study from the study of the history of ideas. My purpose has been to provide the student with materials for the stimulation of critical thought, *not* to provide (as do many anthologies) a sourcebook of all the leading clichés that every educated man should know about moral and social philosophy.

In Part Three, Practical Applications, I have selected several moral and social problems of contemporary practical interest and have generally included at least two opposed philosophical essays on each. Here, it is hoped, the student will see for himself how theory and practice interact, how the theories he has studied in Parts One and Two have a clear and important application to the problems he faces as man and citizen. For the selections illustrate, in my judgment, the immense capacity that philosophical reflection has to clarify and render rational our thinking about matters of importance. Confusion, irrationality, and obscurantism are in some contexts merely humorous. In matters of moral and social importance, however, they are dangerous. And it is the primary task of philosophy to help us in avoiding these intellectual vices.

I should like to close this preface by thanking my colleague Ronald Milo for valuable conversations concerning moral and social philosophy—conversations which have, though he may not have noticed it, immeasurably improved my own capacity to teach and think about these matters. I am also grateful to several of my own teachers who inspired me by example to care about excellence in teaching (Eleanor Weiherman, Maurice Mandelbaum, Frederick Olafson, Lewis White Beck, Robert Holmes, and James Cornman) and to those aggressive graduate teaching assistants who have kept me honest over the years and have forced me constantly to rethink and reorganize my introductory courses. I have particularly valued the assistance in teaching that I have received from Mitchell Axler, George Dawson, and George Panichas. Most of all, however, gratitude is owed to several thousand undergraduate students who have, over the past few years, provided a laboratory wherein various readings could be tested for usefulness in the philosophy classroom. The readings in this volume, with the exception of those published very recently, have all passed this test with flying colors. Apologies, however, are surely owed to those students who had to suffer through reading assignments in those that failed. Finally, I should like to thank Virginia Hickey for her help in preparing the manuscript and my wife, Nancy, for her assistance in correcting the proof.

Jeffrie G. Murphy

Contents

Part One

Moral
Philosophy

1

The Nature of a Moral Problem and the Role of Moral Philosophy

Reading: Plato, Crito

Plato's dialogue *Crito* is a report of an important Socratic conversation. Socrates has been unjustly sentenced to death by an Athenian witchhunt tribunal, and we find him in prison awaiting his execution. His friend, Crito, comes to inform him that an escape can be arranged. Socrates must then face the question (like that faced by draft resisters in our own day), "Under what circumstances, if any, is it morally right to escape one's legal punishment?" Crito offers reasons in favor of escape, Socrates counters these, and then Socrates offers arguments that he takes to be conclusive in favor of his remaining and accepting his punishment of death. The gravity of the issues involved (life and death, personal integrity, the status of the law, and so on) indicates that Socrates is faced with a serious moral problem—having obvious social, political, and legal implications. To resolve the problem, Socrates will not let himself appeal to his subjective feelings or to the authority of common opinion—that is, he rejects *subjectivism* and *relativism* in morals. Rather he insists on appealing to general evaluative principles that can be established on the basis of rational thought. (One of these principles can be interpreted as a formulation of the social contract theory that you will study in Chapter 5.) The attempt to get beyond feelings and convention and to formulate such rational principles has always been the goal of moral philosophy. As you will see later in this book, however, philosophers with this goal have not always reached the same result.

Suggestions for Further Reading

William K. Frankena, *Ethics* (Englewood Cliffs, N.J.: Prentice-Hall, 1963).

Jeffrie G. Murphy, "Violence and the Socratic Theory of Legal Fidelity," in *Aggression and Violence in the History of Ideas* (Proceedings of the Third International Conference of the International Society for the History of Ideas), ed. John Fisher and Philip P. Wiener (Philadelphia: Temple University Press, forthcoming).

Plato, *Euthyphro, Apology,* and *Phaedo* (additional dialogues dealing with the trial and death of Socrates).

Alfred E. Taylor, *Socrates: The Man and His Thought* (Garden City, N.Y.: Doubleday Anchor, 1953).

Anthony D. Woozley, "Socrates on Disobeying the Law," in *The Philosophy of Socrates,* ed. Gregory Vlastos (Garden City, N.Y.: Doubleday Anchor, 1971).

Crito
Plato

Characters

SOCRATES

CRITO

SCENE—The prison of Socrates

SOCRATES. Why have you come at this hour, Crito? Is it not still early?
CRITO. Yes, very early.
SOCR. About what time is it?
CRITO. It is just daybreak.
SOCR. I wonder that the jailer was willing to let you in.

From Plato: *Euthyphro, Apology, Crito,* translated by F. J. Church, revised by Robert D. Cumming, copyright © 1948, 1956, by The Liberal Arts Press, Inc., reprinted by permission of the Bobbs-Merrill Company, Inc. Scholars generally agree that this dialogue, although written by Plato (c. 428–348 B.C.), is primarily a report of the conversation of his teacher Socrates (c. 470–399 B.C.).

CRITO. He knows me now, Socrates; I come here so often, and besides, I have given him a tip.

SOCR. Have you been here long?

CRITO. Yes, some time.

SOCR. Then why did you sit down without speaking? Why did you not wake me at once?

CRITO. Indeed, Socrates, I wish that I myself were not so sleepless and sorrowful. But I have been wondering to see how soundly you sleep. And I purposely did not wake you, for I was anxious not to disturb your repose. Often before, all through your life, I have thought that your temperament was a happy one; and I think so more than ever now when I see how easily and calmly you bear the calamity that has come to you.

SOCR. Nay, Crito, it would be absurd if at my age I were disturbed at having to die.

CRITO. Other men as old are overtaken by similar calamities, Socrates; but their age does not save them from being disturbed by their fate.

SOCR. That is so; but tell me why are you here so early?

CRITO. I am the bearer of sad news, Socrates; not sad, it seems, for you, but for me and for all your friends, both sad and hard to bear; and for none of them, I think, is it as hard to bear as it is for me.

SOCR. What is it? Has the ship come from Delos, at the arrival of which I am to die?

CRITO. No, it has not actually arrived, but I think that it will be here today, from the news which certain persons have brought from Sunium, who left it there. It is clear from their report that it will be here today; and so, Socrates, tomorrow your life will have to end.

SOCR. Well, Crito, may it end well. Be it so, if so the gods will. But I do not think that the ship will be here today.

CRITO. Why do you suppose not?

SOCR. I will tell you. I am to die on the day after the ship arrives, am I not? [1]

CRITO. That is what the authorities say.

SOCR. Then I do not think that it will come today, but tomorrow. I am counting on a dream I had a little while ago in the night, so it seems to be fortunate that you did not wake me.

CRITO. And what was this dream?

SOCR. A fair and beautiful woman, clad in white, seemed to come to me, and call me and say, "O Socrates—

On the third day shall you fertile Phthia reach." [2]

CRITO. What a strange dream, Socrates!

SOCR. But its meaning is clear, at least to me, Crito.

---

[1] Criminals could not be put to death while the sacred ship was away on its voyage.—*Ed.*

[2] Homer, *Iliad,* ix, 363.

CRITO. Yes, too clear, it seems. But, O my good Socrates, I beg you for the last time to listen to me and save yourself. For to me your death will be more than a single disaster; not only shall I lose a friend the like of whom I shall never find again, but many persons who do not know you and me well will think that I might have saved you if I had been willing to spend money, but that I neglected to do so. And what reputation could be more disgraceful than the reputation of caring more for money than for one's friends? The public will never believe that we were anxious to save you, but that you yourself refused to escape.

SOCR. But, my dear Crito, why should we care so much about public opinion? Reasonable men, of whose opinion it is worth our while to think, will believe that we acted as we really did.

CRITO. But you see, Socrates, that it is necessary to care about public opinion, too. This very thing that has happened to you proves that the multitude can do a man not the least, but almost the greatest harm, if he is falsely accused to them.

SOCR. I wish that the multitude were able to do a man the greatest harm, Crito, for then they would be able to do him the greatest good, too. That would have been fine. But, as it is, they can do neither. They cannot make a man either wise or foolish: they act wholly at random.

CRITO. Well, as you wish. But tell me this, Socrates. You surely are not anxious about me and your other friends, and afraid lest, if you escape, the informers would say that we stole you away, and get us into trouble, and involve us in a great deal of expense, or perhaps in the loss of all our property, and, it may be, bring some other punishment upon us besides? If you have any fear of that kind, dismiss it. For of course we are bound to run these risks, and still greater risks than these, if necessary, in saving you. So do not, I beg you, refuse to listen to me.

SOCR. I am anxious about that, Crito, and about much besides.

CRITO. Then have no fear on that score. There are men who, for no very large sum, are ready to bring you out of prison into safety. And then, you know, these informers are cheaply bought, and there would be no need to spend much upon them. My fortune is at your service, and I think that it is adequate; and if you have any feeling about making use of my money, there are strangers in Athens whom you know, ready to use theirs; and one of them, Simmias of Thebes, has actually brought enough for this very purpose. And Cebes and many others are ready, too. And therefore, I repeat, do not shrink from saving yourself on that ground. And do not let what you said in the court—that if you went into exile you would not know what to do with yourself—stand in your way; for there are many places for you to go to, where you will be welcomed. If you choose to go to Thessaly, I have friends there who will make much of you and protect you from any annoyance from the people of Thessaly.

And besides, Socrates, I think that you will be doing what is unjust if you abandon your life when you might preserve it. You are simply playing into your enemies' hands; it is exactly what they wanted—to destroy you. And what is more, to me you seem to be abandoning your children, too. You will leave them to take their chance in life, as far as you are concerned, when you might bring them up and educate them. Most likely their fate will be the usual fate of children who are left orphans. But you ought not to bring children into the world unless you mean to take the trouble of bringing them up and educating them. It seems to me that you are choosing the easy way, and not the way of a good and brave man, as you ought, when you have been talking all your life long of the value that you set upon human excellence. For my part, I feel ashamed both for you and for us who are your friends. Men will think that the whole thing which has happened to you—your appearance in court to face trial, when you need not have appeared at all; the very way in which the trial was conducted; and then last of all this, the crowning absurdity of the whole affair—is due to our cowardice. It will look as if we had shirked the danger out of miserable cowardice; for we did not save you, and you did not save yourself, when it was quite possible to do so if we had been good for anything at all. Take care, Socrates, lest these things be not evil only, but also dishonorable to you and to us. Reflect, then, or rather the time for reflection is past; we must make up our minds. And there is only one plan possible. Everything must be done tonight. If we delay any longer, we are lost. Socrates, I implore you not to refuse to listen to me.

SOCR. My dear Crito, if your anxiety to save me be right, it is most valuable; but if not, the greater it is the harder it will be to cope with. We must reflect, then, whether we are to do as you say or not; for I am still what I always have been—a man who will accept no argument but that which on reflection I find to be truest. I cannot cast aside my former arguments because this misfortune has come to me. They seem to me to be as true as ever they were, and I respect and honor the same ones as I used to. And if we have no better argument to substitute for them, I certainly shall not agree to your proposal, not even though the power of the multitude should scare us with fresh terrors, as children are scared with hobgoblins, and inflict upon us new fines and imprisonments, and deaths. What is the most appropriate way of examining the question? Shall we go back first to what you say about opinions, and ask if we used to be right in thinking that we ought to pay attention to some opinions, and not to others? Were we right in saying so before I was condemned to die, and has it now become apparent that we were talking at random and arguing for the sake of argument, and that it was really nothing but playful nonsense? I am anxious, Crito, to examine our former argument with your help, and to see whether my present circumstance will appear to me to have affected its truth in any way or not; and whether we are to set it aside, or to yield assent to it. Those of us who thought at all seriously always used to say, I think, exactly what I said just now, namely, that we ought to respect some of the opinions which men form, and not others. Tell me, Crito, I beg you, do you not think that they were right? For you in all probability will not have to die tomorrow, and your judgment will not be biased by that circumstance. Reflect, then, do you not think it reasonable to say that we should not respect all the opinions of men but only some, nor the opinions of all men but only of some men? What do you think? Is not this true?

CRITO. It is.

SOCR. And we should respect the good opinions, and not the worthless ones?

CRITO. Yes.

SOCR. But the good opinions are those of the wise, and the worthless ones those of the foolish?

CRITO. Of course.

SOCR. And what did we say about this? Does a man who is in training, and who is serious about it, pay attention to the praise and blame and opinion of all men, or only of the one man who is a doctor or a trainer?

CRITO. He pays attention only to the opinion of the one man.

SOCR. Then he ought to fear the blame and welcome the praise of this one man, not of the multitude?

CRITO. Clearly.

SOCR. Then he must act and exercise, and eat and drink in whatever way the one man who is his director, and who understands the matter, tells him; not as others tell him?

CRITO. That is so.

SOCR. Good. But if he disobeys this one man, and disregards his opinion and his praise, and respects instead what the many say, who understand nothing of the matter, will he not suffer for it?

CRITO. Of course he will.

SOCR. And how will he suffer? In what way and in what part of himself?

CRITO. Of course in his body. That is disabled.

SOCR. You are right. And, Crito, to be brief, is it not the same in everything? And, therefore, in questions of justice and injustice, and of the base and the honorable, and of good and evil, which we are now examining, ought we to follow the opinion of the many and fear that, or the opinion of the one man who understands these matters (if we can find him), and feel more shame and fear before him than before all other men? For if we do not follow him, we shall corrupt and maim that part of us which, we used to say, is improved by justice and disabled by injustice. Or is this not so?

CRITO. No, Socrates, I agree with you.

SOCR. Now, if, by listening to the opinions of those who do not understand, we disable that part of us which is improved by health and corrupted by disease, is our life worth living when it is corrupt? It is the body, is it not?

CRITO. Yes.

SOCR. Is life worth living with the body corrupted and crippled?

CRITO. No, certainly not.

SOCR. Then is life worth living when that part of us which is maimed by injustice and benefited by justice is corrupt? Or do we consider that part of us, whatever it is, which has to do with justice and injustice to be of less consequence than our body?

CRITO. No, certainly not.

SOCR. But more valuable?

CRITO. Yes, much more so.

SOCR. Then, my good friend, we must not think so much of what the many will say of us; we must think of what the one man who understands justice and injustice, and of what truth herself will say of us. And so you are mistaken, to begin with, when you invite us to regard the opinion of the multitude concerning the just and the honorable and the good, and their opposites. But, it may be said, the multitude can put us to death?

CRITO. Yes, that is evident. That may be said, Socrates.

SOCR. True. But, my good friend, to me it appears that the conclusion which we have just reached is the same as our conclusion of former times. Now consider whether we still hold to the belief that we should set the highest value, not on living, but on living well?

CRITO. Yes, we do.

SOCR. And living well and honorably and justly mean the same thing: do we hold to that or not?

CRITO. We do.

SOCR. Then, starting from these premises, we have to consider whether it is just or not for me to try to escape from prison, without the consent of the Athenians. If we find that it is just, we will try; if not, we will give up the idea. I am afraid that considerations of expense, and of reputation, and of bringing up my children, of which you talk, Crito, are only the opinions of the many, who casually put men to death, and who would, if they could, as casually bring them to life again, without a thought. But reason, which is our guide, shows us that we can have nothing to consider but the question which I asked just now—namely, shall we be acting justly if we give money and thanks to the men who are to aid me in escaping, and if we ourselves take our respective parts in my escape? Or shall we in truth be acting unjustly if we do all this? And if we find that we should be acting unjustly, then we must not take any account either of death, or of any other evil that may be the consequence of remaining here, where we are, but only of acting unjustly.

CRITO. I think that you are right, Socrates. But what are we to do?

SOCR. Let us examine this question together, my friend, and if you can contradict anything that I say, do so, and I shall be persuaded. But if you cannot, do not go on repeating to me any longer, my dear friend, that I should escape without the consent of the Athenians. I am very anxious to act with your approval and consent. I do not want you to think me mistaken. But now tell me if you agree with the premise from which I start, and try to answer my questions as you think best.

CRITO. I will try.

SOCR. Ought we never to act unjustly voluntarily? Or may we act unjustly in some ways, and not in others? Is it the case, as we have often agreed in former times, that it is never either good or honorable to act unjustly? Or have all our former conclusions been overturned in these few days; and did we at our age fail to recognize all along, when we were seriously conversing with each other, that we were no better than children? Is not what we used to say most certainly the truth, whether the multitude agrees with us or not? Is not acting unjustly evil and shameful in every case, whether we incur a heavier or a lighter punishment as the consequence? Do we believe that?

CRITO. We do.

SOCR. Then we ought never to act unjustly?

CRITO. Certainly not.

SOCR. If we ought never to act unjustly at all, ought we to repay injustice with injustice, as the multitude thinks we may?

CRITO. Clearly not.

SOCR. Well, then, Crito, ought we to do evil to anyone?

CRITO. Certainly I think not, Socrates.

SOCR. And is it just to repay evil with evil, as the multitude thinks, or unjust?

CRITO. Certainly it is unjust.

SOCR. For there is no difference, is there, between doing evil to a man and acting unjustly?

CRITO. True.

SOCR. Then we ought not to repay injustice with injustice or to do harm to any man, no matter what we may have suffered from him. And in conceding this, Crito, be careful that you do not concede more than you mean. For I know that only a few men hold, or ever will hold, this opinion. And so those who hold it and those who do not have no common ground of argument; they can of necessity only look with contempt on each other's belief. Do you therefore consider very carefully whether or not you agree with me and share my opinion. Are we to start in our inquiry from the premise that it is never right either to act unjustly, or to repay injustice with injustice, or to avenge ourselves on any man who harms us, by harming him in return? Or do you disagree with me and dissent from my premise? I myself have believed in it for a long time, and I believe in it still. But if you differ in any way, explain to me how. If you still hold to our former opinion, listen to my next point.

CRITO. Yes, I hold to it, and I agree with you. Go on.

SOCR. Then, my next point, or rather my next question, is this: Ought a man to carry out his just agreements, or may he shuffle out of them?

CRITO. He ought to carry them out.

SOCR. Then consider. If I escape without the state's consent, shall I be injuring those whom I ought least to injure, or not? Shall I be abiding by my just agreements or not?

CRITO. I cannot answer your question, Socrates. I do not understand it.

SOCR. Consider it in this way. Suppose the laws and the commonwealth were to come and appear to me as I was preparing to run away (if that is the right phrase to describe my escape) and were to ask, "Tell us, Socrates, what have you in your mind to do? What do you mean by trying to escape but to destroy us, the laws and the whole state, so far as you are able? Do you think that a state can exist and not be overthrown, in which the decisions of law are of no force, and are disregarded and undermined by private individuals?" How shall we answer questions like that, Crito? Much might be said, especially by an orator, in defense of the law which makes judicial decisions supreme. Shall I reply, "But the state has injured me by judging my case unjustly?" Shall we say that?

CRITO. Certainly we will, Socrates.

SOCR. And suppose the laws were to reply, "Was that our agreement? Or was it that you would abide by whatever judgments the state should pronounce?" And if we were surprised by their words, perhaps they would say, "Socrates, don't be surprised by our words, but answer us; you yourself are accustomed to ask questions and to answer them. What complaint have you against us and the state, that you are trying to destroy us? Are we not, first of all, your parents? Through us your father took your mother and brought you into the world. Tell us, have you any fault to find with those of us that are the laws of marriage?" "I have none," I should reply. "Or have you any fault to find with those of us that regulate the raising of the child and the education which you, like others, received? Did we not do well in telling your father to educate you in music and athletics?" "You did," I should say. "Well, then, since you were brought into the world and raised and educated by us, how, in the first place, can you deny that you are our child and our slave, as your fathers were before you? And if this be so, do you think that your rights are on a level with ours? Do you think that you have a right to retaliate if we should try to do anything to you? You had not the same rights that your father had, or that your master would have had if you had been a slave. You had no right to retaliate if they ill-treated you, or to answer them if they scolded you, or to strike them back if they struck you, or to repay them evil with evil in any way. And do you think that you may retaliate in the case of your country and its laws? If we try to destroy you, because we think it just, will you in return do all that you can to destroy us, the laws, and your country, and say that in so doing you are acting justly—you, the man who really thinks so much of excellence? Or are you too wise to see that your country is worthier, more to be revered, more sacred, and held in higher honor both by the gods and by all men of understanding, than your father and your mother and all your other ancestors; and that you ought to reverence it, and to submit to it, and to approach it more humbly when it is angry with you than you would approach your father; and either to do whatever it tells you to do or to persuade it to excuse you; and to obey in silence if it orders you to endure flogging or imprisonment, or if it sends you to battle to be wounded or to die? That is just. You must not give way, nor retreat, nor desert your station. In war, and in the court of justice, and everywhere, you must do whatever your state and your country tell you to do, or you must persuade them that their commands are unjust. But it is impious to use violence against your father or your mother; and much more impious to use violence against your country." What answer shall we make, Crito? Shall we say that the laws speak the truth, or not?

CRITO. I think that they do.

SOCR. "Then consider, Socrates," perhaps they would say, "if we are right in saying that by attempting to escape you are attempting an injustice. We brought you into the world, we raised you, we educated you, we gave you and every other citizen a share of all the good things we could. Yet we proclaim that if any man of the Athenians is dissatisfied with us, he may take his goods and go away wherever he pleases; we give that privilege to every man who chooses to avail himself of it, so soon as he has reached manhood, and sees us, the laws, and the administration of our state. No one of us stands in his way or forbids him to take his goods and go wherever he likes, whether it be to an Athenian colony or to any foreign country, if he is dissatisfied with us and with the state. But we say that every man of you who remains here, seeing how we administer justice, and how we govern the state in other matters, has agreed, by the very fact of remaining here, to do whatsoever we tell him. And, we say, he who disobeys us acts unjustly on three counts: he disobeys us who are his parents, and he disobeys us who reared him, and he disobeys us after he has agreed to obey us, without persuading us that we are wrong. Yet we did not tell him sternly to do whatever we told him. We offered him an alternative; we gave him his choice either to obey us or to convince us that we were wrong; but he does neither.

"These are the charges, Socrates, to which we say that you will expose yourself if you do what you intend; and you are more exposed to these charges than other Athenians." And if I were to ask, "Why?" they might retort with justice that I have bound myself by the agreement with them more than other Athenians. They would say, "Socrates, we have very strong evidence that you were satisfied with us and with the state. You would not have been content to stay at home in it more than other Athenians unless you had been satisfied with it more than they. You never went away from Athens to the festivals, nor elsewhere except on military service; you never made other journeys like other men; you had no desire to see other states or other laws; you were contented with us and our state; so strongly did you prefer us, and agree to be governed by us. And what is more, you had children in this city, you found it so satisfactory. Besides, if you had wished, you might at your trial have offered to go into exile. At that time you could have done with the state's consent what you are trying now to do without it. But then you gloried in being willing to die. You said that you preferred death to exile. And now you do not honor those words: you do not respect us, the laws, for you are trying to destroy us; and you are acting just as a miserable slave would act, trying to run away, and breaking the contracts and agreement which you made to live as our citizen. First, therefore, answer this question. Are we right, or are we wrong, in saying that you have agreed not in mere words, but in your actions, to live under our government?" What are we to say, Crito? Must we not admit that it is true?

CRITO. We must, Socrates.

SOCR. Then they would say, "Are you not breaking your contracts and agreements with us? And you were not led to make them by force or by fraud. You did not have to make up your mind in a hurry. You had seventy years in which you might have gone away if you had been dissatisfied with us, or if the agreement had seemed to you unjust. But you preferred neither Sparta nor Crete, though you are fond of saying that they are well governed, nor any other state, either of the Greeks or the Barbarians. You went away from Athens less than the lame and the blind and the crippled. Clearly you, far more than other Athenians, were satisfied with the state, and also with us who are its laws; for who would be satisfied with a state which had no laws? And now will you not abide by your agreement? If you take our advice, you will, Socrates; then you will not make yourself ridiculous by going away from Athens.

"Reflect now. What good will you do yourself or your friends by thus transgressing and breaking your agreement? It is tolerably certain that they, on their part, will at least run the risk of exile, and of losing their civil rights, or of forfeiting their property. You yourself might go to one of the neighboring states, to Thebes or to Megara, for instance—for both of them are well governed—but, Socrates, you will come as an enemy to these governments, and all who care for their city will look askance at you, and think that you are a subverter of law. You will confirm the judges in their opinion, and make it seem that their verdict was a just one. For a man who is a subverter of law may well be supposed to be a corrupter of the young and thoughtless. Then will you avoid well-governed states and civilized men? Will life be worth having, if you do? Will you associate with such men, and converse without shame—about what, Socrates? About the things which you talk of here? Will you tell them that excellence and justice and institutions and law are the most valuable things that men can have? And do you not think that that will be a disgraceful thing for Socrates? You ought to think so. But you will leave these places; you will go to the friends of Crito in Thessaly. For there is found the greatest disorder and license, and very likely they will be delighted to hear of the ludicrous way in which you escaped from prison, dressed up in peasant's clothes, or in some other disguise which people put on when they are running away, and with your appearance altered. But will no one say how you, an old man, with probably only a few more years to live, clung so greedily to life that you dared to break the highest laws? Perhaps not, if you do not annoy them. But if you do, Socrates, you will hear much that will make you blush. You will pass your life as the flatterer and the slave of all men; and what will you be doing but feasting in Thessaly? [3]

---

[3] The Athenians disdained the Thessalians as heavy eaters and drinkers.—*Ed.*

It will be as if you had made a journey to Thessaly for a banquet. And where will be all our old arguments about justice and excellence then? But you wish to live for the sake of your children? You want to bring them up and educate them? What? Will you take them with you to Thessaly, and bring them up and educate them there? Will you make them strangers to their own country, that you may bestow this benefit of exile on them too? Or supposing that you leave them in Athens, will they be brought up and educated better if you are alive, though you are not with them? Yes, your friends will take care of them. Will your friends take care of them if you make a journey to Thessaly, and not if you make a journey to Hades? You ought not to think that, at least if those who call themselves your friends are worth anything at all.

"No, Socrates, be persuaded by us who have reared you. Think neither of children nor of life, nor of any other thing before justice, so that when you come to the other world you may be able to make your defense before the rulers who sit in judgment there. It is clear that neither you nor any of your friends will be happier, or juster, or more pious in this life, if you do this thing, nor will you be happier after you are dead. Now you will go away a victim of the injustice, not of the laws, but of men. But if you repay evil with evil, and injustice with injustice in this shameful way, and break your agreements and covenants with us, and injure those whom you should least injure, yourself and your friends and your country and us, and so escape, then we shall be angry with you while you live, and when you die our brothers, the laws in Hades, will not receive you kindly; for they will know that on earth you did all that you could to destroy us. Listen then to us, and let not Crito persuade you to do as he says."

Be sure, my dear friend Crito, that this is what I seem to hear, as the worshippers of Cybele seem, in their passion, to hear the music of flutes; and the sound of these arguments rings so loudly in my ears, that I cannot hear any other arguments. And I feel sure that if you try to change my mind you will speak in vain. Nevertheless, if you think that you will succeed, speak.

CRITO. I have nothing more to say, Socrates.

SOCR. Then let it be, Crito, and let us do as I say, since the god is our guide.

2

The Claims of Utility

Readings: John Stuart Mill, Utilitarianism
John Rawls, "Two Concepts of Rules"

John Stuart Mill's *Utilitarianism* presents what is surely one of the most plausible and influential of all moral theories. The theory teaches that our fundamental moral obligation is to maximize valuable consequences for as many people as possible and to minimize disvaluable consequences. Most utilitarians agree with Mill that human pleasure or happiness is the most valuable consequence to be maximized and that human pain or misery is the consequence most to be avoided. Thus the essence of utilitarianism was summed up by Jeremy Bentham, Mill's predecessor, in the famous slogan: "The greatest happiness for the greatest number." The theory is *teleological* in that it makes moral evaluation ultimately dependent on consequences or results. (Moral theories, such as those in the next chapter, which regard non-consequential considerations as ultimate are generally called *deontological.*)

Plausible as the theory is, it seems to generate problems. Suppose that we could promote the general happiness in a particular case by punishing an innocent man (scapegoating) or by breaking a promise. Should we then perform these actions? Many people would be tempted to say that there is something morally wrong with these actions that is quite independent of their consequences, that their wrongness can just be seen from their *descriptions* as acts of "breaking a promise" or "punishing the innocent." John Rawls, in his essay "Two Concepts of Rules," attempts to formulate the utilitarian theory in such a way that it will not be defeated by the moral complexity of these kinds of situations. (In part, Chapter V of Mill's essay may also be viewed as such an attempt.) Rawls' essay may thus be regarded as a qualified defense of utilitarianism against certain classic objections.[1]

Suggestions for Further Reading

Michael D. Bayles, ed., *Contemporary Utilitarianism* (Garden City, N.Y.: Doubleday Anchor, 1968).

Jeremy Bentham, *An Introduction to the Principles of Morals and Legislation* (1789).

David Lyons, *Forms and Limits of Utilitarianism* (Oxford: The Clarendon Press, 1965).

H. J. McCloskey, *John Stuart Mill: A Critical Study* (London: Macmillan, 1971).

---

[1] In the judgment of the editor, John Rawls is the most important moral philosopher of the twentieth century. For this reason, several of his essays are included in this volume so that the reader will be able to trace some of the developments in his thought. You will note, for example, that in his essay in the following chapter Rawls goes on to attack against utilitarianism.

Utilitarianism
John Stuart Mill

Chapter I

General Remarks

There are few circumstances among those which make up the present condition of human knowledge more unlike what might have been expected, or more significant of the backward state in which speculation on the most important subjects still lingers, than the little progress which has been made in the decision of the controversy respecting the criterion of right and wrong.

John Stuart Mill (1806–1873) was an extremely influential English moral philosopher and social reformer. He was the author of many books and articles, the most widely read being *On Liberty* (1849) and *Utilitarianism* (1863). For a general study of Mill's philosophy, see H. J. McCloskey, *John Stuart Mill: A Critical Study* (New York: St. Martin's Press, 1970).

From the dawn of philosophy, the question concerning the *summum bonum,* or, what is the same thing, concerning the foundation of morality, has been accounted the main problem in speculative thought, has occupied the most gifted intellects and divided them into sects and schools carrying on a vigorous warfare against one another. And after more than two thousand years the same discussions continue, philosophers are still ranged under the same contending banners, and neither thinkers nor mankind at large seem nearer to being unanimous on the subject than when the youth Socrates listened to the old Protagoras and asserted (if Plato's dialogue be grounded on a real conversation) the theory of utilitarianism against the popular morality of the so-called sophist.

It is true that similar confusion and uncertainty and, in some cases, similiar discordance exist respecting the first principles of all the sciences, not excepting that which is deemed the most certain of them—mathematics, without much impairing, generally indeed without impairing at all, the trustworthiness of the conclusions of those sciences. An apparent anomaly, the explanation of which is that the detailed doctrines of a science are not usually deduced from, nor depend for their evidence upon, what are called its first principles. Were it not so, there would be no science more precarious, or whose conclusions were more insufficiently made out, than algebra, which derives none of its certainty from what are commonly taught to learners as its elements, since these, as laid down by some of its most eminent teachers, are as full of fictions as English law, and of mysteries as theology. The truths which are ultimately accepted as the first principles of a science are really the last results of metaphysical analysis practiced on the elementary notions with which the science is conversant; and their relation to the science is not that of foundations to an edifice, but of roots to a tree, which may perform their office equally well though they be never dug down to and exposed to light. But though in science the particular truths precede the general theory, the contrary might be expected to be the case with a practical art, such as morals or legislation. All action is for the sake of some end, and rules of action, it seems natural to suppose, must take their whole character and color from the end to which they are subservient. When we engage in a pursuit, a clear and precise conception of what we are pursuing would seem to be the first thing we need, instead of the last we are to look forward to. A test of right and wrong must be the means, one would think, of ascertaining what is right or wrong, and not a consequence of having already ascertained it.

The difficulty is not avoided by having recourse to the popular theory of a natural faculty, a sense of instinct, informing us of right and wrong. For—besides that the existence of such a moral instinct is itself one of the matters in dispute—those believers in it who have any pretensions to philosophy have been obliged to abandon the idea that it discerns what is right or wrong in the particular case in hand, as our other senses discern the sight or sound actually present. Our moral faculty, according to all those of its interpreters who are entitled to the name of thinkers, supplies us only with the general principles of moral judgments; it is a branch of our reason, not of our sensitive faculty, and must be looked to for the abstract doctrines of morality, not for perception of it in the concrete. The intuitive, no less than what may be termed the inductive, school of ethics insists on the necessity of general laws. They both agree that the morality of an individual action is not a question of direct perception, but of the application of a law to an individual case. They recognize also, to a great extent, the same moral laws, but differ as to their evidence and the source from which they derive their authority. According to the one opinion, the principles of morals are evident *a priori,* requiring nothing to command assent except that the meaning of the terms be understood. According to the other doctrine, right and wrong, as well as truth and falsehood, are questions of observation and experience. But both hold equally that morality must be deduced from principles; and the intuitive school affirm as strongly as the inductive that there is a science of morals. Yet they seldom attempt to make out a list of the *a priori* principles which are to serve as the premises of the science; still more rarely do they make any effort to reduce those various principles to one first principle or common ground of obligation. They either assume the ordinary precepts of morals as of *a priori* authority, or they lay down as the common groundwork of those maxims some generality much less obviously authoritative than the maxims themselves, and which has never succeeded in gaining popular acceptance. Yet to support their pretensions there ought either to be some one fundamental principle or law at the root of all morality, or, if there be several, there should be a determinate order of precedence among them; and the one principle, or the rule for deciding between the various principles when they conflict, ought to be self-evident.

To inquire how far the bad effects of this deficiency have been mitigated in practice, or to what extent the moral beliefs of mankind have been vitiated or made uncertain by the absence of any distinct recognition of an ultimate standard, would imply a complete survey and criticism of past and present ethical doctrine. It would, however, be easy to show that whatever steadiness or consistency these moral beliefs have attained has been mainly due to the tacit influence of a standard not recognized. Although the nonexistence of an acknowledged first principle has made ethics not so much a guide as a consecration of men's actual sentiments, still, as men's sentiments, both of favor and of aversion, are greatly influenced by what they suppose to be the effects of things upon their happiness, the principle of utility, or, as Bentham latterly called it, the greatest happiness principle, has had a large share in forming the moral doctrines even of those who most scornfully reject its authority. Nor is there any school of thought which refuses to admit that the influence of actions on happiness is a most material and even predominant consideration in many of the details of morals, however unwilling to acknowledge it as the fundamental principle of morality and the source of moral obligation. I might go much further and say that to all those *a priori* moralists who deem it necessary to argue at all, utilitarian arguments are indispensable. It is not my present purpose to criticize these thinkers; but I cannot help referring, for illustration, to a systematic treatise by one of the most illustrious of them, the *Metaphysics of Ethics* by Kant. This remarkable man, whose system of thought will long remain one of the landmarks in the history of philosophical speculation, does, in the treatise in question, lay down a universal first principle as the origin and ground of moral obligation; it is this: "So act that the rule on which thou actest would admit of being adopted as a law by all rational beings." But when he begins to deduce from this precept any of the actual duties of morality, he fails, almost grotesquely, to show that there would be any contradiction, any logical (not to say physical) impossibility, in the adoption by all rational beings of the most outrageously immoral rules of conduct. All he shows is that the *consequences* of their universal adoption would be such as no one would choose to incur.

On the present occasion, I shall, without further discussion of the other theories, attempt to contribute something toward the understanding and appreciation of the "utilitarian" or "happiness" theory, and toward such proof as it is susceptible of. It is evident that this cannot be proof in the ordinary and popular meaning of the term. Questions of ultimate ends are not amenable to direct proof. Whatever can be proved to be good must be so by being shown to be a means to something admitted to be good without proof. The medical art is proved to be good by its conducing to health; but how is it possible to prove that health is good? The art of music is good, for the reason, among others, that it produces pleasure; but what proof is it possible to give that pleasure is good? If, then, it is asserted that there is a comprehensive formula, including all things which are in themselves good, and that whatever else is good is not so as an end but as a means, the formula may be accepted or rejected, but is not a subject of what is commonly understood by proof. We are not, however, to infer that its acceptance or rejection must depend on blind impulse or arbitrary choice. There is a larger meaning of the word "proof," in which this question is as amenable to it as any other of the disputed questions of philosophy. The subject is within the cognizance of the rational faculty; and neither does that faculty deal with it solely in the way of intuition. Considerations may be presented capable of determining the intellect either to give or withhold its assent to the doctrine; and this is equivalent to proof.

We shall examine presently of what nature are these considerations; in what manner they apply to the case, and what rational grounds, therefore, can be given for accepting or rejecting the utilitarian formula. But it is a preliminary condition of rational acceptance or rejection that the formula should be correctly understood. I believe that the very imperfect notion ordinarily formed of its meaning is the chief obstacle which impedes its reception, and that, could it be cleared even from only the grosser misconceptions, the question would be greatly simplified and a large proportion of its difficulties removed. Before, therefore, I attempt to enter into the philosophical grounds which can be given for assenting to the utilitarian standard, I shall offer some illustrations of the doctrine itself, with the view of showing more clearly what it is, distinguishing it from what it is not, and disposing of such of the practical objections to it as either originate in, or are closely connected with, mistaken interpretations of its meaning. Having thus prepared the ground, I shall afterwards endeavor to throw such light as I can call upon the question considered as one of philosophical theory.

Chapter II

What Utilitarianism Is

A passing remark is all that needs be given to the ignorant blunder of supposing that those who stand up for utility as the test of right and wrong use the term in that restricted and merely colloquial sense in which utility is opposed to pleasure. An apology is due to the philosophical opponents of utilitarianism for even the momentary appearance of confounding them with anyone capable of so absurd a misconception; which is the more extraordinary, inasmuch as the contrary accusation, of referring everything to pleasure, and that, too, in its grossest form, is another of the common charges against utilitarianism: and, as has been pointedly remarked by an able writer, the same sort of persons, and often the very same persons, denounce the theory "as impracticably dry when the word 'utility' precedes the word 'pleasure,' and as too practicably voluptuous when the word 'pleasure' precedes the word 'utility.'" Those who know anything about the matter are aware that every writer, from Epicurus to Bentham, who maintained the theory of utility meant by it, not something to be contradistinguished from pleasure, but pleasure itself, together with exemption from pain; and instead of opposing the useful to the agreeable or the ornamental, have always declared that the useful means these, among other things. Yet the common herd, including the herd of writers, not only in newspapers and periodicals, but in books of weight and pretension, are perpetually falling into this shallow mistake. Having caught up the word "utilitarian," while knowing nothing whatever about it but its sound, they habitually express by it the rejection or the neglect of pleasure in some of its forms: of beauty, of ornament, or of amusement. Nor is the term thus ignorantly misapplied solely in disparagement, but occasionally in compliment, as though it implied superiority to frivolity and the mere pleasures of the moment. And this perverted use is the only one in which the word is popularly known, and the one from which the new generation are acquiring their sole notion of its meaning. Those who introduced the word, but who had for many years discontinued it as a distinctive appellation, may well feel themselves called upon to resume it if by doing so they can hope to contribute anything toward rescuing it from this utter degradation.[1]

The creed which accepts as the foundation of morals "utility" or the "greatest happiness principle" holds that actions are right in proportion as they tend to promote happiness; wrong as they tend to produce the reverse of happiness. By happiness is intended pleasure and the absence of pain; by unhappiness, pain and the privation of pleasure. To give a clear view of the moral standard set up by the theory, much more requires to be said; in particular, what things it includes in the ideas of pain and pleasure, and to what extent this is left an open question. But these supplementary explanations do not affect the theory of life on which this theory of morality is grounded—namely, that pleasure and freedom from pain are the only things desirable as ends; and that all desirable things (which are as numerous in the utilitarian as in any other scheme) are desirable either for pleasure inherent in themselves or as means to the promotion of pleasure and the prevention of pain.

Now such a theory of life excites in many minds, and among them in some of the most estimable in feeling and purpose, inveterate dislike. To suppose that life has (as they express it) no higher end than pleasure—no better and nobler object of desire and pursuit—they designate as utterly mean and groveling, as a doctrine worthy only of swine, to whom the followers of Epicurus were, at a very early period, contemptuously likened; and modern holders of the doctrine are occasionally made the subject of equally polite comparisons by its German, French, and English assailants.

When thus attacked, the Epicureans have always answered that it is not they, but their accusers, who represent human nature in a degrading light, since the accusation supposes human beings to be capable of no pleasures except those of which swine are capable. If this supposition were true, the charge could not be gainsaid, but would then be no longer an imputation; for if the sources of pleasure were precisely the same to human beings and to swine, the rule of life which is good enough for the one would be good enough for the other. The comparison of the Epicurean life to that of beasts is felt as degrading, precisely because a beast's pleasures do not satisfy a human being's conceptions of happiness. Human beings have faculties more elevated than the animal appetites and, when once made conscious of them, do not regard anything as happiness which does not include their gratification. I do not, indeed, consider the Epicureans to have been by any means faultless in drawing out their scheme of consequences from the utilitarian prin-

---

[1] The author of this essay has reason for believing himself to be the first person who brought the word "utilitarian" into use. He did not invent it, but adopted it from a passing expression in Mr. Galt's *Annals of the Parish*. After using it as a designation for several years, he and others abandoned it from a growing dislike to anything resembling a badge or watchword of sectarian distinction. But as a name for one single opinion, not a set of opinions—to denote the recognition of utility as a standard, not any particular way of applying it—the term supplies a want in the language, and offers, in many cases, a convenient mode of avoiding tiresome circumlocution.

ciple. To do this in any sufficient manner, many Stoic, as well as Christian, elements require to be included. But there is no known Epicurean theory of life which does not assign to the pleasures of the intellect, of the feelings and imagination, and of the moral sentiments a much higher value as pleasures than to those of mere sensation. It must be admitted, however, that utilitarian writers in general have placed the superiority of mental over bodily pleasures chiefly in the greater permanency, safety, uncostliness, etc., of the former —that is, in their circumstantial advantages rather than in their intrinsic nature. And on all these points utilitarians have fully proved their case; but they might have taken the other and, as it may be called, higher ground with entire consistency. It is quite compatible with the principle of utility to recognize the fact that some kinds of pleasure are more desirable and more valuable than others. It would be absurd that, while in estimating all other things quality is considered as well as quantity, the estimation of pleasure should be supposed to depend on quantity alone.

If I am asked what I mean by difference of quality in pleasures, or what makes one pleasure more valuable than another, merely as a pleasure, except its being greater in amount, there is but one possible answer. Of two pleasures, if there be one to which all or almost all who have experience of both give a decided preference, irrespective of any feeling of moral obligation to prefer it, that is the more desirable pleasure. If one of the two is, by those who are competently acquainted with both, placed so far above the other that they prefer it, even though knowing it to be attended with a greater amount of discontent, and would not resign it for any quantity of the other pleasure which their nature is capable of, we are justified in ascribing to the preferred enjoyment a superiority in quality so far outweighing quantity as to render it, in comparison, of small account.

Now it is an unquestionable fact that those who are equally acquainted with and equally capable of appreciating and enjoying both do give a most marked preference to the manner of existence which employs their higher faculties. Few human creatures would consent to be changed into any of the lower animals for a promise of the fullest allowance of a beast's pleasures; no intelligent human being would consent to be a fool, no instructed person would be an ignoramus, no person of feeling and conscience would be selfish and base, even though they should be persuaded that the fool, the dunce, or the rascal is better satisfied with his lot than they are with theirs. They would not resign what they possess more than he for the most complete satisfaction of all the desires which they have in common with him. If they ever fancy they would, it is only in cases of unhappiness so extreme that to escape from it they would exchange their lot for almost any other, however undesirable in their own eyes. A being of higher faculties requires more to make him happy, is capable probably of more acute suffering, and certainly accessible to it at more points, than one of an inferior type; but in spite of these liabilities, he can never really wish to sink into what he feels to be a lower grade of existence. We may give what explanation we please of this unwillingness; we may attribute it to pride, a name which is given indiscriminately to some of the most and to some of the least estimable feelings of which mankind are capable; we may refer it to the love of liberty and personal independence, an appeal to which was with the Stoics one of the most effective means for the inculcation of it; to the love of power or to the love of excitement, both of which do really enter into and contribute to it; but its most appropriate appellation is a sense of dignity, which all human beings possess in one form or other, and in some, though by no means in exact, proportion to their higher faculties, and which is so essential a part of the happiness of those in whom it is strong that nothing which conflicts with it could be otherwise than momentarily an object of desire to them. Whoever supposes that this preference takes place at a sacrifice of happiness—that the superior being, in anything like equal circumstances, is not happier than the inferior—confounds the two very different ideas of happiness and content. It is indisputable that the being whose capacities of enjoyment are low has the greatest chance of having them fully satisfied; and a highly endowed being will always feel that any happiness which he can look for, as the world is constituted, is imperfect. But he can learn to bear its imperfections, if they are at all bearable; and they will not make him envy the being who is indeed unconscious of the imperfections, but only because he feels not at all the good which those imperfections qualify. It is better to be a human being dissatisfied than a pig satisfied; better to be Socrates dissatisfied than a fool satisfied. And if the fool, or the pig, are of a different opinion, it is because they only know their own side of the question. The other party to the comparison knows both sides.

It may be objected that many who are capable of the higher pleasures occasionally, under the influence of temptation, postpone them to the lower. But this is quite compatible with a full appreciation of the intrinsic superiority of the higher. Men often, from infirmity of character, make their election for the nearer good, though they know it to be the less valuable; and this no less when the choice is between two bodily pleasures than when it is between bodily and mental. They pursue sensual indulgences to the injury of health, though perfectly aware that health is the greater good. It may be further objected that many who begin with youthful enthusiasm for everything noble, as they advance in years, sink into indolence and selfishness. But I do not believe that those who undergo this very common change voluntarily choose the lower description of pleasures in preference to the higher. I believe that, before they devote themselves exclusively to the one, they have already become incapable of the other. Capacity for the nobler feelings is in most natures a very tender plant, easily killed, not only by hostile influences, but by mere want of sustenance; and in the majority of young persons it speedily dies away if the occupations to which their position in life has devoted them, and the society into which it has thrown them, are not favorable to keeping that higher capacity in exercise. Men lose their high aspirations as they lose their intellectual tastes, because they have not time or opportunity for indulging them; and they addict themselves to inferior pleasures, not because they deliberately prefer them, but because they are either the only ones to which they have access or the only ones which they are any longer capable of enjoying. It may be questioned whether anyone who has remained equally susceptible to both classes of pleasures ever knowingly and calmly preferred the lower, though many, in all ages, have broken down in an ineffectual attempt to combine both.

From this verdict of the only competent judges, I apprehend there can be no appeal. On a question which is the best worth having of two pleasures, or which of two modes of existence is the most grateful to the feelings, apart from its moral attributes and from its consequences, the judgment of those who are qualified by knowledge of both, or, if they differ, that of the majority among them, must be admitted as final. And there needs be the less hesitation to accept this judgment respecting the quality of pleasures, since there is no other tribunal to be referred to even on the question of quantity. What means are there of determining which is the acutest of two pains, or the intensest of two pleasurable sensations, except the general suffrage of those who are familiar with both? Neither pains nor pleasures are homogeneous, and pain is always heterogeneous with pleasure. What is there to decide whether a particular pleasure is worth purchasing at the cost of a particular pain, except the feelings and judgment of the experienced? When, therefore, those feelings and judgment declare the pleasures derived from the higher faculties to be preferable *in kind,* apart from the question of intensity, to those of which the animal nature, disjoined from the higher faculties, is susceptible, they are entitled on this subject to the same regard.

I have dwelt on this point as being a necessary part of a perfectly just conception of utility or happiness considered as the directive rule of human conduct. But it is by no means an indispensable condition to the acceptance of the utilitarian standard; for that standard is not the agent's own greatest happiness, but the greatest amount of happiness altogether; and if it may possibly be doubted whether a noble character is always the happier for its nobleness, there can be no doubt that it makes other people happier, and that the world in general is immensely a gainer by it. Utilitarianism, therefore, could only attain its end by the general cultivation of nobleness of character, even if each individual were only benefited by the nobleness of others, and his own, so far as happiness is concerned, were a sheer deduction from the benefit. But the bare enunciation of such an absurdity as this last renders refutation superfluous.

According to the greatest happiness principle, as above explained, the ultimate end, with reference to and for the sake of which all other things are desirable—whether we are considering our own good or that of other people—is an existence exempt as far as possible from pain, and as rich as possible in enjoyments, both in point of quantity and quality; the test of quality and the rule for measuring it against quantity being the preference felt by those who, in their opportunities of experience, to which must be added their habits of self-consciousness and self-observation, are best furnished with the means of comparison. This, being according to the utilitarian opinion the end of human action, is necessarily also the standard of morality, which may accordingly be defined "the rules and precepts for human conduct," by the observance of which an existence such as has been described might be, to the greatest extent possible, secured to all mankind; and not to them only, but, so far as the nature of things admits, to the whole sentient creation.

Against this doctrine, however, arises another class of objectors who say that happiness, in any form, cannot be the rational purpose of human life and action; because, in the first place, it is unattainable; and they contemptuously ask, What right hast thou to be happy?—a question which Mr. Carlyle clinches by the addition, What right, a short time ago, hadst thou even *to be?* Next they say that men can do *without* happiness; that all noble human beings have felt this, and could not have become noble but by learning the lesson of *Entsagen,* or renunciation; which lesson, thoroughly learned and submitted to, they affirm to be the beginning and necessary condition of all virtue.

The first of these objections would go to the root of the matter were it well founded; for if no happiness is to be had at all by human beings, the attainment of it cannot be the end of morality or of any rational conduct. Though, even in that case, something might still be said for the utilitarian theory, since utility includes not solely the pursuit of happiness, but the prevention or mitigation of unhappiness; and if the former aim be chimerical, there will be all the greater scope and more imperative need for the latter, so long at least as mankind think fit to live and do not take refuge in the simultaneous act of suicide recommended under certain conditions by Novalis. When, however, it is thus positively asserted to be impossible that human life should be happy, the assertion, if not something like a verbal quibble, is at least an exaggeration. If by happiness be meant a continuity of highly pleasurable excitement, it is evident enough that this is impossible. A state of exalted pleasure lasts only moments or in some cases, and with some intermissions, hours or days, and is the occasional brilliant flash of enjoyment, not its permanent and steady flame. Of this the philosophers who have taught that happiness is the end of life were as fully aware as those who taunt them. The happiness which they meant was not a life of rapture, but moments of such, in an existence made up of few and transitory pains, many and various pleasures, with a decided predominance of the active over the passive, and having as the foundation of the whole not to expect more from life than it is capable of bestowing. A life thus composed, to those who have been fortunate enough to obtain it, has always appeared worthy of the name of happiness. And such an existence is even now the lot of many during some considerable portion of their lives. The present wretched education and wretched social arrangements are the only real hindrance to its being attainable by almost all.

The objectors perhaps may doubt whether human beings, if taught to consider happiness as the end of life, would be satisfied with such a moderate share of it. But great numbers of mankind have been satisfied with much less. The main constituents of a satisfied life appear to be two, either of which by itself is often found sufficient for the purpose: tranquillity and excitement. With much tranquillity, many find that they can be content with very little pleasure; with much excitement, many can reconcile themselves to a considerable quantity of pain. There is assuredly no inherent impossibility of enabling even the mass of mankind to unite both, since the two are so far from being incompatible that they are in natural alliance, the prolongation of either being a preparation for, and exciting a wish for, the other. It is only those in whom indolence amounts to a vice that do not desire excitement after an interval of repose; it is only those in whom the need of excitement is a disease that feel the tranquillity which follows excitement dull and insipid, instead of pleasurable in direct proportion to the excitement which preceded it. When people who are tolerably fortunate in their outward lot do not find in life sufficient enjoyment to make it valuable to them, the cause generally is caring for nobody but themselves. To those who have neither public nor private affections, the excitements of life are much curtailed, and in any case dwindle in value as the time approaches when all selfish interests must be terminated by death; while those who leave after them objects of personal affection, and especially those who have also cultivated a fellow-feeling with the collective interests of mankind, retain as lively an interest in life on the eve of death as in the vigor of youth and health. Next to selfishness, the principal cause which makes life unsatisfactory is want of mental cultivation. A cultivated mind—I do not mean that of a philosopher, but any mind to which the fountains of knowledge have been opened, and which has been taught, in any tolerable degree, to exercise its faculties—finds sources of inexhaustible interest in all that surrounds it: in the objects of nature, the achievements of art, the imaginations of poetry, the incidents of history, the ways of mankind, past and present, and their prospects in the future. It is possible, indeed, to become indifferent to all this, and that too without having exhausted a thousandth part of it, but only when one has had from the beginning no moral or human interest in these things and has sought in them only the gratification of curiosity.

Now there is absolutely no reason in the nature of things why an amount of mental culture sufficient to give an intelligent interest in these objects of contemplation should not be the inheritance of everyone born in a civilized country. As little is there an inherent necessity that any human being should be a selfish egotist, devoid of every feeling or care but those which center in his own miserable individuality. Something far superior to this is sufficiently common even now, to give ample earnest of what the human species may be made. Genuine private affections and a sincere interest in the public good are possible, though in unequal degrees, to every rightly brought up human being. In a world in which there is so much to interest, so much to enjoy, and so much also to correct and improve, everyone who has this moderate amount of moral and intellectual requisites is capable of an existence which may be called enviable; and unless such a person, through bad laws or subjection to the will of others, is denied the liberty to use the sources of happiness within his reach, he will not fail to find this enviable existence, if he escape the positive evils of life, the great sources of physical and mental suffering—such as indigence, disease, and the unkindness, worthlessness, or premature loss of objects of affection. The main stress of the problem lies, therefore, in the contest with these calamities from which it is a rare good fortune entirely to escape; which, as things now are, cannot be obviated, and often cannot be in any material degree mitigated. Yet no one whose opinion deserves a moment's consideration can doubt that most of the great positive evils of the world are in themselves removable, and will, if human affairs continue to improve, be in the end reduced within narrow limits. Poverty, in any sense implying suffering, may be completely extinguished by the wisdom of society combined with the good sense and providence of individuals. Even that most intractable of enemies, disease, may be indefinitely reduced in dimensions by good physical and moral education and proper control of noxious influences, while the progress of science holds out a promise for the future of still more direct conquests over this detestable foe. And every advance in that direction relieves us from some, not only of the chances which cut short our own lives, but, what concerns us still more, which deprive us of those in whom our happiness is wrapt up. As for vicissitudes of fortune and other disappointments connected with worldly circumstances, these are principally the effect either of gross imprudence, of ill-regulated desires, or of bad or imperfect social institutions. All the grand sources, in short, of human suffering are in a great degree, many of them almost entirely, conquerable by human care and effort; and though their removal is grievously slow—though a long succession of generations will perish in the breach before the conquest is completed, and this world becomes all that, if will and knowledge were not wanting, it might easily be made— yet every mind sufficiently intelligent and generous to bear a part, however small and inconspicuous, in the endeavor will draw a noble enjoyment from the contest itself, which he would not for any bribe in the form of selfish indulgence consent to be without.

And this leads to the true estimation of what is said by the objectors concerning the possibility and the obligation of learning to do without happiness. Unquestionably it is possible to do without happiness; it is done involuntarily by nineteen-twentieths of mankind, even in those parts of our present world which are least deep in barbarism; and it often has to be done voluntarily by the hero or the martyr, for the sake of something which he prizes more than his individual happiness. But this something, what is it, unless the happiness of others or some of the requisites of happiness? It is noble to be capable of resigning entirely one's own portion of happiness, or chances of it; but, after all, this self-sacrifice must be for some end; it is not its own end; and if we are told that its end is not happiness but virtue, which is better than happiness, I ask, would the sacrifice be made if the hero or martyr did not believe that it would earn for others immunity from similar sacrifices? Would it be made if he thought that his renunciation of happiness for himself would produce no fruit for any of his fellow creatures, but to make their lot like his and place them also in the condition of persons who have renounced happiness? All honor to those who can abnegate for themselves the personal enjoyment of life when by such renunciation they contribute worthily to increase the amount of happiness in the world; but he who does it or professes to do it for any other purpose is no more deserving of admiration than the ascetic mounted on his pillar. He may be an inspiriting proof of what men *can* do, but assuredly not an example of what they *should*.

Though it is only in a very imperfect state of the world's arrangements that anyone can best serve the happiness of others by the absolute sacrifice of his own, yet, so long as the world is in that imperfect state, I fully acknowledge that the readiness to make such a sacrifice is the highest virtue which can be found in man. I will add that in this condition of the world, paradoxical as the assertion may be, the conscious ability to do without happiness gives the best prospect of realizing such happiness as is attainable. For nothing except that consciousness can raise a person above the chances of life by making him feel that, let fate and fortune do their worst, they have not power to subdue him; which, once felt, frees him from excess of anxiety concerning the evils of life and enables him, like many a Stoic in the worst times of the Roman Empire, to cultivate in tranquillity the sources of satisfaction accessible to him, without concerning himself about the uncertainty of their duration any more than about their inevitable end.

Meanwhile, let utilitarians never cease to claim the morality of self-devotion as a possession which belongs by as good a right to them as either to the Stoic or to the Transcendentalist. The utilitarian morality does recognize in human beings the power of sacrificing their own greatest good for the good of others. It only refuses to admit that the sacrifice is itself a good. A sacrifice which does not increase or tend to increase the sum total of happiness, it considers as wasted. The only self-renunciation which it applauds is devotion to the happiness, or to some of the means of happiness, of others, either of mankind collectively or of individuals within the limits imposed by the collective interests of mankind.

I must again repeat what the assailants of utilitarianism seldom have the justice to acknowledge, that the happiness which forms the utilitarian standard of what is right in conduct is not the agent's own happiness but that of all concerned. As between his own happiness and that of others, utilitarianism requires him to be as strictly impartial as a disinterested and benevolent spectator. In the golden rule of Jesus of Nazareth, we read the complete spirit of the ethics of utility. "To do as you would be done by," and "to love your neighbor as yourself," constitute the ideal perfection of utilitarian morality. As the means of making the nearest approach to this ideal, utility would enjoin, first, that laws and social arrangements should place the happiness or (as, speaking practically, it may be called) the interest of every individual as nearly as possible in harmony with the interest of the whole; and, secondly, that education and opinion, which have so vast a power over human character, should so use that power as to establish in the mind of every individual an indissoluble association between his own happiness and the good of the whole, especially between his own happiness and the practice of such modes of conduct, negative and positive, as regard for the universal happiness prescribes; so that not only he may be unable to conceive the possibility of happiness to himself, consistently with conduct opposed to the general good, but also that a direct impulse to promote the general good may be in every individual one of the habitual motives of action, and the sentiments connected therewith may fill a large and prominent place in every human being's sentient existence. If the impugners of the utilitarian morality represented it to their own minds in this its true character, I know not what recommendation possessed by any other morality they could possibly affirm to be wanting to it; what more beautiful or more exalted developments of human nature any other ethical system can be supposed to foster, or what springs of action, not accessible to the utilitarian, such systems rely on for giving effect to their mandates.

The objectors to utilitarianism cannot always be charged with representing it in a discreditable light. On the contrary, those among them who entertain anything like a just idea of its disinterested character sometimes find fault with its standard as being too high for humanity. They say it is exacting too much to require that people shall always act from the inducement of promoting the general interests of society. But this is to mistake the very meaning of a standard of morals and confound the rule of action with the motive of it. It is the business of ethics to tell us what are our duties, or by what test we may know them; but no system of ethics requires that the sole motive of all we do shall be a feeling of duty; on the contrary, ninety-nine hundredths of all our actions are done from other motives, and rightly so done if the rule of duty does not condemn them. It is the more unjust to utilitarianism that this particular misapprehension should be made a ground of objection to it, inasmuch as utilitarian moralists have gone beyond almost all others in affirming that the motive has nothing to do with the morality of the action, though much with the worth of the agent. He who saves a fellow creature from drowning does what is morally right, whether his motive be duty or the hope of being paid for his trouble; he who betrays the friend that trusts him is guilty of a crime, even if his object be to serve another friend to whom he is under greater obligations.[2] But to speak only of actions

---

[2] An opponent, whose intellectual and moral fairness it is a pleasure to acknowledge (the Rev. J. Llewellyn Davies), has objected to this passage, saying, "Surely the rightness or wrongness of saving a man from drowning does depend very much upon the motive with which it is done. Suppose that a tyrant, when his enemy jumped into the sea to escape from

done from the motive of duty, and in direct obedience to principle: it is a misapprehension of the utilitarian mode of thought to conceive it as implying that people should fix their minds upon so wide a generality as the world, or society at large. The great majority of good actions are intended not for the benefit of the world, but for that of individuals, of which the good of the world is made up; and the thoughts of the most virtuous man need not on these occasions travel beyond the particular persons concerned, except so far as is necessary to assure himself that in benefiting them he is not violating the rights, that is, the legitimate and authorized expectations, of anyone else. The multiplication of happiness is, according to the utilitarian ethics, the object of virtue: the occasions on which any person (except one in a thousand) has it in his power to do this on an extended scale—in other words, to be a public benefactor—are but exceptional; and on these occasions alone is he called on to consider public utility; in every other case, private utility, the interest or happiness of some few persons, is all he has to attend to. Those alone the influence of whose actions extends to society in general need concern themselves habitually about so large an object. In the case of abstinences indeed—of things which people forbear to do from moral considerations, though the consequences in the particular case might be beneficial —it would be unworthy of an intelligent agent not to be consciously aware that the action is of a class which, if practiced generally, would be generally injurious, and that this is the ground of the obligation to abstain from it. The amount of regard for the public interest implied in this recognition is no greater than is demanded by every system of morals, for they all enjoin to abstain from whatever is manifestly pernicious to society.

The same considerations dispose of another reproach against the doctrine of utility, founded on a still grosser misconception of the purpose of a standard of morality and of the very meaning of the words "right" and "wrong." It is often affirmed that utilitarianism renders men cold and unsympathizing; that it chills their moral feelings toward individuals; that it

---

him, saved him from drowning simply in order that he might inflict upon him more exquisite tortures, would it tend to clearness to speak of that rescue as 'a morally right action'? Or suppose again, according to one of the stock illustrations of ethical inquiries, that a man betrayed a trust received from a friend, because the discharge of it would fatally injure that friend himself or someone belonging to him, would utilitarianism compel one to call the betrayal 'a crime' as much as if it had been done from the meanest motive?"

I submit that he who saves another from drowning in order to kill him by torture afterwards does not differ only in motive from him who does the same thing from duty or benevolence; the act itself is different. The rescue of the man is, in the case supposed, only the necessary first step of an act far more atrocious than leaving him to drown would have been. Had Mr. Davies said, "The rightness or wrongness of saving a man from drowning does depend very much"—not upon the motive, but—"upon the *intention*," no utilitarian would have differed from him. Mr. Davies, by an oversight too common not to be quite venial, has in this case confounded the very different ideas of Motive and Intention. There is no point which utilitarian thinkers (and Bentham pre-eminently) have taken more pains to illustrate than this. The morality of the action depends entirely upon the intention—that is, upon what the agent *wills to do*. But the motive, that is, the feeling which makes him will so to do, if it makes no difference in the act, makes none in the morality: though it makes a great difference in our moral estimation of the agent, especially if it indicates a good or a bad habitual *disposition*—a bent of character from which useful, or from which hurtful actions are likely to arise.

makes them regard only the dry and hard consideration of the consequences of actions, not taking into their moral estimate the qualities from which those actions emanate. If the assertion means that they do not allow their judgment respecting the rightness or wrongness of an action to be influenced by their opinion of the qualities of the person who does it, this is a complaint not against utilitarianism, but against any standard of morality at all; for certainly no known ethical standard decides an action to be good or bad because it is done by a good or a bad man, still less because done by an amiable, a brave, or a benevolent man, or the contrary. These considerations are relevant, not to the estimation of actions, but of persons; and there is nothing in the utilitarian theory inconsistent with the fact that there are other things which interest us in persons besides the rightness and wrongness of their actions. The Stoics, indeed, with the paradoxical misuse of language which was part of their system, and by which they strove to raise themselves above all concern about anything but virtue, were fond of saying that he who has that has everything; that he, and only he, is rich, is beautiful, is a king. But no claim of this description is made for the virtuous man by the utilitarian doctrine. Utilitarians are quite aware that there are other desirable possessions and qualities besides virtue, and are perfectly willing to allow to all of them their full worth. They are also aware that a right action does not necessarily indicate a virtuous character, and that actions which are blamable often proceed from qualities entitled to praise. When this is apparent in any particular case, it modifies their estimation, not certainly of the act, but of the agent. I grant that they are, notwithstanding, of opinion that in the long run the best proof of a good character is good actions; and resolutely refuse to consider any mental disposition as good of which the predominant tendency is to produce bad conduct. This makes them unpopular with many people, but it is an unpopularity which they must share with everyone who regards the distinction between right and wrong in a serious light; and the reproach is not one which a conscientious utilitarian need be anxious to repel.

If no more be meant by the objection than that many utilitarians look on the morality of actions, as measured by the utilitarian standards, with too exclusive a regard, and do not lay sufficient stress upon the other beauties of character which go toward making a human being lovable or admirable, this may be admitted. Utilitarians who have cultivated their moral feelings, but not their sympathies, nor their artistic perceptions, do fall into this mistake; and so do all other moralists under the same conditions. What can be said in excuse for other moralists is equally available for them, namely, that, if there is to be any error, it is better that it should be on that side. As a matter of fact, we may affirm that among utilitarians, as among adherents of other systems, there is every imaginable degree of rigidity and of laxity in the application of their standard; some are even puritanically rigorous, while others are as indulgent as can possibly be desired by sinner or by sentimentalist. But on the whole, a doctrine which brings prominently forward the interest that mankind have in the repression and prevention of conduct which violates the moral law is likely to be inferior to no other in turning the sanctions of opinion against such violations. It is true, the question "What does violate the moral law?" is one on which those who recognize different standards of morality are likely now and then to differ. But difference of opinion on moral questions was not first introduced into the world by utilitarianism, while that doctrine does supply, if not always an easy, at all events a tangible and intelligible, mode of deciding such differences.

It may not be superfluous to notice a few more of the common misapprehensions of utilitarian ethics, even those which are so obvious and gross that it might appear impossible for any person of candor and intelligence to fall into them; since persons, even of considerable mental endowment, often give themselves so little trouble to understand the bearings of any opinion against which they entertain a prejudice, and men are in general so little conscious of this voluntary ignorance as a defect that the vulgarest misunderstandings of ethical doctrines are continually met with in the deliberate writings of persons of the greatest pretensions both to high principle and to philosophy. We not uncommonly hear the doctrine of utility inveighed against as a *godless* doctrine. If it be necessary to say anything at all against so mere an assumption, we may say that the question depends upon what idea we have formed of the moral character of the Deity. If it be a true belief that God desires, above all things, the happiness of his creatures, and that this was his purpose in their creation, utility is not only not a godless doctrine, but more profoundly religious than any other. If it be meant that utilitarianism does not recognize the revealed will of God as the supreme law of morals, I answer that a utilitarian who believes in the perfect goodness and wisdom of *God* necessarily believes that whatever God has thought fit to reveal on the subject of morals must fulfill the requirements of utility in a supreme degree. But others besides utilitarians have been of opinion that the Christian revelation was intended, and is fitted, to inform the hearts and minds of mankind with a spirit which should enable them to find for themselves what is right, and incline them to do it when found, rather than to tell them, except in a very general way, what it is; and that we need a doctrine of ethics, carefully followed out, to *interpret* to us the will of God. Whether this opinion is correct or not, it is superfluous here to discuss; since whatever aid religion, either natural or revealed, can afford to ethical investigation is as open to the utilitarian moralist as to any other. He can use it as the testimony of God to the usefulness or hurtfulness of any given course of action by as good a right as others can use it for the indication of a transcendental law having no connection with usefulness or with happiness.

Again, utility is often summarily stigmatized as an immoral doctrine by giving it the name of "expediency," and taking advantage of the popular use of that term to contrast it with principle. But the expedient, in the sense in which it is opposed to the right, generally means that which is expedient for the particular interest of the agent himself; as when a minister sacrifices the interests of his country to keep himself in place. When it means anything better than this, it means that which is expedient for some immediate object, some temporary purpose, but which violates a rule whose observance is expedient in a much higher degree. The expedient, in this sense, instead of being the same thing with the useful, is a branch of the hurtful. Thus it would often be expedient, for the purpose of getting over some momentary embarrassment, or attaining some object immediately useful to ourselves or others, to tell a lie. But inasmuch as the cultivation in ourselves of a sensitive feeling on the subject of veracity is one of the most useful, and the enfeeblement of that feeling one of the most hurtful, things to which our conduct can be instrumental; and inasmuch as any, even unintentional, deviation from truth does that much toward weakening the trustworthiness of human assertion, which is not only the principal support of all present social well-being, but the insufficiency of which does more than any one thing that can be named to keep back civilization, virtue, everything on which human happiness on the largest scale depends—we feel that the violation, for a present advantage, of a rule of such transcendent expediency is not expedient, and that he who, for the sake of convenience to himself or to some other individual, does what depends on him to deprive mankind of the good, and inflict upon them the evil, involved in the greater or less reliance which they can place in each other's word, acts the part of one of their worst enemies. Yet that even this rule, sacred as it is, admits of possible exceptions is acknowledged by all moralists; the chief of which is when the withholding of some fact (as of information from a malefactor, or of bad news from a person dangerously ill) would save an individual (especially an individual other than oneself) from great and unmerited evil, and when the withholding can only be effected by denial. But in order that the exception may not extend itself beyond the need, and may have the least possible effect in weakening reliance on veracity, it ought to be recognized and, if possible, its limits defined; and, if the principle of utility is good for anything, it must be good for weighing these conflicting utilities against one another and marking out the region within which one or the other preponderates.

Again, defenders of utility often find themselves called upon to reply to such objections as this—that there is not time, previous to action, for calculating and weighing the effects of any line of conduct on the general happiness. This is exactly as if anyone were to say that it is impossible to guide our conduct by Christianity because there is not time, on every occasion on which anything has to be done, to read through the Old and New Testaments. The answer to the objection is that there has been ample time, namely, the whole past duration of the human species. During all that time mankind have been learning by experience the tendencies of actions; on which experience all the prudence as well as all the morality of life are dependent. People talk as if the commencement of this course of experience had hitherto been put off, and as if, at the moment when some man feels tempted to meddle with the property or life of another, he had to begin considering for the first time whether murder and theft are injurious to human happiness. Even then I do not think that he would find the question very puzzling; but, at all events, the matter is now done to his hand. It is truly a whimsical supposition that, if mankind were agreed in considering utility to be the test of morality, they would remain without any agreement as to what *is* useful, and would take no measures for having their notions on the subject taught to the young and enforced by law and opinion. There is no difficulty in proving any ethical standard whatever to work ill if we suppose universal idiocy to be conjoined with it; but on any hypothesis short of that, mankind must by this time have acquired positive beliefs as to the effects of some actions on their happiness; and the beliefs which have thus come down are the rules of morality for the multitude, and for the philosopher until he has succeeded in finding better. That philosophers might easily do this, even now, on many subjects; that the received code of ethics is by no means of divine right; and that mankind have still much to learn as to the effects of actions on the general happiness, I admit or rather earnestly maintain. The corollaries from the principle of utility, like the precepts of every practical art, admit of indefinite improvement, and, in a progressive state of the human mind, their improvement is perpetually going on. But to consider the rules of morality as improvable is one thing; to pass over the intermediate generalization entirely and endeavor to test each individual action directly by the first principle is another. It is a strange notion that the acknowledgment of a first principle is inconsistent with the admission of secondary ones. To inform a traveler respecting the place of his ultimate destination is not to forbid the use of landmarks and direction-posts on the way. The proposition that happiness is the end and aim of morality does not mean that no road ought to be laid down to that goal, or that persons going thither should not be advised to take one direction rather than another. Men really ought to leave off talking a kind of nonsense on this subject, which they would neither talk nor listen to on other matters of practical concernment. Nobody argues that the art of navigation is not founded on astronomy because sailors cannot wait to calculate the Nautical Almanac. Being rational creatures, they go to sea with it ready calculated; and all rational creatures go out upon the sea of life with their minds made up on the common questions of right and wrong, as well as on many of the far more difficult questions of wise and foolish. And this, as long as foresight is a human quality, it is to be presumed they will continue to do. Whatever we adopt as the fundamental principle of morality, we require subordinate principles to apply it by; the impossibility of doing without them, being common to all systems, can afford no argument against any one in particular; but gravely to argue as if no such secondary principles could be had, and as if mankind had remained till now, and always must remain, without drawing any general conclusions from the experience of human life is as high a pitch, I think, as absurdity has ever reached in philosophical controversy.

The remainder of the stock arguments against utilitarianism mostly consist in laying to its charge the common infirmities of human nature, and the general difficulties which embarrass conscientious persons in shaping their course through life. We are told that a utilitarian will be apt to make his own particular case an exception to moral rules, and, when under temptation, will see a utility in the breach of a rule, greater than he will see in its observance. But is utility the only creed which is able to furnish us with excuses for evil-doing and means of cheating our own conscience? They are afforded in abundance by all doctrines which recognize as a fact in morals the existence of conflicting considerations, which all doctrines do that have been believed by sane persons. It is not the fault of any creed, but of the complicated nature of human affairs, that rules of conduct cannot be so framed as to require no exceptions, and that hardly any kind of action can safely be laid down as either always obligatory or always condemnable. There is no ethical creed which does not temper the rigidity of its laws by giving a certain latitude, under the moral responsibility of the agent, for accommodation to peculiarities of circumstances; and under every creed, at the opening thus made, self-deception and dishonest casuistry get in. There exists no moral system under which there do not arise unequivocal cases of conflicting obligation. These are the real difficulties, the knotty points both in the theory of ethics and in the conscientious guidance of personal conduct. They are overcome practically, with greater or with less success, according to the intellect and virtue of the individual; but it can hardly be pretended that anyone will be the less qualified for dealing with them, from possessing an ultimate standard to which conflicting rights and duties can be referred. If utility is the ultimate source of moral obligations, utility may be invoked to decide between them when their demands are incompatible. Though the application of the standard may be difficult, it is better than none at all; while in other systems, the moral laws all claiming independent authority, there is no common umpire entitled to interfere between them; their claims to precedence one over another rest on little better than sophistry, and, unless determined, as they generally are, by the unacknowledged influence of consideration of utility, afford a free scope for the action of personal desires and partialities. We must remember that only in these cases of conflict between secondary principles is it requisite that first principles should be appealed to. There is no case of moral obligation in which some secondary principle is not involved; and if only one, there can seldom be any real doubt which one it is, in the mind of any person by whom the principle itself is recognized.

Chapter III

Of the Ultimate Sanction of the Principle of Utility

The question is often asked, and properly so, in regard to any supposed moral standard—What is its sanction? what are the motives to obey? or, more specifically, what is the source of its obligation? whence does it derive its binding force? It is a necessary part of moral philosophy to provide the answer to this question, which, though frequently assuming the shape of an objection to the utilitarian morality, as if it had some special applicability to that above others, really arises in regard to all standards. It arises, in fact, whenever a person is called on to *adopt* a standard, or refer morality to any basis on which he has not been accustomed to rest it. For the customary morality, that which education and opinion have consecrated, is the only one which presents itself to the mind with the feeling of being *in itself* obligatory; and when a person is asked to believe that this morality *derives* its obligation from some general principle round which custom has not thrown the same halo, the assertion is to him a paradox; the supposed corollaries seem to have a more binding force than the original theorem; the superstructure seems to stand better without than with what is represented as its foundation. He says to himself, I feel that I am bound not to rob or murder, betray or deceive; but why am I bound to promote the general happiness? If my own happiness lies in something else, why may I not give that the preference?

If the view adopted by the utilitarian philosophy of the nature of the moral sense be correct, this difficulty will always present itself until the influences which form moral character have taken the same hold of the principle which they have taken of some of the consequences—until, by the improvement of education, the feeling of unity with our fellow creatures shall be (what it cannot be denied that Christ intended it to be) as deeply rooted in our character, and to our own consciousness as completely a part of our nature, as the horror of crime is in an ordinarily well-brought-up young person. In the meantime, however, the difficulty has no peculiar application to the doctrine of utility, but is inherent in every attempt to analyze morality and reduce it to principles; which, unless the principle is already in men's minds invested with as much sacredness as any of its applications, always seems to divest them of a part of their sanctity.

The principle of utility either has, or there is no reason why it might not have, all the sanctions which belong to any other system of morals. Those sanctions are either external or internal. Of the external sanctions it is not necessary to speak at any length. They are the hope of favor and the fear of displeasure from our fellow creatures or from the Ruler of the universe, along with whatever we may have of sympathy or affection for them, or of love and awe of Him, inclining us to do His will independently of selfish consequences. There is evidently no reason why all these motives for observance should not attach themselves to the utilitarian morality as completely and as powerfully as to any other. Indeed, those of them which refer to our fellow creatures are sure to do so, in proportion to the amount of general intelligence; for whether there be any other ground of moral obligation than the general happiness or not, men do desire happiness; and however imperfect may be their own practice, they desire and commend all conduct in others toward themselves by which they think their happiness is promoted. With regard to the religious motive, if men believe, as most profess to do, in the goodness of God, those who think that conductiveness to the general happiness is the essence or even only the criterion of good must necessarily believe that it is also that which God approves. The whole force therefore of external reward and punishment, whether physical or moral, and whether proceeding from God or from our fellow men, together with all that the capacities of human nature admit of disinterested devotion to either, become available to enforce the utilitarian morality, in proportion as that morality is recognized; and the more powerfully, the more the appliances of education and general cultivation are bent to the purpose.

So far as to external sanctions. The internal sanction of duty, whatever our standard of duty may be, is one and the same—a feeling in our own mind; a pain, more or less intense, attendant on violation of duty, which in properly cultivated moral natures rises, in the more serious cases, into shrinking from it as an impossibility. This feeling, when disinterested and connecting itself with the pure idea of duty, and not with some particular form of it, or with any of the merely accessory circumstances, is the essence of conscience; though in that complex phenomenon as it actually exists, the simple fact is in general all encrusted over with collateral associations derived from sympathy, from love, and still more from fear; from all the forms of religious feeling; from the recollections of childhood and of all our past life; from self-esteem, desire of the esteem of others, and occasionally even self-abasement. This extreme complication is, I apprehend, the origin of the sort of mystical character which, by a tendency of the human mind of which there are many other examples, is apt to be attributed to the idea of moral obligation, and which leads people to believe that the idea cannot possibly attach itself to any other objects than those which, by a supposed mysterious law, are found in our present experience to excite it. Its binding force, however, consists in the existence of a mass of feeling which must be broken through in order to do what violates our standard of right, and which, if we do nevertheless violate that standard, will probably have to be encountered afterwards in the form of remorse. Whatever theory we have of the nature or origin of conscience, this is what essentially constitutes it.

The ultimate sanction, therefore, of all morality (external motives apart) being a subjective feeling in our own minds, I see nothing embarrassing to those whose standard is utility in the question, What is the sanction of that particular standard? We may answer, the same as of all other moral standards —the conscientious feelings of mankind. Undoubtedly this sanction has no binding efficacy on those who do not possess the feelings it appeals to; but neither will these persons be more obedient to any other moral principle than to the utilitarian one. On them morality of any kind has no hold but through the external sanctions. Meanwhile the feelings exist, a fact in human nature, the reality of which, and the great power with which they are capable of acting on those in whom they have been duly cultivated, are proved by experience. No reason has ever been shown why they may not be cultivated to as great intensity in connection with the utilitarian as with any other rule of morals.

There is, I am aware, a disposition to believe that a person who sees in moral obligation a transcendental fact, an objective reality belonging to the province of "things in themselves," is likely to be more obedient to it than one who believes it to be entirely subjective, having its seat in human consciousness only. But whatever a person's opinion may be on this point of ontology, the force he is really urged by is his own subjective feeling, and is exactly measured by its strength. No one's belief that duty is an objective reality is stronger than the belief that God is so; yet the belief in God, apart from the expectation of actual reward and punishment, only operates on conduct through, and in proportion to, the subjective religious feeling. The sanction, so far as it is disinterested, is always in the mind itself; and the notion, therefore, of the transcendental moralists must be that this sanction will not exist *in* the mind unless it is believed to have its root out of the mind; and that if a person is able to say to himself, "That which is restraining me and which is called my conscience is only a feeling in my own mind," he may possibly draw the conclusion that when the feeling ceases the obligation ceases, and that if he find the feeling inconvenient, he may disregard it and endeavor to get rid of it. But is this danger confined to the utilitarian morality? Does the belief that moral obligation has its seat outside the mind make the feeling of it too strong to be got rid of? The fact is so far otherwise that all moralists admit and lament the ease with which, in the generality of minds, conscience can be silenced or stifled. The question, "Need I obey my conscience?" is quite as often put to themselves by persons who never heard of the principle of utility as by its adherents. Those whose conscientious feelings are so weak as to allow of their asking this question, if they answer it affirmatively, will not do so because they believe in the transcendental theory, but because of the external sanctions.

It is not necessary, for the present purpose, to decide whether the feeling of duty is innate or implanted. Assuming it to be innate, it is an open question to what objects it naturally attaches itself; for the philosophic supporters of that theory are now agreed that the intuitive perception is of principles of morality and not of the details. If there be anything innate in the matter, I see no reason why the feeling which is innate should not be that of regard to the pleasures and pains of others. If there is any principle of morals which is intuitively obligatory, I should say it must be that. If so, the intuitive ethics would coincide with the utilitarian, and there would be no further quarrel between them. Even as it is, the intuitive moralists, though they believe that there are other intuitive moral obligations, do already believe this to be one; for they unanimously hold that a large *portion* of morality turns upon the consideration due to the interests of our fellow creatures. Therefore, if the belief in the transcendental origin of moral obligation gives any additional efficacy to the internal sanction, it appears to me that the utilitarian principle has already the benefit of it.

On the other hand, if, as is my own belief, the moral feelings are not innate but acquired, they are not for that reason the less natural. It is natural to man to speak, to reason, to build cities, to cultivate the ground, though these are acquired faculties. The moral feelings are not indeed a part of our nature in the sense of being in any perceptible degree present in all of us; but this, unhappily, is a fact admitted by those who believe the most strenuously in their transcendental origin. Like the other acquired capacities above referred to, the moral faculty, if not a part of our nature, is a natural outgrowth from it; capable, like them, in a certain small degree, of springing up spontaneously; and susceptible of being brought by cultivation to a high degree of development. Unhappily it is also susceptible, by a sufficient use of the external sanctions and of the force of early impressions, of being cultivated in almost any direction, so that there is hardly anything so absurd or so mischievous that it may not, by means of these influences, be made to act on the human mind with all the authority of conscience. To doubt that the same potency might be given by the same means to the principle of utility, even if it had no foundation in human nature, would be flying in the face of all experience.

But moral associations which are wholly of artificial creation, when the intellectual culture goes on, yield by degrees to the dissolving force of analysis; and if the feeling of duty, when associated with utility, would appear equally arbitrary; if there were no leading department of our nature, no powerful class of sentiments, with which that association would harmonize, which would make us feel it congenial and incline us not only to foster it in others (for which we have abundant interested motives), but also to cherish it in ourselves—if there were not, in short, a natural basis of sentiment for utilitarian morality, it might well happen that this association also, even after it had been implanted by education, might be analyzed away.

But there *is* this basis of powerful natural sentiment; and this it is which, when once the general happiness is recognized as the ethical standard, will constitute the strength of the utilitarian morality. This firm foundation is that of the social feelings of mankind—the desire to be in unity with our fellow creatures, which is already a powerful principle in human nature, and happily one of those which tend to become stronger, even without express inculcation, from the influences of advancing civilization. The social state is at once so natural, so necessary, and so habitual to man, that, except in some unusual circumstances or by an effort of voluntary abstraction, he never conceives himself otherwise than as a member of a body; and this association is riveted more and more, as mankind are further removed from the state of savage independence. Any condition, therefore, which is essential to a state of society becomes more and more an inseparable part of every person's conception of the state of things which he is born into, and which is the destiny of a human being. Now society between human beings, except in the relation of master and slave, is manifestly impossible on any other footing than that the interests of all are to be consulted. Society between equals can only exist on the understanding that the interests of all are to be regarded equally. And since in all states of civilization, every person, except an absolute monarch, has equals, everyone is obliged to live on these terms with somebody; and in every age some advance is made toward a state in which it will be impossible to live permanently on other terms with anybody. In this way people grow up unable to conceive as possible to them a state of total disregard of other people's interests. They are under a necessity of conceiving themselves as at least abstaining from all the grosser injuries, and (if only for their own protection) living in a state of constant protest against them. They are also familiar with the fact of co-operating with others and proposing to themselves a collective, not an individual, interest as the aim (at least for the time being) of their actions. So long as they are co-operating, their ends are identified with those of others; there is at least a temporary feeling that the interests of others are their own interests. Not only does all strengthening of social ties, and all healthy growth of society, give to each individual a stronger personal interest in practically consulting the welfare of others, it also leads him to identify his *feelings* more and more with their good, or at least with an even greater degree of practical consideration for it. He comes, as though instinctively, to be conscious of himself as a being who *of course* pays regard to others. The good of others becomes to him a thing naturally and necessarily to be attended to, like any of the physical conditions of our existence. Now, whatever amount of this feeling a person has, he is urged by the strongest motives both of interest and of sympathy to demonstrate it, and to the utmost of his power encourage it in others; and even if he has none of it himself, he is as greatly interested as anyone else that others should have it. Consequently, the smallest germs of the feeling are laid hold of and nourished by the contagion of sympathy and the influences of education; and a complete web of corroborative association is woven round it by the powerful agency of the external sanctions. This mode of conceiving ourselves and human life, as civilization goes on, is felt to be more and more natural. Every step in political improvement renders it more so, by removing the sources of opposition of interest and leveling those inequalities of legal privilege between individuals or classes, owing to which there are large portions of mankind whose happiness it is still practicable to disregard. In an improving state of the human mind, the influences are constantly on the increase which tend to generate in each individual a feeling of unity with all the rest; which, if perfect, would make him never think of, or desire, any beneficial condition for himself in the benefits of which they are not included. If we now suppose this feeling of unity to be taught as a religion, and the whole force of education, of institutions, and of opinion directed, as it once was in the case of religion, to make every person grow up from infancy surrounded on all sides both by the profession and the practice of it, I think that no one who can realize this conception will feel any misgiving about the sufficiency of the ultimate sanction for the happiness morality. To any ethical student who finds the realization difficult, I recommend, as a means of facilitating it, the second of M. Comte's two principal works, the *Traité de politique positive*. I entertain the strongest objections to the system of politics and morals set forth in that treatise, but I think it has superabundantly shown the possibility of giving to the service of humanity, even without the aid of belief in a Providence, both the psychological power and the social efficacy of a religion, making it take hold of human life, and color all thought, feeling, and action in a manner of which the greatest ascendancy ever exercised by any religion may be but a type and foretaste; and of which the danger is, not that it should be insufficient, but that it should be so excessive as to interfere unduly with human freedom and individuality.

Neither is it necessary to the feeling which constitutes the binding force of the utilitarian morality on those who recognize it to wait for those social influences which would make its obligation felt by mankind at large. In the comparatively early state of human advancement in which we now live, a person cannot, indeed, feel that entireness of sympathy with all others which would make any real discordance in the general direction of their conduct in life impossible, but already a person in whom the social feeling is at all developed cannot bring himself to think of the rest of his fellow creatures as struggling rivals with him for the means of happiness, whom he must desire to see defeated in their object in order that he may succeed in his. The deeply rooted conception which every individual even now has of himself as a social being tends to make him feel it one of his natural wants that there should be harmony between his feelings and aims and those of his fellow creatures. If differences of opinion and of mental culture make it impossible for him to share many of their actual feelings—perhaps make him denounce and defy those feelings—he still needs to be conscious that his real aim and theirs do not conflict; that he is not opposing himself to what they really wish for, namely, their own good, but is, on the contrary, promoting it. This feeling in most individuals is much inferior in strength to their selfish feelings, and is often wanting altogether. But to those who have it, it possesses all the characters of a natural feeling. It does not present itself to their minds as a superstition of education or a law despotically imposed by the power of society, but as an attribute which it would not be well for them to be without. This conviction is the ultimate sanction of the greatest happiness morality. This it is which makes any mind of well-developed feelings work with, and not against, the outward motives to care for others, afforded by what I have called the external sanctions; and, when those sanctions are wanting or act in an opposite direction, constitutes in itself a powerful internal binding force, in proportion to the sensitiveness and thoughtfulness of the character, since few but those whose mind is a moral blank could bear to lay out their course of life on the plan of paying no regard to others except so far as their own private interest compels.

Chapter IV

Of What Sort of Proof the Principle of Utility Is Susceptible

It has already been remarked that questions of ultimate ends do not admit of proof, in the ordinary acceptation of the term. To be incapable of proof by reasoning is common to all first principles, to the first premises of our knowledge, as well as to those of our conduct. But the former, being matters of fact, may be the subject of a direct appeal to the faculties which judge of fact—namely, our senses and our internal consciousness. Can an appeal be made to the same faculties on questions of practical ends? Or by what other faculty is cognizance taken of them?

Questions about ends are, in other words, questions about what things are desirable. The utilitarian doctrine is that happiness is desirable, and the only thing desirable, as an end; all other things being only desirable as means to that end. What ought to be required of this doctrine, what conditions is it requisite that the doctrine should fulfill—to make good its claim to be believed?

The only proof capable of being given that an object is visible is that people actually see it. The only proof that a sound is audible is that people hear it; and so of the other sources of our experience. In like manner, I apprehend, the sole evidence it is possible to produce that anything is desirable is that people do actually desire it. If the end which the utilitarian doctrine proposes to itself were not, in theory and in practice, acknowledged to be an end, nothing could ever convince any person that it was so. No reason can be given why the general happiness is desirable, except that each person, so far as he believes it to be attainable, desires his own happiness. This, however, being a fact, we have not only all the proof which the case admits of, but all which it is possible to require, that happiness is a good, that each person's happiness is a good to that person, and the general happiness, therefore, a good to the aggregate of all persons. Happiness has made out its title as *one* of the ends of conduct and, consequently, one of the criteria of morality.

But it has not, by this alone, proved itself to be the sole criterion. To do that, it would seem, by the same rule, necessary to show, not only that people desire happiness, but that they never desire anything else. Now it is palpable that they do desire things which, in common language, are decidedly distinguished from happiness. They desire, for example, virtue and the absence of vice no less really than pleasure and the absence of pain. The desire of virtue is not as universal, but it is as authentic a fact as the desire of happiness. And hence the opponents of the utilitarian standard deem that they have a right to infer that there are other ends of human action besides happiness, and that happiness is not the standard of approbation and disapprobation.

But does the utilitarian doctrine deny that people desire virtue, or maintain that virtue is not a thing to be desired? The very reverse. It maintains not only that virtue is to be desired, but that it is to be desired disinterestedly, for itself. Whatever may be the opinion of utilitarian moralists as to the original conditions by which virtue is made virtue, however they may believe (as they do) that actions and dispositions are only virtuous because they promote another end than virtue, yet this being granted, and it having been decided, from considerations of this description, what *is* virtuous, they not only place virtue at the very head of the things which are good as means to the ultimate end, but they also recognize as a psychological fact the possibility of its being, to the individual, a good in itself, without looking to any end beyond it; and hold that the mind is not in a right state, not in a state conformable to utility, not in the state most conducive to the general happiness, unless it does love virtue in this manner—as a thing desirable in itself, even although, in the individual instance, it should not produce those other desirable consequences which it tends to produce, and on account of which it is held to be virtue. This opinion is not, in the smallest degree, a departure from the happiness principle. The ingredients of happiness are very various, and each of them is desirable in itself, and not merely when considered as swelling an aggregate. The principle of utility does not mean that any given pleasure, as music, for instance, or any given exemption from pain, as for example health, is to be looked upon as means to a collective something termed happiness, and to be desired on that account. They are desired and desirable in and for themselves; besides being means, they are a part of the end. Virtue, according to the utilitarian doctrine, is not naturally and originally part of the end, but it is capable of becoming so; and in those who live it disinterestedly it has become so, and is desired and cherished, not as a means to happiness, but as a part of their happiness.

To illustrate this further, we may remember that virtue is not the only thing originally a means, and which if it were not a means to anything else would be and remain indifferent, but which by association with what it is a means to comes to be desired for itself, and that too with the utmost intensity. What, for example, shall we say of the love of money? There is nothing originally more desirable about money than about any heap of glittering pebbles. Its worth is solely that of the things which it will buy; the desires for other things than itself, which it is a means of gratifying. Yet the love of money is not only one of the strongest moving forces of human life, but money is, in many cases, desired in and for itself; the desire to possess it is often stronger than the desire to use it, and goes on increasing when all the desires which point to ends beyond it, to be compassed by it, are falling off. It may, then, be said truly that money is desired not for the sake of an end, but as part of the end. From being a means to happiness, it has come to be itself a principal ingredient of the individual's conception of happiness. The same may be said of the majority of the great objects of human life: power, for example, or fame, except that to each of these there is a certain amount of immediate pleasure annexed, which has at least the semblance of being naturally inherent in them—a thing which cannot be said of money. Still, however, the strongest natural attraction, both of power and of fame, is the immense aid they give to the attainment of our other wishes; and it is the strong association thus generated between them and all our objects of desire which gives to the direct desire of them the intensity it often assumes, so as in some characters to surpass in strength all other desires. In these cases the means have become a part of the end, and a more important part of it than any of the things which they are means to. What was once desired as an instrument for the attainment of happiness has come to be desired for its own sake. In being desired for its own sake it is, however, desired as *part* of happiness. The person is made, or thinks he would be made, happy by its mere possession; and is made unhappy by failure to obtain it. The desire of it is not a different thing from the desire of happiness any more than the love of music or the desire of health. They are included in happiness. They are some of the elements of which the desire of happiness is made up. Happiness is not an abstract idea but a concrete whole; and these are some of its parts. And the utilitarian standard sanctions and approves their being so. Life would be a poor thing, very ill provided with sources of happiness, if there were not this provision of nature by which things originally indifferent, but conducive to, or otherwise associated with, the satisfaction of our primitive desires, become in themselves sources of pleasure more valuable than the primitive pleasures, both in permanency, in the space of human existence that they are capable of covering, and even in intensity.

Virtue, according to the utilitarian conception, is a good of this description. There was no original desire of it, or motive to it, save its conduciveness to pleasure, and especially to protection from pain. But through the association thus formed it may be felt a good in itself, and desired as such with as great intensity as any other good; and with this difference between it and the love of money, of power, or of fame—that all of these may, and often do, render the individual noxious to the other members of the society to which he belongs, whereas there is nothing which makes him so much a blessing to them as the cultivation of the disinterested love of virtue. And consequently, the utilitarian standard, while it tolerates and approves those other acquired desires, up to the point beyond which they would be more injurious to the general happiness than promotive of it, enjoins and requires the cultivation of the love of virtue up to the greatest strength possible, as being above all things important to the general happiness.

It results from the preceding considerations that there is in reality nothing desired except happiness. Whatever is desired otherwise than as a means to some end beyond itself, and ultimately to happiness, is desired as itself a part of happiness, and is not desired for itself until it has become so. Those who desire virtue for its own sake desire it either because the consciousness of it is a pleasure, or because the consciousness of being without it is a pain, or for both reasons united; as in truth the pleasure and pain seldom exist separately, but almost always together—the same person feeling pleasure in the degree of virtue attained, and pain in not having attained more. If one of these gave him no pleasure, and the other no pain, he would not love or desire virtue, or would desire it only for the other benefits which it might produce to himself or to persons whom he cared for.

We have now, then, an answer to the question, of what sort of proof the principle of utility is susceptible. If the opinion which I have now stated is psychologically true—if human nature is so constituted as to desire nothing which is not either a part of happiness or a means of happiness—we can have no other proof, and we require no other, that these are the only things desirable. If so, happiness is the sole end of human action, and the promotion of it the test by which to judge of all human conduct; from whence it necessarily follows that it must be the criterion of morality, since a part is included in the whole.

And now to decide whether this is really so, whether mankind do desire nothing for itself but that which is a pleasure to them, or of which the absence is a pain, we have evidently arrived at a question of fact and experience, dependent, like all similar questions, upon evidence. It can only be determined by practiced self-consciousness and self-observation, assisted by observation of others. I believe that these sources of evidence, impartially consulted, will declare that desiring a thing and finding it pleasant, aversion to it and thinking of it as painful, are phenomena entirely inseparable or, rather, two parts of the same phenomenon—in strictness of language, two different modes of naming the same psychological fact; that to think of an object as desirable (unless for the sake of its consequences) and to think of it as pleasant are one and the same thing; and that to desire anything except in proportion as the idea of it is pleasant is a physical and metaphysical impossibility.

So obvious does this appear to me that I expect it will hardly be disputed; and the objection made will be, not that desire can possibly be directed to anything ultimately except pleasure and exemption from pain, but that the will is a different thing from desire; that a person of confirmed virtue or any other person whose purposes are fixed carries out his purposes without any thought of the pleasure he has in contemplating them or expects to derive from their fulfillment, and persists in acting on them, even though these pleasures are much diminished by changes in his character or decay of his passive sensibilities, or are outweighed by the pains which the pursuit of the purposes may bring upon him. All this I fully admit and have stated it elsewhere as positively and emphatically as anyone. Will, the active phenomenon, is a different thing from desire, the state of passive sensibility, and, though originally an offshoot from it, may in time take root and detach itself from the parent stock, so much so that in the case of a habitual purpose, instead of willing the thing because we desire it, we often desire it only because we will it. This, however, is but an instance of that familiar fact, the power of habit, and is nowise confined to the case of virtuous actions. Many indifferent things which men originally did from a motive of some sort they continue to do from habit. Sometimes this is done unconsciously, the consciousness coming only after the action; at other times with conscious volition, but volition which has become habitual and is put in operation by the force of habit, in opposition perhaps to the deliberate preference, as often happens with those who have contracted habits of vicious or hurtful indulgence. Third and last comes the case in which the habitual act of will in the individual instance is not in contradiction to the general intention prevailing at other times, but in fulfillment of it, as in the case of the person of confirmed virtue and of all who pursue deliberately and consistently any determinate end. The distinction between will and desire thus understood is an authentic and highly important psychological fact; but the fact consists solely in this—that will, like all other parts of our constitution, is amenable to habit, and that we may will from habit what we no longer desire for itself, or desire only because we will it. It is not the less true that will, in the beginning, is entirely produced by desire, including in that term the repelling influence of pain as well as the attractive one of pleasure. Let us take into consideration no longer the person who has a confirmed will to do right, but him in whom that virtuous will is still feeble, conquerable by temptation, and not to be fully relied on; by what means can it be strengthened? How can the will to be virtuous, where it does not exist in sufficient force, be implanted or awakened? Only by making the person *desire* virtue—by making him think of it in a pleasurable light, or of its absence in a painful one. It is by associating the doing right with pleasure, or the wrong with pain, or by eliciting and impressing and bringing home to the person's experience the pleasure naturally involved in the one or the pain in the other, that it is possible to call forth that will to be virtuous which, when confirmed, acts without any thought of either pleasure or pain. Will is the child of desire, and passes out of the dominion of its parent only to come under that of habit. That which is the result of habit affords no presumption of being intrinsically good; and there would be no reason for wishing that the purpose of virtue should become independent of pleasure and pain were it not that the influence of the pleasurable and painful associations which prompt to virtue is not sufficiently to be depended on for unerring constancy of action until it has acquired the support of habit. Both in feeling and in conduct, habit is the only thing which imparts certainty; and it is because of the importance to others of being able to rely absolutely on one's feelings and conduct, and to oneself of being able to rely on one's own, that the will to do right ought to be cultivated into this habitual independence. In other words, this state of the will is a means to good, not intrinsically a good; and does not contradict the doctrine that nothing is a good to human beings but in so far as it is either itself pleasurable or a means of attaining pleasure or averting pain.

But if this doctrine be true, the principle of utility is proved. Whether it is so or not must now be left to the consideration of the thoughtful reader.

Chapter V

On the Connection Between Justice and Utility

In all ages of speculation one of the strongest obstacles to the reception of the doctrine that utility or happiness is the criterion of right and wrong has been drawn from the idea of justice. The powerful sentiment and apparently clear perception which that word recalls with a rapidity and certainty resembling an instinct have seemed to the majority of thinkers to point to an inherent quality in things; to show that the just must have an existence in nature as something absolute, generically distinct from every variety of the expedient and, in idea, opposed to it, though (as is commonly acknowledged) never, in the long run, disjoined from it in fact.

In the case of this, as of our other moral sentiments, there is no necessary connection between the question of its origin and that of its binding force. That a feeling is bestowed on us by nature does not necessarily legitimate all its promptings. The feeling of justice might be a peculiar instinct, and might yet require, like our other instincts, to be controlled and enlightened by a higher reason. If we have intellectual instincts leading us to judge in a particular way, as well as animal instincts that prompt us to act in a particular way, there is no necessity that the former should be more infallible in their sphere than the latter in theirs; it may as well happen that wrong judgments are occasionally suggested by those, as wrong actions by these. But though it is one thing to believe that we have natural feelings of justice, and another to acknowledge them as an ultimate criterion of conduct, these two opinions are very closely connected in point of fact. Mankind are always predisposed to believe that any subjective feeling, not otherwise accounted for, is a revelation of some objective reality. Our present object is to determine whether the reality to which the feeling of justice corresponds is one which needs any such special revelation, whether the justice or injustice of an action is a thing intrinsically peculiar and distinct from all its other qualities or only a combination of certain of those qualities presented under a peculiar aspect. For the purpose of this inquiry it is practically important to consider whether the feeling itself, of justice and injustice, is *sui generis* like our sensations of color and taste or a derivative feeling formed by a combination of others. And this it is the more essential to examine, as people are in general willing enough to allow that objectively the dictates of justice coincide with a part of the field of general expediency; but inasmuch as the subjective mental feeling of justice is different from that which commonly attaches to simple expediency, and, except in the extreme cases of the latter, is far more imperative in its demands, people find it difficult to see in justice only a particular kind or branch of general utility, and think that its superior binding force requires a totally different origin.

To throw light upon this question, it is necessary to attempt to ascertain what is the distinguishing character of justice, or of injustice; what is the quality, or whether there is any quality, attributed in common to all modes of conduct designated as unjust (for justice, like many other moral attributes, is best defined by its opposite), and distinguishing them from such modes of conduct as are disapproved, but without having that particular epithet of disapprobation applied to them. If in everything which men are accustomed to characterize as just or unjust some one common attribute or collection of attributes is always present, we may judge whether this particular attribute or combination of attributes would be capable of gathering round it a sentiment of that peculiar character and intensity by virtue of the general laws of our emotional constitution, or whether the sentiment is inexplicable and requires to be regarded as a special provision of nature. If we find the former to be the case, we shall, in resolving this question, have resolved also the main problem; if the latter, we shall have to seek for some other mode of investigating it.

To find the common attributes of a variety of objects, it is necessary to begin by surveying the objects themselves in the concrete. Let us therefore advert successively to the various modes of action and arrangements of human affairs which are classed, by universal or widely spread opinion, as just or as unjust. The things well known to excite the sentiments associated with those names are of a very multifarious character. I shall pass them rapidly in review, without studying any particular arrangement.

In the first place, it is mostly considered unjust to deprive anyone of his personal liberty, his property, or any other thing which belongs to him by law. Here, therefore, is one instance of the application of the terms "just" and "unjust" in a perfectly definite sense, namely, that it is just to respect, unjust to violate, the *legal rights* of anyone. But this judgment admits of several exceptions, arising from the other forms in which the notions of justice and injustice present themselves. For example, the person who suffers the deprivation may (as the phrase is) have *forfeited* the rights which he is so deprived of—a case to which we shall return presently. But also—

Secondly, the legal rights of which he is deprived may be rights which *ought* not to have belonged to him; in other words, the law which confers on him these rights may be a bad law. When it is so or when (which is the same thing for our purpose) it is supposed to be so, opinions will differ as to the justice or injustice of infringing it. Some maintain that no law, however bad, ought to be disobeyed by an individual citizen; that his opposition to it, if shown at all, should only be shown in endeavoring to get it altered by competent authority. This opinion (which condemns many of the most illustrious benefactors of mankind, and would often protect pernicious institutions against the only weapons which, in the state of things existing at the time, have any chance of succeeding against them) is defended by those who hold it on grounds of expediency, principally on that of the importance to the common interest of mankind, of maintaining inviolate the sentiment of submission to law. Other persons, again, hold the directly contrary opinion that any law, judged to be bad, may blamelessly be disobeyed, even though it be not judged to be unjust but only inexpedient, while others would confine the license of disobedience to the case of unjust laws; but, again, some say that all laws which are inexpedient are unjust, since every law imposes some restriction on the natural liberty of mankind, which restriction is an injustice unless legitimated by tending to their good. Among these diversities of opinion it seems to be universally admitted that there may be unjust laws, and that law, consequently, is not the ultimate criterion of justice, but may give to one person a benefit, or impose on another an evil, which justice condemns. When, however, a law is thought to be unjust, it seems always to be regarded as being so in the same way in which a breach of law is unjust, namely, by infringing somebody's right, which, as it cannot in this case be a legal right, receives a different appellation and is called a moral right. We may say, therefore, that a second case of injustice consists in taking or withholding from any person that to which he has a *moral right*.

Thirdly, it is universally considered just that each person should obtain that (whether good or evil) which he *deserves,* and unjust that he should obtain a good or be made to undergo an evil which he does not deserve. This is, perhaps, the clearest and most emphatic form in which the idea of justice is conceived by the general mind. As it involves the notion of desert, the question arises what constitutes desert? Speaking in a general way, a person is understood to deserve good if he does right, evil if he does wrong; and in a more particular sense, to deserve good from those to whom he does or has done good, and evil from those to whom he does or has done evil. The precept of returning good for evil has been never regarded as a case of the fulfillment of justice, but as one in which the claims of justice are waived, in obedience to other considerations.

Fourthly, it is confessedly unjust to *break faith* with anyone: to violate an engagement, either express or implied, or disappoint expectations raised by our own conduct, at least if we have raised those expectations knowingly and voluntarily. Like the other obligations of justice already spoken of, this one is not regarded as absolute, but as capable of being overruled by a stronger obligation of justice on the other side, or by such conduct on the part of the person concerned as is deemed to absolve us from our obligation to him and to constitute a *forfeiture* of the benefit which he has been led to expect.

Fifthly, it is, by universal admission, inconsistent with justice to be *partial*—to show favor or preference to one person over another in matters to which favor and preference do not properly apply. Impartiality, however, does not seem to be regarded as a duty in itself, but rather as instrumental to some other duty; for it is admitted that favor and preference are not always censurable, and, indeed, the cases in which they are condemned are rather the exception than the rule. A person would be more likely to be blamed than applauded for giving his family or friends no superiority in good offices over strangers when he could do so without violating any other duty; and no one thinks it unjust to seek one person in preference to another as a friend, connection, or companion. Impartiality where rights are concerned is of course obligatory, but this is involved in the more general obligation of giving to everyone his right. A tribunal, for example, must be impartial because it is bound to award, without regard to any other consideration, a disputed object to the one of two parties who has the right to it. There are other cases in which impartiality means being solely influenced by desert, as with those who, in the capacity of judges, preceptors, or parents, administer reward and punishment as such. There are cases, again, in which it means being solely influenced by consideration for the public interest, as in making a selection among candidates for a government employment. Impartiality, in short, as an obligation of justice, may be said to mean being exclusively influenced by the considerations which it is supposed ought to influence the particular case in hand, and resisting solicitation of any motives which prompt to conduct different from what those considerations would dictate.

Nearly allied to the idea of impartiality is that of *equality,* which often enters as a component part both into the conception of justice and into the practice of it, and, in the eyes of many persons, constitutes its essence. But in this, still more than in any other case, the notion of justice varies in different persons, and always conforms in its variations to their notion of utility. Each person maintains that equality is the dictate of justice, except where he thinks that expediency requires inequality. The justice of giving equal protection to the rights of all is maintained by those who support the most outrageous inequality in the rights themselves. Even in slave countries it is theoretically admitted that the rights of the slave, such as they are, ought to be as sacred as those of the master, and that a tribunal which fails to enforce them with equal strictness is wanting in justice; while, at the same time, institutions which leave to the slave scarcely any rights to enforce are not deemed unjust because they are not deemed inexpedient. Those who think that utility requires distinctions of rank do not consider it unjust that riches and social privileges should be unequally dispensed; but those who think this inequality inexpedient think it unjust also. Whoever thinks that government is necessary sees no injustice in as much inequality as is constituted by giving to the magistrate powers not granted to other people. Even among those who hold leveling doctrines, there are differences of opinion about expediency. Some communists consider it unjust that the produce of the labor of the community should be shared on any other principle than that of exact equality; others think it just that those should receive most whose wants are greatest; while others hold that those who work harder, or who produce more, or whose services are more valuable to the community, may justly claim a larger quota in the division of the produce. And the sense of natural justice may be plausibly appealed to in behalf of every one of these opinions.

Among so many diverse applications of the term "justice," which yet is not regarded as ambiguous, it is a matter of some difficulty to seize the mental link which holds them together, and on which the moral sentiment adhering to the term essentially depends. Perhaps, in this embarrassment, some help may be derived from the history of the word, as indicated by its etymology.

In most if not in all languages, the etymology of the word which corresponds to "just" points distinctly to an origin connected with the ordinances of law. *Justum* is a form of *jussum,* that which has been ordered. *Dikaion* comes directly from *dike,* a suit at law. *Recht,* from which came *right* and *righteous,* is synonymous with law. The courts of justice, the administration of justice, are the courts and the administration of law. *La justice,* in French, is the established term for judicature. I am not committing the fallacy, imputed with some show of truth to Horne Tooke, of assuming that a word must still continue to mean what it originally meant. Etymology is slight evidence of what the idea now signified is, but the very best evidence of how it sprang up. There can, I think, be no doubt that the *idée mère,* the primitive element, in the formation of the notion of justice was conformity to law. It constituted the entire idea among the Hebrews, up to the birth of Christianity; as might be expected in the case of a people whose laws attempted to embrace all subjects on which precepts were required, and who believed those laws to be a direct emanation from the Supreme Being. But other nations, and in particular the Greeks and Romans, who knew that their laws had been made originally, and still continued to be made, by men, were not afraid to admit that those men might make bad laws; might do, by law, the same things, and from the same motives, which if done by individuals without the sanction of law would be called unjust. And hence the sentiment of injustice came to be attached, not to all violations of law, but only to violations of such laws as *ought* to exist, including such as ought to exist but do not, and to laws themselves if supposed to be contrary to what ought to be law. In this manner the idea of law and of its injunctions was still predominant in the notion of justice, even when the laws actually in force ceased to be accepted as the standard of it.

It is true that mankind consider the idea of justice and its obligations as applicable to many things which neither are, nor is it desired that they should be, regulated by law. Nobody desires that laws should interfere with the whole detail of private life; yet everyone allows that in all daily conduct a person may and does show himself to be either just or unjust. But even here, the idea of the breach of what ought to be law still lingers in a modified shape. It would always give us pleasure, and chime in with our feelings of fitness, that acts which we deem unjust should be punished, though we do not always think it expedient that this should be done by the tribunals. We forego that gratification on account of incidental inconveniences. We should be glad to see just conduct enforced and injustice repressed, even in the minutest details, if we were not, with reason, afraid of trusting the magistrate with so unlimited an amount of power over individuals. When we think that a person is bound in justice to do a thing, it is an ordinary form of language to say that he ought to be compelled to do it. We should be gratified to see the obligation enforced by anybody who had the power. If we see that its enforcement by law would be inexpedient, we lament the impossibility, we consider the impunity given to injustice as an evil, and strive to make amends for it by bringing a strong expression of our own and the public disapprobation to bear upon the offender. Thus the idea of legal constraint is still the generating idea of the notion of justice, though undergoing several transformations before that notion as it exists in an advanced state of society becomes complete.

The above is, I think, a true account, as far as it goes, of the origin and progressive growth of the idea of justice. But we must observe that it contains as yet nothing to distinguish that obligation from moral obligation in general. For the truth is that the idea of penal sanction, which is the essence of law, enters not only into the conception of injustice, but into that of any kind of wrong. We do not call anything wrong unless we mean to imply that a person ought to be punished in some way or other for doing it—if not by law, by the opinion of his fellow creatures; if not by opinion, by the reproaches of his own conscience. This seems the real turning point of the distinction between morality and simple expediency. It is a part of the notion of duty in every one of its forms that a person may rightfully be compelled to fulfill it. Duty is a thing which may be *exacted* from a person, as one exacts a debt. Unless we think that it may be exacted from him, we do not call it his duty. Reasons of prudence, or the interest of other people, may militate against actually exacting it, but the person himself, it is clearly understood, would not be entitled to complain. There are other things, on the contrary, which we wish that people should do, which we like or admire them for doing, perhaps dislike or despise them for not doing, but yet admit that they are not bound to do; it is not a case of moral obligation; we do not blame them, that is, we do not think that they are proper objects of punishment. How we come by these ideas of deserving and not deserving punishment will appear, perhaps, in the sequel; but I think there is no doubt that this distinction lies at the bottom of the notions of right and wrong; that we call any conduct wrong, or employ, instead, some other term of dislike or disparagement, according as we think that the person ought, or ought not, be punished for it; and we say it would be right to do so and so, or merely that it would be desirable or laudable, according as we would wish to see the person whom it concerns compelled, or only persuaded and exhorted, to act in that manner.[3]

This, therefore, being the characteristic difference which marks off, not justice, but morality in general from the remaining provinces of expediency and worthiness, the character is still to be sought which distinguishes justice from other branches of morality. Now it is known that ethical writers divide moral duties into two classes, denoted by the ill-chosen expressions, duties of perfect and of imperfect obligation; the latter being those in which, though the act is obligatory, the particular occasions of performing it are left to our choice, as in the case of charity or beneficence, which we are indeed bound to practice but not toward any definite person, nor at any prescribed time. In the more precise language of philosophic jurists, duties of perfect obligation are those duties in virtue of which a correlative *right* resides in some person or persons; duties of imperfect obligation are those moral obligations which do not give birth to any right. I think it will be found that this distinction exactly coincides with that which exists between justice and the other obligations of morality. In our survey of the various popular acceptations of justice, the term appeared generally to involve the idea of a personal right— a claim on the part of one or more individuals, like that which the law gives when it confers a proprietary or other legal right. Whether the injustice consists in depriving a person of a possession, or in breaking faith with him, or in treating him worse than he deserves, or worse than other people who have no greater claims—in each case the supposition implies two things: a wrong done, and some assignable person who is wronged. Injustice may also be done by treating a person better than others; but the wrong in this case is to his competitors, who are also assignable persons. It seems to me that this feature in the case—a right in some person, correlative to the moral obligation—constitutes the specific difference between justice and generosity or beneficence. Justice implies something which it is not only right to do, and wrong not to do, but which some individual person can claim from us as his moral right. No one has a moral right to our generosity or beneficence because we are not morally bound to practice those virtues toward any given individual. And it will be found with respect to this as to every correct definition that the instances which seem to conflict with it are those which most confirm it. For if a moralist attempts, as some have done, to make out that mankind generally, though not any given individual, have a right to all the good we can do them,

---

[3] See this point enforced and illustrated by Professor Bain, in an admirable chapter (entitled "The Ethical Emotions, or the Moral Sense"), of the second of the two treatises composing his elaborate and profound work on the Mind [*The Emotions and the Will*, 1859].

he at once, by that thesis, includes generosity and beneficence within the category of justice. He is obliged to say that our utmost exertions are *due* to our fellow creatures, thus assimilating them to a debt; or that nothing less can be a sufficient *return* for what society does for us, thus classing the case as one of gratitude; both of which are acknowledged cases of justice, and not of the virtue of beneficence; and whoever does not place the distinction between justice and morality in general, where we have now placed it, will be found to make no distinction between them at all, but to merge all morality in justice.

Having thus endeavored to determine the distinctive elements which enter into the composition of the idea of justice, we are ready to enter on the inquiry whether the feeling which accompanies the idea is attached to it by a special dispensation of nature, or whether it could have grown up, by any known laws, out of the idea itself; and, in particular, whether it can have originated in considerations of general expediency.

I conceive that the sentiment itself does not arise from anything which would commonly or correctly be termed an idea of expediency, but that, though the sentiment does not, whatever is moral in it does.

We have seen that the two essential ingredients in the sentiment of justice are the desire to punish a person who has done harm and the knowledge or belief that there is some definite individual or individuals to whom harm has been done.

Now it appears to me that the desire to punish a person who has done harm to some individual is a spontaneous outgrowth from two sentiments, both in the highest degree natural and which either are or resemble instincts: the impulse of self-defense and the feeling of sympathy.

It is natural to resent and to repel or retaliate any harm done or attempted against ourselves or against those with whom we sympathize. The origin of this sentiment it is not necessary here to discuss. Whether it be an instinct or a result of intelligence, it is, we know, common to all animal nature; for every animal tries to hurt those who have hurt, or who it thinks are about to hurt, itself or its young. Human beings, on this point, only differ from other animals in two particulars. First, in being capable of sympathizing, not solely with their offspring, or, like some of the more noble animals, with some superior animal who is kind to them, but with all human, and even with all sentient, beings; secondly, in having a more developed intelligence, which gives a wider range to the whole of their sentiments, whether self-regarding or sympathetic. By virtue of his superior intelligence, even apart from his superior range of sympathy, a human being is capable of apprehending a community of interest between himself and the human society of which he forms a part, such that any conduct which threatens the security of the society generally is threatening to his own, and calls forth his instinct (if instinct it be) of self-defense. The same superiority of intelligence, joined to the power of sympathizing with human beings generally, enables him to attach himself to the collective idea of his tribe, his country, or mankind in such a manner that any act hurtful to them raises his instinct of sympathy and urges him to resistance.

The sentiment of justice, in that one of its elements which consists of the desire to punish, is thus, I conceive, the natural feeling of retaliation or vengeance, rendered by intellect and sympathy applicable to those injuries, that is, to those hurts, which wound us through, or in common with, society at large. This sentiment, in itself, has nothing moral in it; what is moral is the exclusive subordination of it to the social sympathies, so as to wait on and obey their call. For the natural feeling would make us resent indiscriminately whatever anyone does that is disagreeable to us; but, when moralized by the social feeling, it only acts in the directions conformable to the general good: just persons resenting a hurt to society, though not otherwise a hurt to themselves, and not resenting a hurt to themselves, however painful, unless it be of the kind which society has a common interest with them in the repression of.

It is no objection against this doctrine to say that, when we feel our sentiment of justice outraged, we are not thinking of society at large or of any collective interest, but only of the individual case. It is common enough, certainly, though the reverse of commendable, to feel resentment merely because we have suffered pain; but a person whose resentment is really a moral feeling, that is, who considers whether an act is blamable before he allows himself to resent it—such a person, though he may not say expressly to himself that he is standing up for the interest of society, certainly does feel that he is asserting a rule which is for the benefit of others as well as for his own. If he is not feeling this, if he is regarding the act solely as it affects him individually, he is not consciously just; he is not concerning himself about the justice of his actions. This is admitted even by anti-utilitarian moralists. When Kant (as before remarked) propounds as the fundamental principle of morals, "So act that thy rule of conduct might be adopted as a law by all rational beings," he virtually acknowledges that the interest of mankind collectively, or at least of mankind indiscriminately, must be in the mind of the agent when conscientiously deciding on the morality of the act. Otherwise he uses words without a meaning; for that a rule even of utter selfishness could not *possibly* be adopted by all rational beings—that there is any insuperable obstacle in the nature of things to its adoption—cannot be even plausibly maintained. To give any meaning to Kant's principle, the sense put upon it must be that we ought to shape our conduct by a rule which all rational beings might adopt *with benefit to their collective interest*.

To recapitulate: the idea of justice supposes two things—a rule of conduct and a sentiment which sanctions the rule. The first must be supposed common to all mankind and intended for their good. The other (the sentiment) is a desire that punishment may be suffered by those who infringe the rule. There is involved, in addition, the conception of some definite person who suffers by the infringement, whose rights (to use the expression appropriated to the case) are violated by it. And the sentiment of justice appears to me to be the animal desire to repel or retaliate a hurt or damage to oneself or to those with whom one sympathizes, widened so as to include all persons, by the human capacity of enlarged sympathy and the human conception of intelligent self-interest. From the latter elements the feeling derives its morality; from the former, its peculiar impressiveness and energy of self-assertion.

I have, throughout, treated the idea of a *right* residing in the injured person and violated by the injury, not as a separate element in the composition of the idea and sentiment, but as one of the forms in which the other two elements clothe themselves. These elements are a hurt to some assignable person or persons, on the one hand, and a demand for punishment, on the other. An examination of our own minds, I think, will show that these two things include all that we mean when we speak of violation of a right. When we call anything a person's right, we mean that he has a valid claim on society to protect him in the possession of it, either by the force of law or by that of education and opinion. If he has what we consider a sufficient claim, on whatever account, to have something guaranteed to him by society, we say that he has a right to it. If we desire to prove that anything does not belong to him by right, we think this done as soon as it is admitted that society ought not to take measures for securing it to him, but should leave him to chance or to his own exertions. Thus a person is said to have a right to what he can earn in fair professional competition, because society ought not to allow any other person to hinder him from endeavoring to earn in that manner as much as he can. But he has not a right to three hundred a year, though he may happen to be earning it; because society is not called on to provide that he shall earn that sum. On the contrary, if he owns ten thousand pounds three-per-cent stock, he *has* a right to three hundred a year because society has come under an obligation to provide him with an income of that amount.

To have a right, then, is, I conceive, to have something which society ought to defend me in the possession of. If the objector goes on to ask why it ought, I can give him no other reason than general utility. If that expression does not seem to convey a sufficient feeling of the strength of the obligation, nor to account for the peculiar energy of the feeling, it is because there goes to the composition of the sentiment, not a rational only but also an animal element—the thirst for retaliation; and this thirst derives its intensity, as well as its moral justification, from the extraordinarily important and impressive kind of utility which is concerned. The interest involved is that of security, to everyone's feelings the most vital of all interests. All other earthly benefits are needed by one person, not needed by another; and many of them can, if necessary, be cheerfully foregone or replaced by something else; but security no human being can possibly do without; on it we depend for all our immunity from evil and for the whole value of all and every good, beyond the passing moment, since nothing but the gratification of the instant could be of any worth to us if we could be deprived of everything the next instant by whoever was momentarily stronger than ourselves. Now this most indispensable of all necessaries, after physical nutriment, cannot be had unless the machinery for providing it is kept unintermittedly in active play. Our notion, therefore, of the claim we have on our fellow creatures to join in making safe for us the very groundwork of our existence gathers feelings around it so much more intense than those concerned in any of the more common cases of utility that the difference in degree (as is often the case in psychology) becomes a real difference in kind. The claim assumes that character of absoluteness, that apparent infinity and incommensurability with all other considerations which constitute the distinction between the feeling of right and wrong and that of ordinary expediency and inexpediency. The feelings concerned are so powerful, and we count so positively on finding a responsive feeling in others (all being alike interested) that *ought* and *should* grow into *must,* and recognized indispensability becomes a moral necessity, analogous to physical, and often not inferior to it in binding force.

If the preceding analysis, or something resembling it, be not the correct account of the notion of justice—if justice be totally independent of utility, and be a standard *per se,* which the mind can recognize by simple introspection of itself—it is hard to understand why that internal oracle is so ambiguous, and why so many things appear either just or unjust, according to the light in which they are regarded.

We are continually informed that utility is an uncertain standard, which every different person interprets differently, and that there is no safety but in the immutable, ineffaceable, and unmistakable dictates of justice, which carry their evidence in themselves and are independent of the fluctuations of opinion. One would suppose from this that on questions of justice there could be no controversy; that, if we take that for our rule, its application to any given case could leave us in as little doubt as a mathematical demonstration. So far is this from being the fact that there is as much difference of opinion, and as much discussion, about what is just as about what is useful to society. Not only have different nations and individuals different notions of justice, but in the mind of one and the same individual, justice is not some one rule, principle, or maxim, but many which do not always coincide in their dictates, and, in choosing between which, he is guided either by some extraneous standard or by his own personal predilections.

For instance, there are some who say that it is unjust to punish anyone for the sake of example to others, that punishment is just only when intended for the good of the sufferer himself. Others maintain the extreme reverse, contending that to punish persons who have attained years of discretion, for their own benefit, is despotism and injustice, since, if the matter at issue is solely their own good, no one has a right to control their own judgment of it; but that they may justly be punished to prevent evil to others, this being the exercise of the legitimate right of self-defense. Mr. Owen, again, affirms that it is unjust to punish at all, for the criminal did not make his own character; his education and the circumstances which surrounded him have made him a criminal, and for these he is not responsible. All these opinions are extremely plausible; and so long as the question is argued as one of justice simply, without going down to the principles which lie under justice and are the source of its authority, I am unable to see how any of these reasoners can be refuted. For in truth every one of the three builds upon rules of justice confessedly true. The first appeals to the acknowledged injustice of singling out an individual and making him a sacrifice, without his consent, for other people's benefit. The second relies on the acknowledged justice of self-defense and the admitted injustice of forcing one person to conform to another's notions of what constitutes his good. The Owenite invokes the admitted principle that it is unjust to punish anyone for what he cannot help. Each is triumphant so long as he is not compelled to take into consideration any other maxims of justice than the one he has selected; but as soon as their several maxims are brought face to face, each disputant seems to have exactly as much to say for himself as the others. No one of them can carry out his own notion of justice without trampling upon another equally binding. These are difficulties; they have always been felt to be such; and many devices have been invented to turn rather than to overcome them. As a refuge from the last of the three, men imagined what they called the freedom of the will—fancying that they could not justify punishing a man whose will is in a thoroughly hateful state unless it be supposed to have come into that state through no influence of anterior circumstances. To escape from the other difficulties, a favorite contrivance has been the fiction of a contract whereby at some unknown period all the members of society engaged to obey the laws and consented to be punished for any disobedience to them, thereby giving to their legislators the right, which it is assumed they would not otherwise have had, of punishing them, either for their own good or for that of society. This happy thought was considered to get rid of the whole difficulty and to legitimate the infliction of punishment, in virtue of another received maxim of justice, *volenti non fit injuria*—that is not unjust which is done with the consent of the person who is supposed to be hurt by it. I need hardly remark that, even if the consent were not a mere fiction, this maxim is not superior in authority to the others which it is brought in to supersede. It is, on the contrary, an instructive specimen of the loose and irregular manner in which supposed principles of justice grow up. This particular one evidently came into use as a help to the coarse exigencies of courts of law, which are sometimes obliged to be content with very uncertain presumptions, on account of the greater evils which would often arise from any attempt on their part to cut finer. But even courts of law are not able to adhere consistently to the maxim, for they allow voluntary engagements to be set aside on the ground of fraud, and sometimes on that of mere mistake or misinformation.

Again, when the legitimacy of inflicting punishment is admitted, how many conflicting conceptions of justice come to light in discussing the proper apportionment of punishments to offenses. No rule on the subject recommends itself so strongly to the primitive and spontaneous sentiment of justice as the *lex talionis,* an eye for an eye and a tooth for a tooth. Though this principle of the Jewish and of the Mohammedan law has been generally abandoned in Europe as a practical maxim, there is, I suspect, in most minds, a secret hankering after it; and when retribution accidentally falls on an offender in that precise shape, the general feeling of satisfaction evinced bears witness how natural is the sentiment to which this repayment in kind is acceptable. With many, the test of justice in penal infliction is that the punishment should be proportioned to the offense, meaning that it should be exactly measured by the moral guilt of the culprit (whatever be their standard for measuring moral guilt), the consideration what amount of punishment is necessary to deter from the offense having nothing to do with the question of justice, in their estimation; while there are others to whom that consideration is all in all, who maintain that it is not just, at least for man, to inflict on a fellow creature, whatever may be his offenses, any amount of suffering beyond the least that will suffice to prevent him from repeating, and others from imitating, his misconduct.

To take another example from a subject already once referred to. In cooperative industrial association, is it just or not that talent or skill should give a title to superior remuneration? On the negative side of the question it is argued that whoever does the best he can deserves equally well, and ought not in justice to be put in a position of inferiority for no fault of his own; that superior abilities have already advantages more than enough, in the admiration they excite, the personal influence they command, and the internal sources of satisfaction attending them, without adding to these a superior share of the world's goods; and that society is bound in justice rather to make compensation to the less favored for this unmerited inequality of advantages than to aggravate it. On the contrary side it is contended that society receives more from the more efficient laborer; that, his services being more useful, society owes him a larger return for them; that a greater share of the joint result is actually his work, and not to allow his claim to it is a kind of robbery; that, if he is only to receive as much as others, he can only be justly required to produce as much, and to give a smaller amount of time and exertion, proportioned to his superior efficiency. Who shall decide between these appeals to conflicting principles of justice? Justice has in this case two sides to it, which it is impossible to bring into harmony, and the two disputants have chosen opposite sides; the one looks to what it is just that the individual should receive, the other to what it is just that the community should give. Each, from his own point of view, is unanswerable; and any choice between them, on grounds of justice, must be perfectly arbitrary. Social utility alone can decide the preference.

How many, again, and how irreconcilable are the standards of justice to which reference is made in discussing the repartition of taxation. One opinion is that payment to the state should be in numerical proportion to pecuniary means. Others think that justice dictates what they term graduated taxation— taking a higher percentage from those who have more to spare. In point of natural justice a strong case might be made for disregarding means altogether, and taking the same absolute sum (whenever it could be got) from everyone; as the subscribers to a mess or to a club all pay the same sum for the same privileges, whether they can all equally afford it or not. Since the protection (it might be said) of law and government is afforded to and is equally required by all, there is no injustice in making all buy it at the same price. It is reckoned justice, not injustice, that a dealer should charge to all customers the same price for the same article, not a price varying according to their means of payment. This doctrine, as applied to taxation, finds no advocates because it conflicts so strongly with man's feelings of humanity and of social expediency; but the principle of justice which it invokes is as true and as binding as those which can be appealed to against it. Accordingly it exerts a tacit influence on the line of defense employed for other modes of assessing taxation. People feel obliged to argue that the state does more for the rich man than for the poor, as a justification for its taking more from them, though this is in reality not true, for the rich would be far better able to protect themselves, in the absence of law or government, than the poor, and indeed would probably be successful in converting the poor into their slaves. Others, again, so far defer to the same conception of justice as to maintain that all should pay an equal capitation tax for the protection of their persons (these being of equal value to all), and an unequal tax for the protection of their property, which is unequal. To this others reply that the all of one man is as valuable to him as the all of another. From these confusions there is no other mode of extrication than the utilitarian.

Is, then, the difference between the just and the expedient a merely imaginary distinction? Have mankind been under a delusion in thinking that justice is a more sacred thing than policy, and that the latter ought only to be listened to after the former has been satisfied? By no means. The exposition we have given of the nature and origin of the sentiment recognizes a real distinction; and no one of those who profess the most sublime contempt for the consequences of actions as an element in their morality attaches more importance to the distinction than I do. While I dispute the pretensions of any theory which sets up an imaginary standard of justice not grounded on utility, I account the justice which is grounded on utility to be the chief part, and incomparably the most sacred and binding part, of all morality. Justice is a name for certain classes of moral rules which concern the essentials of human well-being more nearly, and are therefore of more absolute obligation, than any other rules for the guidance of life; and the notion which we have found to be of the essence of the idea of justice—that of a right residing in an individual—implies and testifies to this more binding obligation.

The moral rules which forbid mankind to hurt one another (in which we must never forget to include wrongful interference with each other's freedom) are more vital to human well-being than any maxims, however important, which only point out the best mode of managing some department of human affairs. They have also the peculiarity that they are the main element in determining the whole of the social feelings of mankind. It is their observance which alone preserves peace among human beings; if obedience to them were not the rule, and disobedience the exception, everyone would see in everyone else an enemy against whom he must be perpetually guarding himself. What is hardly less important, these are the precepts which mankind have the strongest and the most direct inducements for impressing upon one another. By merely giving to each other prudential instruction or exhortation, they may gain, or think they gain, nothing; in inculcating on each other the duty of positive beneficence, they have an unmistakable interest, but far less in degree; a person may possibly not need the benefits of others, but he always needs that they should not do him hurt. Thus the moralities which protect every individual from being harmed by others, either directly or by being hindered in his freedom of pursuing his own good, are at once those which he himself has most at heart and those which he has the strongest interest in publishing and enforcing by word and deed. It is by a person's observance of these that his fitness to exist as one of the fellowship of human beings is tested and decided; for on that depends his being a nuisance or not to those with whom he is in contact. Now it is these moralities primarily which compose the obligations of justice. The most marked cases of injustice, and those which give the tone to the feeling of repugnance which characterizes the sentiment, are acts of wrongful aggression or wrongful exercise of power over someone; the next are those which consist in wrongfully withholding from him something which is his due—in both cases inflicting on him a positive hurt, either in the form of direct suffering or of the privation of some good which he had reasonable ground, either of a physical or of a social kind, for counting upon.

The same powerful motives which command the observance of these primary moralities enjoin the punishment of those who violate them; and as the impulses of self-defense, of defense of others, and of vengeance are all called forth against such persons, retribution, or evil for evil, becomes closely connected with the sentiment of justice, and is universally included in the idea. Good for good is also one of the dictates of justice; and this, though its social utility is evident, and though it carries with it a natural human feeling, has not at first sight that obvious connection with hurt or injury which, existing in the most elementary cases of just and unjust, is the source of the characteristic intensity of the sentiment. But the connection, though less obvious, is not less real. He who accepts benefits and denies a return of them when needed inflicts a real hurt by disappointing one of the most natural and reasonable of expectations, and one which he must at least tacitly have encouraged, otherwise the benefits would seldom have been conferred. The important rank, among human evils and wrongs, of the disappointment of expectations is shown in the fact that it constitutes the principal criminality of two such highly immoral acts as a breach of friendship and a breach of promise. Few hurts which human beings can sustain are greater, and none wound more, than when that on which they habitually and with full assurance relied fails them in the hour of need; and few wrongs are greater than this mere withholding of good; none excite more resentment, either in the person suffering or in a sympathizing spectator. The principle, therefore, of giving to each what they deserve, that is, good for good as well as evil for evil, is not only included within the idea of justice as we have defined it, but is a proper object of that intensity of sentiment which places the just in human estimation above the simply expedient.

Most of the maxims of justice current in the world, and commonly appealed to in its transactions, are simply instrumental to carrying into effect the principles of justice which we have now spoken of. That a person is only responsible for what he has done voluntarily, or could voluntarily have avoided, that it is unjust to condemn any person unheard; that the punishment ought to be proportioned to the offense, and the like, are maxims intended to prevent the just principle of evil for evil from being perverted to the infliction of evil without that justification. The greater part of these common maxims have come into use from the practice of courts of justice, which have been naturally led to a more complete recognition and elaboration than was likely to suggest itself to others, of the rules necessary to enable them to fulfill their double function—of inflicting punishment when due, and of awarding to each person his right.

That first of judicial virtues, impartiality, is an obligation of justice, partly for the reason last mentioned, as being a necessary condition of the fulfillment of other obligations of justice. But this is not the only source of the exalted rank, among human obligations, of those maxims of equality and impartiality, which, both in popular estimation and in that of the most enlightened, are included among the precepts of justice. In one point of view, they may be considered as corollaries from the principles already laid down. If it is a duty to do to each according to his deserts, returning good for good, as well as repressing evil by evil, it necessarily follows that we should treat all equally well (when no higher duty forbids) who have deserved equally well of *us,* and that society should treat all equally well who have deserved equally well of *it,* that is, who have deserved equally well absolutely. This is the highest abstract standard of social and distributive justice, toward which all institutions and the efforts of all virtuous citizens should be made in the utmost possible degree to converge. But this great moral duty rests upon a still deeper foundation, being a direct emanation from the first principle of morals, and not a mere logical corollary from secondary or derivative doctrines. It is involved in the very meaning of utility, or the greatest happiness principle. That principle is a mere form of words without rational signification unless one person's happiness, supposed equal in degree (with the proper allowance made for kind), is counted for exactly as much as another's. Those conditions being supplied, Bentham's dictum, "everybody to count for one, nobody for more than one," might be written under the principle of utility as an explanatory commentary.[4] The equal claim of everybody to happiness, in the estimation of

---

4 This implication, in the first principle of the utilitarian scheme, of perfect impartiality between persons is regarded by Mr. Herbert Spencer (in his *Social Statics*) as a disproof of the pretensions of utility to be a sufficient guide to right; since (he says) the principle of utility presupposes the anterior principle that everybody has an equal right to happiness. It may be more correctly described as supposing that equal amounts of happiness are equally de-

the moralist and of the legislator, involves an equal claim to all the means of happiness except in so far as the inevitable conditions of human life and the general interest in which that of every individual is included set limits to the maxim; and those limits ought to be strictly construed. As every other maxim of justice, so this is by no means applied or held applicable universally; on the contrary, as I have already remarked, it bends to every person's ideas of social expediency. But in whatever case it is deemed applicable at all, it is held to be the dictate of justice. All persons are deemed to have a *right* to equality of treatment, except when some recognized social expediency requires the reverse. And hence all social inequalities which have ceased to be considered expedient assume the character, not of simple inexpediency, but of injustice, and appear so tyrannical that people are apt to wonder how they ever could have been tolerated—forgetful that they themselves, perhaps, tolerate other inequalities under an equally mistaken notion of expediency, the correction of which would make that which they approve seem quite as monstrous as what they have at last learned to condemn. The entire history of social improvement has been a series of transitions by which one custom or institution after another, from being a supposed primary necessity of social existence, has passed into the rank of a universally stigmatized injustice and tyranny. So it has been with the distinctions of slaves and freemen, nobles and serfs, patricians and plebeians; and so it will be, and in part already is, with the aristocracies of color, race, and sex.

It appears from what has been said that justice is a name for certain moral requirements which, regarded collectively, stand higher in the scale of social utility, and are therefore of more paramount obligation, than any others, though particular cases may occur in which some other social duty is so important as to overrule any one of the general maxims of justice. Thus, to save a life, it may not only be allowable, but a duty, to steal or take by force the necessary food or medicine, or to kidnap and compel to officiate the only

---

sirable, whether felt by the same or different persons. This, however, is not a *pre*supposition, not a premise needful to support the principle of utility, but the very principle itself; for what is the principle of utility if it be not that "happiness" and "desirable" are synonymous terms? If there is any anterior principle implied, it can be no other than this, that the truths of arithmetic are applicable to the valuation of happiness, as of all other measurable quantities.

(Mr. Herbert Spencer, in a private communication on the subject of the preceding note, objects to being considered an opponent of utilitarianism and states that he regards happiness as the ultimate end of morality; but deems that end only partially attainable by empirical generalizations from the observed results of conduct, and completely attainable only by deducing, from the laws of life and the conditions of existence, what kinds of action necessarily tend to produce happiness, and what kinds to produce unhappiness. With the exception of the word "necessarily," I have no dissent to express from this doctrine: and (omitting that word) I am not aware that any modern advocate of utilitarianism is of a different opinion. Bentham, certainly, to whom in the *Social Statics* Mr. Spencer particularly referred, is, least of all writers, chargeable with unwillingness to deduce the effect of actions on happiness from the laws of human nature and the universal conditions of human life. The common charge against him is of relying too exclusively upon such deductions and declining altogether to be bound by the generalizations from specific experience which Mr. Spencer thinks that utilitarians generally confine themselves to. My own opinion (and, as I recollect, Mr. Spencer's) is that in ethics, as in all other branches of scientific study, the consilience of the results of both these processes, each corroborating and verifying the other, is requisite to give to any general proposition the kind and degree of evidence which constitutes scientific proof.)

qualified medical practitioner. In such cases, as we do not call anything justice which is not a virtue, we usually say, not that justice must give way to some other moral principle, but that what is just in ordinary cases is, by reason of that other principle, not just in the particular case. By this useful accommodation of language, the character of indefeasibility attributed to justice is kept up, and we are saved from the necessity of maintaining that there can be laudable injustice.

The considerations which have now been adduced resolve, I conceive, the only real difficulty in the utilitarian theory of morals. It has always been evident that all cases of justice are also cases of expediency; the difference is in the peculiar sentiment which attaches to the former, as contradistinguished from the latter. If this characteristic sentiment has been sufficiently accounted for; if there is no necessity to assume for it any peculiarity of origin; if it is simply the natural feeling of resentment, moralized by being made coextensive with the demands of social good; and if this feeling not only does but ought to exist in all the classes of cases to which the idea of justice corresponds— that idea no longer presents itself as a stumbling block to the utilitarian ethics. Justice remains the appropriate name for certain social utilities which are vastly more important, and therefore more absolute and imperative, than any others are as a class (though not more so than others may be in particular cases); and which, therefore, ought to be, as well as naturally are, guarded by a sentiment, not only different in degree, but also in kind; distinguished from the milder feeling which attaches to the mere idea of promoting human pleasure or convenience at once by the more definite nature of its commands and by the sterner character of its sanctions.

Two Concepts of Rules
John Rawls

In this paper I want to show the importance of the distinction between justifying a practice[1] and justifying a particular action falling under it, and I want to explain the logical basis of this distinction and how it is possible to

From John Rawls, ("Two Concepts of Rules," *The Philosophical Review* 64 (1955), 3–32. Reprinted by permission of *The Philosophical Review* and the author. This is a revision of a paper given at the Harvard Philosophy Club on April 30, 1954. John Rawls, a professor of philosophy at Harvard University, is the author of several important articles in moral and political philosophy and has expanded the argument of these articles in his book *A Theory of Justice* (Cambridge, Mass.: Harvard University Press, 1971).

[1] I use the word "practice" throughout as a sort of technical term meaning any form of activity specified by a system of rules which defines offices, roles, moves, penalties, defenses, and so on, and which gives the activity its structure. As examples one may think of games and rituals, trials and parliaments.

miss its significance. While the distinction has frequently been made,[2] and is now becoming commonplace, there remains the task of explaining the tendency either to overlook it altogether, or to fail to appreciate its importance.

To show the importance of the distinction I am going to defend utilitarianism against those objections which have traditionally been made against it in connection with punishment and the obligation to keep promises. I hope to show that if one uses the distinction in question then one can state utilitarianism in a way which makes it a much better explication of our considered moral judgments than these traditional objections would seem to admit.[3] Thus the importance of the distinction is shown by the way it strengthens the utilitarian view regardless of whether that view is completely defensible or not.

To explain how the significance of the distinction may be overlooked, I am going to discuss two conceptions of rules. One of these conceptions conceals the importance of distinguishing between the justification of a rule or practice and the justification of a particular action falling under it. The other conception makes it clear why this distinction must be made and what is its logical basis.

I

The subject of punishment, in the sense of attaching legal penalties to the violation of legal rules, has always been a troubling moral question.[4] The trouble about it has not been that people disagree as to whether or not punishment is justifiable. Most people have held that, freed from certain abuses, it is an acceptable institution. Only a few have rejected punishment entirely, which is rather surprising when one considers all that can be said against it. The difficulty is with the justification of punishment: various arguments for it have been given by moral philosophers, but so far none of them has won any sort of general acceptance; no justification is without those who detest it. I

---

[2] The distinction is central to Hume's discussion of justice in *A Treatise of Human Nature,* bk. III. pt. 11, esp. secs. 2–4. It is clearly stated by John Austin in the second lecture of *Lectures on Jurisprudence* (4th ed.; London, 1873), I, 116ff. (1st ed., 1832). Also it may be argued that J. S. Mill took it for granted in *Utilitarianism:* on this point cf. J. O. Urmson. "The Interpretation of the Moral Philosophy of J. S. Mill," *Philosophical Quarterly,* vol. III (1953). In addition to the arguments given by Urmson there are several clear statements of the distinction in *A System of Logic* (8th ed.; London, 1872), bk. VI, ch. xii pars. 2, 3, 7. The distinction is fundamental to J. D. Mabbott's important paper, "Punishment," *Mind,* n.s., vol. XLVIII (April, 1939). More recently the distinction has been stated with particular emphasis by S. E. Toulmin in *The Place of Reason in Ethics* (Cambridge, 1950), see esp. ch. xi, where it plays a major part in his account of moral reasoning. Toulmin doesn't explain the basis of the distinction, nor how one might overlook its importance, as I try to in this paper, and in my review of his book (*Philosophical Review,* vol. LX [October, 1951]), as some of my criticisms show, I failed to understand the force of it. See also H. D. Aiken, "The Levels of Moral Discourse," *Ethics,* vol. LXII (1952), A. M. Quinton, "Punishment," *Analysis,* vol. XIV (June, 1954), and P. H. Nowell-Smith, *Ethics* (London, 1954), pp. 236–239, 271–273.

[3] On the concept of explication see the author's paper *Philosophical Review,* vol. LX (April, 1951).

[4] While this paper was being revised, Quinton's appeared; footnote 2 supra. There are several respects in which my remarks are similar to his. Yet as I consider some further questions and rely on somewhat different arguments, I have retained the discussion of punishment and promises together as two test cases for utilitarianism.

hope to show that the use of the aforementioned distinction enables one to state the utilitarian view in a way which allows for the sound points of its critics.

For our purposes we may say that there are two justifications of punishment. What we may call the retributive view is that punishment is justified on the grounds that wrongdoing merits punishment. It is morally fitting that a person who does wrong should suffer in proportion to his wrongdoing. That a criminal should be punished follows from his guilt, and the severity of the appropriate punishment depends on the depravity of his act. The state of affairs where a wrongdoer suffers punishment is morally better than the state of affairs where he does not; and it is better irrespective of any of the consequences of punishing him.

What we may call the utilitarian holds that on the principle that bygones are bygones and that only future consequences are material to present decisions, punishment is justifiable only by reference to the probable consequences of maintaining it as one of the devices of the social order. Wrongs committed in the past are, as such, not relevant considerations for deciding what to do. If punishment can be shown to promote effectively the interest of society it is justifiable, otherwise it is not.

I have stated these two competing views very roughly to make one feel the conflict between them: one feels the force of *both* arguments and one wonders how they can be reconciled. From my introductory remarks it is obvious that the resolution which I am going to propose is that in this case one must distinguish between justifying a practice as a system of rules to be applied and enforced, and justifying a particular action which falls under these rules; utilitarian arguments are appropriate with regard to questions about practices, while retributive arguments fit the application of particular rules to particular cases.

We might try to get clear about this distinction by imagining how a father might answer the question of his son. Suppose the son asks, "Why was *J* put in jail yesterday?" The father answers, "Because he robbed the bank at *B*. He was duly tried and found guilty. That's why he was put in jail yesterday." But suppose the son had asked a different question, namely, "Why do people put other people in jail?" Then the father might answer, "To protect good people from bad people" or "To stop people from doing things that would make it uneasy for all of us; for otherwise we wouldn't be able to go to bed at night and sleep in peace." There are two very different questions here. One question emphasizes the proper name: it asks why *J* was punished rather than someone else, or it asks what he was punished for. The other question asks why we have the institution of punishment: why do people punish one another rather than, say, always forgiving one another?

Thus the father says in effect that a particular man is punished, rather than some other man, because he is guilty, and he is guilty because he broke the law (past tense). In his case the law looks back, the judge looks back, the jury looks back, and a penalty is visited upon him for something he did. That a man is to be punished, and what his punishment is to be, is settled by its being shown that he broke the law and that the law assigns that penalty for the violation of it.

On the other hand we have the institution of punishment itself, and recommend and accept various changes in it, because it is thought by the (ideal) legislator and by those to whom the law applies that, as a part of a system of law impartially applied from case to case arising under it, it will have the consequence, in the long run, of furthering the interests of society.

One can say, then, that the judge and the legislator stand in different positions and look in different directions: one to the past, the other to the future. The justification of what the judge does, *qua* judge, sounds like the retributive view; the justification of what the (ideal) legislator does, *qua* legislator, sounds like the utilitarian view. Thus both views have a point (this is as it should be since intelligent and sensitive persons have been on both sides of the argument); and one's initial confusion disappears once one sees that these views apply to persons holding different offices with different duties, and situated differently with respect to the system of rules that make up the criminal law.[5]

One might say, however, that the utilitarian view is more fundamental since it applies to a more fundamental office, for the judge carries out the legislator's will so far as he can determine it. Once the legislator decides to have laws and to assign penalties for their violation (as things are there must be both the law and the penalty) an institution is set up which involves a retributive conception of particular cases. It is part of the concept of the criminal law as a system of rules that the application and enforcement of these rules in particular cases should be justifiable by arguments of a retributive character. The decision whether or not to use law rather than some other mechanism of social control, and the decision as to what laws to have and what penalties to assign, may be settled by utilitarian arguments; but if one decides to have laws then one has decided on something whose working in particular cases is retributive in form.[6]

The answer, then, to the confusion engendered by the two views of punishment is quite simple: one distinguishes two offices, that of the judge and that of the legislator, and one distinguishes their different stations with respect to the system of rules which make up the law; and then one notes that the different sorts of considerations which would usually be offered as reasons for what is done under the cover of these offices can be paired off with the competing justifications of punishment. One reconciles the two views by the time-honored device of making them apply to different situations.

But can it really be this simple? Well, this answer allows for the apparent intent of each side. Does a person who advocates the retributive view neces-

---

[5] Note the fact that different sorts of arguments are suited to different offices. One way of taking the differences between ethical theories is to regard them as accounts of the reasons expected in different offices.

[6] In this connection see Mabbott, *op. cit.,* pp. 163–164.

sarily advocate, as an *institution,* legal machinery whose essential purpose is to set up and preserve a correspondence between moral turpitude and suffering? Surely not.[7] What retributionists have rightly insisted upon is that no man can be punished unless he is guilty, that is, unless he has broken the law. Their fundamental criticism of the utilitarian account is that, as they interpret it, it sanctions an innocent person's being punished (if one may call it that) for the benefit of society.

On the other hand, utilitarians agree that punishment is to be inflicted only for the violation of law. They regard this much as understood from the concept of punishment itself.[8] The point of the utilitarian account concerns the institution as a system of rules: utilitarianism seeks to limit its use by declaring it justifiable only if it can be shown to foster effectively the good of society. Historically it is a protest against the indiscriminate and ineffective use of the criminal law.[9] It seeks to dissuade us from assigning to penal institutions the improper, if not sacrilegious, task of matching suffering with moral turpitude. Like others, utilitarians want penal institutions designed so that, as far as humanly possible, only those who break the law run afoul of it. They hold that no official should have discretionary power to inflict penalties whenever he thinks it for the benefit of society; for on utilitarian grounds an institution granting such power could not be justified.[10]

The suggested way of reconciling the retributive and the utilitarian justifications of punishment seems to account for what both sides have wanted to say. There are, however, two further questions which arise, and I shall devote the remainder of this section to them.

First, will not a difference of opinion as to the proper criterion of just law make the proposed reconciliation unacceptable to retributionists? Will they not question whether, if the utilitarian principle is used as the criterion, it follows that those who have broken the law are guilty in a way which satisfies

---

[7] On this point see Sir David Ross, *The Right and the Good* (Oxford, 1930), pp. 57–60.

[8] See Hobbes's definition of punishment in *Leviathan,* ch. xxviii; and Bentham's definition in *The Principle of Morals and Legislation,* ch. xii, par. 36, ch. xv, par. 28, and in *The Rationale of Punishment* (London, 1830), bk. I, ch. i. They could agree with Bradley that: "Punishment is punishment only when it is deserved. We pay the penalty, because we owe it, and for no other reason; and if punishment is inflicted for any other reason whatever than because it is merited by wrong, it is a gross immorality, a crying injustice, an abominable crime, and not what it pretends to be." *Ethical Studies* (2nd ed.; Oxford, 1927), pp. 26–27. Certainly by definition it isn't what it pretends to be. The innocent can only be punished by mistake; deliberate "punishment" of the innocent necessarily involves fraud.

[9] Cf. Leon Radzinowicz, *A History of English Criminal Law: The Movement for Reform* 1750–1833 (London, 1948), esp. ch. xi on Bentham.

[10] Bentham discusses how corresponding to a punitory provision of a criminal law there is another provision which stands to it as an antagonist and which needs a name as much as the punitory. He calls it, as one might expect, the *anaetiosostic,* and of it he says: "The punishment of guilt is the object of the former one: the preservation of innocence that of the latter." In the same connection he asserts that it is never thought fit to give the judge the option of deciding whether a thief (that is, a person whom he believes to be a thief, for the judge's belief is what the question must always turn upon) should hang or not, and so the law writes the provision: "The judge shall not cause a thief to be hanged unless he has been duly convicted and sentenced in course of law" (*The Limits of Jurisprudence Defined,* ed. C. W. Everett [New York, 1945], pp. 238–239).

their demand that those punished deserve to be punished? To answer this difficulty, suppose that the rules of the criminal law are justified on utilitarian grounds (it is only for laws that meet his criterion that the utilitarian can be held responsible). Then it follows that the actions which the criminal law specifies as offenses are such that, if they were tolerated, terror and alarm would spread in society. Consequently, retributionists can only deny that those who are punished deserve to be punished if they deny that such actions are wrong. This they will not want to do.

The second question is whether utilitarianism doesn't justify too much. One pictures it as an engine of justification which, if consistently adopted, could be used to justify cruel and arbitrary institutions. Retributionists may be supposed to concede that utilitarians *intend* to reform the law and to make it more humane; that utilitarians do not *wish* to justify any such thing as punishment of the innocent; and that utilitarians may appeal to the fact that punishment presupposes guilt in the sense that by punishment one understands an institution attaching penalties to the infraction of legal rules, and therefore that it is logically absurd to suppose that utilitarians in justifying *punishment* might also have justified punishment (if we may call it that) of the innocent. The real question, however, is whether the utilitarian, in justifying punishment, hasn't used arguments which commit him to accepting the infliction of suffering on innocent persons if it is for the good of society (whether or not one calls this punishment). More generally, isn't the utilitarian committed in principle to accepting many practices which he, as a morally sensitive person, wouldn't want to accept? Retributionists are inclined to hold that there is no way to stop the utilitarian principle from justifying too much except by adding to it a principle which distributes certain rights to individuals. Then the amended criterion is not the greatest benefit of society *simpliciter,* but the greatest benefit of society subject to the constraint that no one's rights may be violated. Now while I think that the classical utilitarians proposed a criterion of this more complicated sort, I do not want to argue that point here.[11] What I want to show is that there is *another* way of preventing the utilitarian principle from justifying too much, or at least of making it much less likely to do so: namely, by stating utilitarianism in a way which accounts for the distinction between the justification of an institution and the justification of a particular action falling under it.

I begin by defining the institution of punishment as follows: a person is said to suffer punishment whenever he is legally deprived of some of the normal rights of a citizen on the ground that he has violated a rule of law, the violation having been established by trial according to the due process of law, provided that the deprivation is carried out by the recognized legal authorities of the state, that the rule of law clearly specifies both the offense and the attached penalty, that the courts construe statutes strictly, and that the statute

---

[11] By the classical utilitarians I understand Hobbes, Hume, Bentham, J. S. Mill, and Sidgwick.

was on the books prior to the time of the offense.[12] This definition specifies what I shall understand by punishment. The question is whether utilitarian arguments may be found to justify institutions widely different from this and such as one would find cruel and arbitrary.

This question is best answered, I think, by taking up a particular accusation. Consider the following from Carritt:

> . . . the utilitarian must hold that we are justified in inflicting pain always and only to prevent worse pain or bring about greater happiness. This, then, is all we need to consider in so-called punishment, which must be purely preventive. But if some kind of very cruel crime becomes common, and none of the criminals can be caught, it might be highly expedient, as an example, to hang an innocent man, if a charge against him could be so framed that he were universally thought guilty; indeed this would only fail to be an ideal instance of utilitarian 'punishment' because the victim himself would not have been so likely as a real felon to commit such a crime in the future; in all other respects it would be perfectly deterrent and therefore felicific.[13]

Carritt is trying to show that there are occasions when a utilitarian argument would justify taking an action which would be generally condemned; and thus that utilitarianism justifies too much. But the failure of Carritt's argument lies in the fact that he makes no distinction between the justification of the general system of rules which constitutes penal institutions and the justification of particular applications of these rules to particular cases by the various officials whose job it is to administer them. This becomes perfectly clear when one asks who the "we" are of whom Carritt speaks. Who is this who has a sort of absolute authority on particular occasions to decide that an innocent man shall be "punished" if everyone can be convinced that he is guilty? Is this person the legislator, or the judge, or the body of private citizens, or what? It is utterly crucial to know who is to decide such matters, and by what authority, for all of this must be written into the rules of the institution. Until one knows these things one doesn't know what the institution is whose justification is being challenged; and as the utilitarian principle applies to the institution one doesn't know whether it is justifiable on utilitarian grounds or not.

Once this is understood it is clear what the countermove to Carritt's argument is. One must describe more carefully what the *institution* is which his example suggests, and then ask oneself whether or not it is likely that having this institution would be for the benefit of society in the long run. One must not content oneself with the vague thought that, when it's a question of *this* case, it would be a good thing if *somebody* did something even if an innocent person were to suffer.

---

[12] All these features of punishment are mentioned by Hobbes; cf. *Leviathan,* ch. xxviii.
[13] *Ethical and Political Thinking* (Oxford, 1947), p. 65.

Try to imagine, then, an institution (which we may call "telishment") which is such that the officials set up by it have authority to arrange a trial for the condemnation of an innocent man whenever they are of the opinion that doing so would be in the best interests of society. The discretion of officials is limited, however, by the rule that they may not condemn an innocent man to undergo such an ordeal unless there is, at the time, a wave of offenses similar to that with which they charge him and telish him for. We may imagine that the officials having the discretionary authority are the judges of the higher courts in consultation with the chief of police, the minister of justice, and a committee of the legislature.

Once one realizes that one is involved in setting up an *institution,* one sees that the hazards are very great. For example, what check is there on the officials? How is one to tell whether or not their actions are authorized? How is one to limit the risks involved in allowing such systematic deception? How is one to avoid giving anything short of complete discretion to the authorities to telish anyone they like? In addition to these considerations, it is obvious that people will come to have a very different attitude towards their penal system when telishment is adjoined to it. They will be uncertain as to whether a convicted man has been punished or telished. They will wonder whether or not they should feel sorry for him. They will wonder whether the same fate won't at any time fall on them. If one pictures how such an institution would actually work, and the enormous risks involved in it, it seems clear that it would serve no useful purpose. A utilitarian justification for this institution is most unlikely.

It happens in general that as one drops off the defining features of punishment one ends up with an institution whose utilitarian justification is highly doubtful. One reason for this is that punishment works like a kind of price system: by altering the prices one has to pay for the performance of actions it supplies a motive for avoiding some actions and doing others. The defining features are essential if punishment is to work in this way; so that an institution which lacks these features, e.g., an institution which is set up to "punish" the innocent, is likely to have about as much point as a price system (if one may call it that) where the prices of things change at random from day to day and one learns the price of something after one has agreed to buy it.[14]

---

[14] The analogy with the price system suggests an answer to the question how utilitarian considerations insure that punishment is proportional to the offense. It is interesting to note that Sir David Ross, after making the distinction between justifying a penal law and justifying a particular application of it, and after stating that utilitarian considerations have a large place in determining the former, still holds back from accepting the utilitarian justification of punishment on the grounds that justice requires that punishment be proportional to the offense, and that utilitarianism is unable to account for this. Cf. *The Right and the Good,* pp. 61–62. I do not claim that utilitarianism can account for this requirement as Sir David might wish, but it happens, nevertheless, that if utilitarian considerations are followed penalties will be proportional to offenses in this sense: the order of offenses according to seriousness can be paired off with the order of penalties according to severity. Also the absolute level of penalties will be as low as possible. This follows from the assumption that people are rational (i.e., that they are able to take into account the "prices" the state puts on actions), the utilitarian rule that a penal system should provide a motive for preferring the less serious offense, and the principle that punishment as such is an evil. All this was carefully worked out by Bentham in *The Principles of Morals and Legislation,* chs. xiii–xv.

If one is careful to apply the utilitarian principle to the institution which is to authorize particular actions, then there is *less* danger of its justifying too much. Carritt's example gains plausibility by its indefiniteness and by its concentration on the particular case. His argument will only hold if it can be shown that there are utilitarian arguments which justify an institution whose publicly ascertainable offices and powers are such as to permit officials to exercise that kind of discretion in particular cases. But the requirement of having to build the arbitrary features of the particular decision into the institutional practice makes the justification much less likely to go through.

II

I shall now consider the question of promises. The objection to utilitarianism in connection with promises seems to be this: it is believed that on the utilitarian view when a person makes a promise the only ground upon which he should keep it, if he should keep it, is that by keeping it he will realize the most good on the whole. So that if one asks the question "Why should I keep *my* promise?" the utilitarian answer is understood to be that doing so in *this* case will have the best consequences. And this answer is said, quite rightly, to conflict with the way in which the obligation to keep promises is regarded.

Now of course critics of utilitarianism are not unaware that one defense sometimes attributed to utilitarians is the consideration involving the practice of promise-keeping.[15] In this connection they are supposed to argue something like this: it must be admitted that we feel strictly about keeping promises, more strictly than it might seem our view can account for. But when we consider the matter carefully it is always necessary to take into account the effect which our action will have on the practice of making promises. The promisor must weigh, not only the effects of breaking his promise on the particular case, but also the effect which his breaking his promise will have on the practice itself. Since the practice is of great utilitarian value, and since breaking one's promise always seriously damages it, one will seldom be justified in breaking one's promise. If we view our individual promises in the wider context of the practice of promising itself we can account for the strictness of the obligation to keep promises. There is always one very strong utilitarian consideration in favor of keeping them, and this will insure that when the question arises as to whether or not to keep a promise it will usually turn out that one should, even where the facts of the particular case taken by itself would seem to justify one's breaking it. In this way the strictness with which we view the obligation to keep promises is accounted for.

---

[15] Ross, *The Right and the Good*, pp. 37–39, and *Foundations of Ethics* (Oxford, 1939), pp. 92–94. I know of no utilitarian who has used this argument except W. A. Pickard-Cambridge in "Two Problems about Duty," *Mind*, n.s., XLI (April, 1932), 153–157, although the argument goes with G. E. Moore's version of utilitarianism in *Principia Ethica* (Cambridge, 1903). To my knowledge it does not appear in the classical utilitarians; and if one interprets their view correctly this is no accident.

Ross has criticized this defense as follows:[16] however great the value of the practice of promising, on utilitarian grounds, there must be some value which is greater, and one can imagine it to be obtainable by breaking a promise. Therefore there might be a case where the promisor could argue that breaking his promise was justified as leading to a better state of affairs on the whole. And the promisor could argue in this way no matter how slight the advantage won by breaking the promise. If one were to challenge the promisor his defense would be that what he did was best on the whole in view of all the utilitarian considerations, which in this case *include* the importance of the practice. Ross feels that such a defense would be unacceptable. I think he is right insofar as he is protesting against the appeal to consequences in general and without further explanation. Yet it is extremely difficult to weigh the force of Ross's argument. The kind of case imagined seems unrealistic and one feels that it needs to be described. One is inclined to think that it would either turn out that such a case came under an exception defined by the practice itself, in which case there would not be an appeal to consequences in general on the particular case, or it would happen that the circumstances were so peculiar that the conditions which the practice presupposes no longer obtained. But certainly Ross is right in thinking that it strikes us as wrong for a person to defend breaking a promise by a general appeal to consequences. For a general utilitarian defense is not open to the promisor: it is not one of the defenses allowed by the practice of making promises.

Ross gives two further counterarguments:[17] First, he holds that it overestimates the damage done to the practice of promising by a failure to keep a promise. One who breaks a promise harms his own name certainly, but it isn't clear that a broken promise always damages the practice itself sufficiently to account for the strictness of the obligation. Second, and more important, I think, he raises the question of what one is to say of a promise which isn't known to have been made except to the promisor and the promisee, as in the case of a promise a son makes to his dying father concerning the handling of the estate.[18] In this sort of case the consideration relating to the practice doesn't weigh on the promisor at all, and yet one feels that this sort of promise is as binding as other promises. The question of the effect which breaking it has on the practice seems irrelevant. The only consequence seems to be that one can break the promise without running any risk of being censured; but the obligation itself seems not the least weakened. Hence it is doubtful whether

---

[16] Ross, *The Right and the Good,* pp. 38–39.

[17] Ross, *ibid.,* p. 39. The case of the nonpublic promise is discussed again in *Foundations of Ethics,* pp. 95–96, 104–105. It occurs also in Mabbott, "Punishment," *op. cit.,* pp. 155–157, and in A. I. Melden, "Two Comments on Utilitarianism," *Philosophical Review,* LX (October, 1951), 519–523, which discusses Carritt's example in *Ethical and Political Thinking,* p. 64.

[18] Ross's example is described simply as that of two men dying alone where one makes a promise to the other. Carritt's example (cf. n. 17 supra) is that of two men at the North Pole. The example in the text is more realistic and is similar to Mabbott's. Another example is that of being told something in confidence by one who subsequently dies. Such cases need not be "desert-island arguments" as Nowell-Smith seems to believe (cf. his *Ethics,* pp. 239–244).

the effect on the practice ever weighs in the particular case; certainly it cannot account for the strictness of the obligation where it fails to obtain. It seems to follow that a utilitarian account of the obligation to keep promises cannot be successfully carried out.

From what I have said in connection with punishment, one can foresee what I am going to say about these arguments and counterarguments. They fail to make the distinction between the justification of a practice and the justification of a particular action falling under it, and therefore they fall into the mistake of taking it for granted that the promisor, like Carritt's official, is entitled without restriction to bring utilitarian considerations to bear in deciding whether to keep *his* promise. But if one considers what the practice of promising is one will see, I think, that it is such as not to allow this sort of general discretion to the promisor. Indeed, the point of the practice is to abdicate one's title to act in accordance with utilitarian and prudential considerations in order that the future may be tied down and plans coordinated in advance. There are obvious utilitarian advantages in having a practice which denies to the promisor, as a defense, any general appeal to the utilitarian principle in accordance with which the practice itself may be justified. There is nothing contradictory, or surprising, in this: utilitarian (or aesthetic) reasons might properly be given in arguing that the game of chess, or baseball, is satisfactory just as it is, or in arguing that it should be changed in various respects, but a player in a game cannot properly appeal to such considerations as reasons for his making one move rather than another. It is a mistake to think that if the practice is justified on utilitarian grounds then the promisor must have complete liberty to use utilitarian arguments to decide whether or not to keep his promise. The practice forbids this general defense; and it is a purpose of the practice to do this. Therefore what the above arguments presuppose—the idea that if the utilitarian view is accepted then the promisor is bound if, and only if, the application of the utilitarian principle to his own case shows that keeping it is best on the whole—is false. The promisor is bound because he promised: weighing the case on its merits is not open to him.[19]

Is this to say that in particular cases one cannot deliberate whether or not to keep one's promise? Of course not. But to do so is to deliberate whether the various excuses, exceptions and defenses, which are understood by, and which constitute an important part of, the practice, apply to one's own case.[20] Various defenses for not keeping one's promise are allowed, but among them there isn't the one that, on general utilitarian grounds, the promisor (truly) thought his action best on the whole, even though there may be the defense that the consequences of keeping one's promise would have been *extremely* severe. While there are too many complexities here to consider all the neces-

---

[19] What I have said in this paragraph seems to me to coincide with Hume's important discussion in the *Treatise of Human Nature*, bk. III, pt. 11, sec. 5; and also sec. 6, par. 8.

[20] For a discussion of these, see H. Sidgwick, *The Methods of Ethics* (6th ed.: London, 1901), bk. III, ch. vi.

sary details, one can see that the general defense isn't allowed if one asks the following question: what would one say of someone who, when asked why he broke his promise, replied simply that breaking it was best on the whole? Assuming that his reply is sincere, and that his belief was reasonable (i.e., one need not consider the possibility that he was mistaken), I think that one would question whether or not he knows what it means to say "I promise" (in the appropriate circumstances). It would be said of someone who used this excuse without further explanation that he didn't understand what defenses the practice, which defines a promise, allows to him. If a child were to use this excuse one would correct him; for it is part of the way one is taught the concept of a promise to be corrected if one uses this excuse. The point of having the practice would be lost if the practice did allow this excuse.

It is no doubt part of the utilitarian view that every practice should admit the defense that the consequences of abiding by it would have been extremely severe; and utilitarians would be inclined to hold that some reliance on people's good sense and some concession to hard cases is necessary. They would hold that a practice is justified by serving the interests of those who take part in it; and as with any set of rules there is understood a background of circumstances under which it is expected to be applied and which need not—indeed which cannot—be fully stated. Should these circumstances change, then even if there is no rule which provides for the case, it may still be in accordance with the practice that one be released from one's obligation. But this sort of defense allowed by a practice must not be confused with the general option to weigh each particular case on utilitarian grounds which critics of utilitarianism have thought it necessarily to involve.

The concern which utilitarianism raises by its justification of punishment is that it may justify too much. The question in connection with promises is different: it is how utilitarianism can account for the obligation to keep promises at all. One feels that the recognized obligation to keep one's promise and utilitarianism are incompatible. And to be sure, they are incompatible if one interprets the utilitarian view as necessarily holding that each person has complete liberty to weigh every particular action on general utilitarian grounds. But must one interpret utilitarianism in this way? I hope to show that, in the sorts of cases I have discussed, one cannot interpret it in this way.

III

So far I have tried to show the importance of the distinction between the justification of a practice and the justification of a particular action falling under it by indicating how this distinction might be used to defend utilitarianism against two long-standing objections. One might be tempted to close the discussion at this point by saying that utilitarian considerations should be understood as applying to practices in the first instance and not to particular actions falling under them except insofar as the practices admit of it. One might say that in this modified form it is a better account of our considered moral opinions and let it go at that. But to stop here would be to neglect the interesting question as to how one can fail to appreciate the significance of this rather obvious distinction and can take it for granted that utilitarianism has the consequence that particular cases may always be decided on general utilitarian grounds.[21] I want to argue that this mistake may be connected with misconceiving the logical status of the rules of practices; and to show this I am going to examine two conceptions of rules, two ways of placing them within the utilitarian theory.

The conception which conceals from us the significance of the distinction I am going to call the summary view. It regards rules in the following way: one supposes that each person decides what he shall do in particular cases by applying the utilitarian principle; one supposes further that different people will decide the same particular case in the same way and that there will be recurrences of cases similar to those previously decided. Thus it will happen that in cases of certain kinds the same decision will be made either by the same person at different times or by different persons at the same time. If a case occurs frequently enough one supposes that a rule is formulated to cover that sort of case. I have called this conception the summary view because rules are pictured as summaries of past decisions arrived at by the *direct* application of the utilitarian principle to particular cases. Rules are regarded as reports that cases of a certain sort have been found on *other* grounds to be properly decided in a certain way (although, of course, they do not *say* this).

There are several things to notice about this way of placing rules within the utilitarian theory.[22]

---

[21] So far as I can see it is not until Moore that the doctrine is expressly stated in this way. See, for example, *Principia Ethica*, p. 147, where it is said that the statement "I am morally bound to perform this action" is identical with the statement "*This action* will produce the greatest possible amount of good in the Universe" (my italics). It is important to remember that those whom I have called the classical utilitarians were largely interested in social institutions. They were among the leading economists and political theorists of their day, and they were not infrequently reformers interested in practical affairs. Utilitarianism historically goes together with a coherent view of society, and is not simply an ethical theory, much less an attempt at philosophical analysis in the modern sense. The utilitarian principle was quite naturally thought of, and used, as a criterion for judging social institutions (practices) and as a basis for urging reforms. It is not clear, therefore, how far it is necessary to amend utilitarianism in its classical form. For a discussion of utilitarianism as an integral part of a theory of society, see L. Robbins, *The Theory of Economic Policy in English Classical Political Economy* (London, 1952).

[22] This footnote should be read after sec. 3 and presupposes what I have said there. It provides a few references to statements by leading utilitarians of the summary conception. In general it appears that when they discussed the logical features of rules the summary conception prevailed and that it was typical of the way they talked about moral rules. I cite a rather lengthy group of passages from Austin as a full illustration.

John Austin in his *Lectures on Jurisprudence* meets the objection that deciding in accordance with the utilitarian principle case by case is impractical by saying that this is a misinterpretation of utilitarianism. According to the utilitarian view ". . . our conduct would conform to *rules* inferred from the tendencies of actions, but would not be determined by a direct resort to the principle of general utility. Utility would be the test of our conduct, ultimately, but not immediately: the immediate test of the rules to which our conduct would conform, but not the immediate test of specific or individual actions. Our rules would be fashioned on utility: our conduct, on our rules" (vol. I, p. 116). As to how one decides on the tendency of an action he says: "If we would try the tendency of a specific or individual act, we must not contemplate the act as if it were single and insulated, but must look at the class of acts to which it belongs. We must suppose that acts of the class were generally done or

1. The point of having rules derives from the fact that similar cases tend to recur and that one can decide cases more quickly if one records past decisions in the form of rules. If similar cases didn't recur, one would be required to apply the utilitarian principle directly, case by case, and rules reporting past decisions would be of no use.

---

omitted, and consider the probable effect upon the general happiness or good. We must guess the consequences which would follow, if the class of acts were general; and also the consequences which would follow, if they were generally omitted. We must then compare the consequences on the positive and negative sides, and determine on which of the two the *balance* of advantage lies. . . . If we truly try the tendency of a specific or individual act, we try the tendency of the class to which that act belongs. The *particular* conclusion which we draw, with regard to the single act, implies a *general* conclusion embracing all similar acts. . . . To the rules thus inferred, and lodged in the memory, our conduct would conform *immediately* if it were truly adjusted to utility" (*ibid.,* p. 117). One might think that Austin meets the objection by stating the practice conception of rules; and perhaps he did intend to. But it is not clear that he has stated this conception. Is the generality he refers to of the statistical sort? This is suggested by the notion of tendency. Or does he refer to the utility of setting up a practice? I don't know; but what suggests the summary view is his subsequent remarks. He says: "To consider the specific consequences of single or individual acts, would *seldom* [my italics] consist with that ultimate principle" (*ibid.,* p. 117). But would one ever do this? He continues: ". . . this being admitted, the necessity of pausing and calculating, which the objection in question supposes, is an imagined necessity. To preface each act or forbearance by a conjecture and comparison of consequences, were clearly *superfluous* [my italics] and mischievous. It were clearly superfluous, inasmuch as the *results of that process* [my italics] would be embodied in a known *rule.* It were clearly mischievous, inasmuch as the *true* result would be expressed by that rule, whilst the process would probably be faulty, if it were done on the spur of the occasion" (*ibid.,* pp. 117–118). He goes on: "If our experience and observation of particulars were not *generalized,* our experience and observation of particulars would seldom avail us in *practice.* . . . The inferences suggested to our minds by repeated experience and observation are, therefore, drawn into *principles,* or compressed into *maxims.* These we carry about us ready for use, and apply to individual cases promptly . . . without reverting to the process by which they were obtained; or without recalling, and arraying before our minds, the numerous and intricate considerations of which they are *handy abridgments* [my italics]. . . . True theory is a *compendium* of particular truths. . . . Speaking then, generally, human conduct is inevitably *guided* [my italics] by *rules,* or by *principles* or *maxims*" (*ibid.,* pp. 117–118). I need not trouble to show how all these remarks incline to the summary view. Further, when Austin comes to deal with cases "of comparatively rare occurrence" he holds that specific considerations may outweigh the general. "Looking at the reasons from which we had inferred the rule, it were absurd to think it inflexible. We should therefore dismiss the *rule;* resort directly to the *principle* upon which our rules were fashioned; and calculate *specific* consequences to the best of our knowledge and ability" (*ibid.,* pp. 120–121). Austin's view is interesting because it shows how one may come close to the practice conception and then slide away from it.

In *A System of Logic,* bk. VI, ch. xii, par. 2, Mill distinguishes clearly between the position of judge and legislator and in doing so suggests the distinction between the two concepts of rules. However, he distinguishes two positions to illustrate the difference between cases where one is to apply a rule already established and cases where one must formulate a rule to govern subsequent conduct. It's the latter case that interests him and he takes the "maxim of policy" of a legislator as typical of rules. In par. 3 the summary conception is very clearly stated. For example, he says of rules of conduct that they should be taken provisionally, as they are made for the most numerous cases. He says that they "point out" the manner in which it is least perilous to act; they serve as an "admonition" that a certain mode of conduct has been found suited to the most common occurrences. In *Utilitarianism,* ch. ii, par. 24, the summary conception appears in Mill's answer to the same objection Austin considered. Here he speaks of rules as "corollaries" from the principle of utility; these "secondary" rules are compared to "landmarks" and "direction-posts." They are based on long experience and so make it unnecessary to apply the utilitarian principle to each case. In par. 25 Mill refers to the task of the utilitarian principle in adjudicating between competing moral rules. He talks here as if one then applies the utilitarian principle directly to the particular case. On the practice view one would rather use the principle to decide which of the ways that make the practice consistent is the best. It should be noted that while in par. 10 Mill's definition of utilitarianism makes the utilitarian principle apply to morality, i.e., to the rules and precepts of human conduct, the definition in par. 2 uses the phrase "actions are right in *proportion*

2. The decisions made on particular cases are logically prior to rules. Since rules gain their point from the need to apply the utilitarian principle to many similar cases, it follows that a particular case (or several cases similar to it) may exist whether or not there is a rule covering that case. We are pictured as recognizing particular cases prior to there being a rule which covers them, for it is only if we meet with a number of cases of a certain sort that we formulate a rule. Thus we are able to describe a particular case as a particular case of the requisite sort whether there is a rule regarding *that* sort of case or not. Put another way: what the *A*'s and the *B*'s refer to in rules of the form 'Whenever *A* do *B*' may be described as *A*'s and *B*'s whether or not there is the rule 'Whenever *A* do *B*,' or whether or not there is any body of rules which make up a practice of which that rule is a part.

To illustrate this consider a rule, or maxim, which could arise in this way: suppose that a person is trying to decide whether to tell someone who is fatally ill what his illness is when he had been asked to do so. Suppose the person to reflect and then decide, on utilitarian grounds, that he should not answer truthfully; and suppose that on the basis of this and other like occasions he formulates a rule to the effect that when asked by someone fatally ill what his illness is, one should not tell him. The point to notice is that someone's being fatally ill and asking what his illness is, and someone's telling him, are things that can be described as such whether or not there is this rule. The performance of the action to which the rule refers doesn't require the stage-setting of a practice of which this rule is a part. This is what is meant by saying that on the summary view particular cases are logically prior to rules.

3. Each person is in principle always entitled to reconsider the correctness of a rule and to question whether or not it is proper to follow it in a particular case. As rules are guides and aids, one may ask whether in past decisions there might not have been a mistake in applying the utilitarian principle to get the rule in question, and wonder whether or not it is best in this case. The reason for rules is that people are not able to apply the utilitarian principle effortlessly and flawlessly; there is need to save time and to post a guide. On this view a

---

as they tend to promote happiness" [my italics] and this inclines towards the summary view. In the last paragraph of the essay "On the Definition of Political Economy," *Westminster Review* (October, 1836), Mill says that it is only in art, as distinguished from science, that one can properly speak of exceptions. In a question of practice, if something is fit to be done "in the majority of cases" then it is made the rule. "We may . . . in talking of art *unobjectionably* speak of the *rule* and the *exception,* meaning by the rule the cases in which there exists a preponderance . . . of inducements for acting in a particular way; and by the exception, the cases in which the preponderance is on the contrary side." These remarks, too, suggest the summary view.

In Moore's *Principia Ethica,* ch. v, there is a complicated and difficult discussion of moral rules. I will not examine it here except to express my suspicion that the summary conception prevails. To be sure, Moore speaks frequently of the utility of rules as generally followed, and of actions as generally practiced, but it is possible that these passages fit the statistical notion of generality which the summary conception allows. This conception is suggested by Moore's taking the utilitarian principle as applying directly to particular actions (pp. 147–148) and by his notion of a rule as something indicating which of the few alternatives likely to occur to anyone will generally produce a greater total good in the immediate future (p. 154). He talks of an "ethical law" as a prediction, and as a generalization (pp. 146, 155). The summary conception is also suggested by his discussion of exceptions (pp. 162–163) and of the force of examples of breaching a rule (pp. 163–164).

society of rational utilitarians would be a society without rules in which each person applied the utilitarian principle directly and smoothly, and without error, case by case. On the other hand, ours is a society in which rules are formulated to serve as aids in reaching these ideally rational decisions on particular cases, guides which have been built up and tested by the experience of generations. If one applies this view to rules, one is interpreting them as maxims, as "rules of thumb"; and it is doubtful that anything to which the summary conception did apply would be called a *rule*. Arguing as if one regarded rules in this way is a mistake one makes while doing philosophy.

4. The concept of a *general* rule takes the following form. One is pictured as estimating on what percentage of the cases likely to arise a given rule may be relied upon to express the correct decision, that is, the decision that would be arrived at if one were to correctly apply the utilitarian principle case by case. If one estimates that by and large the rule will give the correct decision, or if one estimates that the likelihood of making a mistake by applying the utilitarian principle directly on one's own is greater than the likelihood of making a mistake by following the rule, and if these considerations held of persons generally, then one would be justified in urging its adoption as a general rule. In this way *general* rules might be accounted for on the summary view. It will still make sense, however, to speak of applying the utilitarian principle case by case, for it was by trying to foresee the results of doing this that one got the initial estimates upon which acceptance of the rule depends. That one is taking a rule in accordance with the summary conception will show itself in the naturalness with which one speaks of the rule as a guide, or as a maxim, or as a generalization from experience, and as something to be laid aside in extraordinary cases where there is no assurance that the generalization will hold and the case must therefore be treated on its merits. Thus there goes with this conception the notion of a particular exception which renders a rule suspect on a particular occasion.

The other conception of rules I will call the practice conception. On this view rules are pictured as defining a practice. Practices are set up for various reasons, but one of them is that in many areas of conduct each person's deciding what to do on utilitarian grounds case by case leads to confusion, and that the attempt to coordinate behavior by trying to foresee how others will act is bound to fail. As an alternative one realizes that what is required is the establishment of a practice, the specification of a new form of activity; and from this one sees that a practice necessarily involves the abdication of full liberty to act on utilitarian and prudential grounds. It is the mark of a practice that being taught how to engage in it involves being instructed in the rules which define it, and that appeal is made to those rules to correct the behavior of those engaged in it. Those engaged in a practice recognize the rules as defining it. The rules cannot be taken as simply describing how those engaged in the practice in fact behave: it is not simply that they act as if they were obeying the rules. Thus it is essential to the notion of a practice that the rules are publicly known and understood as definitive; and it is essential also that the rules of a practice can be taught and can be acted upon to yield a coherent practice. On this conception, then, rules are not generalizations from the decision of individuals applying the utilitarian principle directly and independently to recurrent particular cases. On the contrary, rules define a practice and are themselves the subject of the utilitarian principle.

To show the important differences between this way of fitting rules into the utilitarian theory and the previous way, I shall consider the differences between the two conceptions on the points previously discussed.

1. In contrast with the summary view, the rules of practices are logically prior to particular cases. This is so because there cannot be a particular case of an action falling under a rule of a practice unless there is the practice. This can be made clearer as follows: in a practice there are rules setting up offices, specifying certain forms of action appropriate to various offices, establishing penalties for the breach of rules, and so on. We may think of the rules of a practice as defining offices, moves, and offenses. Now what is meant by saying that the practice is logically prior to particular cases is this: given any rule which specifies a form of action (a move), a particular action which would be taken as falling under this rule given that there is the practice would not be *described as* that sort of action unless there was the practice. In the case of actions specified by practices it is logically impossible to perform them outside the stage setting provided by those practices, for unless there is the practice, and unless the requisite proprieties are fulfilled, whatever one does, whatever movements one makes, will fail to count as a form of action which the practice specifies. What one does will be described in some *other* way.

One may illustrate this point from the game of baseball. Many of the actions one performs in a game of baseball one can do by oneself or with others whether there is the game or not. For example, one can throw a ball, run, or swing a peculiarly shaped piece of wood. But one cannot steal base, or strike out, or draw a walk, or make an error, or balk; although one can do certain things which appear to resemble these actions such as sliding into a bag, missing a grounder and so on. Striking out, stealing a base, balking, etc., are all actions which can only happen in a game. No matter what a person did, what he did would not be described as stealing a base or striking out or drawing a walk unless he could also be described as playing baseball, and for him to be doing this presupposes the rule-like practice which constitutes the game. The practice is logically prior to particular cases: unless there is the practice the terms referring to actions specified by it lack a sense.[23]

2. The practice view leads to an entirely different conception of the au-

---

[23] One might feel that it is a mistake to say that a practice is logically prior to the forms of action it specifies on the grounds that if there were never any instances of actions falling under a practice then we should be strongly inclined to say that there wasn't the practice either. Blue-prints for a practice do not make a practice. That there is a practice entails that there are instances of people having been engaged and now being engaged in it (with suitable qualifications). This is correct, but it doesn't hurt the claim that any given particular instance of a form of action specified by a practice presupposes the practice. This isn't so on the summary picture, as each instance must be "there" prior to the rules, so to speak, as something from which one gets the rule by applying the utilitarian principle to it directly.

thority which each person has to decide on the propriety of following a rule in particular cases. To engage in a practice, to perform those actions specified by a practice, means to follow the appropriate rules. If one wants to do an action which a certain practice specifies then there is no way to do it except to follow the rules which define it. Therefore, it doesn't make sense for a person to raise the question whether or not a rule of a practice correctly applies to *his* case where the action he contemplates is a form of action defined by a practice. If someone were to raise such a question, he would simply show that he didn't understand the situation in which he was acting. If one wants to perform an action specified by a practice, the only legitimate question concerns the nature of the practice itself ("How do I go about making a will?").

This point is illustrated by the behavior expected of a player in games. If one wants to play a game, one doesn't treat the rules of the game as guides as to what is best in particular cases. In a game of baseball if a batter were to ask "Can I have four strikes?" it would be assumed that he was asking what the rule was; and if, when told what the rule was, he were to say that he meant that on this occasion he thought it would be best on the whole for him to have four strikes rather than three, this would be most kindly taken as a joke. One might contend that baseball would be a better game if four strikes were allowed instead of three; but one cannot picture the rules as guides to what is best on the whole in particular cases, and question their applicability to particular cases as particular cases.

3 and 4. To complete the four points of comparison with the summary conception, it is clear from what has been said that rules of practices are not guides to help one decide particular cases correctly as judged by some higher ethical principle. And neither the quasi-statistical notion of generality, nor the notion of a particular exception, can apply to the rules of practices. A more or less general rule of a practice must be a rule which according to the structure of the practice applies to more or fewer of the kinds of cases arising under it; or it must be a rule which is more or less basic to the understanding of the practice. Again, a particular case cannot be an exception to a rule of a practice. An exception is rather a qualification or a further specification of the rule.

It follows from what we have said about the practice conception of rules that if a person is engaged in a practice, and if he is asked why *he* does what *he* does, or if he is asked to defend what he does, then his explanation, or defense, lies in referring the questioner to the practice. He cannot say of *his* action, if it is an action specified by a practice, that he does it rather than some other because he thinks it is best on the whole.[24] When a man engaged in a practice is queried about his action he must assume that the questioner either doesn't know that he is engaged in it ("Why are you in a hurry to pay him?" "I promised to pay him today") or doesn't know what the practice is.

---

[24] A philosophical joke (in the mouth of Jeremy Bentham): "When I run to the other wicket after my partner has struck a good ball I do so because it is best on the whole."

One doesn't so much justify one's particular action as explain, or show, that it is in accordance with the practice. The reason for this is that it is only against the stage-setting of the practice that one's particular action is described as it is. Only by reference to the practice can one *say* what one is doing. To explain or to defend one's own action, as a particular action, one fits it into the practice which defines it. If this is not accepted it's a sign that a different question is being raised as to whether one is justified in accepting the practice, or in tolerating it. When the challenge is to the practice, citing the rules (saying what the practice is) is naturally to no avail. But when the challenge is to the particular action defined by the practice, there is nothing one can do but refer to the rules. Concerning particular actions there is only a question for one who isn't clear as to what the practice is, or who doesn't know that it is being engaged in. This is to be contrasted with the case of a maxim which may be taken as pointing to the correct decision on the case as decided on *other* grounds, and so giving a challenge on the case a sense by having it question whether these other grounds really support the decision on this case.

If one compares the two conceptions of rules I have discussed, one can see how the summary conception misses the significance of the distinction between justifying a practice and justifying actions falling under it. On this view rules are regarded as guides whose purpose it is to indicate the ideally rational decision on the given particular case which the flawless application of the utilitarian principle would yield. One has, in principle, full option to use the guides or to discard them as the situation warrants without one's moral office being altered in any way: whether one discards the rules or not, one always holds the office of a rational person seeking case by case to realize the best on the whole. But on the practice conception, if one holds an office defined by a practice then questions regarding one's actions in this office are settled by reference to the rules which define the practice. If one seeks to question these rules, then one's office undergoes a fundamental change: one then assumes the office of one empowered to change and criticize the rules, or the office of a reformer, and so on. The summary conception does away with the distinction of offices and the various forms of argument appropriate to each. On that conception there is one office and so no offices at all. It therefore obscures the fact that the utilitarian principle must, in the case of actions and offices defined by a practice, apply to the practice, so that general utilitarian arguments are not available to those who act in offices so defined.[25]

---

[25] How do these remarks apply to the case of the promise known only to father and son? Well, at first sight the son certainly holds the office of promisor, and so he isn't allowed by the practice to weigh the particular case on general utilitarian grounds. Suppose instead that he wishes to consider himself in the office of one empowered to criticize and change the practice, leaving aside the question as to his right to move from his previously assumed office to another. Then he may consider utilitarian arguments as applied to the practice; but once he does this he will see that there are such arguments for not allowing a general utilitarian defense in the practice for this sort of case. For to do so would make it impossible to ask for and to give a kind of promise which one often wants to be able to ask for and to give. Therefore he will not want to change the practice, and so as a promisor he has no option but to keep his promise.

Some qualifications are necessary in what I have said. First, I may have talked of the summary and the practice conceptions of rules as if only one of them could be true of rules, and if true of any rules, then necessarily true of *all* rules. I do not, of course, mean this. (It is the critics of utilitarianism who make this mistake insofar as their arguments against utilitarianism presuppose a summary conception of the rules of practices.) Some rules will fit one conception, some rules the other; and so there are rules of practices (rules in the strict sense), and maxims and "rules of thumb."

Secondly, there are further distinctions that can be made in classifying rules, distinctions which should be made if one were considering other questions. The distinctions which I have drawn are those most relevant for the rather special matter I have discussed, and are not intended to be exhaustive.

Finally, there will be many border-line cases about which it will be difficult, if not impossible, to decide which conception of rules is applicable. One expects border-line cases with any concept, and they are especially likely in connection with such involved concepts as those of a practice, institution, game, rule, and so on. Wittgenstein has shown how fluid these notions are.[26] What I have done is to emphasize and sharpen two conceptions for the limited purpose of this paper.

IV

What I have tried to show by distinguishing between two conceptions of rules is that there is a way of regarding rules which allows the option to consider particular cases on general utilitarian grounds; whereas there is another conception which does not admit of such discretion except insofar as the rules themselves authorize it. I want to suggest that the tendency while doing philosophy to picture rules in accordance with the summary conception is what may have blinded moral philosophers to the significance of the distinction between justifying a practice and justifying a particular action falling under it; and it does so by misrepresenting the logical force of the reference to the rules in the case of a challenge to a particular action falling under a practice, and by obscuring the fact that where there is a practice, it is the practice itself that must be the subject of the utilitarian principle.

It is surely no accident that two of the traditional test cases of utilitarianism, punishment and promises, are clear cases of practices. Under the influence of the summary conception it is natural to suppose that the officials of a penal system, and one who has made a promise, may decide what to do in particular cases on utilitarian grounds. One fails to see that a general discretion to decide particular cases on utilitarian grounds is incompatible with the concept of a practice; and that what discretion one does have is itself defined by the practice (e.g., a judge may have discretion to determine the penalty within certain limits). The traditional objections to utilitarianism which I have dis-

---

[26] *Philosophical Investigations* (Oxford, 1953), I, pars. 65–71, for example.

cussed presuppose the attribution to judges, and to those who have made promises, of a plenitude of moral authority to decide particular cases on utilitarian grounds. But once one fits utilitarianism together with the notion of a practice, and notes that punishment and promising are practices, then one sees that this attribution is logically precluded.

That punishment and promising are practices is beyond question. In the case of promising this is shown by the fact that the form of words "I promise" is a performative utterance which presupposes the stage-setting of the practice and the proprieties defined by it. Saying the words "I promise" will only be promising given the existence of the practice. It would be absurd to interpret the rules about promising in accordance with the summary conception. It is absurd to say, for example, that the rule that promises should be kept could have arisen from its being found in past cases to be best on the whole to keep one's promise; for unless there were already the understanding that one keeps one's promises as part of the practice itself there couldn't have been any cases of promising.

It must, of course, be granted that the rules defining promising are not codified, and that one's conception of what they are necessarily depends on one's moral training. Therefore it is likely that there is considerable variation in the way people understand the practice, and room for argument as to how it is best set up. For example, differences as to how strictly various defenses are to be taken, or just what defenses are available, are likely to arise amongst persons with different backgrounds. But irrespective of these variations it belongs to the concept of the practice of promising that the general utilitarian defense is not available to the promisor. That this is so accounts for the force of the traditional objection which I have discussed. And the point I wish to make is that when one fits the utilitarian view together with the practice conception of rules, as one must in the appropriate cases, then there is nothing in that view which entails that there must be such a defense, either in the practice of promising, or in any other practice.

Punishment is also a clear case. There are many actions in the sequence of events which constitute someone's being punished which presuppose a practice. One can see this by considering the definition of punishment which I gave when discussing Carritt's criticism of utilitarianism. The definition there stated refers to such things as the normal rights of a citizen, rules of law, due process of law, trials and courts of law, statutes, etc., none of which can exist outside the elaborate stage-setting of a legal system. It is also the case that many of the actions for which people are punished presuppose practices. For example, one is punished for stealing, for trespassing, and the like, which presuppose the institution of property. It is impossible to say what punishment is, or to describe a particular instance of it, without referring to offices, actions, and offenses specified by practices. Punishment is a move in an elaborate legal game and presupposes the complex of practices which make up the legal order. The same thing is true of the less formal sorts of punishment: a parent or guardian or someone in proper authority may punish a child, but no one else can.

There is one mistaken interpretation of what I have been saying which it is worthwhile to warn against. One might think that the use I am making of the distinction between justifying a practice and justifying the particular actions falling under it involves one in a definite social and political attitude in that it leads to a kind of conservatism. It might seem that I am saying that for each person the social practices of his society provide the standard of justification for his actions; therefore let each person abide by them and his conduct will be justified.

This interpretation is entirely wrong. The point I have been making is rather a logical point. To be sure, it has consequences in matters of ethical theory; but in itself it leads to no particular social or political attitude. It is simply that where a form of action is specified by a practice there is no justification possible of the particular action of a particular person save by reference to the practice. In such cases the action is what it is in virtue of the practice and to explain it is to refer to the practice. There is no inference whatsoever to be drawn with respect to whether or not one should accept the practices of one's society. One can be as radical as one likes but in the case of actions specified by practices the objects of one's radicalism must be the social practices and people's acceptance of them.

I have tried to show that when we fit the utilitarian view together with the practice conception of rules, where this conception is appropriate,[27] we can formulate it in a way which saves it from several traditional objections. I have further tried to show how the logical force of the distinction between justifying a practice and justifying an action falling under it is connected with the practice conception of rules and cannot be understood as long as one regards the rules of practices in accordance with the summary view. Why, when doing philosophy, one may be inclined to so regard them, I have not discussed. The reasons for this are evidently very deep and would require another paper.

---

[27] As I have already stated, it is not always easy to say where the conception is appropriate. Nor do I care to discuss at this point the general sorts of cases to which it does apply except to say that one should not take it for granted that it applies to many so-called "moral rules." It is my feeling that relatively few actions of the moral life are defined by practices and that the practice conception is more relevant to understanding legal and legal-like arguments than it is to the more complex sort of moral arguments. Utilitarianism must be fitted to different conceptions of rules depending on the case, and no doubt the failure to do this has been one source of difficulty in interpreting it correctly.

3

The Claims of Justice

Readings: Immanuel Kant, Fundamental Principles of the Metaphysic of Morals
John Rawls, "Justice as Fairness"

Fundamental to the moral outlook of most men is a commitment to the value of justice. A commitment to utility involves an attempt to maximize certain benefits; a commitment to justice involves an attempt to ensure that whatever benefits are maximized will be *fairly distributed*. Liberty is a basic human benefit, and fundamental to the idea of justice is the thought that it is wrong to claim for oneself a liberty in action that it would not be reasonable to extend to others in similar circumstances. Slavery may be regarded as a paradigm of an unjust practice, for it involves giving a liberty to some (the slaveholders) that is incompatible with a like liberty for others (the slaves). It is an institution which, regardless of the benefits it may provide, stands condemned by the defender of justice just because it involves the exploitation of some persons for the benefit of others. It disregards the rights and dignity of certain persons to make them instruments or means to the welfare of others.

In his *Fundamental Principles,* Immanuel Kant attempts to raise this commitment to justice above the level of intuition, maintaining that the fundamental principles of justice (various forms of what he calls "The Categorical Imperative") would be a part of the nature of any fully rational being. The fundamental idea here is that the value of justice can be derived from the concept of *rationality*. In contrast to Mill, who attempts a limited defense of justice in Chapter V of *Utilitarianism* by arguing that justice serves utility, Kant believes that his argument demonstrates the value of justice quite independently of any consequentialist notions—for example, the capacity of justice to promote the general happiness.

After reading Kant, one has to admit that he really does not establish the logical connection he desires between justice and rationality. He leaves only a promissory note that such a derivation is possible. In his "Justice as Fairness," John Rawls, after analyzing the concept of justice, attempts to do the job that Kant left undone: to demonstrate logically that fully rational beings would (a) choose principles of justice to order their lives and (b) choose such principles over all other principles—particularly utilitarian principles. Rawls attempts to demonstrate that a fundamental commitment to justice is incompatible with a fundamental commitment to utility and, *a fortiori,* that the former is not reducible to the latter. Thus Mill's attempt in Chapter V of *Utilitarianism* was perhaps in vain.[1]

Kant does more than simply examine the value of justice, however. Worries about justice, like worries about utility, are concerned with what *actions* it is right to perform. And this worry is certainly an important part of morality. But there are additional moral worries as well. First, there is the question of the morality, not of actions, but of *agents* or *persons.* The question here is, "What makes a man a morally good (bad) or praiseworthy (blameworthy) man?" The actions he performs are certainly relevant, but Kant wants to argue that a man's *motives* are absolutely central to such a determination. Except for a brief footnote in Chapter II of *Utilitarianism,* Mill does not seem concerned with this sort of issue.

Another question, concerning what might be called the presuppositions of morality, is the following: What must the world be like for morality to have a point or make sense? Kant suggests that, at a minimum, it must be a world in which human beings have free will, God exists, and there is personal immortality.[2] Although most philosophers would now be skeptical about the latter two claims, there certainly does seem to be some point in the first. If, like stones, men had no control over their behavior, then the whole enterprise of directing moral advice or praise and blame to them would seem, to say the least, stupid. This does not show that men do have free will, only that morality is in bad shape if they do not. Kant takes comfort in the belief that because human freedom cannot be disproved it may safely be postulated.

---

[1] It is interesting to note that Rawls' model of rational choice is drawn from social contract theory, and thus his article provides a useful prelude for the readings in Chapter 5 of this book. When the student comes to that chapter, it would be well to reread the Rawls selection.

[2] The latter two presuppositions of morality are explored by Kant in his *Critique of Practical Reason* (1788).

Suggestions for Further Reading

H. B. Acton, *Kant's Moral Philosophy* (London: Macmillan, 1970).

Jeffrie G. Murphy, *Kant: The Philosophy of Right* (London: Macmillan, 1970).

John Rawls, *A Theory of Justice* (Cambridge, Mass.: Harvard University Press, 1971).

Peter Winch, *Moral Integrity* (Oxford: Basil Blackwell, 1968).

Fundamental Principles of the Metaphysic of Morals
Immanuel Kant

Ancient Greek philosophy was divided into three sciences: Physics, Ethics, and Logic. This division is perfectly suitable to the nature of the thing; and the only improvement that can be made in it is to add the principle on which it is based, so that we may both satisfy ourselves of its completeness, and also be able to determine correctly the necessary subdivisions.

All rational knowledge is either *material* or *formal*: the former considers some object, the latter is concerned only with the form of the understanding and of the reason itself, and with the universal laws of thought in general without distinction of its objects. Formal philosophy is called logic. Material philosophy, however, which has to do with determinate objects and the laws to which they are subject, is again twofold; for these laws are either laws of *nature* or of *freedom*. The science of the former is physics, that of the latter, ethics; they are also called *natural philosophy* and *moral philosophy* respectively.

Logic cannot have any empirical part—that is, a part in which the universal and necessary laws of thought should rest on grounds taken from experience; otherwise it would not be logic, that is, a canon for the understanding or the reason, valid for all thought, and capable of demonstration. Natural and moral philosophy, on the contrary, can each have their empirical part, since the former has to determine the laws of nature as an object of experi-

Immanuel Kant (1724–1804) was surely the greatest philosopher of the German Enlightenment, and many would consider him to be the greatest philosopher of all time. He wrote in all the major areas of philosophy, and his influence is still widely felt. The work included here was written in 1785 and was translated into English by Thomas K. Abbott in 1873. Because Kant's writing is extremely difficult, it is sometimes helpful to consult a commentator; see, for example, J. G. Murphy, *Kant: The Philosophy of Right* (London: Macmillan, 1970).

ence, the latter the laws of the human will, so far as it is affected by nature; the former, however, being laws according to which everything does happen, the latter, laws according to which everything ought to happen. Ethics, however, must also consider the conditions under which what ought to happen frequently does not.

We may call all philosophy *empirical,* so far as it is based on grounds of experience; on the other hand, that which delivers its doctrines from *a priori* principles alone we may call *pure* philosophy. When the latter is merely formal, it is *logic*; if it is restricted to definite objects of the understanding, it is *metaphysic*.

In this way there arises the idea of a twofold metaphysic—a *metaphysic of nature* and a *metaphysic of morals.* Physics will thus have an empirical and also a rational part. It is the same with ethics; but here the empirical part might have the special name of *practical anthropology,* the name *morality* being appropriated to the rational part.

All trades, arts, and handiworks have gained by division of labor, namely, when, instead of one man doing everything, each confines himself to a certain kind of work distinct from others in the treatment it requires, so as to be able to perform it with greater facility and in the greatest perfection. Where the different kinds of work are not so distinguished and divided, where everyone is a jack-of-all-trades, there manufactures remain still in the greatest barbarism. It might deserve to be considered whether pure philosophy in all its parts does not require a man specially devoted to it, and whether it would not be better for the whole business of science if those who, to please the tastes of the public, are wont to blend the rational and empirical elements together, mixed in all sorts of proportions unknown to themselves, and who call themselves independent thinkers, giving the name of minute philosophers to those who apply themselves to the rational part only—if these, I say, were warned not to carry on two employments together which differ widely in the treatment they demand, for each of which perhaps a special talent is required, and the combination of which in one person only produces bunglers. But I only ask here whether the nature of science does not require that we should always carefully separate the empirical from the rational part, and prefix to physics proper (or empirical physics) a metaphysic of nature, and to practical anthropology a metaphysic of morals, which must be carefully cleared of everything empirical so that we may know how much can be accomplished by pure reason in both cases, and from what sources it draws this its *a priori* teaching, and that whether the latter inquiry is conducted by all moralists (whose name is legion), or only by some who feel a calling thereto.

As my concern here is with moral philosophy, I limit the question suggested to this: whether it is not of the utmost necessity to construct a pure moral philosophy, perfectly cleared of everything which is only empirical, and which belongs to anthropology? For that such a philosophy must be possible is evident from the common idea of duty and of the moral laws. Everyone must admit that if a law is to have moral force, that is, to be the basis of an obligation, it must carry with it absolute necessity; that, for example, the precept, "Thou shalt not lie," is not valid for men alone, as if other rational beings had no need to observe it; and so with all the other moral laws properly so called; that, therefore, the basis of obligation must not be sought in the nature of man, or in the circumstances in the world in which he is placed, but *a priori* simply in the conceptions of pure reason; and although any other precept which is founded on principles of mere experience may be in certain respects universal, yet in as far as it rests even in the least degree on an empirical basis, perhaps only as to a motive, such a precept, while it may be a practical rule, can never be called a moral law.

Thus not only are moral laws with their principles essentially distinguished from every other kind of practical knowledge in which there is anything empirical, but all moral philosophy rests wholly on its pure part. When applied to man, it does not borrow the least thing from the knowledge of man himself (anthropology), but gives laws *a priori* to him as a rational being. No doubt these laws require a judgment sharpened by experience, in order, on the one hand, to distinguish in what cases they are applicable, and, on the other, to procure for them access to the will of the man, and effectual influence on conduct; since man is acted on by so many inclinations that, though capable of the idea of a practical pure reason, he is not so easily able to make it effective *in concreto* in his life.

A metaphysic of morals is therefore indispensably necessary, not merely for speculative reasons, in order to investigate the sources of the practical principles which are to be found *a priori* in our reason, but also because morals themselves are liable to all sorts of corruption as long as we are without that clue and supreme canon by which to estimate them correctly. For in order that an action should be morally good, it is not enough that it *conform* to the moral law, but it must also be done *for the sake of the law,* otherwise that conformity is only very contingent and uncertain; since a principle which is not moral, although it may now and then produce actions conformable to the law, will also often produce actions which contradict it. Now it is only in a pure philosophy that we can look for the moral law in its purity and genuineness (and, in a practical matter, this is of the utmost consequence): we must, therefore, begin with pure philosophy (metaphysic), and without it there cannot be any moral philosophy at all. That which mingles these pure principles with the empirical does not deserve the name of philosophy (for what distinguishes philosophy from common rational knowledge is that it treats in separate sciences what the latter only comprehends confusedly); much less does it deserve that of moral philosophy, since by this confusion it even spoils the purity of morals themselves and counteracts its own end.

Let it not be thought, however, that what is here demanded is already extant in the propaedeutic prefixed by the celebrated Wolf to his moral philosophy, namely, his so-called *general practical philosophy,* and that, therefore, we have not to strike into an entirely new field. Just because it was to be a general practical philosophy, it has not taken into consideration a will of any particular kind—say, one which should be determined solely from *a priori* principles without any empirical motives, and which we might call a pure will —but volition in general, with all the actions and conditions which belong to it in this general signification. By this it is distinguished from a metaphysic of morals, just as general logic, which treats of the acts and canons of thought *in general,* is distinguished from transcendental philosophy, which treats of the particular acts and canons of *pure* thought, that is, that whose cognitions are altogether *a priori.* For the metaphysic of morals has to examine the idea and the principles of a possible *pure* will, and not the acts and conditions of human volition generally, which for the most part are drawn from psychology. It is true that moral laws and duty are spoken of in the general practical philosophy (contrary indeed to all fitness). But this is no objection, for in this respect also the authors of that science remain true to their idea of it; they do not distinguish the motives which are prescribed as such by reason alone altogether *a priori,* and which are properly moral, from the empirical motives which the understanding raises to general conceptions merely by comparison of experiences; but without noticing the difference of their sources, and looking on them all as homogeneous, they consider only their greater or less amount. It is in this way they frame their notion of *obligation,* which, though anything but moral, is all that can be asked for in a philosophy which passes no judgment at all on the origin of all possible practical concepts, whether they are *a priori* or only *a posteriori.*

Intending to publish hereafter a metaphysic of morals, I issue in the first instance these fundamental principles. Indeed there is properly no other foundation for it than the *critical examination of a pure practical reason*; just as that of metaphysics is the critical examination of the pure speculative reason, already published. But in the first place the former is not so absolutely necessary as the latter, because in moral concerns human reason can easily be brought to a high degree of correctness and completeness, even in the commonest understanding, while on the contrary in its theoretic but pure use it is wholly dialectical; and in the second place, if the critique of a pure practical reason is to be complete, it must be possible at the same time to show its identity with the speculative reason in a common principle, for it can ultimately be only one and the same reason which has to be distinguished merely in its application. I could not, however, bring it to such completeness here without introducing considerations of a wholly different kind, which would be perplexing to the reader. On this account I have adopted the title of *Fundamental Principles of the Metaphysic of Morals* instead of that of a *critical examination of the pure practical reason.*

But in the third place, since a metaphysic of morals, in spite of the discouraging title, is yet capable of being presented in a popular form, and one adapted to the common understanding, I find it useful to separate from it this preliminary treatise on its fundamental principles, in order that I may not hereafter have need to introduce these necessarily subtle discussions into a book of a more simple character.

The present treatise is, however, nothing more than the investigation and establishment of *the supreme principle of morality,* and this alone constitutes a study complete in itself, and one which ought to be kept apart from every other moral investigation. No doubt, my conclusions on this weighty question, which has hitherto been very unsatisfactorily examined, would receive much light from the application of the same principle to the whole system, and would be greatly confirmed by the adequacy which it exhibits throughout; but I must forego this advantage, which indeed would be after all more gratifying than useful, since the easy applicability of a principle and its apparent adequacy give no very certain proof of its soundness, but rather inspire a certain partiality, which prevents us from examining and estimating it strictly in itself, and without regard to consequences.

I have adopted in this work the method which I think most suitable, proceeding analytically from common knowledge to the determination of its ultimate principle, and again descending synthetically from the examination of this principle and its sources to the common knowledge in which we find it employed. The division will, therefore, be as follows:

1. *First section:* Transition from the common rational knowledge of morality to the philosophical.
2. *Second section:* Transition from popular moral philosophy to the metaphysic of morals.
3. *Third section:* Final step from the metaphysic of morals to the critique of the pure practical reason.

First Section

Transition from the Common Rational Knowledge of Morality to the Philosophical

Nothing can possibly be conceived in the world, or even out of it, which can be called good without qualification, except a *good will.* Intelligence, wit, judgment, and the other *talents* of the mind, however they may be named, or courage, resolution, perseverance, as qualities of temperament, are undoubtedly good and desirable in many respects; but these gifts of nature may also become extremely bad and mischievous if the will which is to make use of them, and which, therefore, constitutes what is called *character,* is not good. It is the same with the *gifts of fortune.* Power, riches, honor, even health, and the general well-being and contentment with one's condition which is called *happiness,* inspire pride, and often presumption, if there is not a good will to correct the influence of these on the mind, and with this also to rectify the whole principle of acting, and adapt it to its end. The sight of a being who is not adorned with a single feature of a pure and good will, enjoying unbroken prosperity, can never give pleasure to an impartial rational spectator. Thus a good will appears to constitute the indispensable condition even of being worthy of happiness.

There are even some qualities which are of service to this good will itself, and may facilitate its action, yet which have no intrinsic unconditional value, but always presuppose a good will, and this qualifies the esteem that we justly have for them, and does not permit us to regard them as absolutely good. Moderation in the affections and passions, self-control, and calm deliberation are not only good in many respects, but even seem to constitute part of the intrinsic worth of the person; but they are far from deserving to be called good without qualification, although they have been so unconditionally praised by the ancients. For without the principles of a good will, they may become extremely bad; and the coolness of a villain not only makes him far more dangerous, but also directly makes him more abominable in our eyes than he would have been without it.

A good will is good not because of what it performs or effects, not by its aptness for the attainment of some proposed end, but simply by virtue of the volition—that is, it is good in itself, and considered by itself is to be esteemed much higher than all that can be brought about by it in favor of any inclination, nay, even of the sum-total of all inclinations. Even if it should happen that, owing to special disfavor of fortune, or the niggardly provision of a step-motherly nature, this will should wholly lack power to accomplish its purpose, if with its greatest efforts it should yet achieve nothing, and there should remain only the good will (not, to be sure, a mere wish, but the summoning of all means in our power), then, like a jewel, it would still shine by its own light, as a thing which has its whole value in itself. Its usefulness or fruitlessness can neither add to nor take away anything from this value. It would be, as it were, only the setting to enable us to handle it the more conveniently in common commerce, or to attract to it the attention of those who are not yet connoisseurs, but not to recommend it to true connoisseurs, or to determine its value.

There is, however, something so strange in this idea of the absolute value of the mere will, in which no account is taken of its utility, that notwithstanding the thorough assent of even common reason to the idea, yet a suspicion must arise that it may perhaps really be the product of mere high-flown fancy, and that we may have misunderstood the purpose of nature in assigning reason as the governor of our will. Therefore we will examine this idea from this point of view.

In the physical constitution of an organized being, that is, a being adapted suitably to the purposes of life, we assume it as a fundamental principle that no organ for any purpose will be found but what is also the fittest and best adapted for that purpose. Now in a being which has reason and a will, if the proper object of nature were its *conservation,* its *welfare,* in a word, its *happiness,* then nature would have hit upon a very bad arrangement in selecting the reason of the creature to carry out this purpose. For all the actions which the creature has to perform with a view to this purpose, and the whole rule of its conduct, would be far more surely prescribed to it by instinct, and that end would have been attained thereby much more certainly than it ever can be by reason. Should reason have been communicated to this favored creature over and above, it must only have served it to contemplate the happy constitution of its nature, to admire it, to congratulate itself thereon, and to feel thankful for it to the beneficent cause, but not that it should subject its desires to that weak and delusive guidance, and meddle bunglingly with the purpose of nature. In a word, nature would have taken care that reason should not break forth into *practical exercise,* nor have the presumption, with its weak insight, to think out for itself the plan of happiness and of the means of attaining it. Nature would not only have taken on herself the choice of the ends but also of the means, and with wise foresight would have entrusted both to instinct.

And, in fact, we find that the more a cultivated reason applies itself with deliberate purpose to the enjoyment of life and happiness, so much the more does the man fail of true satisfaction. And from this circumstance there arises in many, if they are candid enough to confess it, a certain degree of *misology,* that is, hatred of reason, especially in the case of those who are most experienced in the use of it, because after calculating all the advantages they derive —I do not say from the invention of all the arts of common luxury, but even from the sciences (which seem to them to be after all only a luxury of the understanding)—they find that they have, in fact, only brought more trouble on their shoulders rather than gained in happiness; and they end by envying rather than despising the more common stamp of men who keep closer to the guidance of mere instinct, and do not allow their reason much influence on their conduct. And this we must admit, that the judgment of those who would very much lower the lofty eulogies of the advantages which reason gives us in regard to the happiness and satisfaction of life, or who would even reduce them below zero, is by no means morose or ungrateful to the goodness with which the world is governed, but that there lies at the root of these judgments the idea that our existence has a different and far nobler end, for which, and not for happiness, reason is properly intended, and which must, therefore, be regarded as the supreme condition to which the private ends of man must, for the most part, be postponed.

For as reason is not competent to guide the will with certainty in regard to its objects and the satisfaction of all our wants (which it to some extent even multiplies), this being an end to which an implanted instinct would have led with much greater certainty; and since, nevertheless, reason is imparted to us as a practical faculty, that is, as one which is to have influence on the *will,* therefore, admitting that nature generally in the distribution of her capacities has adapted the means to the end, its true destination must be to produce a *will,* not merely good as a *means* to something else, but *good in itself,* for which reason was absolutely necessary. This will then, though not indeed the sole and complete good, must be the supreme good and the condition of every other, even of the desire of happiness. Under these circumstances, there is nothing inconsistent with the wisdom of nature in the fact that the cultivation of the reason, which is requisite for the first and unconditional purpose, does in many ways interfere, at least in this life, with the attainment of the second, which is always conditional—namely, happiness. Nay, it may even reduce it to nothing, without nature thereby failing of her purpose. For reason recognizes the establishment of a good will as its highest practical destination, and in attaining this purpose is capable only of a satisfaction of its own proper kind, namely, that from the attainment of an end, which end again is determined by reason only, notwithstanding that this may involve many a disappointment to the ends of inclination.

We have then to develop the notion of a will which deserves to be highly esteemed for itself, and is good without a view to anything further, a notion which exists already in the sound natural understanding, requiring rather to be cleared up than to be taught, and which in estimating the value of our actions always takes the first place and constitutes the condition of all the rest. In order to do this, we will take the notion of duty, which includes that of a good will, although implying certain subjective restrictions and hindrances. These, however, far from concealing it or rendering it unrecognizable, rather bring it out by contrast and make it shine forth so much the brighter.

I omit here all actions which are already recognized as inconsistent with duty, although they may be useful for this or that purpose, for with these the question whether they are done *from duty* cannot arise at all, since they even conflict with it. I also set aside those actions which really conform to duty, but to which men have *no* direct *inclination,* performing them because they are impelled thereto by some other inclination. For in this case we can readily distinguish whether the action which agrees with duty is done *from duty* or from a selfish view. It is much harder to make this distinction when the action accords with duty, and the subject has besides a *direct* inclination to it. For example, it is always a matter of duty that a dealer should not overcharge an inexperienced purchaser; and wherever there is much commerce the prudent tradesman does not overcharge, but keeps a fixed price for everyone, so that a child buys of him as well as any other. Men are thus *honestly* served; but this is not enough to make us believe that the tradesman has so acted from duty and from principles of honesty; his own advantage required it; it is out of the question in this case to suppose that he might besides have a direct inclination in favor of the buyers, so that, as it were, from love he should give no advantage to one over another. Accordingly the action was done neither from duty nor from direct inclination, but merely with a selfish view.

On the other hand, it is a duty to maintain one's life; and, in addition, everyone has also a direct inclination to do so. But on this account the often anxious care which most men take for it has no intrinsic worth, and their maxim has no moral import. They preserve their life *as duty requires,* no doubt, but not *because duty requires.* On the other hand, if adversity and hopeless sorrow have completely taken away the relish for life, if the unfortunate one, strong in mind, indignant at his fate rather than desponding or dejected, wishes for death, and yet preserves his life without loving it—not from inclination or fear, but from duty—then his maxim has a moral worth.

To be beneficent when we can is a duty; and besides this, there are many minds so sympathetically constituted that, without any other motive of vanity or self-interest, they find a pleasure in spreading joy around them, and can take delight in the satisfaction of others so far as it is their own work. But I maintain that in such a case an action of this kind, however proper, however amiable it may be, has nevertheless no true moral worth, but is on a level with other inclinations, for example, the inclination to honor, which, if it is happily directed to that which is in fact of public utility and accordant with duty, and consequently honorable, deserves praise and encouragement, but not esteem. For the maxim lacks the moral import, namely, that such actions be done *from duty,* not from inclination. Put the case that the mind of that philanthropist was clouded by sorrow of his own, extinguishing all sympathy with the lot of others, and that while he still has the power to benefit others in distress, he is not touched by their trouble because he is absorbed with his own; and now suppose that he tears himself out of this dead insensibility and performs the action without any inclination to it, but simply from duty, then first has his action its genuine moral worth. Further still, if nature has put little sympathy in the heart of this or that man, if he, supposed to be an upright man, is by temperament cold and indifferent to the sufferings of others, perhaps because in respect of his own he is provided with the special gift of patience and fortitude, and supposes, or even requires, that others should have the same—and such a man would certainly not be the meanest product of nature—but if nature had not specially framed him for a philanthropist, would he not still find in himself a source from whence to give himself a far higher worth than that of a good-natured temperament could be? Unquestionably. It is just in this that the moral worth of the character is brought out which is incomparably the highest of all, namely, that he is beneficent, not from inclination, but from duty.

To secure one's own happiness is a duty, at least indirectly; for discontent with one's condition, under a pressure of many anxieties and amidst unsatisfied wants, might easily become a great *temptation to transgression of duty.* But here again, without looking to duty, all men have already the strongest and most intimate inclination to happiness, because it is just in this idea that all inclinations are combined in one total. But the precept of happiness is often of such a sort that it greatly interferes with some inclinations, and yet a man cannot form any definite and certain conception of the sum of satisfaction of all of them which is called happiness. It is not then to be wondered at that a single inclination, definite both as to what it promises and as to the time within which it can be gratified, is often able to overcome such a fluctuating idea, and that a gouty patient, for instance, can choose to enjoy what he likes, and to suffer what he may, since, according to his calculation, on this occasion at least, he has [only] not sacrificed the enjoyment of the present moment to a possibly mistaken expectation of a happiness which is supposed to be found in health. But even in this case, if the general desire for happiness did not influence his will, and supposing that in his particular case health was not a necessary element in this calculation, there yet remains in this, as in all other cases, this law—namely, that he should promote his happiness not from inclination but from duty, and by this would his conduct first acquire true moral worth.

It is in this manner, undoubtedly, that we are to understand those passages of Scripture also in which we are commanded to love our neighbor, even our enemy. For love, as an affection, cannot be commanded, but beneficence for duty's sake may, even though we are not impelled to it by any inclination—nay, are even repelled by a natural and unconquerable aversion. This is *practical* love, and not *pathological*—a love which is seated in the will, and not in the propensions of sense—in principles of action and not of tender sympathy; and it is this love alone which can be commanded.

The second proposition is: That an action done from duty derives its moral worth; *not from the purpose* which is to be attained by it, but from the maxim by which it is determined, and therefore does not depend on the realization of the object of the action, but merely on the *principle of volition* by which the action has taken place, without regard to any object of desire. It is clear from what precedes that the purposes which we may have in view in our actions, or their effects regarded as ends and springs of the will, cannot give to actions any unconditional or moral worth. In what, then, can their worth lie if it is not to consist in the will and in reference to its expected effect? It cannot lie anywhere but in the *principle of the will* without regard to the ends which can be attained by the action. For the will stands between its *a priori* principle, which is formal, and its *a posteriori* spring, which is material, as between two roads, and as it must be determined by something, it follows that it must be determined by the formal principle of volition when an action is done from duty, in which case every material principle has been withdrawn from it.

The third proposition, which is a consequence of the two preceding, I would express thus: *Duty is the necessity of acting from respect for the law.* I may have *inclination* for an object as the effect of my proposed action, but I cannot have *respect* for it just for this reason that it is an effect and not an energy of will. Similarly, I cannot have respect for inclination, whether my own or another's; I can at most, if my own, approve it; if another's, sometimes even love it, that is, look on it as favorable to my own interest. It is only what is connected with my will as a principle, by no means as an effect —what does not subserve my inclination, but overpowers it, or at least in case of choice excludes it from its calculation—in other words, simply the law of itself, which can be an object of respect, and hence a command. Now an action done from duty must wholly exclude the influence of inclination, and with it every object of the will, so that nothing remains which can determine the will except objectively the *law,* and subjectively *pure respect* for this practical law, and consequently the maxim[1] that I should follow this law even to the thwarting of all my inclinations.

Thus the moral worth of an action does not lie in the effect expected from it, nor in any principle of action which requires to borrow its motive from this expected effect. For all these effects—agreeableness of one's condition, and even the promotion of the happiness of others—could have been also brought about by other causes, so that for this there would have been no need of the will of a rational being; whereas it is in this alone that the supreme and unconditional good can be found. The pre-eminent good which we call moral can therefore consist in nothing else than *the conception of law* in itself, *which certainly is only possible in a rational being,* in so far as this conception, and not the expected effect, determines the will. This is a good which is already present in the person who acts accordingly, and we have not to wait for it to appear first in the result.[2]

But what sort of law can that be the conception of which must determine the will, even without paying any regard to the effect expected from it, in order that this will may be called good absolutely and without qualification? As I have deprived the will of every impulse which could arise to it from obedience to any law, there remains nothing but the universal conformity of its actions to law in general, which alone is to serve the will as a principle, that is, I am never to act otherwise than so *that I could also will that my maxim should become a universal law.* Here, now, it is the simple conformity to law in general, without assuming any particular law applicable to certain

---

[1] A *maxim* is the subjective principle of volition. The objective principle (i.e., that which would also serve subjectively as a practical principle to all rational beings if reason had full power over the faculty of desire) is the practical *law.*

[2] It might be here objected to me that I take refuge behind the word *respect* in an obscure feeling, instead of giving a distinct solution of the question by a concept of the reason. But although respect is a feeling, it is not a feeling *received* through influence, but is *self-wrought* by a rational concept, and, therefore, is specifically distinct from all feelings of the former kind, which may be referred either to inclination or fear. What I recognize immediately as a law for me, I recognize with respect. This merely signifies the consciousness that my will is *subordinate* to a law, without the intervention of other influences on my sense. The immediate determination of the will by the law, and the consciousness of this, is called *respect,* so that this is regarded as an *effect* of the law on the subject, and not as the *cause* of it. Respect is properly the conception of a worth which thwarts my self-love. Accordingly it is something which is considered neither as an object of inclination nor of fear, although it has something analogous to both. The *object* of respect is the *law* only, that is, the law which we impose on *ourselves,* and yet recognize as necessary in itself. As a law, we are subjected to it without consulting self-love; as imposed by us on ourselves, it is a result of our will. In the former aspect it has an analogy to fear, in the latter to inclination. Respect for a person is properly only respect for the law (of honesty, etc.) of which he gives us an example. Since we also look on the improvement of our talents as a duty, we consider that we see in a person of talents, as it were, the *example of a law* (viz., to become like him in this by exercise), and this constitutes our respect. All so-called moral *interest* consists simply in *respect* for the law.

actions, that serves the will as its principle, and must so serve it if duty is not to be a vain delusion and a chimerical notion. The common reason of men in its practical judgments perfectly coincides with this, and always has in view the principle here suggested. Let the question be, for example: May I when in distress make a promise with the intention not to keep it? I readily distinguish here between the two significations which the question may have: whether it is prudent or whether it is right to make a false promise? The former may undoubtedly often be the case. I see clearly indeed that it is not enough to extricate myself from a present difficulty by means of this subterfuge, but it must be well considered whether there may not hereafter spring from this lie much greater inconvenience than that from which I now free myself, and as, with all my supposed *cunning,* the consequences cannot be so easily foreseen but that credit once lost may be much more injurious to me than any mischief which I seek to avoid at present, it should be considered whether it would not be more *prudent* to act herein according to a universal maxim, and to make it a habit to promise nothing except with the intention of keeping it. But it is soon clear to me that such a maxim will still only be based on the fear of consequences. Now it is a wholly different thing to be truthful from duty, and to be so from apprehension of injurious consequences. In the first case, the very notion of the action already implies a law for me; in the second case, I must first look about elsewhere to see what results may be combined with it which would affect myself. For to deviate from the principle of duty is beyond all doubt wicked; but to be unfaithful to my maxim of prudence may often be very advantageous to me, although to abide by it is certainly safer. The shortest way, however, and an unerring one, to discover the answer to this question whether a lying promise is consistent with duty, is to ask myself, Should I be content that my maxim (to extricate myself from difficulty by a false promise) should hold good as a universal law, for myself as well as for others; and should I be able to say to myself, "Every one may make a deceitful promise when he finds himself in a difficulty from which he cannot otherwise extricate himself"? Then I presently become aware that, while I can will the lie, I can by no means will that lying should be a universal law. For with such a law there would be no promises at all, since it would be in vain to allege my intention in regard to my future actions to those who would not believe this allegation, or if they over-hastily did so, would pay me back in my own coin. Hence my maxim, as soon as it should be made a universal law, would necessarily destroy itself.

I do not, therefore, need any far-reaching penetration to discern what I have to do in order that my will may be morally good. Inexperienced in the course of the world, incapable of being prepared for all its contingencies, I only ask myself: Canst thou also will that thy maxim should be a universal law? If not, then it must be rejected, and that not because of a disadvantage accruing from it to myself or even to others, but because it cannot enter as a principle into a possible universal legislation, and reason extorts from me immediate respect for such legislation. I do not indeed as yet *discern* on what this respect is based (this the philosopher may inquire), but at least I understand this—that it is an estimation of the worth which far outweighs all worth of what is recommended by inclination, and that the necessity of acting from *pure* respect for the practical law is what constitutes duty, to which every other motive must give place because it is the condition of a will being good *in itself,* and the worth of such a will is above everything.

Thus, then, without quitting the moral knowledge of common human reason, we have arrived at its principle. And although, no doubt, common men do not conceive it in such an abstract and universal form, yet they always have it really before their eyes and use it as the standard of their decision. Here it would be easy to show how, with this compass in hand, men are well able to distinguish, in every case that occurs, what is good, what bad, conformably to duty or inconsistent with it, if, without in the least teaching them anything new, we only, like Socrates, direct their attention to the principle they themselves employ; and that, therefore, we do not need science and philosophy to know what we should do to be honest and good, yea, even wise and virtuous. Indeed we might well have conjectured beforehand that the knowledge of what every man is bound to do, and therefore also to know, would be within the reach of every man, even the commonest. Here we cannot forbear admiration when we see how great an advantage the practical judgment has over the theoretical in the common understanding of men. In the latter, if common reason ventures to depart from the laws of experience and from the perceptions of the senses, it falls into mere inconceivabilities and self-contradictions, at least into a chaos of uncertainty, obscurity, and instability. But in the practical sphere it is just when the common understanding excludes all sensible springs from practical laws that its power of judgment begins to show itself to advantage. It then becomes even subtle, whether it be that it chicanes with its own conscience or with other claims respecting what is to be called right, or whether it desires for its own instruction to determine honestly the worth of actions; and, in the latter case, it may even have as good a hope of hitting the mark as any philosopher whatever can promise himself. Nay, it is almost more sure of doing so, because the philosopher cannot have any other principle, while he may easily perplex his judgment by a multitude of considerations foreign to the matter, and so turn aside from the right way. Would it not therefore be wiser in moral concerns to acquiesce in the judgment of common reason, or at most only to call in philosophy for the purpose of rendering the system of morals more complete and intelligible, and its rules more convenient for use (especially for disputation), but not so as to draw off the common understanding from its happy simplicity, or to bring it by means of philosophy into a new path of inquiry and instruction?

Innocence is indeed a glorious thing; only, on the other hand, it is very sad that it cannot well maintain itself, and is easily seduced. On this account even wisdom—which otherwise consists more in conduct than in knowledge —yet has need of science, not in order to learn from it, but to secure for its precepts admission and permanence. Against all the commands of duty which reason represents to man as so deserving of respect, he feels in himself a powerful counterpoise in his wants and inclinations, the entire satisfaction of which he sums up under the name of happiness. Now reason issues its commands unyieldingly, without promising anything to the inclinations, and, as it were, with disregard and contempt for these claims, which are so impetuous and at the same time so plausible, and which will not allow themselves to be suppressed by any command. Hence there arises a natural *dialectic,* that is, a disposition to argue against these strict laws of duty and to question their validity, or at least their purity and strictness; and, if possible, to make them more accordant with our wishes and inclinations, that is to say, to corrupt them at their very source and entirely to destroy their worth—a thing which even common practical reason cannot ultimately call good.

Thus is the *common reason of man* compelled to go out of its sphere and to take a step into the field of a *practical philosophy,* not to satisfy any speculative want (which never occurs to it as long as it is content to be mere sound reason), but even on practical grounds, in order to attain in it information and clear instruction respecting the source of its principle, and the correct determination of it in opposition to the maxims which are based on wants and inclinations, so that it may escape from the perplexity of opposite claims, and not run the risk of losing all genuine moral principles through the equivocation into which it easily falls. Thus, when practical reason cultivates itself, there insensibly arises in it a dialectic which forces it to seek aid in philosophy, just as happens to it in its theoretic use; and in this case, therefore, as well as in the other, it will find rest nowhere but in a thorough critical examination of our reason.

Second Section

Transition from Popular Moral Philosophy to the Metaphysic of Morals

If we have hitherto drawn our notion of duty from the common use of our practical reason, it is by no means to be inferred that we have treated it as an empirical notion. On the contrary, if we attend to the experience of men's conduct, we meet frequent and, as we ourselves allow, just complaints that one cannot find a single certain example of the disposition to act from pure duty. Although many things are done in *conformity* with what *duty* prescribes, it is nevertheless always doubtful whether they are done strictly *from duty,* so as to have a moral worth. Hence there have at all times been philosophers who have altogether denied that this disposition actually exists at all in human actions, and have ascribed everything to a more or less refined self-love. Not that they have on that account questioned the soundness of the conception of morality; on the contrary, they spoke with sincere regret of the frailty and corruption of human nature, which, though noble enough to take as its rule an idea so worthy of respect, is yet too weak to follow it; and employs reason, which ought to give it the law only for the purpose of providing for the interest of the inclinations, whether singly or at the best in the greatest possible harmony with one another.

In fact, it is absolutely impossible to make out by experience with complete certainty a single case in which the maxim of an action, however right in itself, rested simply on moral grounds and on the conception of duty. Sometimes it happens that with the sharpest self-examination we can find nothing beside the moral principle of duty which could have been powerful enough to move us to this or that action and to so great a sacrifice; yet we cannot from this infer with certainty that it was not really some secret impulse of self-love, under the false appearance of duty, that was the actual determining cause of the will. We like then to flatter ourselves by falsely taking credit for a more noble motive; whereas in fact we can never, even by the strictest examination, get completely behind the secret springs of action, since, when the question is of moral worth, it is not with the actions which we see that we are concerned, but with those inward principles of them which we do not see.

Moreover, we cannot better serve the wishes of those who ridicule all morality as a mere chimera of human imagination overstepping itself from vanity, than by conceding to them that notions of duty must be drawn only from experience (as from indolence, people are ready to think is also the case with all other notions); for this is to prepare for them a certain triumph. I am willing to admit out of love of humanity that even most of our actions are correct, but if we look closer at them we everywhere come upon the dear self which is always prominent, and it is this they have in view, and not the strict command of duty, which would often require self-denial. Without being an enemy of virtue, a cool observer, one that does not mistake the wish for good, however lively, for its reality, may sometimes doubt whether true virtue is actually found anywhere in the world, and this especially as years increase and the judgment is partly made wiser by experience, and partly also more acute in observation. This being so, nothing can secure us from falling away altogether from our ideas of duty, or maintain in the soul a well-grounded respect for its law, but the clear conviction that although there should never have been actions which really sprang from such pure sources, yet whether this or that takes place is not at all the question; but that reason of itself, independent on all experience, ordains what ought to take place, that accordingly actions of which perhaps the world has hitherto never given an example, the feasibility even of which might be very much doubted by one who founds everything on experience, are nevertheless inflexibly commanded by reason;

that, for example, even though there might never yet have been a sincere friend, yet not a whit the less is pure sincerity in friendship required of every man, because, prior to all experience, this duty is involved as duty in the idea of a reason determining the will by *a priori* principles.

When we add further that, unless we deny that the notion of morality has any truth or reference to any possible object, we must admit that its law must be valid, not merely for men, but for all *rational creatures generally,* not merely under certain contingent conditions or with exceptions, but *with absolute necessity,* then it is clear that no experience could enable us to infer even the possibility of such apodictic laws. For with what right could we bring into unbounded respect as a universal precept for every rational nature that which perhaps holds only under the contingent conditions of humanity? Or how could laws of the determination of *our* will be regarded as laws of the determination of the will of rational beings generally, and for us only as such, if they were merely empirical and did not take their origin wholly *a priori* from pure but practical reason?

Nor could anything be more fatal to morality than that we should wish to derive it from examples. For every example of it that is set before me must be first itself tested by principles of morality, whether it is worthy to serve as an original example, that is, as a pattern, but by no means can it authoritatively furnish the conception of morality. Even the Holy One of the Gospels must first be compared with our ideal of moral perfection before we can recognize Him as such; and so He says of Himself, "Why call ye Me [whom you see] good; none is good [the model of good] but God only [whom ye do not see]?" But whence have we the conception of God as the supreme good? Simply from the *idea* of moral perfection, which reason frames *a priori* and connects inseparably with the notion of a free will. Imitation finds no place at all in morality, and examples serve only for encouragement, that is, they put beyond doubt the feasibility of what the law commands, they make visible that which the practical rule expresses more generally, but they can never authorize us to set aside the true original which lies in reason, and to guide ourselves by examples.

If then there is no genuine supreme principle of morality but what must rest simply on pure reason, independent on all experience, I think it is not necessary even to put the question whether it is good to exhibit these concepts in their generality (*in abstracto*) as they are established *a priori* along with the principles belonging to them, if our knowledge is to be distinguished from the *vulgar* and to be called philosophical. In our times indeed this might perhaps be necessary; for if we collected votes, whether pure rational knowledge separated from everything empirical, that is to say, metaphysic of morals, or whether popular practical philosophy is to be preferred, it is easy to guess which side would preponderate.

This descending to popular notions is certainly very commendable if the ascent to the principles of pure reason has first taken place and been satisfactorily accomplished. This implies that we first *found* Ethics on Metaphysics, and then, when it is firmly established, procure a *hearing* for it by giving it a popular character. But it is quite absurd to try to be popular in the first inquiry, on which the soundness of the principles depends. It is not only that this proceeding can never lay claim to the very rare merit of a true *philosophical popularity,* since there is no art in being intelligible if one renounces all thoroughness of insight; but also it produces a disgusting medley of compiled observations and half-reasoned principles. Shallow pates enjoy this because it can be used for everyday chat, but the sagacious find in it only confusion, and being unsatisfied and unable to help themselves, they turn away their eyes, while philosophers, who see quite well through this delusion, are little listened to when they call men off for a time from this pretended popularity in order that they might be rightfully popular after they have attained a definite insight.

We need only look at the attempts of moralists in that favorite fashion, and we shall find at one time the special constitution of human nature (including, however, the idea of a rational nature generally), at one time perfection, at another happiness, here moral sense, there fear of God, a little of this and a little of that, in marvellous mixture, without its occurring to them to ask whether the principles of morality are to be sought in the knowledge of human nature at all (which we can have only from experience); and, if this is not so—if these principles are to be found altogether *a priori* free from everything empirical, in pure rational concepts only, and nowhere else, not even in the smallest degree—then rather to adopt the method of making this a separate inquiry, as pure practical philosophy, or (if one may use a name so decried) as metaphysic of morals,[3] to bring it by itself to completeness, and to require the public, which wishes for popular treatment, to await the issue of this undertaking.

Such a metaphysic of morals, completely isolated, not mixed with any anthropology, theology, physics, or hyperphysics, and still less with occult qualities (which we might call hypophysical), is not only an indispensable substratum of all sound theoretical knowledge of duties, but is at the same time a desideratum of the highest importance to the actual fulfilment of their precepts. For the pure conception of duty, unmixed with any foreign addition of empirical attractions, and, in a word, the conception of the moral law, exercises on the human heart, by way of reason alone (which first becomes aware with this that it can of itself be practical), an influence so much more powerful than all other springs[4] which may be derived from the field of

---

[3] Just as pure mathematics are distinguished from applied, pure logic from applied, so if we choose we may also distinguish pure philosophy of morals (metaphysic) from applied (viz., applied to human nature). By this designation we are also at once reminded that moral principles are not based on properties of human nature, but must subsist *a priori* of themselves, while from such principles practical rules must be capable of being deduced for every rational nature, and accordingly for that of man.

[4] I have a letter from the late excellent Sulzer, in which he asks me what can be the reason that moral instruction, although containing much that is convincing for the reason, yet accomplishes so little? My answer was postponed in order that I might make it complete. But it is simply this, that the teachers themselves have not got their own notions clear, and

experience that in the consciousness of its worth it despises the latter, and can by degrees become their master; whereas a mixed ethics, compounded partly of motives drawn from feelings and inclinations, and partly also of conceptions of reason, must make the mind waver between motives which cannot be brought under any principle, which lead to good only by mere accident, and very often also to evil.

From what has been said, it is clear that all moral conceptions have their seat and origin completely *a priori* in the reason, and that, moreover, in the commonest reason just as truly as in that which is in the highest degree speculative; that they cannot be obtained by abstraction from any empirical, and therefore merely contingent, knowledge; that it is just this purity of their origin that makes them worthy to serve as our supreme practical principle, and that just in proportion as we add anything empirical, we detract from their genuine influence and from the absolute value of actions; that it is not only of the greatest necessity, in a purely speculative point of view, but is also of the greatest practical importance, to derive these notions and laws from pure reason, to present them pure and unmixed, and even to determine the compass of this practical or pure rational knowledge, that is, to determine the whole faculty of pure practical reason; and, in doing so, we must not make its principles dependent on the particular nature of human reason, though in speculative philosophy this may be permitted, or may even at times be necessary; but since moral laws ought to hold good for every rational creature, we must derive them from the general concept of a rational being. In this way, although for its *application* to man morality has need of anthropology, yet, in the first instance, we must treat it independently as pure philosophy, that is, as metaphysic, complete in itself (a thing which in such distinct branches of science is easily done); knowing well that, unless we are in possession of this, it would not only be vain to determine the moral element of duty in right actions for purposes of speculative criticism, but it would be impossible to base morals on their genuine principles, even for common practical purposes, especially of moral instruction, so as to produce pure moral dispositions, and to engraft them on men's minds to the promotion of the greatest possible good in the world.

But in order that in this study we may not merely advance by the natural steps from the common moral judgment (in this case very worthy of respect) to the philosophical, as has been already done, but also from a popular philosophy, which goes no further than it can reach by groping with the help

---

when they endeavor to make up for this by raking up motives of moral goodness from every quarter, trying to make their physic right strong, they spoil it. For the commonest understanding shows that if we imagine, on the one hand, an act of honesty done with steadfast mind, apart from every view to advantage of any kind in this world or another, and even under the greatest temptations of necessity or allurement, and, on the other hand, a similar act which was affected, in however low a degree, by a foreign motive, the former leaves far behind and eclipses the second; it elevates the soul, and inspires the wish to be able to act in like manner oneself. Even moderately young children feel this impression, and one should never represent duties to them in any other light.

of examples, to metaphysic (which does not allow itself to be checked by anything empirical and, as it must measure the whole extent of this kind of rational knowledge, goes as far as ideal conceptions, where even examples fail us), we must follow and clearly describe the practical faculty of reason, from the general rules of its determination to the point where the notion of duty springs from it.

Everything in nature works according to laws. Rational beings alone have the faculty of acting according *to the conception* of laws—that is, according to principles, that is, have a *will*. Since the deduction of actions from principles requires *reason,* the will is nothing but practical reason. If reason infallibly determines the will, then the actions of such a being which are recognized as objectively necessary are subjectively necessary also, that is, the will is a faculty to choose *that only* which reason independent on inclination recognizes as practically necessary, that is, as good. But if reason of itself does not sufficiently determine the will, if the latter is subject also to subjective conditions (particular impulses) which do not always coincide with the objective conditions, in a word, if the will does not *in itself* completely accord with reason (which is actually the case with men), then the actions which objectively are recognized as necessary are subjectively contingent, and the determination of such a will according to objective laws is *obligation,* that is to say, the relation of the objective laws to a will that is not thoroughly good is conceived as the determination of the will of a rational being by principles of reason, but which the will from its nature does not of necessity follow.

The conception of an objective principle, in so far as it is obligatory for a will, is called a command (of reason), and the formula of the command is called an Imperative.

All imperatives are expressed by the word *ought* [or *shall*], and thereby indicate the relation of an objective law of reason to a will which from its subjective constitution is not necessarily determined by it (an obligation). They say that something would be good to do or to forbear, but they say it to a will which does not always do a thing because it is conceived to be good to do it. That is practically *good,* however, which determines the will by means of the conceptions of reason, and consequently not from subjective causes, but objectively, that is, on principles which are valid for every rational being as such. It is distinguished from the *pleasant* as that which influences the will only by means of sensation from merely subjective causes, valid only for the sense of this or that one, and not as a principle of reason which holds for every one.[5]

---

[5] The dependence of the desires on sensations is called inclination, and this accordingly always indicates a *want.* The dependence of a contingently determinable will on principles of reason is called an *interest.* This, therefore, is found only in the case of a dependent will which does not always of itself conform to reason; in the Divine will we cannot conceive any interest. But the human will can also *take an interest* in a thing without therefore acting *from interest.* The former signifies the *practical* interest in the action, the latter the *pathological* in the object of the action. The former indicates only dependence of the will on principles of reason in themselves, the second, dependence on principles of reason for the

A perfectly good will would therefore be equally subject to objective laws (viz., laws of good), but could not be conceived as *obliged* thereby to act lawfully, because of itself from its subjective constitution it can only be determined by the conception of good. Therefore no imperatives hold for the Divine will, or in general for a *holy* will; *ought* is here out of place because the volition is already of itself necessarily in unison with the law. Therefore imperatives are only formulae to express the relation of objective laws of all volition to the subjective imperfection of the will of this or that rational being, for example, the human will.

Now all *imperatives* command either *hypothetically* or *categorically*. The former represent the practical necessity of a possible action as means to something else that is willed (or at least which one might possibly will). The categorical imperative would be that which represented an action as necessary of itself without reference to another end, that is, as objectively necessary.

Since every practical law represents a possible action as good, and on this account, for a subject who is practically determinable by reason as necessary, all imperatives are formulae determining an action which is necessary according to the principle of a will good in some respects. If now the action is good only as a means *to something else,* then the imperative is *hypothetical;* if it is conceived as good *in itself* and consequently as being necessarily the principle of a will which of itself conforms to reason, then it is *categorical.*

Thus the imperative declares what action possible by me would be good, and presents the practical rule in relation to a will which does not forthwith perform an action simply because it is good, whether because the subject does not always know that it is good, or because, even if it knows this, yet its maxims might be opposed to the objective principles of practical reason.

Accordingly the hypothetical imperative only says that the action is good for some purpose, *possible* or *actual.* In the first case it is a *problematical,* in the second an *assertorial* practical principle. The categorical imperative which declares an action to be objectively necessary in itself without reference to any purpose, that is, without any other end, is valid as an *apodictic* (practical) principle.

Whatever is possible only by the power of some rational being may also be conceived as a possible purpose of some will; and therefore the principles of action as regards the means necessary to attain some possible purpose are in fact infinitely numerous. All sciences have a practical part consisting of problems expressing that some end is possible for us, and of imperatives directing how it may be attained. These may, therefore, be called in general imperatives of *skill.* Here there is no question whether the end is rational and good, but only what one must do in order to attain it. The precepts for the

---

sake of inclination, reason supplying only the practical rules how the requirement of the inclination may be satisfied. In the first case the action interests me; in the second the object of the action (because it is pleasant to me). We have seen in the first section that in an action done from duty we must look not to the interest in the object, but only to that in the action itself, and in its rational principle (viz., the law).

physician to make his patient thoroughly healthy, and for a poisoner to ensure certain death, are of equal value in this respect, that each serves to effect its purpose perfectly. Since in early youth it cannot be known what ends are likely to occur to us in the course of life, parents seek to have their children taught a *great many things,* and provide for their *skill* in the use of means for all sorts of arbitrary ends, of none of which can they determine whether it may not perhaps hereafter be an object to their pupil, but which it is at all events *possible* that he might aim at; and this anxiety is so great that they commonly neglect to form and correct their judgment on the value of the things which may be chosen as ends.

There is *one* end, however, which may be assumed to be actually such to all rational beings (so far as imperatives apply to them, viz., as dependent beings), and, therefore, one purpose which they not merely *may* have, but which we may with certainty assume that they all actually *have* by a natural necessity, and this is *happiness.* The hypothetical imperative which expresses the practical necessity of an action as means to the advancement of happiness is *assertorial.* We are not to present it as necessary for an uncertain and merely possible purpose, but for a purpose which we may presuppose with certainty and *a priori* in every man, because it belongs to his being. Now skill in the choice of means to his own greatest well-being may be called *prudence,*[6] in the narrowest sense. And thus the imperative which refers to the choice of means to one's own happiness, that is, the precept of prudence, is still always *hypothetical;* the action is not commanded absolutely, but only as means to another purpose.

Finally, there is an imperative which commands a certain conduct immediately, without having as its condition any other purpose to be attained by it. This imperative is *categorical.* It concerns not the matter of the action, or its intended result, but its form and the principle of which it is itself a result; and what is essentially good in it consists in the mental disposition, let the consequence be what it may. This imperative may be called that of *morality.*

There is a marked distinction also between the volitions on these three sorts of principles in the *dissimilarity* of the obligation of the will. In order to mark this difference more clearly, I think they would be most suitably named in their order if we said they are either *rules* of skill, or *counsels* of prudence, or *commands* (*laws*) of morality. For it is *law* only that involves the conception of an *unconditional* and objective necessity, which is consequently universally valid; and commands are laws which must be obeyed, that is, must be followed, even in opposition to inclination. *Counsels,* indeed, involve necessity, but one which can only hold under a contingent subjective condition,

---

[6] The word *prudence* is taken in two senses: in the one it may bear the name of knowledge of the world, in the other that of private prudence. The former is a man's ability to influence others so as to use them for his own purposes. The latter is the sagacity to combine all these purposes for his own lasting benefit. This latter is properly that to which the value even of the former is reduced, and when a man is prudent in the former sense, but not in the latter, we might better say of him that he is clever and cunning, but, on the whole, imprudent.

viz., they depend on whether this or that man reckons this or that as part of his happiness; the categorical imperative, on the contrary, is not limited by any condition, and as being absolutely, although practically, necessary may be quite properly called a command. We might also call the first kind of imperatives *technical* (belonging to art), the second *pragmatic*[7] (belonging to welfare), the third *moral* (belonging to free conduct generally, that is, to morals).

Now arises the question, how are all these imperatives possible? This question does not seek to know how we can conceive the accomplishment of the action which the imperative ordains, but merely how we can conceive the obligation of the will which the imperative expresses. No special explanation is needed to show how an imperative of skill is possible. Whoever wills the end wills also (so far as reason decides his conduct) the means in his power which are indispensably necessary thereto. This proposition is, as regards the volition, analytical; for in willing an object as my effect there is already thought the causality of myself as an acting cause, that is to say, the use of the means; and the imperative educes from the conception of volition of an end the conception of actions necessary to this end. Synthetical propositions must no doubt be employed in defining the means to a proposed end; but they do not concern the principle, the act of the will, but the object and its realization. For example, that in order to bisect a line on an unerring principle I must draw from its extremities two intersecting arcs; this no doubt is taught by mathematics only in synthetical propositions; but if I know that it is only by this process that the intended operation can be performed, then to say that if I fully will the operation, I also will the action required for it, is an analytical proposition; for it is one and the same thing to conceive something as an effect which I can produce in a certain way, and to conceive myself as acting in this way.

If it were only equally easy to give a definite conception of happiness, the imperatives of prudence would correspond exactly with those of skill, and would likewise be analytical. For in this case as in that, it could be said whoever wills the end wills also (according to the dictate of reason necessarily) the indispensable means thereto which are in his power. But, unfortunately, the notion of happiness is so indefinite that although every man wishes to attain it, yet he never can say definitely and consistently what it is that he really wishes and wills. The reason of this is that all the elements which belong to the notion of happiness are altogether empirical, that is, they must be borrowed from experience, and nevertheless the idea of happiness requires an absolute whole, a maximum of welfare in my present and all future circumstances. Now it is impossible that the most clear-sighted and

---

[7] It seems to me that the proper signification of the word *pragmatic* may be most accurately defined in this way. For *sanctions* are called pragmatic which flow properly, not from the law of the states as necessary enactments, but from *precaution* for the general welfare. A history is composed pragmatically when it teaches *prudence*, that is, instructs the world how it can provide for its interests better, or at least as well as the men of former time.

at the same time most powerful being (supposed finite) should frame to himself a definite conception of what he really wills in this. Does he will riches, how much anxiety, envy, and snares might he not thereby draw upon his shoulders? Does he will knowledge and discernment, perhaps it might prove to be only an eye so much the sharper to show him so much the more fearfully the evils that are now concealed from him and that cannot be avoided, or to impose more wants on his desires, which already give him concern enough. Would he have long life? Who guarantees to him that it would not be a long misery? Would he at least have health? How often has uneasiness of the body restrained from excesses into which perfect health would have allowed one to fall, and so on? In short, he is unable, on any principle, to determine with certainty what would make him truly happy; because to do so he would need to be omniscient. We cannot therefore act on any definite principles to secure happiness, but only on empirical counsels, for example, of regimen, frugality, courtesy, reserve, etc., which experience teaches do, on the average, most promote well-being. Hence it follows that the imperatives of prudence do not, strictly speaking, command at all, that is, they cannot present actions objectively as practically *necessary;* that they are rather to be regarded as counsels than precepts of reason, that the problem to determine certainly and universally what action would promote the happiness of a rational being is completely insoluble, and consequently no imperative respecting it is possible which should, in the strict sense, command to do what makes happy; because happiness is not an ideal of reason but of imagination, resting solely on empirical grounds, and it is vain to expect that these should define an action by which one could attain the totality of a series of consequences which is really endless. This imperative of prudence would, however, be an analytical proposition if we assume that the means to happiness could be certainly assigned; for it is distinguished from the imperative of skill only by this that in the latter the end is merely *possible,* in the former it is *given;* as, however, both only ordain the means to that which we suppose to be willed as an end, it follows that the imperative which ordains the willing of the means to him who wills the end is in both cases analytical. Thus there is no difficulty in regard to the possibility of an imperative of this kind either.

On the other hand, the question, how the imperative of *morality* is possible, is undoubtedly one, the only one, demanding a solution, as this is not at all hypothetical, and the objective necessity which it presents cannot rest on any hypothesis, as is the case with the hypothetical imperatives. Only here we must never leave out of consideration that we *cannot* make out *by any example,* in other words, empirically, whether there is such an imperative at all; but it is rather to be feared that all those which seem to be categorical may yet be at bottom hypothetical. For instance, when the precept is: Thou shalt not promise deceitfully; and it is assumed that the necessity of this is not a mere counsel to avoid some other evil, so that it should mean: Thou shalt not make a lying promise, lest if it become known thou shouldst destroy thy credit, but that an action of this kind must be regarded as evil in itself, so that the imperative of the prohibition is categorical; then we cannot show with certainty in any example that the will was determined merely by the law, without any other spring of action, although it may appear to be so. For it is always possible that fear of disgrace, perhaps also obscure dread of other dangers, may have a secret influence on the will. Who can prove by experience the non-existence of a cause when all that experience tells us is that we do not perceive it? But in such a case the so-called moral imperative, which as such appears to be categorical and unconditional, would in reality be only a pragmatic precept, drawing our attention to our own interests, and merely teaching us to take these into consideration.

We shall therefore have to investigate *a priori* the possibility of a categorical imperative, as we have not in this case the advantage of its reality being given in experience, so that [the elucidation of] its possibility should be requisite only for its explanation, not for its establishment. In the meantime it may be discerned beforehand that the categorical imperative alone has the purport of a practical law; all the rest may indeed be called *principles* of the will but not laws, since whatever is only necessary for the attainment of some arbitrary purpose may be considered as in itself contingent, and we can at any time be free from the precept if we give up the purpose; on the contrary, the unconditional command leaves the will no liberty to choose the opposite, consequently it alone carries with it that necessity which we require in a law.

Secondly, in the case of this categorical imperative or law of morality, the difficulty (of discerning its possibility) is a very profound one. It is an *a priori* synthetical practical proposition;[8] and as there is so much difficulty in discerning the possibility of speculative propositions of this kind, it may readily be supposed that the difficulty will be no less with the practical.

In this problem we will first inquire whether the mere conception of a categorical imperative may not perhaps supply us also with the formula of it, containing the proposition which alone can be a categorical imperative; for even if we know the tenor of such an absolute command, yet how it is possible will require further special and laborious study, which we postpone to the last section.

When I conceive a hypothetical imperative, in general I do not know beforehand what it will contain until I am given the condition. But when I conceive a categorical imperative, I know at once what it contains. For as the imperative contains besides the law only the necessity that the maxims[9]

---

[8] I connect the act with the will without presupposing any condition resulting from any inclination, but *a priori,* and therefore necessarily (though only objectively, that is, assuming the idea of a reason possessing full power over all subjective motives). This is accordingly a practical proposition which does not deduce the willing of an action by mere analysis from another already presupposed (for we have not such a perfect will), but connects it immediately with the conception of the will of a rational being, as something not contained in it.

[9] A "maxim" is a subjective principle of action, and must be distinguished from the *objective principle,* namely, practical law. The former contains the practical rule set by reason according to the conditions of the subject (often its ignorance or its inclinations), so that it is the principle on which the subject *acts;* but the law is the objective principle valid for every rational being, and is the principle on which it *ought to act*—that is an imperative.

shall conform to this law, while the law contains no conditions restricting it, there remains nothing but the general statement that the maxim of the action should conform to a universal law, and it is this conformity alone that the imperative properly represents as necessary.

There is therefore but one categorical imperative, namely, this: *Act only on that maxim whereby thou canst at the same time will that it should become a universal law.*

Now if all imperatives of duty can be deduced from this one imperative as from their principle, then, although it should remain undecided whether what is called duty is not merely a vain notion, yet at least we shall be able to show what we understand by it and what this notion means.

Since the universality of the law according to which effects are produced constitutes what is properly called *nature* in the most general sense (as to form)—that is, the existence of things so far as it is determined by general laws—the imperative of duty may be expressed thus: *Act as if the maxim of thy action were to become by thy will a universal law of nature.*

We will now enumerate a few duties, adopting the usual division of them into duties to ourselves and to others, and into perfect and imperfect duties.[10]

1. A man reduced to despair by a series of misfortunes feels wearied of life, but is still so far in possession of his reason that he can ask himself whether it would not be contrary to his duty to himself to take his own life. Now he inquires whether the maxim of his action could become a universal law of nature. His maxim is: From self-love I adopt it as a principle to shorten my life when its longer duration is likely to bring more evil than satisfaction. It is asked then simply whether this principle founded on self-love can become a universal law of nature. Now we see at once that a system of nature of which it should be a law to destroy life by means of the very feeling whose special nature it is to impel to the improvement of life would contradict itself, and therefore could not exist as a system of nature; hence that maxim cannot possibly exist as a universal law of nature, and consequently would be wholly inconsistent with the supreme principle of all duty.

2. Another finds himself forced by necessity to borrow money. He knows that he will not be able to repay it, but sees also that nothing will be lent to him unless he promises stoutly to repay it in a definite time. He desires to make this promise, but he has still so much conscience as to ask himself: Is it not unlawful and inconsistent with duty to get out of a difficulty in this way? Suppose, however, that he resolves to do so, then the maxim of his action would be expressed thus: When I think myself in want of money, I will borrow money and promise to repay it, although I know that I never can do so. Now this principle of self-love or of one's own advantage may perhaps

---

[10] It must be noted here that I reserve the division of duties for a future *metaphysic of morals;* so that I give it here only as an arbitrary one (in order to arrange my examples). For the rest, I understand by a perfect duty one that admits no exception in favor of inclination, and then I have not merely external but also internal perfect duties. This is contrary to the use of the word adopted in the schools; but I do not intend to justify it here, as it is all one for my purpose whether it is admitted or not.

be consistent with my whole future welfare; but the question now is, Is it right? I change then the suggestion of self-love into a universal law, and state the question thus: How would it be if my maxim were a universal law? Then I see at once that it could never hold as a universal law of nature, but would necessarily contradict itself. For supposing it to be a universal law that every-one when he thinks himself in a difficulty should be able to promise whatever he pleases, with the purpose of not keeping his promise, the promise itself would become impossible, as well as the end that one might have in view in it, since no one would consider that anything was promised to him, but would ridicule all such statements as vain pretenses.

3. A third finds in himself a talent which with the help of some culture might make him a useful man in many respects. But he finds himself in comfortable circumstances and prefers to indulge in pleasure rather than to take pains in enlarging and improving his happy natural capacities. He asks, however, whether his maxim of neglect of his natural gifts, besides agreeing with his inclination to indulgence, agrees also with what is called duty. He sees then that a system of nature could indeed subsist with such a universal law, although men (like the South Sea islanders) should let their talents rest and resolve to devote their lives merely to idleness, amusement, and propaga-tion of their species—in a word, to enjoyment; but he cannot possibly *will* that this should be a universal law of nature, or be implanted in us as such by a natural instinct. For, as a rational being, he necessarily wills that his faculties be developed, since they serve him, and have been given him, for all sorts of possible purposes.

4. A fourth, who is in prosperity, while he sees that others have to con-tend with great wretchedness and that he could help them, thinks: What con-cern is it of mine? Let everyone be as happy as Heaven pleases, or as he can make himself; I will take nothing from him nor even envy him, only I do not wish to contribute anything to his welfare or to his assistance in distress! Now no doubt, if such a mode of thinking were a universal law, the human race might very well subsist, and doubtless even better than in a state in which everyone talks of sympathy and good-will, or even takes care occa-sionally to put it into practice, but, on the other side, also cheats when he can, betrays the rights of men, or otherwise violates them. But although it is possible that a universal law of nature might exist in accordance with that maxim, it is impossible to *will* that such a principle should have the universal validity of a law of nature. For a will which resolved this would contradict itself, inasmuch as many cases might occur in which one would have need of the love and sympathy of others, and in which, by such a law of nature, sprung from his own will, he would deprive himself of all hope of the aid he desires.

These are a few of the many actual duties, or at least what we regard as such, which obviously fall into two classes on the one principle that we have laid down. We must be *able to will* that a maxim of our action should be a universal law. This is the canon of the moral appreciation of the action generally. Some actions are of such a character that their maxim cannot without contradiction be even *conceived* as a universal law of nature, far from it being possible that we should *will* that it *should* be so. In others, this intrinsic impossibility is not found, but still it is impossible to *will* that their maxim should be raised to the universality of a law of nature, since such a will would contradict itself. It is easily seen that the former violate strict or rigorous (inflexible) duty; the latter only laxer (meritorious) duty. Thus it has been completely shown by these examples how all duties depend as regards the nature of the obligation (not the object of the action) on the same principle.

If now we attend to ourselves on occasion of any transgression of duty, we shall find that we in fact do not will that our maxim should be a universal law, for that is impossible for us; on the contrary, we will that the opposite should remain a universal law, only we assume the liberty of making an *exception* in our own favor or (just for this time only) in favor of our inclination. Consequently, if we considered all cases from one and the same point of view, namely, that of reason, we should find a contradiction in our own will, namely, that a certain principle should be objectively necessary as a universal law, and yet subjectively should not be universal, but admit of exceptions. As, however, we at one moment regard our action from the point of view of a will wholly conformed to reason, and then again look at the same action from the point of view of a will affected by inclination, there is not really any contradiction, but an antagonism of inclination to the precept of reason, whereby the universality of the principle is changed into a mere generality, so that the practical principle of reason shall meet the maxim half way. Now, although this cannot be justified in our own impartial judgment, yet it proves that we do really recognize the validity of the categorical imperative and (with all respect for it) only allow ourselves a few exceptions which we think unimportant and forced from us.

We have thus established at least this much—that if duty is a conception which is to have any import and real legislative authority for our actions, it can only be expressed in categorical, and not at all in hypothetical, imperatives. We have also, which is of great importance, exhibited clearly and definitely for every practical application the content of the categorical imperative, which must contain the principle of all duty if there is such a thing at all. We have not yet, however, advanced so far as to prove *a priori* that there actually is such an imperative, that there is a practical law which commands absolutely of itself and without any other impulse, and that the following of this law is duty.

With the view of attaining to this it is of extreme importance to remember that we must not allow ourselves to think of deducing the reality of this principle from the *particular attributes of human nature*. For duty is to be a practical, unconditional necessity of action; it must therefore hold for all rational beings (to whom an imperative can apply at all), and *for this reason only* be also a law for all human wills. On the contrary, whatever is deduced from certain feelings and propensions, nay, even, if possible, from any particular tendency proper to human reason, and which need not necessarily hold for the will of every rational being—this may indeed supply us with a maxim but not with a law; with a subjective principle on which we may have a propension and inclination to act, but not with an objective principle on which we should be *enjoined* to act, even though all our propensions, inclinations, and natural dispositions were opposed to it. In fact, the sublimity and intrinsic dignity of the command in duty are so much the more evident, the less the subjective impulses favor it and the more they oppose it, without being able in the slightest degree to weaken the obligation of the law or to diminish its validity.

Here then we see philosophy brought to a critical position, since it has to be firmly fixed, notwithstanding that it has nothing to support it in heaven or earth. Here it must show its purity as absolute director of its own laws, not the herald of those which are whispered to it by an implanted sense or who knows what tutelary nature. Although these may be better than nothing, yet they can never afford principles dictated by reason, which must have their source wholly *a priori* and thence their commanding authority, expecting everything from the supremacy of the law and the due respect for it, nothing from inclination, or else condemning the man to self-contempt and inward abhorrence.

Thus every empirical element is not only quite incapable of being an aid to the principle of morality, but is even highly prejudicial to the purity of morals; for the proper and inestimable worth of an absolutely good will consists just in this that the principle of action is free from all influence of contingent grounds, which alone experience can furnish. We cannot too much or too often repeat our warning against this lax and even mean habit of thought which seeks for its principle among empirical motives and laws; for human reason in its weariness is glad to rest on this pillow, and in a dream of sweet illusions (in which, instead of Juno, it embraces a cloud) it substitutes for morality a bastard patched up from limbs of various derivation, which looks like anything one chooses to see in it; only not like virtue to one who has once beheld her in her true form.[11]

The question then is this: Is it a necessary law *for all rational beings* that they should always judge of their actions by maxims of which they can themselves will that they should serve as universal laws? If it is so, then it must be connected (altogether *a priori*) with the very conception of the will of a rational being generally. But in order to discover this connection we must, however reluctantly, take a step into metaphysic, although into a domain of it which is distinct from speculative philosophy—namely, the metaphysic of morals. In a practical philosophy, where it is not the reasons of what *happens*

---

[11] To behold virtue in her proper form is nothing else but to contemplate morality stripped of all admixture of sensible things and of every spurious ornament of reward or self-love. How much she then eclipses everything else that appears charming to the affections, every one may readily perceive with the least exertion of his reason, if it be not wholly spoiled for abstraction.

that we have to ascertain, but the laws of what *ought to happen,* even although it never does, that is, objective practical laws, there it is not necessary to inquire into the reasons why anything pleases or displeases, how the pleasure of mere sensation differs from taste, and whether the latter is distinct from a general satisfaction of reason; on what the feeling of pleasure or pain rests, and how from it desires and inclinations arise, and from these again maxims by the cooperation of reason; for all this belongs to an empirical psychology, which would constitute the second part of physics, if we regard physics as the *philosophy* of nature, so far as it is based on *empirical laws.* But here we are concerned with objective practical laws, and consequently with the relation of the will to itself so far as it is determined by reason alone, in which case whatever has reference to anything empirical is necessarily excluded; since if *reason of itself alone* determines the conduct (and it is the possibility of this that we are now investigating), it must necessarily do so *a priori.*

The will is conceived as a faculty of determining oneself to action *in accordance with the conception of certain laws.* And such a faculty can be found only in rational beings. Now that which serves the will as the objective ground of its self-determination is the *end,* and if this is assigned by reason alone, it must hold for all rational beings. On the other hand, that which merely contains the ground of possibility of the action of which the effect is the end, this is called the *means.* The subjective ground of the desire is the *spring,* the objective ground of the volition is the *motive;* hence the distinction between subjective ends which rest on springs, and objective ends which depend on motives valid for every rational being. Practical principles are *formal* when they abstract from all subjective ends; they are *material* when they assume these, and therefore particular, springs of action. The ends which a rational being proposes to himself at pleasure as *effects* of his actions (material ends) are all only relative, for it is only their relation to the particular desires of the subject that gives them their worth, which therefore cannot furnish principles universal and necessary for all rational beings and for every volition, that is to say, practical laws. Hence all these relative ends can give rise only to hypothetical imperatives.

Supposing, however, that there were something *whose existence* has *in itself* an absolute worth, something which, being *an end in itself,* could be a source of definite laws, then in this and this alone would lie the source of a possible categorical imperative, that is, a practical law.

Now I say: man and generally any rational being *exists* as an end in himself, *not merely as a means* to be arbitrarily used by this or that will, but in all his actions, whether they concern himself or other rational beings, must be always regarded at the same time as an end. All objects of the inclinations have only a conditional worth; for if the inclinations and the wants founded on them did not exist, then their object would be without value. But the inclinations themselves, being sources of want, are so far from having an absolute worth for which they should be desired that, on the contrary, it must be the universal wish of every rational being to be wholly free from them. Thus the worth of any object which is *to be acquired* by our action is always conditional. Beings whose existence depends not on our will but on nature's, have nevertheless, if they are nonrational beings, only a relative value as means, and are therefore called *things;* rational beings, on the contrary, are called *persons,* because their very nature points them out as ends in themselves, that is, as something which must not be used merely as means, and so far therefore restricts freedom of action (and is an object of respect). These, therefore, are not merely subjective ends whose existence has a worth *for us* as an effect of our action, but *objective ends,* that is, things whose existence is an end in itself—an end, moreover, for which no other can be substituted, which they should subserve *merely* as means, for otherwise nothing whatever would possess *absolute worth;* but if all worth were conditioned and therefore contingent, then there would be no supreme practical principle of reason whatever.

If then there is a supreme practical principle or, in respect of the human will, a categorical imperative, it must be one which, being drawn from the conception of that which is necessarily an end for everyone because it is *an end in itself,* constitutes an *objective* principle of will, and can therefore serve as a universal practical law. The foundation of this principle is: *rational nature exists as an end in itself.* Man necessarily conceives his own existence as being so; so far then this is a *subjective* principle of human actions. But every other rational being regards its existence similarly, just on the same rational principle that holds for me;[12] so that it is at the same time an objective principle from which as a supreme practical law all laws of the will must be capable of being deduced. Accordingly the practical imperative will be as follows: *So act as to treat humanity, whether in thine own person or in that of any other, in every case as an end withal, never as means only.* We will now inquire whether this can be practically carried out.

To abide by the previous examples:

First, under the head of necessary duty to oneself: He who contemplates suicide should ask himself whether his action can be consistent with the idea of humanity *as an end in itself.* If he destroys himself in order to escape from painful circumstances, he uses a person merely as *a mean* to maintain a tolerable condition up to the end of life. But a man is not a thing, that is to say, something which can be used merely as means, but must in all his actions be always considered as an end in himself. I cannot, therefore, dispose in any way of a man in my own person so as to mutilate him, to damage or kill him. (It belongs to ethics proper to define this principle more precisely, so as to avoid all misunderstanding, for example, as to the amputation of the limbs in order to preserve myself; as to exposing my life to danger with a view to preserve it, etc. This question is therefore omitted here.)

Secondly, as regards necessary duties, or those of strict obligation, to-

---

[12] This proposition is here stated as a postulate. The ground of it will be found in the concluding section.

wards others: He who is thinking of making a lying promise to others will see at once that he would be using another man *merely as a mean,* without the latter containing at the same time the end in himself. For he whom I propose by such a promise to use for my own purposes cannot possibly assent to my mode of acting towards him, and therefore cannot himself contain the end of this action. This violation of the principle of humanity in other men is more obvious if we take in examples of attacks on the freedom and property of others. For then it is clear that he who transgresses the rights of men intends to use the person of others merely as means, without considering that as rational beings they ought always to be esteemed also as ends, that is, as beings who must be capable of containing in themselves the end of the very same action.[13]

Thirdly, as regards contingent (meritorious) duties to oneself: It is not enough that the action does not violate humanity in our own person as an end in itself, it must also *harmonize with* it. Now there are in humanity capacities of greater perfection which belong to the end that nature has in view in regard to humanity in ourselves as the subject; to neglect these might perhaps be consistent with the *maintenance* of humanity as an end in itself, but not with the *advancement* of this end.

Fourthly, as regards meritorious duties towards others: The natural end which all men have is their own happiness. Now humanity might indeed subsist although no one should contribute anything to the happiness of others, provided he did not intentionally withdraw anything from it; but after all, this would only harmonize negatively, not positively, with *humanity as an end in itself,* if everyone does not also endeavor, as far as in him lies, to forward the ends of others. For the ends of any subject which is an end in himself ought as far as possible to be *my* ends also, if that conception is to have its *full* effect with me.

This principle that humanity and generally every rational nature is *an end in itself* (which is the supreme limiting condition of every man's freedom of action), is not borrowed from experience, *first,* because it is universal, applying as it does to all rational beings whatever, and experience is not capable of determining anything about them; *secondly,* because it does not present humanity as an end to men (subjectively), that is, as an object which men do of themselves actually adopt as an end; but as an objective end which must as a law constitute the supreme limiting condition of all our subjective ends, let them be what we will; it must therefore spring from pure reason. In fact the objective principle of all practical legislation lies (according to the first principle) in *the rule* and its form of universality which makes it

---

[13] Let it not be thought that the common: *quad tibi non vis fieri,* etc., could serve here as the rule or principle. For it is only a deduction from the former, though with several limitations; it cannot be a universal law, for it does not contain the principle of duties to oneself, nor of the duties of benevolence to others (for many a one would gladly consent that others should not benefit him, provided only that he might be excused from showing benevolence to them), nor finally that of duties of strict obligation to one another, for on this principle the criminal might argue against the judge who punishes him, and so on.

capable of being a law (say, for example, a law of nature); but the *subjective* principle is in the *end;* now by the second principle, the subject of all ends is each rational being inasmuch as it is an end in itself. Hence follows the third practical principle of the will, which is the ultimate condition of its harmony with the universal practical reason, viz., the idea of *the will of every rational being as a universally legislative will.*

On this principle all maxims are rejected which are inconsistent with the will being itself universal legislator. Thus the will is not subject to the law, but so subject that it must be regarded *as itself giving the law,* and on this ground only subject to the law (of which it can regard itself as the author).

In the previous imperatives, namely, that based on the conception of the conformity of actions to general laws, as in a *physical system of nature,* and that based on the universal *prerogative* of rational beings as *ends* in themselves —these imperatives just because they were conceived as categorical excluded from any share in their authority all admixture of any interest as a spring of action; they were, however, only *assumed* to be categorical, because such an assumption was necessary to explain the conception of duty. But we could not prove independently that there are practical propositions which command categorically, nor can it be proved in this section; one thing, however, could be done, namely, to indicate in the imperative itself, by some determinate expression, that in the case of volition from duty all interest is renounced, which is the specific criterion of categorical as distinguished from hypothetical imperatives. This is done in the present (third) formula of the principle, namely, in the idea of the will of every rational being as a *universally legislating will.*

For although a will *which is subject to laws* may be attached to this law by means of an interest, yet a will which is itself a supreme lawgiver, so far as it is such, cannot possibly depend on any interest, since a will so dependent would itself still need another law restricting the interest of its self-love by the condition that it should be valid as universal law.

Thus the *principle* that every human will is *a will which in all its maxims gives universal laws,*[14] provided it be otherwise justified, would be very *well adapted* to be the categorical imperative, in this respect, namely, that just because of the idea of universal legislation it is *not based on any interest,* and therefore it alone among all possible imperatives can be *unconditional.* Or still better, converting the proposition, if there is a categorical imperative (that is, a law for the will of every rational being), it can only command that everything be done from maxims of one's will regarded as a will which could at the same time will that it should itself give universal laws, for in that case only the practical principle and the imperative which it obeys are unconditional, since they cannot be based on any interest.

Looking back now on all previous attempts to discover the principle of

---

[14] I may be excused from adducing examples to elucidate this principle, as those which have already been used to elucidate the categorical imperative and its formula would all serve for the like purpose here.

morality, we need not wonder why they all failed. It was seen that man was bound to laws by duty, but it was not observed that the laws to which he is subject are *only those of his own giving,* though at the same time they are *universal,* and that he is only bound to act in conformity with his own will— a will, however, which is designed by nature to give universal laws. For when one has conceived man only as subject to a law (no matter what), then this law required some interest, either by way of attraction or constraint, since it did not originate as a law from *his own* will, but this will was according to a law obliged by *something else* to act in a certain manner. Now by this necessary consequence all the labor spent in finding a supreme principle of *duty* was irrevocably lost. For men never elicited duty, but only a necessity of acting from a certain interest. Whether this interest was private or otherwise, in any case the imperative must be conditional, and could not by any means be capable of being a moral command. I will therefore call this the principle of *Autonomy* of the will, in contrast with every other which I accordingly reckon as *Heteronomy*.

The conception of every rational being as one which must consider itself as giving in all the maxims of its will universal laws, so as to judge itself and its actions from this point of view—this conception leads to another which depends on it and is very fruitful, namely, that of a *kingdom of ends.*

By a "kingdom" I understand the union of different rational beings in a system by common laws. Now since it is by laws that ends are determined as regards their universal validity, hence, if we abstract from the personal differences of rational beings, and likewise from all the content of their private ends, we shall be able to conceive all ends combined in a systematic whole (including both rational beings as ends in themselves, and also the special ends which each may propose to himself), that is to say, we can conceive a kingdom of ends, which on the preceding principles is possible.

For all rational beings come under the *law* that each of them must treat itself and all others *never merely as means,* but in every case *at the same time as ends in themselves.* Hence results a systematic union of rational beings by common objective laws, that is, a kingdom which may be called a kingdom of ends, since what these laws have in view is just the relation of these beings to one another as ends and means. It is certainly only an ideal.

A rational being belongs as a *member* to the kingdom of ends when, although giving universal laws in it, he is also himself subject to these laws. He belongs to it *as sovereign* when, while giving laws, he is not subject to the will of any other.

A rational being must always regard himself as giving laws either as member or as sovereign in a kingdom of ends which is rendered possible by the freedom of will. He cannot, however, maintain the latter position merely by the maxims of his will, but only in case he is a completely independent being without wants and with unrestricted power adequate to his will.

Morality consists then in the reference of all action to the legislation which alone can render a kingdom of ends possible. This legislation must be capable of existing in every rational being, and of emanating from his will, so that the principle of this will is never to act on any maxim which could not without contradiction be also a universal law, and accordingly always so to act *that the will could at the same time regard itself as giving in its maxims universal laws.* If now the maxims of rational beings are not by their own nature coincident with this objective principle, then the necessity of acting on it is called practical necessitation, that is, *duty.* Duty does not apply to the sovereign in the kingdom of ends, but it does to every member of it and to all in the same degree.

The practical necessity of acting on this principle, that is, duty, does not rest at all on feelings, impulses, or inclinations, but solely on the relation of rational beings to one another, a relation in which the will of a rational being must always be regarded as *legislative,* since otherwise it could not be conceived as *an end in itself.* Reason then refers every maxim of the will, regarding it as legislating universally, to every other will and also to every action towards oneself; and this not on account of any other practical motive or any future advantage, but from the ideas of the *dignity* of a rational being, obeying no law but that which he himself also gives.

In the kingdom of ends everything has either *value* or *dignity.* Whatever has a value can be replaced by something else which is *equivalent;* whatever on the other hand, is above all value, and therefore admits of no equivalent, has a dignity.

Whatever has reference to the general inclinations and wants of mankind has a *market value;* whatever, without presupposing a want, corresponds to a certain taste, that is, to a satisfaction in the mere purposeless play of our faculties, has a *fancy value;* but that which constitutes the condition under which alone anything can be an end in itself, this has not merely a relative worth, that is, value, but an intrinsic worth, that is, *dignity.*

Now morality is the condition under which alone a rational being can be an end in himself, since by this alone it is possible that he should be a legislating member in the kingdom of ends. Thus morality, and humanity as capable of it, is that which alone has dignity. Skill and diligence in labor have a market value; wit, lively imagination, and humor have fancy value; on the other hand, fidelity to promises, benevolence from principle (not from instinct), have an intrinsic worth. Neither nature nor art contains anything which in default of these it could put in their place, for their worth consists not in the effects which spring from them, not in the use and advantage which they secure, but in the disposition of mind, that is, the maxims of the will which are ready to manifest themselves in such actions, even though they should not have the desired effect. These actions also need no recommendation from any subjective taste or sentiment, that they may be looked on with immediate favor and satisfaction; they need no immediate propension or feeling for them; they exhibit the will that performs them as an object of an immediate respect, and nothing but reason is required to *impose* them on the will; not to *flatter* it into them, which, in the case of duties, would be a contradiction. This estimation therefore shows that the worth of such a disposition is dignity, and places it infinitely above all value, with which it cannot for a moment be brought into comparison or competition without as it were violating its sanctity.

What then is it which justifies virtue or the morally good disposition, in making such lofty claims? It is nothing less than the privilege it secures to the rational being of participating in the giving of universal laws, by which it qualifies him to be a member of a possible kingdom of ends, a privilege to which he was already destined by his own nature as being an end in himself, and on that account legislating in the kingdom of ends; free as regards all laws of physical nature, and obeying those only which he himself gives, and by which his maxims can belong to a system of universal law to which at the same time he submits himself. For nothing has any worth except what the law assigns it. Now the legislation itself which assigns the worth of everything must for that very reason possess dignity, that is, an unconditional incomparable worth; and the word *respect* alone supplies a becoming expression for the esteem which a rational being must have for it. *Autonomy* then is the basis of the dignity of human and of every rational nature.

The three modes of presenting the principle of morality that have been adduced are at bottom only so many formulae of the very same law, and each of itself involves the other two. There is, however, a difference in them, but it is rather subjectively than objectively practical, intended, namely, to bring an idea of the reason nearer to intuition (by means of a certain analogy), and thereby nearer to feeling. All maxims, in fact, have—

1. A *form,* consisting in universality; and in this view the formula of the moral imperative is expressed thus, that the maxims must be so chosen as if they were to serve as universal laws of nature.

2. A *matter,* namely, an end, and here the formula says that the rational being, as it is an end by its own nature and therefore an end in itself, must in every maxim serve as the condition limiting all merely relative and arbitrary ends.

3. A *complete characterization* of all maxims by means of that formula, namely, that all maxims ought, by their own legislation, to harmonize with a possible kingdom of ends as with a kingdom of nature.[15] There is a progress here in the order of the categories of *unity* of the form of the will (its universality), *plurality* of the matter (the objects, that is, the ends), and *totality* of the system of these. In forming our moral *judgment* of actions it is better to proceed always on the strict method, and start from the general formula of the categorical imperative: *Act according to a maxim which can at the same time make*

---

[15] Teleology considers nature as a kingdom of ends; ethics regards a possible kingdom of ends as a kingdom of nature. In the first case, the kingdom of ends is a theoretical idea, adopted to explain what actually is. In the latter it is a practical idea, adopted to bring about that which is not yet, but which can be realized by our conduct, namely, if it conforms to this idea.

itself a universal law. If, however, we wish to gain an *entrance* for the moral law, it is very useful to bring one and the same action under the three specified conceptions, and thereby as far as possible to bring it nearer to intuition.

We can now end where we started at the beginning, namely, with the conception of a will unconditionally good. *That will* is *absolutely good* which cannot be evil—in other words, whose maxim, if made a universal law, could never contradict itself. This principle, then, is its supreme law: *Act always on such a maxim as thou canst at the same time will to be a universal law;* this is the sole condition under which a will can never contradict itself; and such an imperative is categorical. Since the validity of the will as a universal law for possible actions is analogous to the universal connection of the exist-ence of things by general laws, which is the formal notion of nature in general, the categorical imperative can also be expressed thus: *Act on maxims which can at the same time have for their object themselves as universal laws of nature.* Such then is the formula of an absolutely good will.

Rational nature is distinguished from the rest of nature by this that it sets before itself an end. This end would be the matter of every good will. But since in the idea of a will that is absolutely good without being limited by any condition (of attaining this or that end) we must abstract wholly from every end *to be effected* (since this would make every will only relatively good), it follows that in this case the end must be conceived, not as an end to be effected, but as an *independently* existing end. Consequently it is con-ceived only negatively, that is, as that which we must never act against, and which, therefore, must never be regarded merely as means, but must in every volition be esteemed as an end likewise. Now this end can be nothing but the subject of all possible ends, since this is also the subject of a possible abso-lutely good will; for such a will cannot without contradiction be postponed to any other object. This principle: So act in regard to every rational being (thyself and others) that he may always have place in thy maxim as an end in himself, is accordingly essentially identical with this other: Act upon a maxim which, at the same time, involves its own universal validity for every rational being. For that in using means for every end I should limit my maxim by the condition of its holding good as a law for every subject, this comes to the same thing as that the fundamental principle of all maxims of action must be that the subject of all ends, that is, the rational being himself, be never employed merely as means, but as the supreme condition restricting the use of all means—that is, in every case as an end likewise.

It follows incontestably that, to whatever laws any rational being may be subject, he being an end in himself must be able to regard himself as also legislating universally in respect of these same laws, since it is just this fitness of his maxims for universal legislation that distinguishes him as an end in himself; also it follows that this implies his dignity (prerogative) above all mere physical beings, that he must always take his maxims from the point of view which regards himself, and likewise every other rational being, as law-giving beings (on which account they are called persons). In this way a world of rational beings (*mundus intelligibilis*) is possible as a kingdom of ends, and this by virtue of the legislation proper to all persons as members. Therefore, every rational being must so act as if he were by his maxims in every case a legislating member in the universal kingdom of ends. The formal principle of these maxims is: So act as if thy maxim were to serve likewise as the universal law (of all rational beings). A kingdom of ends is thus only possible on the analogy of a kingdom of nature, the former, however, only by maxims—that is, self-imposed rules—the latter only by the laws of efficient causes acting under necessitation from without. Nevertheless, although the system of nature is looked upon as a machine, yet so far as it has reference to rational beings as its ends, it is given on this account the name of a kingdom of nature. Now such a kingdom of ends would be actually realized by means of maxims conforming to the canon which the categorical imperative prescribes to all rational beings, *if they were universally followed*. But although a rational being, even if he punctually follows this maxim himself, cannot reckon upon all others being therefore true to the same, nor expect that the kingdom of nature and its orderly arrangements shall be in harmony with him as a fitting member, so as to form a kingdom of ends to which he himself contributes, that is to say, that it shall favor his expectation of happiness, still that law: Act according to the maxims of a member of a merely possible kingdom of ends legislating in it universally, remains in its full force inasmuch as it commands categorically. And it is just in this that the paradox lies; that the mere dignity of man as a rational creature, without any other end or advantage to be attained thereby, in other words, respect for a mere idea, should yet serve as an inflexible precept of the will, and that it is precisely in this independence of the maxim on all such springs of action that its sublimity consists; and it is this that makes every rational subject worthy to be a legislative member in the kingdom of ends, for otherwise he would have to be conceived only as subject to the physical law of his wants. And although we should suppose the kingdom of nature and the kingdom of ends to be united under one sovereign, so that the latter kingdom thereby ceased to be a mere idea and acquired true reality, then it would no doubt gain the accession of a strong spring, but by no means any increase of its intrinsic worth. For this sole absolute lawgiver must, notwithstanding this, be always conceived as estimating the worth of rational beings only by their disinterested behavior, as prescribed to themselves from that idea [the dignity of man] alone. The essence of things is not altered by their external relations, and that which, abstracting from these, alone constitutes the absolute worth of man is also that by which he must be judged, whoever the judge may be, and even by the Supreme Being. *Morality,* then, is the relation of actions to the autonomy of the will, that is, to the potential universal legislation by its maxims. An action that is consistent with the autonomy of the will is *permitted;* one that does not agree therewith is *forbidden.* A will whose maxims necessarily coincide with the laws of autonomy is a *holy* will, good absolutely. The dependence of a will not absolutely good on the principle of autonomy (moral necessitation) is obligation. This, then, cannot be applied to a holy being. The objective necessity of actions from obligation is called *duty*.

From what has just been said, it is easy to see how it happens that, although the conception of duty implies subjection to the law, we yet ascribe a certain *dignity* and sublimity to the person who fulfills all his duties. There is not, indeed, any sublimity in him, so far as he is *subject* to the moral law; but inasmuch as in regard to that very law he is likewise a *legislator,* and on that account alone subject to it, he has sublimity. We have also shown above that neither fear nor inclination, but simply respect for the law, is the spring which can give actions a moral worth. Our own will, so far as we suppose it to act only under the condition that its maxims are potentially universal laws, this ideal will which is possible to us is the proper object of respect; and the dignity of humanity consists just in this capacity of being universally legislative, though with the condition that it is itself subject to this same legislation.

The Autonomy of the Will as the Supreme Principle of Morality

Autonomy of the will is that property of it by which it is a law to itself (independently on any property of the objects of volition). The principle of autonomy then is: Always so to choose that the same volition shall comprehend the maxims of our choice as a universal law. We cannot prove that this practical rule is an imperative, that is, that the will of every rational being is necessarily bound to it as a condition, by a mere analysis of the conceptions which occur in it, since it is a synthetical proposition; we must advance beyond the cognition of the objects to a critical examination of the subject, that is, of the pure practical reason, for this synthetic proposition which commands apodictically must be capable of being cognized wholly *a priori*. This matter, however, does not belong to the present section. But that the principle of autonomy in question is the sole principle of morals can be readily shown by mere analysis of the conceptions of morality. For by this analysis we find that its principle must be a categorical imperative, and that what this commands is neither more nor less than this very autonomy.

Heteronomy of the Will as the Source of All Spurious Principles of Morality

If the will seeks the law which is to determine it *anywhere else* than in the fitness of its maxims to be universal laws of its own dictation, consequently if it goes out of itself and seeks this law in the character of any of its objects, there always results *heteronomy*. The will in that case does not give itself the law, but it is given by the object through its relation to the will. This relation, whether it rests on inclination or on conceptions of reason, only admits of hypothetical imperatives: I ought to do something *because I wish for something else*. On the contrary, the moral, and therefore categorical, imperative says: I ought to do so and so, even though I should not wish for anything else. For example, the former says: I ought not to lie if I would retain my reputation; the latter says: I ought not to lie although it should not bring me the least discredit. The latter therefore must so far abstract from all objects that they shall have no *influence* on the will, in order that practical reason (will) may not be restricted to administering an interest not belonging to it, but may simply show its own commanding authority as the supreme legislation. Thus, for example, I ought to endeavor to promote the happiness of others, not as if its realization involved any concern of mine (whether by immediate inclination or by any satisfaction indirectly gained through reason), but simply because a maxim which excludes it cannot be comprehended as a universal law in one and the same volition.

Classification

Of All Principles of Morality Which
Can Be Founded on the Conception of Heteronomy

Here as elsewhere human reason in its pure use, so long as it was not critically examined, has first tried all possible wrong ways before it succeeded in finding the one true way.

All principles which can be taken from this point of view are either *empirical* or *rational*. The *former,* drawn from the principle of *happiness,* are built on physical or moral feelings; the *latter,* drawn from the principle of *perfection,* are built either on the rational conception of perfection as a possible effect, or on that of an independent perfection (the will of God) as the determining cause of our will.

Empirical principles are wholly incapable of serving as a foundation for moral laws. For the universality with which these should hold for all rational beings without distinction, the unconditional practical necessity which is thereby imposed on them is lost when their foundation is taken from the *particular constitution of human nature* or the accidental circumstances in which it is placed. The principle of *private happiness,* however, is the most objectionable, not merely because it is false, and experience contradicts the supposition that prosperity is always proportioned to good conduct, nor yet merely because it contributes nothing to the establishment of morality—since it is quite a different thing to make a prosperous man and a good man, or to make one prudent and sharp-sighted for his own interests, and to make him virtuous—but because the springs it provides for morality are such as rather undermine it and destroy its sublimity, since they put the motives to virtue and to vice in the same class, and only teach us to make a better calculation, the specific difference between virtue and vice being entirely extinguished. On the other hand, as to moral feeling, this supposed special sense,[16] the appeal

---

[16] I class the principle of moral feeling under that of happiness, because every empirical interest promises to contribute to our well-being by the agreeableness that a thing affords, whether it be immediately and without a view to profit, or whether profit be regarded. We must likewise, with Hutcheson, class the principle of sympathy with the happiness of others under his assumed moral sense.

to it is indeed superficial when those who cannot *think* believe that *feeling* will help them out, even in what concerns general laws; and besides, feelings which naturally differ infinitely in degree cannot furnish a uniform standard of good and evil, nor has anyone a right to form judgments for others by his own feelings; nevertheless this moral feeling is nearer to morality and its dignity in this respect that it pays virtue the honor of ascribing to her *immediately* the satisfaction and esteem we have for her, and does not, as it were, tell her to her face that we are not attached to her by her beauty but by profit.

Among the *rational* principles of morality, the ontological conception of *perfection,* notwithstanding its defects, is better than the theological conception which derives morality from a Divine absolutely perfect will. The former is, no doubt, empty and indefinite, and consequently useless for finding in the boundless field of possible reality the greatest amount suitable for us; moreover, in attempting to distinguish specifically the reality of which we are now speaking from every other, it inevitably tends to turn in a circle and cannot avoid tacitly presupposing the morality which it is to explain; it is nevertheless preferable to the theological view, first, because we have no intuition of the Divine perfection, and can only deduce it from our own conceptions the most important of which is that of morality, and our explanation would thus be involved in a gross circle; and, in the next place, if we avoid this, the only notion of the Divine will remaining to us is a conception made up of the attributes of desire of glory and dominion, combined with the awful conceptions of might and vengeance, and any system of morals erected on this foundation would be directly opposed to morality.

However, if I had to choose between the notion of the moral sense and that of perfection in general (two systems which at least do not weaken morality, although they are totally incapable of serving as its foundation), then I should decide for the latter, because it at least withdraws the decision of the question from the sensibility and brings it to the court of pure reason; and although even here it decides nothing, it at all events preserves the indefinite idea (of a will good in itself) free from corruption, until it shall be more precisely defined.

For the rest I think I may be excused here from a detailed refutation of all these doctrines; that would only be superfluous labor, since it is so easy, and is probably so well seen even by those whose office requires them to decide for one of those theories (because their hearers would not tolerate suspension of judgment). But what interests us more here is to know that the prime foundation of morality laid down by all these principles is nothing but heteronomy of the will, and for this reason they must necessarily miss their aim.

In every case where an object of the will has to be supposed, in order that the rule may be prescribed which is to determine the will, there the rule is simply heteronomy; the imperative is conditional, namely, *if* or *because* one wishes for this object, one should act so and so; hence it can never command morally, that is, categorically. Whether the object determines the will by means of inclination, as in the principle of private happiness, or by means of reason directed to objects of our possible volition generally, as in the principle of perfection, in either case the will never determines itself *immediately* by the conception of the action, but only by the influence which the foreseen effect of the action has on the will; *I ought to do something, on this account, because I wish for something else;* and here there must be yet another law assumed in me as its subject, by which I necessarily will this other thing, and this law again requires an imperative to restrict this maxim. For the influence which the conception of an object within the reach of our faculties can exercise on the will of the subject in consequence of its natural properties, depends on the nature of the subject, either the sensibility (inclination and taste) or the understanding and reason, the employment of which is by the peculiar constitution of their nature attended with satisfaction. It follows that the law would be, properly speaking, given by nature, and as such it must be known and proved by experience, and would consequently be contingent, and therefore incapable of being an apodictic practical rule, such as the moral rule must be. Not only so, but it is *inevitably only heteronomy;* the will does not give itself the law, but it is given by a foreign impulse by means of a particular natural constitution of the subject adapted to receive it. An absolutely good will, then, the principle of which must be a categorical imperative, will be indeterminate as regards all objects, and will contain merely the *form of volition* generally, and that as autonomy, that is to say, the capability of the maxims of every good will to make themselves a universal law, is itself the only law which the will of every rational being imposes on itself, without needing to assume any spring or interest as a foundation.

How such a synthetical practical a priori *proposition is possible,* and why it is necessary, is a problem whose solution does not lie within the bounds of the metaphysic of morals; and we have not here affirmed its truth, much less professed to have a proof of it in our power. We simply showed by the development of the universally received notion of morality that an autonomy of the will is inevitably connected with it, or rather is its foundation. Whoever then holds morality to be anything real, and not a chimerical idea without any truth, must likewise admit the principle of it that is here assigned. This section, then, like the first, was merely analytical. Now to prove that morality is no creation of the brain, which it cannot be if the categorical imperative and with it the autonomy of the will is true, and as an *a priori* principle absolutely necessary, this supposes the *possibility of a synthetic use of pure practical reason,* which, however, we cannot venture on without first giving a critical examination of this faculty of reason. In the concluding section we shall give the principal outlines of this critical examination as far as is sufficient for our purpose.

Third Section

Transition from the Metaphysic of Morals to the Critique of Pure Practical Reason

The Concept of Freedom Is the Key that Explains the Autonomy of the Will

The *will* is a kind of causality belonging to living beings in so far as they are rational, and *freedom* would be this property of such causality that it can be efficient, independently on foreign causes *determining* it; just as *physical necessity* is the property that the causality of all irrational beings has of being determined to activity by the influence of foreign causes.

The preceding definition of freedom is *negative,* and therefore unfruitful for the discovery of its essence; but it leads to a *positive* conception which is so much the more full and fruitful. Since the conception of causality involves that of laws, according to which, by something that we call cause, something else, namely, the effect, must be produced [laid down]; hence, although freedom is not a property of the will depending on physical laws, yet it is not for that reason lawless; on the contrary, it must be a causality acting according to immutable laws, but of a peculiar kind; otherwise a free will would be an absurdity. Physical necessity is a heteronomy of the efficient causes, for every effect is possible only according to this law—that something else determines the efficient cause to exert its causality. What else then can freedom of the will be but autonomy, that is, the property of the will to be a law to itself? But the proposition: The will is in every action a law to itself, only expresses the principle to act on no other maxim than that which can also have as an object itself as a universal law. Now this is precisely the formula of the categorical imperative and is the principle of morality, so that a free will and a will subject to moral laws are one and the same.

On the hypothesis, then, of freedom of the will, morality together with its principle follows from it by mere analysis of the conception. However, the latter is a synthetic proposition, viz., an absolutely good will is that whose maxim can always include itself regarded as a universal law; for this property of its maxim can never be discovered by analyzing the conception of an absolutely good will. Now such synthetic propositions are only possible in this way —that the two cognitions are connected together by their union with a third in which they are both to be found. The *positive* concept of freedom furnishes this third cognition, which cannot, as with physical cause, be the nature of the sensible world (in the concept of which we find conjoined the concept of something in relation as cause to *something else* as effect). We cannot now at once show what this third is to which freedom points us, and of which we have an idea *a priori,* nor can we make intelligible how the concept of freedom is shown to be legitimate from principles of pure practical reason, and with it the possibility of a categorical imperative; but some further preparation is required.

Freedom

Must Be Presupposed as a
Property of the Will of All Rational Beings

It is not enough to predicate freedom of our own will, from whatever reason, if we have not sufficient grounds for predicating the same of all rational beings. For as morality serves as a law for us only because we are *rational beings,* it must also hold for all rational beings; and as it must be deduced simply from the property of freedom, it must be shown that freedom also is a property of all rational beings. It is not enough, then, to prove it from certain supposed experiences of human nature (which indeed is quite impossible, and it can only be shown *a priori*), but we must show that it belongs to the activity of all rational beings endowed with a will. Now I say every being that cannot act except *under the idea of freedom* is just for that reason in a practical point of view really free, that is to say, all laws which are inseparably connected with freedom have the same force for him as if his will had been shown to be free in itself by a proof theoretically conclusive.[17] Now I affirm that we must attribute to every rational being which has a will that it has also the idea of freedom and acts entirely under this idea. For in such a being we conceive a reason that is practical, that is, has causality in reference to its objects. Now we cannot possibly conceive a reason consciously receiving a bias from any other quarter with respect to its judgments, for then the subject would ascribe the determination of its judgment not to its own reason, but to an impulse. It must regard itself as the author of its principles independent of foreign influences. Consequently, as practical reason or as the will of a rational being it must regard itself as free, that is to say, the will of such a being cannot be a will of its own except under the idea of freedom. This idea must therefore in a practical point of view be ascribed to every rational being.

Of the Interest Attaching to the Ideas of Morality

We have finally reduced the definite conception of morality to the idea of freedom. This latter, however, we could not prove to be actually a property of ourselves or of human nature; only we saw that it must be presupposed if we would conceive a being as rational and conscious of its causality in respect of its actions, that is, as endowed with a will; and so we find that on just the

---

[17] I adopt this method of assuming freedom merely *as an idea* which rational beings suppose in their actions, in order to avoid the necessity of proving it in its theoretical aspect also. The former is sufficient for my purpose; for even though the speculative proof should not be made out, yet a being that cannot act except with the idea of freedom is bound by the same laws that would oblige a being who was actually free. Thus we can escape here from the onus which presses on the theory.

same grounds we must ascribe to every being endowed with reason and will this attribute of determining itself to action under the idea of its freedom.

Now it resulted also from the presupposition of this idea that we became aware of a law that the subjective principles of action, that is, maxims, must also be so assumed that they can also hold as objective, that is, universal principles, and so serve as universal laws of our own dictation. But why, then, should I subject myself to this principle and that simply as a rational being, thus also subjecting to it all other beings endowed with reason? I will allow that no interest *urges* me to this, for that would not give a categorical imperative, but I must *take* an interest in it and discern how this comes to pass; for this "I ought" is properly an "I would," valid for every rational being, provided only that reason determined his actions without any hindrance. But for beings that are in addition affected as we are by springs of a different kind, namely, sensibility, and in whose case that is not always done which reason alone would do, for these that necessity is expressed only as an "ought," and the subjective necessity is different from the objective.

It seems, then, as if the moral law, that is, the principle of autonomy of the will, were properly speaking only presupposed in the idea of freedom, and as if we could not prove its reality and objective necessity independently. In that case we should still have gained something considerable by at least determining the true principle more exactly than had previously been done; but as regards its validity and the practical necessity of subjecting oneself to it, we should not have advanced a step. For if we were asked why the universal validity of our maxim as a law must be the condition restricting our actions, and on what we ground the worth which we assign to this manner of acting—a worth so great that there cannot be any higher interest—and if we were asked further how it happens that it is by this alone a man believes he feels his own personal worth, in comparison with which that of an agreeable or disagreeable condition is to be regarded as nothing, to these questions we could give no satisfactory answer.

We find indeed sometimes that we can take an interest in a personal quality which does not involve any interest of external condition, provided this quality makes us capable of participating in the condition in case reason were to effect the allotment; that is to say, the mere being worthy of happiness can interest of itself even without the motive of participating in this happiness. This judgment, however, is in fact only the effect of the importance of the moral law which we before presupposed (when by the idea of freedom we detach ourselves from every empirical interest); but that we ought to detach ourselves from these interests, that is, to consider ourselves as free in action and yet as subject to certain laws, so as to find a worth simply in our own person which can compensate us for the loss of everything that gives worth to our condition, this we are not yet able to discern in this way, nor do we see how it is possible so to act—in other words, *whence the moral law derives its obligation.*

It must be freely admitted that there is a sort of circle here from which it seems impossible to escape. In the order of efficient causes we assume ourselves free, in order that in the order of ends we may conceive ourselves as subject to moral laws; and we afterwards conceive ourselves as subject to these laws because we have attributed to ourselves freedom of will; for freedom and self-legislation of will are both autonomy, and therefore are reciprocal conceptions, and for this very reason one must not be used to explain the other or give the reason of it, but at most only for logical purposes to reduce apparently different notions of the same object to one single concept (as we reduce different fractions of the same value to the lowest terms).

One resource remains to us, namely, to inquire whether we do not occupy different points of view when by means of freedom we think ourselves as causes efficient *a priori,* and when we form our conception of ourselves from our actions as effects which we see before our eyes.

It is a remark which needs no subtle reflection to make, but which we may assume that even the commonest understanding can make, although it be after its fashion by an obscure discernment of judgment which it calls feeling, that all the "ideas" that come to us involuntarily (as those of the senses) do not enable us to know objects otherwise than as they affect us; so that what they may be in themselves remains unknown to us, and consequently that as regards "ideas" of this kind even with the closest attention and clearness that the understanding can apply to them, we can by them only attain to the knowledge of *appearances,* never to that of *things in themselves.* As soon as this distinction has once been made (perhaps merely in consequence of the difference observed between the ideas given us from without, and in which we are passive, and those that we produce simply from ourselves, and in which we show our own activity), then it follows of itself that we must admit and assume behind the appearance something else that is not an appearance, namely, the things in themselves; although we must admit that, as they can never be known to us except as they affect us, we can come no nearer to them, nor can we ever know what they are in themselves. This must furnish a distinction, however crude, between a *world of sense* and the *world of understanding,* of which the former may be different according to the difference of the sensuous impressions in various observers, while the second which is its basis always remains the same. Even as to himself, a man cannot pretend to know what he is in himself from the knowledge he has by internal sensation. For as he does not as it were create himself, and does not come by the conception of himself *a priori* but empirically, it naturally follows that he can obtain his knowledge even of himself only by the inner sense, and consequently only through the appearances of his nature and the way in which his consciousness is affected. At the same time, beyond these characteristics of his own subject, made up of mere appearances, he must necessarily suppose something else as their basis, namely, his *ego,* whatever its characteristics in itself may be. Thus in respect to mere perception and receptivity of sensations he must reckon himself as belonging to the *world of sense;* but in respect of whatever there may be of pure activity in him (that which reaches consciousness immediately and not through affecting the senses), he must reckon himself as belonging to the *intellectual world,* of which, however, he has no further knowledge. To such a conclusion the reflecting man must come with respect to all the things which can be presented to him; it is probably to be met with even in persons of the commonest understanding, who, as is well known, are very much inclined to suppose behind the objects of the senses something else invisible and acting of itself. They spoil it, however, by presently sensualizing this invisible again, that is to say, wanting to make it an object of intuition, so that they do not become a whit the wiser.

Now man really finds in himself a faculty by which he distinguishes himself from everything else, even from himself as affected by objects, and that is *reason.* This being pure spontaneity is even elevated above the *understanding.* For although the latter is a spontaneity and does not, like sense, merely contain intuitions that arise when we are affected by things (and are therefore passive), yet it cannot produce from its activity any other conceptions than those which merely serve *to bring the intuitions of sense under rules,* and thereby to unite them in one consciousness, and without this use of the sensibility it could not think at all; whereas, on the contrary, reason shows so pure a spontaneity in the case of what I call "ideas" [Ideal Conceptions] that it thereby far transcends everything that the sensibility can give it, and exhibits its most important function in distinguishing the world of sense from that of understanding, and thereby prescribing the limits of the understanding itself.

For this reason a rational being must regard himself *qua* intelligence (not from the side of his lower faculties) as belonging not to the world of sense, but to that of understanding; hence he has two points of view from which he can regard himself, and recognize laws of the exercise of his faculties, and consequently of all his actions; *first,* so far as he belongs to the world of sense, he finds himself subject to laws of nature (heteronomy); *secondly,* as belonging to the intelligible world, under laws which, being independent of nature, have their foundation not in experience but in reason alone.

As a reasonable being, and consequently belonging to the intelligible world, man can never conceive the causality of his own will otherwise than on condition of the idea of freedom, for independence on the determining causes of the sensible world (an independence which reason must always ascribe to itself) is freedom. Now the idea of freedom is inseparably connected with the conception of *autonomy,* and this again with the universal principle of morality which is ideally the foundation of all actions of *rational* beings, just as the law of nature is of all phenomena.

Now the suspicion is removed which we raised above, that there was a latent circle involved in our reasoning from freedom to autonomy, and from this to the moral law, viz., that we laid down the idea of freedom because of the moral law only that we might afterwards in turn infer the latter from freedom, and that consequently we could assign no reason at all for this law, but could only [present] it as a *petitio principii* which well-disposed minds would gladly concede to us, but which we could never put forward as a provable proposition. For now we see that when we conceive ourselves as free we transfer ourselves into the world of understanding as members of it, and recognize the autonomy of the will with its consequence, morality; whereas, if we conceive ourselves as under obligation, we consider ourselves as belonging to the world of sense, and at the same time to the world of understanding.

How Is a Categorical Imperative Possible?

Every rational being reckons himself *qua* intelligence as belonging to the world of understanding, and it is simply as an efficient cause belonging to that world that he calls his causality a *will*. On the other side, he is also conscious of himself as a part of the world of sense in which his actions, which are mere appearances [phenomena] of that causality, are displayed; we cannot, however, discern how they are possible from this causality which we do not know; but instead of that, these actions as belonging to the sensible world must be viewed as determined by other phenomena, namely, desires and inclinations. If therefore I were only a member of the world of understanding, then all my actions would perfectly conform to the principle of autonomy of the pure will; if I were only a part of the world of sense, they would necessarily be assumed to conform wholly to the natural law of desires and inclinations, in other words, to the heteronomy of nature. (The former would rest on morality as the supreme principle, the latter on happiness.) Since, however, *the world of understanding contains the foundation of the world of sense, and consequently of its laws also,* and accordingly gives the law to my will (which belongs wholly to the world of understanding) directly, and must be conceived as doing so, it follows that, although on the one side I must regard myself as a being belonging to the world of sense, yet, on the other side, I must recognize myself, as an intelligence, as subject to the law of the world of understanding, that is, to reason, which contains this law in the idea of freedom, and therefore as subject to the autonomy of the will; consequently I must regard the laws of the world of understanding as imperatives for me, and the actions which conform to them as duties.

And thus what makes categorical imperatives possible is this—that the idea of freedom makes me a member of an intelligible world, in consequence of which, if I were nothing else, all my actions *would* always conform to the autonomy of the will; but as I at the same time intuit myself as a member of the world of sense, they *ought* so to conform, and this *categorical* "ought" implies a synthetic *a priori* proposition, inasmuch as besides my will as affected by sensible desires there is added further the idea of the same will, but as belonging to the world of the understanding, pure and practical of itself, which contains the supreme condition according to reason of the former will; precisely as to the intuitions of sense there are added concepts of the understanding which of themselves signify nothing but regular form in general, and in this way synthetic *a priori* propositions become possible, on which all knowledge of physical nature rests.

The practical use of common human reason confirms this reasoning. There is no one, not even the most consummate villain, provided only that he is otherwise accustomed to the use of reason, who, when we set before him examples of honesty of purpose, of steadfastness in following good maxims, of sympathy and general benevolence (even combined with great sacrifices of advantages and comfort), does not wish that he might also possess these qualities. Only on account of his inclinations and impulses he cannot attain this in himself, but at the same time he wishes to be free from such inclinations which are burdensome to himself. He proves by this that he transfers himself in thought with a will free from the impulses of the sensibility into an order of things wholly different from that of his desires in the field of the sensibility; since he cannot expect to obtain by that wish any gratification of his desires, nor any position which would satisfy any of his actual or supposable inclinations (for this would destroy the preeminence of the very idea which wrests that wish from him), he can only expect a greater intrinsic worth of his own person. This better person, however, he imagines himself to be when he transfers himself to the point of view of a member of the world of the understanding, to which he is involuntarily forced by the idea of freedom, that is, of independence on *determining* causes of the world of sense; and from this point of view he is conscious of a good will, which by his own confession constitutes the law for the bad will that he possesses as a member of the world of sense— a law whose authority he recognizes while transgressing it. What he morally "ought" is then what he necessarily "would" as a member of the world of the understanding, and is conceived by him as an "ought" only inasmuch as he likewise considers himself as a member of the world of sense.

On the Extreme Limits of All Practical Philosophy

All men attribute to themselves freedom of will. Hence come all judgments upon actions as being such as *ought to have been done,* although they *have not been* done. However, this freedom is not a conception of experience, nor can it be so, since it still remains, even though experience shows the contrary of what on supposition of freedom are conceived as its necessary consequences. On the other side, it is equally necessary that everything that takes place should be fixedly determined according to laws of nature. This necessity of nature is likewise not an empirical conception, just for this reason that it involves the notion of necessity and consequently of *a priori* cognition. But this conception of a system of nature is confirmed by experience; and it must even be inevitably presupposed if experience itself is to be possible, that is, a connected knowledge of the objects of sense resting on general laws. Therefore freedom is only an *idea* [Ideal Conception] of *reason,* and its objective reality in itself is doubtful; while nature is a *concept* of the *understanding* which proves, and must necessarily prove, its reality in examples of experience.

There arises from this a dialectic of reason, since the freedom attributed to the will appears to contradict the necessity of nature, and, placed between these two ways, reason for *speculative purposes* finds the road of physical necessity much more beaten and more appropriate than that of freedom; yet for *practical purposes* the narrow footpath of freedom is the only one on which it is possible to make use of reason in our conduct; hence it is just as impossible for the subtlest philosophy as for the commonest reason of men to argue away freedom. Philosophy must then assume that no real contradiction will be found between freedom and physical necessity of the same human actions, for it cannot give up the conception of nature any more than that of freedom.

Nevertheless, even though we should never be able to comprehend how freedom is possible, we must at least remove this apparent contradiction in a convincing manner. For if the thought of freedom contradicts either itself or nature, which is equally necessary, it must in competition with physical necessity be entirely given up.

It would, however, be impossible to escape this contradiction if the thinking subject, which seems to itself free, conceived itself *in the same sense* or in *the very same relation* when it calls itself free as when in respect of the same action it assumes itself to be subject to the law of nature. Hence it is an indispensable problem of speculative philosophy to show that its illusion respecting the contradiction rests on this that we think of man in a different sense and relation when we call him free, and when we regard him as subject to the laws of nature as being part and parcel of nature. It must therefore show that not only *can* both these very well coexist, but that both must be thought *as necessarily united* in the same subject, since otherwise no reason could be given why we should burden reason with an idea which, though it may possibly *without contradiction* be reconciled with another that is sufficiently established, yet entangles us in a perplexity which sorely embarrasses reason in its theoretic employment. This duty, however, belongs only to speculative philosophy, in order that it may clear the way for practical philosophy. The philosopher, then, has no option whether he will remove the apparent contradiction or leave it untouched; for in the latter case the theory respecting this would be *bonum vacans* into the possession of which the fatalist would have a right to enter, and chase all morality out of its supposed domain as occupying it without title.

We cannot, however, as yet say that we are touching the bounds of practical philosophy. For the settlement of that controversy does not belong to it; it only demands from speculative reason that it should put an end to the discord in which it entangles itself in theoretical questions, so that practical reason may have rest and security from external attacks which might make the ground debatable on which it desires to build.

The claims to freedom of will made even by common reason are founded on the consciousness and the admitted supposition that reason is independent of merely subjectively determined causes which together constitute what belongs to sensation only, and which consequently come under the general designation of sensibility. Man considering himself in this way as an intelligence places himself thereby in a different order of things and in a relation to determining grounds of a wholly different kind when on the one hand he thinks of himself as an intelligence endowed with a will, and consequently with causality, and when on the other he perceives himself as a phenomenon in the world of sense (as he really is also), and affirms that his causality is subject to external determination according to laws of nature. Now he soon becomes aware that both can hold good, nay, must hold good at the same time. For there is not the smallest contradiction in saying that a *thing in appearance* (belonging to the world of sense) is subject to certain laws on which the very same *as a thing* or being *in itself* is independent; and that he must conceive and think of himself in this two-fold way, rests as to the first on the consciousness of himself as an object affected through the senses, and as to the second on the consciousness of himself as an intelligence, that is, as independent of sensible impressions in the employment of his reason (in other words as belonging to the world of understanding).

Hence it comes to pass that man claims the possession of a will which takes no account of anything that comes under the head of desires and inclinations, and on the contrary conceives actions as possible to him, nay, even as necessary, which can only be done by disregarding all desires and sensible inclinations. The causality of such actions lies in him as an intelligence and in the laws of effects and actions [which depend] on the principles of an intelligible world, of which indeed he knows nothing more than that in it pure reason alone independent on sensibility gives the law; moreover, since it is only in that world, as an intelligence, that he is his proper self (being as man only the appearance of himself), those laws apply to him directly and categorically, so that the incitements of inclinations and appetites (in other words, the whole nature of the world of sense) cannot impair the laws of his volition as an intelligence. Nay, he does not even hold himself responsible for the former or ascribe them to his proper self, that is, his will; he only ascribes to his will any indulgence which he might yield them if he allowed them to influence his maxims to the prejudice of the rational laws of the will.

When practical reason *thinks* itself into a world of understanding, it does not thereby transcend its own limits, as it would if it tried to enter it by *intuition* or *sensation*. The former is only a negative thought in respect of the world of sense, which does not give any laws to reason in determining the will, and is positive only in this single point that this freedom as a negative characteristic is at the same time conjoined with a (positive) faculty and even with a causality of reason, which we designate a will, namely, a faculty of so acting that the principle of the actions shall conform to the essential character of a rational motive, that is, the condition that the maxim have universal validity as a law. But were it to borrow an *object of will,* that is, a motive, from the world of understanding, then it would overstep its bounds and pretend to be acquainted with something of which it knows nothing. The conception of a world of the understanding is then only a *point of view* which reason finds itself compelled to take outside the appearances in order to *conceive itself as practical,* which would not be possible if the influences of the sensibility had a determining power on man, but which is necessary unless he is to be denied the consciousness of himself as an intelligence, and consequently as a rational cause, energizing by reason, that is, operating freely. This thought certainly involves the idea of an order and a system of laws different from that of the mechanism of nature which belongs to the sensible world; and it makes the conception of an intelligible world necessary (that is to say, the whole system of rational beings as things in themselves). But it does not in the least authorize us to think of it further than as to its *formal* condition only, that is, the universality of the maxims of the will as laws, and consequently the autonomy of the latter, which alone is consistent with its freedom; whereas, on the contrary, all laws that refer to a definite object give heteronomy, which only belongs to laws of nature, and can only apply to the sensible world.

But reason would overstep all its bounds if it undertook to *explain how* pure reason can be practical, which would be exactly the same problem as to explain *how freedom is possible.*

For we can explain nothing but that which we can reduce to laws the object of which can be given in some possible experience. But freedom is a mere *idea* [ideal conception], the objective reality of which can in no wise be shown according to laws of nature, and consequently not in any possible experience; and for this reason it can never be comprehended or understood because we cannot support it by any sort of example or analogy. It holds good only as a necessary hypothesis of reason in a being that believes itself conscious of a will, that is, of a faculty distinct from mere desire (namely, a faculty of determining itself to action as an intelligence, in other words, by laws of reason independently on natural instincts). Now where determination according to laws of nature ceases, there all *explanation* ceases also, and nothing remains but *defense,* that is, the removal of the objections of those who pretend to have seen deeper into the nature of things, and thereupon boldly declare freedom impossible. We can only point out to them that the supposed contradiction that they have discovered in it arises only from this that in order to be able to apply the law of nature to human actions, they must necessarily consider man as an appearance; then when we demand of them that they should also think of him *qua* intelligence as a thing in itself, they still persist in considering him in this respect also as an appearance. In this view it would no doubt be a contradiction to suppose the causality of the same subject (that is, his will) to be withdrawn from all the natural laws of the sensible world. But this contradiction disappears if they would only bethink themselves and admit, as is reasonable, that behind the appearances there must also lie at their root (although hidden) the things in themselves, and that we cannot expect the laws of these to be the same as those that govern their appearances.

The subjective impossibility of explaining the freedom of the will is identical with the impossibility of discovering and explaining an interest [18] which man can take in the moral law. Nevertheless he does actually take an interest in it, the basis of which in us we call the moral feeling, which some have falsely assigned as the standard of our moral judgment, whereas it must rather be viewed as the *subjective* effect that the law exercises on the will, the objective principle of which is furnished by reason alone.

In order, indeed, that a rational being who is also affected through the senses should will what reason alone directs such beings that they ought to will, it is no doubt requisite that reason should have a power *to infuse a feeling of pleasure* or satisfaction in the fulfilment of duty, that is to say, that it should have a causality by which it determines the sensibility according to its own principles. But it is quite impossible to discern, that is, to make it intelligible *a priori,* how a mere thought, which itself contains nothing sensible, can itself produce a sensation of pleasure or pain; for this is a particular kind of causality of which, as of every other causality, we can determine nothing whatever *a priori;* we must only consult experience about it. But as this cannot supply us with any relation of cause and effect except between two objects of experience, whereas in this case, although indeed the effect produced lies within experience, yet the cause is supposed to be pure reason acting through mere ideas which offer no object to experience, it follows that for us men it is quite impossible to explain how and why the *universality of the maxim as a law,* that is, morality, interests. This only is certain, that it is not *because it interests* us that it has validity for us (for that would be heteronomy and dependence of practical reason on sensibility, namely, on a feeling as its principle, in which case it could never give moral laws), but that it interests us because it is valid for us as men, inasmuch as it had its source in our will as intelligences, in other words in our proper self, *and what belongs to mere appearance is necessarily subordinated by reason to the nature of the thing in itself.*

The question, then, How a categorical imperative is possible, can be answered to this extent that we can assign the only hypothesis on which it is possible, namely, the idea of freedom; and we can also discern the necessity of this hypothesis, and this is sufficient for the *practical exercise* of reason, that is, for the conviction of the *validity of this imperative,* and hence of the moral law; but how this hypothesis itself is possible can never be discerned by any human reason. On the hypothesis, however, that the will of an intelligence is free, its *autonomy,* as the essential formal condition of its determination, is a

---

[18] Interest is that by which reason becomes practical, that is, a cause determining the will. Hence we say of rational beings only that they take an interest in a thing; irrational beings only feel sensual appetites. Reason takes a direct interest in action, then, only when the universal validity of its maxims is alone sufficient to determine the will. Such an interest alone is pure. But if it can determine the will only by means of another object of desire or on the suggestion of a particular feeling of the subject, then Reason takes only an indirect interest in the action; and as Reason by itself without experience cannot discover either objects of the will or a special feeling actuating it, this latter interest would only be empirical, and not a pure rational interest. The logical interest of Reason (namely, to extend its insight) is never direct, but presupposes purposes for which reason is employed.

necessary consequence. Moreover, this freedom of will is not merely quite *possible* as a hypothesis (not involving any contradiction to the principle of physical necessity in the connection of the phenomena of the sensible world) as speculative philosophy can show; but further, a rational being who is conscious of a causality through reason, that is to say, of a will (distinct from desires), must *of necessity* make it practically, that is, in idea, the condition of all his voluntary actions. But to explain how pure reason can be of itself practical without the aid of any spring of action that could be derived from any other source, that is, how the mere principle of the *universal validity of all its maxims as laws* (which would certainly be the form of a pure practical reason) can of itself supply a spring, without any matter (object) of the will in which one could antecedently take any interest; and how it can produce an interest which would be called purely *moral;* or in other words, *how pure reason can be practical*—to explain this is beyond the power of human reason, and all the labor and pains of seeking an explanation of it are lost.

It is just the same as if I sought to find out how freedom itself is possible as the causality of a will. For then I quit the ground of philosophical explanation, and I have no other to go upon. I might indeed revel in the world of intelligences which still remains to me, but although I have an *idea* of it which is well founded, yet I have not the least *knowledge* of it, nor can I ever attain to such knowledge with all the efforts of my natural faculty of reason. It signifies only a something that remains over when I have eliminated everything belonging to the world of sense from the actuating principles of my will, serving merely to keep in bounds the principle of motives taken from the field of sensibility; fixing its limits and showing that it does not contain all in all within itself, but that there is more beyond it; but this something more I know no further. Of pure reason which frames this ideal, there remains after the abstraction of all matter, that is, knowledge of objects, nothing but the form, namely, the practical law of the universality of the maxims, and in conformity with this the conception of reason in reference to a pure world of understanding as a possible efficient cause, that is, a cause determining the will. There must here be a total absence of springs unless this idea of an intelligible world is itself the spring, or that in which reason primarily takes an interest; but to make this intelligible is precisely the problem that we cannot solve.

Here now is the extreme limit of all moral inquiry, and it is of great importance to determine it even on this account in order that reason may not, on the one hand, to the prejudice of morals, seek about in the world of sense for the supreme motive and an interest comprehensible but empirical; and on the other hand, that it may not impotently flap its wings without being able to move in the (for it) empty space of transcendent concepts which we call the intelligible world, and so lose itself amidst chimeras. For the rest, the idea of a pure world of understanding as a system of all intelligences, and to which we ourselves as rational beings belong (although we are likewise on the other side members of the sensible world), this remains always a useful and legitimate idea for the purposes of rational belief, although all knowledge stops at its threshold, useful, namely, to produce in us a lively interest in the moral law by means of the noble ideal of a universal kingdom of *ends in themselves* (rational beings), to which we can belong as members then only when we carefully conduct ourselves according to the maxims of freedom as if they were laws of nature.

Concluding Remark

The speculative employment of reason *with respect to nature* leads to the absolute necessity of some supreme cause of *the world;* the practical employment of reason *with a view to freedom* leads also to absolute necessity, but only *of the laws of the actions* of a rational being as such. Now it is an essential *principle* of reason, however employed, to push its knowledge to a consciousness of its *necessity* (without which it would not be rational knowledge). It is, however, an equally essential *restriction* of the same reason that it can neither discern the *necessity* of what is or what happens, nor of what ought to happen, unless a condition is supposed on which it is or happens or ought to happen. In this way, however, by the constant inquiry for the condition, the satisfaction of reason is only further and further postponed. Hence it unceasingly seeks the unconditionally necessary, and finds itself forced to assume it, although without any means of making it comprehensible to itself, happy enough if only it can discover a conception which agrees with this assumption. It is therefore no fault in our deduction of the supreme principle of morality, but an objection that should be made to human reason in general, that it cannot enable us to conceive the absolute necessity of an unconditional practical law (such as the categorical imperative must be). It cannot be blamed for refusing to explain this necessity by a condition, that is to say, by means of some interest assumed as a basis, since the law would then cease to be a moral law, that is, a supreme law of freedom. And thus while we do not comprehend the practical unconditional necessity of the moral imperative, we yet comprehend its *incomprehensibility,* and this is all that can be fairly demanded of a philosophy which strives to carry its principles up to the very limit of human reason.

Justice as Fairness
John Rawls

1. It might seem at first sight that the concepts of justice and fairness are the same, and that there is no reason to distinguish them, or to say that one

is more fundamental than the other. I think that this impression is mistaken. In this paper I wish to show that the fundamental idea in the concept of justice is fairness; and I wish to offer an analysis of the concept of justice from this point of view. To bring out the force of this claim, and the analysis based upon it, I shall then argue that it is this aspect of justice for which utilitarianism, in its classical form, is unable to account but which is expressed, even if misleadingly, by the idea of the social contract.

To start with I shall develop a particular conception of justice by stating and commenting upon two principles which specify it, and by considering the circumstances and conditions under which they may be thought to arise. The principles defining this conception, and the conception itself, are, of course, familiar. It may be possible, however, by using the notion of fairness as a framework, to assemble and to look at them in a new way. Before starting this conception, however, the following preliminary matters should be kept in mind.

Throughout I consider justice only as a virtue of social institutions, or what I shall call practices.[1] The principles of justice are regarded as formulating restrictions as to how practices may define positions and offices, and assign thereto powers and liabilities, rights and duties. Justice as a virtue of particular actions or of persons I do not take up at all. It is important to distinguish these various subjects of justice, since the meaning of the concept varies according to whether it is applied to practices, particular actions, or persons. These meanings are, indeed, connected, but they are not identical. I shall confine my discussion to the sense of justice as applied to practices, since this sense is the basic one. Once it is understood, the other senses should go quite easily.

Justice is to be understood in its customary sense as representing but *one* of the many virtues of social institutions, for these may be antiquated, inefficient, degrading, or any number of other things, without being unjust. Justice is not to be confused with an all inclusive vision of a good society; it is only one part of any such conception. It is important, for example, to distinguish that sense of equality which is an aspect of the concept of justice from that sense of equality which belongs to a more comprehensive social ideal. There may well be inequalities which one concedes are just, or at least not unjust, but which, nevertheless, one wishes, on other grounds, to do away

---

From John Rawls, "Justice as Fairness," *The Philosophical Review* 67 (1958), 164–194. Reprinted by permission of *The Philosophical Review* and the author. The last paragraph of Section 3 has been extensively revised. An abbreviated version of this paper (less than one-half the length) was presented in a symposium with the same title at the American Philosophical Association, Eastern Division, December 28, 1957, and appeared in the *Journal of Philosophy*, LIV, 653–662.

[1] I use the word "practice" throughout as a sort of technical term meaning any form of activity specified by a system of rules which defines offices, roles, moves, penalties, defenses, and so on, and which gives the activity its structure. As examples one may think of games and rituals, trials and parliaments, markets and systems of property. I have attempted a partial analysis of the notion of a practice in a paper "Two Concepts of Rules," *Philosophical Review*, LXIV (1955), 3–32.

with. I shall focus attention, then, on the usual sense of justice in which it is essentially the elimination of arbitrary distinctions and the establishment, within the structure of a practice, of a proper balance between competing claims.

Finally, there is no need to consider the principles discussed below as *the* principles of justice. For the moment it is sufficient that they are typical of a family of principles normally associated with the concept of justice. The way in which the principles of this family resemble one another, as shown by the background against which they may be thought to arise, will be made clear by the whole of the subsequent argument.

2. The conception of justice which I want to develop may be stated in the form of two principles as follows: first, each person participating in a practice, or affected by it, has an equal right to the most extensive liberty compatible with a like liberty for all; and second, inequalities are arbitrary unless it is reasonable to expect that they will work out for everyone's advantage, and provided the positions and offices to which they attach, or from which they may be gained, are open to all. These principles express justice as a complex of three ideas: liberty, equality, and reward for services contributing to the common good.[2]

The term "person" is to be construed variously depending on the circumstances. On some occasions it will mean human individuals, but in others it may refer to nations, provinces, business firms, churches, teams, and so on. The principles of justice apply in all these instances, although there is a certain logical priority to the case of human individuals. As I shall use the term "person," it will be ambiguous in the manner indicated.

The first principle holds, of course, only if other things are equal: that is, while there must always be a justification for departing from the initial position of equal liberty (which is defined by the pattern of rights and duties, powers and liabilities, established by a practice), and the burden of proof is placed on him who would depart from it, nevertheless, there can be, and often there is, a justification for doing so. Now, that similar particular cases, as defined by a practice, should be treated similarly as they arise, is part of the very concept of a practice; it is involved in the notion of an activity in accordance with rules.[3] The first principle expresses an analogous conception, but as applied to the structure of practices themselves. It holds, for example, that there

---

[2] These principles are, of course, well-known in one form or another and appear in many analyses of justice even where the writers differ widely on other matters. Thus if the principle of equal liberty is commonly associated with Kant (see *The Philosophy of Law,* tr. by W. Hastie, Edinburgh, 1887, pp. 56 f.), it may be claimed that it can also be found in J. S. Mill's *On Liberty* and elsewhere, and in many other liberal writers. Recently H. L. A. Hart has argued for something like it in his paper "Are There Any Natural Rights?," *Philosophical Review,* LXIV (1955), 175–191. The injustice of inequalities which are not won in return for a contribution to the common advantage is, of course, widespread in political writings of all sorts. The conception of justice here discussed is distinctive, if at all, only in selecting these two principles in this form; but for another similar analysis, see the discussion by W. D. Lamont, *The Principles of Moral Judgment* (Oxford, 1946), ch. v.

[3] This point was made by Sidgwick, *Methods of Ethics,* 6th ed. (London, 1901). Bk. III, ch. v. sec. 1. It has recently been emphasized by Sir Isaiah Berlin in a symposium, "Equality," *Proceedings of the Aristotelian Society,* n.s. LVI (1955–56), 305 f.

is a presumption against the distinctions and classifications made by legal systems and other practices to the extent that they infringe on the original and equal liberty of the persons participating in them. The second principle defines how this presumption may be rebutted.

It might be argued at this point that justice requires only an equal liberty. If, however, a greater liberty were possible for all without loss or conflict, then it would be irrational to settle on a lesser liberty. There is no reason for circumscribing rights unless their exercise would be incompatible, or would render the practice defining them less effective. Therefore no serious distortion of the concept of justice is likely to follow from including within it the concept of the greatest equal liberty.

The second principle defines what sorts of inequalities are permissible; it specifies how the presumption laid down by the first principle may be put aside. Now by inequalities it is best to understand not *any* differences between offices and positions, but differences in the benefits and burdens attached to them either directly or indirectly, such as prestige and wealth, or liability to taxation and compulsory services. Players in a game do not protest against there being different positions, such as batter, pitcher, catcher, and the like, nor to there being various privileges and powers as specified by the rules; nor do the citizens of a country object to there being the different offices of government such as president, senator, governor, judge, and so on, each with their special rights and duties. It is not differences of this kind that are normally thought of as inequalities, but differences in the resulting distribution established by a practice, or made possible by it, of the things men strive to attain or avoid. Thus they may complain about the pattern of honors and rewards set up by a practice (e.g., the privileges and salaries of government officials) or they may object to the distribution of power and wealth which results from the various ways in which men avail themselves of the opportunities allowed by it (e.g., the concentration of wealth which may develop in a free price system allowing large entrepreneurial or speculative gains).

It should be noted that the second principle holds that an inequality is allowed only if there is reason to believe that the practice with the inequality, or resulting in it, will work for the advantage of *every* party engaging in it. Here it is important to stress that *every* party must gain from the inequality. Since the principle applies to practices, it implies that the representative man in every office or position defined by a practice, when he views it as a going concern, must find it reasonable to prefer his condition and prospects with the inequality to what they would be under the practice without it. The principle excludes, therefore, the justification of inequalities on the grounds that the disadvantages of those in one position are outweighed by the greater advantages of those in another position. This rather simple restriction is the main modification I wish to make in the utilitarian principle as usually understood. When coupled with the notion of a practice, it is a restriction of consequence,[4] and

---

[4] In the paper referred to above, footnote 2, I have tried to show the importance of taking practices as the proper subject of the utilitarian principle. The criticisms of so-called "restricted

one which some utilitarians, e.g., Hume and Mill, have used in their discussions of justice without realizing apparently its significance, or at least without calling attention to it.[5] Why it is a significant modification of principle, changing one's conception of justice entirely, the whole of my argument will show.

Further, it is also necessary that the various offices to which special benefits or burdens attach are open to all. It may be, for example, to the common advantage, as just defined, to attach special benefits to certain offices. Perhaps by doing so the requisite talent can be attracted to them and encouraged to give its best efforts. But any offices having special benefits must be won in a fair competition in which contestants are judged on their merits. If some offices were not open, those excluded would normally be justified in feeling unjustly treated, even if they benefited from the greater efforts of those who were allowed to compete for them. Now if one can assume that offices are open, it is necessary only to consider the design of practices themselves and how they jointly, as a system, work together. It will be a mistake to focus attention on the varying relative positions of particular persons, who may be known to us by their proper names, and to require that each such change, as a once for all transaction viewed in isolation, must be in itself just. It is the system of practices which is to be judged, and judged from a general point of view: unless one is prepared to criticize it from the standpoint of a representative man holding some particular office, one has no complaint against it.

3. Given these principles one might try to derive them from a priori principles of reason, or claim that they were known by intuition. These are familiar enough steps and, at least in the case of the first principle, might be

---

utilitarianism" by J. J. C. Smart, "Extreme and Restricted Utilitarianism," *Philosophical Quarterly,* VI (1956), 344–354, and by H. J. McCloskey, "An Examination of Restricted Utilitarianism," *Philosophical Review,* LXVI (1957), 466–485, do not affect my argument. These papers are concerned with the very general proposition, which is attributed (with what justice I shall not consider) to S. E. Toulmin and P. H. Nowell-Smith (and in the case of the latter paper, also, apparently, to me); namely, the proposition that particular moral actions are justified by appealing to moral rules, and moral rules in turn by reference to utility. But clearly I meant to defend no such view. My discussion of the concept of rules as maxims is an explicit rejection of it. What I did argue was that, in the *logically special* case of practices (although actually quite a common case) where the rules have special features and are not moral rules at all but legal rules or rules of games and the like (except, perhaps, in the case of promises), there is a peculiar force to the distinction between justifying particular actions and justifying the system of rules themselves. Even then I claimed only that restricting the utilitarian principle to practices as defined strengthened it. I did not argue for the position that this amendment alone is sufficient for a complete defense of utilitarianism as a general theory of morals. In this paper I take up the question as to how the utilitarian principle itself must be modified, but here, too, the subject of inquiry is not all of morality at once, but a limited topic, the concept of justice.

[5] It might seem as if J. S. Mill, in paragraph 36 of Chapter v of *Utilitarianism,* expressed the utilitarian principle in this modified form, but in the remaining two paragraphs of the chapter, and elsewhere, he would appear not to grasp the significance of the change. Hume often emphasizes that *every* man must benefit. For example, in discussing the utility of general rules, he holds that they are requisite to the "well-being of every individual"; from a stable system of property "every individual person must find himself a gainer in balancing the account. . . ." "Every member of society is sensible of this interest; everyone expresses this sense to his fellows along with the resolution he has taken of squaring his actions by it, on the conditions that others will do the same." *A Treatise of Human Nature,* Bk. III, Pt. II, Section II, paragraph 22.

made with some success. Usually, however, such arguments, made at this point, are unconvincing. They are not likely to lead to an understanding of the basis of the principles of justice, not at least as principles of justice. I wish, therefore, to look at the principle in a different way.

Imagine a society of persons amongst whom a certain system of practices is *already* well established. Now suppose that by and large they are mutually self-interested; their allegiance to their established practices is normally founded on the prospect of self-advantage. One need not assume that, in all senses of the term "person," the persons in this society are mutually self-interested. If the characterization as mutually self-interested applies when the line of division is the family, it may still be true that members of families are bound by ties of sentiment and affection and willingly acknowledge duties in contradiction to self-interest. Mutual self-interestedness in the relations between families, nations, churches, and the like, is commonly associated with intense loyalty and devotion on the part of individual members. Therefore, one can form a more realistic conception of this society if one thinks of it as consisting of mutually self-interested families, or some other association. Further, it is not necessary to suppose that these persons are mutually self-interested under all circumstances, but only in the usual situations in which they participate in their common practices.

Now suppose also that these persons are rational: they know their own interests more or less accurately; they are capable of tracing out the likely consequences of adopting one practice rather than another; they are capable of adhering to a course of action once they have decided upon it; they can resist present temptations and the enticements of immediate gain; and the bare knowledge or perception of the difference between their condition and that of others is not, within certain limits and in itself, a source of great dissatisfaction. Only the last point adds anything to the usual definition of rationality. This definition should allow, I think, for the idea that a rational man would not be greatly downcast from knowing, or seeing, that others are in a better position than himself, unless he thought their being so was the result of injustice, or the consequence of letting chance work itself out for no useful common purpose, and so on. So if these persons strike us as unpleasantly egoistic, they are at least free in some degree from the fault of envy.[6]

Finally, assume that these persons have roughly similar needs and interests, or needs and interests in various ways complementary, so that fruitful cooperation amongst them is possible; and suppose that they are sufficiently equal in power and ability to guarantee that in normal circumstances none is able to dominate the others. This condition (as well as the others) may seem

---

[6] It is not possible to discuss here this addition to the usual conception of rationality. If it seems peculiar, it may be worth remarking that it is analogous to the modification of the utilitarian principle which the argument as a whole is designed to explain and justify. In the same way that the satisfaction of interests, the representative claims of which violate the principles of justice, is not a reason for having a practice (see sec. 7), unfounded envy, within limits, need not be taken into account.

excessively vague; but in view of the conception of justice to which the argument leads, there seems no reason for making it more exact here.

Since these persons are conceived as engaging in their common practices, which are already established, there is no question of our supposing them to come together to deliberate as to how they will set these practices up for the first time. Yet we can imagine that from time to time they discuss with one another whether any of them has a legitimate complaint against their established institutions. Such discussions are perfectly natural in any normal society. Now suppose that they have settled on doing this in the following way. They first try to arrive at the principles by which complaints, and so practices themselves, are to be judged. Their procedure for this is to let each person propose the principles upon which he wishes his complaints to be tried with the understanding that, if acknowledged, the complaints of others will be similarly tried, and that no complaints will be heard at all until everyone is roughly of one mind as to how complaints are to be judged. They each understand further that the principles proposed and acknowledged on this occasion are binding on future occasions. Thus each will be wary of proposing a principle which would give him a peculiar advantage, in his present circumstances, supposing it to be accepted. Each person knows that he will be bound by it in future circumstances the peculiarities of which cannot be known, and which might well be such that the principle is then to his disadvantage. The idea is that everyone should be required to make *in advance* a firm commitment, which others also may reasonably be expected to make, and that no one be given the opportunity to tailor the canons of a legitimate complaint to fit his own special condition, and then to discard them when they no longer suit his purpose. Hence each person will propose principles of a general kind which will, to a large degree, gain their sense from the various applications to be made of them, the particular circumstances of which being as yet unknown. These principles will express the conditions in accordance with which each is the least unwilling to have his interests limited in the design of practices, given the competing interests of the others, on the supposition that the interests of others will be limited likewise. The restrictions which would so arise might be thought of as those a person would keep in mind if he were designing a practice in which his enemy were to assign him his place.

The two main parts of this conjectural account have a definite significance. The character and respective situations of the parties reflect the typical circumstances in which questions of justice arise. The procedure whereby principles are proposed and acknowledged represents constraints, analogous to those of having a morality, whereby rational and mutually self-interested persons are brought to act reasonably. Thus the first part reflects the fact that questions of justice arise when conflicting claims are made upon the design of a practice and where it is taken for granted that each person will insist, as far as possible, on what he considers his rights. It is typical of cases of justice to involve persons who are pressing on one another their claims, between which a fair balance or equilibrium must be found. On the other hand, as expressed by the second part, having a morality must at least imply the acknowledgment of principles as impartially applying to one's own conduct as well as to another's, and moreover principles which may constitute a constraint, or limitation, upon the pursuit of one's own interests. There are, of course, other aspects of having a morality: the acknowledgment of moral principles must show itself in accepting a reference to them as reasons for limiting one's claims, in acknowledging the burden of providing a special explanation, or excuse, when one acts contrary to them, or else in showing shame and remorse and a desire to make amends, and so on. It is sufficient to remark here that having a morality is analogous to having made a firm commitment in advance; for one must acknowledge the principles of morality even when to one's disadvantage.[7] A man whose moral judgments always coincided with his interests could be suspected of having no morality at all.

Thus the two parts of the foregoing account are intended to mirror the kinds of circumstances in which questions of justice arise and the constraints which having a morality would impose upon persons so situated. In this way one can see how the acceptance of the principles of justice might come about, for given all these conditions as described, it would be natural if the two principles of justice were to be acknowledged. Since there is no way for anyone to win special advantages for himself, each might consider it reasonable to acknowledge equality as an initial principle. There is, however, no reason why they should regard this position as final; for if there are inequalities which satisfy the second principle, the immediate gain which equality would allow can be considered as intelligently invested in view of its future return. If, as is quite likely, these inequalities work as incentives to draw out better efforts, the members of this society may look upon them as concessions to human nature: they, like us, may think that people ideally should want to serve one another. But as they are mutually self-interested, their acceptance of these inequalities is merely the acceptance of the relations in which they actually stand, and a recognition of the motives which lead them to engage in their common practices. *They* have no title to complain of one another. And so provided that the conditions of the principle are met, there is no reason why they should not allow such inequalities. Indeed, it would be short-sighted of them to do so, and could result, in most cases, only from their being dejected by the bare knowledge, or perception, that others are better situated. Each person will, however, insist on an advantage to himself, and so on a common advantage, for none is willing to sacrifice anything for the others.

These remarks are not offered as a rigorous proof that persons conceived and situated as the conjectural account supposes, and required to adopt the

---

[7] The idea that accepting a principle as a moral principle implies that one generally acts on it, failing a special explanation, has been stressed by R. M. Hare, *The Language of Morals* (Oxford, 1952). His formulation of it needs to be modified, however, along the lines suggested by P. L. Gardiner, "On Assenting to a Moral Principle," *Proceedings of the Aristotelian Society,* n.s. LV (1953), 23–44. See also C. K. Grant, "Akrasia and the Criteria of Assent to Practical Principles," *Mind,* LXV (1956), 400–407, where the complexity of the criteria for assent is discussed.

procedure described, would settle on the two principles of justice. For such a proof a more elaborate and formal argument would have to be given; there remain certain details to be filled in, and various alternatives to be ruled out. The argument should, however, be taken as a proof, or as a sketch of a proof; for the proposition I seek to establish is a necessary one, that is, it is intended as a theorem: namely, that when mutually self-interested and rational persons confront one another in typical circumstances of justice, and when they are required by a procedure expressing the constraints of having a morality to jointly acknowledge principles by which their claims on the design of their common practices are to be judged, they will settle on these two principles as restrictions governing the assignment of rights and duties, and thereby accept them as limiting their rights against one another. It is this theorem which accounts for these principles as principles of justice, and explains how they come to be associated with this moral concept. Moreover this theorem is analogous to those about human conduct in other branches of social thought. That is, a simplified situation is described in which rational persons pursuing certain ends and related to one another in a definite way, are required to act subject to certain limitations; then, given this situation, it is shown that they will act in a certain manner. Failure to so act would imply that one or more of the assumptions does not obtain. The foregoing account aims to establish, or to sketch, a theorem in this sense; the aim of the argument is to show the basis for saying that the principles of justice may be regarded as those principles which arise when the constraints of having a morality are imposed upon rational persons in typical circumstances of justice.

4. These ideas are, of course, connected with a familiar way of thinking about justice which goes back at least to the Greek Sophists, and which regards the acceptance of the principles of justice as a compromise between persons of roughly equal power who would enforce their will on each other if they could, but who, in view of the equality of forces amongst them and for the sake of their own peace and security, acknowledge certain forms of conduct insofar as prudence seems to require. Justice is thought of as a pact between rational egoists the stability of which is dependent on a balance of power and a similarity of circumstances.[8] While the previous account is connected with this

---

[8] Perhaps the best known statement of this conception is that given by Glaucon at the beginning of Book II of Plato's *Republic*. Presumably it was, in various forms, a common view among the Sophists; but that Plato gives a fair representation of it is doubtful. See K. R. Popper, *The Open Society and Its Enemies*, rev. ed. (Princeton, 1950), pp. 112–118. Certainly Plato usually attributes to it a quality of manic egoism which one feels must be an exaggeration; on the other hand, see the Melian Debate in Thucydides, *The Peloponnesian War*, Book V, ch. VII, although it is impossible to say to what extent the views expressed there reveal any current philosophical opinion. Also in this tradition are the remarks of Epicurus on justice in *Principal Doctrines*, XXXI–XXXVIII. In modern times elements of the conception appear in a more sophisticated form in Hobbes' *The Leviathan* and in Hume's *A Treatise of Human Nature*, Book III, Pt. II, as well as in the writings of the school of natural law such as Pufendorf's *De jure naturae et gentium*. Hobbes and Hume are especially instructive. For Hobbes's argument see Howard Warrender's *The Political Philosophy of Hobbes* (Oxford, 1957). W. J. Baumol's *Welfare Economics and the Theory of the State* (London, 1952), is valuable in showing the wide applicability of Hobbes's fundamental idea (interpreting his natural law as principles of prudence), although in this book it is traced back only to Hume's *Treatise*.

tradition, and with its most recent variant, the theory of games,[9] it differs from it in several important respects which, to forestall misinterpretations, I will set out here.

First, I wish to use the previous conjectural account of the background of justice as a way of analyzing the concept. I do not want, therefore, to be interpreted as assuming a general theory of human motivation: when I suppose that the parties are mutually self-interested, and are not willing to have their (substantial) interests sacrificed to others, I am referring to their conduct and motives as they are taken for granted in cases where questions of justice ordinarily arise. Justice is the virtue of practices where there are assumed to be competing interests and conflicting claims, and where it is supposed that persons will press their rights on each other. That persons are mutually self-interested in certain situations and for certain purposes is what gives rise to the question of justice in practices covering those circumstances. Amongst an association of saints, if such a community could really exist, the disputes about justice could hardly occur; for they would all work selflessly together for one end, the glory of God as defined by their common religion, and reference to this end would settle every question of right. The justice of practices does not come up until there are several different parties (whether we think of these as individuals, associations, or nations and so on, is irrelevant) who do press their claims on one another, and who do regard themselves as representatives of interests which deserve to be considered. Thus the previous account involves no general theory of human motivation. Its intent is simply to incorporate into the conception of justice the relations of men to one another which set the stage for questions of justice. It makes no difference how wide or general these relations are, as this matter does not bear on the analysis of the concept.

Again, in contrast to the various conceptions of the social contract, the several parties do not establish any particular society or practice; they do not covenant to obey a particular sovereign body or to accept a given constitution.[10] Nor do they, as in the theory of games (in certain respects a marvelously sophisticated development of this tradition), decide on individual strategies adjusted to their respective circumstances in the game. What the parties do is to *jointly* acknowledge certain principles of appraisal relating to their common *practices* either as already established or merely proposed. They accede to standards of judgment, not to a given practice; they do not make any specific agreement, or bargain, or adopt a particular strategy. The subject of their acknowledgment is, therefore, very general indeed; it is simply the acknowledgment of certain principles of judgment, fulfilling certain general

---

[9] See J. von Neumann and O. Morgenstern, *The Theory of Games and Economic Behavior,* 2nd ed. (Princeton, 1947). For a comprehensive and not too technical discussion of the developments since, see R. Duncan Luce and Howard Raiffa, *Games and Decisions: Introduction and Critical Survey* (New York, 1957). Chs. vi and xiv discuss the developments most obviously related to the analysis of justice.

[10] For a general survey see J. W. Gough, *The Social Contract,* 2nd ed. (Oxford, 1957), and Otto von Gierke, *The Development of Political Theory,* tr. by B. Freyd (London, 1939), Pt. II, ch. ii.

conditions, to be used in criticizing the arrangement of their common affairs. The relations of mutual self-interest between the parties who are similarly circumstanced mirror the conditions under which questions of justice arise, and the procedure by which the principles of judgment are proposed and acknowledged reflects the constraints of having a morality. Each aspect, then, of the preceding hypothetical account serves the purpose of bringing out a feature of the notion of justice. One could, if one liked, view the principles of justice as the "solution" of this highest order "game" of adopting, subject to the procedure described, principles of argument for all coming particular "games" whose peculiarities one can in no way foresee. But this comparison, while no doubt helpful, must not obscure the fact that this highest order "game" is of a special sort.[11] Its significance is that its various pieces represent aspects of the concept of justice.

Finally, I do not, of course, conceive the several parties as necessarily coming together to establish their common practices for the first time. Some institutions may, indeed, be set up *de novo;* but I have framed the preceding account so that it will apply when the full complement of social institutions already exists and represents the result of a long period of development. Nor is the account in any way fictitious. In any society where people reflect on their institutions they will have an idea of what principles of justice would be acknowledged under the conditions described, and there will be occasions when questions of justice are actually discussed in this way. Therefore if their practices do not accord with these principles, this will affect the quality of their social relations. For in this case there will be some recognized situations wherein the parties are mutually aware that one of them is being forced to accept what the other would concede is unjust. The foregoing analysis may

---

[11] The difficulty one gets into by a mechanical application of the theory of games to moral philosophy can be brought out by considering among several possible examples, R. B. Braithwaite's study, *Theory of Games as a Tool for the Moral Philosopher* (Cambridge, 1955). On the analysis there given, it turns out that the fair division of playing time between Matthew and Luke depends on their preferences, and these in turn are connected with the instruments they wish to play. Since Matthew has a threat advantage over Luke, arising purely from the fact that Matthew, the trumpeter, prefers both of them playing at once to neither of them playing, whereas Luke, the pianist, prefers silence to cacophony, Matthew is alloted 26 evenings of play to Luke's 17. If the situation were reversed, the threat advantage would be with Luke. See pp. 36 f. But now we have only to suppose that Matthew is a jazz enthusiast who plays the drums, and Luke a violinist who plays sonatas, in which case it will be fair, on this analysis, for Matthew to play whenever and as often as he likes, assuming, of course, as it is plausible to assume, that he does not care whether Luke plays or not. Certainly something has gone wrong. To each according to his threat advantage is hardly the principle of fairness. What is lacking is the concept of morality, and it must be brought into the conjectural account in some way or other. In the text this is done by the form of the procedure whereby principles are proposed and acknowledged (Section 3). If one starts directly with the particular case as known, and if one accepts as given and definitive the preferences and relative positions of the parties, whatever they are, it is impossible to give an analysis of the moral concept of fairness. Braithwaite's use of the theory of games, insofar as it is intended to analyze the concept of fairness, is, I think, mistaken. This is not, of course, to criticize in any way the theory of games as a mathematical theory, to which Braithwaite's book certainly contributes, nor as an analysis of how rational (and amoral) egoists might behave (and so as an analysis of how people sometimes actually do behave). But it is to say that if the theory of games is to be used to analyze moral concepts, its formal structure must be interpreted in a special and general manner as indicated in the text. Once we do this, though, we are in touch again with a much older tradition.

then be thought of as representing the actual quality of relations between persons as defined by practices accepted as just. In such practices the parties will acknowledge the principles on which it is constructed, and the general recognition of this fact shows itself in the absence of resentment and in the sense of being justly treated. Thus one common objection to the theory of the social contract, its apparently historical and fictitious character, is avoided.

5. That the principles of justice may be regarded as arising in the manner described illustrates an important fact about them. Not only does it bring out the idea that justice is a primitive moral notion in that it arises once the concept of morality is imposed on mutually self-interested agents similarly circumstanced, but it emphasizes that, fundamental to justice, is the concept of fairness which relates to right dealing between persons who are cooperating with or competing against one another, as when one speaks of fair games, fair competition, and fair bargains. The question of fairness arises when free persons, who have no authority over one another, are engaging in a joint activity and amongst themselves settling or acknowledging the rules which define it and which determine the respective shares in its benefits and burdens. A practice will strike the parties as fair if none feels that, by participating in it, they or any of the others are taken advantage of, or forced to give in to claims which they do not regard as legitimate. This implies that each has a conception of legitimate claims which he thinks it reasonable for others as well as himself to acknowledge. If one thinks of the principles of justice as arising in the manner described, then they do define this sort of conception. A practice is just or fair, then, when it satisfies the principles which those who participate in it could propose to one another for mutual acceptance under the afore-mentioned circumstances. Persons engaged in a just, or fair, practice can face one another openly and support their respective positions, should they appear questionable, by reference to principles which it is reasonable to expect each to accept.

It is this notion of the possibility of mutual acknowledgment of principles by free persons who have no authority over one another which makes the concept of fairness fundamental to justice. Only if such acknowledgment is possible can there be true community between persons in their common practices; otherwise their relations will appear to them as founded to some extent on force. If, in ordinary speech, fairness applies more particularly to practices in which there is a choice whether to engage or not (e.g., in games, business competition), and justice to practices in which there is no choice (e.g., in slavery), the element of necessity does not render the conception of mutual acknowledgment inapplicable, although it may make it much more urgent to change unjust than unfair institutions. For one activity in which one can always engage is that of proposing and acknowledging principles to one another supposing each to be similarly circumstanced; and to judge practices by the principles so arrived at is to apply the standard of fairness to them.

Now if the participants in a practice accept its rules as fair, and so have no complaint to lodge against it, there arises a prima facie duty (and a corresponding prima facie right) of the parties to each other to act in accordance with the practice when it falls upon them to comply. When any number of persons engage in a practice, or conduct a joint undertaking according to rules, and thus restrict their liberty, those who have submitted to these restrictions when required have the right to a similar acquiescence on the part of those who have benefited by their submission. These conditions will obtain if a practice is correctly acknowledged to be fair, for in this case all who participate in it will benefit from it. The rights and duties so arising are special rights and duties in that they depend on previous actions voluntarily undertaken, in this case on the parties having engaged in a common practice and knowingly accepted its benefits.[12] It is not, however, an obligation which presupposes a deliberate performative act in the sense of a promise, or contract, and the like.[13] An unfortunate mistake of proponents of the idea of the social contract was to suppose that political obligation does require some such act, or at least to use language which suggests it. It is sufficient that one has knowingly participated in and accepted the benefits of a practice acknowledged to be fair. This prima facie obligation may, of course, be overridden: it may happen, when it comes one's turn to follow a rule, that other considerations will justify not doing so. But one cannot, in general, be released from this obligation by denying the justice of the practice only when it falls on one to obey. If a person rejects a practice, he should, so far as possible, declare his intention in advance, and avoid participating in it or enjoying its benefits.

This duty I have called that of fair play, but it should be admitted that to refer to it in this way is, perhaps, to extend the ordinary notion of fairness. Usually acting unfairly is not so much the breaking of any particular rule, even if the infraction is difficult to detect (cheating), but taking advantage of loop-holes or ambiguities in rules, availing oneself of unexpected or special circumstances which make it impossible to enforce them, insisting that rules be enforced to one's advantage when they should be suspended, and more generally, acting contrary to the intention of a practice. It is for this reason that one speaks of the sense of fair play: acting fairly requires more than simply being able to follow rules; what is fair must often be felt, or perceived, one wants to say. It is not, however, an unnatural extension of the duty of fair play to have it include the obligation which participants who have knowingly accepted the benefits of their common practice owe to each other to act in accordance with it when their performance falls due; for it is usually considered unfair if someone accepts the benefits of a practice but refuses to do his part in maintaining it. Thus one might say of the tax-dodger that he violates the duty of fair play: he accepts the benefits of government but will not do his part in releasing resources to it; and members of labor unions often

---

[12] For the definition of this prima facie duty, and the idea that it is a special duty, I am indebted to H. L. A. Hart. See his paper "Are There Any Natural Rights?," *Philosophical Review*, LXIV (1955), 185 f.

[13] The sense of "performative" here is to be derived from J. L. Austin's paper in the symposium, "Other Minds," *Proceedings of the Aristotelian Society*, Supplementary Volume (1916), pp. 170–174.

say that fellow workers who refuse to join are being unfair: they refer to them as "free riders," as persons who enjoy what are the supposed benefits of unionism, higher wages, shorter hours, job security, and the like, but who refuse to share in its burdens in the form of paying dues, and so on.

The duty of fair play stands beside other prima facie duties such as fidelity and gratitude as a basic moral notion; yet it is not to be confused with them.[14] These duties are all clearly distinct, as would be obvious from their definitions. As with any moral duty, that of fair play implies a constraint on self-interest in particular cases; on occasion it enjoins conduct which a rational egoist strictly defined would not decide upon. So while justice does not require of anyone that he sacrifice his interests in that *general position* and procedure whereby the principles of justice are proposed and acknowledged, it may happen that in particular situations, arising in the context of engaging in a practice, the duty of fair play will often cross his interests in the sense that he will be required to forego particular advantages which the peculiarities of his circumstances might permit him to take. There is, of course, nothing surprising in this. It is simply the consequence of the firm commitment which the parties may be supposed to have made, or which they would make, in the general position, together with the fact that they have participated in and accepted the benefits of a practice which they regard as fair.

Now the acknowledgment of this constraint in particular cases, which is manifested in acting fairly or wishing to make amends, feeling ashamed, and the like, when one has evaded it, is one of the forms of conduct by which participants in a common practice exhibit their recognition of each other as persons with similar interests and capacities. In the same way that, failing a special explanation, the criterion for the recognition of suffering is helping one who suffers, acknowledging the duty of fair play is a necessary part of the criterion for recognizing another as a person with similar interests and feelings as oneself.[15] A person who never under any circumstances showed a wish to help others in pain would show, at the same time, that he did not recognize that they were in pain; nor could he have any feelings of affection or friendship for anyone; for having these feelings implies, failing special circumstances,

---

[14] This, however, commonly happens. Hobbes, for example, when invoking the notion of a "tacit covenant," appeals not to the natural law that promises should be kept but to his fourth law of nature, that of gratitude. On Hobbes's shift from fidelity to gratitude, see Warrender, *op. cit.*, pp. 51–52, 233–237. While it is not a serious criticism of Hobbes, it would have improved his argument had he appealed to the duty of fair play. On his premises he is perfectly entitled to do so. Similarly Sidgwick thought that a principle of justice, such as every man ought to receive adequate requital for his labor, is like gratitude universalized. See *Methods of Ethics*, Bk. III, ch. v, Sec. 5. There is a gap in the stock of moral concepts used by philosophers into which the concept of the duty of fair play fits quite naturally.

[15] I am using the concept of criterion here in what I take to be Wittgenstein's sense. See *Philosophical Investigations* (Oxford, 1953); and Norman Malcolm's review, "Wittgenstein's *Philosophical Investigations*," *Philosophical Review*, LXIII (1954), 543–547. That the response of compassion, under appropriate circumstances, is part of the criterion for whether or not a person understands what "pain" means, is, I think, in the *Philosophical Investigations*. The view in the text is simply an extension of this idea. I cannot, however, attempt to justify it here. Similar thoughts are to be found, I think, in Max Scheler, *The Nature of Sympathy*, tr. by Peter Heath (New Haven, 1954). His way of writing is often so obscure that I cannot be certain.

that he comes to their aid when they are suffering. Recognition that another is a person in pain shows itself in sympathetic action; this primitive natural response of compassion is one of those responses upon which the various forms of moral conduct are built.

Similarly, the acceptance of the duty of fair play by participants in a common practice is a reflection in each person of the recognition of the aspirations and interests of the others to be realized by their joint activity. Failing a special explanation, their acceptance of it is a necessary part of the criterion for their recognizing one another as persons with similar interests and capacities, as the conception of their relations in the general position suppose them to be. Otherwise they would show no recognition of one another as persons with similar capacities and interests, and indeed, in some cases perhaps hypothetical, they would not recognize one another as persons at all, but as complicated objects involved in a complicated activity. To recognize another as a person one must respond to him and act towards him in certain ways; and these ways are intimately connected with the various prima facie duties. Acknowledging these duties in *some* degree, and so having the elements of morality, is not a matter of choice, or of intuiting moral qualities, or a matter of the expression of feeling or attitudes (the three interpretations between which philosophical opinion frequently oscillates); it is simply the possession of one of the forms of conduct in which the recognition of others as persons is manifested.

These remarks are unhappily obscure. Their main purpose here, however, is to forestall, together with the remarks in Section 4, the misinterpretation that on the view presented, the acceptance of justice and the acknowledgment of the duty of fair play depends in every day life solely on there being a *de facto* balance of forces between the parties. It would indeed be foolish to underestimate the importance of such a balance in securing justice; but it is not the only basis thereof. The recognition of one another as persons with similar interests and capacities engaged in a common practice must, failing a special explanation, show itself in the acceptance of the principles of justice and the acknowledgment of the duty of fair play.

The conception at which we have arrived, then, is that the principles of justice may be thought of as arising once the constraints of having a morality are imposed upon rational and mutually self-interested parties who are related and situated in a special way. A practice is just if it is in accordance with the principles which all who participate in it might reasonably be expected to propose or to acknowledge before one another when they are similarly circumstanced and required to make a firm commitment in advance without knowledge of what will be their peculiar condition, and thus when it meets standards which the parties could accept as fair should occasion arise for them to debate its merits. Regarding the participants themselves, once persons knowingly engage in a practice which they acknowledge to be fair and accept the benefits of doing so, they are bound by the duty of fair play to follow the rules when it comes their turn to do so, and this implies a limitation on their pursuit of self-interest in particular cases.

Now one consequence of this conception is that, where it applies, there is no moral value in the satisfaction of a claim incompatible with it. Such a claim violates the conditions of reciprocity and community amongst persons, and he who presses it, not being willing to acknowledge it when pressed by another, has no grounds for complaint when it is denied; whereas he against whom it is pressed can complain. As it cannot be mutually acknowledged it is a resort to coercion; granting the claim is possible only if one party can compel acceptance of what the other will not admit. But it makes no sense to concede claims the denial of which cannot be complained of in preference to claims the denial of which can be objected to. Thus in deciding on the justice of a practice it is not enough to ascertain that it answers to wants and interests in the fullest and most effective manner. For if any of these conflict with justice, they should not be counted, as their satisfaction is no reason at all for having a practice. It would be irrelevant to say, even if true, that it resulted in the greatest satisfaction of desire. In tallying up the merits of a practice one must toss out the satisfaction of interests the claims of which are incompatible with the principles of justice.

6. The discussion so far has been excessively abstract. While this is perhaps unavoidable, I should now like to bring out some of the features of the conception of justice as fairness by comparing it with the conception of justice in classical utilitarianism as represented by Bentham and Sidgwick, and its counterpart in welfare economics. This conception assimilates justice to benevolence and the latter in turn to the most efficient design of institutions to promote the general welfare. Justice is a kind of efficiency.[16]

Now it is said occasionally that this form of utilitarianism puts no restrictions on what might be a just assignment of rights and duties in that there might be circumstances which, on utilitarian grounds, would justify institutions highly offensive to our ordinary sense of justice. But the classical utilitarian conception is not totally unprepared for this objection. Beginning with

---

[16] While this assimilation is implicit in Bentham's and Sidgwick's moral theory, explicit statements of it as applied to justice are relatively rare. One clear instance in *The Principles of Morals and Legislation* occurs in ch. x, footnote 2 to section XL: ". . . justice, in the only sense in which it has a meaning, is an imaginary personage, feigned for the convenience of discourse, whose dictates are the dictates of utility, applied to certain particular cases. Justice, then, is nothing more than an imaginary instrument, employed to forward on certain occasions, and by certain means, the purposes of benevolence. The dictates of justice are nothing more than a part of the dictates of benevolence, which, on certain occasions, are applied to certain subjects. . . ." Likewise in *The Limits of Jurisprudence Defined,* ed. by C. W. Everett (New York, 1945), pp. 117 f., Bentham criticizes Grotius for denying that justice derives from utility; and in *The Theory of Legislation,* ed. by C. K. Ogden (London, 1931), p. 3, he says that he uses the words "just" and "unjust" along with other words "simply as collective terms including the ideas of certain pains or pleasures." That Sidgwick's conception of justice is similar to Bentham's is admittedly not evident from his discussion of justice in Book III, ch. v of *Methods of Ethics.* But it follows, I think, from the moral theory he accepts. Hence C. D. Broad's criticisms of Sidgwick in the matter of distribution justice in *Five Types of Ethical Theory* (London, 1930), pp. 249–253, do not rest in a misinterpretation.

the notion that the general happiness can be represented by a social utility function consisting of a sum of individual utility functions with identical weights (this being the meaning of the maxim that each counts for one and no more than one),[17] it is commonly assumed that the utility functions of individuals are similar in all essential respects. Differences between individuals are ascribed to accidents of education and upbringing, and they should not be taken into account. This assumption, coupled with that of diminishing marginal utility, results in a prima facie case for equality, e.g., of equality in the distribution of income during any given period of time, laying aside indirect effects on the future. But even if utilitarianism is interpreted as having such restrictions built into the utility function, and even if it is supposed that these restrictions have in practice much the same result as the application of the principles of justice (and appear, perhaps, to be ways of expressing these principles in the language of mathematics and psychology), the fundamental idea is very different from the conception of justice as fairness. For one thing, that the principles of justice should be accepted is interpreted as the contingent result of a higher order administrative decision. The form of this decision is regarded as being similar to that of an entrepreneur deciding how much to produce of this or that commodity in view of its marginal revenue, or to that of someone distributing goods to needy persons according to the relative urgency of their wants. The choice between practices is thought of as being made on the basis of the allocation of benefits and burdens to individuals (these being measured by the present capitalized value of their utility over the full period of the practice's existence), which results from the distribution of rights and duties established by a practice.

Moreover, the individuals receiving these benefits are not conceived as being related in any way: they represent so many different directions in which limited resources may be allocated. The value of assigning resources to one direction rather than another depends solely on the preferences and interests of individuals as individuals. The satisfaction of desire has its value irrespective of the moral relations between persons, say as members of a joint undertaking, and of the claims which, in the name of these interests, they are prepared to make on one another;[18] and it is this value which is to be taken

---

[17] This maxim is attributed to Bentham by J. S. Mill in *Utilitarianism*, ch. v, paragraph 36. I have not found it in Bentham's writings, nor seen such a reference. Similarly James Bonar, *Philosophy and Political Economy* (London, 1893), p. 234 n. But it accords perfectly with Bentham's ideas. See the hitherto unpublished manuscript in David Baumgardt, *Bentham and the Ethics of Today* (Princeton, 1952), Appendix IV. For example, "the total value of the stock of pleasure belonging to the whole community is to be obtained by multiplying the number expressing the value of it as respecting any one person, by the number expressing the multitude of such individuals" (p. 556).

[18] An idea essential to the classical utilitarian conception of justice. Bentham is firm in his statement of it: "It is only upon that principle [the principle of asceticism], and not from the principle of utility, that the most abominable pleasure which the vilest of malefactors ever reaped from his crime would be reprobated, if it stood alone. The case is, that it never does stand alone; but is necessarily followed by such a quantity of pain (or, what comes to the same thing, such a chance for a certain quantity of pain) that the pleasure in comparison of it, is as nothing; and this is the true and sole, but perfectly sufficient, reason for making it a ground for punishment" (*The Principles of Morals and Legislation*, ch. ii, sec. iv. See

into account by the (ideal) legislator who is conceived as adjusting the rules of the system from the center so as to maximize the value of the social utility function.

It is thought that the principles of justice will not be violated by a legal system so conceived provided these executive decisions are correctly made. In this fact the principles of justice are said to have their derivation and explanation; they simply express the most important general features of social institutions in which the administrative problem is solved in the best way. These principles have, indeed, a special urgency because, given the facts of human nature, so much depends on them; and this explains the peculiar quality of the moral feelings associated with justice.[19] This assimilation of justice to a higher order executive decision, certainly a striking conception, is central to classical utilitarianism; and it also brings out its profound individualism, in one sense of this ambiguous word. It regards persons as so many *separate* directions in which benefits and burdens may be assigned; and the value of the satisfaction or dissatisfaction of desire is not thought to depend in any way on the moral relations in which individuals stand, or on the kinds of claims which they are willing, in the pursuit of their interests, to press on each other.

7. Many social decisions are, of course, of an administrative nature. Certainly this is so when it is a matter of social utility in what one may call its ordinary sense: that is, when it is a question of the efficient design of social institutions for the use of common means to achieve common ends. In this case either the benefits and burdens may be assumed to be impartially distributed, or the question of distribution is misplaced, as in the instance of maintaining public order and security or national defense. But as an interpretation of the basis of the principles of justice, classical utilitarianism is mistaken. It *permits* one to argue, for example, that slavery is unjust on the grounds that the advantages to the slaveholder as slaveholder do not counterbalance the disadvantages to the slave and to society at large burdened by a comparatively inefficient system of labor. Now the conception of justice as fairness, when applied to the practice of slavery with its offices of slaveholder and slave, would not allow one to consider the advantages of the slaveholder in the first place. As that office is not in accordance with principles which

---

also ch. x, sec. x, footnote 1). The same point is made in *The Limits of Jurisprudence Defined*, pp. 115 f. Although much recent welfare economics, as found in such important works as I. M. D. Little, *A Critique of Welfare Economics*, 2nd ed. (Oxford, 1957) and K. J. Arrow, *Social Choice and Individual Values* (New York, 1951), dispenses with the idea of cardinal utility, and uses instead the theory of ordinal utility as stated by J. R. Hicks, *Value and Capital*, 2nd ed. (Oxford, 1946), Pt. I, it assumes with utilitarianism that individual preferences have value as such, and so accepts the idea being criticized here. I hasten to add, however, that this is no objection to it as a means of analyzing economic policy, and for that purpose it may, indeed, be a necessary simplifying assumption. Nevertheless it is an assumption which cannot be made in so far as one is trying to analyze moral concepts, especially the concept of justice, as economists would, I think, agree. Justice is usually regarded as a separate and distinct part of any comprehensive criterion of economic policy. See, for example, Tibor Scitovsky, *Welfare and Competition* (London, 1952), pp. 59–69, and Little, *op. cit.*, ch. VII.

[19] See J. S. Mill's argument in *Utilitarianism*, ch. v, pars. 16–25.

could be mutually acknowledged, the gains accruing to the slaveholder, assuming them to exist, cannot be counted as in *any* way mitigating the injustice of the practice. The question whether these gains outweigh the disadvantages to the slave and to society cannot arise, since in considering the justice of slavery these gains have no weight at all which requires that they be overridden. Where the conception of justice as fairness applies, slavery is *always* unjust.

I am not, of course, suggesting the absurdity that the classical utilitarians approved of slavery. I am only rejecting a type of argument which their view allows them to use in support of their disapproval of it. The conception of justice as derivative from efficiency implies that judging the justice of a practice is always, in principle at least, a matter of weighing up advantages and disadvantages, each having an intrinsic value or disvalue as the satisfaction of interests, irrespective of whether or not these interests necessarily involve acquiescence in principles which could not be mutually acknowledged. Utilitarianism cannot account for the fact that slavery is always unjust, nor for the fact that it would be recognized as irrelevant in defeating the accusation of injustice for one person to say to another, engaged with him in a common practice and debating its merits, that nevertheless it allowed of the greatest satisfaction of desire. The charge of injustice cannot be rebutted in this way. If justice were derivative from a higher order executive efficiency, this would not be so.

But now, even if it is taken as established that, so far as the ordinary conception of justice goes, slavery is always unjust (that is, slavery by definition violates commonly recognized principles of justice), the classical utilitarian would surely reply that these principles, as other moral principles subordinate to that of utility, are only generally correct. It is simply for the most part true that slavery is less efficient than other institutions; and while common sense may define the concept of justice so that slavery is unjust, nevertheless, where slavery would lead to the greatest satisfaction of desire, it is not wrong. Indeed, it is then right, and for the very same reason that justice, as ordinarily understood, is usually right. If, as ordinarily understood, slavery is always unjust, to this extent the utilitarian conception of justice might be admitted to differ from that of common moral opinion. Still the utilitarian would want to hold that, as a matter of moral principle, his view is correct in giving no special weight to considerations of justice beyond that allowed for by the general presumption of effectiveness. And this, he claims, is as it should be. The every day opinion is morally in error, although, indeed, it is a useful error, since it protects rules of generally high utility.

The question, then, relates not simply to the analysis of the concept of justice as common sense defines it, but the analysis of it in the wider sense as to how much weight considerations of justice, as defined, are to have when laid against other kinds of moral considerations. Here again I wish to argue that reasons of justice have a *special* weight for which only the conception of justice as fairness can account. Moreover, it belongs to the concept of justice that they do have this special weight. While Mill recognized that this was so, he thought that it could be accounted for by the special urgency of the moral feelings which naturally support principles of such high utility. But it is a mistake to resort to the urgency of feeling; as with the appeal to intuition, it manifests a failure to pursue the question far enough. The special weight of considerations of justice can be explained from the conception of justice as fairness. It is only necessary to elaborate a bit what has already been said as follows.

If one examines the circumstances in which a certain tolerance of slavery is justified, or perhaps better, excused, it turns out that these are of a rather special sort. Perhaps slavery exists as an inheritance from the past and it proves necessary to dismantle it piece by piece; at times slavery may conceivably be an advance on previous institutions. Now while there may be some excuse for slavery in special conditions, it is never an excuse for it that it is sufficiently advantageous to the slaveholder to outweigh the disadvantages to the slave and to society. A person who argues in this way is not perhaps making a wildly irrelevant remark; but he is guilty of a moral fallacy. There is disorder in his conception of the ranking of moral principles. For the slaveholder, by his own admission, has no moral title to the advantages which he receives as a slaveholder. He is no more prepared than the slave to acknowledge the principle upon which is founded the respective positions in which they both stand. Since slavery does not accord with principles which they could mutually acknowledge, they each may be supposed to agree that it is unjust: it grants claims which it ought not to grant and in doing so denies claims which it ought not to deny. Amongst persons in a general position who are debating the form of their common practices, it cannot, therefore, be offered as a reason for a practice that, in conceding these very claims that ought to be denied, it nevertheless meets existing interests more effectively. By their very nature the satisfaction of these claims is without weight and cannot enter into any tabulation of advantages and disadvantages.

Furthermore, it follows from the concept of morality that, to the extent that the slaveholder recognizes his position vis-à-vis the slave to be unjust, he would not choose to press his claims. His not wanting to receive his special advantages is one of the ways in which he shows that he thinks slavery is unjust. It would be fallacious for the legislator to suppose, then, that it is a ground for having a practice that it brings advantages greater than disadvantages, if those for whom the practice is designed, and to whom the advantages flow, acknowledge that they have no moral title to them and do not wish to receive them.

For these reasons the principles of justice have a special weight; and with respect to the principle of the greatest satisfaction of desire, as cited in the general position amongst those discussing the merits of their common practices, the principles of justice have an absolute weight. In this sense they are not contingent; and this is why their force is greater than can be accounted for by the general presumption (assuming that there is one) of the effectiveness, in the utilitarian sense, of practices which in fact satisfy them.

If one wants to continue using the concepts of classical utilitarianism, one will have to say, to meet this criticism, that at least the individual or social utility functions must be so defined that no value is given to the satisfaction of interests the representative claims of which violate the principles of justice. In this way it is no doubt possible to include these principles within the form of the utilitarian conception; but to do so is, of course, to change its inspiration altogether as a moral conception. For it is to incorporate within it principles which cannot be understood on the basis of a higher order executive decision aiming at the greatest satisfaction of desire.

It is worth remarking, perhaps, that this criticism of utilitarianism does not depend on whether or not the two assumptions, that of individuals having similar utility functions and that of diminishing marginal utility, are interpreted as psychological propositions to be supported or refuted by experience, or as moral and political principles expressed in a somewhat technical language. There are, certainly, several advantages in taking them in the latter fashion.[20] For one thing, one might say that this is what Bentham and others really meant by them, at least as shown by how they were used in arguments for social reform. More importantly, one could hold that the best way to defend the classical utilitarian view is to interpret these assumptions as moral and political principles. It is doubtful whether, taken as psychological propositions, they are true of men in general as we know them under normal conditions. On the other hand, utilitarians would not have wanted to propose them merely as practical working principles of legislation, or as expedient maxims to guide reform, given the egalitarian sentiments of modern society.[21] When pressed they might well have invoked the idea of a more or less equal capacity of men in relevant respects if given an equal chance in a just society. But if the argument above regarding slavery is correct, then granting these assumptions as moral and political principles makes no difference. To view individuals as equally fruitful lines for the allocation of benefits, even as a matter of moral principle, still leaves the mistaken notion that the satisfaction of desire has value in itself irrespective of the relations between persons as members of a common practice, and irrespective of the claims upon one another which the satisfaction of interests represents. To see the error of this idea one must give up the conception of justice as an executive decision altogether and refer to the notion of justice as fairness: that participants

---

[20] See D. G. Ritchie, *Natural Rights* (London, 1894), pp. 95 ff., 249 ff. Lionel Robbins has insisted on this point on several occasions. See *An Essay on the Nature and Significance of Economic Science*, 2nd ed. (London, 1935), pp. 134–43, "Interpersonal Comparisons of Utility: A Comment," *Economic Journal*, XLVIII (1938), 635–41, and more recently, "Robertson on Utility and Scope," *Economica*, n.s. XX (1953), 108 f.

[21] As Sir Henry Maine suggested Bentham may have regarded them. See *The Early History of Institutions* (London, 1875), pp. 398 ff.

in a common practice be regarded as having an original and equal liberty and that their common practices be considered unjust unless they accord with principles which persons so circumstanced and related could freely acknowledge before one another, and so could accept as fair. Once the emphasis is put upon the concept of the mutual recognition of principles by participants in a common practice the rules of which are to define their several relations and give form to their claims on one another, then it is clear that the granting of a claim the principle of which could not be acknowledged by each in the general position (that is, in the position in which the parties propose and acknowledge principles before one another) is not a reason for adopting a practice. Viewed in this way, the background of the claim is seen to exclude it from consideration; that it can represent a value in itself arises from the conception of individuals as separate lines for the assignment of benefits, as isolated persons who stand as claimants on an administrative or benevolent largesse. Occasionally persons do so stand to one another; but this is not the general case, nor, more importantly, is it the case when it is a matter of the justice of practices themselves in which participants stand in various relations to be appraised in accordance with standards which they may be expected to acknowledge before one another. Thus however mistaken the notion of the social contract may be as history, and however far it may overreach itself as a general theory of social and political obligation, it does express, suitably interpreted, an essential part of the concept of justice.[22]

8. By way of conclusion I should like to make two remarks: first, the original modification of the utilitarian principle (that it require of practices that the offices and positions defined by them be equal unless it is reasonable to suppose that the representative man in *every* office would find the inequality to his advantage), slight as it may appear at first sight, actually has a different conception of justice standing behind it. I have tried to show how this is so by developing the concept of justice as fairness and by indicating how this notion involves the mutual acceptance, from a general position, of the principles on which a practice is founded, and how this in turn requires the exclusion from consideration of claims violating the principles of justice. Thus the slight alteration of principle reveals another family of notions, another way of looking at the concept of justice.

Second, I should like to remark also that I have been dealing with the *concept* of justice. I have tried to set out the kinds of principles upon which judgments concerning the justice of practices may be said to stand. The analysis will be successful to the degree that it expresses the principles involved in these judgments when made by competent persons upon deliberation and

---

[22] Thus Kant was not far wrong when he interpreted the original contract merely as an "Idea of Reason"; yet he still thought of it as a *general* criterion of right and as providing a general theory of political obligation. See the second part of the essay, "On the Saying 'That may be right in theory but has no value in practice' " (1793), in *Kant's Principles of Politics,* tr. by W. Hastie (Edinburgh, 1891). I have drawn on the contractarian tradition not for a general theory of political obligation but to clarify the concept of justice.

reflection.[23] Now every people may be supposed to have the concept of justice, since in the life of every society there must be at least some relations in which the parties consider themselves to be circumstanced and related as the concept of justice as fairness requires. Societies will differ from one another not in having or in failing to have this notion but in the range of cases to which they apply it and in the emphasis which they give to it as compared with other moral concepts.

A firm grasp of the concept of justice itself is necessary if these variations, and the reasons for them, are to be understood. No study of the development of moral ideas and of the differences between them is more sound than the analysis of the fundamental moral concepts upon which it must depend. I have tried, therefore, to give an analysis of the concept of justice which should apply generally, however large a part the concept may have in a given morality, and which can be used in explaining the course of men's thoughts about justice and its relations to other moral concepts. How it is to be used for this purpose is a large topic which I cannot, of course, take up here. I mention it only to emphasize that I have been dealing with the concept of justice itself and to indicate what use I consider such an analysis to have.

---

[23] For a further discussion of the idea expressed here, see my paper, "Outline of a Decision Procedure for Ethics," in *The Philosophical Review*, LX (1951), 177–197. For an analysis, similar in many respects but using the notion of the ideal observer instead of that of the considered judgment of a competent person, see Roderick Firth, "Ethical Absolutism and the Ideal Observer," *Philosophy and Phenomenological Research*, XII (1952), 317–345. While the similarities between these two discussions are more important than the differences, an analysis based on the notion of a considered judgment of a competent person, as it is based on a kind of judgment, may prove more helpful in understanding the features of moral judgment than an analysis based on the notion of an ideal observer, although this remains to be shown. A man who rejects the conditions imposed on a considered judgment of a competent person could no longer profess to *judge* at all. This seems more fundamental than his rejecting the conditions of observation, for these do not seem to apply, in an ordinary sense, to making a moral judgment.

Part Two

Social Philosophy

4

The Nature of Society and Law

Reading: Stanley I. Benn and Richard S. Peters, "Society and Types of Social Regulation"

Much of social philosophy may be viewed as applied moral philosophy—that is, the attempt to spell out the political and legal implications of certain moral theories such as utilitarianism or Kantianism. Equally important, however, is the prior task of analyzing the basic *concepts* involved in the understanding of society, politics, and law—for example, *authority, sovereignty,* and *representation.* (These concepts will be dealt with in later chapters by, for example, Hobbes and Dickinson.) In this chapter, two contemporary philosophers analyze what could be regarded as the most basic concepts of all: *society* and *law.* What is a society, and how does a society differ, for example, from a random aggregate collection of persons? What makes a rule a legal rule, and how does a legal rule differ, for example, from rules of custom, etiquette and morality? Benn and Peters explore these questions, and others, in the following selection. Clarity on the issues they discuss will aid one considerably in understanding and assessing the complex analytical and evaluative theories put forth in later chapters by such writers as Hobbes and Marx.

Suggestion for Further Reading

H. L. A. Hart, *The Concept of Law* (Oxford: The Clarendon Press, 1961).

Society and Types of Social Regulation
Stanley I. Benn and Richard S. Peters

Social Wholes

Man, said Aristotle, is a political animal. He lives in society and is thereby able to survive, to talk, and to develop a culture. This is no doubt true, but the initial difficulty in theorizing about society is to be clear what we are talking about. If an ornithologist says that woodpeckers live in trees there is little to puzzle us. For trees and birds are easily picked out; they have definite contours; they move about; they have parts which mutually influence one another so as to make them both recognizable wholes. But when a social theorist tells us that men live in society, the matter is more puzzling. We are not inclined to dispute what he says, but it is not quite clear what he is saying. For though men are recognizable wholes like birds, societies are not wholes of the same order at all. The way in which a man lives in a society is quite different from the way in which a woodpecker lives in a tree. For membership of a society does not necessarily imply residence in some larger spatial whole. What then does it imply?

The first and obvious observation to make is that there is no such thing as society. By this is meant, firstly, that men are members of various societies rather than of society, and, secondly, that societies are not things in the ordinary sense of "thing." The most obvious characteristic of a thing is that it is spatially extended with recognizable contours. Yet quite obviously such a criterion does not fit the Society for the Propagation of Christian Knowledge. Indeed, very few societies conform to this criterion. For all members would have to be present at a given place—a rare occurrence at even the annual general meeting of any society. The fact, however, that societies are not things

---

Reprinted with permission of The Macmillan Company and George Allen and Unwin Ltd. from *The Principles of Political Thought* (originally: *Social Principles and the Democratic State*) by Stanley I. Benn and Richard S. Peters. Copyright © 1959 by George Allen and Unwin Ltd. First Free Press paperback edition 1965. Stanley I. Benn, until recently lecturer in government at the University of Southampton, is now at the Australian National University, Canberra. Richard S. Peters is professor of philosophy of education at the University of London Institute of Education.

in the obvious sense of the word "thing" need not worry us unduly; for neither are minds, and yet we all think that we have got them—except, perhaps, behaviourists. People palpably are things—though, of course, things of a special sort—and when we speak of societies we are using language to pick out types of order which make an intelligible pattern of the activities which people share with one another. As a matter of fact we have to be taught to recognize forms of order which seem obviously given to us, as the psychologists have shown. Language itself makes possible a new level of life; by initiation into it we are also introduced to the contours of our environment. We learn words for cats, cars and clouds. And the process of learning the word is part of the process of learning the type of order intimated by it.

The trouble, however, about societies is that they are *not* given for us to recognize in the obvious way in which trees, toads, and turnips are. What we call a social whole is largely a matter of our construction; for the conventions of our language mirror the social forms which we develop. Of course, our selectivity and constructiveness enter into all our classifications, but in the case of social wholes much less is given and much more is constructed.

Consider, for instance, the case of social classes about which so much has been written since Marx popularized this way of grouping people together. His notion of class presupposed a highly sophisticated theory about the relation of people to the means of production. The proletarian class, for example, were those who sold their labour but owned none of the means of production. Yet others, who did not share Marx's theory about the significance for social life of people's relationship to the means of production, held that it was more fruitful to define a social class in terms, perhaps, of people's education or occupation. The point is that such ways of grouping people together presuppose all sorts of assumptions which are highly disputable.[1] If there are such wholes, they obviously are not palpable wholes.

It is, as a matter of fact, a cardinal mistake to assume that just because we have terms like "nations," "state," and "social class," there need be any one type of order that is properly referred to by the word. People still hotly dispute about whether any recognizable type of order is referred to by the term "nation" at all. Words are only tools for communication. Provided that we understand what other people mean when they use words, it is idle, unless we are writing a dictionary, to insist that one way of using the words is alone correct. For students of society an interest in terminology should take the form of asking what theory about society the terms are being used to state. This, as a matter of fact, is a very difficult attitude to maintain. For our hopes and fears, our desires and dreads, are much more easily aroused by theories about man than by theories about Nature. It is significant that the sciences which were the first to develop were those which dealt with the stars—the bodies most remote from man. And even astronomy itself developed in the

---

[1] For discussion of this and related points about social wholes and the methods of the social sciences, see K. R. Popper, *The Poverty of Historicism* (1957).

face of strong opposition because of the emotional and religious significance of the behaviour of the heavenly bodies. It was not until the nineteenth century that men achieved the degree of detachment necessary to study themselves scientifically. So when we talk about states, nations, social classes, and other such postulated types of order, it is very difficult to detach our emotions from our analysis; for holding on to a definition of "social class" or "nation" is too often a way of defending our valuations rather than of getting clearer about the facts.

Nature and Convention

So far it has been shown how much human constructiveness helps to form the contours which we recognize in our social environment, and it has been intimated how difficult it is to separate our valuations from an analysis of society. These two difficulties in achieving a detached description of society may both be in part due to one of the outstanding differences between our social and physical environments. The order discernible in the natural world —the constitution of a crystal or a sponge, the rotation of the earth around the sun, the way in which lead melts at a certain temperature—is universal and not dependent on human desire or decision. Human decision enters, of course, in the choice of an order, in the way in which we select and group what is given. The laws of nature, after all, are human utterances or human marks on paper. Nature is what is the case—concrete particular facts; it does not consist in generalizations made about such occurrences. But whether or not these laws are true depends upon facts which are independent of human decision. No Act of Parliament can alter the constitution of a crystal or the laws of planetary motion. The order of society, on the other hand, is only maintained because of certain rules or norms which are very variable and which depend upon human desire and decision. This is not to say that all such rules have been consciously thought out and instituted; for what we call customs quite obviously have not. It is to say, rather, that such rules are expressive of human desires and aversions and that they are the sorts of things which can be altered by human decision. If men cease to think that divorce is always wrong, then marriage laws, which introduce a form of order into a certain area of human behaviour, can be changed. The vital difference between these forms of order is concealed by the fact that in English we use the word "law" for both. We speak of marriage laws and of the laws of planetary motion. This often obscures the crucial point that whereas laws, in the legal sense, *prescribe* what ought to be, laws of Nature only *describe* what is invariably the case.

This distinction is a trifle over-simplified, but, perhaps a consideration of one or two complications will make it clearer. It will be said that the distinction is not clear because we can, on the one hand, alter the course of Nature, and on the other hand, we can develop laws about social orders. Both these assertions are true but they do not affect the crux of the distinction. Of course, we can tinker with Nature and introduce alterations. We do this every time we make a table, build a bridge or dam a river. But in making these alterations what we can do is limited by the properties and modes of change of the objects which the laws of Nature describe and explain. We cannot suddenly introduce large quantities of arsenic into an organism and expect the organism to live unless, because of our further knowledge of the properties of arsenic and organisms, we also introduce an antidote. When we adopt the interventionist attitude to Nature we are only successful if we have a thorough knowledge of the things with which we are dealing. Scientific laws tell us what we cannot do. Now psychologists and social scientists attempt to discover similar properties of human nature—the limitations imposed on our decisions by the material with which we have to work. Every system of social order grows up on a foundation of human nature. The problem is to discover which properties of human nature are universal and unalterable. Similarly, we can try, like the sociologists, to develop descriptive laws about the conditions under which normative orders of a certain sort develop, just as psychologists can make generalizations about the conditions under which people tend to conform to rules, or to deviate from them, about the different ways in which rules can be handed on from parents to children, and about the various "needs" which rule-following satisfies. These laws resemble those in any natural science; but they just happen to be laws *about* rule-following. In the same way the sociologist can try to develop laws about the conditions under which scientific laws tend to emerge. But the admissions do not affect the basic distinction between natural laws which hold because of facts independent of human decision and normative laws which can cease to hold if human beings so decide.

This distinction between normative rules and scientific laws, which is here regarded as basic in our understanding of society, was made explicit comparatively late in the history of thought—probably in Europe in the eighteenth century. In primitive thought not only are these forms of order lumped together, but the sort of order discernible in our social environment is taken as the universal type. The regularities of Nature are laid down or ordained in the same kind of way as social codes. We still hear relics of this more primitive way of thinking when people speak of the laws of motion *governing* the movement of the planets. To the primitive mind Nature is peopled with gods and spirits who are responsible for different departments. If there is a storm at sea, Poseidon is angry. If the crops fail, Ceres must be placated. Elaborate rituals are performed to ensure that the customary order of Nature is maintained. When, with the development of abstract thought, all-pervasive forms of order are discerned, then men tend to suppose that this is instituted by some all-powerful agent. Plato, for instance, conjectured that in everything some kind of geometrical order was manifest, and added that God everywhere does geometry. The implicit assumption of this mode of thought is that any form of order presupposes an orderer. Hume's *Dialogues Concerning Natural Religion,* published in 1779, were a landmark in the history of thought in that

Hume emphasized that there were different forms of order—that of a vegetable, of a house, of a commonwealth, of a mind—and showed conclusively that just because some forms of order presuppose an orderer, it cannot be inferred that all forms of order do. The order of the world, he suggested satirically, is just as likely to have developed spontaneously like that of a vegetable as to have been consciously instituted like that of a house.

In the light of this distinction;[2] which took so long to develop, between what is natural and what is normative, we can become clearer about what constitutes a human society. Men, of course, like the rest of Nature, have certain natural ways of behaving. Psychological theories about universal, unalterable and, perhaps innate, tendencies (e.g. doctrines of human instincts) are attempts to sketch what these ways of behaving are. But imposed on these tendencies and providing the social conditions under which they operate are all kinds of normative rules which introduce order of a different kind. This order can only persist if it does not violate the unalterable properties of human nature. Indeed a frequent criticism of revolutionary reforms is that they take no account of human nature. What we call a human society is a number of individuals bound together by such an order of normative rules. They behave predictably in relation to one another because of this normative system. These rules define the rights and duties which they have towards one another, the ends which they may pursue, and the ways in which it is legitimate to pursue them.

Men, then, are rule-following animals; they perform predictably in relation to one another and form what is called a social system to a large extent because they accept systems of rules which are variable and alterable by human decision. Indeed we cannot really bring out what we mean by a human action without recourse to standards laying down what are accepted as ends and what are efficient and socially appropriate ways of attaining them. Actions like buying a watch or signing a contract are not just movements of the body; they are movements which we make to bring about ends which are defined largely in terms of man-made standards. They can be performed more or less intelligently as well as more or less correctly, which implies standards of social appropriateness.[3] They are not just things that happen like the blowing of the wind or the falling of the snow.

---

[2] For a fuller treatment of the distinction between nature and convention, see K. R. Popper, *The Open Society and Its Enemies,* Vol. 1, Ch. 5 (1957).

[3] For elaboration of the point that the concept of "action" involves the notion of standards and cannot, therefore be analysed in terms of mere movements, responses to stimuli, and so on, see R. S. Peters, *The Concept of Motivation* (1958), passim—especially Ch. 1.

Authority and Other Forms of Social Regulation

Rules and standards are passed on and originated to a large extent by means of speech, which has a most important regulatory function in the life of men, and which makes possible a quite distinctive form of life. The artifice of speech introduces systems of order into human life which make no sense in the forest or the farmyard. For what human beings do can be described as "right" or "correct," and things are done just because they are right or correct. And together with the notion of "rightness" develops the necessity of *procedures* for deciding what these standards are and whether or not they are being conformed to. And this is very closely linked with the idea of "authority." For such standards being man-made, alterable, and, to a certain extent, arbitrary, procedures are necessary in some spheres at least, for deciding what standards are to be maintained, who is to originate them, who is to decide about their application to particular cases, and who is entitled to introduce changes. Where we find such an arrangement for originators or umpires in the realm of rules, we are in the sphere of "authority." For the concept of "authority," is obviously derived from the old concepts of "auctor" and "auctoritas," which referred to a producing, inventing or cause in the sphere of opinion, counsel or command.[4]

Now in some spheres of social life it is imperative to have such "auctores" who are producers or originators of orders, pronouncements, and decisions. It is also the case that in social life, whether we like it or not, there are such "auctores" to whom commands, decisions and pronouncements are to be traced back in any factual survey of how social regulation is brought about. The authority structure is very much part of what we mean by terms like "a social system," and, to a large extent, accounts for its continuance as a whole while its members pass away. It would be difficult to understand what is meant by an army, a state, or the Roman Catholic Church without an understanding of the concept of "authority." Indeed Hobbes relied on the notion of "authority" to give an analysis of how it comes about that there is a social system rather than a multitude of men,[5] and recently de Jouvenel has seen in "authority" an all-pervasive bond that integrates men into purposeful groups.[6]

But in spite of the pervasiveness of authority and of the indispensability of the concept in the analysis of social systems, we think it important to stress that the concept is itself rather a complex one. Hobbes and de Jouvenel, for instance, were using it in different ways. It is also important to guard against

---

[4] There is a great deal more to be said about the concept of "authority" which is not strictly relevant to the theme presented in this chapter. See R. S. Peters, *Authority*, in symposium on the subject in Proc. Aristotelian Soc., Supp. Vol. XXXII (1958).

[5] T. Hobbes, *Leviathan* (Ed. Oakeshott), pp. 105–106.

[6] B. de Jouvenel, *Sovereignty* (1957), pp. 29–31.

making the sphere of authority co-extensive with that of social regulation, as is done by de Jouvenel amongst others. In our view the use of authority should be clearly distinguished from other techniques of social regulation like the use of moral guidance on the one hand and the use of various forms of power on the other. Let us briefly consider each of these points in turn.

Types of Authority

We must first of all note that "authority" is used both as a *de jure* and as a *de facto* concept. (Hobbes illustrates the first use, de Jouvenel the second.) In its *de jure* sense it implies a set of procedural rules which determine who shall be the "auctor" and about what—as when we speak of those "in authority," "the authorities," or "an authority." In its *de facto* sense it involves reference to a man whose word in fact goes in some sphere—as when we say "he exercised authority over his men."

One of the great services done by the sociologist Max Weber has been to stress the *different* types of normative systems which are connected with different types of authority *de jure*. For legitimacy may be bestowed in different ways on the commands or decisions or pronouncements issuing from an "auctor." In what Weber called a legal-rational system the claim to legitimacy rests on "a belief in the 'legality' of patterns of normative rules and the right of those elevated to authority under such rules to issue commands." [7] There is also traditional authority "resting on an established belief in the sanctity of immemorial traditions and the legitimacy of the status of those exercising authority under them." There are most important and interesting differences between these types of authority—but in both cases to speak of "the authorities" or "those in authority" is to proclaim that on certain matters certain people are entitled, licensed, commissioned or have a right to be "auctores." And the right is bestowed by a set pattern of rules.

This type of authority is to be distinguished carefully from other types of authority where the right derives from personal history, personal credentials, and personal achievements, an extreme form of which Weber took account of when he dealt with "charismatic authority"—"resting on devotion to the specific and exceptional sanctity, heroism or exemplary character of an individual person, and of the normative patterns or order revealed or ordained by him." [8] Weber, of course, was thinking primarily of the outstanding religious and military leaders like Jesus and Napoleon. He therefore pitched his account rather high and personal authority was decked with the trappings of vocation, miracles, and revelation. Nevertheless there is something distinctive about the

---

[7] M. Weber, *Theory of Economic and Social Organization* (tr. Talcott Parsons, 1947), pp. 300–301.

[8] *Op. cit.*, p. 301.

charismatic leader which he shares in an exaggerated form with other natural leaders who exercise authority in virtue of personal claims and personal characteristics. For the reference to personal characteristics is a way of establishing that a man has a right to make pronouncements and issue commands because he is a special sort of person. And, although in some societies a man who sees visions and goes into trance states is in danger of electric shock treatment, in other societies pointing to such peculiarities of personal biography are ways of establishing a man as *an* authority in certain spheres.

We usually speak of a man being "an authority" in the sphere of pronouncements rather than that of commands and decisions where reference to "the authorities" or "those in authority" is more natural. Thus we speak of a man being "an authority" on art, music, nuclear physics, or the Bible. Such a man has not been put in authority; he does not hold authority according to any system of rules. But because of his training, competence, and success in this sphere, he comes to be regarded as an authority. He has a right to make pronouncements. And his right derives from his *personal* history and achievements in a specific sphere. These more mundane cases of where we speak of a man being "an authority" are similar, in this respect, to Weber's charismatic authority, where the legitimacy also is regarded as grounded in personal characteristics.

Authority and Power

So far we have distinguished the different grounds of entitlement which are involved in speaking of a man being "in authority" or "an authority." But we also speak of a man exercising authority over another man in a purely *de facto* sense. And although as a matter of fact he usually does this because he is in authority over him or because he is regarded as an authority, this is not necessarily the case. There is the Admirable Crichton situation, for instance. Or we might say that a man exercised authority over others if, during a crisis like a fire in a cinema, he rose to his feet and told everyone to file out quietly, and everybody in fact obeyed him, even though he was not the cinema manager or a fireman and was a complete stranger to all present. In such a case a man would exercise authority even though he was not in authority.

We are inclined to say that this would be an exercise of authority because the basic features of the concept fit even this situation. The audience files out just because he says so. Equal weight must here be given to the "he" and the "says." To exercise authority over another is to get him to do things by giving orders to him, or by making pronouncements and decisions. It is inseparable from the use of *speech*. Hens, it is said, have a pecking order; but there is no hen *in* authority over other hens, neither does one hen *exercise* authority over other hens. Their system looks like a pure power system. They give no orders, make no pronouncements, and have no rules bestowing legitimacy. The main function of the term "authority," when it is used in its *de facto* sense of "exercising authority," is therefore to stress the regulation of behaviour by means of speech and symbolic gesture as distinct from the use of power. In other words it has its meaning by contrast with other ways of regulating behaviour that do make sense in the forest or farmyard.

This is to reject the more usual attempts to analyze "authority" in terms of power as exemplified, for instance, by Weldon, who claimed that "authority" means power exercised with the general approval of those concerned.[9] For often, what we want to bring out when we say that men are "in authority" or "exercise authority" over other men is that they get their way or ought to get their way by means other than those of force, threats, propaganda, and other ways of exercising power. It is only when a system of authority breaks down or a given individual loses his authority that there must be recourse to power if conformity is to be ensured.[10] The ability to exercise power may, of course, be a necessary condition for the exercise of authority under certain circumstances. It may also be a ground of entitlement as in the old saying "no legitimacy without power." But a necessary condition for the exercise of authority or a ground of entitlement to it should not be confused with what "authority" *means*.

Authority, Science, and Morality

We have claimed that the implication of saying that a man is "in authority" or "exercises authority" is that others do what he says just because he says so. The stress so far in our elucidation of this has been on "says." But in other contexts it is equally important to stress the "he," the existence of an "auctor" or originator in the sphere of decision, pronouncement or command. For in some such spheres the notion of there being an "auctor" is anathema; not all decisions or pronouncements are authoritative. Perhaps commands must always be authoritative, the very concept of "command" or "order" implying this. For commands, roughly speaking, are the sorts of regulatory utterances for which no reasons need to be given. Questions of course can be raised about a man's right to issue commands; but granted that he is entitled to give them and is not straying from his field of competence, there is no further question of justifying them. Indeed the tone of voice in which they are given bears witness to this.

Commands, however, are not the only sort of authoritative utterance. There are also decisions and pronouncements. And, as we have pointed out, not all these are authoritative. Indeed there is a long tradition which stresses

---

[9] T. D. Weldon, *The Vocabulary of Politics* (1953), p. 56.
[10] See B. de Jouvenel, *op. cit.*, Chs. 2 and 3.

the incompatability between authority and certain specific human enterprises like science and morality. For it would be held that in science the importance of the "auctor" or originator is at a minimum, it never being justifiable in scientific institutions to set up an individual or body who will either be the originator of pronouncements or who will decide finally on the truth of pronouncements made. The procedural rules of science lay it down, roughly speaking, that hypotheses must be decided on by looking at the evidence, not by appealing to a man. There are also, and can be, no rules to decide who will be the originators of scientific theories.

In a similar way, as we shall maintain later, a rule cannot be a moral one if it is to be accepted just because someone has laid it down or made a decision between competing alternatives. Reasons must be given for it, not originators or umpires produced. Of course, in both enterprises provisional authorities can be consulted. But there are usually good reasons for this choice and their pronouncements are never to be regarded as final just because they have made them. In science and morality there are no appointed judges or policemen. This is one of the ways in which life in the laboratory differs from life in the army and law courts.

The Development of Types of Social Regulation

So far we have distinguished between natural laws and normative rules and have suggested that what we call societies are individuals bound together by varying patterns of normative rules. We have also suggested that the concept of "authority" is intimately connected with the regulation of behaviour by means of such rules in a social system. For in certain spheres of social life it is imperative to have originators or umpires, men whose pronouncements and decisions determine what rule is to be followed or what interpretation of a rule adopted. In considering the different rules of *procedure* from which men derive their right to be "auctores" in different spheres we had occasion to mention Weber's distinction between legal and traditional rules; we also made a contrast between the fields where authorities are appropriate and the fields of scientific pronouncements and moral decisions, where there can be no authorities. More must now be said about the distinctions implicit in our account of these different types of social regulation.

In some simple and cohesive types of social system a man's behaviour is regulated almost entirely by the roles deriving from his status in society—as a father, a husband, a warrior, or a hunter. But in our modern type of social system our duties are not all so derivable from our station in life. There are, in addition, rules of an all-pervasive character like those relating to non-injury, respect for property, veracity, gratitude to benefactors, unselfishness, and fair play. These very general rules'which are binding on all who live in a given area are usually referred to as social codes.

But we do not regard such social codes as being all of a piece; for we distinguish between customs and traditions, laws, moral rules, and religious rules. We would say, for instance, that it is traditional or customary for a man to walk on the outside of a woman on a pavement; but this is not a law, neither is it a moral duty. Primitive people make no such distinctions, as social regulation in pre-literate societies is comparatively undifferentiated. Indeed, if an anthropologist were to ask one of his subjects whether the prohibition on incest were a moral, legal, religious, or customary rule, he would be greeted with blank incomprehension.

How then do we make these distinctions? Surely, they presuppose, on the part of the people who make them, a certain degree of consciousness of *procedures,* of differences in formal rules by means of which substantive rules like "contracts ought to be kept" or "debts ought to be paid" are decided upon. It is, surely, such differences in procedures that lie behind the distinctions, which obviously are not simply in terms of the content of the rule. The prohibition on incest, for example, is a moral, legal, religious, and customary rule, and the fact that we can say that it exemplifies all these different types of rule shows that it is not the content alone which decides its status.[11] What, then, is the criterion of distinction?

The Emergence of Law

Perhaps the best way of arriving at a general understanding of these distinctions is to say very briefly how they probably arose. In small, preliterate or semi-literate, self-contained societies norms tend to be quite undifferentiated. The lives of the people are regulated by a system of rules which are thought to have been handed down from time immemorial. The question of justifying the rules does not arise. They are part of the order of the world like the movement of the sun or the properties of fire. When, however, social change or social expansion develops—perhaps in a society by the sea that trades with other societies, or in a society that conquers or is conquered by others—the system of local rules proves inadequate either because new contingencies have arisen or because some overall system of rules is necessary for societies to fuse with one another. At such times a system of what we call law tends to arise. This differs from custom in that it is usually written down, it issues from a determinate source like a king, and it is supported by determinate sanctions. Literate societies often hold in reverence someone who

---

[11] Students requiring a fuller consideration of the major social codes should consult a textbook like R. M. MacIver and C. Page, *Society* (1949), Bk. 11, Part 1.

is assumed to have been their first great law-giver—Lycurgus of Sparta, Solon of Athens, and so on. Custom, of course, is not abrogated. Sections of it—usually those which are of most far-reaching social importance—are merely clarified and codified. But the life of the individual continues to be determined by countless customs which have not been converted into laws.

In our society right up to the seventeenth century custom was the predominant form of social control together with the Common Law which was intermediary between custom and law. A man's status and the roles which he had to play in the various departments of life were prescribed by rules handed down from time immemorial. Economic life was static and secure, regulated by the guild system which blocked undue competition and self-assertion. There was little social mobility, and the world view propagated by the Church assigned a proper place to everything in the divine order of things. But with the growth of international commerce in the fourteenth and fifteenth centuries, with the invention of printing and the improvement of communications, a new individualistic order gradually began to take shape. Social life became more and more characterised by acquisitiveness, the pursuit of power, and the striving for honour.[12] Life, indeed, became rather like a race, as the great seventeenth century philosopher, Thomas Hobbes, pictured it. Thrift, efficiency, and hard work became virtues of the rising middle class. Individual effort and initiative, as well as traditional status, came to determine a man's place. In the religion of Protestantism much was made of the priesthood of all believers; the individual was confronted with God without the intermediaries of the Church hierarchy; he had to make his lonely way in quest of salvation by his own individual effort.

The rise of individualism brought about great gains in the field of liberty, self-discipline, and personal responsibility. But these were achieved, to a certain extent, by the loss of the sense of security that goes with a small close-knit traditional society. The need for a new kind of security was almost universally met by the development of a new form of social control—the strengthening and extension of the powers of the king. The nation state emerged with the increase in statute law as the method of social control appropriate to it. And in most countries acute controversy developed about the proper relationship between the individual and this new form of social control which Hobbes aptly dubbed "Leviathan." [13] What rights had the king over his subjects against the king? What made his authority legitimate? On what grounds were they justified in resisting his decrees? How could the insistent demands for the liberty of the subject be reconciled with the obvious need for security? These are the crucial questions of social philosophy. They tend to arise acutely only at a time of social change and intellectual bewilderment; for philosophy is intellectual unrest made explicit. In periods like that of the seventeenth cen-

---

[12] For stimulating sketches on this background, see R. H. Tawney, *Religion and the Rise of Capitalism* (1926), Ch. I, Sec. 1, and Ch. IV, Sec. 1, and E. Fromm, *The Fear of Freedom* (1942), Ch. III.

[13] See R. S. Peters, *Hobbes* (1956), Ch. VIII.

tury in England men were confused and undecided about how they stood in relation to this new form of social control that was developing. And it was at this period that the distinctions between the major forms of social control began to be hammered out.

Law, in the order that was passing, was closely related to custom in that it was thought to be a *declaration* of existing custom. *The law* was there to discover—a kind of appurtenance of the people—as it applied to particular circumstances. With the development in England of Common Law or the King's law this view still persisted. The king and his courts never *made* laws; they declared what the law was. Common Law was intermediary between custom and law in that the judges, in declaring the law, did so by attempting to make explicit the customs of the realm. Parliament itself was regarded as only a kind of court rather than as a law-making body. But when James I claimed that law was simply his command and that customary law was only valid because his silence denoted his assent, and when later on in the seventeenth century the Long Parliament indulged in an unprecedented amount of legislation, it became increasingly clear that laws were not simply declarations of existing custom. For where was the precedent for a parliament prolonging its own life by statute? Was law then, as Hobbes suggested, "the word of him that by right hath command over others"? Our analysis of "authority" helps to explain this suggested connection between "authority" and "command." For commands, roughly speaking, are the sorts of regulatory utterances for which no reasons need to be given. A man can only give a command if, like a king, he is in a position of authority or if he exerts authority in a *de facto* sense. For as an occupant of an office or as a status holder he has a right to make decisions which are binding and to issue orders. Authority, however, is not exercised *only* in the giving of commands. There are also the spheres of making pronouncements and decisions. Behaviour or opinion in these spheres is regulated by the utterance of a man which carries with it the obligation for others to accept, follow, or obey. The claim put forward by Hobbes that law is command is right in stressing the connection between law and authority but wrong in conceiving of commands as the only form of authoritative utterance. A law is obviously an *authoritative* utterance; but it does not follow that it is a command. Further clarifications of such problems about the status of law must, however, await our third chapter.

The Emergence of Morality

The rise of individualism was also manifest in another distinction which was as old as Socrates and those others who had been the mouthpieces of the individualist movement in Greece in the fifth and fourth centuries B.C. This was the difference between a moral rule on the one hand and a custom or law on the other. Socrates and his followers insisted that the individual should accept only those rules which he himself could justify. It was not enough to adopt traditional standards secondhand because they were sanctified by immemorial custom or laid down by some authority. After all, times change, and authorities disagree. Even the law might be unjust and, although in general the individual should obey the laws of his state, these laws might conflict with his conscience, his own reasoned conviction about what was right and wrong.

This critical rejection or acceptance of custom or law is what is distinctive of morality, just as the critical attitude to theories about Nature is what is distinctive about science. The germ of both morality and science emerged at about the same time; they were manifestations of the emergence of individualism. For, with the development of trade and the interchange of ideas between societies, it came to be realized (and made explicit by writers like Herodotus) that men lived under a bewilderingly different number of laws and customs just as they accepted quite different theories of Nature. The individual like Socrates or Protagoras who reflected on this diversity was thrown back on himself; authorities had to be challenged and the truth arrived at. Men began to proclaim that, whatever their civic allegiances, there was a bond between them as reasonable beings. The concept of the individual and respect for the individual as an individual developed. In the dispute about Nature and convention, which can be found in the writings of Plato and Protagoras, this distinction was implicit;[14] for it was held by some that all men shared in a certain common "nature" whatever conventions they happened to live under. Later on, with the breakdown of the autonomous city states and the consequent decline in the importance of man's duty as a citizen, the notion developed of a universal system of rules binding on all men in virtue of their nature as rational beings. This universal system of rules or law of nature[15] as it was called was contrasted with the laws and customs of particular states. The Stoics, who were the first to formulate this conception of natural law with explicitness, spoke of man as a citizen of the world as well as of a particular state. As rational beings men occupied a cosmic status and were equal, whatever their civic status; and as rational beings they could not doubt that contracts ought to be kept, life and property respected, and that justice should prevail between men. These were the sorts of rules that could be justified in any society whatsoever. Thus the Stoics, who flourished after the conquests of Alexander and the cosmopolitan tendencies which he fostered, developed with greater explicitness the implications of the Socratic tradition. They began to systematize what we now call a moral code. For the characteristic of a moral rule is that it should be regarded as universally applicable and rationally acceptable to the individual.

---

[14] One of the earliest discussions of this is in Bks. 1 and 2 of Plato's *Republic*.

[15] For fuller treatment of the concept of the "law of nature" at this period, see G. H. Sabine, *History of Political Theory* (1951), Ch. VIII.

The notion of such an ideal universal code persisted in Rome through the influence of the Stoics. It exerted a simplifying and humanising influence on the Roman law of nations—a practical system of law developed to regulate dealings with those foreign cities with which Rome was brought into contact through her commercial and military expansion. With the coming of Christianity, cosmopolitanism and egalitarianism found a more dynamic and emotional form of expression. Later, with the development of theology, the system of natural law came to be regarded by Aquinas as a selection from God's rules which could be rationally discerned and which did not need to be supernaturally revealed. It was appealed to by the more philosophically minded of the clergy to humanise, and often to condemn, current laws and customs.

The heyday of natural law, however, was the post-Renaissance growth of individualism.[16] The Renaissance, as has often been said, focused interest on man as an individual. The law of Nature was thought to be rooted in man as an individual rather than derivative from his ecclesiastical or civic status. Hence its appeal at this time. Also, at a time of acute religious controversy it appealed to reasonable men, like Grotius in Holland, who wanted peace and toleration; for it suggested a set of rules which were rationally acceptable and unaffected by the revelations and authoritative claims of rival religious sects. The law of Nature was also a godsend to those rising representatives of the middle class who feared the absolutist ambitions of the rulers of the developing nation states; for the law of Nature provided a system of universal principles binding on king and subject alike to which appeal could be made in calling in question the justice of laws.

It was in this kind of context that moral philosophy grew and flourished. For moral philosophy is the attempt to find criteria in virtue of which rules can be rationally justified.[17] It presupposes a critical attitude to rules and the refusal to equate what is right with what is laid down by custom, law or any other authoritative source. This attitude is only possible in an individualist era where the distinction is made between man as a citizen of a state and man as an individual belonging to other societies and able to criticize the laws and customs in which he has been nurtured. In our second chapter we shall give a brief outline of the criteria suggested for distinguishing a moral rule from a custom. So far we have claimed only that a moral rule differs from a custom in that it has been critically examined in accordance with some criterion other than the degree to which it is generally accepted or the competence of the authority prescribing it. In the same way scientific laws become differentiated from a mass of heterogeneous assumptions about the world. They emerged as those assumptions which stood up to observational tests. The task of moral philosophy is to make explicit the test in the sphere of normative rules which corresponds to that of the observational test in the sphere of descriptions of

---

[16] A. D'Entreves, *Natural Law* (1951), should be consulted for an account of the development of natural law.

[17] See L. T. Hobhouse, *Morals in Evolution* (7th ed. M. Ginsberg, 1951), Chs. VI, VII.

Nature. For what we call moral rules are those that have emerged from an undifferentiated mass of normative rules after a certain kind of test has been applied to them.

Morality and Religion

Of course, the distinction between man as an individual and man as a member of a state was enormously helped by Christianity with its stress on the brotherhood of man and the distinction between man as a subject of temporal authorities and man as a child of God. Indeed, the very existence of the Church institutionalised this distinction. Protestantism especially emphasised the conscience of the individual in his endeavour to find out what was right by searching the Scriptures and his own heart. Catholicism inhibited the development of morality by its stress on the authority of the church hierarchy in matters of right and wrong. This raises the question of how moral rules are to be distinguished from religious ones—a very difficult question in view of their similarity of content. Probably the answer would be that a rule is specifically religious if it is thought to have been laid down by some divinely inspired individual or group of individuals or if the individual himself regards the rule as revealed to him personally by God, and if the divine nature of its origin is thought to be the justification for obeying it. A religious rule does not have the same connection with man's reason as is usually claimed for moral rules; it depends much more on the authority of a man. This suggested criterion raises the fundamental question of the existence of God and of the criteria possible for claiming that God's will has been revealed. As this book makes no attempt to enter the field of the philosophy of religion, the problems connected with this suggested criterion of distinction will not be further explored.

We have, in this introductory chapter, suggested that the important respect in which society differs from Nature is that its order is largely the product of systems of normative rules. We then showed how the concept of "authority" is intimately connected with the regulation of behaviour within such a social system. We claimed, however, that the sphere of authority is to be distinguished from the sphere of power on the one hand and the sphere of moral regulation on the other. We then embarked on a brief description of the contexts in which the distinction between law, custom, and morality arose. We can now proceed to examine in more detail the criteria assumed in making these distinctions.

5

Individualism and the Social Contract

Readings: Thomas Hobbes, Leviathan (abridged)
F. A. Hayek, "The Principles of a Liberal Social Order"

Thomas Hobbes may be viewed as one of the philosophical founders of classical liberalism. Given that he is a known authoritarian in politics, this claim may sound initially absurd. However, certain basic claims in his social and political theory are central to all forms of liberalism. Two of the most important are the following:

1. Government and law are not goods in themselves but are rather, since coercive, intrinsically evil. They are only to be tolerated because they prevent some, even greater evil (in Hobbes's case, this evil is regarded as the anarchical state of nature, which is a war of all against all and wherein life is "brutish, nasty and short").

2. The basic values that society and government serve can be ascribed to individual atomistic man in total abstraction from any society. All social values are totally reducible to values of individuals (the basic values, in Hobbes's view, being the avoidance of pain and death). Man is only contingently, and not necessarily or essentially, a social and political animal. He enters society only because he sees it as instrumental to values he can have and understand in isolation. This

general outlook may be regarded as a radical commitment to *individualism* in social and political theory. Given the close tie between classical liberalism and economic capitalism, C. B. Macpherson has called this a commitment to "possessive individualism."

One of the fascinations of Hobbes's general theory is his attempt to present it in a deductive geometrical form wherein most of his claims are to be regarded as theorems founded on certain basic axioms. Hobbes begins by developing a theory of human nature—a theory concerning those basic facts that are true of man as he is in himself independent of any social or conventional or institutional conditioning. According to Hobbes, natural man is a complex causal mechanism driven by *self-interest*. (This theory is generally called *psychological egoism*.) This self-interest exhibits itself primarily in desires to preserve the organism against pain and death. Each man attempts to gain power over others to help in avoiding pain and death at their hands, and this results in a ruthless struggle for power which, given the approximate equality of all men in strength and ability, no one can win. A state of war results. Since all rational egoists can see that such a struggle, since it cannot be won, increases the likelihood of pain and death for everyone, it should be possible to persuade them to do whatever is necessary for peace (security from pain and death). According to Hobbes, the only way to attain a certain peace is to set up an arbitrary and absolute authority (the sovereign leviathan) to resolve controversy and thus end violent conflict. Hobbes's questionable theory of knowledge and language supports this outlook because it maintains that a man's only contact with the world is through sense impressions (phantasms) and the names he gives them; that is, men have no direct acquaintance with the world as it really is. This being so, the result is a position of epistemological skepticism concerning the external world. Because men can only be acquainted with their own mental contents, they can never be sure that they know the world as it really is or that they genuinely communicate with their fellows (since they cannot be sure that the name they give a sense impression is the same that others give theirs). Thus there is no genuinely right or correct answer to any interpersonal dispute (all knowledge, according to Hobbes, is limited to definitions); and thus to secure peace men must simply resolve their disputes by accepting the arbitrary decision of some authority.

Hobbes is not, it should be pointed out, making a historical claim that there really was at one time such a state of nature or war. Rather he imagines what the world would be like without law or government, calls this the state of nature, and paints such a dire picture of it that we can see the value of law and government in a fresh light. Similarly with Hobbes's talk about a social contract. He is not claiming that there was a time when men actually signed a contract or made a covenant to enter civil society. Rather he uses the concept of a contract or covenant as a model of rational decision: A rule or institution is rational to adopt if and only if it would necessarily be contracted for by a group of enlightened egoists meeting together to choose rules for their mutual regulation. (For a contemporary elaboration of this idea, reread the selection from Rawls in Chapter 3.) According to Hobbes, such rational creatures would contract for absolute government.

Now most subsequent individualistic contractarians (for example, Locke, Kant, and Rawls) have not been absolutists or authoritarians. This is not because they disagree with Hobbes's methodological strategy, however, but is generally because they disagree with him on the facts concerning human nature. Hobbes, many would argue, is just wrong in supposing that all men care about avoiding pain and death more than they care about anything else. Some value their dignity or liberty or property more and will risk pain and death to preserve these values. Thus Locke, for example, holding a more charitable view of human nature, argues that rational men would contract only for a government which did more than preserve their lives. Such a government would also have to preserve certain other values (sometimes called natural or human *rights*) such as liberty and property. Locke, however, still agrees with Hobbes on the basic points (a) that government is only instrumentally useful in providing men with what they value and (b) that these values or rights are "natural" in that they are socially independent and can intelligibly be understood and ascribed to man without any reference to rules, conventions, or (to use Rawls' term) practices. This idea that man's nature can be understood in total isolation from society will be challenged in the next chapter by Marx.

Hobbes also holds the liberal theory of obedience to law and revolution —that men owe obedience to the legal system only insofar as it serves the basic purposes that it is supposed to serve *for them*. According to Hobbes, this basic purpose is to protect men from pain and death. When government can no longer do this adequately, a man's obligation to it ceases and it can be resisted. Of course even fairly terrible governments can do a fairly decent job of keeping their citizens alive and free from gross pain, and thus Hobbes's account does not perhaps provide as many opportunities for justified rebellion or revolution as some would like. But it is still, in form, the same theory to be offered by "revolutionists" like Locke, the only difference being that Locke conceives government's purposes to involve much more than security against pain and death. This being so, government has more opportunities to fail and thus be legitimately resisted.

The second selection in this chapter, F. A. Hayek's "The Principles of a Liberal Social Order," develops radical individualism (including *laissez-faire* capitalism) in an *anti-authoritarian* spirit. According to Hobbes, peace or security is the only genuinely important social value. According to Hayek, more is required: peace, justice, and liberty. Hayek also insists on one feature of classical liberalism that is totally missing from Hobbes—the demand that government be limited by the rule of law. Otherwise men cannot be protected from the abuse of political power, a kind of abuse that Hobbes quite stupidly minimizes.[1] Despite his brilliance, Hobbes was not able to anticipate the wisdom of Lord Acton's famous maxim: "Power corrupts; absolute power corrupts absolutely." To protect against this form of corruption is central to most forms of liberalism and is emphasized by Hayek. (These issues will be explored further in Chapter 10 on the values of democracy.)

Suggestions for Further Reading

Sir Ernest Barker, ed., *The Social Contract* (Oxford: Oxford University Press, 1962). This work contains selections from Locke, Hume and Rousseau.

Bernard H. Baumrin, ed., *Hobbes's Leviathan: Interpretation and Criticism* (Belmont, Calif.: Wadsworth, 1969).

F. A. Hayek, *The Constitution of Liberty* (Chicago: University of Chicago Press, 1960).

C. B. Macpherson, *The Political Theory of Possessive Individualism* (Oxford: Oxford University Press, 1962).

A. I. Melden, ed., *Human Rights* (Belmont, Calif.: Wadsworth, 1970).

Richard S. Peters, *Hobbes* (Baltimore: Penguin Books, 1956).

Robert Paul Wolff, *In Defense of Anarchism* (New York: Harper Torchbooks, 1970).

---

[1] We might also note, in anticipation of Chapter 6, that Marx too appears insufficiently concerned with this kind of abuse—an abuse that paved the way for Stalinism.

Leviathan
Thomas Hobbes

Nature (the Art whereby God hath made and governes the World) is by the *Art* of man, as in many other things, so in this also imitated, that it can make an Artificiall Animal. For seeing life is but a motion of Limbs, the beginning whereof is in some principall part within; why may we not say, that all *Automata* (Engines that move themselves by springs and wheeles as doth a watch) have an artificiall life? For what is the *Heart,* but a *Spring;* and the *Nerves,* but so many *Strings;* and the *Joynts,* but so many *Wheeles,* giving

---

Thomas Hobbes (1588–1679) was an English philosopher whose works in social and political philosophy are widely acknowledged to be among the most important and original works ever produced in this field. He is also a literary master of the English language. *Leviathan* was first published in 1651. Its complete title is: *Leviathan, or the Matter, Forme and Power of a Common-wealth Ecclesiasticall and Civil.* For a good general study of Hobbes's philosophy, see Richard Peters, *Hobbes* (Baltimore: Penguin Books, 1968). For later writings on social contract theory, see Sir Ernest Barker, ed. *Social Contract* (Oxford: Oxford University Press, 1962).

motion to the whole Body, such as was intended by the Artificer? *Art* goes yet further, imitating that Rationall and most excellent worke of Nature, *Man.* For by Art is created that great LEVIATHAN called a COMMON-WEALTH, or STATE, (in latine CIVITAS) which is but an Artificiall Man; though of greater stature and strength than the Naturall, for whose protection and defense it was intended; and in which, the *Soveraignty* is an Artificiall *Soul,* as giving life and motion to the whole body; The *Magistrates,* and other *Officers* of Judicature and Execution, artificiall *Joynts; Reward* and *Punishment* (by which fastned to the seate of the Soveraignty, every joynt and member is moved to performe his duty) are the *Nerves,* that do the same in the Body Naturall; The *Wealth* and *Riches* of all the particular members, are the *Strength; Salus Populi* (the *peoples safety*) its *Businesse; Counsellors,* by whom all things needfull for it to know, are suggested unto it, are the *Memory; Equity* and *Lawes,* an artificiall *Reason* and *Will; Concord, Health; Sedition, Sicknesse;* and *Civill war, Death.* Lastly, the *Pacts* and *Covenants,* by which the parts of this Body Politique were at first made, set together, and united, resemble that *Fiat,* or the *Let us make man,* pronounced by God in the Creation.

To describe the Nature of this Artificiall man, I will consider

First, the *Matter* thereof, and the *Artificer;* both which is *Man.*

Secondly, *How,* and by what *Covenants* it is made; what are the *Rights* and just *Power* or *Authority* of a *Soveraigne;* and what it is that *preserveth* and *dissolveth* it. . . .

Concerning the first, there is a saying much usurped of late, That *Wisedome* is acquired, not by reading of *Books,* but of *Men.* Consequently whereunto, those persons, that for the most part can give no other proof of being wise, take great delight to shew what they think they have read in men, by uncharitable censures of one another behind their backs. But there is another saying not of late understood, by which they might learn truly to read one another, if they would take the pains; and that is, *Nosce teipsum, Read thy self:* which was not meant, as it is now used, to countenance, either the barbarous state of men in power, towards their inferiors; or to encourage men of low degree, to a sawcie behaviour towards their betters; But to teach us, that for the similitude of the thoughts, and Passions of one man, to the thoughts, and Passions of another, whosoever looketh into himself, and considereth what he doth, when he does *think, opine, reason, hope, feare,* &c, and upon what grounds; he shall thereby read and know, what are the thoughts, and Passions of all other men, upon the like occasions. I say the similitude of *Passions,* which are the same in all men, *desire, feare, hope,* &c; not the similitude of *the objects* of the Passions, which are the things *desired, feared, hoped,* &c: for these the constitution individuall, and particular education do so vary, and they are so easie to be kept from our knowledge, that the characters of mans heart, blotted and confounded as they are, with dissembling, lying, counterfeiting, and erroneous doctrines, are legible onely to him that searcheth hearts. And though by mens actions wee do discover their designe sometimes; yet to do it without comparing them with our own, and distinguishing all circumstances, by which the case may come to be altered, is to decypher without a key, and be for the most part deceived, by too much trust, or by too much diffidence; as he that reads, is himself a good or evil man.

But let one man read another by his actions never so perfectly, it serves him onely with his acquaintance, which are but few. He that is to govern a whole Nation, must read in himself, not this, or that particular man; but Mankind: which though it be hard to do, harder than to learn any Language, or Science; yet, when I shall have set down my own reading orderly, and perspicuously, the pains left another, will be onely to consider, if he also find not the same in himself. For this kind of Doctrine, admitteth no other Demonstration.

Part I

Of Man

Chap. I

Of Sense

Concerning the Thoughts of man, I will consider them first *Singly,* and afterwards in *Trayne,* or dependance upon one another. *Singly,* they are every one a *Representation* or *Apparence,* of some quality, or other Accident of a body without us; which is commonly called an *Object.* Which Object worketh on the Eyes, Eares, and other parts of mans body; and by diversity of working, produceth diversity of Apparences.

The Originall of them all, is that which we call SENSE; (For there is no conception in a mans mind, which hath not at first, totally, or by parts, been begotten upon the organs of Sense.) The rest are derived from that originall. . . .

Chap. IV

Of Speech

. . . The most noble and profitable invention of all other, was that of SPEECH, consisting of *Names* or *Appellations,* and their Connexion; whereby men register their Thoughts; recall them when they are past; and also declare them one to another for mutuall utility and conversation; without which, there had been amongst men, neither Common-wealth, nor Society, nor Contract, nor Peace, no more than amongst Lyons, Bears, and Wolves. . . .

The generall use of Speech, is to transferre our Mentall Discourse, into Verbal; or the Trayne of our Thoughts, into a Trayne of Words; and that for two commodities; whereof one is, the Registring of the Consequences of our Thoughts; which being apt to slip out of our memory, and put us to a new labour, may again be recalled, by such words as they were marked by. So that the first use of names, is to serve for *Markes,* or *Notes* of remembrance. Another is, when many use the same words, to signifie (by their connexion and order,) one to another, what they conceive, or think of each matter; and also what they desire, feare, or have any other passion for. And for this use they are called *Signes.* Speciall uses of Speech are these; First, to Register, what by cogitation, wee find to be the cause of any thing, present or past; and what we find things present or past may produce, or effect: which in summe, is acquiring of Arts. Secondly, to shew to others that knowledge which we have attained; which is, to Counsell, and Teach one another. Thirdly, to make known to others our wills, and purposes, that we may have the mutuall help of one another. Fourthly, to please and delight our selves, and others, by playing with our words, for pleasure or ornament, innocently.

To these Uses, there are also foure correspondent Abuses. First, when men register their thoughts wrong, by the inconstancy of the signification of their words; by which they register for their conceptions, that which they never conceived; and so deceive themselves. Secondly, when they use words metaphorically; that is, in other sense than that they are ordained for; and thereby deceive others. Thirdly, when by words they declare that to be their will, which is not. Fourthly, when they use them to grieve one another: for seeing nature hath armed living creatures, some with teeth, some with horns, and some with hands, to grieve an enemy, it is but an abuse of Speech, to grieve him with the tongue, unlesse it be one whom wee are obliged to govern; and then it is not to grieve, but to correct and amend.

The manner how Speech serveth to the remembrance of the consequence of causes and effects, consisteth in the imposing of *Names,* and the *Connexion* of them. . . .

When two Names are joyned together into a Consequence, or Affirmation; as thus, *A man is a living creature;* or thus, *if he be a man, he is a living creature,* If the later name *Living creature,* signifie all that the former name *Man* signifieth, then the affirmation, or consequence is *true;* otherwise *false.* For *True* and *False* are attributes of Speech, not of Things. And where Speech is not, there is neither *Truth* nor *Falshood. Errour* there may be, as when wee expect that which shall not be; or suspect what has not been: but in neither case can a man be charged with Untruth.

Seeing then that *truth* consisteth in the right ordering of names in our affirmations, a man that seeketh precise *truth,* had need to remember what every name he uses stands for; and to place it accordingly; or else he will find himselfe entangled in words, as a bird in lime-twiggs; the more he struggles, the more belimed. And therefore in Geometry, (which is the onely Science that it hath pleased God hitherto to bestow on mankind,) men begin at settling the significations of their words; which settling of significations, they call *Definitions;* and place them in the beginning of their reckoning.

By this it appears how necessary it is for any man that aspires to true Knowledge, to examine the Definitions of former Authors; and either to correct them, where they are negligently set down; or to make them himselfe. For the errours of Definitions multiply themselves, according as the reckoning proceeds; and lead men into absurdities, which at last they see, but cannot avoyd, without reckoning anew from the beginning; in which lyes the foundation of their errours. From whence it happens, that they which trust to books, do as they that cast up many little summs into a greater, without considering whether those little summes were rightly cast up or not; and at last finding the errour visible, and not mistrusting their first grounds, know not which way to cleere themselves; but spend time in fluttering over their bookes; as birds that entring by the chimney, and finding themselves inclosed in a chamber, flutter at the false light of a glasse window, for want of wit to consider which way they came in. So that in the right Definition of Names, lyes the first use of Speech; which is the Acquisition of Science: And in wrong, or no Definitions, lyes the first abuse; from which proceed all false and senslesse Tenets; which make those men that take their instruction from the authority of books, and not from their own meditation, to be as much below the condition of ignorant men, as men endued with true Science are above it. For between true Science, and erroneous Doctrines, Ignorance is in the middle. Naturall sense and imagination, are not subject to absurdity. Nature it selfe cannot erre: and as men abound in copiousnesse of language; so they become more wise, or more mad than ordinary. Nor is it possible without Letters for any man to become either excellently wise, or (unless his memory be hurt by disease, or ill constitution of organs) excellently foolish. For words are wise mens counters, they do but reckon by them: but they are the mony of fooles, that value them by the authority of an *Aristotle,* a *Cicero,* or a *Thomas,* or any other Doctor whatsoever, if but a man. . . .

Chap. V

Of Reason, *and* Science

When a man *Reasoneth,* hee does nothing else but conceive a summe totall, from *Addition* of parcels; or conceive a Remainder, from *Substraction* of one summe from another: which (if it be done by Words,) is conceiving of the consequence of the names of all the parts, to the name of the whole; or from the names of the whole and one part, to the name of the other part. And though in some things, (as in numbers,) besides *Adding* and *Substracting,* men name other operations, as *Multiplying* and *Dividing;* yet they are the same; for Multiplication, is but Adding together of things equall; and Division, but Substracting of one thing, as often as we can. These operations are not incident to Numbers onely, but to all manner of things that can be added together, and taken one out of another. For as Arithmeticians teach to adde and substract in *numbers;* so the Geometricians teach the same in *lines, figures* (solid and superficiall,) *angles, proportions, times,* degrees of *swiftnesse, force, power,* and the like; The Logicians teach the same in *Consequences of words;* adding together *two Names,* to make an *Affirmation;* and *two Affirmations,* to make a *Syllogisme;* and *many Syllogismes* to make a *Demonstration;* and from the *summe,* or *Conclusion of a Syllogisme,* they substract one *Proposition,* to finde the other. Writers of Politiques, adde together *Pactions,* to find mens *duties;* and Lawyers, *Lawes,* and *facts,* to find what is *right* and *wrong* in the actions of private men. In summe, in what matter soever there is place for *addition* and *substraction,* there also is place for *Reason;* and where these have no place, there *Reason* has nothing at all to do.

Out of all which we may define, (that is to say determine,) what that is, which is meant by this word *Reason,* when wee reckon it amongst the Faculties of the mind. For REASON, in this sense, is nothing but *Reckoning* (that is, Adding and Substracting) of the Consequences of generall names agreed upon, for the *marking* and *signifying* of our thoughts; I say *marking* them, when we reckon by our selves; and *signifying,* when we demonstrate, or approve our reckonings to other men.

And as in Arithmetique, unpractised men must, and Professors themselves may often erre, and cast up false; so also in any other subject of Reasoning, the ablest, most attentive, and most practised men, may deceive themselves, and inferre false Conclusions; Not but that Reason it selfe is always Right Reason, as well as Arithmetique is a certain and infallible Art: But no one mans Reason, nor the Reason of any one number of men, makes the certaintie; no more than an account is therefore well cast up, because a great many men have unanimously approved it. And therfore, as when there is a controversy in an account, the parties must by their own accord, set up for right Reason, the Reason of some Arbitrator, or Judge, to whose sentence they will both stand, or their controversie must either come to blowes, or be undecided, for want of a right Reason constituted by Nature; so is it also in all debates of what kind soever: And when men that think themselves wiser than all others, clamor and demand right Reason for judge; yet seek no more, but that things should be determined, by no other mens reason but their own, it is as intolerable in the society of men, as it is in play after trump is turned, to use for trump on every occasion, that suite whereof they have most in their hand. For they do nothing els, that will have every of their passions, as it comes to bear sway in them, to be taken for right Reason, and that in their own controversies: bewraying their want of right Reason, by the claym they lay to it.

The Use and End of Reason, is not the finding of the summe, and truth of one, or a few consequences, remote from the first definitions, and settled significations of names; but to begin at these; and proceed from one consequence to another. For there can be no certainty of the last Conclusion, without a certainty of all those Affirmations and Negations, on which it was grounded, and inferred. As when a master of a family, in taking an account,

casteth up the summs of all the bills of expence, into one sum; and not regarding how each bill is summed up, by those that give them in account; nor
what it is he payes for; he advantages himself no more, than if he allowed the
account in grosse, trusting to every of the accountants skill and honesty: so
also in Reasoning of all other things, he that takes up conclusions on the trust
of Authors, and doth not fetch them from the first Items in every Reckoning,
(which are the significations of names settled by definitions), loses his labour;
and does not know any thing; but onely beleeveth.

When a man reckons without the use of words, which may be done in
particular things, (as when upon the sight of any one thing, wee conjecture
what was likely to have preceded, or is likely to follow upon it;) if that which
he thought likely to follow, followes not; or that which he thought likely to
have preceded it, hath not preceded it, this is called ERROR; to which even the
most prudent men are subject. But when we Reason in Words of generall signification, and fall upon a generall inference which is false; though it be commonly called *Error,* it is indeed an ABSURDITY, or senselesse Speech. For Error
is but a deception, in presuming that somewhat is past, or to come; of which,
though it were not past, or not to come; yet there was no impossibility discoverable. But when we make a generall assertion, unlesse it be a true one, the
possibility of it is unconceivable. And words whereby we conceive nothing but
the sound, are those we call *Absurd, Insignificant,* and *Non-sense.* And therefore if a man should talk to me of a *round Quadrangle;* or *accidents of Bread
in Cheese;* or *Immateriall Substances;* or of *A free Subject; A free-Will;* or any
Free, but free from being hindred by opposition, I should not say he were in
an Errour; but that his words were without meaning; that is to say, Absurd. . . .

By this it appears that Reason is not as Sense, and Memory, borne with
us; nor gotten by Experience onely; as Prudence is; but attayned by Industry;
first in apt imposing of Names; and secondly by getting a good and orderly
Method in proceeding from the Elements, which are Names, to Assertions
made by Connexion of one of them to another; and so to Syllogismes, which
are the Connexions of one Assertion to another, till we come to a knowledge
of all the Consequences of names appertaining to the subject in hand; and that
is it, men call SCIENCE. And whereas Sense and Memory are but knowledge
of Fact, which is a thing past, and irrevocable; *Science* is the knowledge of
Consequences, and dependance of one fact upon another: by which, out of
that we can presently do, we know how to do something else when we will,
or the like, another time: Because when we see how any thing comes about,
upon what causes, and by what manner; when the like causes come into our
power, wee see how to make it produce the like effects. . . .

But yet they that have no *Science,* are in better, and nobler condition with
their naturall Prudence; than men, that by mis-reasoning, or by trusting them
that reason wrong, fall upon false and absurd generall rules. For ignorance of
causes, and of rules, does not set men so farre out of their way, as relying on

false rules, and taking for causes of what they aspire to, those that are not so, but rather causes of the contrary.

To conclude, The Light of humane minds is Perspicuous Words, but by exact definitions first snuffed, and purged from ambiguity; *Reason* is the *pace;* Encrease of *Science,* the *way;* and the Benefit of man-kind, the *end.* And on the contrary, Metaphors, and senslesse and ambiguous words, are like *ignes fatui;* and reasoning upon them, is wandering amongst innumerable absurdities; and their end, contention, and sedition, or contempt. . . .

Chap. VI

Of the Interiour Beginnings of
Voluntary Motions: commonly called the Passions.
And the Speeches by which they are expressed

There be in Animals, two sorts of *Motions* peculiar to them: One called *Vitall;* begun in generation, and continued without interruption through their whole life; such as are the *course* of the *Bloud,* the *Pulse,* the *Breathing,* the *Concoction, Nutrition, Excretion,* &c; to which Motions there needs no help of Imagination: The other is *Animall motion,* otherwise called *Voluntary motion;* as to *go,* to *speak,* to *move* any of our limbes, in such manner as is first fancied in our minds. That Sense, is Motion in the organs and interiour parts of mans body, caused by the action of the things we See, Heare, &c; And that Fancy is but the Reliques of the same Motion, remaining after Sense, has been already sayd in the first and second Chapters. And because *going, speaking,* and the like Voluntary motions, depend alwayes upon a precedent thought of *whither, which way,* and *what;* it is evident, that the Imagination is the first internall beginning of all Voluntary Motion. And although unstudied men, doe not conceive any motion at all to be there, where the thing moved is invisible; or the space it is moved in, is (for the shortnesse of it) insensible; yet that doth not hinder, but that such Motions are. For let a space be never so little, that which is moved over a greater space, whereof that little one is part, must first be moved over that. These small beginnings of Motion, within the body of Man, before they appear in walking, speaking, striking, and other visible actions, are commonly called ENDEAVOUR.

This Endeavour, when it is toward something which causes it, is called APPETITE, or DESIRE; the later, being the generall name; and the other, oftentimes restrayned to signifie the Desire of Food, namely *Hunger* and *Thirst.* And when the Endeavour is fromward something, it is generally called AVERSION. These words *Appetite,* and *Aversion* we have from the *Latines;* and they both of them signifie the motions, one of approaching, the other of retiring. So also do the Greek words for the same, which are ὁρμὴ, and ἀφορμὴ. For Nature it selfe does often presse upon men those truths, which afterwards, when they look for somewhat beyond Nature, they stumble at. For the Schooles find in meere Appetite to go, or move, no actuall Motion at all: but because some Motion they must acknowledge, they call it Metaphoricall Motion; which is but an absurd speech: for though Words may be called metaphoricall; Bodies, and Motions cannot.

That which men Desire, they are also sayd to LOVE: and to HATE those things, for which they have Aversion. So that Desire, and Love, are the same thing; save that by Desire, we alwayes signifie the Absence of the Object; by Love, most commonly the Presence of the same. So also by Aversion, we signifie the Absence; and by Hate, the Presence of the Object.

Of Appetites, and Aversions, some are born with men; as Appetite of food, Appetite of excretion, and exoneration, (which may also and more properly be called Aversions, from somewhat they feele in their Bodies;) and some other Appetites, not many. The rest, which are Appetites of particular things, proceed from Experience, and triall of their effects upon themselves, or other men. For of things wee know not at all, or believe not to be, we can have no further Desire, than to tast and try. But Aversion wee have for things, not onely which we know have hurt us; but also that we do not know whether they will hurt us, or not.

Those things which we neither Desire, nor Hate, we are said to *Contemne:* CONTEMPT being nothing else but an immobility, or contumacy of the Heart, in resisting the action of certain things; and proceeding from that the Heart is already moved otherwise, by other more potent objects; or from want of experience of them.

And because the constitution of a mans Body, is in continuall mutation; it is impossible that all the same things should alwayes cause in him the same Appetites, and Aversions: much lesse can all men consent, in the Desire of almost any one and the same Object.

But whatsoever is the object of any mans Appetite or Desire; that is it, which he for his part calleth *Good:* And the object of his Hate, and Aversion, *Evill;* And of his Contempt, *Vile,* and *Inconsiderable.* For these words of Good, Evill, and Contemptible, are ever used with relation to the person that useth them: There being nothing simply and absolutely so; nor any common Rule of Good and Evill, to be taken from the nature of the objects themselves; but from the Person of the man (where there is no Common-wealth;) or, (in a Common-wealth,) from the Person that representeth it; or from an Arbitrator or Judge, whom men disagreeing shall by consent set up, and make his sentence the Rule thereof. . . .

As, in Sense, that which is really within us, is (as I have sayd before) onely Motion, caused by the action of externall objects, but in apparence; to the Sight, Light and Colour; to the Eare, Sound; to the Nostrill, Odour, &c: so, when the action of the same object is continued from the Eyes, Eares, and other organs to the Heart; the reall effect there is nothing but Motion, or Endeavour; which consisteth in Appetite, or Aversion, to, or from the object moving. But the apparence, or sense of that motion, is that wee either call DELIGHT, or TROUBLE OF MIND.

This Motion, which is called Appetite, and for the apparence of it *Delight,* and *Pleasure,* seemeth to be, a corroboration of Vitall motion, and a help thereunto; and therefore such things as caused Delight, were not improperly called *Jucunda,* (*à Juvando,*) from helping or fortifying; and the contrary, *Molesta, Offensive,* from hindering, and troubling the motion vitall.

Pleasure therefore, (or *Delight,*) is the apparence, or sense of Good; and *Molestation* or *Displeasure,* the apparence, or sense of Evill. And consequently all Appetite, Desire, and Love, is accompanied with some Delight more or lesse; and all Hatred, and Aversion, with more or lesse Displeasure and Offence. . . .

When in the mind of man, Appetites, and Aversions, Hopes, and Feares, concerning one and the same thing, arise alternately; and divers good and evill consequences of the doing, or omitting the thing propounded, come successively into our thoughts; so that sometimes we have an Appetite to it; sometimes an Aversion from it; sometimes Hope to be able to do it; sometimes Despaire, or Feare to attempt it; the whole summe of Desires, Aversions, Hopes and Fears, continued till the thing be either done, or thought impossible, is that we call DELIBERATION.

Therefore of things past, there is no *Deliberation;* because manifestly impossible to be changed: nor of things known to be impossible, or thought so; because men know, or think such Deliberation vain. But of things impossible, which we think possible, we may Deliberate; not knowing it is in vain. And it is called *Deliberation;* because it is a putting an end to the *Liberty* we had of doing, or omitting, according to our own Appetite, or Aversion.

This alternate Succession of Appetites, Aversions, Hopes and Fears, is no lesse in other living Creatures then in Man: and therefore Beasts also Deliberate.

Every *Deliberation* is then sayd to *End,* when that whereof they Deliberate, is either done, or thought impossible; because till then wee retain the liberty of doing, or omitting, according to our Appetite, or Aversion.

In *Deliberation,* the last Appetite, or Aversion, immediately adhæring to the action, or to the omission thereof, is that wee call the WILL; the Act, (not the faculty,) of *Willing.* And Beasts that have *Deliberation,* must necessarily also have *Will.* The Definition of the *Will,* given commonly by the Schooles, that it is a *Rationall Appetite,* is not good. For if it were, then could there be no Voluntary Act against Reason. For a *Voluntary Act* is that, which proceedeth from the *will,* and no other. But if in stead of a Rationall Appetite, we shall say an Appetite resulting from a precedent Deliberation, then the Definition is the same that I have given here. *Will* therefore *is the last Appetite in Deliberating.* And though we say in common Discourse, a man had a Will once to do a thing, that neverthelesse he forbore to do; yet that is properly but an Inclination, which makes no Action Voluntary; because the action depends not of it, but of the last Inclination, or Appetite. For if the intervenient Appetites, make any action Voluntary; then by the same Reason all intervenient Aversions, should make the same action Involuntary; and so one and the same action, should be both Voluntary & Involuntary.

By this it is manifest, that not onely actions that have their beginning from Covetousnesse, Ambition, Lust, or other Appetites to the thing propounded; but also those that have their beginning from Aversion, or Feare of those consequences that follow the omission, are *voluntary actions*.

The formes of Speech by which the Passions are expressed, are partly the same, and partly different from those, by which wee expresse our Thoughts. And first generally all Passions may be expressed *Indicatively;* as *I love, I feare, I joy, I deliberate, I will, I command:* but some of them have particular expressions by themselves, which neverthelesse are not affirmations, unlesse it be when they serve to make other inferences, besides that of the Passion they proceeded from. Deliberation is expressed *Subjunctively;* which is a speech proper to signifie suppositions, with their consequences; as, *If this be done, then this will follow;* and differs not from the language of Reasoning, save that Reasoning is in generall words; but Deliberation for the most part is of Particulars. The language of Desire, and Aversion, is *Imperative;* as *Do this, forbeare that;* which when the party is obliged to do, or forbeare, is *Command;* otherwise *Prayer;* or els *Counsell.* The language of Vain-Glory, of Indignation, Pitty and Revengefulness, *Optative:* But of the Desire to know, there is a peculiar expression, called *Interrogative;* as, *What is it, when shall it, how is it done,* and *why so?* other language of the Passions I find none: For Cursing, Swearing, Reviling, and the like, do not signifie as Speech; but as the actions of a tongue accustomed.

These formes of Speech, I say, are expressions, or voluntary significations of our Passions: but certain signes they be not; because they may be used arbitrarily, whether they that use them, have such Passions or not. The best signes of Passions present, are either in the countenance, motions of the body, actions, and ends, or aimes, which we otherwise know the man to have.

And because in Deliberation, the Appetites, and Aversions are raised by foresight of the good and evill consequences, and sequels of the action whereof we Deliberate; the good or evill effect thereof dependeth on the foresight of a long chain of consequences, of which very seldome any man is able to see to the end. But for so farre as a man seeth, if the Good in those consequences, be greater than the Evill, the whole chaine is that which Writers call *Apparent,* or *Seeming Good.* And contrarily, when the Evill exceedeth the Good, the whole is *Apparent,* or *Seeming Evill:* so that he who hath by Experience, or Reason, the greatest and surest prospect of Consequences, Deliberates best himself; and is able when he will, to give the best counsell unto others.

Continuall successe in obtaining those things which a man from time to time desireth, that is to say, continuall prospering, is that men call FELICITY; I mean the Felicity of this life. For there is no such thing as perpetuall Tranquillity of mind, while we live here; because Life it selfe is but Motion, and can never be without Desire, nor without Feare, no more than without Sense. What kind of Felicity God hath ordained to them that devoutly honour him, a man shall no sooner know, than enjoy; being joyes, that now are as incomprehensible, as the word of School-men *Beatificall Vision* is unintelligible.

The forme of Speech whereby men signifie their opinion of the Goodnesse of any thing, is PRAISE. That whereby they signifie the power and greatnesse of any thing, is MAGNIFYING. And that whereby they signifie the opinion they have of a mans Felicity, is by the Greeks called μακαρισμός, for which wee have no name in our tongue. And thus much is sufficient for the present purpose, to have been said of the PASSIONS. . . .

Chap. X

Of Power, Worth, Dignity, Honour *and* Worthiness

The Power *of a Man,* (to take it Universally,) is his present means, to obtain some future apparent Good. And is either *Originall,* or *Instrumentall.*

Naturall Power, is the eminence of the Faculties of Body, or Mind: as extraordinary Strength, Forme, Prudence, Arts, Eloquence, Liberality, Nobility. *Instrumentall* are those Powers, which acquired by these, or by fortune, are means and Instruments to acquire more: as Riches, Reputation, Friends, and the secret working of God, which men call Good Luck. For the nature of Power, is in this point, like to Fame, increasing as it proceeds; or like the motion of heavy bodies, which the further they go, make still the more hast.

The Greatest of humane Powers, is that which is compounded of the Powers of most men, united by consent, in one person, Naturall, or Civill, that has the use of all their Powers depending on his will; such as is the Power of a Common-wealth: Or depending on the wills of each particular; such as is the Power of a Faction, or of divers factions leagued. Therefore to have servants, is Power; To have friends, is Power: for they are strengths united.

Also Riches joyned with liberality, is Power; because it procureth friends, and servants: Without liberality, not so; because in this case they defend not; but expose men to Envy, as a Prey.

Reputation of power, is Power; because it draweth with it the adhærence of those that need protection.

So is Reputation of love of a mans Country, (called Popularity,) for the same Reason.

Also, what quality soever maketh a man beloved, or feared of many; or the reputation of such quality, is Power; because it is a means to have the assistance, and service of many.

Good successe is Power; because it maketh reputation of Wisdome, or good fortune; which makes men either feare him, or rely on him.

Affability of men already in power, is encrease of Power; because it gaineth love.

Reputation of Prudence in the conduct of Peace or War, is Power; because to prudent men, we commit the government of our selves, more willingly than to others.

Nobility is Power, not in all places, but onely in those Common-wealths, where it has Priviledges: for in such priviledges consisteth their Power.

Eloquence is power; because it is seeming Prudence.

Forme is Power; because being a promise of Good, it recommendeth men to the favour of women and strangers.

The Sciences, are small Power; because not eminent; and therefore, not acknowledged in any man; nor are at all, but in a few; and in them, but of a few things. For Science is of that nature, as none can understand it to be, but such as in a good measure have attayned it.

Arts of publique use, as Fortification, making of Engines, and other Instruments of War; because they conferre to Defence, and Victory, are Power: And though the true Mother of them, be Science, namely the Mathematiques; yet, because they are brought into the Light, by the hand of the Artificer, they be esteemed (the Midwife passing with the vulgar for the Mother,) as his issue.

The *Value,* or WORTH of a man, is as of all other things, his Price; that is to say, so much as would be given for the use of his Power: and therefore is not absolute; but a thing dependant on the need and judgement of another.[1] An able conductor of Souldiers, is of great Price in time of War present, or imminent; but in Peace not so. A learned and uncorrupt Judge, is much Worth in time of Peace; but not so much in War. And as in other things, so in men, not the seller, but the buyer determines the Price. For let a man (as most men do,) rate themselves as the highest Value they can; yet their true Value is no more than it is esteemed by others.

The manifestation of the Value we set on one another, is that which is commonly called Honouring, and Dishonouring. To Value a man at a high rate, is to *Honour* him; at a low rate, is to *Dishonour* him. But high, and low, in this case, is to be understood by comparison to the rate that each man setteth on himselfe. . . .

Chap. XI

Of the difference of Manners

By Manners, I mean not here, Decency of behaviour; as how one man should salute another, or how a man should wash his mouth, or pick his teeth before company, and such other points of the *Small Moralls;* But those qualities of man-kind, that concern their living together in Peace, and Unity. To which end we are to consider, that the Felicity of this life, consisteth not in the repose of a mind satisfied. For there is no such *Finis ultimus,* (utmost ayme,) nor *Summum Bonum,* (greatest Good,) as is spoken of in the Books of the old Morall Philosophers. Nor can a man any more live, whose Desires are at an end, than he, whose Senses and Imaginations are at a stand. Felicity is a continuall progresse of the desire, from one object to another; the attaining of the former, being still but the way to the later. The cause whereof is, That the object of mans desire, is not to enjoy once onely, and for one instant

---

[1] [From CHAP. XXIV: "For a mans Labour also, is a commodity exchangeable for benefit, as well as any other thing."]

of time; but to assure for ever, the way of his future desire. And therefore the voluntary actions, and inclinations of all men, tend, not only to the procuring, but also to the assuring of a contented life; and differ onely in the way: which ariseth partly from the diversity of passions, in divers men; and partly from the difference of the knowledge, or opinion each one has of the causes, which produce the effect desired.

So that in the first place, I put for a generall inclination of all mankind, a perpetuall and restlesse desire of Power after power, that ceaseth onely in Death. And the cause of this, is not alwayes that a man hopes for a more intensive delight, than he has already attained to; or that he cannot be content with a moderate power: but because he cannot assure the power and means to live well, which he hath present, without the acquisition of more. And from hence it is, that Kings, whose power is greatest, turn their endeavours to the assuring it at home by Lawes, or abroad by Wars: and when that is done, there succeedeth a new desire; in some, of Fame from new Conquest; in others, of ease and sensuall pleasure; in others, of admiration, or being flattered for excellence in some art, or other ability of the mind.

Competition of Riches, Honour, Command, or other power, enclineth to Contention, Enmity, and War: Because the way of one Competitor, to the attaining of his desire, is to kill, subdue, supplant, or repell the other. Particularly, competition of praise, enclineth to a reverence of Antiquity. For men contend with the living, not with the dead; to these ascribing more than due, that they may obscure the glory of the other.

Desire of Ease, and sensuall Delight, disposeth men to obey a common Power: Because by such Desires, a man doth abandon the protection might be hoped for from his own Industry, and labour. Fear of Death, and Wounds, disposeth to the same; and for the same reason. On the contrary, needy men, and hardy, not contented with their present condition; as also, all men that are ambitious of Military command, are enclined to continue the causes of warre; and to stirre up trouble and sedition: for there is no honour Military but by warre; nor any such hope to mend an ill game, as by causing a new shuffle.

Desire of Knowledge, and Arts of Peace, enclineth men to obey a common Power: For such Desire, containeth a desire of leasure; and consequently protection from some other Power than their own.

Desire of Praise, disposeth to laudable actions, such as please them whose judgement they value; for of those men whom we contemn, we contemn also the Praises. Desire of Fame after death does the same. And though after death, there be no sense of the praise given us on Earth, as being joyes, that are either swallowed up in the unspeakable joyes of Heaven, or extinguished in the extreme torments of Hell: yet is not such Fame vain; because men have a present delight therein, from the foresight of it, and of the benefit that may rebound thereby to their posterity: which though they now see not, yet they imagine; and any thing that is pleasure in the sense, the same also is pleasure in the imagination. . . .

Chap. XIII

Of the Naturall Condition *of Mankind,*
as concerning their Felicity, and Misery

Nature hath made men so equall, in the faculties of body, and mind; as that though there bee found one man sometimes manifestly stronger in body, or of quicker mind than another; yet when all is reckoned together, the difference between man, and man, is not so considerable, as that one man can thereupon claim to himselfe any benefit, to which another may not pretend, as well as he. For as to the strength of body, the weakest has strength enough to kill the strongest, either by secret machination, or by confederacy with others, that are in the same danger with himselfe.

And as to the faculties of the mind, (setting aside the arts grounded upon words, and especially that skill of proceeding upon generall, and infallible rules, called Science; which very few have, and but in few things; as being not a native faculty, born with us; nor attained, (as Prudence,) while we look after somewhat els,) I find yet a greater equality amongst men, than that of strength. For Prudence, is but Experience; which equall time, equally bestowes on all men, in those things they equally apply themselves unto. That which may perhaps make such equality incredible, is but a vain concept of ones owne wisdome, which almost all men think they have in a greater degree, than the Vulgar; that is, than all men but themselves, and a few others, whom by Fame, or for concurring with themselves, they approve. For such is the nature of men, that howsoever they may acknowledge many others to be more witty, or more eloquent, or more learned; Yet they will hardly believe there be many so wise as themselves: For they see their own wit at hand, and other mens at a distance. But this proveth rather that men are in that point equall, than unequall. For there is not ordinarily a greater signe of the equall distribution of any thing, than that every man is contented with his share.

From this equality of ability, ariseth equality of hope in the attaining of our Ends. And therefore if any two men desire the same thing, which neverthelesse they cannot both enjoy, they become enemies; and in the way to their End, (which is principally their owne conservation, and sometimes their delectation only,) endeavour to destroy, or subdue one an other. And from hence it comes to passe, that where an Invader hath no more to feare, than an other mans single power; if one plant, sow, build, or possesse a convenient Seat, others may probably be expected to come prepared with forces united, to dispossesse, and deprive him, not only of the fruit of his labour, but also of his life, or liberty. And the Invader again is in the like danger of another.

And from this diffidence of one another, there is no way for any man to secure himselfe, so reasonable, as Anticipation; that is, by force, or wiles, to master the persons of all men he can, so long, till he see no other power great enough to endanger him: And this is no more than his own conservation requireth, and is generally allowed. Also because there be some, that taking pleasure in contemplating their own power in the acts of conquest, which they pursue farther than their security requires; if others, that otherwise would be glad to be at ease within modest bounds, should not by invasion increase their power, they would not be able, long time, by standing only on their defence, to subsist. And by consequence, such augmentation of dominion over men, being necessary to a mans conservation, it ought to be allowed him.

Againe, men have no pleasure, (but on the contrary a great deale of griefe) in keeping company, where there is no power able to over-awe them all. For every man looketh that his companion should value him, at the same rate he sets upon himselfe: And upon all signes of contempt, or undervaluing, naturally endeavours, as far as he dares (which amongst them that have no common power, to keep them in quiet, is far enough to make them destroy each other,) to extort a greater value from his contemners, by dommage; and from others, by the example.

So that in the nature of man, we find three principall causes of quarrell. First, Competition; Secondly, Diffidence; Thirdly, Glory.

The first, maketh men invade for Gain; the second, for Safety; and the third, for Reputation. The first use Violence, to make themselves Masters of other mens persons, wives, children, and cattell; the second, to defend them; the third, for trifles, as a word, a smile, a different opinion, and any other signe of undervalue, either direct in their Persons, or by reflexion in their Kindred, their Friends, their Nation, their Profession, or their Name.

Hereby it is manifest, that during the time men live without a common Power to keep them all in awe, they are in that condition which is called Warre; and such a warre, as is of every man, against every man. For WARRE, consisteth not in Battell onely, or the act of fighting; but in a tract of time, wherein the Will to contend by Battell is sufficiently known: and therefore the notion of *Time,* is to be considered in the nature of Warre; as it is in the nature of Weather. For as the nature of Foule weather, lyeth not in a showre or two of rain; but in an inclination thereto of many dayes together: So the nature of War, consisteth not in actuall fighting; but in the known disposition thereto, during all the time there is no assurance to the contrary. All other time is PEACE.

Whatsoever therefore is consequent to a time of Warre, where every man is Enemy to every man; the same is consequent to the time, wherein men live without other security, than what their own strength, and their own invention shall furnish them withall. In such condition, there is no place for Industry; because the fruit thereof is uncertain: and consequently no Culture of the Earth; no Navigation, nor use of the commodities that may be imported by Sea; no commodious Building; no Instruments of moving, and removing such things as require much force; no Knowledge of the face of the Earth; no account of Time; no Arts; no Letters; no Society; and which is worst of all, continuall feare, and danger of violent death; And the life of man, solitary, poore, nasty, brutish, and short.

It may seem strange to some man, that has not well weighed these things; that Nature should thus dissociate, and render men apt to invade, and destroy one another: and he may therefore, not trusting to this Inference, made from the Passions, desire perhaps to have the same confirmed by Experience. Let him therefore consider with himselfe, when taking a journey, he armes himselfe, and seeks to go well accompanied; when going to sleep, he locks his dores; when even in his house he locks his chests; and this when he knows there bee Lawes, and publike Officers, armed, to revenge all injuries shall bee done him; what opinion he has of his fellow subjects, when he rides armed; of his fellow Citizens, when he locks his dores; and of his children, and servants, when he locks his chests. Does he not there as much accuse mankind by his actions, as I do by my words? But neither of us accuse mans nature in it. The Desires, and other Passions of man, are in themselves no Sin. No more are the Actions, that proceed from those Passions, till they know a Law that forbids them: which till Lawes be made they cannot know: nor can any Law be made, till they have agreed upon the Person that shall make it.

It may peradventure be thought, there was never such a time, nor condition of warre as this; and I believe it was never generally so, over all the world: but there are many places, where they live so now. For the savage people in many places of *America,* except the government of small Families, the concord whereof dependeth on naturall lust, have no government at all; and live at this day in that brutish manner, as I said before. Howsoever, it may be perceived what manner of life there would be, where there were no common Power to feare; by the manner of life, which men that have formerly lived under a peacefull government, use to degenerate into, in a civill Warre.

But though there had never been any time, wherein particular men were in a condition of warre one against another; yet in all times, Kings, and Persons of Soveraigne authority, because of their Independency, are in continuall jealousies, and in the state and posture of Gladiators; having their weapons pointing, and their eyes fixed on one another; that is, their Forts, Garrisons, and Guns upon the Frontiers of their Kingdomes; and continuall Spyes upon their neighbours; which is a posture of War. But because they uphold thereby, the Industry of their Subjects; there does not follow from it, that misery, which accompanies the Liberty of particular men.

To this warre of every man against every man, this also is consequent; that nothing can be Unjust. The notions of Right and Wrong, Justice and Injustice have there no place. Where there is no common Power, there is no Law: where no Law, no Injustice. Force, and Fraud, are in warre the two Cardinall vertues. Justice, and Injustice are none of the Faculties neither of the Body, nor Mind. If they were, they might be in a man that were alone in the world, as well as his Senses, and Passions. They are Qualities, that relate to men in Society, not in Solitude. It is consequent also to the same condition, that there be no Propriety, no Dominion, no *Mine* and *Thine* distinct; but onely that to be every mans that he can get; and for so long, as he can keep it. And thus much for the ill condition, which man by meer Nature is actually placed in; though with a possibility to come out of it, consisting partly in the Passions, partly in his Reason.

The Passions that encline men to Peace, are Feare of Death; Desire of such things as are necessary to commodious living; and a Hope by their Industry to obtain them. And Reason suggesteth convenient Articles of Peace, upon which men may be drawn to agreement. These Articles, are they, which otherwise are called the Lawes of Nature: whereof I shall speak more particularly, in the two following Chapters.

Chap. XIV

Of the first and second Naturall Lawes, *and of* Contracts

The Right of Nature, which Writers commonly call *Jus Naturale,* is the Liberty each man hath, to use his own power, as he will himselfe, for the preservation of his own Nature; that is to say, of his own Life; and consequently, of doing any thing, which in his own Judgement, and Reason, hee shall conceive to be the aptest means thereunto.

By LIBERTY, is understood, according to the proper signification of the word, the absence of externall Impediments: which Impediments, may oft take away part of a mans power to do what hee would; but cannot hinder him from using the power left him, according as his judgement, and reason shall dictate to him.

A LAW OF NATURE, (*Lex Naturalis,*) is a Precept, or generall Rule, found out by Reason, by which a man is forbidden to do, that, which is destructive of his life, or taketh away the means of preserving the same; and to omit, that, by which he thinketh it may be best preserved. For though they that speak of this subject, use to confound *Jus,* and *Lex, Right* and *Law;* yet they ought to be distinguished; because RIGHT, consisteth in liberty to do, or to forbeare; Whereas LAW, determineth, and bindeth to one of them: so that Law, and Right, differ as much, as Obligation, and Liberty; which in one and the same matter are inconsistent.

And because the condition of Man, (as hath been declared in the precedent Chapter) is a condition of Warre of every one against every one; in which case every one is governed by his own Reason; and there is nothing he can make use of, that may not be a help unto him, in preserving his life against his enemyes; It followeth, that in such a condition, every man has a Right to every thing; even to one anothers body. And therefore, as long as this naturall Right of every man to every thing endureth, there can be no security to any man, (how strong or wise soever he be,) of living out the time, which Nature ordinarily alloweth men to live. And consequently it is a precept, or generall rule of Reason, *That every man, ought to endeavour Peace, as farre as he has hope of obtaining it; and when he cannot obtain it, that he may seek, and use, all helps, and advantages of Warre.* The first branch of which Rule, containeth the first, and Fundamentall Law of Nature; which is, *to seek Peace, and follow it.* The Second, the summe of the Right of Nature; which is, *By all means we can, to defend our selves.*

From this Fundamentall Law of Nature, by which men are commanded to endeavour Peace, is derived this second Law; *That a man be willing, when others are so too, as farre-forth, as for Peace, and defence of himself he shall think it necessary, to lay down this right to all things; and be contented with so much liberty against other men, as he would allow other men against himselfe.* For as long as every man holdeth this Right, of doing any thing he liketh; so long are all men in the condition of Warre. But if other men will not lay down their Right, as well as he; then there is no Reason for any one, to devest himselfe of his: For that were to expose himselfe to Prey, (which no man is bound to) rather than to dispose himselfe to Peace. This is that Law of the Gospell; *Whatsoever you require that others should do to you, that do ye to them.* And that Law of all men, *Quod tibi fieri non vis, alteri ne feceris.*

To *lay downe* a mans *Right* to any thing, is to *devest* himselfe of the *Liberty,* of hindring another of the benefit of his own Right to the same. For he that renounceth, or passeth away his Right, giveth not to any other man a Right which he had not before; because there is nothing to which every man had not Right by Nature: but onely standeth out of his way, that he may enjoy his own originall Right, without hindrance from him; not without hindrance from another. So that the effect which redoundeth to one man, by another mans defect of Right, is but so much diminution of impediments to the use of his own Right originall.

Right is layd aside, either by simply Renouncing it; or by Transferring it to another. By *Simply* Renouncing; when he cares not to whom the benefit thereof redoundeth. By Transferring; when he intendeth the benefit thereof to some certain person, or persons. And when a man hath in either manner abandoned, or granted away his Right; then is he said to be Obliged, or Bound, not to hinder those, to whom such Right is granted, or abandoned, from the benefit of it: and that he *Ought,* and it is his Duty, not to make voyd that voluntary act of his own; and that such hindrance is Injustice, and Injury, as being *Sine Jure;* the Right being before renounced, or transferred. So that *Injury,* or *Injustice,* in the controversies of the world, is somewhat like to that, which in the disputations of Scholers is called *Absurdity.* For as it is there called an Absurdity, to contradict what one maintained in the Beginning: so in the world, it is called Injustice, and Injury, voluntarily to undo that, which from the beginning he had voluntarily done. The way by which a man either simply Renounceth, or Transferreth his Right, is a Declaration, or Signification, by some voluntary and sufficient signe, or signes, that he doth so Renounce, or Transferre; or hath so Renounced, or Transferred the same, to him that accepteth it. And these Signes are either Words onely, or Actions onely; or (as it happeneth most often) both Words and Actions. And the same are the Bonds, by which men are bound, and obliged: Bonds, that have their strength, not from their own Nature, (for nothing is more easily broken than a mans word,) but from Feare of some evill consequence upon the rupture.

Whensoever a man Transferreth his Right, or Renounceth it; it is either in consideration of some Right reciprocally transferred to himselfe; or for some other good he hopeth for thereby. For it is a voluntary act: and of the voluntary acts of every man, the object is some *Good to himselfe*. And therefore there be some Rights, which no man can be understood by any words, or other signes, to have abandoned, or transferred. As first a man cannot lay down the right of resisting them, that assault him by force, to take away his life; because he cannot be understood to ayme thereby, at any Good to himselfe. The same may be sayd of Wounds, and Chayns, and Imprisonment; both because there is no benefit consequent to such patience; as there is to the patience of suffering another to be wounded, or imprisoned: as also because a man cannot tell, when he seeth men proceed against him by violence, whether they intend his death or not. And lastly the motive, and end for which this renouncing, and transferring of Right is introduced, is nothing else but the security of a mans person, in his life, and in the means of so preserving life, as not to be weary of it. And therefore if a man by words, or other signes, seem to despoyle himselfe of the End, for which those signes were intended; he is not to be understood as if he meant it, or that it was his will; but that he was ignorant of how such words and actions were to be interpreted.

The mutuall transferring of Right, is that which men call Contract.

There is difference, between transferring of Right to the Thing; and transferring, or tradition, that is, delivery of the Thing it selfe. For the Thing may be delivered together with the Translation of the Right; as in buying and selling with ready mony; or exchange of goods, or lands: and it may be delivered some time after.

Again, one of the Contractors, may deliver the Thing contracted for on his part, and leave the other to perform his part at some determinate time after, and in the mean time be trusted; and then the Contract on his part, is called Pact, or Covenant: Or both parts may contract now, to performe hereafter: in which cases, he that is to performe in time to come, being trusted, his performance is called *Keeping of Promise,* or Faith; and the fayling of performance (if it be voluntary) *Violation of Faith.*

When the transferring of Right, is not mutuall; but one of the parties transferreth, in hope to gain thereby friendship, or service from another, or from his friends; or in hope to gain the reputation of Charity, or Magnanimity; or to deliver his mind from the pain of compassion; or in hope of reward in heaven; This is not Contract, but Gift, Free-gift, Grace: which words signifie one and the same thing.

Signes of Contract, are either *Expresse,* or *by Inference.* Expresse, are words spoken with understanding of what they signifie: And such words are either of the time *Present,* or *Past;* as, *I Give, I Grant, I have Given, I have Granted, I will that this be yours:* Or of the future; as, *I will Give, I will Grant:* which words of the future, are called Promise.

Signes by Inference, are sometimes the consequence of Words; sometimes the consequence of Silence; sometimes the consequence of Actions; sometimes the consequence of Forbearing an Action: and generally a signe by Inference, of any Contract, is whatsoever sufficiently argues the will of the Contractor.

Words alone, if they be of the time to come, and contain a bare promise, are an insufficient signe of a Free-gift and therefore not obligatory. For if they be of the time to Come, as, *To morrow I will Give,* they are a signe I have not given yet, and consequently that my right is not transferred, but remaineth till I transferre it by some other Act. But if the words be of the time Present, or Past, as, *I have given, or do give to be delivered to morrow,* then is my to morrows Right given away to day; and that by the vertue of the words, though there were no other argument of my will. And there is a great difference in the signification of these words, *Volo hoc tuum esse cras,* and *Cras dabo;* that is, between *I will that this be thine to morrow,* and, *I will give it thee to morrow:* For the word *I will,* in the former manner of speech, signifies an act of the will Present; but in the later, it signifies a promise of an act of the will to Come: and therefore the former words, being of the Present, transferre a future right; the later, that be of the Future, transferre nothing. But if there be other signes of the Will to transferre a Right, besides Words; then, though the gift be Free, yet may the Right be understood to passe by words of the future: as if a man propound a Prize to him that comes first to the end of a race, The gift is Free; and though the words be of the Future, yet the Right passeth: for if he would not have his words so be understood, he should not have let them runne.

In Contracts, the right passeth, not onely where the words are of the time Present, or Past; but also where they are of the Future: because all Contract is mutuall translation, or change of Right; and therefore he that promiseth onely, because he hath already received the benefit for which he promiseth, is to be understood as if he intended the Right should passe: for unlesse he had been content to have his words so understood, the other would not have performed his part first. And for that cause, in buying, and selling, and other acts of Contract, a Promise is equivalent to a Covenant; and therefore obligatory.

He that performeth first in the case of a Contract, is said to MERIT that which he is to receive by the performance of the other; and he hath it as *Due.* Also when a Prize is propounded to many, which is to be given to him onely that winneth; or mony is thrown amongst many, to be enjoyed by them that catch it; though this be a Free gift; yet so to Win, or so to Catch, is to *Merit,* and to have it as DUE. For the Right is transferred in the Propounding of the Prize, and in throwing down the mony; though it be not determined to whom, but by the Event of the contention. But there is between these two sorts of Merit, this difference, that In Contract, I Merit by vertue of my own power, and the Contractors need; but in this case of Free gift, I am enabled to Merit onely by the benignity of the Giver: In Contract, I merit at the Contractors hand that hee should depart with his right; In this case of Gift, I Merit not that the giver should part with his right; but that when he has parted with it, it should be mine, rather than anothers. And this I think to be the meaning of that distinction of the Schooles, between *Meritum congrui,* and *Meritum con-*

digni. For God Almighty, having promised Paradise to those men (hoodwinkt with carnall desires,) that can walk through this world according to the Precepts, and Limits prescribed by him; they say, he that shall so walk, shall Merit Paradise *Ex congruo.* But because no man can demand a right to it, by his own Righteousnesse, or any other power in himselfe, but by the Free Grace of God onely; they say, no man can Merit Paradise *ex condigno.* This I say, I think is the meaning of that distinction; but because Disputers do not agree upon the signification of their own termes of Art, longer than it serves their turn; I will not affirme any thing of their meaning: onely this I say; when a gift is given indefinitely, as a prize to be contended for, he that winneth Meriteth, and may claime the Prize as Due.

If a Covenant be made, wherein neither of the parties performe presently, but trust one another; in the condition of meer Nature, (which is a condition of Warre of every man against every man,) upon any reasonable suspition, it is Voyd: But if there be a common Power set over them both, with right and force sufficient to compell performance; it is not Voyd. For he that performeth first, has no assurance the other will performe after; because the bonds of words are too weak to bridle mens ambition, avarice, anger, and other Passions, without the feare of some coerceive Power; which in the condition of meer Nature, where all men are equall, and judges of the justnesse of their own fears cannot possibly be supposed. And therefore he which performeth first, does but betray himselfe to his enemy; contrary to the Right (he can never abandon) of defending his life, and means of living.

But in a civill estate, where there is a Power set up to constrain those that would otherwise violate their faith, that feare is no more reasonable; and for that cause, he which by the Covenant is to perform first, is obliged so to do.

The cause of feare, which maketh such a Covenant invalid, must be alwayes something arising after the Covenant made; as some new fact, or other signe of the Will not to performe: else it cannot make the Covenant voyd. For that which could not hinder a man from promising, ought not to be admitted as a hindrance of performing.

He that transferreth any Right, transferreth the Means of enjoying it, as farre as lyeth in his power. As he that selleth Land, is understood to transferre the Herbage, and whatsoever growes upon it; Nor can he that sells a Mill turn away the Stream that drives it. And they that give to a man the Right of government in Soveraignty, are understood to give him the right of levying mony to maintain Souldiers; and of appointing Magistrates for the administration of Justice. . . .

Covenants entred into by fear, in the condition of meer Nature, are obligatory. For example, if I Covenant to pay a ransome, or service for my life, to an enemy; I am bound by it. For it is a Contract, wherein one receiveth the benefit of life; the other is to receive mony, or service for it; and consequently, where no other Law (as in the condition, of meer Nature) forbiddeth the performance, the Covenant is valid. Therefore Prisoners of warre, if trusted with the payment of their Ransome, are obliged to pay it: And if a weaker Prince, make a disadvantageous peace with a stronger, for feare; he is bound to keep it; unlesse (as hath been sayd before) there ariseth some new, and just cause of feare, to renew the war. And even in Common-wealths, if I be forced to redeem my selfe from a Theefe by promising him mony, I am bound to pay it, till the Civill Law discharge me. For whatsoever I may lawfully do without Obligation, the same I may lawfully Covenant to do through feare: and what I lawfully Covenant, I cannot lawfully break. . . .

A Covenant not to defend my selfe from force, by force, is always voyd. For (as I have shewed before) no man can transferre, or lay down his Right to save himselfe from Death, Wounds, and Imprisonment, (the avoyding whereof is the onely End of laying down any Right, and therefore the promise of not resisting force, in no Covenant transferreth any right; nor is obliging). For though a man may Covenant thus, *Unlesse I do so, or so, kill me;* he cannot Covenant thus, *Unlesse I do so, or so, I will not resist you, when you come to kill me.* For man by nature chooseth the lesser evill, which is danger of death in resisting; rather than the greater, which is certain and present death in not resisting. And this is granted to be true by all men, in that they lead Criminals to Execution, and Prison, with armed men, notwithstanding that such Criminals have consented to the Law, by which they are condemned. . . .

Chap. XV

Of other Lawes of Nature

From that law of Nature, by which we are obliged to transferre to another, such Rights, as being retained, hinder the peace of Mankind, there followeth a Third; which is this, *That men performe their Covenants made:* without which, Covenants are in vain, and but Empty words; and the Right of all men to all things remaining, wee are still in the condition of Warre.

And in this law of Nature, consisteth the Fountain and Originall of JUS-TICE. For where no Covenant hath preceded, there hath no Right been transferred, and every man has right to every thing; and consequently, no action can be Unjust. But when a Covenant is made, then to break it is *Unjust:* And the definition of INJUSTICE, is no other than *the not Performance of Covenant.* And whatsoever is not Unjust, is *Just.*

But because Covenants of mutuall trust, where there is a feare of not performance on either part, (as hath been said in the former Chapter,) are invalid; though the Originall of Justice be the making of Covenants; yet Injustice actually there can be none, till the cause of such feare be taken away; which while men are in the naturall condition of Warre, cannot be done. Therefore before the names of Just, and Unjust can have place, there must be some coercive Power, to compell men equally to the performance of their Covenants, by the terrour of some punishment, greater than the benefit they expect by the breach of their Covenant; and to make good that Propriety, which by mutuall Contract men acquire, in recompence of the universall Right they abandon: and such power there is none before the erection of a Common-wealth. And this is also to be gathered out of the ordinary definition of Justice in the Schooles: For they say, that *Justice is the constant Will of giving to every man his own.* And therefore where there is no *Own,* that is, no Propriety, there is no Injustice; and where there is no coërceive Power erected, that is, where there is no Common-wealth, there is no Propriety; all men having Right to all things: Therefore where there is no Common-wealth, there nothing is Unjust. So that the nature of Justice, consisteth in keeping of valid Covenants: but the Validity of Covenants begins not but with the Constitution of a Civill Power, sufficient to compell men to keep them: And then it is also that Propriety begins.

The Foole hath sayd in his heart, there is no such thing as Justice; and sometimes also with his tongue; seriously alleaging, that every mans conservation, and contentment, being committed to his own care, there could be no reason, why every man might not do what he thought conduced thereunto: and therefore also to make, or not make; keep, or not keep Covenants, was not against Reason, when it conduced to ones benefit. He does not therein deny, that there be Covenants; and that they are sometimes broken, sometimes kept; and that such breach of them may be called Injustice, and the observance of them Justice: but he questioneth, whether Injustice, taking away the feare of God, (for the same Foole hath said in his heart there is no God,) may not sometimes stand with that Reason, which dictateth to every man his own good; and particularly then, when it conduceth to such a benefit, as shall put a man in a condition, to neglect not onely the dispraise, and revilings, but also the power of other men. The Kingdome of God is gotten by violence: but what if it could be gotten by unjust violence? were it against Reason so to get it, when it is impossible to receive hurt by it? and if it be not against Reason, it is not against Justice: or else Justice is not to be approved for good. From such reasoning as this, Succesfull wickednesse hath obtained the name of Vertue: and some that in all other things have disallowed the violation of Faith; yet have allowed it, when it is for the getting of a Kingdome. And the Heathen that believed, that *Saturn* was deposed by his son *Jupiter,* believed neverthelesse the same *Jupiter* to be the avenger of Injustice: Somewhat like to a piece of Law in *Cokes* Commentaries on *Litleton;* where he sayes, If the right Heire of the Crown be attainted of Treason; yet the Crown shall descend to him, and *eo instante* the Atteynder be voyd: From which instances a man will be very prone to inferre; that when the Heire apparent of a Kingdome, shall kill him that is in possession, though his father; you may call it Injustice, or by what other name you will; yet it can never be against Reason, seeing all the voluntary actions of men tend to the benefit of themselves; and those actions are most Reasonable, that conduce most to their ends. This specious reasoning is neverthelesse false.

For the question is not of promises mutuall, where there is no security of performance on either side; as when there is no Civill Power erected over the parties promising; for such promises are no Covenants: But either where one of the parties has performed already; or where there is a Power to make him performe; there is the question whether it be against reason, that is, against the benefit of the other to performe, or not. And I say it is not against reason. For the manifestation whereof, we are to consider; First, that when a man doth a thing, which notwithstanding any thing can be foreseen, and reckoned on, tendeth to his own destruction, howsoever some accident which he could not expect, arriving may turne it to his benefit; yet such events do not make it reasonably or wisely done. Secondly, that in a condition of Warre, wherein every man to every man, for want of a common Power to keep them all in awe, is an Enemy, there is no man can hope by his own strength, or wit, to defend himselfe from destruction, without the help of Confederates; where every one expects the same defence by the Confederation, that any one else does: and therefore he which declares he thinks it reason to deceive those that help him, can in reason expect no other means of safety, than what can be had from his own single Power. He therefore that breaketh his Covenant, and consequently declareth that he thinks he may with reason do so, cannot be received into any Society, that unite themselves for Peace and Defence, but by the errour of them that receive him; nor when he is received, be re-tayned in it, without seeing the danger of their errour; which errours a man cannot reasonably reckon upon as the means of his security: and therefore if he be left, or cast out of Society, he perisheth; and if he live in Society, it is by the errours of other men, which he could not foresee, nor reckon upon; and consequently against the reason of his preservation; and so, as all men that contribute not to his destruction, forbear him only out of ignorance of what is good for themselves.

As for the Instance of gaining the secure and perpetuall felicity of Heaven, by any way; it is frivolous: there being but one way imaginable; and that is not breaking, but keeping of Covenant.

And for the other Instance of attaining Soveraignty by Rebellion; it is manifest, that though the event follow, yet because it cannot reasonably be expected, but rather the contrary; and because by gaining it so, others are taught to gain the same in like manner, the attempt thereof is against reason. Justice therefore, that is to say, Keeping of Covenant, is a Rule of Reason, by which we are forbidden to do any thing destructive to our life; and conse-quently a Law of Nature.

There be some that proceed further; and will not have the Law of Nature, to be those Rules which conduce to the preservation of mans life on earth; but to the attaining of an eternall felicity after death; to which they think the breach of Covenant may conduce; and consequently be just and reasonable; (such are they that think it a work of merit to kill, or depose, or rebell against, the Soveraigne Power constituted over them by their own consent). But be-cause there is no naturall knowledge of mans estate after death; much lesse of the reward that is then to be given to breach of Faith; but onely a beliefe grounded upon other mens saying, that they know it supernaturally, or that they know those, that knew them, that knew others, that knew it supernaturally; Breach of Faith cannot be called a Precept of Reason, or Nature.

Others, that allow for a Law of Nature, the keeping of Faith, do neverthelesse make exception of certain persons; as Heretiques, and such as use not to performe their Covenant to others: And this also is against reason. For if any fault of a man, be sufficient to discharge our Covenant made; the same ought in reason to have been sufficient to have hindred the making of it.

The names of Just, and Injust, when they are attributed to Men, signifie one thing; and when they are attributed to Actions, another. When they are attributed to Men, they signifie Conformity, or Inconformity of Manners, to Reason. But when they are attributed to Actions, they signifie the Conformity, or Inconformity to Reason, not of Manners, or manner of life, but of particular Actions. A Just man therefore, is he that taketh all the care he can, that his Actions may be all Just: and an Unjust man, is he that neglecteth it. And such men are more often in our Language stiled by the names of Righteous, and Unrighteous; then Just, and Unjust; though the meaning be the same. Therefore a Righteous man, does not lose that Title, by one, or a few unjust Actions, that proceed from sudden Passion, or mistake of Things, or Persons: nor does an Unrighteous man, lose his character, for such Actions, as he does, or forbeares to do, for feare: because his Will is not framed by the Justice, but by the apparent benefit of what he is to do. That which gives to humane Actions the relish of Justice, is a certain Noblenesse or Gallantnesse of courage, (rarely found,) by which a man scorns to be beholding for the contentment of his life, to fraud, or breach of promise. This Justice of the Manners, is that which is meant, where Justice is called a Vertue; and Injustice a Vice.

But the Justice of Actions denominates men, not Just, but *Guiltlesse:* and the Injustice of the same, (which is also called Injury,) gives them but the name of *Guilty.*

Again, the Injustice of Manners, is the disposition, or aptitude to do Injurie; and is Injustice before it proceed to Act; and without supposing any individuall person injured. But the Injustice of an Action, (that is to say Injury,) supposeth an individuall person Injured; namely him, to whom the Covenant was made: And therefore many times the injury is received by one man, when the dammage redoundeth to another. As when the Master commandeth his servant to give mony to a stranger; if it be not done, the Injury is done to the Master, whom he had before Covenanted to obey; but the dammage redoundeth to the stranger, to whom he had no Obligation; and therefore could not Injure him. And so also in Common-wealths, private men may remit to one another their debts; but not robberies or other violences, whereby they are endammaged; because the detaining of Debt, is an Injury to themselves; but Robbery and Violence, are Injuries to the Person of the Commonwealth.

Whatsoever is done to a man, conformable to his own Will signified to the doer, is no Injury to him. For if he that doeth it, hath not passed away his originall right to do what he please, by some Antecedent Covenant, there is no breach of Covenant; and therefore no Injury done him. And if he have; then his Will to have it done being signified, is a release of that Covenant: and so again there is no Injury done him.

Justice of Actions, is by Writers divided into *Commutative,* and *Distributive:* and the former they say consisteth in proportion Arithmeticall; the later in proportion Geometricall. Commutative therefore, they place in the equality of value of the things contracted for; And Distributive, in the distribution of equall benefit, to men of equall merit. As if it were Injustice to sell dearer than we buy; or to give more to a man than he merits. The value of all things contracted for, is measured by the Appetite of the Contractors: and therefore the just value, is that which they be contented to give. And Merit (besides that which is by Covenant, where the performance on one part, meriteth the performance of the other part, and falls under Justice Commutative, not Distributive,) is not due by Justice; but is rewarded of Grace onely. And therefore this distinction, in the sense wherein it useth to be expounded, is not right. To speak properly, Commutative Justice, is the Justice of a Contractor; that is, a Performance of Covenant, in Buying, and Selling; Hiring, and Letting to Hire; Lending, and Borrowing; Exchanging, Bartering, and other acts of Contract.

And Distributive Justice, the Justice of an Arbitrator; that is to say, the act of defining what is Just. Wherein, (being trusted by them that make him Arbitrator,) if he performe his Trust, he is said to distribute to every man his own: and this is indeed Just Distribution, and may be called (though improperly) Distributive Justice; but more properly Equity; which also is a Law of Nature, as shall be shewn in due place. . . .

[At this point, Hobbes sketches sixteen additional laws of nature which are, in comparison with the first three, trivial and uninteresting with the exception of number 17—that no man should act as judge in any controversy to which he is a party.]

These are the Lawes of Nature, dictating Peace, for a means of the conservation of men in multitudes; and which onely concern the doctrine of Civill Society. There be other things tending to the destruction of particular men; as Drunkenness, and all other parts of Intemperance; which may therefore also be reckoned amongst those things which the Law of Nature hath forbidden; but are not necessary to be mentioned, nor are pertinent enough to this place.

And though this may seem too subtile a deduction of the Lawes of Nature, to be taken notice of by all men; whereof the most part are too busie in getting food, and the rest too negligent to understand; yet to leave all men unexcusable, they have been contracted into one easie sum, intelligible, even to the meanest capacity; and that is, *Do not that to another, which thou wouldest not have done to thy selfe;* which sheweth him, that he has no more to do in learning the Lawes of Nature, but, when weighing the actions of other men with his own, they seem too heavy, to put them into the other part of the ballance, and his own into their place, that his own passions, and selfe-love, may adde nothing to the weight; and then there is none of these Lawes of Nature that will not appear unto him very reasonable.

The Lawes of Nature oblige *in foro interno;* that is to say, they bind to a desire they should take place: but *in foro externo;* that is, to the putting them in act, not alwayes. For he that should be modest, and tractable, and performe all he promises, in such time, and place, where no man els should do so, should but make himselfe a prey to others, and procure his own certain ruine, contrary to the ground of all Lawes of Nature, which tend to Natures preservation. And again, he that having sufficient Security, that others shall observe the same Lawes towards him, observes them not himselfe, seeketh not Peace, but War; & consequently the destruction of his Nature by Violence.

And whatsoever Lawes bind *in foro interno,* may be broken, not onely by a fact contrary to the Law but also by a fact according to it, in case a man think it contrary. For though his Action in this case, be according to the Law; yet his Purpose was against the Law; which where the Obligation is *in foro interno,* is a breach.

The Lawes of Nature are Immutable and Eternall; For Injustice, Ingratitude, Arrogance, Pride, Iniquity, Acception of persons, and the rest, can never be made lawfull. For it can never be that Warre shall preserve life, and Peace destroy it.

The same Lawes, because they oblige onely to a desire, and endeavour, I mean an unfeigned and constant endeavour, are easie to be observed. For in that they require nothing but endeavour; he that endeavoureth their performance, fulfilleth them; and he that fulfilleth the Law, is Just.

And the Science of them, is the true and onely Morall Philosophy. For Morall Philosophy is nothing else but the Science of what is *Good,* and *Evill,* in the conversation, and Society of mankind. *Good,* and *Evill,* are names that signifie our Appetites, and Aversions; which in different tempers, customes, and doctrines of men, are different: And divers men, differ not onely in their Judgement, on the senses of what is pleasant, and unpleasant to the tast, smell, hearing, touch, and sight; but also of what is conformable, or disagreeable to Reason, in the actions of common life. Nay, the same man, in divers times, differs from himselfe; and one time praiseth, that is, calleth Good, what another time he dispraiseth, and calleth Evil: From whence arise Disputes, Controversies, and at last War. And therefore so long a man is in the condition of meer Nature, (which is a condition of War,) as private Appetite is the measure of Good, and Evill: and consequently all men agree on this, that Peace is Good, and therefore also the way, or means of Peace, which (as I have shewed before) are *Justice, Gratitude, Modesty, Equity, Mercy,* & the rest of the Laws of Nature, are good; that is to say, *Morall Vertues;* and their contrarie *Vices,* Evill. Now the science of Vertue and Vice, is Morall Philosophie; and therfore the true Doctrine of the Lawes of Nature, is the true Morall Philosophie. But the Writers of Morall Philosophie, though they acknowledge the same Vertues and Vices; Yet not seeing wherein consisted their Goodnesse; nor that they come to be praised, as the meanes of peaceable, sociable, and comfortable living; place them in a mediocrity of passions: as if not the Cause, but the Degree of daring, made Fortitude; or not the Cause, but the Quantity of a gift, made Liberality.

These dictates of Reason, men use to call by the name of Lawes; but improperly: for they are but Conclusions, or Theoremes concerning what conduceth to the conservation and defence of themselves; wheras Law, properly is the word of him, that by right hath command over others. But yet if we consider the same Theoremes, as delivered in the word of God, that by right commandeth all things; then are they properly called Lawes.

Chap. XVI

Of Persons, Authors, *and things Personated*

. . . A Multitude of men, are made *One* Person, when they are by one man, or one Person, Represented; so that it be done with the consent of every one of that Multitude in particular. For it is the *Unity* of the Representer, not the *Unity* of the Represented, that maketh the Person *One*. And it is the Representer that beareth the Person, and but one Person: And *Unity,* cannot otherwise be understood in Multitude.

And because the Multitude naturally is not *One,* but *Many;* they cannot be understood for one; but many Authors, of every thing their Representative faith, or doth in their name; Every man giving their common Representer, Authority from himselfe in particular; and owning all the actions the Representer doth, in case they give him Authority without stint: Otherwise, when they limit him in what, and how farre he shall represent them, none of them owneth more, than they gave him commission to Act. . . .

Part II

Of Common-wealth

Chap. XVII

Of the Causes, Generation, and Definition of a Common-Wealth

The finall Cause, End, or Designe of men, (who naturally love Liberty, and Dominion over others,) in the introduction of that restraint upon themselves, (in which wee see them live in Common-wealths,) is the foresight of their own preservation, and of a more contented life thereby; that is to say, of getting themselves out from that miserable condition of Warre, which is necessarily consequent (as hath been shewn) to the naturall Passions of men, when there is no visible Power to keep them in awe, and tye them by feare of punishment to the performance of their Covenants, and observation of those Lawes of Nature set down in the fourteenth and fifteenth Chapters.

For the Lawes of Nature (as *Justice, Equity, Modesty, Mercy,* and (in summe) *doing to others, as wee would be done to,*) of themselves, without the terrour of some Power, to cause them to be observed, are contrary to our naturall Passions, that carry us to Partiality, Pride, Revenge, and the like. And Covenants, without the Sword, are but Words, and of no strength to secure a man at all. Therefore notwithstanding the Lawes of Nature, (which every one hath then kept, when he has the will to keep them, when he can do it safely,) if there be no Power erected, or not great enough for our security; every man will and may lawfully rely on his own strength and art, for caution against all other men. And in all places, where men have lived by small Families, to robbe and spoyle one another, has been a Trade, and so farre from being reputed against the Law of Nature, that the greater spoyles they gained, the greater was their honour; and men observed no other Lawes therein, but the Lawes of Honour; that is, to abstain from cruelty, leaving to men their lives, and instruments of husbandry. And as small Familyes did then; so now do Cities and Kingdomes which are but greater Families (for their own security) enlarge their Dominions, upon all pretences of danger, and fear of Invasion, or assistance that may be given to Invaders, endeavour as much as they can, to subdue, or weaken their neighbours, by open force, and secret arts, for want of other Caution, justly; and are remembred for it in after ages with honour.

Nor is it the joyning together of a small number of men, that gives them this security; because in small numbers, small additions on the one side or the other, make the advantage of strength so great, as is sufficient to carry the Victory; and therefore gives encouragement to an Invasion. The Multitude sufficient to confide in for our Security, is not determined by any certain number, but by comparison with the Enemy we feare; and is then sufficient, when the odds of the Enemy is not of so visible and conspicuous moment, to determine the event of warre, as to move him to attempt.

And be there never so great a Multitude; yet if their actions be directed according to their particular judgements, and particular appetites, they can expect thereby no defence, nor protection, neither against a Common enemy, nor against the injuries of one another. For being distracted in opinions concerning the best use and application of their strength, they do not help, but hinder one another; and reduce their strength by mutuall opposition to nothing: whereby they are easily, not onely subdued by a very few that agree together; but also when there is no common enemy, they make warre upon each other, for their particular interests. For if we could suppose a great Multitude of men to consent in the observation of Justice, and other Lawes of Nature, without a common Power to keep them all in awe; we might as well suppose all Man-kind to do the same; and then there neither would be, nor need to be any Civill Government, or Common-wealth at all; because there would be Peace without subjection.

Nor is it enough for the security, which men desire should last all the time of their life, that they be governed, and directed by one judgement, for a limited time; as in one Battell, or one Warre. For though they obtain a Victory by their unanimous endeavour against a forraign enemy; yet afterwards, when either they have no common enemy, or he that by one part is held for an enemy, is by another part held for a friend, they must needs by the difference of their interests dissolve, and fall again into a Warre amongst themselves.

It is true, that certain living creatures, as Bees, and Ants, live sociably one with another, (which are therefore by *Aristotle* numbred amongst Politicall creatures;) and yet have no other direction, than their particular judgements and appetites; nor speech, whereby one of them can signifie to another, what he thinks expedient for the common benefit: and therefore some man may perhaps desire to know, why Man-kind cannot do the same. To which I answer,

First, that men are continually in competition for Honour and Dignity, which these creatures are not; and consequently amongst men there ariseth on that ground, Envy and Hatred, and finally Warre; but amongst these not so.

Secondly, that amongst these creatures, the Common good differeth not from the Private; and being by nature enclined to their private, they procure thereby the common benefit. But man, whose Joy consisteth in comparing himselfe with other men, can relish nothing but what is eminent.

Thirdly, that these creatures, having not (as man) the use of reason, do not see, nor think they see any fault, in the administration of their common businesse: whereas amongst men, there are very many, that thinke themselves wiser, and abler to govern the Publique, better than the rest; and these strive to reforme and innovate, one this way, another that way; and thereby bring it into Distraction and Civill warre.

Fourthly, that these creatures, though they have some use of voice, in making knowne to one another their desires, and other affections; yet they want that art of words, by which some men can represent to others, that which is Good, in the likenesse of Evill; and Evill, in the likeness of Good; and augment, or diminish the apparent greatnesse of Good and Evill; discontenting men, and troubling their Peace at their pleasure.

Fifthly, irrationall creatures cannot distinguish betweene *Injury,* and *Dammage;* and therefore as long as they be at ease, they are not offended with their fellowes: whereas Man is then most troublesome, when he is most at ease: for then it is that he loves to shew his Wisdome, and controule the Actions of them that governe the Common-wealth.

Lastly, the agreement of these creatures is Naturall; that of men, is by Covenant only, which is Artificiall: and therefore it is no wonder if there be somewhat else required (besides Covenant) to make their Agreement constant and lasting; which is a Common Power, to keep them in awe, and to direct their actions to the Common Benefit.

The only way to erect such a Common Power, as may be able to defend them from the invasion of Forraigners, and the injuries of one another, and thereby to secure them in such sort, as that by their owne industrie, and by the fruites of the Earth, they may nourish themselves and live contentedly; is, to conferre all their power and strength upon one Man, or upon one Assembly of men, that may reduce all their Wills, by plurality of voices, unto one Will: which is as much as to say, to appoint one man, or Assembly of men, to beare their Person; and every one to owne, and acknowledge himselfe to be Author of whatsoever he that so beareth their Person, shall Act, or cause to be Acted, in those things which concerne the Common Peace and Safetie; and therein to submit their Wills, every one to his Will, and their Judgements, to his Judgment. This is more than Consent, or Concord; it is a reall Unitie of them all, in one and the same Person, made by Covenant of every man with every man, in such manner, as if every man should say to every man, *I Authorise and give up my Right of Governing my selfe, to this Man, or to this Assembly of men, on this condition, that thou give up thy Right to him, and Authorise all his Actions in like manner.* This done, the Multitude so united in one Person, is called a COMMON-WEALTH, in latine CIVITAS. This is the Generation of that great LEVIATHAN, or rather (to speake more reverently) of that *Mortall God,* to which wee owe under the *Immortall God,* our peace and defence. For by this Authoritie, given him by every particular man in the Common-Wealth, he hath the use of so much Power and Strength conferred on him, that by terror thereof, he is inabled to forme the wills of them all, to Peace at home, and mutuall ayd against their enemies abroad. And in him consisteth the Essence of the Common-wealth; which (to define it,) is *One Person, of whose Acts a great Multitude, by mutuall Covenants one with another, have made themselves every one the Author, to the end he may use the strength and means of them all, as he shall think expedient, for their Peace and Common Defence.*

And he that carryeth this Person, is called SOVERAIGNE, and said to have *Soveraigne Power;* and every one besides, his SUBJECT.

The attaining to this Soveraigne Power, is by two wayes. One, by Naturall force; as when a man maketh his children, to submit themselves, and their children to his government, as being able to destroy them if they refuse; or by Warre subdueth his enemies to his will, giving them their lives on that condition. The other, is when men agree amongst themselves, to submit to some Man, or Assembly of men, voluntarily, on confidence to be protected by him against all others. This later, may be called a Politicall Common-wealth or Common-wealth by *Institution;* and the former, a Common-wealth by *Acquisition.* And first, I shall speak of a Common-wealth by Institution.

Chap. XVIII

Of the Rights *of Soveraignes by Institution*

A *Common-wealth* is said to be *Instituted,* when a *Multitude* of men do Agree, and *Covenant, every one, with every one,* that to whatsoever *Man,* or *Assembly of Men,* shall be given by the major part, the *Right* to *Present* the

Person of them all, (that is to say, to be their *Representative;*) every one, as well he that *Voted for it,* as he that *Voted against it,* shall *Authorise* all the Actions and Judgements, of that Man, or Assembly of men, in the same manner, as if they were his own, to the end, to live peaceably amongst themselves, and be protected against other men.

From this Institution of a Common-wealth are derived all the *Rights,* and *Facultyes* of him, or them, on whom the Soveraigne Power is conferred by the consent of the People assembled.

First, because they Covenant, it is to be understood, they are not obliged by former Covenant to any thing repugnant hereunto. And Consequently they that have already Instituted a Common-wealth, being thereby bound by Covenant, to own the Actions, and Judgements of one, cannot lawfully make a new Covenant, amongst themselves, to be obedient to any other, in any thing whatsoever, without his permission. And therefore, they that are subjects to a Monarch, cannot without his leave cast off Monarchy, and return to the confusion of a disunited Multitude; nor transferre their Person from him that beareth it, to another Man, or other Assembly of men: for they are bound, every man to every man, to Own, and be reputed Author of all, that he that already is their Soveraigne, shall do, and judge fit to be done: so that any one man dissenting, all the rest should break their Covenant made to that man, which is injustice: and they have also every man given the Soveraignty to him that beareth their Person; and therefore if they depose him, they take from him that which is his own, and so again it is injustice. Besides, if he that attempteth to depose his Soveraign, be killed, or punished by him for such attempt, he is author of his own punishment, as being by the Institution, Author of all his Soveraign shall do: And because it is injustice for a man to do any thing, for which he may be punished by his own authority, he is also upon that title, unjust. And whereas some men have pretended for their disobedience to their Soveraign, a new Covenant, made, not with men, but with God; this also is unjust: for there is no Covenant with God, but by mediation of some body that representeth Gods Person; which none doth but Gods Lieutenant, who hath the Soveraignty under God. But this pretence of Covenant with God, is so evident a lye, even in the pretenders own consciences, that it is not onely an act of an unjust, but also of a vile, and unmanly disposition.

Secondly, Because the Right of bearing the Person of them all, is given to him they make Soveraigne, by Covenant onely of one to another, and not of him to any of them; there can happen no breach of Covenant on the part of the Soveraigne; and consequently none of his Subjects, by any pretence of forfeiture, can be freed from his Subjection. That he which is made Soveraigne maketh no Covenant with his Subjects beforehand, is manifest; because either he must make it with the whole multitude, as one party to the Covenant; or he must make a severall Covenant with every man. With the whole, as one party, it is impossible; because as yet they are not one Person: and if he make so many severall Covenants as there be men, those Covenants after he hath the

Soveraignty are voyd, because what act soever can be pretended by any one of them for breach thereof, is the act both of himselfe, and of all the rest, because done in the Person, and by the Right of every one of them in particular. Besides, if any one, or more of them, pretend a breach of the Covenant made by the Soveraigne at his Institution; and others, or one other of his Subjects, or himselfe alone, pretend there was no such breach, there is in this case, no Judge to decide the controversie: it returns therefore to the Sword again; and every man recovereth the right of Protecting himselfe by his own strength, contrary to the designe they had in the Institution. It is therefore in vain to grant Soveraignty by way of precedent Covenant. The opinion that any Monarch receiveth his Power by Covenant, that is to say on Condition, proceedeth from want of understanding this easie truth, that Covenants being but words, and breath, have no force to oblige, contain, constrain, or protect any man, but what it has from the publique Sword; that is, from the untyed hands of that Man, or Assembly of men that hath the Soveraignty, and whose actions are avouched by them all, and performed by the strength of them all, in him united. But when an Assembly of men is made Soveraigne; then no man imagineth any such Covenant to have past in the Institution; for no man is so dull as to say, for example, the People of *Rome,* made a Covenant with the Romans, to hold the Soveraignty on such or such conditions; which not performed, the Romans might lawfully depose the Roman People. That men see not the reason to be alike in a Monarchy, and in a Popular Government, proceedeth from the ambition of some, that are kinder to the government of an Assembly, whereof they may hope to participate, than of Monarchy, which they despair to enjoy.

Thirdly, because the major part hath by consenting voices declared a Soveraigne; he that dissented must now consent with the rest; that is, be contented to avow all the actions he shall do, or else justly be destroyed by the rest. For if he voluntarily entered into the Congregation of them that were assembled, he sufficiently declared thereby his will (and therefore tacitely covenanted) to stand to what the major part should ordayne: and therefore if he refuse to stand thereto, or make Protestation against any of their Decrees, he does contrary to his Covenant, and therefore unjustly. And whether he be of the Congregation, or not; and whether his consent be asked, or not, he must either submit to their decrees, or be left in the condition of warre he was in before; wherein he might without injustice be destroyed by any man whatsoever.

Fourthly, because every Subject is by this Institution Author of all the Actions, and Judgments of the Soveraigne Instituted; it followes, that whatsoever he doth, it can be no injury to any of his Subjects; nor ought he to be by any of them accused of Injustice. For he that doth any thing by authority from another, doth therein no injury to him by whose authority he acteth: But by this Institution of a Common-wealth, every particular man is Author of all the Soveraigne doth; and consequently he that complaineth of injury from his Soveraigne, complaineth of that whereof he himselfe is Author; and therefore ought not to accuse any man but himselfe; no nor himselfe of injury; because to do injury to ones selfe, is impossible. It is true that they that have Soveraigne power, may commit Iniquity; but not Injustice, or Injury in the proper signification.

Fifthly, and consequently to that which was sayd last, no man that hath Soveraigne power can justly be put to death, or otherwise in any manner by his Subjects punished. For seeing every Subject is Author of the actions of his Soveraigne; he punisheth another, for the actions committed by himselfe.

And because the End of this Institution, is the Peace and Defence of them all; and whosoever has right to the End, has right to the Means; it belongeth of Right, to whatsoever Man, or Assembly that hath the Soveraignty, to be Judge both of the meanes of Peace and Defence; and also of the hindrances, and disturbances of the same; and to do whatsoever he shall think necessary to be done, both before hand, for the preserving of Peace and Security, by prevention of Discord at home and Hostility from abroad; and, when Peace and Security are lost, for the recovery of the same. And therefore,

Sixthly, it is annexed to the Soveraignty, to be Judge of what Opinions and Doctrines are averse, and what conducing to Peace; and consequently, on what occasions, how farre, and what, men are to be trusted withall, in speaking to Multitudes of people; and who shall examine the Doctrines of all bookes before they be published. For the Actions of men proceed from their Opinions; and in the well governing of Opinions, consisteth the well governing of mens Actions, in order to their Peace, and Concord. And though in matter of Doctrine, nothing ought to be regarded but the Truth; yet this is not repugnant to regulating of the same by Peace. For Doctrine repugnant to Peace, can no more be True, than Peace and Concord can be against the Law of Nature. It is true, that in a Common-wealth, where by the negligence, or unskilfullnesse of Governours, and Teachers, false Doctrines are by time generally received; the contrary Truths may be generally offensive: Yet the most sudden, and rough busling in of a new Truth, that can be, does never breake the Peace, but only somtimes awake the Warre. For those men that are so remissely governed, that they dare take up Armes, to defend, or introduce an Opinion, are still in Warre; and their condition not Peace, but only a Cessation of Armes for feare of one another; and they live as it were, in the precincts of battaile continually. It belongeth therefore to him that hath the Soveraign Power, to be Judge, or constitute all Judges of Opinions and Doctrines, as a thing necessary to Peace, thereby to prevent Discord and Civill Warre.

Seventhly, is annexed to the Soveraigntie, the whole power of prescribing the Rules, whereby every man may know, what Goods he may enjoy and what Actions he may doe, without being molested by any of his fellow Subjects: And this is it men call *Propriety*. For before constitution of Soveraign Power (as hath already been shewn) all men had right to all things; which necessarily causeth Warre: and therefore this Proprietie, being necessary to Peace, and depending on Soveraign Power, is the Act of that Power, in order to the publique peace. These Rules of Propriety (or *Meum* and *Tuum*) and of *Good, Evill, Lawfull,* and *Unlawfull* in the actions of Subjects, are the Civill Lawes, that is to say, the Lawes of each Common-wealth in particular; though the name of Civill Law be now restrained to the antient Civill Lawes of the City of *Rome;* which being the head of a great part of the World, her Lawes at that time were in these parts the Civill Law.

Eighthly, is annexed to the Soveraigntie, the Right of Judicature; that is to say, of hearing and deciding all Controversies, which may arise concerning Law, either Civill, or Naturall, or concerning Fact. For without the decision of Controversies, there is no protection of one Subject, against the injuries of another; the Lawes concerning *Meum* and *Tuum* are in vaine; and to every man remaineth, from the naturall and necessary appetite of his own conservation, the right of protecting himselfe by his private strength, which is the condition of Warre; and contrary to the end for which every Common-wealth is instituted.

Ninthly, is annexed to the Soveraignty, the Right of making Warre, and Peace with other Nations, and Common-wealths; that is to say, of Judging when it is for the publique good, and how great forces are to be assembled, armed, and payd for that end; and to levy mony upon the Subjects, to defray the expenses thereof. For the Power by which the people are to be defended, consisteth in their Armies; and the strength of an Army, in the union of their strength under one Command; which Command the Soveraign Instituted, therefore hath; because the command of the *Militia,* without other Institution, maketh him that hath it Soveraign. And therefore whosoever is made Generall of an Army, he that hath the Soveraign Power is alwayes Generallissimo.

Tenthly, is annexed to the Soveraignty, the choosing of all Councellours, Ministers, Magistrates, and Officers, both in Peace, and War. For seeing the Soveraign is charged with the End, which is the common Peace and Defence; he is understood to have Power to use such Means, as he shall think most fit for his discharge.

Eleventhly, to the Soveraign is committed the Power of Rewarding with riches, or honour; and of Punishing with corporall, or pecuniary punishment, or with ignominy every Subject according to the Law he hath formerly made; or if there be no Law made, according as he shall judge most to conduce to the encouraging of men to serve the Common-wealth, or deterring of them from doing dis-service to the same.

Lastly, considering what values men are naturally apt to set upon themselves; what respect they look for from others; and how little they value other men; from whence continually arise amongst them, Emulation, Quarrells, Factions, and at last Warre, to the destroying of one another, and diminution of their strength against a Common Enemy; It is necessary that there be Lawes of Honour, and a publique rate of the worth of such men as have deserved, or are able to deserve well of the Common-wealth; and that there be force in the hands of some or other, to put those Lawes in execution. But it hath already been shewn, that not onely the whole *Militia,* or forces of the Common-wealth; but also the Judicature of all Controversies, is annexed to the Soveraignty. To the Soveraign therefore it belongeth also to give titles of Honour; and to appoint what Order of place, and dignity, each man shall hold; and what signes of respect, in publique or private meetings, they shall give to one another.

These are the Rights, which make the Essence of Soveraignty; and which are the markes, whereby a man may discern in what Man, or Assembly of men, the Soveraign Power is placed, and resideth. For these are incommunicable, and inseparable. The Power to coyn Mony; to dispose of the estate and persons of Infant heires; to have præemption in Markets; and all other Statute Prærogatives, may be transferred by the Soveraign; and yet the Power to protect his Subjects be retained. But if he transferre the *Militia,* he retains the Judicature in vain, for want of execution of the Lawes: Or if he grant away the Power of raising Mony; the *Militia* is in vain: or if he give away the government of Doctrines, men will be frighted into rebellion with the feare of Spirits. And so if we consider any one of the said Rights, we shall presently see, that the holding of all the rest, will produce no effect, in the conservation of Peace and Justice, the end for which all Common-wealths are Instituted. And this division is it, whereof it is said, *a Kingdome divided in it selfe cannot stand*: For unless this division precede, division into opposite Armies can never happen. If there had not first been an opinion received of the greatest part of *England,* that these Powers were divided between the King, and the Lords, and the House of Commons, the people had never been divided, and fallen into this Civill Warre; first between those that disagreed in Politiques; and after between the Dissenters about the liberty of Religion; which have so instructed men in this point of Soveraign Right, that there be few now (in *England,*) that do not see, that these Rights are inseparable, and will be so generally acknowledged, at the next return of Peace; and so continue, till their miseries are forgotten; and no longer, except the vulgar be better taught than they have hitherto been.

And because they are essentiall and inseparable Rights, it follows necessarily, that in whatsoever, words any of them seem to be granted away, yet if the Soveraign Power it selfe be not in direct termes renounced, and the name of Soveraign no more given by the Grantees to him that Grants them, the Grant is voyd: for when he has granted all he can, if we grant back the Soveraignty, all is restored, as inseparably annexed thereunto.

This great Authority being Indivisible, and inseparably annexed to the Soveraignty, there is little ground for the opinion of them, that say of Soveraign Kings, though they be *singulis majores,* of greater Power than every one of their Subjects, yet they be *Universis minores,* of lesse power than them all together. For if by *all together,* they mean not the collective body as one person, then *all together,* and *every one,* signifie the same; and the speech is absurd. But if by *all together,* they understand them as one Person (which person the Soveraign bears,) then the power of all together, is the same with the Soveraigns power; and so again the speech is absurd: which absurdity they see well enough, when the Soveraignty is in an Assembly of the people; but in a Monarch they see it not; and yet the power of Soveraignty is the same in whomsoever it be placed.

And as the Power, so also the Honour of the Soveraign, ought to be greater, than that of any, or all the Subjects. For in the Soveraignty is the fountain of Honour. The dignities of Lord, Earle, Duke, and Prince are his Creatures. As in the presence of the Master, the Servants are equall, and without any honour at all; So are the Subjects, in the presence of the Soveraign. And though they shine some more, some lesse, when they are out of his sight; yet in his presence, they shine no more than the Starres in presence of the Sun.

But a man may here object, that the Condition of Subjects is very miserable; as being obnoxious to the lusts, and other irregular passions of him, or them that have so unlimited a Power in their hands. And commonly they that live under a Monarch, think it the fault of Monarchy; and they that live under the government of Democracy, or other Soveraign Assembly, attribute all the inconvenience to that forme of Common-wealth; whereas the Power in all formes, if they be perfect enough to protect them, is the same; not considering that the estate of Man can never be without some incommodity or other; and that the greatest, that in any forme of Government can possibly happen to the people in generall, is scarce sensible, in respect of the miseries, and horrible calamities, that accompany a Civill Warre; or that dissolute condition of masterlesse men, without subjection to Lawes, and a coërcive Power to tye their hands from rapine, and revenge: nor considering that the greatest pressure of Soveraign Governours, proceedeth not from any delight, or profit they can expect in the dammage, or weakening of their Subjects, in whose vigor, consisteth their own strength and glory; but in the restiveness of themselves, that unwillingly contributing to their own defence, make it necessary for their Governours to draw from them what they can in time of Peace, that they may have means on any emergent occasion, or sudden need, to resist, or take advantage on their Enemies. For all men are by nature provided of notable multiplying glasses, (that is their Passions and Self-love,) through which, every little payment appeareth a great grievance; but are destitute of those prospective glasses, (namely Morall and Civill Science,) to see a farre off the miseries that hang over them, and cannot without such payments be avoyded.

Chap. XIX

Of the severall Kinds of Common-wealth *by Institution, and of Succession to the Soveraigne Power*

The difference of Common-wealths, consisteth in the difference of the Soveraign, or the Person representative of all and every one of the Multitude. And because the Soveraignty is either in one Man, or in an Assembly of more than one; and into that Assembly either Every man hath right to enter, or not every one, but Certain men distinguished from the rest; it is manifest, there can be but Three kinds of Common-wealth. For the Representative must needs be One man, or More: and if more, then it is the Assembly of All, or but of a Part. When the Representative is One man, then is the Common-wealth a MONARCHY: when an Assembly of All that will come together, then it is a DEMOCRACY, or Popular Common-wealth: when an Assembly of a Part onely, then it is called an ARISTOCRACY. Other kind of Common-wealth there can be none: for either One, or More, or All must have the Soveraign Power (which I have shewn to be indivisible) entire.

There be other names of Government, in the Histories, and books of Policy; as *Tyranny,* and *Oligarchy:* But they are not the names of other Formes of Government, but of the same Formes misliked. For they that are discontented under *Monarchy,* call it *Tyranny;* and they that are displeased with *Aristocracy,* called it *Oligarchy:* So also, they which find themselves grieved under a *Democracy,* call it *Anarchy,* (which signifies want of Govern-ment;) and yet I think no man believes, that want of Government, is any new kind of Government: nor by the same reason ought they to believe, that the Government is of one kind, when they like it, and another, when they mislike it, or are oppressed by the Governours.

It is manifest, that men who are in absolute liberty, may, if they please, give Authority to One man, to represent them every one; as well as give such Authority to any Assembly of men whatsoever; and consequently may sub-ject themselves, if they think good, to a Monarch, as absolutely, as to any other Representative. Therefore, where there is already erected a Soveraign Power, there can be no other Representative of the same people, but onely to certain particular ends, by the Soveraign limited. For that were to erect two Soveraigns; and every man to have his person represented by two Actors, that by opposing one another, must needs divide that Power, which (if men will live in Peace) is indivisible; and thereby reduce the Multitude into the condition of Warre, contrary to the end for which all Soveraignty is instituted. And therefore as it is absurd, to think that a Soveraign Assembly, inviting the People of their Dominion, to send up their Deputies, with power to make known their Advise, or Desires, should therefore hold such Deputies, rather than themselves, for the absolute Representative of the people: so it is absurd also, to think the same in a Monarchy. And I know not how this so manifest a truth, should of late be so little observed; that in a Monarchy, he that had the Soveraignty from a descent of 600 years, was alone called Soveraign, had the title of Majesty from every one of his Subjects, and was unquestionably taken by them for their King; was notwithstanding never considered as their Representative; that name without contradiction passing for the title of those men, which at his command were sent up by the people to carry their Peti-tions, and give him (if he permitted it) their advise. Which may serve as an admonition, for those that are the true, and absolute Representative of a People, to instruct men in the nature of that Office, and to take heed how they admit of any other generall Representation upon any occasion whatso-ever, if they mean to discharge the truth committed to them.

The difference between these three kindes of Common-wealth, consisteth not in the difference of Power; but in the difference of Convenience, or Aptitude to produce the Peace, and Security of the people; for which end they were instituted. And to compare Monarchy with the other two, we may observe; First, that whosoever beareth the Person of the people, or is one of that Assembly that bears, it, beareth also his own naturall Person. And though he be carefull in his politique Person to procure the common interest; yet he is more, or no lesse carefull to procure the private good of himselfe, his family, kindred and friends; and for the most part, if the publique interest chance to crosse the private, he preferrs the private: for the Passions of men, are commonly more potent than their Reason. From whence it follows, that where the publique and private interest are most closely united, there is the publique most advanced. Now in Monarchy, the private interest is the same with the publique. The riches, power, and honour of a Monarch arise onely from the riches, strength and reputation of his Subjects. For no King can be rich, nor glorious, nor secure; whose Subjects are either poore, or contemptible, or too weak through want, or dissention, to maintain a war against their enemies: Whereas in a Democracy, or Aristocracy, the publique prosperity conferres not so much to the private fortune of one that is corrupt, or ambitious, as doth many times a perfidious advice, a treacherous action, or a Civill warre.

Secondly, that a Monarch receiveth counsell of whom, when, and where he pleaseth; and consequently may heare the opinion of men versed in the matter about which he deliberates, of what rank or quality soever, and as long before the time of action, and with as much secrecy, as he will. But when a Soveraigne Assembly has need of Counsell, none are admitted but such as have a Right thereto from the beginning; which for the most part are of those who have beene versed more in the acquisition of Wealth than of Knowledge; and are to give their advice in long discourses, which may, and do commonly excite men to action, but not governe them in it. For the *Understanding* is by the flame of the Passions, never enlightened, but dazzled: Nor is there any place, or time, wherein an Assemblie can receive Counsell with secrecie, because of their owne Multitude.

Thirdly, that the Resolutions of a Monarch, are subject to no other Inconstancy, than that of Humane Nature; but in Assemblies, besides that of Nature, there ariseth an Inconstancy from the Number. For the absence of a few, that would have the Resolution once taken, continue firme, (which may happen by security, negligence, or private impediments,) or the diligent appearance of a few of the contrary opinion, undoes to day, all that was concluded yesterday.

Fourthly, that a Monarch cannot disagree with himselfe, out of envy, or interest; but an Assembly may; and that to such a height, as may produce a Civill Warre.

Fifthly, that in Monarchy there is this inconvenience; that any Subject, by the power of one man, for the enriching of a favourite or flatterer, may be deprived of all he possesseth; which I confesse is a great and inevitable inconvenience. But the same may as well happen, where the Soveraigne Power is in an Assembly: For their power is the same; and they are as subject to evill Counsell, and to be seduced by Orators, as a Monarch by Flatterers; and becoming one an others Flatterers, serve one anothers Covetousnesse and Ambition by turnes. And whereas the Favorites of Monarchs, are few, and they have none els to advance but their owne Kindred; the Favorites of an Assembly, are many; and the Kindred much more numerous, than of any Monarch. Besides, there is no Favourite of a Monarch, which cannot as well succour his friends, as hurt his enemies: But Orators, that is to say, Favourites of Soveraigne Assemblies, though they have great power to hurt, have little to save. For to accuse, requires lesse Eloquence (such is mans Nature) than to excuse; and condemnation, than absolution more resembles Justice.

Sixthly, that it is an inconvenience in Monarchie, that the Soveraigntie may descend upon an Infant, or one that cannot discerne between Good and Evill: and consisteth in this, that the use of his Power, must be in the hand of another Man, or of some Assembly of men, which are to governe by his right, and in his name; as Curators, and Protectors of his Person, and Authority. But to say there is inconvenience, in putting the use of the Soveraign Power, into the hand of a Man, or an Assembly of men; is to say that all Government is more Inconvenient, than Confusion, and Civill Warre. And therefore all the danger that can be pretended, must arise from the Contention of those, that for an office of so great honour, and profit, may become Competitors. To make it appear, that this inconvenience, proceedeth not from that forme of Government we call Monarchy, we are to consider, that the precedent Monarch, hath appointed who shall have the Tuition of his Infant Successor, either expressely by Testament, or tacitly, by not controlling the Custome in that case received: And then such inconvenience (if it happen) is to be attributed, not to the Monarchy, but to the Ambition, and Injustice of the Subjects; which in all kinds of Government, where the people are not well instructed in their Duty, and the Rights of Soveraignty, is the same. Or else the precedent Monarch, hath not at all taken order for such Tuition; And then the Law of Nature hath provided this sufficient rule, That the Tuition shall be in him, that hath by Nature most interest in the preservation of the Authority of the Infant, and to whom least benefit can accrue by his death, or diminution. For seeing every man by nature seeketh his own benefit, and promotion; to put an Infant into the power of those, that can promote themselves by his destruction, or dammage, is not Tuition, but Trechery. So that sufficient provision being taken, against all just quarrell, about the Government under a Child, if any contention arise to the disturbance of the publique Peace, it is not to be attributed to the forme of Monarchy, but to the ambition of Subjects, and ignorance of their Duty. On the other side, there is no great Common-wealth, the Soveraignty whereof is in a great Assembly, which is not, as to consultations of Peace, and Warre, and making of Lawes, in the same condition, as if the Government were in a Child. For as a Child wants the judgement to dissent from counsell given him, and is thereby necessitated to take the advise of them, or him, to whom he is committed: So an Assembly wanteth the liberty, to dissent from the counsell of the major part, be it good, or bad. And as a Child has need of a Tutor, or Protector, to preserve his Person, and Authority: So also (in great Common-wealths,) the Soveraign Assembly, in all great dangers and troubles, have need of *Custodes libertatis;* that is of Dictators, or Protectors of their Authoritie; which are as much as Temporary Monarchs; to whom for a time, they may commit the entire exercise of their Power; and have (at the end of that time) been oftner deprived thereof, than Infant Kings, by their Protectors, Regents, or any other Tutors.

Though the Kinds of Soveraigntie be, as I have now shewn, but three; that is to say, Monarchie, where One Man has it; or Democracie, where the generall Assembly of Subjects hath it; or Aristocracie, where it is in an Assembly of certain persons nominated, or otherwise distinguished from the rest: Yet he that shall consider the particular Common-wealthes that have been, and are in the world, will not perhaps easily reduce them to three, and may thereby be inclined to think there be other Formes, arising from these mingled together. As for example, Elective Kingdomes; where Kings have the Soveraigne Power put into their hands for a time; or Kingdomes, wherein the King hath a power limited: which Governments, are nevertheless by most Writers called Monarchie. Likewise if a Popular, or Aristocraticall Common-wealth, subdue an Enemies Countrie, and govern the same, by a President, Procurator, or other Magistrate; this may seeme perhaps at first sight, to be a Democraticall, or Aristocraticall Government. But it is not so. For Elective Kings, are not Soveraignes, but Ministers of the Soveraigne; nor limited Kings Soveraignes, but Ministers of them that have the Soveraigne Power: Nor are those Provinces which are in subjection to a Democracie, or Aristocracie of another Common-wealth, Democratically, or Aristocratically governed, but Monarchically.

And first, concerning an Elective King, whose power is limited to his life, as it is in many places of Christendome at this day; or to certaine Yeares or Moneths, as the Dictators power amongst the Romans; If he have Right to appoint his Successor, he is no more Elective but Hereditary. But if he have no Power to elect his Successor, then there is some other Man, or Assembly known, which after his decease may elect a new, or else the Common-wealth dieth, and dissolveth with him, and returneth to the condition of Warre. If it be known who have the power to give the Soveraigntie after his death, it is known also that the Soveraigntie was in them before: For none have right to give that which they have not right to possesse, and keep to themselves, if they think good. But if there be none that can give the Soveraigntie, after the decease of him that was first elected; then has he power, nay he is obliged by the Law of Nature, to provide, by establishing his Successor, to keep those that had trusted him with the Government, from relapsing into the miserable condition of Civill warre. And consequently he was, when elected, a Soveraign absolute.

Secondly, that King whose power is limited, is not superiour to him, or them that have the power to limit it; and he that is not superiour, is not su-preme; that is to say not Soveraign. The Soveraignty therefore was alwaies in that Assembly which had the Right to Limit him; and by consequence the government not Monarchy, but either Democracy, or Aristocracy; as of old time in *Sparta;* where the Kings had a priviledge to lead their Armies; but the Soveraignty was in the *Ephori.*

Thirdly, whereas heretofore the Roman People, governed the land of *Judea* (for example) by a President; yet was not *Judea* therefore a Democ-racy; because they were not governed by any Assembly, into which, any of them, had right to enter; nor by an Aristocracy; because they were not gov-erned by any Assembly, into which, any man could enter by their Election: but they were governed by one Person, which though as to the people of *Rome* was an Assembly of the people, or Democracy; yet as to people of *Judea,* which had no right at all of participating in the government, was a Monarch. For though where the people are governed by an Assembly, chosen by them-selves out of their own number, the government is called a Democracy, or Aristocracy; yet when they are governed by an Assembly, not of their own choosing, 'tis a Monarchy; not of *One* man, over another man; but of one people, over another people.

Of all these Formes of Government, the matter being mortall, so that not onely Monarchs, but also whole Assemblies dy, it is necessary for the con-servation of the peace of men, that as there was order taken for an Artificiall Man, so there be order also taken, for an Artificiall Eternity of life; without which, men that are governed by an Assembly, should return into the condi-tion of Warre in every age; and they that are governed by One man, as soon as their Governour dyeth. This artificiall Eternity, is that which men call the Right of *Succession.*

There is no perfect forme of Government, where the disposing of the Succession is not in the present Soveraign. For if it be in any other particular Man, or private Assembly, it is in a person subject, and may be assumed by the Soveraign at his pleasure; and consequently the Right is in himselfe. And if it be in no particular man, but left to a new choyce; then is the Common-wealth dissolved; and the Right is in him that can get it; contrary to the in-tention of them that did Institute the Common-wealth, for their perpetuall, and not temporary security.

In a Democracy, the whole Assembly cannot faile, unlesse the Multitude that are to be governed faile. And therefore questions of the right of Succes-sion, have in that forme of Government no place at all.

In an Aristocracy, when any of the Assembly dyeth, the election of an-other into his room belongeth to the Assembly, as the Soveraign, to whom belongeth the choosing of all Counsellours, and Officers. For that which the Representative doth, as Actor, every one of the Subjects doth, as Author. And though the Soveraign Assembly, may give Power to others, to elect new men, for supply of their Court; yet it is still by their Authority, that the

Election is made; and by the same it may (when the publique shall require it) be recalled.

The greatest difficultie about the right of Succession, is in Monarchy: And the difficulty ariseth from this, that at first sight, it is not manifest who is to appoint the Successor; nor many times, who it is whom he hath appointed. For in both these cases, there is required a more exact ratiocination, than every man is accustomed to use. As to the question, who shall appoint the Successor, of a Monarch that hath the Soveraign Authority; that is to say, who shall determine of the right of Inheritance, (for Elective Kings and Princes have not the Soveraign Power in propriety, but in use only,) we are to consider, that either he that is in possession, has right to dispose of the Succession, or else that right is again in the dissolved Multitude. For the death of him that hath the Soveraign power in propriety, leaves the Multitude without any Soveraign at all; that is, without any Representative in whom they should be united, and be capable of doing any one action at all: And therefore they are incapable of Election of any new Monarch; every man having equall right to submit himselfe to such as he thinks best able to protect him, or if he can, protect himselfe by his owne sword; which is a returne to Confusion, and to the condition of a War of every man against every man, contrary to the end for which Monarchy had its first Institution. Therefore it is manifest, that by the Institution of Monarchy, the disposing of the Successor, is alwaies left to the Judgment and Will of the present Possessor.

And for the question (which may arise sometimes) who it is that the Monarch in possession, hath designed to the succession and inheritance of his power; it is determined by his expresse Words, and Testament; or by other tacite signes sufficient.

By expresse Words, or Testament, when it is declared by him in his life time, *viva voce,* or by Writing; as the first Emperours of *Rome* declared who should be their Heires. For the word Heire does not of it selfe imply the Children, or nearest Kindred of a man; but whomsoever a man shall any way declare, he would have to succeed him in his Estate. If therefore a Monarch declare expresly, that such a man shall be his Heire, either by Word or Writing, then is that man immediately after the decease of his Predecessor, Invested in the right of being Monarch.

But where Testament, and expresse Words are wanting, other naturall signes of the Will are to be followed: whereof the one is Custome. And therefore where the Custome is, that the next of Kindred absolutely succeedeth, there also the next of Kindred hath right to the Succession; for that, if the will of him that was in posession had been otherwise, he might easily have declared the same in his life time. And likewise where the Custome is, that the next of the Male Kindred succeedeth, there also the right of Succession is in the next of the Kindred Male, for the same reason. And so it is if the Custome were to advance the Female. For whatsoever Custome a man may by a word controule, and does not, it is a naturall signe he would have that Custome stand.

But where neither Custome, nor Testament hath preceded, there it is to be understood, First, that a Monarchs will is, that the government remain Monarchicall; because he hath approved that government in himselfe. Secondly, that a Child of his own, Male, or Female, be preferred before any other; because men are presumed to be more enclined by nature, to advance their own children, than the children of other men; and of their own, rather a Male than a Female; because men, are naturally fitter than women, for actions of labour and danger. Thirdly, where his own Issue faileth, rather a Brother than a stranger; and so still the neerer in bloud, rather than the more remote, because it is alwayes presumed that the neerer of kin, is the neerer in affection; and 'tis evident that a man receives alwayes, by reflexion, the most honour from the greatnesse of his neerest kindred.

But if it be lawfull for a Monarch to dispose of the Succession by words of Contract, or Testament, men may perhaps object a great inconvenience: for he may sell, or give his Right of governing to a stranger; which, because strangers (that is, men not used to live under the same government, nor speaking the same language) do commonly undervalue one another, may turn to the oppression of his Subjects; which is indeed a great inconvenience: but it proceedeth not necessarily from the subjection to a strangers government, but from the unskilfulnesse of the Governours, ignorant of the true rules of Politiques. And therefore the Romans when they had subdued many Nations, to make their Government digestible, were wont to take away that grievance, as much as they thought necessary, by giving sometimes to whole Nations, and sometimes to Principall men of every Nation they conquered, not onely the Privileges, but also the Name of Romans; and took many of them into the Senate, and Offices of charge, even in the Roman City. And this was it our most wise King, King *James,* aymed at, in endeavouring the Union of his two Realms of *England* and *Scotland.* Which if he could have obtained, had in all likelihood prevented the Civill warres, which make both those Kingdomes at this present, miserable. It is not therefore any injury to the people, for a Monarch to dispose of the Succession by Will; though by the fault of many Princes, it hath been sometimes found inconvenient. Of the lawfulnesse of it, this also is an argument, that whatsoever inconvenience can arrive by giving a Kingdome to a stranger, may arrive also by so marrying with strangers, as the Right of Succession may descend upon them: yet this by all men is accounted lawfull.

Chap. XX

Of Dominion Paternall *and* Despoticall

A *Common-wealth* by *Acquisition,* is that, where the Soveraign Power is acquired by Force; And it is acquired by force, when men singly, or many together by plurality of voyces, for fear of death, or bonds, do authorise all the actions of that Man, or Assembly, that hath their lives and liberty in his Power.

And this kind of Dominion, or Soveraignty, differeth from Soveraignty by Institution, onely in this, That men who choose their Soveraign, do it for fear of one another, and not of him whom they Institute: But in this case, they subject themselves, to him they are afraid of. In both cases they do it for fear: which is to be noted by them, that hold all such Covenants, as proceed from fear of death, or violence, voyd: which if it were true, no man, in any kind of Common-wealth, could be obliged to Obedience. It is true, that in a Common-wealth once Instituted, or acquired, Promises proceeding from fear of death, or violence, are no Covenants, nor obliging, when the thing promised is contrary to the Lawes; But the reason is not, because it was made upon fear, but because he that promiseth, hath no right in the thing promised. Also, when he may lawfully performe, and doth not, it is not the Invalidity of the Covenant, that absolveth him, but the Sentence of the Soveraign. Otherwise, whensoever a man lawfully promiseth, he unlawfully breaketh: But when the Soveraign, who is the Actor, acquitteth him, then he is acquitted by him that exorted the promise, as by the Author of such absolution.

But the Rights, and Consequences of Soveraignty, are the same in both. His Power cannot, without his consent, be Transferred to another: He cannot Forfeit it: He cannot be Accused by any of his Subjects, of Injury: He cannot be Punished by them: He is Judge of what is necessary for Peace; and Judge of Doctrines: He is Sole Legislator; and Supreme Judge of Controversies; and of the Times, and Occasions of Warre, and Peace: to him it belongeth to choose Magistrates, Counsellours, Commanders, and all other Officers, and Ministers; and to determine of Rewards, and Punishments, Honour, and Order. The reasons whereof, are the same which are alledged in the precedent Chapter, for the same Rights, and Consequences of Soveraignty by Institution. . . .

Chap. XXI

Of the Liberty of Subjects

LIBERTY, or FREEDOME, signifieth (properly) the absence of Opposition; (by Opposition, I mean externall Impediments of motion;) and may be applyed no lesse to Irrationall, and Inanimate creatures, than to Rationall. For whatsoever is so tyed, or environed, as it cannot move, but within a certain space, which space is determined by the opposition of some externall body, we say it hath not Liberty to go further. And so of all living creatures, whilest they are imprisoned, or restrained, with walls, or chayns; and of the water whilest it is kept in by banks, or vessels, that otherwise would spread it selfe into a larger space, we use to say, they are not at Liberty, to move in such manner, as without those externall impediments they would. But when the impediment of motion, is in the constitution of the thing it selfe, we use not to say, it wants the Liberty; but the Power to move; as when a stone lyeth still, or a man is fastned to his bed by sicknesse.

And according to this proper, and generally received meaning of the word,

A FREE-MAN, *is he, that in those things, which by his strength and wit he is able to do, is not hindred to doe what he has a will to.* But when the words *Free,* and *Liberty,* are applyed to any thing but *Bodies,* they are abused; for that which is not subject to Motion, is not subject to Impediment: And therefore, when 'tis said (for example) The way is free, no liberty of the way is signified, but of those that walk in it without stop. And when we say a Guift is free, there is not meant any liberty of the Guift, but of the Giver, that was not bound by any law, or Covenant to give it. So when we *speak freely,* it is not the liberty of voice, or pronunciation, but of the man, whom no law hath obliged to speak otherwise then he did. Lastly, from the use of the word *Freewill,* no liberty can be inferred to the will, desire, or inclination, but the liberty of the man; which consisteth in this, that he finds no stop, in doing what he has the will, desire, or inclination to doe.

Feare and Liberty are consistent; as when a man throweth his goods into the Sea for *feare* the ship should sink, he doth it neverthelesse very willingly, and may refuse to doe it if he will: It is therefore the action, of one that was *free:* so a man sometimes pays his debt, only for *feare* of Imprisonment, which because no body hindred him from detaining, was the action of a man at *liberty.* And generally all actions which men doe in Common-wealths, for *feare* of the law, or actions, which the doers had *liberty* to omit.

Liberty and *Necessity* are Consistent: As in the water, that hath not only *liberty,* but a *necessity* of descending by the Channel: so likewise in the Actions which men voluntarily doe; which (because they proceed from their will) proceed from *liberty;* and yet because every act of mans will, and every desire, and inclination proceedeth from some cause, and that from another cause, which causes in a continuall chaine (whose first link in the hand of God the first of all causes) proceed from *necessity.* So that to him that could see the connexion of those causes, the *necessity* of all mens voluntary actions, would appeare manifest. And therefore God, that seeth, and disposeth all things, seeth also that the *liberty* of man in doing what he will, is accompanied with the *necessity* of doing that which God will, & no more, nor lesse. For though men may do many things, which God does not command, nor is therefore Author of them; yet they can have no passion, nor appetite to any thing, of which appetite Gods will is not the cause. And did not his will assure the *necessity* of mans will, and consequently of all that on mans will dependeth, the *liberty* of men would be a contradiction, and impediment to the omnipotence and *liberty* of God. And this shall suffice, (as to the matter in hand) of that naturall *liberty,* which only is properly called *liberty.*

But as men, for the atteyning of peace, and conservation of themselves thereby, have made an Artificiall Man, which we call a Common-wealth; so also have they made Artificiall Chains, called *Civill Lawes,* which they themselves, by mutuall covenants, have fastened at one end, to the lips of that Man, or Assembly, to whom they have given the Soveraigne Power; and at the other end to their own Ears. These Bonds in their own nature but weak, may neverthelesse be made to hold, by the danger, though not by the difficulty of breaking them.

In relation to these Bonds only it is, that I am to speak now, of the *Liberty* of *Subjects*. For seeing there is no Common-wealth in the world, wherein there be Rules enough set down, for the regulating of all the actions, and words of men, (as being a thing impossible:) it followeth necessarily, that in all kinds of actions, by the laws prætermitted, men have the Liberty, of doing what their own reasons shall suggest, for the most profitable to themselves. For if we take Liberty in the proper sense, for corporall Liberty; that is to say, freedome from chains, and prison, it were very absurd for men to clamor as they doe, for the Liberty they so manifestly enjoy. Againe, if we take Liberty, for an exemption from Lawes, it is no lesse absurd, for men to demand as they doe, that Liberty, by which all other men may be masters of their lives. And yet as absurd as it is, this is it they demand; not knowing that the Lawes are of no power to protect them, without a Sword in the hands of a man, or men, to cause those laws to be put in execution. The Liberty of a Subject, lyeth therefore only in those things, which in regulating their actions, the Soveraign hath prætermitted: such as is the Liberty to buy, and sell, and otherwise contract with one another; to choose their own aboad, their own diet, their own trade of life, and institute their children as they themselves think fit; & the like.

Neverthelesse we are not to understand, that by such Liberty, the Soveraign Power of life, and death, is either abolished, or limited. For it has been already shewn, that nothing the Soveraign Representative can doe to a Subject, on what pretence soever, can properly be called Injustice, or Injury; because every Subject is Author of every act the Soveraign doth; so that he never wanteth Right to any thing, otherwise, than as he himself is the Subject of God, and bound thereby to observe the laws of Nature. And therefore it may, and doth often happen in Common-wealths, that a Subject may be put to death, by the command of the Soveraign Power; and yet neither doe the other wrong: As when *Jeptha* caused his daughter to be sacrificed: In which, and the like cases, he that so dieth, had Liberty to doe the action, for which he is neverthelesse, without Injury put to death. And the same holdeth also in a Soveraign Prince, that putteth to death an Innocent Subject. For though the action be against the law of Nature, as being contrary to Equitie, (as was the killing of *Uriah,* by *David;*) yet it was not an Injurie to *Uriah;* but to *God.* Not to *Uriah,* because the right to doe what he pleased, was given him by *Uriah* himself: And yet to *God,* because *David* was *Gods* Subject; and prohibited all Iniquitie by the law of Nature. Which distinction, *David* himself, when he repented the fact, evidently confirmed, saying, *To thee only have I sinned.* In the same manner, the people of *Athens,* when they banished the most potent of their Common-wealth for ten years, thought they committed no Injustice; and yet they never questioned what crime he had done; but what hurt he would doe: Nay they commanded the banishment of they knew not whom; and every Citizen bringing his Oystershell into the market place, written with the name of him he desired should be banished, without actuall accusing him, sometimes banished an *Aristides,* for his reputation of Justice; And sometimes a scurrilous Jester, as *Hyperbolus,* to make a Jest of it. And yet a man cannot say, the Soveraign People of *Athens* wanted right to banish them; or an *Athenian* the Libertie to Jest, or to be Just.

The Libertie, whereof there is so frequent, and honourable mention, in the Histories, and Philosophy of the Antient Greeks, and Romans, and in the writings, and discourse of those that from them have received all their learning in the Politiques, is not the Libertie of Particular men; but the Libertie of the Common-wealth: which is the same with that, which every man then should have, if there were no Civil Laws, nor Common-wealth at all. And the effects of it also be the same. For as amongst masterlesse men, there is perpetuall war, of every man against his neighbour; no inheritance, to transmit to the Son, nor to expect from the Father; no propriety of Goods, or Lands; no security; but a full and absolute Libertie in every Particular man: So in States, and Common-wealths not dependent on one another, every Common-wealth, (not every man) has an absolute Libertie, to doe what it shall judge (that is to say, what that Man, or Assemblie that representeth it, shall judge) most conducing to their benefit. But withall, they live in the condition of a perpetuall war, and upon the confines of battel, with their frontiers armed, and canons planted against their neighbours round about. The *Athenians,* and *Romanes* were free; that is, free Common-wealths: not that any particular men had the Libertie to resist their own Representative; but that their Representative had the Libertie to resist, or invade other people. There is written on the Turrets of the city of *Luca* in great characters at this day, the word *LIBERTAS;* yet no man can thence inferre, that a particular man has more Libertie, or Immunitie from the service of the Common-wealth there, than in *Constantinople.* Whether a Common-wealth be Monarchicall, or Popular, the Freedome is still the same.

But it is an easy thing, for men to be deceived, by the specious name of Libertie; and for want of Judgement to distinguish, mistake that for their Private Inheritance, and Birth right, which is the right of the Publique only. And when the same errour is confirmed by the authority of men in reputation for their writings in this subject, it is no wonder if it produce sedition, and change of Government. In these westerne parts of the world, we are made to receive our opinions concerning the Institution, and Rights of Common-wealths, from *Aristotle, Cicero,* and other men, Greeks and Romanes, that living under Popular States, derived those Rights, not from the Principles of Nature, but transcribed them into their books, out of the Practice of their own Common-wealths, which were Popular; as the Grammarians describe the Rules of Language, out of the Practise of the time; or the Rules of Poetry, out of the Poems of *Homer* and *Virgil.* And because the Athenians were taught, (to keep them from desire of changing their Government,) that they were Freemen, and all that lived under Monarchy were slaves; therefore *Aristotle* puts it down in his *Politiques, In democracy,* Liberty *is to be supposed: for 'tis commonly held, that no man is* Free *in any other Government.* And as *Aristotle;* so *Cicero,* and other Writers have grounded their Civill doctrine, on the opinions of the Romans, who were taught to hate Monarchy, at first, by them that having deposed their Soveraign, shared amongst them the Soveraignty of *Rome;* and afterwards by their Successors. And by reading of these Greek, and Latine Authors, men from their childhood have gotten a habit (under a false shew of Liberty,) of favouring tumults, and of licentious controlling the actions of their Soveraigns; and again of controlling those controllers, with the effusion of so much blood; as I think I may truly say, there was never any thing so deerly bought, as these Western parts have bought the learning of the Greek and Latine tongues.

To come now to the particulars of the true Liberty of a Subject; that is to say, what are the things, which though commanded by the Soveraign, he may neverthelesse, without Injustice, refuse to do; we are to consider, what Rights we passe away, when we make a Common-wealth; or (which is all one,) what Liberty we deny our selves, by owning all the Actions (without exception) of the Man, or Assembly we make our Soveraign. For in the act of our *Submission,* consisteth both our *Obligation,* and our *Liberty;* which must therefore be inferred by arguments taken from thence; there being no Obligation on any man, which ariseth not from some Act of his own; for all men equally, are by Nature Free. And because such arguments, must either be drawn from the expresse words, *I Authorise all his Actions,* or from the Intention of him that submitteth himselfe to his Power, (which Intention is to be understood by the End for which he so submitteth;) The Obligation, and Liberty of the Subject, is to be derived, either from those Words, (or others equivalent;) or else from the End of the Institution of Soveraignty; namely, the Peace of the Subjects within themselves, and their Defence against a common Enemy.

First therefore, seeing Soveraignty by Institution, is by Covenant of every one to every one; and Soveraignty by Acquisition, by Covenants of the Vanquished to the Victor, or Child to the Parent; It is manifest, that every Subject has Liberty in all those things, the right whereof cannot by Covenant be transferred. I have shewn before in the 14. Chapter, that Covenants, not to defend a mans own body, are voyd. Therefore,

If the Soveraign command a man (though justly condemned,) to kill, wound, or mayme himselfe; or not to resist those that assault him; or to abstain from the use of food, ayre, medicine, or any other thing, without which he cannot live; yet hath that man the Liberty to disobey.

If a man be interrogated by the Soveraign, or his Authority, concerning a crime done by himselfe, he is not bound (without assurance of Pardon) to confesse it; because no man (as I have shewn in the same Chapter) can be obliged by Covenant to accuse himselfe.

Again, the Consent of a Subject to Soveraign Power, is contained in these words, *I Authorise, or take upon me, all his actions;* in which there is no restriction at all, of his own former naturall Liberty: For by allowing him to *kill me,* I am not bound to kill my selfe when he commands me. 'Tis one thing to say, *Kill me, or my fellow, if you please;* another thing to say, *I will kill my selfe, or my fellow.* It followeth therefore, that

No man is bound by the words themselves, either to kill himselfe, or any other man; And consequently, that the Obligation a man may sometimes have, upon the Command of the Soveraign to execute any dangerous, or dishonourable Office, dependeth not on the Words of our Submission; but on the Intention; which is to be understood by the End thereof. When therefore our refusall to obey, frustrates the End for which the Soveraignty was ordained; then there is no Liberty to refuse: otherwise there is.

Upon this ground, a man that is commanded as a Souldier to fight against the enemy, though his Soveraign have Right enough to punish his refusall with death, may neverthelesse in many cases refuse, without Injustice; as when he substituteth a sufficient Souldier in his place: for in this case he deserteth not the service of the Common-wealth. And there is allowance to be made for naturall timorousnesse, not onely to women, (of whom no such dangerous duty is expected,) but also to men of feminine courage. When Armies fight, there is on one side, or both, a running away; yet when they do it not out of trechery, but fear, they are not esteemed to do it unjustly, but dishonourably. For the same reason, to avoyd battell, is not Injustice, but Cowardise. But he that inrowleth himselfe a Souldier, or taketh imprest mony, taketh away the excuse of a timorous nature; and is obliged, not onely to go to the battell, but also not to run from it, without his Captaines leave. And when the Defence of the Common-wealth, requireth at once the help of all that are able to bear Arms, every one is obliged; because otherwise the Institution of the Common-wealth, which they have not the purpose, or courage to preserve, was in vain.

To resist the Sword of the Common-wealth, in defence of another man, guilty, or innocent, no man hath Liberty; because such Liberty, takes away from the Soveraign, the means of Protecting us; and is therefore destructive of the very essence of Government. But in case a great many men together, have already resisted the Soveraign Power unjustly, or committed some Capitall crime, for which every one of them expecteth death, whether have they not the Liberty then to joyn together, and assist, and defend one another? Certainly they have: For they but defend their lives, which the Guilty man may as well do, as the Innocent. There was indeed injustice in the first breach of their duty; Their bearing of Arms subsequent to it, though it be to maintain what they have done, is no new unjust act. And if it be onely to defend their persons, it is not unjust at all. But the offer of Pardon taketh from them, to whom it is offered, the plea of self-defence, and maketh their perseverance in assisting, or defending the rest, unlawfull.

As for other Lyberties, they depend on the silence of the Law. In cases where the Soveraign has prescribed no role, there the Subject hath the liberty to do, or forbeare, according to his own discretion. And therefore such Liberty is in some places more, and in some lesse; and in some times more, in other times lesse, according as they that have the Soveraignty shall think most convenient. As for Example, there was a time, when in *England* a man might enter in to his own Land, (and dispossesse such as wrongfully possessed it) by force. But in after-times, that Liberty of Forcible entry, was taken away by a Statute made (by the King) in Parliament. And in some places of the world, men have the Liberty of many wives: in other places, such Liberty is not allowed.

If a Subject have a controversie with his Soveraigne, of Debt, or of right of possession of lands or goods, or concerning any service required at his hands, or concerning any penalty corporall, or pecuniary, grounded on a precedent Law; He hath the same Liberty to sue for his right, as if it were against a Subject; and before such Judges, as are appointed by the Soveraign. For seeing the Soveraign demandeth by force of a former Law, and not by vertue of his Power; he declareth thereby, that he requireth no more, than shall appear to be due by that Law. The sute therefore is not contrary to the will of the Soveraign; and consequently the Subject hath the Liberty to demand the hearing of his Cause; and sentence, according to that Law. But if he demand, or take any thing by pretence of his Power; there lyeth, in that case, no action of Law: for all that is done by him in Vertue of his Power, is done by the Authority of every subject, and consequently, he that brings an action against the Soveraign, brings it against himselfe.

If a Monarch, or Soveraign Assembly, grant a Liberty to all, or any of his Subjects; which Grant standing, he is disabled to provide for their safety, the Grant is voyd; unlesse he directly renounce, or transferre the Soveraignty to another. For in that he might openly, (if it had been his will,) and in plain termes, have renounced, or transferred it, and did not; it is to be understood it was not his will; but that the Grant proceeded from ignorance of the repugnancy between such a Liberty and the Soveraign Power; and therefore the Soveraignty is still retayned; and consequently all those Powers, which are necessary to the exercising thereof; such as are the Power of Warre, and Peace, of Judicature, of appointing Officers, and Councellours, of levying Mony, and the rest named in the 18th Chapter.

The Obligation of Subjects to the Soveraign, is understood to last as long, and no longer, than the power lasteth, by which he is able to protect them. For the right men have by Nature to protect themselves, when none else can protect them, can by no Covenant be relinquished. The Soveraignty is the Soule of the Common-wealth; which once departed from the Body, the members doe no more receive their motion from it. The end of Obedience is Protection; which, wheresoever a man seeth it, either in his own, or in anothers sword, Nature applyeth his obedience to it, and his endeavour to maintain it. And though Soveraignty, in the intention of them that make it, be immortall; yet is it in its own nature, not only subject to violent death, by forreign war; but also through the ignorance, and passions of men, it hath in it, from the very institution, many seeds of a naturall mortality, by Intestine Discord.

If a Subject be taken prisoner in war; or his person, or his means of life be within the Guards of the enemy, and hath his life and corporall Libertie given him, on condition to be Subject to the Victor, he hath Libertie to accept the condition; and having accepted it, is the subject of him that took him; because he had no other way to preserve himselfe. The case is the same, if he be deteined on the same termes, in a forraign country. But if a man be held in prison, or bonds, or is not trusted with the libertie of his bodie; he cannot be understood to be bound by Covenant to subjection; and therefore may, if he can, make his escape by any means whatsoever.

If a Monarch shall relinquish the Soveraignty, both for himself, and his heires; His Subjects returne to the absolute Libertie of Nature; because, though Nature may declare who are his Sons, and who are the nerest of his Kin; yet it dependeth on his own will, (as hath been said in the precedent chapter,) who shall be his Heyr. If therefore he will have no Heyre, there is no Soveraignty, nor Subjection. The case is the same, if he dye without known Kindred, and without declaration of his Heyre. For then there can no Heyre be known, and consequently no Subjection be due.

If the Soveraign Banish his Subject; during the Banishment, he is not Subject. But he that is sent on a message, or hath leave to travell, is still Subject; but it is, by Contract between Soveraigns, not by vertue of the covenant of Subjection. For whosoever entreth into anothers dominion, is Subject to all the Lawes thereof; unlesse he have a privilege by the amity of the Soveraigns, or by speciall licence.

If a Monarch subdued by war, render himself Subject to the Victor; his Subjects are delivered from their former obligation, and become obliged to the Victor. But if he be held prisoner, or have not the liberty of his own Body; he is not understood to have given away the Right of Soveraigntie; and therefore his Subjects are obliged to yield obedience to the Magistrates formerly placed, governing not in their own name, but in his. For, his Right remaining, the question is only of the Administration; that is to say, of the Magistrates and Officers; which, if he have not means to name, he is supposed to approve those, which he himself had formerly appointed. . . .

Chap. XXIX

Of those things that Weaken, or tend
to the Dissolution *of a Common-wealth*

Though nothing can be immortall, which mortals make; yet, if men had the use of reason they pretend to, their Common-wealths might be secured, at least, from perishing by internall diseases. For by the nature of their Institution, they are designed to live, as long as Man-kind, or as the Lawes of Nature, or as Justice it selfe, which gives them life. Therefore when they come to be dissolved, not by externall violence, but intestine disorder, the fault is not in men, as they are the *Matter;* but as they are the *Makers,* and orderers of them. For men, as they become at last weary of irregular justling, and hewing one another, and desire with all their hearts, to conforme themselves into one firme and lasting edifice; so for want, both of the art of making fit Lawes, to square their actions by, and also of humility, and patience, to suffer the rude and combersome points of their present greatnesse to be taken off, they cannot without the help of a very able Architect, be compiled, into any other than a crasie building, such as hardly lasting out their own time, must assuredly fall upon the heads of their posterity.

Amongst the *Infirmities* therefore of a Common-wealth, I will reckon in the first place, those that arise from an Imperfect Institution, and resemble the diseases of a naturall body, which proceed from a Defectuous Procreation.

Of which, this is one, *That a man to obtain a Kingdome, is sometimes content with lesse Power, than to the Peace, and defence of the Common-wealth is necessarily required.* From whence it commeth to passe, that when the exercise of the Power layd by, is for the publique safety to be resumed, it hath the resemblance of an unjust act; which disposeth great numbers of men (when occasion is presented) to rebell; In the same manner as the bodies of children, gotten by diseased parents, are subject either to untimely death, or to purge the ill quality, derived from their vicious conception, by breaking out into biles and scabbs. And when Kings deny themselves some such necessary Power, it is not alwayes (though sometimes) out of ignorance of what is necessary to the office they undertake; but many times out of a hope to recover the same again at their pleasure: Wherein they reason not well; because such as will hold them to their promises, shall be maintained against them by forraign Common-wealths; who in order to the good of their own Subjects let slip few occasions to *weaken* the estate of their Neighbours. So was *Thomas Becket* Archbishop of *Canterbury,* supported against *Henry* the Second, by the Pope; the subjection of Ecclesiastiques to the Common-wealth, having been dispensed with by *William the Conquerour* at his reception, when he took an Oath, not to infringe the liberty of the Church. And so were the *Barons,* whose power was by *William Rufus* (to have their help in transferring the Succession from his Elder brother, to himselfe,) encreased to a degree, inconsistent with the Soveraign Power, maintained in their Rebellion against King *John,* by the French.

Nor does this happen in Monarchy onely. For whereas the stile of the antient Roman Common-wealth, was, *The Senate, and People of Rome;* neither Senate, nor People pretended to the whole Power; which first caused the seditions, of *Tiberius Gracchus, Caius Gracchus, Lucius Saturninus,* and others; and afterwards the warres between the Senate and the People, under *Marius* and *Sylla;* and again under *Pompey* and *Cæsar,* to the Extinction of their Democracy, and the setting up of Monarchy.

The people ot *Athens* bound themselves but from one onely Action; which was, that no man on pain of death should propound the renewing of the warre for the Island of *Salamis;* And yet thereby, if *Solon* had not caused to be given out he was mad, and afterwards in gesture and habit of a mad-man, and in verse, propounded it to the People that flocked about him, they had had an enemy perpetually in readinesse, even at the gates of their Citie; such dammage, or shifts, are all Common-wealths forced to, that have their Power never so little limited.

In the second place, I observe the *Diseases* of a Common-wealth, that proceed from the poyson of seditious doctrines; whereof one is, *That every private man is Judge of Good and Evill actions.* This is true in the condition of meer Nature, where there are no Civill Lawes; and also under Civill Government, in such cases as are not determined by the Law. But otherwise, it is manifest, that the measure of Good and Evill actions, is the Civill Law; and the Judge the Legislator, who is alwayes Representative of the Common-wealth. From this false doctrine, men are disposed to debate with themselves, and dispute the commands of the Common-wealth; and afterwards to obey, or disobey them, as in their private judgements they shall think fit. Whereby the Common-wealth is distracted and *Weakened*.

Another doctrine repugnant to Civill Society, is, that *whatsoever a man does against his Conscience, is Sinne;* and it dependeth on the presumption of making himself judge of Good and Evill. For a mans Conscience, and his Judgement is the same thing; and as the Judgement, so also the Conscience may be erroneous. Therefore, though he that is subject to no Civill Law, sinneth in all he does against his Conscience, because he has no other rule to follow but his own reason; yet it is not so with him that lives in a Common-wealth; because the Law is the publique Conscience, by which he hath already undertaken to be guided. Otherwise in such diversity, as there is of private Consciences, which are but private opinions, the Common-wealth must needs be distracted, and no man dare to obey the Soveraign Power, farther than it shall seem good in his own eyes.

It hath been also commonly taught, *That Faith and Sanctity, are not to be attained by Study and Reason, but by supernaturall Inspiration, or Infusion,* which granted, I see not why any man should render a reason of his Faith; or why every Christian should not be also a Prophet; or why any man should take the Law of his Country, rather than his own Inspiration, for the rule of his action. And thus wee fall again into the fault of taking upon us to Judge of Good and Evill; or to make Judges of it, such private men as pretend to be supernaturally Inspired, to the Dissolution of all Civill Government. Faith comes by hearing, and hearing by those accidents, which guide us into the presence of them that speak to us; which accidents are all contrived by God Almighty; and yet are not supernaturall, but onely, for the great number of them that concurre to every effect, unobservable. Faith, and Sanctity, are indeed not very frequent; but yet they are not Miracles, but brought to passe by education, discipline, correction, and other naturall wayes, by which God worketh them in his elect, at such time as he thinketh fit. And these three opinions, pernicious to Peace and Government, have in this part of the world, proceeded chiefly from the tongues, and pens of unlearned Divines; who joyning the words of Holy Scripture together, otherwise than is agreeable to reason, do what they can, to make men think, that Sanctity and Naturall Reason, cannot stand together.

A fourth opinion, repugnant to the nature of a Common-wealth, is this, *That he that hath the Soveraign Power, is subject to the Civill Lawes.* It is true, that Soveraigns are all subjects to the Lawes of Nature; because such lawes be Divine, and cannot by any man, or Common-wealth be abrogated. But to those Lawes which the Soveraign himselfe, that is, which the Common-wealth maketh, he is not subject. For to be subject to Lawes, is to be subject to the Common-wealth, that is to the Soveraign Representative, that is to himselfe; which is not subjection, but freedome from the Lawes. Which errour, because it setteth the Lawes above the Soveraign, setteth also a Judge above him, and a Power to punish him; which is to make a new Soveraign; and again for the same reason a third, to punish the second; and so continually without end, to the Confusion, and Dissolution of the Common-wealth.

A Fifth doctrine, that tendeth to the Dissolution of a Common-wealth, is, *That every private man has an absolute Propriety in his Goods; such, as excludeth the Right of the Soveraign.* Every man has indeed a Propriety that excludes the Right of every other Subject: And he has it onely from the Soveraign Power; without the protection whereof, every other man should have equall Right to the same. But if the Right of the Soveraign also be excluded, he cannot performe the office they have put him into; which is, to defend them both from forraign enemies, and from the injuries of one another; and consequently there is no longer a Common-wealth.

And if the Propriety of Subjects, exclude not the Right of the Soveraign Representative to their Goods; much lesse to their offices of Judicature, or Execution, in which they Represent the Soveraign himselfe.

There is a Sixth doctrine, plainly, and directly against the essence of a Common-wealth; and 'tis this, *That the Soveraign Power may be divided.* For what is it to divide the Power of a Common wealth, but to Dissolve it; for Powers divided mutually destroy each other. And for these doctrines, men are chiefly beholding to some of those, that making profession of the Lawes, endeavour to make them depend upon their own learning, and not upon the Legislative Power.

And as False Doctrine, so also often-times the Example of different Government in a neighbouring Nation, disposeth men to alteration of the forme already setled. So the people of the Jewes were stirred up to reject God, and to call upon the Prophet *Samuel,* for a King after the manner of the Nations: So also the lesser Cities of *Greece,* were continually disturbed, with seditions of the Aristocraticall, and Democraticall factions; one part of almost every Common-wealth, desiring to imitate the Lacedæmonians; the other, the Athenians. And I doubt not, but many men, have been contented to see the late troubles in *England,* out of an imitation of the Low Countries; supposing there needed no more to grow rich, than to change, as they had done, the forme of their Government. For the constitution of mans nature, is of it selfe subject to desire novelty: When therefore they are provoked to the same, by the neighbourhood also of those that have been enriched by it, it is almost impossible for them, not to be content with those that solicite them to change; and love the first beginnings, though they be grieved with the continuance of disorder; like hot blouds, that having gotten the itch, tear themselves with their own nayles, till they can endure the smart no longer.

And as to Rebellion in particular against Monarchy; one of the most frequent causes of it, is the Reading of the books of Policy, and Histories of the antient Greeks, and Romans; from which, young men, and all others that are unprovided of the Antidote of solid Reason, receiving a strong, and delightfull impression, of the great exploits of warre, achieved by the Conductors of their Armies, receive withall a pleasing Idea, of all they have done besides; and imagine their great prosperity, not to have proceeded from the æmulation of particular men, but from the vertue of their popular forme of government: Not considering the frequent Seditions, and Civill warres, produced by the imperfection of their Policy. From the reading, I say, of such books, men have undertaken to kill their Kings, because the Greek and Latine writers, in their books, and discourses of Policy, make it lawfull, and laudable, for any man so to do; provided before he do it, he call him Tyrant. For they say not *Regicide,* that is, killing of a King, but *Tyrannicide,* that is, killing of a Tyrant is lawfull. From the same books, they that live under a Monarch conceive an opinion, that the Subjects in a Popular Common-wealth enjoy Liberty; but that in a Monarchy they are all Slaves. I say, they that live under a Monarchy conceive such an opinion; not they that live under a Popular Government: for they find no such matter. In summe, I cannot imagine, how anything can be more prejudiciall to a Monarchy, than the allowing of such books to be publikely read, without present applying such correctives of discreet Masters, as are fit to take away their Venime: Which Venime I will not doubt to compare to the biting of a mad Dogge, which is a disease the Physicians call *Hydrophobia,* or *fear of Water.* For as he that is so bitten, has a continuall torment of thirst, and yet abhorreth water; and is in such an estate, as if the poyson endeavoured to convert him into a Dogge: So when a Monarchy is once bitten to the quick, by those Democraticall writers, that continually snarle at that estate; it wanteth nothing more than a strong Monarch, which neverthelesse out of a certain *Tyrannophobia,* or feare of being strongly governed, when they have him, they abhorre.

As there have been Doctors, that hold there be three Soules in a man; so there be also that think there may be more Soules, (that is, more Soveraigns,) than one, in a Common-wealth; and set up a *Supremacy* against the *Soveraignty; Canons* against *Lawes;* and a *Ghostly Authority* against the *Civill;* working on mens minds, with words and distinctions, that of themselves signifie nothing, but bewray (by their obscurity) that there walketh (as some think invisibly) another Kingdome, as it were a Kingdome of Fayries, in the dark. Now seeing it is manifest, that the Civill Power, and the Power of the Common-wealth is the same thing; and that Supremacy, and the Power of making

Canons, and granting Faculties, implyeth a Common-wealth; it followeth, that where one is Soveraign, another Supreme; where one can make Lawes, and another make Canons; there must needs be two Common-wealths, of one & the same Subjects; which is a Kingdome divided in it selfe, and cannot stand. For notwithstanding the insignificant distinction of *Temporall,* and *Ghostly,* they are still two Kingdomes, and every Subject is subject to two Masters. For seeing the *Ghostly* Power challengeth the Right to declare what is Sinne it challengeth by consequence to declare what is Law, (Sinne being nothing but the transgression of the Law;) and again, the Civill Power challenging to declare what is Law, every Subject must obey two Masters, who both will have their Commands be observed as Law; which is impossible. Or, if it be but one Kingdome, either the *Civill,* which is the Power of the Common-wealth, must be subordinate to the *Ghostly,* and then there is no Soveraignty but the *Ghostly;* or the *Ghostly* must be subordinate to the *Temporall* and then there is no *Supremacy* but the *Temporall.* When therefore these two Powers oppose one another, the Common-wealth cannot but be in great danger of Civill warre, and Dissolution. For the *Civill* Authority being more visible, and standing in the cleerer light of naturall reason cannot choose but draw to it in all times a very considerable part of the people: And the *Spirituall,* though it stand in the darknesse of Schoole distinctions, and hard words; yet because the fear of Darknesse, and Ghosts, is greater than other fears, cannot want a party sufficient to Trouble, and sometimes to Destroy a Common-wealth. And this is a Disease which not unfitly may be compared to the Epilepsie, or Falling-sicknesse (which the Jewes took to be one kind of possession by Spirits) in the Body Naturall. For as in this Disease, there is an unnaturall spirit, or wind in the head that obstructeth the roots of the Nerves, and moving them violently, taketh away the motion which naturally they should have from the power of the Soule in the Brain, and thereby causeth violent, and irregular motions (which men call Convulsions) in the parts; insomuch as he that is seized therewith, falleth down sometimes into the water, and sometimes into the fire, as a man deprived of his senses; so also in the Body Politique, when the Spirituall power, moveth the Members of a Common-wealth, by the terrour of punishments, and hope of rewards (which are the Nerves of it,) otherwise than by the Civill Power (which is the Soule of the Common-wealth) they ought to be moved; and by strange, and hard words suffocates their understanding, it must needs thereby Distract the people, and either Overwhelm the Common-wealth with Oppression, or cast it into the Fire of a Civill warre.

Sometimes also in the meerly Civill government, there be more than one Soule: As when the Power of levying mony, (which is the Nutritive faculty,) has depended on a generall Assembly; the Power of conduct and command, (which is the Motive faculty,) on one man; and the Power of making Lawes, (which is the Rationall faculty,) on the accidentall consent, not onely of those two, but also of a third; This endangereth the Common-wealth, somtimes for want of consent to good Lawes; but most often for want of such Nourishment, as is necessary to Life, and Motion. For although few perceive, that such

government, is not government, but division of the Common-wealth into three
Factions, and call it mixt Monarchy; yet the truth is, that it is not one independent Common-wealth, but three independent Factions; nor one Representative Person, but three. In the Kingdome of God, there may be three Persons
independent, without breach of unity in God that Reigneth; but where men
Reigne, that be subject to diversity of opinions, it cannot be so. And therefore
if the King bear the person of the People, and the generall Assembly bear also
the person of the People, and another Assembly bear the person of a Part of
the people, they are not one Person, nor one Soveraign, but three Persons, and
three Soveraigns.

To what Disease in the Naturall Body of man, I may exactly compare
this irregularity of a Common-wealth, I know not. But I have seen a man,
that had another man growing out of his side, with an head, armes, breast, and
stomach, of his own: If he had had another man growing out of his other side,
the comparison might then have been exact.

Hitherto I have named such Diseases of a Common-wealth, as are of the
greatest, and most present danger. There be other, not so great; which neverthelesse are not unfit to be observed. As first, the difficulty of raising Mony,
for the necessary uses of the Common-wealth; especially in the approach of
warre. This difficulty ariseth from the opinion, that every Subject hath of a
Propriety in his lands and goods, exclusive of the Soveraigns Right to the use
of the same. From whence it commeth to passe, that the Soveraign Power,
which foreseeth the necessities and dangers of the Common-wealth, (finding
the passage of mony to the publique Treasure obstructed, by the tenacity of
the people,) whereas it ought to extend it selfe, to encounter, and prevent such
dangers in their beginnings, contracteth it selfe as long as it can, and when it
cannot longer, struggles with the people by stratagems of Law, to obtain little
summes, which not sufficing, he is fain at last violently to open the way for
present supply, or Perish; and being put often to these extremities, at last
reduceth the people to their due temper; or else the Common-wealth must
perish. Insomuch as we may compare this Distemper very aptly to an Ague;
wherein, the fleshy parts being congealed, or by venomous matter obstructed;
the Veins which by their naturall course empty themselves into the Heart, are
not (as they ought to be) supplyed from the Arteries, whereby there succeedeth at first a cold contraction, and trembling of the limbes; and afterwards
a hot, and strong endeavour of the Heart, to force a passage for the Bloud;
and before it can do that, contenteth it selfe with the small refreshments of
such things as coole for a time, till (if Nature be strong enough) it break at
last the contumacy of the parts obstructed, and dissipateth the venome into
sweat; or (if Nature be too weak) the Patient dyeth.

Again, there is sometimes in a Common-wealth, a Disease, which re-
sembleth the Pleurisie; and that is, when the Treasure of the Common-wealth,
flowing out of its due course, is gathered together in too much abundance, in
one, or a few private men, by Monopolies, or by Farmes of the Publique
Revenues; in the same manner as the Blood in a Pleurisie, getting into the

Membrane of the breast, breedeth there an Inflammation, accompanied with a Fever, and painfull stitches.

Also, the Popularity of a potent Subject, (unlesse the Common-wealth have very good caution of his fidelity,) is a dangerous Disease; because the people (which should receive their motion from the Authority of the Soveraign,) by the flattery, and by the reputation of an ambitious man, are drawn away from their obedience to the Lawes, to follow a man, of whose vertues, and designes they have no knowledge. And this is commonly of more danger in a Popular Government, than in a Monarchy; because an Army is of so great force, and multitude, as it may easily be made believe, they are the People. By this means it was, that *Julius Cæsar,* who was set up by the People against the Senate, having won to himselfe the affections of his Army, made himselfe Master, both of Senate and People. And this proceeding of popular, and ambitious men, is plain Rebellion; and may be resembled to the effects of Witchcraft.

Another infirmity of a Common-wealth, is the immoderate greatnesse of a Town, when it is able to furnish out of its own Circuit, the number, and expence of a great Army: As also the great number of Corporations; which are as it were many lesser Common-wealths in the bowels of a greater, like wormes in the entrayles of a naturall man. To which may be added, the Liberty of Disputing against absolute Power, by pretenders to Politicall Prudence; which though bred for the most part in the Lees of the people; yet animated by False Doctrines, are perpetually medling with the Fundamentall Lawes, to the molestation of the Common-wealth; like the little Wormes, which Physicians call *Ascarides.*

We may further adde, the insatiable appetite, or *Bulimia,* of enlarging Dominion; with the incurable *Wounds* thereby many times received from the enemy; And the *Wens,* of ununited conquests, which are many times a burthen, and with lesse danger lost, than kept; As also the *Lethargy* of Ease, and *Consumption* of Riot and Vain Expence.

Lastly, when in a warre (forraign, or intestine,) the enemies get a final Victory; so as (the forces of the Common-wealth keeping the field no longer) there is no farther protection of Subjects in their loyalty; then is the Commonwealth DISSOLVED, and every man at liberty to protect himselfe by such courses as his own discretion shall suggest unto him. For the Sovereign, is the publique Soule, giving Life and Motion to the Common-wealth; which expiring, the Members are governed by it no more, than the Carcasse of a man, by his departed (though Immortall) Soule. For though the Right of a Soveraign Monarch cannot be extinguished by the act of another; yet the Obligation of the members may. For he that wants protection, may seek it anywhere; and when he hath it, is obliged (without fraudulent pretence of having submitted himselfe out of fear,) to protect his Protection as long as he is able. But when the Power of an Assembly is once suppressed, the Right of the same perisheth utterly; because the Assembly it selfe is extinct; and consequently, there is no possibility for the Soveraignty to re-enter. . . .

[Parts III and IV, *Of a Christian Commonwealth* and *Of Darknesse* are here omitted entirely.]

A Review, *and* Conclusion

. . . And thus I have brought to an end my Discourse of Civill and Ecclesiasticall Government, occasioned by the disorders of the present time, without partiality, without application, and without other designe, than to set before mens eyes the mutuall Relation between Protection and Obedience; of which the condition of Humane Nature, and the Laws Divine, (both Naturall and Positive) require an inviolable observation. And though in the revolution of States, there can be no very good Constellation for Truths of this nature to be born under, (as having an angry aspect from the dissolvers of an old Government, and seeing but the backs of them that erect a new;) yet I cannot think it will be condemned at this time, either by the Publique Judge of Doctrine, or by any that desires the continuance of Publique Peace. And in this hope I return to my interrupted Speculation of Bodies Naturall; wherein, (if God give me health to finish it,) I hope the Novelty will as much please, as in the Doctrine of this Artificiall Body it useth to offend. For such Truth, as opposeth no mans profit, nor pleasure, is to all men welcome.

The Principles of a Liberal Social Order
F. A. Hayek

1. By 'liberalism' I shall understand here the conception of a desirable political order which in the first instance was developed in England from the time of the Old Whigs in the later part of the seventeenth century to that of Gladstone at the end of the nineteenth. David Hume, Adam Smith, Edmund Burke, T. B. Macaulay and Lord Acton may be regarded as its typical representatives in England. It was this conception of individual liberty under the law which in the first instance inspired the liberal movements on the Continent and which became the basis of the American political tradition.

A paper submitted to the Tokyo Meeting of the Mont Pélèrin Society, September 1966, and published in *Il Politico,* December 1966. From *Studies in Philosophy, Politics and Economics,* copyright 1967 by F. A. Hayek. Reprinted by permission of The University of Chicago Press, Routledge & Kegan Paul Ltd., and the author. F. A. Hayek, a philosopher and economist, has written widely in social, political, and economic theory. Perhaps his most important work is *The Constitution of Liberty* (Chicago: University of Chicago Press, 1960). Formerly of the University of London and the University of Chicago, Hayek is now a professor of economics at the University of Freiburg. Often called a conservative, he prefers to be regarded as a liberal in the classical sense. He places a high value on economic liberty, but he also (unlike some modern conservatives) stresses other liberties, such as freedom of speech and the press.

A few of the leading political thinkers in those countries like B. Constant and A. de Tocqueville in France, Immanuel Kant, Friedrich von Schiller and Wilhelm von Humboldt in Germany, and James Madison, John Marshall and Daniel Webster in the United States belong wholly to it.

2. This liberalism must be clearly distinguished from another, originally Continental European tradition, also called 'liberalism' of which what now claims this name in the United States is a direct descendant. This latter view, though beginning with an attempt to imitate the first tradition, interpreted it in the spirit of a constructivist rationalism prevalent in France and thereby made of it something very different, and in the end, instead of advocating limitations on the powers of government, ended up with the ideal of the unlimited powers of the majority. This is the tradition of Voltaire, Rousseau, Condorcet and the French Revolution which became the ancestor of modern socialism. English utilitarianism has taken over much of this Continental tradition and the late-nineteenth-century British liberal party, resulting from a fusion of the liberal Whigs and the utilitarian Radicals, was also a product of this mixture.

3. Liberalism and democracy, although compatible, are not the same. The first is concerned with the extent of governmental power, the second with who holds this power. The difference is best seen if we consider their opposites: the opposite of liberalism is totalitarianism, while the opposite of democracy is authoritarianism. In consequence, it is at least possible in principle that a democratic government may be totalitarian and that an authoritarian government may act on liberal principles. The second kind of 'liberalism' mentioned before has in effect become democratism rather than liberalism and, demanding *unlimited* power of the majority, has become essentially anti-liberal.

4. It should be specially emphasized that the two political philosophies which both describe themselves as 'liberalism' and lead in a few respects to similar conclusions, rest on altogether different philosophical foundations. The first is based on an evolutionary interpretation of all phenomena of culture and mind and on an insight into the limits of the powers of the human reason. The second rests on what I have called 'constructivist' rationalism, a conception which leads to the treatment of all cultural phenomena as the product of deliberate design, and on the belief that it is both possible and desirable to reconstruct all grown institutions in accordance with a preconceived plan. The first kind is consequently reverent of tradition and recognizes that all knowledge and all civilization rests on tradition, while the second type is contemptuous of tradition because it regards an independently existing reason as capable of designing civilization. (Cf. the statement by Voltaire: 'If you want good laws, burn those you have and make new ones.') The first is also an essentially modest creed, relying on abstraction as the only available means to extend the limited powers of reason, while the second refuses to recognize any such limits and believes that reason alone can prove the desirability of particular concrete arrangements.

(It is a result of this difference that the first kind of liberalism is at least not incompatible with religious beliefs and has often been held and even been developed by men holding strong religious beliefs, while the 'Continental' type of liberalism has always been antagonistic to all religion and politically in constant conflict with organized religions.)

5. The first kind of liberalism, which we shall henceforth alone consider, is itself not the result of a theoretical construction but arose from the desire to extend and generalize the beneficial effects which unexpectedly had followed on the limitations placed on the powers of government out of sheer distrust of the rulers. Only after it was found that the unquestioned greater personal liberty which the Englishman enjoyed in the eighteenth century had produced an unprecedented material prosperity were attempts made to develop a systematic theory of liberalism, attempts which in England never were carried very far while the Continental interpretations largely changed the meaning of the English tradition.

6. Liberalism thus derives from the discovery of a self-generating or spontaneous order in social affairs (the same discovery which led to the recognition that there existed an object for theoretical social sciences), an order which made it possible to utilize the knowledge and skill of all members of society to a much greater extent than would be possible in any order created by central direction, and the consequent desire to make as full use of these powerful spontaneous ordering forces as possible.

7. It was thus in their efforts to make explicit the principles of an order already existing but only in an imperfect form that Adam Smith and his followers developed the basic principles of liberalism in order to demonstrate the desirability of their general application. In doing this they were able to presuppose familiarity with the common law conception of justice and with the ideals of the rule of law and of government under the law which were little understood outside the Anglo-Saxon world; with the result that not only were their ideas not fully understood outside the English-speaking countries, but that they ceased to be fully understood even in England when Bentham and his followers replaced the English legal tradition by a constructivist utilitarianism derived more from Continental rationalism than from the evolutionary conception of the English tradition.

8. The central concept of liberalism is that under the enforcement of universal rules of just conduct, protecting a recognizable private domain of individuals, a spontaneous order of human activities of much greater complexity will form itself than could ever be produced by deliberate arrangement, and that in consequence the coercive activities of government should be limited to the enforcement of such rules, whatever other services government may at the same time render by administering those particular resources which have been placed at its disposal for those purposes.

9. The distinction between a *spontaneous order* based on abstract rules which leave individuals free to use their own knowledge for their own purposes, and an *organization or arrangement* based on commands, is of central importance for the understanding of the principles of a free society and must

in the following paragraphs be explained in some detail, especially as the spontaneous order of a free society will contain many organizations (including the biggest organization, government), but the two principles of order cannot be mixed in any manner we may wish.

10. The first peculiarity of a spontaneous order is that by using its order-ing forces (the regularity of the conduct of its members) we can achieve an order of a much more complex set of facts than we could ever achieve by deliberate arrangement, but that, while availing ourselves of this possibility of inducing an order of much greater extent than we otherwise could, we at the same time limit our power over the details of that order. We shall say that when using the former principle we shall have power only over the abstract character but not over the concrete detail of that order.

11. No less important is the fact that, in contrast to an organization, neither has a spontaneous order a purpose nor need there be agreement on the concrete results it will produce in order to agree on the desirability of such an order, because, being independent of any particular purpose, it can be used for, and will assist in the pursuit of, a great many different, divergent and even conflicting individual purposes. Thus the order of the market, in particular, rests not on common purposes but on reciprocity, that is on the reconciliation of different purposes for the mutual benefit of the participants.

12. The conception of the common welfare or of the public good of a free society can therefore never be defined as a sum of known particular re-sults to be achieved, but only as an abstract order which as a whole is not oriented on any particular concrete ends but provides merely the best chance for any member selected at random successfully to use his knowledge for his purposes. Adopting a term of Professor Michael Oakeshott (London), we may call such a free society a *nomocratic* (law-governed) as distinguished from an unfree *telocratic* (purpose-governed) social order.

13. The great importance of the spontaneous order or nomocracy rests on the fact that it extends the possibility of peaceful co-existence of men for their mutual benefit beyond the small group whose members have concrete common purposes, or were subject to a common superior, and that it thus made the appearance of the Great or Open Society possible. This order which has progressively grown beyond the organizations of the family, the horde, the clan and the tribe, the principalities and even the empire or national state, and has produced at least the beginning of a world society, is based on the adoption—without and often against the desire of political authority—of rules which came to prevail because the groups who observed them were more successful; and it has existed and grown in extent long before men were aware of its existence or understood its operation.

14. The spontaneous order of the market, based on reciprocity or mutual benefits, is commonly described as an economic order; and in the vulgar sense of the term 'economic' the Great Society is indeed held together entirely by what are commonly called economic forces. But it is exceedingly misleading, and has become one of the chief sources of confusion and misunderstanding,

to call this order an economy as we do when we speak of a national, social, or world economy. This is at least one of the chief sources of most socialist endeavour to turn the spontaneous order of the market into a deliberately run organization serving an agreed system of common ends.

15. An economy in the strict sense of the word in which we can call a household, a farm, an enterprise or even the financial administration of government an economy, is indeed an organization or a deliberate arrangement of a given stock of resources in the service of a unitary order of purposes. It rests on a system of coherent decisions in which a single view of the relative importance of the different competing purposes determines the uses to be made of the different resources.

16. The spontaneous order of the market resulting from the interaction of many such economies is something so fundamentally different from an economy proper that it must be regarded as a great misfortune that it has ever been called by the same name. I have become convinced that this practice so constantly misleads people that it is necessary to invent a new technical term for it. I propose that we call this spontaneous order of the market a *catallaxy* in analogy to the term 'catallactics', which has often been proposed as a substitute for the term 'economics'. (Both 'catallaxy' and 'catallactics' derive from the ancient Greek verb *katallattein* which, significantly, means not only 'to barter' and 'to exchange' but also 'to admit into the community' and 'to turn from enemy into friend'.)

17. The chief point about the catallaxy is that, as a spontaneous order, its orderliness does *not* rest on its orientation on a single hierarchy of ends, and that, therefore, it will *not* secure that for it as a whole the more important comes before the less important. This is the chief cause of its condemnation by its opponents, and it could be said that most of the socialist demands amount to nothing less than that the catallaxy should be turned into an economy proper (i.e., the purposeless spontaneous order into a purpose-oriented organization) in order to assure that the more important be never sacrificed to the less important. The defence of the free society must therefore show that it is due to the fact that we do not enforce a unitary scale of concrete ends, nor attempt to secure that some particular view about what is more and what is less important governs the whole of society, that the members of such a free society have as good a chance successfully to use their individual knowledge for the achievement of their individual purposes as they in fact have.

18. The extension of an order of peace beyond the small purpose-oriented organization became thus possible by the extension of purpose-independent ('formal') rules of just conduct to the relations with other men who did not pursue the same concrete ends or hold the same values except those abstract rules—rules which did not impose obligations for particular actions (which always presuppose a concrete end) but consisted solely in prohibitions from infringing the protected domain of each which these rules enable us to determine. Liberalism is therefore inseparable from the institution

of private property which is the name we usually give to the material part of this protected individual domain.

19. But if liberalism presupposes the enforcement of rules of just conduct and expects a desirable spontaneous order to form itself only if appropriate rules of just conduct are in fact observed, it also wants to restrict the *coercive* powers of government to the enforcement of such rules of just conduct, including at least one prescribing a positive duty, namely, the rule requiring citizens to contribute according to uniform principles not only to the cost of enforcing those rules but also to the costs of the non-coercive service functions of government which we shall presently consider. Liberalism is therefore the same as the demand for the rule of law in the classical sense of the term according to which the coercive functions of government are strictly limited to the enforcement of uniform rules of law, meaning uniform rules of just conduct towards one's fellows. (The 'rule of law' corresponds here to what in German is called *materieller Rechtsstaat* as distinguished from the mere *formelle Rechtsstaat* which requires only that each act of government is authorized by legislation, whether such a law consists of a general rule of just conduct or not.)

20. Liberalism recognizes that there are certain other services which for various reasons the spontaneous forces of the market may not produce or may not produce adequately, and that for this reason it is desirable to put at the disposal of government a clearly circumscribed body of resources with which it can render such services to the citizens in general. This requires a sharp distinction between the coercive powers of government, in which its actions are strictly limited to the enforcement of rules of just conduct and in the exercise of which all discretion is excluded, and the provision of services by government, for which it can use only the resources put at its disposal for this purpose, has no coercive power or monopoly, but in the use of which resources it enjoys wide discretion.

21. It is significant that such a conception of a liberal order has arisen only in countries in which, in ancient Greece and Rome no less than in modern Britain, justice was conceived as something to be discovered by the efforts of judges or scholars and not as determined by the arbitrary will of any authority; that it always had difficulty in taking roots in countries in which law was conceived primarily as the product of deliberate legislation, and that it has everywhere declined under the joint influence of legal positivism and of democratic doctrine, both of which know no other criterion of justice than the will of the legislator.

22. Liberalism has indeed inherited from the theories of the common law and from the older (pre-rationalist) theories of the law of nature, and also presupposes, a conception of justice which allows us to distinguish between such rules of just individual conduct as are implied in the conception of the 'rule of law' and are required for the formation of a spontaneous order on the one hand, and all the particular commands issued by authority for the

purpose of organization on the other. This essential distinction has been made explicit in the legal theories of two of the greatest philosophers of modern times, David Hume and Immanuel Kant, but has not been adequately restated since and is wholly uncongenial to the governing legal theories of our day.

23. The essential points of this conception of justice are (a) that justice can be meaningfully attributed only to human action and not to any state of affairs as such without reference to the question whether it has been, or could have been, deliberately brought about by somebody; (b) that the rules of justice have essentially the nature of prohibitions, or, in other words, that injustice is really the primary concept and the aim of rules of just conduct is to prevent unjust action; (c) that the injustice to be prevented is the infringement of the protected domain of one's fellow men, a domain which is to be ascertained by means of these rules of justice; and (d) that these rules of just conduct which are in themselves negative can be developed by consistently applying to whatever such rules a society has inherited the equally negative test of universal applicability—a test which, in the last resort, is nothing else than the self-consistency of the actions which these rules allow if applied to the circumstances of the real world. These four crucial points must be developed further in the following paragraphs.

24. *Ad(a)*: Rules of just conduct can require the individual to take into account in his decisions only such consequences of his actions as he himself can foresee. The concrete results of the catallaxy for particular people are, however, essentially unpredictable; and since they are not the effect of anyone's design or intentions, it is meaningless to describe the manner in which the market distributed the good things of this world among particular people as just or unjust. This, however, is what the so-called 'social' or 'distributive' justice aims at in the name of which the liberal order of law is progressively destroyed. We shall later see that no test or criteria have been found or can be found by which such rules of 'social justice' can be assessed, and that, in consequence, and in contrast to the rules of just conduct, they would have to be determined by the arbitrary will of the holders of power.

25. *Ad(b)*: No particular human action is fully determined without a concrete purpose it is meant to achieve. Free men who are to be allowed to use their own means and their own knowledge for their own purposes must therefore not be subject to rules which tell them what they must positively do, but only to rules which tell them what they must not do; except for the discharge of obligations an individual has voluntarily incurred, the rules of just conduct thus merely delimit the range of permissible actions but do not determine the particular actions a man must take at a particular moment. (There are certain rare exceptions to this, like actions to save or protect life, prevent catastrophes, and the like, where either rules of justice actually do require, or would at least generally be accepted as just rules if they required, some positive action. It would lead far to discuss here the position of such rules in the system.) The generally negative character of the rules of just conduct, and the corresponding primacy of the injustice which is prohibited,

has often been noticed but scarcely ever been thought through to its logical consequences.

26. *Ad(c)*: The injustice which is prohibited by rules of just conduct is any encroachment on the protected domain of other individuals, and they must therefore enable us to ascertain what is the protected sphere of others. Since the time of John Locke it is customary to describe this protected domain as property (which Locke himself had defined as 'the life, liberty, and possessions of a man'). This term suggests, however, a much too narrow and purely material conception of the protected domain which includes not only material goods but also various claims on others and certain expectations. If the concept of property is, however, (with Locke) interpreted in this wide sense, it is true that law, in the sense of rules of justice, and the institution of property are inseparable.

27. *Ad(d)*: It is impossible to decide about the justice of any one particular rule of just conduct except within the framework of a whole system of such rules, most of which must for this purpose be regarded as unquestioned: values can always be tested only in terms of other values. The test of the justice of a rule is usually (since Kant) described as that of its 'universalizability', i.e., of the possibility of willing that the rules should be applied to all instances that correspond to the conditions stated in it (the 'categorical imperative'). What this amounts to is that in applying it to any concrete circumstances it will not conflict with any other accepted rules. The test is thus in the last resort one of the compatibility or non-contradictoriness of the whole system of rules, not merely in a logical sense but in the sense that the system of actions which the rules permit will not lead to conflict.

28. It will be noticed that only purpose-independent ('formal') rules pass this test because, as rules which have originally been developed in small, purpose-connected groups ('organizations') are progressively extended to larger and larger groups and finally universalized to apply to the relations between any members of an Open Society who have no concrete purposes in common and merely submit to the same abstract rules, they will in this process have to shed all references to particular purposes.

29. The growth from the tribal organization, all of whose members served common purposes, to the spontaneous order of the Open Society in which people are allowed to pursue their own purposes in peace, may thus be said to have commenced when for the first time a savage placed some goods at the boundary of his tribe in the hope that some member of another tribe would find them and leave in turn behind some other goods to secure the repetition of the offer. From the first establishment of such a practice which served reciprocal but not common purposes, a process has been going on for millennia which, by making rules of conduct independent of the particular purposes of those concerned, made it possible to extend these rules to ever wider circles of undetermined persons and eventually might make possible a universal peaceful order of the world.

30. The character of those universal rules of just individual conduct,

which liberalism presupposes and wishes to improve as much as possible, has been obscured by confusion with that other part of law which determines the organization of government and guides it in the administration of the resources placed at its disposal. It is a characteristic of liberal society that the private individual can be coerced to obey only the rules of private and criminal law; and the progressive permeation of private law by public law in the course of the last eighty or hundred years, which means a progressive replacement of rules of conduct by rules of organization, is one of the main ways in which the destruction of the liberal order has been effected. A German scholar (Franz Böhm) has for this reason recently described the liberal order very justly as the private law society.

31. The difference between the order at which the rules of conduct of private and criminal law aim, and the order at which the rules of organization of public law aim, comes out most clearly if we consider that rules of conduct will determine an order of action only in combination with the particular knowledge and aims of the acting individuals, while the rules of organization of public law determine directly such concrete action in the light of particular purposes, or, rather, give some authority power to do so. The confusion between rules of conduct and rules of organization has been assisted by an erroneous identification of what is often called the 'order of law' with the order of actions, which in a free system is not fully determined by the system of laws but merely presupposes such system of laws as one of the conditions required for its formation. Not every system of rules of conduct which secures uniformity of action (which is how the 'order of law' is frequently interpreted) will, however, secure an order of action in the sense that the actions permitted by the rules will not conflict.

32. The progressive displacement of the rules of conduct of private and criminal law by a conception derived from public law is the process by which existing liberal societies are progressively transformed into totalitarian societies. This tendency has been most explicitly seen and supported by Adolf Hitler's 'crown jurist' Carl Schmitt who consistently advocated the replacement of the 'normative' thinking of liberal law by a conception of law which regards as its purpose the 'concrete order formation'.

33. Historically this development has become possible as a result of the fact that the same representative assemblies have been charged with the two different tasks of laying down rules of individual conduct and laying down rules and giving orders concerning the organization and conduct of government. The consequence of this has been that the term 'law' itself, which in the older conception of the 'rule of law' had meant only rules of conduct equally applicable to all, came to mean any rule of organization or even any particular command approved by the constitutionally appointed legislature. Such a conception of the rule of law which merely demands that a command be legitimately issued and not that it be a rule of justice equally applicable to all (what the Germans call the merely *formelle Rechtsstaat*), of course no longer provides any protection of individual freedom.

34. If it was the nature of the constitutional arrangements prevailing in all Western democracies which made this development possible, the driving force which guided it in the particular direction was the growing recognition that the application of uniform or equal rules to the conduct of individuals who were in fact very different in many respects, inevitably produced very different results for the different individuals; and that in order to bring about by government action a reduction in these unintended but inevitable differences in the material position of different people, it would be necessary to treat them not according to the same but according to different rules. This gave rise to a new and altogether different conception of justice, namely that usually described as 'social' or 'distributive' justice, a conception of justice which did not confine itself to rules of conduct for the individual but aimed at particular results for particular people, and which therefore could be achieved only in a purpose-governed organization but not in a purpose-independent spontaneous order.

35. The concepts of a 'just price', a 'just remuneration' or a 'just distribution of incomes' are of course very old; it deserves notice, however, that in the course of the efforts of two thousand years in which philosophers have speculated about the meaning of these concepts, not a single rule has been discovered which would allow us to determine what is in this sense just in a market order. Indeed the one group of scholars which have most persistently pursued the question, the schoolmen of the later middle ages and early modern times, were finally driven to define the just price or wage as that price or wage which would form itself on a market in the absence of fraud, violence or privilege—thus referring back to the rules of just conduct and accepting as a just result whatever was brought about by the just conduct of all individuals concerned. This negative conclusion of all the speculations about 'social' or 'distributive' justice was, as we shall see, inevitable, because a just remuneration or distribution has meaning only within an organization whose members act under command in the service of a common system of ends, but can have no meaning whatever in a catallaxy or spontaneous order which can have no such common system of ends.

36. A state of affairs as such, as we have seen, cannot be just or unjust as a mere fact. Only in so far as it has been brought about designedly or could be so brought about does it make sense to call just or unjust the actions of those who have created it or permitted it to arise. In the catallaxy, the spontaneous order of the market, nobody can foresee, however, what each participant will get, and the results for particular people are not determined by anyone's intentions; nor is anyone responsible for particular people getting particular things. We might therefore question whether a deliberate choice of the market order as the method for guiding economic activities, with the unpredictable and in a great measure chance incidence of its benefits, is a just decision, but certainly not whether, once we have decided to avail ourselves of the catallaxy for that purpose, the particular results it produces for particular people are just or unjust.

37. That the concept of justice is nevertheless so commonly and readily applied to the distribution of incomes is entirely the effect of an erroneous anthropomorphic interpretation of society as an organization rather than as a spontaneous order. The term 'distribution' is in this sense quite as misleading as the term 'economy', since it also suggests that something is the result of deliberate action which in fact is the result of spontaneous ordering forces. Nobody distributes income in a market order (as would have to be done in an organization) and to speak, with respect to the former, of a just or unjust distribution is therefore simple nonsense. It would be less misleading to speak in this respect of a 'dispersion' rather than a 'distribution' of incomes.

38. All endeavours to secure a 'just' distribution must thus be directed towards turning the spontaneous order of the market into an organization or, in other words, into a totalitarian order. It was this striving after a new conception of justice which produced the various steps by which rules of organization ('public law'), which were designed to make people aim at particular results, came to supersede the purpose-independent rules of just individual conduct, and which thereby gradually destroyed the foundations on which a spontaneous order must rest.

39. The ideal of using the coercive powers of government to achieve 'positive' (i.e., social or distributive) justice leads, however, not only necessarily to the destruction of individual freedom, which some might not think too high a price, but it also proves on examination a mirage or an illusion which cannot be achieved in any circumstances, because it presupposes an agreement on the relative importance of the different concrete ends which cannot exist in a great society whose members do not know each other or the same particular facts. It is sometimes believed that the fact that most people today desire social justice demonstrates that this ideal has a determinable content. But it is unfortunately only too possible to chase a mirage, and the consequence of this is always that the result of one's striving will be utterly different from what one had intended.

40. There can be no rules which determine how much everybody 'ought' to have unless we make some unitary conception of relative 'merits' or 'needs' of the different individuals, for which there exists no objective measure, the basis of a central allocation of all goods and services—which would make it necessary that each individual, instead of using *his* knowledge for *his* purposes, were made to fulfil a duty imposed upon him by somebody else, and were remunerated according to how well he has, in the opinion of others, performed this duty. This is the method of remuneration appropriate to a closed organization, such as an army, but irreconcilable with the forces which maintain a spontaneous order.

41. It ought to be freely admitted that the market order does not bring about any close correspondence between subjective merit or individual needs and rewards. It operates on the principle of a combined game of skill and chance in which the results for each individual may be as much determined by circumstances wholly beyond his control as by his skill or effort. Each is

remunerated according to the value his particular services have to the particular people to whom he renders them, and this value of his services stands in no necessary relation to anything which we could appropriately call his merits and still less to his needs.

42. It deserves special emphasis that, strictly speaking, it is meaningless to speak of a value 'to society' when what is in question is the value of some services to certain people, services which may be of no interest to anybody else. A violin virtuoso presumably renders services to entirely different people from those whom a football star entertains, and the maker of pipes altogether different people from the maker of perfumes. The whole conception of a 'value to society' is in a free order as illegitimate an anthropomorphic term as its description as 'one economy' in the strict sense, as an entity which 'treats' people justly or unjustly, or 'distributes' among them. The results of the market process for particular individuals are neither the result of anybody's will that they should have so much, nor even foreseeable by those who have decided upon or support the maintenance of this kind of order.

43. Of all the complaints about the injustice of the results of the market order the one which appears to have had the greatest effect on actual policy, and to have produced a progressive destruction of the equal rules of just conduct and their replacement by a 'social' law aiming at 'social justice', however, was not the extent of the inequality of the rewards, nor their disproportion with recognizable merits, needs, efforts, pains incurred, or whatever else has been chiefly stressed by social philosophers, but the demands for protection against an undeserved descent from an already achieved position. More than by anything else the market order has been distorted by efforts to protect groups from a decline from their former position; and when government interference is demanded in the name of 'social justice' this now means, more often than not, the demand for the protection of the existing relative position of some group. 'Social justice' has thus become little more than a demand for the protection of vested interests and the creation of new privilege, such as when in the name of social justice the farmer is assured 'parity' with the industrial worker.

44. The important facts to be stressed here are that the positions thus protected were the result of the same sort of forces as those which now reduce the relative position of the same people, that their position for which they now demand protection was no more deserved or earned than the diminished position now in prospect for them, and that their former position could in the changed position be secured to them only by denying to others the same chances of ascent to which they owed their former position. In a market order the fact that a group of persons has achieved a certain relative position cannot give them a claim in justice to maintain it, because this cannot be defended by a rule which could be equally applied to all.

45. The aim of economic policy of a free society can therefore never be to assure particular results to particular people, and its success cannot be measured by any attempt at adding up the value of such particular results. In

this respect the aim of what is called 'welfare economics' is fundamentally mistaken, not only because no meaningful sum can be formed of the satisfactions provided for different people, but because its basic idea of a maximum of need-fulfilment (or a maximum social product) is appropriate only to an economy proper which serves a single hierarchy of ends, but not to the spontaneous order of a catallaxy which has no common concrete ends.

46. Though it is widely believed that the conception of an optimal economic policy (or any judgment whether one economic policy is better than another) presupposes such a conception of maximizing aggregate real social income (which is possible only in value terms and therefore implies an illegitimate comparison of the utility to different persons), this is in fact not so. An optimal policy in a catallaxy may aim, and ought to aim, at increasing the chances of any member of society taken at random of having a high income, or, what amounts to the same thing, the chance that, whatever his share in total income may be, the real equivalent of this share will be as large as we know how to make it.

47. This condition will be approached as closely as we can manage, irrespective of the dispersion of incomes, if everything which is produced is being produced by persons or organizations who can produce it more cheaply than (or at least as cheaply as) anybody who does not produce it, and is sold at a price lower than that at which it would be possible to offer it for anybody who does not in fact so offer it. (This allows for persons or organizations to whom the costs of producing one commodity or service are lower than they are for those who actually produce it and who still produce something else instead, because their comparative advantage in that other production is still greater; in this case the total costs of their producing the first commodity would have to include the loss of the one which is not produced.)

48. It will be noticed that this optimum does not presuppose what economic theory calls 'perfect competition' but only that there are no obstacles to the entry into each trade and that the market functions adequately in spreading information about opportunities. It should also be specially observed that this modest and achievable goal has never yet been fully achieved because at all times and everywhere governments have both restricted access to some occupations and tolerated persons and organizations deterring others from entering occupations when this would have been to the advantage of the latter.

49. This optimum position means that as much will be produced of whatever combination of products and services is in fact produced as can be produced by any method that we know, because we can through such a use of the market mechanism bring more of the dispersed knowledge of the members of society into play than by any other. But it will be achieved only if we leave the share in the total, which each member will get, to be determined by the market mechanism and all its accidents, because it is only through the market determination of incomes that each is led to do what this result requires.

50. We owe, in other words, our chances that our unpredictable share

in the total product of society represents as large an aggregate of goods and services as it does to the fact that thousands of others constantly submit to the adjustments which the market forces on them; and it is consequently also our duty to accept the same kind of changes in our income and position, even if it means a decline in our accustomed position and is due to circumstances we could not have foreseen and for which we are not responsible. The conception that we have 'earned' (in the sense of morally deserved) the income we had when we were more fortunate, and that we are therefore entitled to it so long as we strive as honestly as before and had no warning to turn elsewhere, is wholly mistaken. Everybody, rich or poor, owes his income to the outcome of a mixed game of skill and chance, the aggregate result of which and the shares in which are as high as they are only because we have agreed to play that game. And once we have agreed to play the game and profited from its results, it is a moral obligation on us to abide by the results even if they turn against us.

51. There can be little doubt that in modern society all but the most unfortunate and those who in a different kind of society might have enjoyed a legal privilege, owe to the adoption of that method an income much larger than they could otherwise enjoy. There is of course no reason why a society which, thanks to the market, is as rich as modern society should not provide *outside the market* a minimum security for all who in the market fall below a certain standard. Our point was merely that considerations of justice provide no justification for 'correcting' the results of the market and that justice, in the sense of treatment under the same rules, requires that each takes what a market provides in which every participant behaves fairly. There is only a justice of individual conduct but not a separate 'social justice'.

52. We cannot consider here the legitimate tasks of government in the administration of the resources placed at its disposal for the rendering of services to the citizens. With regard to these functions, for the discharge of which the government is given money, we will here only say that in exercising them government should be under the same rules as every private citizen, that it should possess no monopoly for a particular service of the kind, that it should discharge these functions in such a manner as not to disturb the much more comprehensive spontaneously ordered efforts of society, and that the means should be raised according to a rule which applies uniformly to all. (This, in my opinion, precludes an overall progression of the burden of taxation of the individuals, since such a use of taxation for purposes of redistribution could be justified only by such arguments as we have just excluded.) In the remaining paragraphs we shall be concerned only with some of the functions of government for the discharge of which it is given not merely money but power to enforce rules of private conduct.

53. The only part of these coercive functions of government which we can further consider in this outline are those which are concerned with the preservation of a functioning market order. They concern primarily the conditions which must be provided by law to secure the degree of competition

required to steer the market efficiently. We shall briefly consider this question first with regard to enterprise and then with regard to labour.

54. With regard to enterprise the first point which needs underlining is that it is more important that government refrain from assisting monopolies than that it combat monopoly. If today the market order is confined only to a part of the economic activities of men, this is largely the result of deliberate government restrictions of competition. It is indeed doubtful whether, if government consistently refrained from creating monopolies and from assisting them through protective tariffs and the character of the law of patents for inventions and of the law of corporations, there would remain an element of monopoly significant enough to require special measures. What must be chiefly remembered in this connection is, firstly, that monopolistic positions are always undesirable but often unavoidable for objective reasons which we cannot or do not wish to alter; and, secondly, that all government-supervised monopolies tend to become government-protected monopolies which will persist when their justification has disappeared.

55. Current conceptions of anti-monopoly policy are largely misguided by the application of certain conceptions developed by the theory of perfect competition which are irrelevant to conditions where the factual presuppositions of the theory of perfect competition are absent. The theory of perfect competition shows that if on a market the number of buyers and sellers is sufficiently large to make it impossible for any one of them deliberately to influence prices, such quantities will be sold at prices which will equal marginal costs. This does not mean, however, that it is either possible or even necessarily desirable everywhere to bring about a state of affairs where large numbers buy and sell the same uniform commodity. The idea that in situations where we cannot, or do not wish to, bring about such a state, the producers should be held to conduct themselves as if perfect competition existed, or to sell at a price which would rule under perfect competition, is meaningless, because we do not know what would be the particular conduct required, or the price which would be formed, if perfect competition existed.

56. Where the conditions for perfect competition do not exist, what competition still can and ought to be made to achieve is nevertheless very remarkable and important, namely the conditions described in paragraphs 46–49 above. It was pointed out then that this state will tend to be approached if nobody can be prevented by government or others to enter any trade or occupation he desired.

57. This condition would, I believe, be approached as closely as it is possible to secure this if, *firstly,* all agreements to restrain trade were without exception (not prohibited, but merely) made void and unenforceable, and, *secondly,* all discriminatory or other aimed actions towards an actual or potential competitor intended to make him observe certain rules of market conduct were to make him liable for multiple damages. It seems to me that such a modest aim would produce a much more effective law than actual prohibitions under penalties, because no exceptions need to be made from such a declara-

tion as invalid or unenforceable of all contracts in restraint of trade, while, as experience has shown, the more ambitious attempts are bound to be qualified by so many exceptions as to make them much less effective.

58. The application of this same principle that all agreements in restraint of trade should be invalid and unenforceable and that every individual should be protected against all attempts to enforce them by violence or aimed discrimination, is even more important with regard to labour. The monopolistic practices which threaten the functioning of the market are today much more serious on the side of labour than on the side of enterprise, and the preservation of the market order will depend, more than on anything else, on whether we succeed in curbing the latter.

59. The reason for this is that the developments in this field are bound to force government, and are already forcing many governments, into two kinds of measures which are wholly destructive of the market order: attempts authoritatively to determine the appropriate incomes of the various groups (by what is called an 'incomes policy') and efforts to overcome the wage 'rigidities' by an inflationary monetary policy. But since this evasion of the real issue by only temporarily effective monetary means must have the effect that those 'rigidities' will constantly increase, they are a mere palliative which can only postpone but not solve the central problem.

60. Monetary and financial policy is outside the scope of this paper. Its problems were mentioned only to point out that its fundamental and in the present situation insoluble dilemmas cannot be solved by any monetary means but only by a restoration of the market as an effective instrument for determining wages.

61. In conclusion, the basic principles of a liberal society may be summed up by saying that in such a society all coercive functions of government must be guided by the overruling importance of what I like to call THE THREE GREAT NEGATIVES: PEACE, JUSTICE AND LIBERTY. Their achievement requires that in its coercive functions government shall be confined to the enforcement of such prohibitions (stated as abstract rules) as can be equally applied to all, and to exacting under the same uniform rules from all a share of the costs of the other, noncoercive services it may decide to render to the citizens with the material and personal means thereby placed at its disposal.

6

The Organic
Theory of Society
and Marxism

*Readings: Karl Marx, "Alienation and
Its Overcoming in Communism"
Steven Lukes, "Alienation and Anomie"*

"It is not the consciousness of men that determines their social being but
rather their social being that determines their consciousness." This famous
statement by Marx may be viewed as a total repudiation of the whole way
of thinking that lies behind the social and political theory (represented in this
book by Hobbes, for example) of individualistic contractarianism. For Marx is
here expressing his commitment to what is generally called an organic conception of the relation between man and society, a conception wherein man
is *defined* as a social and political animal. Men are to be understood as related to each other in society, not as random members of an aggregate collection, but rather as internally related parts of an organism.

To understand this point, we might recall Hobbes's fundamental outlook.
Hobbes argued that one does political theory by first examining the nature of
man as he is in atomistic isolation from his fellows and from any form of
social institutions. Once we have discovered this nature (Hobbes regarded
it as selfish and competitive), we may then design a society and government
as a kind of *machine* that will best serve man's natural purposes. The view
is a mechanical rather than an organic model of man's relation to society.

Organic theorists reject this conception entirely. They argue that the qualities the individualist attributes to man as natural are in fact derived from man as he has been observed in a particular social setting—that is, as a product of a certain kind of education and general conditioning. Thus Marx argues that man is not naturally selfish and competitive but is rather *taught* to be so and (since it is a condition for his very survival) *reinforced* to be so only in capitalistic society. Man is naturally (before corruption by certain institutions) a *species being*—that is, a being bound up with his fellows in relations of sympathy, respect, and mutual aid. To drive this general point home, the organic theorist enjoys noting that an individualist such as Hobbes argues that men enter society (that is, create institutions and laws) by making a *contract* to do so. Hobbes argues in this way without seeming to notice that the concept of a contract can only be understood within, and not prior to, a context of institutional rules.

This general outlook generates great optimism in much organic political theory. Hobbes, constructing his theory on the least favorable set of assumptions about man, plans for the worst and constructs the terrible leviathan of sovereignty. Many (although by no means all) organic theorists, however, do not suppose that man will necessarily remain as we now find him; there is hope for change and improvement. If man is greedy and competitive, this may be due to the character of the society in which he was brought up. If we could then radically restructure society, we might have a chance of educating and improving men thereby.[1]

This general conception of social and political philosophy was first anticipated by Plato and Aristotle and was given its most powerful modern formulation by Rousseau, Feuerbach, and Hegel. Marx, however, by coupling the theory with certain empirical scientific claims in economics and sociology, was able to mold this tradition into a powerful philosophical and political movement.

The selections from Marx in this chapter are drawn from his early (1844) manuscripts on the concept of *alienation*. According to Marx, men and the societies in which they live are at their worst if their relationships are alienated. And note well that alienation is a property, not of men themselves, but of their *relationships*. Thus unlike Hobbes (who regarded individual pain and death as the worst things imaginable), Marx describes the basic social pathology with a concept that cannot even be understood except insofar as man is regarded as a social being, for alienation is a defect, not of men *simpliciter*, but of their social relationships.

What is alienation? A relationship (say between a man and his children) can be regarded as alienated if (1) it involves *estrangement* or *separation,* (2) those estranged feel *powerless* to overcome their estrangement, and (3) the estrangement is to be viewed as a *defect,* as in some sense undesirable or

---

[1] One strong form of the organic theory, sometimes called *collectivism,* holds that man's only function is to serve the state. This unattractive fascistic view is often attributed to Marx by militant anti-Communists but all textual evidence is against his ever having held it.

unnatural. Thus a voluntary divorce between a couple involves estrangement but may not be alienated since it may not satisfy conditions (2) and (3). The separation of inability to communicate between a man and his dog is a separation the dog and the man are powerless to overcome, but it is not alienation because it fails to satisfy condition (3)—noncommunication between men and animals being perfectly normal and not viewed as a defect. However, a father and son who are estranged through lack of communication and who lack the resources to overcome the estrangement can be regarded as alienated from each other since such a relationship is defective—that is, not a fitting or proper or desirable relation between members of a family.

Now what is of primary interest to Marx is alienation of *labor*—that is, the various ways a worker can be alienated (from his product, his work, himself, and other men) in the context of economic production. Marx tends to believe that all forms of human alienation are at root a function of the alienation of labor (a facet of his economic determinism) and that this pathology arises only in capitalistic societies whose economic systems rest on the market theory of value, the division of labor, private property, and money. And this belief provides the background for his later (and certainly more famous) writings on revolution, for Marx (as a part of his so-called "union of theory and practice") believes that the findings of social science are relevant to political philosophy—even to the evaluative or normative aspect. Since alienation is the worst state of social relations possible (an evaluative claim), and since capitalism causes alienation (an empirical scientific claim), man has only one hope: a revolution that will overthrow the system of bourgeois capitalism and replace it with a social system that will eliminate greed and competition and thereby rehumanize mankind, a social system wherein man's true individuality and creativity will often be expressed with and through his fellows and never at their expense. Communist revolutions have often been rationalized by such an argument, and so it is interesting to note the abysmal failure of at least many of them in ending even economic alienation—not to mention other forms of human alienation. The important question here, of course, is the following: Does this show that Marx is wrong or rather that what often passes for Marxism or communism has little to do with what Marx had in mind? (In this regard, it is perhaps worth noting that near the end of his life Marx denied he was a Marxist.) This point is mentioned only to help the student avoid what is in America one common but silly line of reasoning—since Soviet Russia has a society that is something less than wonderful, and since Soviet Russia calls itself Marxist, it follows that Marx is a man with nothing to teach us. One might as well reason from the defects in American democracy that there is nothing to learn from such writers as Locke, Jefferson, and Mill; or that, since authority can be abused, Hobbes has nothing to tell us about the values of political authority.

Marx's general outlook on the relation of man and society was developed (and elaborated on by later writers, such as Herbert Marcuse whom you will read in Chapter 10) into a critique of the liberal idea of freedom or liberty. According to the Marxist interpretation of traditional liberalism, one is free to the extent that one has the opportunity of getting one's needs and desires (wants) satisfied. However, Marxists are inclined to call this an illusory "bourgeois freedom," for many of these needs and desires, they will argue, are *artificial* (constituting what Marx called the "fetishism of commodities"). They have been conditioned into people by a particular repressive social system to make members of that system pliant and cooperative. (A crude example: A Marxist might claim that if a worker is given a color television and an automobile, he is likely to stop noticing that his routine job is dehumanizing.) This idea has perhaps been overdone in recent radical writing, but perhaps there is something in it worth taking seriously and thinking about. At any rate, the present chapter will provide useful background for the later consideration of Marcuse.[2]

In the closing article, Steven Lukes analyzes the concept of alienation in great detail and contrasts it with Émile Durkheim's concept of *anomie.* According to Durkheim, individuals experience anomie (a condition of extreme free-floating anxiety and dread over the awesome responsibilities that freedom involves) when social alienation (particularly that resulting from the division of labor) is absent. Thus perhaps alienation is in some sense a good thing. Lukes tries to sort out the status of the various claims in Marx and Durkheim (for example, which are empirical, which are conceptual, and which are evaluative) and tries to deal with the question of how, if at all, one may rationally choose between competing theories of this nature.

Suggestions for Further Reading

Shlomo Avineri, *The Social and Political Thought of Karl Marx* (Cambridge: Cambridge University Press, 1968).

Émile Durkheim, *Suicide: A Study in Sociology,* ed. George Simpson (Glencoe, Ill.: The Free Press, 1951).

Émile Durkheim, *Division of Labor,* ed. George Simpson (Glencoe, Ill.: The Free Press, 1933).

Bertell Ollmann, *Alienation: Marx's Conception of Man in Capitalist Society* (Cambridge: Cambridge University Press, 1971).

Richard Schacht, *Alienation* (Garden City, N.Y.: Doubleday, 1970).

Peter Winch, "Man and Society in Hobbes and Rousseau," in *Hobbes and Rousseau,* ed. Maurice Cranston and Richard S. Peters (Garden City, N.Y.: Doubleday Anchor, 1972).

---

[2] There is a danger, of course, that the hasty use of such concepts as "bourgeois freedom" will result in throwing out much that had value in the bourgeois revolution—for example, the attempt to limit by law the power of rulers. Without some such notion as the "rule of law," it is difficult to provide a theoretical apparatus for the opposition of Stalinism.

Alienation and Its
Overcoming in Communism
Karl Marx

Marx's now widely known *Economic and Philosophical Manuscripts,* written in Paris in 1844, were never intended for publication. Here he developed his first detailed analysis of the processes of estrangement and alienation characteristic of bourgeois society and capitalist production.

Beginning with the presuppositions of the political economists, Marx examined first the alienated condition of the laborers as seen in (1) their relation to the product of their activity; (2) the process of labor itself; (3) the relation of the laborer to nature; (4) the relation of man to man; and (5) their relation to the human potential for freedom and creation. The basis of this condition Marx located in the private property relationship characterized by the reduction of human activity to wage labor as merely one commodity among others. That is, this represents the nearly total dehumanization of the laborer.

In response to this negation of the potentialities of humanity, Marx examines Communism as a proposed solution to this alienation, distinguishing carefully between "vulgar" Communism (determined by the abstract negation of private property and thus still under its sway) and positive Communism, the "real appropriation of human nature through and for man." He discusses the historical basis of Communism and envisions positive Communism as being quite other than a merely utopian dream. It is, rather, to be realized in history through the revolutionary action of the proletariat.

He also examines the foundation of the capitalist process of production in the division of labor and in the social process of exchange characterized and facilitated by money, the (im)moral implications of which Marx sees in what he terms its "fetish" character. This is to claim that in bourgeois society the traditional values have all been debased and replaced by the simple lust for money.

From *Karl Marx: The Essential Writings,* edited by Frederic L. Bender. Compilation and introductory remarks copyright 1972 by Frederic L. Bender. Reprinted by permission of Harper & Row, Publishers. Copyrighted translations of the various sections have also been used by permission, and proper citations may be found on the first page of each section. Karl Marx (1818–1883) made important contributions to philosophy, sociology, and economic theory. He is generally regarded as the philosophical founder of Communism. His best known writings are *Capital* (Vol. I, 1867 and 1873; Vol. II, 1885; and Vol. III, 1894) and (with Friedrich Engels) *The Communist Manifesto* (1848). For secondary reading, see *Alienation: Marx's Conception of Man in Capitalist Society* by Bertell Ollmann (Cambridge: Cambridge University Press, 1971).

The selections are taken from Marx's manuscripts of 1844, most from the so-called Economic and Philosophical Manuscripts first edited by D. Riazanov in 1932, and the concluding selection of "Truly Human Production" from Marx's notes on James Mill's *Treatise on Political Economy*.

Alienated Labor[1]

The first of the *Economic and Philosophical Manuscripts,* from which this selection is taken, is entitled "Alienated Labor." We see Marx's first expression of the concept which forms the cornerstone of his subsequent critique of the capitalist production process and of the bourgeois political economy which remains within its orbit: political economy is unable to detach itself from acquiescence in the alienation of labor which forms the basis of capitalistic enterprise. The selection portrays the important shift from a discussion of political problems to the more fundamental level of labor (= human activity), as well as Marx's newly developed concern with matters of *Praxis* (activity) in addition to philosophy and political theory.

We have begun from the presuppositions of political economy. We have accepted its terminology and its laws. We presupposed private property, the separation of labor, capital and land, as also of wages, profit and rent, the division of labor, competition, the concept of exchange value, etc. From political economy itself, in its own words, we have shown that the worker sinks to the level of a commodity, and to a most miserable commodity; that the misery of the worker increases with the power and volume of his production; that the necessary result of competition is the accumulation of capital in a few hands, and thus a restoration of monopoly in a more terrible form; and finally that the distinction between capitalist and landlord, and between agricultural laborer and industrial worker, must disappear and the whole of society divide into the two classes of property *owners* and propertyless *workers*.

Political economy begins with the fact of private property; it does not explain it. It conceives the *material process* of private property, as this occurs in reality, in general and abstract formulas which then serve it as laws. It does not *comprehend* these laws; that is, it does not show how they arise out of the nature of private property. Political economy provides no explanation of the basis of the distinction of labor from capital, of capital from land. When, for example, the relation of wages to profits is defined, this is explained in terms of the interests of capitalists; in other words, what should be explained is assumed. Similarly, competition is referred to at every point and is explained in terms of external conditions. Political economy tells us

---

[1] From *Marx's Concept of Man,* ed. by Erich Fromm, trans. by T. B. Bottomore (London: C. A. Watts & Co. Ltd., 1961). Reprinted by permission.

nothing about the extent to which these external and apparently accidental conditions are simply the expression of a necessary development. We have seen how exchange itself seems an accidental fact. The only moving forces which political economy recognizes are *avarice* and the *war between the avaricious, competition.* . . .

Thus we have now to grasp the real connection between this whole system of alienation—private property, acquisitiveness, the separation of labor, capital and land, exchange and competition, value and the devaluation of man, monopoly and competition—and the system of *money.*

Let us not begin our explanation, as does the economist, from a legendary primordial condition. Such a primordial condition does not explain anything; it merely removes the question into a gray and nebulous distance. It asserts as a fact or event what it should deduce, namely, the necessary relation between two things; for example, between the division of labor and exchange. . . .

We shall begin from a *contemporary* economic fact. The worker becomes poorer the more wealth he produces and the more his production increases in power and extent. The worker becomes an ever cheaper commodity the more goods he creates. The *devaluation* of the human world increases in direct relation with the *increase in value* of the world of things. Labor does not only create goods; it also produces itself and the worker as a *commodity,* and indeed in the same proportion as it produces goods.

This fact simply implies that the object produced by labor, its product, now stands opposed to it as an *alien* being, as a *power independent* of the producer. The product of labor is labor which has been embodied in an object and turned into a physical thing; this product is an *objectification* of labor. The performance of work is at the same time its objectification. The performance of work appears in the sphere of political economy as a *vitiation* of the worker, objectification as a *loss* and as *servitude* to the object, and appropriation as *alienation.*

So much does the performance of work appear as vitiation that the worker is vitiated to the point of starvation. So much does objectification appear as loss of the object that the worker is deprived of the most essential things not only of life but also of work. Labor itself becomes an object which he can acquire only by the greatest effort and with unpredictable interruptions. So much does the appropriation of the object appear as alienation that the more objects the worker produces the fewer he can possess and the more he falls under the domination of his product, of capital.

All these consequences follow from the fact that the worker is related to the *product of his labor* as to an *alien* object. For it is clear on this presupposition that the more the worker expends himself in work the more powerful becomes the world of objects which he creates in face of himself, the poorer he becomes in his inner life, and the less he belongs to himself. It is just the same as in religion. The more of himself man attributes to God the less he has left in himself. The worker puts his life into the object, and his life then belongs no longer to himself but to the object. The greater his activity, therefore, the less he possesses. What is embodied in the product of his labor is no longer his own. The greater this product is, therefore, the more he is diminished. The *alienation* of the worker in his product means not only that his labor becomes an object, assumes an *external* existence, but that it exists independently, *outside* himself, and alien to him, and that it stands opposed to him as an autonomous power. The life which he has given to the object sets itself against him as an alien and hostile force.

Let us now examine more closely the phenomenon of *objectification,* the worker's production and the *alienation* and *loss* of the object it produces, which is involved in it. The worker can create nothing without *nature,* without the *sensuous external world.* The latter is the material in which his labor is realized, in which it is active, out of which and through which it produces things.

But just as nature affords the *means of existence* of labor in the sense that labor cannot *live* without objects upon which it can be exercised, so also it provides the *means of existence* in a narrower sense; namely the means of physical existence for the *worker* himself. Thus, the more the worker *appropriates* the external world of sensuous nature by his labor the more he deprives himself of *means of existence,* in two respects: first, that the sensuous external world becomes progressively less an object belonging to his labor, and secondly, that it becomes progressively less a means of existence in the direct sense, a means for the physical subsistence of the worker.

In both respects, therefore, the worker becomes a slave of the object; first, in that he receives an *object of work,* i.e., receives *work,* and secondly that he receives *means of subsistence.* Thus the object enables him to exist, first as a *worker* and secondly, as a *physical subject.* The culmination of this enslavement is that he can only maintain himself as a *physical subject* so far as he is a *worker,* and that it is only as a *physical subject* that he is a worker.

(The alienation of the worker in his object is expressed as follows in the laws of political economy: the more the worker produces the less he has to consume; the more value he creates the more worthless he becomes; the more refined his product the more crude and misshapen the worker; the more civilized the product the more barbarous the worker; the more powerful the work the more feeble the worker; the more the work manifests intelligence the more the worker declines in intelligence and becomes a slave of nature.)

Political economy conceals the alienation in the nature of labor insofar as it does not examine the direct relationship between the worker (work) *and production.* Labor certainly produces marvels for the rich, but it produces privation for the worker. It produces palaces, but hovels for the worker. It produces beauty, but deformity for the worker. It replaces labor by machinery, but it casts some of the workers back into a barbarous kind of work and turns the others into machines. It produces intelligence, but also stupidity and cretinism for the workers.

The direct relationship of labor to its products is the relationship of the worker to the objects of his production. The relationship of property owners to the objects of production and to production itself is merely a *consequence* of this first relationship and confirms it. We shall consider this second aspect later.

Thus when we ask what is the important relationship of labor, we are concerned with the relationship of the *worker* to production.

So far we have considered the alienation of the worker only from one aspect; namely, *his relationship with the products of his labor.* However, alienation appears not only in the result, but also in the *process,* of *production,* within *productive activity* itself. How could the worker stand in an alien relationship to the product of his activity if he did not alienate himself in the act of production itself? The product is indeed only the *résumé* of activity, of production. Consequently, if the product of labor is alienation, production itself must be active alienation—the alienation of activity and the activity of alienation. The alienation of the object of labor merely summarizes the alienation in the work activity itself.

What constitutes the alienation of labor? First, that the work is *external* to the worker, that it is not part of his nature; and that, consequently, he does not fulfill himself in his work but denies himself, has a feeling of misery rather than well-being, does not develop freely his mental and physical energies but is physically exhausted and mentally debased. The worker therefore feels himself at home only during his leisure time, whereas to work he feels homeless. His work is not voluntary but imposed, *forced labor.* It is not the satisfaction of a need, but only a *means* for satisfying other needs. Its alien character is clearly shown by the fact that as soon as there is no physical or other compulsion it is avoided like a plague. External labor, labor in which man alienates himself, is a labor of self-sacrifice, of mortification. Finally, the external character of work for the worker is shown by the fact that it is not his own work but work for someone else, that in work he does not belong to himself but to another person. . . .

We arrive at the result that man (the worker) feels himself to be freely active only in his animal functions—eating, drinking and procreating, or at most also in his dwelling and in personal adornment—while in his human functions he is reduced to an animal. The animal becomes human and the human becomes animal.

Eating, drinking and procreating are of course also genuine human functions. But abstractly considered, apart from the environment of other human activities, and turned into final and sole ends, they are animal functions.

We have now considered the act of alienation of practical human activity, labor, from two aspects: (1) the relationship of the worker to the *product of labor* as an alien object which dominates him. This relationship is at the same time the relationship to the sensuous external world, to natural objects, as an alien and hostile world; (2) the relationship of labor to the *act of production* within *labor.* This is the relationship of the worker to his own activity as something alien and not belonging to him, activity as suffering (passivity), strength as powerlessness, creation as emasculation, the *personal* physical and mental energy of the worker, his personal life (for what is life but activity?) as an activity which is directed against himself, independent of him and not belonging to him. This is *self-alienation* as against the above-mentioned alienation of the *thing*.

We have now to infer a third characteristic of *alienated labor* from the two we have considered.

Man is a species-being not only in the sense that he makes the community (his own as well as those of other things) his object both practically and theoretically, but also (and this is simply another expression for the same thing) in the sense that he treats himself as the present, living species, as a *universal* and consequently free being.

Species-life, for man as for animals, has its physical basis in the fact that man (like animals) lives from inorganic nature, and since man is more universal than an animal so the range of inorganic nature from which he lives is more universal. Plants, animals, minerals, air, light, etc., constitute, from the theoretical aspect, a part of human consciousness as objects of natural science and art; they are man's spiritual inorganic nature, his intellectual means of life, which he must first prepare for enjoyment and perpetuation. So also, from the practical aspect they form a part of human life and activity. In practice man lives only from these natural products, whether in the form of food, heating, clothing, housing, etc. The universality of man appears in practice in the universality which makes the whole of nature into his inorganic body: (1) as a direct means of life; and equally (2) as the material object and instrument of his life activity. Nature is the *inorganic body* of man; that is to say, nature excluding the human body itself. To say that man *lives* from nature means that nature is his *body* with which he must remain in a continuous interchange in order not to die. The statement that the physical life and mental life of man, and nature, are interdependent means simply that nature is interdependent with itself, for man is a part of nature.

Since alienated labor: (1) alienates nature from man; and (2) alienates man from himself, from his own active function, his life activity; so it alienates him from the species. It makes *species-life* into a means of individual life. In the first place it alienates species-life and individual life, and secondly, it turns the latter, as an abstraction, into the purpose of the former, also in its abstract and alienated form.

For labor, *life activity, productive life,* now appear to man only as *means* for the satisfaction of a need, the need to maintain his physical existence. Productive life is, however, species-life. It is life creating life. In the type of life activity resides the whole character of a species, its species-character; and free, conscious activity is the species-character of human beings. Life itself appears only as a *means of life*.

The animal is one with its life activity. It does not distinguish the activity from itself. It is *its activity*. But man makes his life activity itself an object of his will and consciousness. He has a conscious life activity. It is not a determination with which he is completely identified. Conscious life activity distinguishes man from the life activity of animals. Only for this reason is he a species-being. Or rather, he is only a self-conscious being, i.e., his own life is an object for him, because he is a species-being. Only for this reason is his activity free activity. Alienated labor reverses the relationship, in that man because he is a self-conscious being makes his life activity, his *being,* only a means for his *existence*.

The practical construction of an *objective world,* the *manipulation* of inorganic nature, is the confirmation of man as a conscious species-being, i.e., a being who treats the species as his own being or himself as a species-being. Of course, animals also produce. They construct nests, dwellings, as in the case of bees, beavers, ants, etc. But they only produce what is strictly necessary for themselves or their young. They produce only in a single direction, while man produces universally. They produce only under the compulsion of direct physical need, while man produces when he is free from physical need and only truly produces in freedom from such need. Animals produce only themselves, while man reproduces the whole of nature. The products of animal production belong directly to their physical bodies, while man is free in face of his product. Animals construct only in accordance with the standards and needs of the species to which they belong, while man knows how to produce in accordance with the standards of every species and knows how to apply the appropriate standard to the object. Thus man constructs also in accordance with the laws of beauty.

It is just in his work upon the objective world that man really proves himself as a *species-being*. This production is his active species-life. By means of it nature appears as *his* work and his reality. The object of labor is, therefore, the *objectification of man's species-life;* for he no longer reproduces himself merely intellectually, as in consciousness, but actively and in a real sense, and he sees his own reflection in a world which he has constructed. While, therefore, alienated labor takes away the object of production from man, it also takes away his *species-life,* his real objectivity as a species-being, and changes his advantage over animals into a disadvantage in so far as his inorganic body, nature, is taken from him.

Just as alienated labor transforms free and self-directed activity into a means, so it transforms the species-life of man into a means of physical existence.

Consciousness, which man has from his species, is transformed through alienation so that species-life becomes only a means for him.

(3) Thus alienated labor turns the *species-life of man,* and also nature as his mental species-property, into an *alien* being and into a *means* for his *individual existence*. It alienates from man his own body, external nature, his mental life and his *human* life.

(4) A direct consequence of the alienation of man from the product of

his labor, from his life activity and from his species-life is that *man* is *alienated* from other *men.* When man confronts himself he also confronts *other* men. What is true of man's relationship to his work, to the product of his work and to himself, is also true of his relationship to other men to their labor and to the objects of their labor.

In general, the statement that man is alienated from his species-life means that each man is alienated from others, and that each of the others is likewise alienated from human life.

Human alienation, and above all the relation of man to himself, is first realized and expressed in the relationship between each man and other men. Thus in the relationship of alienated labor every man regards other men according to the standards and relationships in which he finds himself placed as a worker. . . .

Let us now examine further how this concept of alienated labor must express and reveal itself in reality. If the product of labor is alien to me and confronts me as an alien power, to whom does it belong? . . .

If the product of labor does not belong to the worker, but confronts him as an alien power, this can only be because it belongs to *a man other than the worker.* If his activity is a torment to him it must be a source of enjoyment and pleasure to another. . . . Only man himself can be this alien power over men.

Consider the earlier statement that the relation of man to himself is first realized, objectified, through his relation to other men. If therefore he is related to the product of his labor, his objectified labor, as to an *alien,* hostile, powerful and independent object, he is related in such a way that another alien, hostile, powerful and independent man is the lord of this object. If he is related to his own activity as to unfree activity, then he is related to it as activity in the service, and under the domination, coercion and yoke, of another man.

Every self-alienation of man, from himself and from nature, appears in the relation which he postulates between other men and himself and nature. . . . In the real world of practice this self-alienation can only be expressed in the real, practical relation of man to his fellow-men. The medium through which alienation occurs is itself a *practical* one. Through alienated labor, therefore, man not only produces his relation to the object and to the process of production as to alien and hostile men; he also produces the relation of other men to his production and his product, and the relation between himself and other men. Just as he creates his own production as a vitiation, a punishment, and his own product as a loss, as a product which does not belong to him, so he creates the domination of the nonproducer over production and its product. As he alienates his own activity, so he bestows upon the stranger an activity which is not his own. . . .

Thus, through alienated labor the worker creates the relation of another man, who does not work and is outside the work process, to this labor. The relation of the worker to work also produces the relation of the capitalist (or whatever one likes to call the lord of labor) to work. *Private property* is therefore the product, the necessary result, of *alienated labor,* of the external relation of the worker to nature and to himself.

Private property is thus derived from the analysis of the concept of *alienated labor;* that is, alienated man, alienated labor, alienated life, and estranged man.

We have, of course, derived the concept of *alienated labor* (*alienated life*) from political economy, from an analysis of the *movement of private property*. But the analysis of this concept shows that although private property appears to be the basis and cause of alienated labor, it is rather a consequence of the latter, just as the gods are *fundamentally* not the cause but the product of confusions of human reason. At a later stage, however, there is a reciprocal influence.

Only in the final stage of the development of private property is its secret revealed, namely, that it is on one hand the *product* of alienated labor, and on the other hand the *means* by which labor is alienated, the *realization of this alienation*.

This elucidation throws light upon several unresolved controversies:

(1) Political economy begins with labor as the real soul of production and then goes on to attribute nothing to labor and everything to private property. Proudhon, faced by this contradiction, has decided in favor of labor against private property. We perceive, however, that this apparent contradiction is the contradiction of *alienated labor* with itself and that political economy has merely formulated the laws of alienated labor.

We also observe, therefore, that *wages* and *private property* are identical, for wages, like the product or object of labor, labor itself remunerated, are only a necessary consequence of the alienation of labor. In the wage system labor appears not as an end in itself but as the servant of wages. . . .

An enforced *increase in wages* (disregarding the other difficulties, and especially that such an anomaly could only be maintained by force) would be nothing more than a *better remuneration of slaves,* and would not restore, either to the worker or to the work, their human significance and worth.

Even the *equality of incomes* which Proudhon demands would only change the relation of the present-day worker to his work into a relation of all men to work. Society would then be conceived as an abstract capitalist.

(2) From the relation of alienated labor to private property it also follows that the emancipation of society from private property, from servitude, takes the political form of the *emancipation of the workers;* not in the sense that only the latter's emancipation is involved, but because this emancipation includes the emancipation of humanity as a whole. For all human servitude is involved in the relation of the worker to production, and all the types of servitude are only modifications or consequences of this relation. . . .

Forms of Private Property [2]

The Second of the *Economic and Philosophical Manuscripts,* "The Relationship of Private Property," continues the discussion of alienated labor; but it focuses on the nature of the historical transition from the large-scale landownership characteristic of the feudal era to the modern capitalistic ownership based upon movable property and wage labor. Marx contrasts the claims made by both these parties and discusses the reasons for the triumph of the bourgeoisie.

The worker is the subjective manifestation of the fact that capital is man wholly lost to himself, just as capital is the objective manifestation of the fact that labor is man lost to himself. However, the *worker* has the misfortune to be a *living* capital, a capital with needs, which forfeits its interest and consequently its livelihood every moment that it is not at work. As capital, the *value* of the worker varies according to supply and demand, and his *physical existence,* his *life,* was and is considered as a supply of goods, similar to any other goods. The worker produces capital and capital produces him. Thus he produces himself, and man as a *worker,* as a *commodity,* is the product of the whole process. Man is simply a *worker,* and as a worker his human qualities only exist for the sake of capital which is *alien* to him. . . . As soon as it occurs to capital—either necessarily or voluntarily—not to exist any longer for the worker, he no longer exists for himself; he has *no* work, *no* wage, and since he exists only as a *worker* and not as a *human being,* he may as well let himself be buried, starve, etc. The worker is only a worker when he exists as capital *for himself,* and he only exists as capital when *capital* is there *for him.* The existence of capital is *his* existence, his life, since it determines the content of his life independently of him. Political economy thus does not recognize the unoccupied worker, the working man so far as he is outside this work relationship. . . . The needs of the worker are thus reduced to the need to maintain him *during work,* so that the race of workers does not die out. Consequently, wages have exactly the same significance as the *maintenance* of any other productive instrument, and as the *consumption of capital* in general so that it can reproduce itself with interest. . . .

Production does not only produce man as a *commodity,* the *human commodity,* man in the form of a *commodity;* in conformity with this situation it produces him as a *mentally* and *physically dehumanized* being. . . . Its product is the *self-conscious* and *self-acting commodity* . . . the human commodity. . . . The true end of production is not the number of workers a given capital maintains, but the amount of interest it earns, the total annual saving. It was . . . a great and logical advance in recent English political

[2] From *Marx's Concept of Man,* ed. by Erich Fromm, trans. by T. B. Bottomore (London: C. A. Watts & Co. Ltd., 1961). Reprinted by permission.

economy that, while establishing *labor* as the only principle of political economy, it clearly . . . observed that as a rule the capitalist could *only* increase his gains by the depression of wages and vice versa. The *normal* relation is seen to be not the defrauding of the consumer, but the mutual cheating of capitalist and worker. . . . On the one hand, there is the production of human activity as *labor,* that is, as an activity which is alien to itself, to man and to nature, and thus alien to consciousness and to the realization of human life; the *abstract* existence of man as a mere *working man* who therefore plunges every day from his fulfilled nothingness into absolute nothingness, into social, and thus real, nonexistence. On the other hand, there is the production of objects of human labor as *capital,* in which every natural and social characteristic of the object is *dissolved,* in which private property has lost its natural and social quality (and has thereby lost all political and social disguise and no longer even *appears* to be involved with human relationships), and in which the *same* capital remains the *same* in the most varied natural and social conditions, which have no relevance to its *real* content. . . .

The *distinction* between capital and land, profit and ground rent, and the distinction of both from wages, *industry, agriculture, immovable and movable* private property, is a *historical* distinction, not one inscribed in the nature of things. It is a *fixed* stage in the formation and development of the antithesis between capital and labor. In industry, etc., as opposed to immovable landed property, only the mode of origin and the antithesis to agriculture through which industry has developed, is expressed. As a *particular* kind of labor, as a more *significant, important and comprehensive* distinction it exists only so long as industry (town life) is established in opposition to landed property (aristocratic feudal life) and still bears the characteristics of this contradiction in itself in the form of monopolies, crafts, guilds, corporations, etc. In such a situation, labor still appears to have a *social* meaning, still has the significance of *genuine* communal life, and has not yet progressed to *neutrality* in relation to its content, to full self-sufficient being, i.e., to abstraction from all other existence and thus to *liberated* capital.

But the necessary *development* of labor is liberated *industry,* constituted for itself alone, and *liberated capital.* The power of industry over its opponent is shown by the rise of *agriculture* as a real industry, whereas formerly most of the work was left to the soil itself and to the *slave* of the soil through whom the land cultivated itself. With the transformation of the slave into a *free* worker, i.e., into a *hireling,* the landowner himself is transformed into a lord of industry, a capitalist. . . .

Recollecting their contrasting origins and descent the landowner recognizes the capitalist as his insubordinate, liberated and enriched slave of yesterday, and sees himself as a *capitalist* who is threatened by him. The capitalist sees the landowner as the idle, cruel and egotistical lord of yesterday; he knows that he injures him as a capitalist, and yet that industry is responsible for his present social significance, for his possession and pleasures. He regards the landowner as the antithesis of *free* enterprise and of *free capital* which is independent of every natural limitation. This opposition is extremely bitter and each side expresses the truth about the other. . . . The landowner emphasizes the noble lineage of his property, feudal souvenirs, reminiscences, the poetry of recollection, his open-hearted character, his political importance, etc., and when he talks in economic terms asserts that agriculture *alone* is productive. At the same time he portrays his opponent as a sly, bargaining, deceitful, mercenary, rebellious, heartless and soulless individual, an extortionate, pimping, servile, smooth, flattering, desiccated rogue, without honor, principles, poetry or anything else, who is alienated from the community which he freely trades away, and who breeds, nourishes and cherishes competition and along with it poverty, crime and the dissolution of all social bonds. . . .

Movable property, for its part, points to the miracle of modern industry and development. It is the child, the legitimate, native-born son, of the modern age. It pities its opponent as a simpleton, *ignorant* of his own nature (and this is entirely true), who wishes to replace moral capital and free labor by crude, immoral coercion and serfdom. It depicts him as a Don Quixote who, under the appearance of *directness, decency,* the *general interest,* and *stability,* conceals his incapacity for development, greedy self-indulgence, selfishness, sectional interest and evil intention. It exposes him as a cunning *monopolist;* it pours cold water upon his reminiscences, his poetry and his romanticism, by a historical and satirical recital of the baseness, cruelty, degradation, prostitution, infamy, anarchy and revolt, of which the romantic castles were the workshops.

It (movable property) claims to have won political freedom for the people, to have removed the chains which bound civil society, to have linked together different worlds, to have established commerce which promotes friendship between peoples, to have created a pure morality and an agreeable culture. It has given the people, in place of their crude wants, civilized needs and the means of satisfying them. But the landowner—this idle grain speculator—raises the price of the people's basic necessities of life and thereby forces the capitalist to raise wages without being able to increase productivity, so hindering and ultimately arresting the growth of national income and the accumulation of capital upon which depends the creation of work for the people and of wealth for the country. He brings about a general decline, and parasitically exploits *all* the advantages of modern civilization without making the least contribution to it, and without abandoning any of his feudal prejudices. . . . Everything which he can really bring forward in justification is true only of the *cultivator of the land* (the capitalist and the laborers) of whom the landowner is rather the *enemy;* thus he testifies against himself. *Without* capital, landed property is lifeless and worthless matter. It is indeed the civilized victory of movable property to have discovered and created human labor as the source of wealth, in place of the lifeless thing. . . .

From the *real* course of development . . . there follows the necessary victory of the *capitalist,* i.e., of developed private property, over undeveloped, immature private property, the *landowner*. In general, movement must triumph over immobility, overt self-conscious baseness over concealed, unconscious baseness, *avarice* over *self-indulgence,* the avowedly restless and able self-interest of *enlightenment* over the local, worldly-wise, simple, idle and fantastic *self-interest of superstition,* and *money* over the other forms of private property. . . .

Private Property Versus Communism[3]

The Third Manuscript of the *Economic and Philosophical Manuscripts,* a discussion of "Private Property and Communism," is one of the most important works of Marx's developmental period in that he here, for the first time, takes up in depth the concept of Communism as the solution to the historically given problem of the alienation of labor. The basis of the discussion is soon revealed to be that of actualizing the nature of man (which Marx terms "socialist man") as one who recognizes in world history the process of his own self-creation. Thus the problem of man's actualization becomes one to be directly faced in a concrete historical context. Considering the fact that the conditions of alienated labor create a deformed subhuman type, the solution is posed in terms of a communism which is not merely the "abstract" negation of private property (a fault of which Marx accuses the communists of his day), but of the positive supersession, or the "negation of the negation," of private property. Thus, we see that for Marx Communism is not merely another political or economic doctrine; it is rather proposed as the practical solution to the problem of actualizing the potential of human nature itself in terms of the conditions of labor in their given historical situation.

The supersession of self-estrangement follows the same course as self-estrangement. *Private property* is first considered only from its objective aspect, but with labor conceived as its essence. . . . Fourier, in accord with the Physiocrats, regards *agricultural labor* as being at least the exemplary kind of labor. Saint-Simon asserts on the contrary that *industrial labor* as such is the essence of labor, and consequently he desires the *exclusive* rule of the industrialists and an amelioration of the condition of the workers. Finally, *communism* is the *positive* expression of the abolition of private property, and in the first place of universal private property. In taking this relation in its *universal aspect* communism is (1) in its first form, only the generalization and fulfillment of the relation. As such it appears in a double form; the domi-

---

[3] From *Marx's Concept of Man,* ed. by Erich Fromm, trans. by T. B. Bottomore (London: C. A. Watts & Co. Ltd., 1961). Reprinted by permission.

nation of material property looms so large that it aims to destroy everything which is incapable of being possessed by everyone as private property. It wishes to eliminate talent, etc., by *force*. Immediate physical possession seems to it the unique goal of life and existence. The role of *worker* is not abolished, but is extended to all men. The relation of private property remains the relation of the community to the world of things. Finally, this tendency to oppose general private property to private property is expressed in an animal form; *marriage* (which is incontestably a form of *exclusive private property*) is contrasted with the community of women, in which women become communal and common property. One may say that this idea of the *community of women* is the *open secret* of this entirely crude and unreflective communism. Just as women are to pass from marriage to universal prostitution, so the whole world of wealth (i.e., the objective being of man) is to pass from the relation of exclusive marriage with the private owner to the relation of universal prostitution with the community. This communism, which negates the *personality* of man in every sphere, is only the logical expression of private property, which is this negation. Universal *envy* setting itself up as a power is only a camouflaged form of cupidity which reestablishes itself and satisfies itself in a different way. The thoughts of every individual private property are *at least* directed against any *wealthier* private property, in the form of envy and the desire to reduce everything to a common level; so that this envy and leveling in fact constitute the essence of competition. Crude communism is only the culmination of such envy and leveling-down on the basis of a *preconceived* minimum. How little this abolition of private property represents a genuine appropriation is shown by the abstract negation of the whole world of culture and civilization, and the regression to the *unnatural* simplicity of the poor and wantless individual who has not only not surpassed private property but has not yet even attained to it.

The community is only a community of *work* and of *equality of wages* paid out by the communal capital, by the *community* as universal capitalist. The two sides of the relation are raised to a *supposed* universality; *labor* as a condition in which everyone is placed, and *capital* as the acknowledged universality and power of the community.

In the relationship with *woman,* as the prey and the handmaid of communal lust, is expressed the infinite degradation in which man exists for himself; for the secret of this relationship finds its *unequivocal,* incontestable, *open* and revealed expression in the relation of man to woman and in the way in which the *direct* and *natural* species relationship is conceived. The immediate, natural and necessary relation of human being to human being is also the *relation* of *man* to *woman*. In this *natural* species relationship man's relation to nature is directly his relation to man, and his relation to man is directly his relation to nature, to his own *natural* function. Thus, in this relation is *sensuously* revealed, reduced to an observable *fact,* the extent to which human nature has become nature for man and to which nature has become human nature for him. From this relationship man's whole level of development can be assessed. It follows from the character of this relationship how far *man* has become, and has understood himself as, a *species-being,* a *human being.* The relation of man to woman is the *most natural* relation of human being to human being. It indicates, therefore, how far man's *natural* behavior has become *human,* and how far his *human* essence has become a *natural* essence for him, how far his *human* nature has become *nature* for *him.* It also shows how far man's *needs* have become *human* needs, and consequently how far the other person, as a person, has become one of his needs, and to what extent he is in his individual existence at the same time a social being. The first positive annulment of private property, crude communism, is therefore only a *phenomenal form* of the infamy of private property representing itself as positive community.

(2) Communism (a) still political in nature, democratic or despotic; (b) with the abolition of the state, yet still incomplete and influenced by private property, that is, by the alienation of man. In both forms communism is already aware of being the reintegration of man, his return to himself, the supersession of man's self-alienation. But since it has not yet grasped the positive nature of private property, or the *human* nature of needs, it is still captured and contaminated by private property. It has well understood the concept, but not the essence.

(3) *Communism* is the *positive* abolition of *private property,* of *human self-alienation,* and thus the real *appropriation* of *human* nature through and for man. It is, therefore, the return of man himself as a *social,* i.e., really human, being, a complete and conscious return which assimilates all the wealth of previous development. Communism as a fully developed naturalism is humanism and as a fully developed humanism is naturalism. It is the *definitive* resolution of the antagonism between man and nature, and between man and man. It is the true solution of the conflict between existence and essence, between objectification and self-affirmation, between freedom and necessity, between individual and species. It is the solution of the riddle of history and knows itself to be this solution.

Thus the whole historical development, both the *real* genesis of communism (the birth of its empirical existence) and its thinking consciousness, is its comprehended and conscious process of becoming; whereas the other, still undeveloped communism seeks in certain historical forms opposed to private property, a *historical* justification founded upon what already exists, and to this end tears out of their context isolated elements of this development. . . .

It is easy to understand the necessity which leads the whole revolutionary movement to find its empirical, as well as its theoretical, basis in the development of *private property,* and more precisely of the economic system.

This material, directly *perceptible* private property is the material and sensuous expression of *alienated human* life. Its movement—production and consumption—is the *sensuous* manifestation of the movement of all previous production, i.e., the realization or reality of man. Religion, the family, the state, law, morality, science, art, etc., are only *particular* forms of production and come under its general law. The positive supersession of *private property* as the appropriation of *human* life is therefore the *positive* supersession of all alienation, and the return of man from religion, the family, the state, etc., to his *human,* i.e., *social* life. Religious alienation as such occurs only in the sphere of *consciousness,* in the inner life of man, but economic alienation is that of *real life* and its supersession therefore affects both aspects. Of course, the development in different nations has a different beginning according to whether the actual and *established* life of the people is more in the realm of mind or more in the external world, is a real or ideal life. Communism begins where atheism begins, but atheism is at the outset still far from being communism; indeed it is still for the most part an abstraction. Thus the philanthropy of atheism is at first only an abstract *philosophical* philanthropy, whereas that of communism is at once *real* and oriented towards *action.*

We have seen how, on the assumption that private property has been positively superseded, man produces man, himself and then other men; how the object which is the direct activity of his personality is at the same time his existence for other men and their existence for him. Similarly, the material of labor and man himself as a subject are the starting point as well as the result of this movement (and because there must be this starting point private property is a historical necessity). Therefore, the *social* character is the universal character of the whole movement; *as* society itself produces *man* as *man,* so it is *produced* by him. Activity and mind are social in their content as well as in their *origin;* they are *social* activity and *social* mind. The *human* significance of nature only exists for *social* man, because only in this case is nature a *bond* with other *men,* the basis of his existence for others and of their existence for him. Only then is nature the *basis* of his own *human* experience and a vital element of human reality. The *natural* existence of man has here become his *human* existence and nature itself has become human for him. Thus *society* is the accomplished union of man with nature, the veritable resurrection of nature, the realized naturalism of man and the realized humanism of nature.

Social activity and social mind by no means exist *only* in the form of activity or mind which is directly communal. Nevertheless, communal activity and mind, i.e., activity and mind which express and confirm themselves directly in a *real association* with other men, occur everywhere where this *direct* expression of sociability arises from the content of the activity or corresponds to the nature of mind.

Even when I carry out *scientific* work, etc., an activity which I can seldom conduct in direct association with other men, I perform a *social,* because *human,* act. It is not only the material of my activity—such as the language itself which the thinker uses—which is given to me as a social product. *My own existence* is a social activity. For this reason, what I myself produce I produce for society, and with the consciousness of acting as a social being. . . .

It is above all necessary to avoid postulating "society" once again as an abstraction confronting the individual. The individual *is* the *social being*. The manifestation of his life—even when it does not appear directly in the form of a communal manifestation, accomplished in association with other men—is therefore a manifestation and affirmation of *social life*. Individual human life and species-life are not *different things,* even though the mode of existence of individual life is necessarily either a more *specific* or a more *general* mode of species-life, or that of species-life a more *specific* or more *general* mode of individual life.

In his *species-consciousness* man confirms his real *social life,* and reproduces his real existence in thought; while conversely, species-life confirms itself in species-consciousness and exists for itself in its universality as a thinking being. Though man is a unique individual—and it is just his particularity which makes him an individual, a really *individual* communal being—he is equally the *whole,* the ideal whole, the subjective existence of society as thought and experienced. He exists in reality as the representation and the real mind of social existence, and as the sum of human manifestation of life.

Thought and being are indeed *distinct,* but they also form a unity. *Death* seems to be a harsh victory of the species over the individual and to contradict their unity; but the particular individual is only a *determinate species-being* and as such he is mortal.

(4) Just as *private property* is only the sensuous expression of the fact that man is at the same time an *objective* fact for himself and becomes an alien and nonhuman object for himself; just as his manifestation of life is also his alienation of life and his self-realization a loss of reality, the emergence of an *alien* reality; so the positive supersession of private property, i.e., the *sensuous* appropriation of the human essence and of human life, of objective man and of human *creations,* by and for man, should not be taken only in the sense of *immediate,* exclusive *enjoyment,* or only in the sense of *possession* or *having.* Man appropriates his manifold being in an all-inclusive way, and thus as a whole man. All his *human* relations to the world—seeing, hearing, smelling, testing, touching, thinking, observing, feeling, desiring, acting, loving —in short all the organs of his individuality, like the organs which are directly communal in form are, in their objective action (their *action in relation to the object*) the appropriation of this object, the appropriation of human reality. The way in which they react to the object is the confirmation of *human reality.*[4] It is human effectiveness and human *suffering,* for suffering humanly considered is an enjoyment of the self for man.

Private property has made us so stupid and partial that an object is only *ours* when we have it, when it exists for us as capital or when it is directly eaten, drunk, worn, inhabited, etc., in short, *utilized* in some way; although private property itself only conceives these various forms of possession as

---

[4] It is therefore just as varied as the determinations of human nature and activities are diverse.

means of life, and the life for which they serve as means is the *life* of *private property*—labor and creation of capital.

Thus *all* the physical and intellectual senses have been replaced by the simple alienation of *all* these senses; the sense of *having.* The human being had to be reduced to this absolute poverty in order to be able to give birth to all his inner wealth. . . .

The supersession of private property is therefore the complete *emancipation* of all the human qualities and senses. It is this emancipation because these qualities and senses have become *human,* from the subjective as well as the objective point of view. The eye has become a *human* eye when its *object* has become a *human,* social object, created by man and destined for him. The senses have therefore become directly theoreticians in practice. They relate themselves to the thing for the sake of the thing, but the thing itself is an *objective human* relation to itself and to man, and vice versa.[5] Need and enjoyment have thus lost their *egoistic* character, and nature has lost its mere *utility* by the fact that its utilization has become *human* utilization.

Similarly, the senses and minds of other men have become my *own* appropriation. Thus besides these direct organs, *social* organs are constituted, in the form of society; for example, activity in direct association with others has become an organ for the manifestation of life and a mode of appropriation of *human* life.

It is evident that the human eye appreciates things in a different way from the crude, nonhuman eye, the human *ear* differently from the crude ear. As we have seen, it is only when the object becomes a *human* object, or objective *humanity,* that man does not become lost in it. This is only possible when the object becomes a *social* object, and when he himself becomes a social being and society becomes a being for him in this object.

On the one hand, it is only when objective reality everywhere becomes for man in society the reality of human faculties, human reality, and thus the reality of his own faculties, that all *objects* become for him the *objectification of himself.* The objects then confirm and realize his individuality, they are *his own* objects, i.e., man himself becomes the object. *The manner in which* these objects become his own depends upon the *nature of the object* and the nature of the corresponding faculty; for it is precisely the *determinate character* of this relation which constitutes the specific *real* mode of affirmation. The object is not the same for the *eye* as for the *ear,* for the ear as for the eye. The *distinctive character* of each faculty is precisely its *characteristic* essence and thus also the characteristic mode of its objectification, of its *objectively real, living being.* It is therefore not only in thought, but through *all* the senses that man is affirmed in the objective world.

Let us next consider the subjective aspect. Man's musical sense is only awakened by music. The most beautiful music has no meaning for the non-

---

[5] In practice I can only relate myself in a human way to a thing when the thing is related in a human way to man.

musical ear, is not an object for it, because my object can only be the confirmation of one of my own faculties. It can only be so for me in so far as my faculty exists for itself as a subjective capacity, because the meaning of an object for me extends only as far as the sense extends (only makes sense for an appropriate sense). For this reason, the *senses* of social man are *different* from those of nonsocial man. It is only through the objectively deployed wealth of the human being that the wealth of subjective *human* sensibility (a musical ear, an eye which is sensitive to the beauty of form, in short, senses which are capable of human satisfaction and which confirm themselves as human faculties) is cultivated or created. For it is not only the five senses, but also the so-called spiritual senses, the practical senses (desiring, loving, etc.), in brief, human sensibility and the human character of the senses, which can only come into being through the existence of *its* object, through humanized nature. The cultivation of the five senses is the work of all previous history. Sense which is subservient to crude needs has only a restricted meaning. For a starving man the human form of food does not exist, but only its abstract character as food. It could just as well exist in the most crude form, and it is impossible to say in what way this feeding-activity would differ from that of animals. The needy man, burdened with cares, has no appreciation of the most beautiful spectacle. The dealer in minerals sees only their commercial value, not their beauty or their particular characteristics; he has no mineralogical sense. Thus, the objectification of the human essence, both theoretically and practically, is necessary in order to *humanize* man's *senses,* and also to create the *human senses* corresponding to all the wealth of human and natural being.

Just as society at its beginnings finds, through the development of *private property* with its wealth and poverty (both intellectual and material), the materials necessary for this *cultural development, so* the fully constituted society produces man in all the plenitude of his being, the wealthy man endowed with all the senses, as an enduring reality. It is only in a social context that subjectivism and objectivism, spiritualism and materialism, activity and passivity, cease to be antinomies and thus cease to exist as such antinomies. The resolution of the *theoretical* contradictions is possible *only* through *practical* means, only through the practical energy of man. Their resolution is not by any means, therefore, only a problem of knowledge, but is a *real* problem of life which philosophy was unable to solve precisely because it saw there a purely theoretical problem.

It can be seen that the history of *industry* and industry as it *objectively* exists is an open book of the *human faculties,* and a human *psychology* which can be sensuously apprehended. This history has not so far been conceived in relation to human *nature,* but only from a superficial utilitarian point of view, since in the condition of alienation it was only possible to conceive real human faculties and *human* species-action in the form of general human existence, as religion, or as history in its abstract, general aspect as politics, art and literature, etc. *Everyday material industry* (which can be conceived as part of that general development; or equally, the general development can be conceived as a *specific* part of industry since all human activity up to the present has been labor, i.e., industry, self-alienated activity) shows us, in the form of *sensuous useful objects,* in an alienated form, the *essential human faculties* transformed into objects. No psychology for which this book, i.e., the most sensibly present and accessible part of history, remains closed, can become a *real* science with a genuine content. What is to be thought of a science which stays aloof from this enormous field of human labor and which does not feel its own inadequacy even though this great wealth of human activity means nothing to it except perhaps what can be expressed in the single phrase—"needs," "common need"?

The *natural sciences* have developed a tremendous activity and have assembled an ever-growing mass of data. But philosophy has remained alien to these sciences just as they have remained alien to philosophy. Their momentary *rapprochement* was only a *fantastic* illusion. There was a desire for union but the power to effect it was lacking. Historiography itself only takes natural science into account incidentally, regarding it as a factor making for enlightenment, for practical utility and for particular great discoveries. But natural science has penetrated all the more *practically* into human life through industry. It has transformed human life and prepared the emancipation of humanity even though its immediate effect was to accentuate the dehumanization of man. *Industry* is the actual historical relationship of nature, and thus of natural science, to man. If industry is conceived as the *exoteric* manifestation of the essential human *faculties,* the *human* essence of nature and the *natural* essence of man can also be understood. Natural science will then abandon its abstract materialist, or rather idealist, orientation, and will become the basis of a *human* science, just as it has already become—though in an alienated form—the basis of actual human life. One basis for life and another for science is *a priori* a falsehood. Nature, as it develops in human history, in the act of genesis of human society, is the *actual* nature of man; thus nature, as it develops through industry, though in an *alienated* form, is truly *anthropological* nature.

Sense experience (see Feuerbach) must be the basis of all science. Science is *only genuine* science when it proceeds from sense experience, in the two forms of *sense perception* and *sensuous* need; i.e., only when it proceeds from nature. The whole of history is a preparation for "man" to become an object of *sense perception,* and for the development of human needs (the needs of man as such). History itself is a *real* part of *natural history,* of the development of nature into man. Natural science will one day incorporate the science of man, just as the science of man will incorporate natural science; there will be a *single* science.

Man is the direct object of natural science, because directly *perceptible nature* is for man directly human sense experience (an identical expression) as the *other person* who is directly presented to him in a sensuous way. His own sense experience only exists as human sense experience for himself through the *other person*. But *nature* is the direct object of the *science of man*. The first object for man—man himself—is nature, sense experience; and the particular sensuous human faculties, which can only find objective realization in *natural* objects, can only attain self-knowledge in the science of natural being. The element of thought itself, the element of the living manifestation of thought, *language*, is sensuous in nature. The *social* reality of nature and *human* natural science or the *natural science of man*, are identical expressions.

It will be seen from this how, in place of the *wealth* and *poverty* of political economy, we have the *wealthy* man and the plenitude of *human* need. The wealthy man is at the same time one who *needs* a complex of human manifestations of life, and whose own self-realization exists as an inner necessity, a *need*. Not only the *wealth* but also the *poverty* of man acquires, in a socialist perspective, a *human* and thus a social meaning. Poverty is the passive bond which leads man to experience a need for the greatest wealth, the *other* person. The sway of the objective entity within me, the sensuous outbreak of my life-activity, is the passion which here becomes the *activity* of my being.

(5) A being does not regard himself as independent unless he is his own master, and he is only his own master when he owes his existence to himself. A man who lives by the favor of another considers himself a dependent being. But I live completely by another person's favor when I owe to him not only the continuance of my life but also *its creation;* when he is its *source*. My life has necessarily such a cause outside itself if it is not my own creation. The idea of *creation* is thus one which it is difficult to eliminate from popular consciousness. This consciousness is *unable to conceive* that nature and man exist on their own account, because such an existence contradicts all the tangible facts of practical life. . . .

But it is easy indeed to say to the particular individual what Aristotle said: You are engendered by your father and mother, and consequently it is the coitus of two human beings, a human species-act, which has produced the human being. You see therefore that even in a physical sense man owes his existence to man. Consequently, it is not enough to keep in view only one of the two aspects, the *infinite* progression, and to ask further: who engendered my father and my grandfather? You must also keep in mind the *circular movement* which is perceptible in that progression, according to which man, in the act of generation, reproduces himself; thus *man* always remains the subject. But you will reply: I grant you this circular movement, but you must in turn concede the progression, which leads even further to the point where I ask: who created the first man and nature as a whole? I can only reply: your question is itself a product of abstraction. Ask yourself how you arrive at that question. Ask yourself whether your question does not arise from a point of view to which I cannot reply because it is a perverted one. Ask yourself whether that progression exists as such for rational thought. If you ask a question about the creation of nature and man you abstract from nature and man. You suppose them *nonexistent* and you want me to demonstrate that they *exist*. I reply: give up your abstraction and at the same time you abandon your question. Or else, if you want to maintain your abstraction, be consistent, and if you think of man and nature as nonexistent think of yourself too as nonexistent, for you are also man and nature. Do not think, do not ask me any questions, for as soon as you think and ask questions your *abstraction* from the existence of nature and man becomes meaningless. Or are you such an egoist that you conceive everything as nonexistent and yet want to exist yourself?

You may reply: I do not want to conceive the nothingness of nature, etc.; I only ask you about the act of its creation, just as I ask the anatomist about the formation of bones, etc.

Since, however, for socialist man, the *whole of what is called world history* is nothing but the creation of man by human labor, and the emergence of nature for man, he therefore has the evident and irrefutable proof of his *self-creation,* of his *origins.* Once the essence of man and of nature, man as a natural being and nature as a human reality, has become evident in practical life, in sense experience, the quest for an *alien* being, a being above man and nature (a quest which is an avowal of the unreality of man and nature) becomes impossible in practice. *Atheism,* as a denial of this unreality, is no longer meaningful, for atheism is a *negation of God* and seeks to assert by this negation the *existence of man.* Socialism no longer requires such a roundabout method; it begins from the *theoretical* and *practical sense perception* of man and nature as essential beings. It is positive human *self-consciousness,* no longer a self-consciousness attained through the negation of religion; just as the *real life* of man is positive and no longer attained through the negation of private property, through *communism.* Communism is the phase of negation of the negation and is, consequently, for the next stage of historical development, a real and necessary factor in the emancipation and rehabilitation of man. Communism is the necessary form and the dynamic principle of the immediate future, but communism is not itself the goal of human development —the form of human society.

The Perversion of Human Needs [6]

Directly following the preceding selection, Marx enters into a discussion of "Needs, Production, and Division of Labor," in which he elaborates upon the perverse nature of social relations under capitalism and briefly contrasts it with a communistic form of association. He then discusses the political economists' treatment of the division of labor and of their facile way of ignoring its dehumanizing effects.

---

[6] From *Marx's Concept of Man,* ed. by Erich Fromm, trans. by T. B. Bottomore (London: C. A. Watts & Co. Ltd., 1961). Reprinted by permission.

We have seen what importance should be attributed, in a socialist perspective, to the *wealth of* human needs, and consequently also to a *new mode of production* and to a new *object* of production. A new manifestation of *human* powers and a new enrichment of the human being. Within the system of private property it has the opposite meaning. Every man speculates upon creating a *new* need in another in order to force him to a new sacrifice, to place him in a new dependence, and to entice him into a new kind of pleasure and thereby into economic ruin. Everyone tries to establish over others an *alien* power in order to find there the satisfaction of his own egoistic need. With the mass of objects, therefore, there also increases the realm of alien entities to which man is subjected. Every new product is a new *potentiality* of mutual deceit and robbery. Man becomes increasingly poor as a man; he has increasing need of *money* in order to take possession of the hostile being. The power of his *money* diminishes directly with the growth of the quantity of production, i.e., his need increases with the increasing *power* of money. The need for money is therefore the real need created by the modern economy, and the only need which it creates. The *quantity* of money becomes increasingly its only important quality. Just as it reduces every entity to its abstraction, so it reduces itself in its own development to a *quantitative* entity. Excess and immoderation become its true standard. This is shown subjectively, partly in the fact that the expansion of production and of needs becomes an *ingenious* and always *calculating* subservience to inhuman, depraved, unnatural, and *imaginary* appetites. Private property does not know how to change crude need into *human* need; its *idealism* is *fantasy, caprice* and *fancy.* No eunuch flatters his tyrant more shamefully or seeks by more infamous means to stimulate his jaded appetite, in order to gain some favor, than does the eunuch of industry, the entrepreneur, in order to acquire a few silver coins or to charm the gold from the purse of his dearly beloved neighbor. (Every product is a bait by means of which the individual tries to entice the essence of the other person, his money. Every real or potential need is a weakness which will draw the bird into the lime. Universal exploitation of human communal life. As every imperfection of man is a bond with heaven, a point from which his heart is accessible to the priest, so every want is an opportunity for approaching one's neighbor, with an air of friendship, and saying, "Dear friend, I will give you what you need, but you know the *conditio sine qua non.* You know what ink you must use in signing yourself over to me. I shall swindle you while providing your enjoyment.") The entrepreneur accedes to the most depraved fancies of his neighbor, plays the role of pander between him and his needs, awakens unhealthy appetites in him, and watches for every weakness in order, later, to claim the remuneration for this labor of love.

This alienation is shown in part by the fact that the refinement of needs and of the means to satisfy them produces as its counterpart a bestial savagery, a complete, primitive and abstract simplicity of needs; or rather, that it simply reproduces itself in its opposite sense. For the worker even the need for fresh air ceases to be a need. Man returns to the cave dwelling again, but it is now poisoned by the pestilential breath of civilization. The worker has only a *precarious* right to inhabit it, for it has become an alien dwelling which may suddenly not be available, or from which he may be evicted if he does not pay the rent. He has to *pay* for this mortuary. The dwelling full of light which Prometheus, in Aeschylus, indicates as one of the great gifts by which he has changed savages into men, ceases to exist for the worker. Light, air, and the simplest *animal* cleanliness cease to be human needs. *Filth,* this corruption and putrefaction which runs in the *sewers* of civilization (this is to be taken literally) becomes the *element in which man lives.* Total and *unnatural* neglect, putrified nature, becomes the *element in which he lives.* None of his senses exist any longer, either in a human form, or even in a *nonhuman,* animal form. The crudest *methods* and (and *instruments*) of human labor reappear; thus the *tread-mill* of the Roman slaves has become the mode of production and mode of existence of many English workers. It is not enough that man should lose his human needs; even animal needs disappear. The Irish no longer have any need but that of *eating—eating potatoes*. But France and England already possess in every industrial town a *little* Ireland. Savages and animals have at least the need for hunting, exercise and companionship. But the simplification of machinery and of work is used to make workers out of those who are just growing up, who are still immature, *children,* while the worker himself has become a child deprived of all care. Machinery is adapted to the weakness of the human being, in order to turn the weak human being into a machine.

The fact that the growth of needs and of the means to satisfy them results in a lack of needs and of means is demonstrated in several ways by the economist (and by the capitalist; in fact, it is always *empirical* businessmen we refer to when we speak of economists, who are their *scientific* self-revelation and existence). First, by reducing the needs of the worker to the miserable necessities required for the maintenance of his physical existence, and by reducing his activity to the most abstract mechanical movements, the economist asserts that man has no needs, for activity or enjoyment, beyond that; and yet he declares that this kind of life is a *human* way of life. Secondly, by reckoning as the general standard of life (general because it is applicable to the mass of men) the *most impoverished* life conceivable, he turns the worker into a being who has neither senses nor needs, just as he turns his activity into a pure abstraction from all activity. Thus all working class *luxury* seems to him blameworthy, and everything which goes beyond the most abstract need (whether it be a passive enjoyment or a manifestation of personal activity) is regarded as a *luxury*. Political economy, the science of *wealth,* is therefore, at the same time, the science of renunciation, of privation and of saving, which actually succeeds in depriving man of fresh *air* and of physical *activity*. This science of a marvelous industry is at the same time the science of *asceticism*. Its true ideal is the *ascetic* but *usurious* miser and the *ascetic* but *productive* slave. Its moral ideal is the *worker* who takes a part of his wages to the savings bank. It has even found a servile art to embody this favorite idea, which has been produced in a sentimental manner on the stage. Thus, despite its worldly and pleasure-seeking appearance, it is a truly moral science, the most moral of all sciences. Its principal thesis is the renunciation of life and of human needs. The less you eat, drink, buy books, go to the theatre or to balls, or to the public house, and the less you think, love, theorize, sing, paint, fence, etc., the more you will be able to save and the *greater* will become your treasure which neither moth nor dust will corrupt—your *capital.* The less you *are,* the less you express your life, the more you *have,* the greater is your *alienated* life and the greater is the saving of your alienated being. Everything which the economist takes from you in the way of life and humanity, he restores to you in the form of *money* and *wealth.* And everything which you are unable to do, your money can do for you; it can eat, drink, go to the ball and to the theatre. It can acquire art, learning, historical treasures, political power; and it can travel. It *can* appropriate all these things for you, can purchase everything; it is the true *opulence.* . . .

You must not only be abstemious in the satisfaction of your direct senses, such as eating, etc., but also in your participation in general interests, your sympathy, trust, etc., if you wish to be economical and to avoid being ruined by illusions.

Everything which you own must be made *venal,* i.e., useful. Suppose I ask the economist: am I acting in accordance with economic laws if I earn money by the sale of my body, by prostituting it to another person's lust (in France, the factory workers call the prostitution of their wives and daughters the *n*th hour of work, which is literally true); or if I sell my friend to the Moroccans (and the direct sale of men occurs in all civilized countries in the form of trade in conscripts)? He will reply: you are not acting contrary to my laws, but you must take into account what Cousin Morality and Cousin Religion have to say. My *economic* morality and religion have no objection to make, but. . . . But whom then should we believe, the economist or the moralist? The morality of political economy is *gain,* work, thrift and sobriety —yet political economy promises to satisfy my needs. The political economy of morality is the riches of a good conscience, of virtue, etc., but how can I be virtuous if I am not alive and how can I have a good conscience if I am not aware of anything? The nature of alienation implies that each sphere applies a different and contradictory norm, that morality does not apply the same norm as political economy, etc., because each of them is a particular alienation of man; each is concentrated upon a specific area of alienated activity and is itself alienated from the other[s]. . . .

The bearing of political economy upon morals is either arbitrary and accidental and thus lacking any scientific basis or character, a mere *sham,* or it is *essential* and can then only be a relation between economic laws and morals. . . . Moreover, the antithesis between morals and political economy is itself only *apparent;* there is an antithesis and equally no antithesis. Political economy expresses, *in its own fashion,* the moral laws.

The absence of needs, as the principle of political economy, is shown in the most *striking* way in its *theory of population.* There are *too many* men.

The very existence of man is a pure luxury, and if the worker is *"moral"* he will be *economical* in procreation. (Mill proposes that public commendation should be given to those who show themselves abstemious in sexual relations, and public condemnation to those who sin against the sterility of marriage. Is this not the moral doctrine of asceticism?) The production of men appears as a public misfortune.

The significance which production has in relation to the wealthy is *revealed* in the significance which it has for the poor. . . . The *crude* need of the worker is a much greater source of profit than the *refined* need of the wealthy. The cellar dwellings in London bring their landlords more than do the palaces; i.e., they constitute *greater wealth* as far as the landlord is concerned and thus, in economic terms, greater *social* wealth.

Just as industry speculates upon the refinement of needs so also it speculates upon their *crudeness,* and upon their artificially produced crudeness whose true soul therefore is *self-stupefaction,* the *illusory* satisfaction of needs, a civilization *within* the crude barbarism of need. The English gin-shops are therefore *symbolical* representations of private property. Their *luxury* reveals the real relation of industrial luxury and wealth to man. They are therefore rightly the only Sunday enjoyment of the people. . . .

We have already seen how the economist establishes the unity of labor and capital in various ways: (1) capital is *accumulated* labor; (2) the purpose of capital within production—partly the reproduction of capital with profit, partly capital as raw material (material of labor), partly capital as itself a *working instrument* (the machine is fixed capital which is identical with labor)—is *productive work;* (3) the worker is capital; (4) wages form part of the costs of capital; (5) for the worker, labor is the reproduction of his life-capital; (6) for the capitalist, labor is a factor in the activity of his capital.

Finally (7) the economist postulates the original unity of capital and labor as the unity of capitalist and worker. This is the original paradisaical condition. How these two factors, as two persons, spring at each other's throats is for the economist a *fortuitous* occurrence, which therefore requires only to be explained by external circumstances. . . .

If we now characterize *communism* itself (for as negation of the negation, as the appropriation of human existence which mediates itself with itself through the negation of private property, it is not the *true,* self-originating position, but rather one which begins from private property) . . .[7] The alienation of human life remains and a much greater alienation remains the more one is conscious of it as such can only be accomplished by the establishment of communism. In order to supersede the *idea* of private property communist *ideas* are sufficient but *genuine* communist activity is necessary in order to supersede *real* private property. History will produce it, and the development which we already recognize in *thought* as self-transcending will in

---

[7] A part of the page is torn away here, and there follow fragments of six lines which are insufficient to reconstruct the passage—*Tr. Note*

reality involve a severe and protracted process. We must, however, consider it an advance that we have previously acquired an awareness of the limited nature and the goal of the historical development and can see beyond it.

When communist *artisans* form associations teaching and propaganda are their first aims. But their association itself creates a new need—the need for society—and what appeared to be a means has become an end. The most striking results of this practical development are to be seen when French socialist workers meet together. Smoking, eating and drinking are no longer simply means of bringing people together. Society, association, entertainment which also has society as its aim, is sufficient for them; the brotherhood of man is no empty phrase but a reality, and the nobility of man shines forth upon us from their toilworn bodies. . . .

We said above that man is regressing to the *cave dwelling,* but in an alienated, malignant form. The savage in his cave (a natural element which is freely offered for his use and protection) does not feel himself a stranger; on the contrary he feels as much at home as a *fish* in water. But the cellar dwelling of the poor man is a hostile dwelling, "an alien, constricting power which only surrenders itself to him in exchange for blood and sweat." He cannot regard it as his home, as a place where he might at last say, "here I am at home." Instead, he finds himself in *another person's* house, the house of a *stranger* who lies in wait for him every day and evicts him if he does not pay the rent. He is also aware of the contrast between his own dwelling and a human dwelling such as exists in *that other world,* the heaven of wealth.

Alienation is apparent not only in the fact that *my* means of life belong to *someone else,* that *my* desires are the unattainable possession of *someone else,* but that everything is *something different* from itself, that my activity is *something else,* and finally (and this is also the case for the capitalist) that *an inhuman power* rules over everything. There is a kind of wealth which is inactive, prodigal and devoted to pleasure, the beneficiary of which *behaves* as an *ephemeral,* aimlessly active individual who regards the slave labor of others, human *blood and sweat,* as the prey of his cupidity and sees mankind, and himself, as a sacrificial and superfluous being. Thus he acquires a contempt for mankind, expressed in the form of arrogance and the squandering of resources which would support a hundred human lives, and also in the form of the infamous illusion that his unbridled extravagance and endless unproductive consumption is a condition for the *labor* and *subsistence* of others. He regards the realization of the *essential powers* of man only as the realization of his own disorderly life, his whims and his capricious, bizarre ideas. Such wealth, however, which sees wealth merely as a means, as something to be consumed, and which is therefore both master and slave, generous and mean, capricious, presumptuous, conceited, refined, cultured, and witty, has not yet discovered *wealth* as a wholly *alien power* but sees in it its own power and enjoyment rather than wealth. . . .

Society, as it appears to the economist, is *civil society,* in which each individual is a totality of needs and only exists for another person, as another exists for him, in so far as each becomes a means for the other. The economist (like politics in its *rights of man*) reduces everything to man, i.e., to the individual, whom he deprives of all characteristics in order to classify him as a capitalist or a worker.

The *division of labor* is the economic expression of the *social character of labor* within alienation. Or, since *labor* is only an expression of human activity within alienation, of life activity as alienation of life, the *division of labor* is nothing but the *alienated* establishment of human activity as a *real species-activity* or *the activity of man as a species-being.* . . .

The whole of modern political economy is agreed, however, upon the fact that division of labor and wealth of production, division of labor and accumulation of capital, are mutually determining; and also that liberated and autonomous private property alone can produce the most effective and extensive division of labor.

Adam Smith's argument may be summarized as follows: the division of labor confers upon labor an unlimited capacity to produce. It arises from the *propensity to exchange and barter,* a specifically human propensity which is probably not fortuitous but determined by the use of reason and speech. The motive of those who engage in exchange is not humanity but *egoism.* The diversity of human talents is more the effect than the cause of the division of labor, i.e., of exchange. Furthermore, it is only the latter which makes this diversity useful. The particular qualities of the different tribes within an animal species are by nature more pronounced than the differences between the aptitudes and activities of human beings. But since animals are not able to exchange, the diversity of qualities in animals of the same species but of different tribes is of no benefit to any individual animal. Animals are unable to combine the various qualities of their species, or to contribute to the *common* advantage and comfort of the species. It is otherwise with *men,* whose most diverse talents and forms of activity are useful to each other, *because* they can bring their *different* products together in a common stock, from which each man can buy. As the division of labor arises from the propensity to *exchange,* so it develops and is limited by the *extent of exchange,* by the *extent of the market.* In developed conditions every man is a *merchant* and society is a *commercial association.* Say regards *exchange* as fortuitous and not fundamental. Society could exist without it. It becomes indispensable in an advanced state of society. Yet *production* cannot take place *without it.* The division of labor is a *convenient* and *useful* means, a skillful deployment of human powers for social wealth, but it diminishes the *capacity of each person* taken *individually.* The last remark is an advance on the part of Say. . . .

The consideration of *division of labor* and *exchange* is of the greatest interest, since they are the *perceptible, alienated* expression of human *activity* and *capacities* as the activity and capacities *proper to a species.* . . .

The *division of labor* and *exchange* are the two *phenomena* which lead the economist to vaunt the social character of his science, while in the same

breath he unconsciously expresses the contradictory nature of his science—
the establishment of society through unsocial, particular interests.

The factors we have to consider are as follows: the *propensity to exchange*
—whose basis is egoism—is regarded as the cause of the reciprocal effect of
the division of labor. Say considers exchange as being not *fundamental* to the
nature of society. Wealth and production are explained by the division of labor
and exchange. The impoverishment and denaturing of individual activity
through the division of labor are admitted. Exchange and division of labor
are recognized as the sources of the great *diversity of human talents,* a diversity which in turn becomes useful as a result of exchange. . . . Further, the
division of labor is limited by the *market*. Human labor is simple *mechanical
motion;* the major part is done by the material properties of the objects. The
smallest possible number of operations must be allocated to each individual.
Fission of labor and concentration of capital; the nullity of individual production and the mass production of wealth. Meaning of free private property in
the division of labor.

The Destructive Power of Money [8]

> Marx advances the thesis that money is the alienated form of labor
> process as well as a "disruptive power," which undermines all social
> relations. This argument is presented in the present selection, the first
> part of which is taken from Marx's notes of 1844 on James Mill's *Treatise
> of Political Economy,* and the second part is from the Third of the
> *Economic and Philosophical Manuscripts* of the same year.

The essence of money is not primarily that it externalizes property, but
that the *mediating activity* or process—the *human* and social act in which
man's products reciprocally complement one another—becomes *alienated*
and takes on the quality of a *material thing,* money, external to man. By ex-
ternalizing this mediating activity, man is active only as he is lost and dehumanized. The very *relationship* of things and the human dealings with them
become an operation beyond and above man. Through this *alien mediation*
man regards his will, his activity, and his relationships to others as a power
independent of himself and of them—instead of man himself being the mediator for man. His slavery thus reaches a climax. It is clear that this *mediator*
becomes an *actual god,* for the mediator is the *actual power* over that which
he mediates to me. His worship becomes an end in itself. Apart from this

[8] First part from *Writings of the Young Marx on Philosophy and Society,* by Loyd D.
Easton and Kurt H. Guddat. Copyright © 1967 by Loyd D. Easton and Kurt H. Guddat.
Reprinted by permission of Doubleday & Company, Inc. Second part from *Marx's Concept
of Man,* ed. by Erich Fromm, trans. by T. B. Bottomore (London: C. A. Watts & Co. Ltd.,
1961). Reprinted by permission.

mediation, objects lose their value. They have value only insofar as they *represent* it while originally it appeared that the mediation would have value only insofar as *it* represents *objects*. This inversion of the original relationship is necessary. The *mediation,* therefore, is the lost, alienated *essence* of private property, exteriorated and *externalized* private property, just as it is the *externalized exchange* of human production with human production, the *externalized* species-activity of man. All qualities involved in this activity are transmitted to the mediator. Man as separated from this mediator thus becomes so much the poorer as the mediator becomes *richer.* . . .

Why must private property end up in *money?* Because man as a social being must resort to *exchange* and because exchange—under the presupposition of private property—must end up in value. The mediating process of man making exchanges is no social, no *human process,* no human relationship; rather, it is the *abstract relationship* of private property to private property, and this *abstract* relationship is the *value* whose actual existence as value is primarily *money.* Because men making exchanges do not relate to one another as men, *things* lose the significance of being human and personal property. The social relationship of private property to private property is a relationship in which private property has alienated itself. The reflexive existence of this relationship, money, is thus the externalization of private property, an abstraction from its *specific* and personal nature. . . .

[. . . Money is] the *pander* between need and object, between human life and the means of subsistence. But *that which* mediates *my* life mediates also the existence of other men for me. It is for me the *other* person.

> Why, Zounds! Both hands and feet are, truly—
> And head and virile forces—thine:
> Yet all that I indulge in newly,
> Is't thence less wholly mine?
> If I've six stallions in my stall,
> Are not their forces also lent me?
> I speed along completest man of all,
> As though my feet were four-and-twenty.
>   (Goethe, *Faust*—Mephistopheles) [9]

Shakespeare in *Timon of Athens:*

> Gold? yellow, glittering, precious gold? No, gods,
> I am no idle votarist: roots, you clear heavens!
> Thus much of this will make black, white; foul, fair;
> Wrong, right; base, noble; old, young; coward, valiant.

---

[9] Goethe, *Faust.* Part I, Scene 4. This passage is taken from the translation by Bayard Taylor; the Modern Library, New York, 1950.—*Tr. Note*

......Why this
Will lug your priests and servants from your sides;
Pluck stout men's pillows from below their heads:
This yellow slave
Will knit and break religions; bless th' accurst;
Make the hoar leprosy ador'd; place thieves,
And give them title, knee, and approbation,
With senators on the bench: this is it
That makes the wappen'd widow wed again;
She whom the spital-house and ulcerous sores
Would cast the gorge at, this embalms and spices
To th' April day again. Come, damned earth,
Thou common whore of mankind, that putt'st odds
Among the rout of nations, I will make thee
Do thy right nature.[10]

And later on:

O thou sweet king-killer, and dear divorce
'Twixt natural son and sire! Thou bright defiler
Of Hymen's purest bed! thou valiant Mars!
Thou ever young, fresh, loved, and delicate wooer,
Whose blush doth thaw the consecrated snow
That lies on Dian's lap! thou visible god,
That solder'st close impossibilities,
And mak'st them kiss! that speak'st with every tongue,
To every purpose! O thou touch of hearts!
Think, thy slave man rebels; and by the virtue
Set them into confounding odds, that beasts
May have the world in empire! [11]

Shakespeare portrays admirably the nature of *money*. To understand him, let us begin by expounding the passage from Goethe.

That which exists for me through the medium of *money*, that which I can pay for (i.e., which money can buy), that I *am,* the possessor of the money. My own power is as great as the power of money. The properties of money are my own (the possessor's) properties and faculties. What I *am* and *can do* is, therefore, not at all determined by my individuality. I *am* ugly, but I can buy the *most beautiful* woman for myself. Consequently, I am not *ugly,* for the effect of *ugliness,* its power to repel, is annulled by money. As an individual I am *lame,* but money provides me with twenty-four legs. Therefore, I am not lame. I am a detestable, dishonorable, unscrupulous and stupid

---

[10] Shakespeare, *Timon of Athens.* Act IV, Scene 3. Marx quotes from the Schlegel-Tieck translation.—*Tr. Note*
[11] *Ibid.*

man, but money is honored and so also is its possessor. Money is the highest good, and so its possessor is good. Besides, money saves me the trouble of being dishonest; therefore, I am presumed honest. I am *stupid,* but since money is the *real mind* of all things, how should its possessor be stupid? Moreover, he can buy talented people for himself, and is not he who has power over the talented more talented than they? I who can have, through the power of money, *everything* for which the human heart longs, do I not possess all human abilities? Does not my money, therefore, transform all my incapacities into their opposites?

If *money* is the bond which binds me to *human* life, and society to me, and which links me with nature and man, is it not the bond of all *bonds?* Is it not, therefore, also the universal agent of separation? It is the real means of both *separation* and *union,* the galvano-*chemical* power of society.

Shakespeare emphasizes particularly two properties of money: (1) it is the visible deity, the transformation of all human and natural qualities into their opposites, the universal confusion and inversion of things; it brings incompatibles into fraternity; (2) it is the universal whore, the universal pander between men and nations.

The power to confuse and invert all human and natural qualities, to bring about fraternization of incompatibles, the *divine* power of money, resides in its *character* as the alienated and self-alienating species-life of man. It is the alienated *power* of *humanity.*

What I as a *man* am unable to do, and thus what all my individual faculties are unable to do, is made possible for me by *money.* Money, therefore, turns each of these faculties into something which it is not, into its *opposite.*

If I long for a meal, or wish to take the mail coach because I am not strong enough to go on foot, money provides the meal and the mail coach; i.e., it transforms my desires from representations into *realities,* from imaginary being into *real being.* In meditating thus, money is a *genuinely creative* power.

Demand also exists for the individual who has no money, but his demand is a mere creature of the imagination which has no effect, no existence for me, for a third party . . . and which thus remains *unreal* and *without object.* The difference between effective demand, supported by money, and ineffective demand, based upon my need, my passion, my desire, etc., is the difference between *being* and *thought,* between the merely *inner* representation and the representation which exists outside as a *real object.*

If I have no money for travel I have no *need*—no real and self-realizing need—for travel. If I have a *vocation* for study but no money for it, then I have *no* vocation, i.e., no *effective, genuine* vocation. Conversely, if I really have *no* vocation for study, but have money and the urge for it, then I have an *effective* vocation. *Money* is the external, universal *means* and *power* (not derived from man as man or from human society as society) to change *representation* into *reality* and *reality* into *mere representation.* It transforms *real human and natural faculties* into mere abstract representations, i.e., *im-*

perfections and tormenting chimeras; and on the other hand, it transforms *real imperfections and fancies,* faculties which are really impotent and which exist only in the individual's imagination, into *real faculties and powers.* In this respect, therefore, money is the general inversion of *individualities,* turning them into their opposites and associating contradictory qualities with their qualities.

Money, then, appears as a *disruptive* power for the individual and for the social bonds, which claim to be self-subsistent *entities.* It changes fidelity into infidelity, love into hate, hate into love, virtue into vice, vice into virtue, servant into master, stupidity into intelligence and intelligence into stupidity.

Since money, as the existing and active concept of value, confounds and exchanges everything, it is the universal *confusion and transposition* of all things, the inverted world, the confusion and transposition of all natural and human qualities.

He who can purchase bravery is brave, though a coward. Money is not exchanged for a particular quality, a particular thing, or a specific human faculty, but for the whole objective world of man and nature. Thus, from the standpoint of its possessor, it exchanges every quality and object for every other, even though they are contradictory. It is the fraternization of incompatibles; it forces contraries to embrace.

Let us assume *man* to be *man,* and his relation to the world to be a human one. Then love can only be exchanged for love, trust for trust, etc. If you wish to enjoy art you must be an artistically cultivated person; if you wish to influence other people you must be a person who really has a stimulating and encouraging effect upon others. Every one of your relations to man and to nature must be a *specific expression,* corresponding to the object of your will, of your *real individual* life. If you love without evoking love in return, i.e., if you are not able, by the *manifestation* of yourself as a loving person, to make yourself a *beloved person,* then your love is impotent and a misfortune.

Alienated Labor Versus Truly Human Production [12]

This selection is also taken from Marx's notes and comments on Mill's *Treatise*; it directly contrasts alienated labor under capitalism with the concept of labor which would not be so alienated. This is a crucial discussion, for it explores in more detail than elsewhere the positive nature of Marx's communist ideal.

[12] From *Writings of the Young Marx on Philosophy and Society,* by Loyd D. Easton and Kurt H. Guddat. Copyright © 1967 by Loyd D. Easton and Kurt H. Guddat. Reprinted by permission of Doubleday & Company, Inc.

. . . The exchange of human activity within production itself as well as the exchange of *human products* with one another is equivalent to the *generic activity* and generic spirit whose actual, conscious, and authentic existence is *social* activity and *social* satisfaction. As *human* nature is the *true common life* of man, men through the activation of their *nature create* and produce a human *common life,* a social essence which is no abstractly universal power opposed to the single individual, but is the essence or nature of every single individual, his own activity, his own life, his own spirit, his own wealth. *Authentic common life* arises not through reflection; rather it comes about from the *need* and *egoism* of individuals, that is, immediately from the activation of their very existence. It is not up to man whether this common life exists or not. However, so long as man does not recognize himself as man and does not organize the world humanly, this *common life* appears in the form of *alienation,* because its *subject,* man, is a being alienated from itself. Men as actual, living, particular individuals, not in an abstraction, *constitute* this common life. It is, therefore, *what* men are. To say that *man* alienates himself is the same as saying that the *society* of this alienated man is the caricature of his *actual common life,* of his true generic life. His activity, therefore, appears as torment, his own creation as a force alien to him, his wealth as poverty, the *essential bond* connecting him with other men as something unessential so that the separation from other men appears as his true existence. His life appears as the sacrifice of his life, the realization of his nature as the diminution of his life, his production as the production of his destruction, his power over the object as the power of the object over him; the master of his creation appears as its slave.

Political economy understands the *common life of man,* the self-activating *human* essence and mutual redintegration toward generic and truly human life, in the form of *exchange* and *commerce. Society,* says Destutt de Tracy, is a *series of multilateral exchanges.* It is constituted by this movement of multilateral integration. *Society,* says Adam Smith, is a *commercial enterprise.* Each of its members is a *merchant.* It is evident that political economy *establishes* an *alienated* form of social intercourse as the *essential, original,* and definitive human form.

Economics—like the actual process itself—proceeds from the *relationship of man to man* and from the relationship of one *property owner to another.* Let us presuppose man as *property owner,* that is, an exclusive possessor who maintains his personality and distinguishes himself from other men and relates himself to them through this exclusive possession. Private property is his personal existence, his *distinguishing* and hence essential existence. The *loss* or *relinquishing* of private property, then, is an *externalization of man* as well as of *private property.* We are concerned here only with the latter. When I yield my private property to another person, it ceases being mine. It becomes something independent of me and *outside* my sphere, something *external* to me. I *externalize* my private property. So far as I am concerned, it is *externalized* private property. I see it only as something generally *externalized;*

I only transcend my *personal* relationship to it; and I return it to the *elemental* forces of nature when I externalize it only in relation to myself. It only becomes externalized *private property* as it ceases being *my* private property without ceasing to be *private property* in general, that is, when it acquires the same relationship to *another* man *outside* of me, as it had to me—in a word, when it becomes the *private property* of *another* man. Apart from the situation of *force,* what causes me to externalize *my* private property to another person? Economics answers correctly: *need* and *want.* The other person is also a property owner, but of *another object* which I lack and which I neither can nor want to be without, an object which to me seems to be something *needed* for the redintegration of my existence and the realization of my nature.

The bond relating the two property owners to each other is the *specific nature of the object.* The fact that either property owner desires and wants objects makes him aware that he has another *essential* relationship to objects outside of property and that he is not the particular being he takes himself to be but rather a *total* being whose wants have a relationship of *inner* property to the products of the labor of the other person. For the need of an object is the most evident and irrefutable proof that the object belongs to *my* nature and that the existence of the object for me and its *property* are the property appropriate to my essence. Both owners are thus impelled to relinquish their property, but in such a way that at the same time they reaffirm that property; or they are impelled to relinquish that property within the relationship of private property. Each thus externalizes a part of his property in the other person.

The *social* relationship of both owners is thus the *mutuality of externalization,* the relationship of externalization on both sides—or *externalization* as the relationship of both owners—while in simple private property *externalization* takes place only one-sidedly, in relationship to itself.

Exchange or *barter,* therefore, is the social, generic act, the common essence, the social intercourse and integration of man within *private property,* and the external, the *externalized* generic act. For that very reason it appears as *barter.* And hence it is likewise the opposite of the *social* relationship.

Through the mutual externalization or alienation of private property, *private property* itself has been determined as *externalized* private property. First of all it has ceased being the product of labor and being the exclusive, distinctive personality of its owner because the owner has externalized it; it has been removed from the owner whose product it was and has acquired a personal significance for the person who did *not* produce it. It has lost its personal significance for the owner. In the second place it has been related to and equated with another private property. A private property of a *different* nature has taken its place, just as it itself takes the position of a private property of a *different* nature. On both sides, then, private property appears as a representative of private property of a different nature, as the *equivalence* of another natural product. Both sides are so related that each represents the existence of the *other* and they mutually serve as *substitutes* for themselves and the other. The existence of private property as such has thus become a *substitute,* an *equivalent.* Instead of its immediate self-unity it exists only in relationship to *something else.* As an *equivalent* its existence is no longer something peculiarly appropriate to it. It has become *value* and immediately exchange value. Its existence as *value* is a determination of *itself,* different from its immediate existence, outside of its specific nature, and *externalized* —only a *relative* existence. . . .

The relationship of exchange being presupposed, *labor immediately* becomes *wage-labor.* This relationship of alienated labor reaches its apex only by the fact (1) that on the one side *wage-labor,* the product of the laborer, stands in no *immediate* relationship to his need and to his *status* but is rather determined in both directions through social combinations alien to the laborer; (2) that the *buyer* of the product is not himself productive but exchanges what has been produced by others. In the crude form of *externalized* private property, *barter,* each of the two private owners produces what his need, his inclination, and the existing raw material induces him to produce. They exchange only the surplus of their production. To be sure, labor was for each one the immediate *source of his subsistence;* at the same time, however, it was also the confirmation of his *individual existence.* Through exchange, his *labor* has partly become his *source of income.* The purpose and existence of labor have changed. The product is created as *value, exchange value,* and an *equivalent* and no longer because of its immediate personal relationship to the producer. The more varied production becomes—in other words, the more varied the needs become on the one hand and the more one-sided the producer's output becomes on the other—the more does his labor fall into the category of *wage-labor,* until it is eventually nothing but wage-labor and until it becomes entirely *incidental* and *unessential* whether the producer immediately enjoys and needs his product and whether the *activity,* the action of labor itself, is his self-satisfaction and the realization of his natural dispositions and spiritual aims.

The following elements are contained in *wage-labor:* (1) the chance relationship and alienation of labor from the laboring subject; (2) the chance relationship and alienation of labor from its object; (3) the determination of the laborer through social needs which are an alien compulsion to him, a compulsion to which he submits out of egoistic need and distress—these social needs are merely a source of providing the necessities of life for him, just as he is merely a slave for them; (4) the maintenance of his individual existence appears to the worker as the *goal* of his activity and his real action is only a means; he lives to acquire the means of *living.*

The greater and the more articulated the social power is within the relationship of private property, the more *egoistic* and asocial man becomes, the more he becomes alienated from his own nature.

Just as the mutual exchange of products of *human activity* appears as *trading* and *bargaining,* so does the mutual redintegration and exchange of the activity itself appear as the *division of labor* making man as far as possible an

abstract being, an automaton, and transforming him into a spiritual and physical monster.

Precisely the unity of human labor is regarded as being its *division* because
its social nature comes into being only as its opposite, in the form of alienation.
The *division of labor* increases with civilization.

Within the presupposition of the division of labor, the product and material of private property gradually acquire for the individual the significance
of an *equivalent*. He no longer exchanges his *surplus,* and he can become *indifferent* to the object of his production. He no longer immediately exchanges
his product for the product he *needs*. The equivalent becomes an equivalent in
money which is the immediate result of wage-labor and the *medium* of exchange.

The complete domination of the alienated object *over* man is evident in
money and the complete disregard of the nature of the material, the specific
nature of private property as well as the personality of the proprietor.

What formerly was the domination of one person over another has now
become the general domination of the *thing* over the *person,* the domination
of the product over the producer. Just as the determination of the *externalization* of private property lay in the *equivalent* and in value, so is *money* the
sensuous, self-objectified existence of this *externalization*. . . .

It is the basic presupposition of private property that man *produces* only
in order to *own*. The purpose of production is to *own*. It not only has such a
useful purpose; it also has a *selfish* purpose. Man only produces in order to
own something for himself. The object of his production is the objectification
of his *immediate,* selfish *need*. Man—in his wild, barbaric condition—determines his production by the *extent* of his immediate need whose content is the
immediately produced object itself.

In that condition man produces *no more* than he immediately needs. The
limit of his need is the *limit of his production*. Demand and supply coincide.
Production is *determined* by need. Either no exchange takes place or the
exchange is reduced to the exchange of man's labor for the product of his
labor, and this exchange is the latent form (the germ) of real exchange.

As soon as exchange occurs, there is an overproduction beyond the immediate boundary of ownership. But this overproduction does not exceed
selfish need. Rather it is only an *indirect* way of satisfying a need which finds
its objectification in the production of another person. Production has become
a *source of income,* labor for profit. While formerly need determined the extent of production, now production, or rather the *owning of the product,* determines how far needs can be satisfied.

I have produced for myself and not for you, just as you have produced
for yourself and not for me. The result of my production as such has as little
direct connection with you as the result of your production has with me, that
is, our production is not production of man for man as man, not *socialized*
production. No one is gratified by the product of another. Our mutual pro-

duction means nothing for us as human beings. Our exchange, therefore, cannot be the mediating movement in which it would be acknowledged that my product means anything for you because it is an *objectification* of your being, your need. *Human nature* is not the bond of our production for each other. Exchange can only set in *motion* and confirm the *relationship* which each of us has to his own product and to the production of the other person. Each of us sees in his product only his *own* objectified self-interest and in the product of another person, *another* self-interest which is independent, alien, and objectified.

As a human being, however, you do have a human relation to my product; you *want* my product. It is the object of your desire and your will. But your want, desire, and will for my product are impotent. In other words, your *human* nature, necessarily and intimately related to my human production, is not your *power,* not your sharing in this production, because the *power* of human nature is not acknowledged in my production. Rather it is in the *bond* which makes you dependent upon me because it makes you dependent on my product. It is far from being the *means* of giving you *power* over my production; rather it is the *means* of giving me power over you.

When I produce *more* than I can consume, I subtly *reckon* with your need. I produce only the *semblance* of a surplus of the object. In truth I produce a *different* object, the object of your production which I plan to exchange for this surplus, an exchange already accomplished in thought. My *social* relationship with you and my labor for your want is just plain *deception* and our mutual redintegration is *deception* just as well. Mutual pillaging is its base. Its background is the intent to pillage, to defraud. Since our exchange is selfish on your side as well as mine and since every self-interest attempts to surpass that of another person, we necessarily attempt to defraud each other. The power I give my object over yours, however, requires your *acknowledgment* to become real. Our mutual acknowledgment of the mutual power of our objects is a battle and the one with more insight, energy, power, and cleverness is the winner. If my physical strength suffices, I pillage you directly. If there is no physical power, we mutually dissemble and the more adroit comes out on top. It makes no difference for the *entire* relationship who the winner is, for the *ideal* and *intended* victory takes place on both sides; in his own judgment each of the two has overcome the other.

On both sides exchange necessarily requires the *object* of mutual production and mutual ownership. The ideal relationship to the mutual objects of our production is our mutual need. But the *real* and *truly effective* relationship is only the mutually *exclusive ownership* of mutual production. It is your *object,* the *equivalent* of my object, that gives your want for my object *value, dignity,* and *efficacy* for me. Our mutual product, therefore, is the *means,* the *intermediary,* the *instrument,* the *acknowledged power* of our mutual needs. Your *demand* and the *equivalent of your property* are terms which for me are *synonymous* and equally valid, and your demand is effective only when it has an effect on me. Without this effect your demand is merely an unsatisfied effort on your part and without consequence for me. You have no relationship to my object as a human being because I *myself* have no human relation to it. But the *means* is the *real power* over an object, and we mutually regard our product as the *power* each one has over the other and over himself. In other words, our own product is turned against us. It appeared to be our property, but actually we are its property. We ourselves are excluded from *true* property because our *property* excludes the other human being.

Our objects in their relation to one another constitute the only intelligible language we use with one another. We would not understand a human language, and it would remain without effect. On the one hand, it would be felt and spoken as a plea, as begging, and as *humiliation* and hence uttered with shame and with a feeling of supplication; on the other hand, it would be heard and rejected as *effrontery* or *madness*. We are so much mutually alienated from human nature that the direct language of this nature is an *injury to human dignity* for us, while the alienated language of objective values appears as justified, self-confident, and self-accepted human dignity.

To be sure, from your point of view your product is an *instrument*, a *means* for the appropriation of my product and for the satisfaction of your need. But from my point of view it is the *goal* of our exchange. I regard you as a means and instrument for the production of this object, that is, my goal, and much more so than I regard you as related to my object. But (1) each of us actually *does* what the other thinks he is doing. You actually made yourself the means, the instrument, and the producer of *your* own object in order to appropriate mine; (2) for you, your own object is only the *sensuous shell* and *concealed form* of my object; its production *means* and *expressly* is the *acquisition* of my object. You indeed become the *means* and *instrument* of your object; your greed is the *slave* of this object, and you performed slavish services so that the object is never again a remission of your greed. This mutual servitude to the object is actually manifested to us at the beginning of its development as the relationship of *lordship* and *slavery,* and is only the *crude* and *frank* expression of our *essential* relationship.

Our *mutual* value is the *value* of our mutual objects for us. Man himself, therefore, is mutually *valueless* for us.

Suppose we had produced things as human beings: in his production each of us would have *twice affirmed* himself and the other. (1) In my *production* I would have objectified my *individuality* and its *particularity,* and in the course of the activity I would have enjoyed an individual *life;* in viewing the object I would have experienced the individual joy of knowing my personality as an *objective, sensuously perceptible,* and *indubitable* power. (2) In your satisfaction and your use of my product I would have had the *direct* and conscious satisfaction that my work satisfied a *human* need, that it objectified *human* nature, and that it created an object appropriate to the need of another *human* being. (3) I would have been the *mediator* between you and the species and you would have experienced me as a redintegration of your own nature and a necessary part of your self; I would have been affirmed in your thought as well as your love. (4) In my individual life I would have directly created your life; in my individual activity I would have immediately *confirmed* and *realized* my true *human* and *social* nature.

Our productions would be so many mirrors reflecting our nature.

What happens so far as I am concerned would also apply to you.

Let us summarize the various factors in the supposition above:

My labor would be a *free manifestation of life* and an *enjoyment of life.* Under the presupposition of private property it is an *externalization of life* because I work *in order to live* and provide for myself the *means* of living. Working *is not* living.

Furthermore, in my labor the *particularity* of my individuality would be affirmed because my *individual* life is affirmed. Labor then would be *true, active property.* Under the presupposition of private property my individuality is externalized to the point where I *hate* this *activity* and where it is a *torment* for me. Rather it is then only the *semblance* of an activity, only a *forced* activity, imposed upon me only by *external* and accidental necessity and *not* by an *internal* and *determined* necessity.

My labor can appear in my object only according to its nature; it cannot appear as something *different* from itself. My labor, therefore, is manifested as the objective, sensuous, perceptible, and indubitable expression of my *self-loss* and my *powerlessness.*

Alienation and Anomie
Steven Lukes

Both Marx and Durkheim were profound critics of industrial society in nineteenth-century Europe. What is striking is the markedly different bases of their criticisms of the ills of their societies, which can best be brought out by a careful consideration of the different assumptions and implications that belong to the two concepts of alienation and anomie, which they respectively employed.[1] These concepts were elaborated by the two thinkers in their earliest writings and remain implicit as basic and integral elements in their developed social theories. Thus a study of the differing perspectives which they

From *Philosophy, Politics and Society,* Third Series, edited by Peter Laslett and W. G. Runciman. Copyright 1967 by Basil Blackwell Ltd. Reprinted by permission of A. D. Peters and Company. Steven Lukes is a fellow of Balliol College, Oxford.

[1] For other discussions of these concepts, treating them together but in ways rather different both from one another and from that adopted here, see J. Horton, 'The Dehumanisation of Anomie and Alienation', *British Journal of Sociology,* XV, 4, December 1964, and E. H. Mizruchi, 'Alienation and Anomie', in I. L. Horowitz (ed.), *The New Sociology: Essays in Social Science and Social Theory* (New York, 1964).

manifest should be fruitful. I shall argue: first, that they are both socio-psychological concepts, embodying hypotheses about specific relationships between social conditions and individual psychological states; second, that they differ precisely in the sorts of hypotheses they embody; and third, that this difference derives in part from a fundamental divergence in the views of human nature they presuppose. Fourthly, I shall examine the nature of that divergence, and in particular the extent to which the dispute is an empirical one. I shall conclude by asking to what extent such approaches to the analysis of society remain relevant and important today.

First, however, I need to make the negative point that contemporary uses of the notions of alienation and anomie, while claiming to derive from Marx and Durkheim, are not for our purposes a useful starting point. 'Alienation' in particular has achieved considerable and widespread contemporary currency, but it has become debased in consequence. Its evident resonance for 'neo-Marxist' thinkers, in both the West and the East, for existentialist philosophers and theologians, for psychiatrists and industrial sociologists, for *déraciné* artists and intellectuals and student rebels, has meant that it has been widely extended and altered in the interests of a number of contemporary preoccupations; as a result the core of Marx's concept has been lost.[2] 'Anomie' has been less widely used, but it too has achieved a new life, within American social science. In particular, Robert Merton's paper 'Social Structure and Anomie'[3] (published 1938) has led to an extensive literature of conceptual refinement and empirical research, chiefly concerned with 'deviance' in all its forms.[4] But here too, much of the original meaning of the concept has been lost: in particular, most writers have followed Merton in discarding Durkheim's theory of human nature.

Furthermore, modern versions of these concepts vary widely in the range of their empirical reference. In the work of sociologists they are often taken as synonymous or else one is taken to be a sub-type of the other. Thus Nettler, Seeman and Scott in recent attempts to develop typologies of alienation count anomie as a variant, while Srole[5] counts alienation as a variant of anomie.

---

[2] Robert Nisbet writes: 'The hypothesis of alienation has reached an extraordinary degree of importance. It has become nearly as prevalent as the doctrine of enlightened self-interest was two generations ago' (*The Quest for Community,* New York, 1953, p. 15). There is even an 'alienation reader' (E. and M. Josephson, *Man Alone,* New York, 1962).

[3] R. K. Merton, *Social Theory and Social Structure* (Glencoe, revised edition, 1957), ch. IV.

[4] According to a recent article on the subject (H. McClosky and J. H. Schaar, 'Psychological Dimensions of Anomy', *American Sociological Review,* 30, 1965) there have been since Merton's paper first appeared about 35 papers on 'anomy'. 'In addition, the concept has been used in a large number of books and essays and applied to discussions of an astonishing variety of topics, ranging from delinquency among the young to apathy among the old, and including along the way such matters as political participation, status aspirations, the behaviour of men in prisons, narcotics addiction, urbanization, race relations, social change, and suicide'. *Art. cit.,* p. 14.

[5] G. Nettler, 'A Measure of Alienation', *American Sociological Review,* 22, 1957. M. Seeman, 'On the Meaning of Alienation', *American Sociological Review,* 24, 1959. M. B. Scott, 'The Social Sources of Alienation', *Inquiry,* 6, 1963. L. Srole, 'Social Integration and Certain Corollaries', *American Sociological Review,* 21, 1956.

Worse, there has been endless dispute in the case of both concepts about whether they are to be taken as sociological or psychological or as socio-psychological and, if the last, in what sense. Thus Merton defines 'the socio-logical concept of anomie' as 'a breakdown in the cultural structure, occurring particularly when there is an acute disjunction between the cultural norms and goals and the socially structured capacities of members of the group to act in accord with them',[6] and Robin Williams observes that 'Anomie as a social condition has to be defined independently of the psychological states thought to accompany normlessness and normative conflict'; while, for ex-ample, Riesman, MacIver, Lasswell and Srole[7] take it to refer to a state of mind. Similarly, 'alienation' is sometimes taken to refer to an objective social condition, which is to be identified independently of people's feelings and beliefs, as in the work of Lukacs and those who follow him: men live within 'reified' and 'fetishist' social forms and the task is precisely to make them *conscious* of their history, which is 'in part the product, evidently uncon-scious until now, of the activity of men themselves, and in part the succession of the processes in which the forms of this activity, the relations of man with himself (with nature and with other men) are transformed';[8] on the other hand, very many writers take alienation to be a state of mind (e.g., existential-ist writers, theologians, psychiatrists, American sociologists). One writer even takes alienation to be synonymous with frustration of any kind, arguing that it 'lies in every direction of human experience where basic emotional desire is frustrated'.[9]

Concepts can embody hypotheses and, in the case of these two concepts, when the focus is sociological there is frequently assumed to be a psychological correlate, and vice versa. Thus, e.g., Merton classifies the psychological states resulting from sociological anomie, while others make assumptions about the social causes of psychological anomie; similarly, Marxist sociologists make assumptions about the psychological effects of alienated social forms, while, e.g., Erich Fromm sees the psychological state of alienation as a function of market society.

A basic unclarity thus exists about the range of reference of each of these concepts and, even where the concepts are clearly used to embody hypotheses about relationships between social conditions and mental states, the very diversity of such hypotheses makes an analytical comparison of the concepts in their modern forms unmanageable in a short space. Where 'alien-ation' can mean anything from 'bureaucratic rules which stifle initiative and deprive individuals of all communication among themselves and of all infor-

---

[6] *Op. cit.*, ch. V, p. 162.

[7] R. Williams, *American Society* (New York, 1951), p. 537. D. Riesman, *The Lonely Crowd* (New Haven, 1950), p. 287. R. MacIver, *The Ramparts We Guard* (New York, 1950), pp. 84–85. H. Lasswell, 'The Threat to Privacy' in R. MacIver (ed.), *Conflict of Loyalties* (New York, 1952), and Srole, *Loc. cit.*, p. 712.

[8] G. Lukacs, *Histoire de Classe et Conscience de Classe* (Paris, 1960), p. 230.

[9] L. Feuer, 'What Is Alienation? The Career of a Concept', *New Politics*, 1962, p. 132.

mation about the institutions in which they are situated'[10] to 'a mode of experience in which the person experiences himself as an alien',[11] and where 'anomie' can extend from the malintegration of the cultural and social structure to 'the state of mind of one who has been pulled up by his moral roots',[12] then the time has come either to abandon the concepts or return to their origins for guidance.

I

Marx distinguishes four aspects of alienated labour: (1) 'the relationship of the worker to the *product of labour* as an alien object which dominates him'. Thus, 'the more the worker expends himself in work the more powerful becomes the world of objects which he creates in face of himself, the poorer he becomes in his inner life, and the less he belongs to himself'; (2) 'the relationship of labour to the *act of production*', with the result that 'the work is *external* to the worker, that it is not part of his nature; and that, consequently, he does not fulfil himself in his work but denies himself, has a feeling of misery rather than wellbeing, does not develop freely his mental and physical energies but is physically exhausted and mentally debased. The worker, therefore, feels himself at home only during his leisure time, whereas at work he feels homeless. His work is not voluntary but imposed, *forced labour*. It is not the satisfaction of a need, but only a *means* for satisfying other needs'; (3) The alienation of man from himself as a 'species-being', from 'his own active function, his life-activity', which is 'free, conscious activity'. Man is thus alienated from 'his own body, external nature, his mental life and his *human* life'; (4) The alienation of man 'from other *men*. When man confronts himself he also confronts other men . . . in the relationship of alienated labour every man regards other men according to the standards and relationships in which he finds himself placed as a worker.' Social relations 'are not relations between individual and individual, but between worker and capitalist, between farmer and landlord, etc.' Further, men's lives are divided up into different spheres of activity, where conflicting standards apply: 'The nature of alienation implies that each sphere applies a different and contradictory norm, that morality does not apply the same norm as political economy, etc., because each of them is a particular alienation of man; each is concentrated upon a specific area of alienated activity and is itself alienated from the other.'

'Alienation' thus refers to the relationship of the individual to elements of his social and natural environment and to his state of mind, or relationship with himself. Marx contends that 'the division of labour . . . impoverishes the worker and makes him into a machine', that 'the division of labour offers

---

[10] C. Lefort in 'Marxisme et Sociologie', *Les Cahiers du Centre d'Etudes Socialistes*, 34–35, 1963, p. 24.

[11] E. Fromm, *The Sane Society* (New York, 1955), p. 120.

[12] MacIver, *The Ramparts We Guard*, p. 84.

us the first example of how . . . man's own deed becomes an alien power opposed to him, which enslaves him instead of being controlled by him. For as soon as labour is distributed, each man has a particular exclusive sphere of activity, which is forced upon him and from which he cannot escape.' In conditions where men must work for the increase of wealth, labour is 'harmful and deleterious'; the division of labour, which develops in such conditions, causes the worker to become 'even more completely dependent . . . upon a particular, extremely one-sided mechanical kind of labour'. All the aspects of alienation are seen to derive from the worker's role in production: his view of his work, his products, the institutions of his society, other men and himself. In general, the capitalist economic system 'perfects the worker and degrades the man'. Thus Marx's socio-psychological hypothesis concerning alienation is that it increases in proportion to the growing division of labour under capitalism, where men are forced to confine themselves to performing specialized functions within a system they neither understand nor control.

Durkheim uses 'anomie' in *The Division of Labour* to characterize the pathological state of the economy, 'this sphere of collective life [which] is, in large part, freed from the moderating action of regulation', where 'latent or active, the state of war is necessarily chronic' and 'each individual finds himself in a state of war with every other'. In *Suicide* it is used to characterize the pathological mental state of the individual who is insufficiently regulated by society and suffers from 'the malady of infinite aspiration': 'unregulated emotions are adjusted neither to one another nor to the conditions they are supposed to meet: they must therefore conflict with one another most painfully'. It is accompanied by 'weariness', 'disillusionment', 'disturbance, agitation and discontent', 'anger' and 'irritated disgust with life'. In extreme cases this condition leads a man to commit suicide, or homicide. It is aggravated by sudden crises, both economic disasters and 'the abrupt growth of power and wealth': with increased prosperity, for instance, anomie '. . . is heightened by passions being less disciplined, precisely when they need more discipline'. Anomie is the peculiar disease of modern industrial man, 'sanctified' both by orthodox economists and by extreme socialists. Industry, 'instead of being still regarded as a means to an end transcending itself, has become the supreme end of individuals and societies alike'. Anomie is accepted as normal, indeed 'a mark of moral distinction', and 'it is everlastingly repeated that it is man's nature to be eternally dissatisfied, constantly to advance, without relief or rest, toward an indefinite goal'. Religion, governmental power over the economy and occupational groups have lost their moral force. Thus 'appetites have become freed of any limiting authority' and 'from top to bottom of the ladder, greed is aroused without knowing where to find ultimate foothold. Nothing can calm it, since its goal is far beyond all it can attain'. The lives of 'a host of individuals are passed in the industrial and commercial sphere', where 'the greater part of their existence is passed divorced from any moral influence . . . the manufacturer, the merchant, the workman, the employee, in carrying on his occupation, is aware of no influence set about him to check his egoism'.[13]

'Anomie', like 'alienation', thus also refers first to the relationship of the individual to elements of his social environment and second to his state of mind. Durkheim initially thought that the division of labour itself has a 'natural' tendency to provide the necessary regulative force, that it produces solidarity because 'it creates among men an entire system of rights and duties which link them together in a durable way', for 'functions, when they are sufficiently in contact with one another, tend to stabilize and regulate themselves'. Anomie is prevalent because of the rapid growth of the market and big industry, for since 'these changes have been accomplished with extreme rapidity, the interests in conflict have not yet had time to be equilibrated'; also there is the harmful existence of 'the still very great inequality in the external conditions of the struggle'. Later he came to believe that it was primarily due to the lack of occupational groups which would regulate economic life by establishing 'occupational ethics and law in the different economic occupations': anomie 'springs from the lack of collective forces at certain points in society; that is, of groups established for the regulation of social life'. Both explanations are consistent with Durkheim's socio-psychological hypothesis concerning anomie, which is that it is a function of the rapid growth of the economy in industrial society which has occurred without a corresponding growth in the forces which could regulate it.

II

Alienation and anomie have in common the formal characteristic that they each have a multiple reference to: (1) social phenomena (states of society, its institutions, rules and norms); (2) individual states of mind (beliefs, desires, attitudes, etc.); (3) a hypothesized empirical relationship between (1) and (2); and (4) a presupposed picture of the 'natural' relationship between (1) and (2). Thus, whereas Marx sees capitalism as a compulsive social system, which narrows men's thoughts, places obstacles in the way of their desires and denies the realization of 'a world of productive impulses and faculties', Durkheim sees it as a state of moral anarchy in the economic sphere, where men's thoughts and desires are insufficiently controlled and where the individual is not 'in harmony with his condition'. We will later notice the extent to which (3) is related to (4) in the two cases. Let us here concentrate on (3), and in particular on the difference between the hypotheses in question.

Compare what the two thinkers have to say about the division of labour.

---

[13] Durkheim, *Professional Ethics and Civic Morals,* tr. C. Brookfield (London, 1957), p. 12. This quotation, incidentally, confirms that, despite Durkheim's attempt to distinguish 'anomie' from 'egoism' in *Suicide,* they are not in the end conceptually distinct. See B. D. Johnson, 'Durkheim's One Cause of Suicide', *American Sociological Review,* 30, 6, 1965, pp. 882–886.

For Marx it is *in itself* the major contributing factor in alienation, in all its forms, and not just for the worker but for all men. All men are alienated under the division of labour (for, as he says, 'capital and labour are two sides of one and the same relation' and 'all human servitude is involved in the relation of the worker to production, and all the types of servitude are only modifications or consequences of this relation'). Men have to enter into 'definite relations that are indispensable and independent of their wills', they are forced to play determined roles within the economic system, and, in society as a whole, they are dehumanized by social relations which take on 'an independent existence' and which determine not only what they do, but the very structure of their thought, their images of themselves, their products, their activities and other men. Alienated man is dehumanized by being conditioned and constrained to see himself, his products, his activities and other men in economic, political, religious and other categories—in terms which deny his and their human possibilities.

Durkheim sees the division of labour as being (when properly regulated) the source of solidarity in modern industrial society: the prevalence of anomie is due to a lag in the growth of the relevant rules and institutions. Interdependence of functions (plus occupational groups) should lead to growing solidarity and a sense of community, although the division of labour in advanced societies is also (ideally) accompanied by the growth of the importance of the individual personality and the development of values such as justice and equality. For Durkheim the economic functions of the division of labour are 'trivial in comparison with the moral effect it produces'. By means of it 'the individual becomes aware of his dependence upon society; from it comes the forces which keep him in check and restrain him'. When educating a child, it is 'necessary to get him to like the idea of circumscribed tasks and limited horizons', for in modern society 'man is destined to fulfil a special function in the social organism, and, consequently, he must learn in advance how to play this role'. The division of labour does not normally degrade the individual 'by making him into a machine': it merely requires that in performing his special function 'he feels he is serving something'. Moreover, 'if a person has grown accustomed to vast horizons, total views, broad generalities, he cannot be confined, without impatience, within the strict limits of a special task'.

By now it should be apparent that alienation, in Marx's thinking, is, *in part,* what characterizes precisely those states of the individual and conditions of society which Durkheim sees as the solution to anomie: namely, where men are socially determined and constrained, when they must conform to social rules which are independent of their wills and are conditioned to think and act within the confines of specialized roles. Whereas anomic man is, for Durkheim, the unregulated man who needs rules to live by, limits to his desires, 'circumscribed tasks' to perform and 'limited horizons' for his thoughts, alienated man is, for Marx, a man in the grip of a system, who 'cannot escape' from a 'particular, exclusive sphere of activity which is forced upon him'.[14]

Whence does this difference derive? In part, obviously, from the fact that Marx and Durkheim wrote at different periods about different stages of industrial society. Also it is clear that Marx was concerned chiefly to describe the alienated worker, while Durkheim saw economic anomie as primarily characterizing employers. But there is also a theoretical difference that is striking and important: these concepts offer opposite and incompatible analyses of the relation of the individual to society.

Compare Marx's statements that 'it is above all necessary to avoid postulating "society" once again as an abstraction confronting the individual' and that communism creates the basis for 'rendering it impossible that anything should exist independently of individuals' with Durkheim's that society is 'a reality from which everything that matters to us flows', that it 'transcends the individual's consciousness' and that it 'has all the characteristics of a moral authority that imposes respect'. Marx begins from the position that the independent or 'reified' and determining character of social relationships and norms is precisely what characterizes human 'pre-history' and will be abolished by the revolutionary transition to a 'truly-human' society, whereas Durkheim assumes the 'normality' of social regulation, the lack of which leads to the morbid, self-destructive state of 'non-social' or Hobbesian anarchy evident in unregulated capitalism. Social constraint is for Marx a denial and for Durkheim a condition of human freedom and self-realization.

III

It is my contention that one can only make sense of the empirical relationships postulated between social conditions and individual mental states which are held to constitute alienation and anomie by taking into account what Marx and Durkheim see as the 'natural' (or 'human' or 'normal' or 'healthy') condition of the individual in society. Alienation and anomie do not identify themselves, as it were, independently of the theories from which they derive: witness the diversity of contemporary uses of the terms, discussed above. They are, in fact, only identifiable if one knows what it would be *not* to be alienated or anomic, that is, if one applies a standard specifying 'natural' states of institutions, rules and norms and individual mental states. Moreover, this standard must be external. That is, neither the individual mental states nor the social conditions studied can provide that standard, for they themselves are to be evaluated for their degree of alienation and anomie.

Thus despite recent attempts to divest these concepts of their nonempirical

---

[14] But Durkheim obviously did not want to see men treated as commodities or as appendages to machines. (See *Division of Labour,* pp. 371–373), and Marx had much to say, especially in Vol. III of *Capital,* about avarice and unregulated desires prevalent under capitalism (see also his account of 'raw communism' in the 1844 manuscripts).

presuppositions,[15] they are in their original form an inextricable fusion of fact and value, so that one cannot eliminate the latter while remaining faithful to the original concepts.

The standard specifying the 'natural' condition of the individual in society involves, in each case, a theory of human nature. Marx's view of man is of a being with a wide range of creative potentialities, or 'species powers' whose 'self-realization exists as an inner necessity, a need'. In the truly human society there will be 'a new manifestation of *human* powers and a new enrichment of the human being', when 'man appropriates his manifold being in an all-inclusive way, and thus is a whole man'. Man needs to develop all his faculties in a context where neither the natural nor the social environment are constraining: 'objects then confirm his individuality . . . the wealth of subjective human sensibility . . . is cultivated or created' and 'the practical relations of everyday life offer to man none but perfectly intelligible and reasonable relations with regard to his fellow men and to nature'. With the end of the division of labour, there will be an end to 'the exclusive concentration of artistic talent in particular individuals and its suppression in the broad mass'. The 'detail worker of today', with 'nothing more to perform than a partial social function', will be superseded by 'an individual with an all-round development, one for whom various social functions are alternative modes of activity'.[16] Furthermore, with the end of the social determination of 'abstract' individual roles, man's relationship with man and with woman will become fully human, that is, fully reciprocal and imbued with respect for the uniqueness of the individual. As Marx says, 'the relation of man to woman is the most *natural* relation of human being to human being. . . . It also shows how far man's needs have become human needs, and consequently how far the other person, as a person, has become one of his needs, and to what extent he is in his individual existence at the same time a social being.' Thus Marx assumes that the full realization of human powers and 'the return of man himself as a *social,* i.e., really human, being' can only take place in a world in which man is free to apply himself to whatever activity he chooses and where his activities and his way of seeing himself and other men are not dictated by a system within which he and they play specified roles.

Durkheim saw human nature as essentially in need of limits and discipline. His view of man is of a being with potentially limitless and insatiable desires, who needs to be controlled by society. He writes:

---

[15] See e.g., B. F. Dohrenwend, 'Egoism, Altruism, Anomie and Fatalism: A Conceptual Analysis of Durkheim's Types', *American Sociological Review,* 24, 1959, p. 467, where anomie is described as 'ambiguous . . . indistinct . . . and infused with value judgments about what is "good" and "bad" ', and e.g., Seeman, *op. cit.*

[16] Cf. the famous passage from the *German Ideology* in which Marx writes of 'communist society, where no one has one exclusive sphere of activity but each can become accomplished in any branch he wishes' and where it is 'possible for me to hunt in the morning, fish in the afternoon, rear cattle in the evening, criticize after dinner, just as I have a mind, without ever becoming hunter, fisherman, shepherd or critic'. See also *Capital* (Moscow, 1959), I, pp. 483–484 and Engels, *Anti-Dühring* (Moscow, 1959), pp. 403 and 409. On the other hand, Marx seems to have changed his attitude at the end of his life to a concern with leisure in the 'realm of freedom'.

> To limit man, to place obstacles in the path of his free development, is this not to prevent him from fulfilling himself? But . . . this limitation is a condition of our happiness and moral health. Man, in fact, is made for life in a determinate, limited environment. . . .

'Health' for man in society is a state where 'a regulative force' plays 'the same role for moral needs which the organism plays for physical needs', which makes men 'contented with their lot, while stimulating them moderately to improve it' and results in that 'calm, active happiness . . . which characterizes health for societies as well as for individuals'. Durkheim's picture of a healthy society in modern Europe is of a society that is organized and meritocratic, with equality of opportunity and personal liberty, where men are attached to intermediary groups by stable loyalties rather than being atomized units caught in an endemic conflict, and where they fulfil determinate functions in an organized system of work, where they conform in their mental horizons, their desires and ambitions to what their role in society demands and where there are clear-cut rules defining limits to desire and ambition in all spheres of life. There should be 'rules telling each of the workers his rights and duties, not vaguely in general terms but in precise detail' and 'each in his sphere vaguely realizes the extreme limit set to his ambitions and aspires to nothing beyond . . . he respects regulations and is docile to collective authority, that is, has a wholesome moral constitution'. Man must be governed by a 'conscience superior to his own, the superiority of which he feels': men cannot assign themselves the 'law of justice' but 'must receive it from an authority which they respect and to which they yield spontaneously'. Society alone 'as a whole or through the agency of one of its organs, can play this moderating role'. It alone can 'stipulate law' and 'set the point beyond which the passions must not go'; and it alone 'can estimate the reward to be prospectively offered to every class of human functionary, in the name of the common interest'.

IV

The doctrines of Marx and Durkheim about human nature are representative of a long and distinguished tradition of such doctrines in the history of political and social theory. The difference between them is also representative of that tradition (and parallel differences can be traced back to the Middle Ages). Doctrines of this general type can be seen to underlie, for example, the work of Hobbes, Rousseau, the Utopian Socialists and Freud; and it is evident that, in large measure, Durkheim sides with Hobbes and Freud where Marx sides with Rousseau and the Utopians. For the former, man is a bundle of desires, which need to be regulated, tamed, repressed, manipulated and given direction for the sake of social order, whereas, for the latter, man is still an angel, rational and good, who requires a rational and good society in which to develop his essential nature—a 'form of association in which each, while uniting himself with all, may still obey himself alone. . . .' [17] For the former, coercion, external authority, and restraint are necessary and desirable for social order and individual happiness; for the latter, they are an offence against reason and an attack upon freedom.

I want here to ask two difficult questions. First, how is one to understand Marx's and Durkheim's theories of human nature, and, in particular, what is their logical and epistemological status? And, second, how is one to account for their divergence?

Statements about human nature can be construed in many different ways. They commonly include such terms as 'need', 'real self', 'real will', 'basic desires', 'human potentialities', 'human powers', 'normal', 'healthy', and so on. Statements of this sort might be taken to refer to: (1) man as existing before or apart from society, (2) man considered analytically, with those factors due to the influence of society abstracted, (3) man considered in an *a priori* manner, i.e. according to some *a priori* definition, (4) man considered from the point of view of features which seem to be common to men in all known societies, (5) man considered from the point of view of features which are held to characterize him in certain specifiable social conditions as opposed to others.[18]

My suggestion is that very often, and in particular in the cases I am dis-cussing, the last is the most accurate way to read statements about human nature. It is, in general, not absurd to take statements about human needs, 'real' wants, potentialities and so on as asserting that individuals in situation S are unable to experience satisfactions that situation S_1 is held to make possible for them and which they would experience and value highly. Now, it is, in my view, not necessary that such statements refer to actual *discontents* of individuals in situation S: both Marx and Durkheim, for example, were clear that individuals could acquiesce in and even value highly their alienated or anomic condition. What is required is that, once they are in S_1, they experience satisfactions unavailable in S.

Thus far it is evidently an empirical matter. It is an empirical and testable question (1) whether the satisfactions in question are precluded in S; (2) whether they would be available in S_1, and (3) whether they would be actually experienced by individuals in S_1 and would be important and valuable to them. (1) can in principle be investigated directly. To take easy examples, it is not difficult to show that work on the assembly line precludes work-satisfaction or that the life of the highly ambitious businessman precludes a mental condition of harmonious contentment. (2) and (3) can be investigated indirectly or directly. To do so indirectly would involve looking at evidence available in S and, indeed, in other societies, which provides a strong presumption in their favour. Thus Marx can write of what happens

---

[17] J.-J. Rousseau, *The Social Contract,* tr. G. D. H. Cole (London, 1913), p. 12.

[18] These possibilities are distinguished for analytical purposes. Clearly, in most actual cases they are combined. Rousseau, for instance, combines (1) and (2), while Pareto combines (2) and (4). I shall in the end argue that Marx and Durkheim combine (4) and (5).

when 'communist artisans form associations'. When 'French socialist workers meet together', he writes, 'society, association, entertainment which also has society as its aim, is sufficient for them: the brotherhood of man is no empty phrase but a reality, and the nobility of man shines forth upon us from their toil-worn bodies'. And he writes in *The Holy Family* that one 'must be acquainted with the studiousness, the craving for knowledge, the moral energy and the unceasing urge for development of the French and English workers to be able to form an idea of the *human* nobleness of that movement'. Durkheim can appeal to countless examples of cohesive social groups—primitive tribes, medieval guilds, rural Catholic communities, the Jews, and to the evidence of, e.g., differential suicide rates. He compares, for instance, the poor with the rich and argues that 'everything that enforces subordination attenuates the effects of [anomie]. At least the horizon of the lower classes is limited by those above them, and for this same reason their desires are more modest. Those who have only empty space above them are almost inevitably lost in it. . . .' *Direct* investigation of (2) and (3) can be pursued only by social experiment. Thus the final test for Marx's theory of human nature is the communist revolution; and that for Durkheim's is the institution of a kind of centralized guild-socialism.

We have analysed statements about human nature as empirical statements (in this case, hypothetical predictions) about the condition of man in S_1. But our analysis is as yet incomplete, for they also involve the affirmation that this condition is privileged—that it is evaluated as preferable to all other conditions. How is one to analyse this evaluation: is it also empirical, that is, a ranking in accordance with what men actually want, or is it nonempirical—a mere exhortation to look at the world in one way rather than another?

If it is empirical, the question arises: by *whom* is the condition of man in S_1 said to be preferred—which men's wants are relevant here? If one believes, as Marx and Durkheim did, that man is largely conditioned by social circumstances, that new needs are generated by the historical process, that his very picture of himself and others is a function of his situation, then the problem becomes even more acute, for no one is in a position genuinely to compare and evaluate alternatives, like Mill's wise man deciding between higher and lower pleasures. An appeal to men in S_1 is self-defeating, for it carries the presumption that their evaluations are privileged, which is what is at issue. An appeal to men in S will not do either, for they would not ordinarily have the necessary evidence, and, again, why should their judgments be privileged? Worse still, what criteria are appropriate? If men in S_1 are satisfied, fulfilled, contented in certain ways, what is privileged about judgments which value these states rather than others?

Both Marx and Durkheim *thought* that they had found solid empirical ground upon which to base statements about human nature. They both had a picture of history as a process of the progressive emergence of the individual and both thought that man's potentiality for individual autonomy and for genuine community with others (both of which they envisaged differently) was frustrated by existing social forms. They thought that they had found conclusive evidence for their respective views of human nature in present and past societies: they assumed that, despite the continual generation of new needs throughout history, men's fundamental aspirations, more or less hidden, and the conditions of their ultimate happiness had always been and would continue to be the same. They were both impressed by the growth of industrialism and by the possibilities it had opened up for human fulfilment[19] and they believed that men were, despite the present, and temporary, obstacles, increasingly becoming (and would continue to become) what they had it in them to be; one could identify *this* by looking at their miseries and sufferings, as well as at their strivings and aspirations towards 'human' or 'healthy' forms of life, and at historical examples of societies or institutions in which alienation or anomie were less severe or even absent. Yet this evidence about men's wants is itself selected and interpreted, and that requires a prior perspective, providing criteria of selection and interpretation.

It would seem, therefore, that statements about human nature, such as those examined here, are partly empirical and partly not. One can often get a long way with support of the empirical part, for evidence of all kinds is relevant to the question what men's lives would be like in alternative circumstances. The hypothetical prediction about S_1 may be verifiable; at least one would know how to verify it, and one could in principle point to evidence which strongly supports it. The claim, however, that life in S_1 is to be judged superior, though it may rest on an appeal to evidence about men's wants, is ultimately non-empirical, for that evidence has been selected and interpreted in the light of the claim. Which men's wants and which of their wants has already been decided. Moreover, the claim of superiority does not follow logically from the evidence: one must add the premise that certain wants and satisfactions are more 'human' or 'healthy' than others. In the end what is required is a perspective and an initial set of evaluations.

It is precisely here that Marx and Durkheim differed radically. Marx wrote that the 'socialist perspective' attributed importance to 'the wealth of human needs, and consequently also to a *new mode of production* and to a new *object* of production' as well as to a 'new manifestation of human powers and a new enrichment of the human being'. He began from an image of man in society, where a morality of duty would be unnecessary because irrelevant, an image in which *aesthetic* criteria were of predominant importance in assessing the quality of man's relationship with the natural and social world.[20]

---

[19] As Marx says, 'The history of *industry* and industry as it *objectively* exists is an *open* book of the *human faculties*' (*Early Writings*, ed. T. B. Bottomore, London, 1963, p. 162); and, as Durkheim says, 'society is, or tends to be, essentially industrial' (*Division of Labour*, ed. G. Simpson, Glencoe, 1933, p. 3) and what characterizes its morality is 'that there is something more human, and therefore more rational' about modern, organized societies (*ibid.*, p. 407).

[20] This image is, I would argue, ultimately Romantic in origin. Compare the following from Schiller's *Briefe ueber die aesthetische Erziehung des Menschen*: '. . . enjoyment is separated from labour, the means from the end, exertion from recompense. Eternally *fettered* only to a single little fragment of the whole, man fashions himself only as a fragment; ever hearing only the monotonous whirl of the wheel which he turns, he never displays the full harmony of his

Yet where Marx wrote in the *Theses on Feurbach* from 'the standpoint of . . . human society', Durkheim argued in the *Rules of Sociological Method* that it was 'no longer a matter of pursuing desperately an objective that retreats as one advances but of working with steady perseverance to maintain the normal state, of re-establishing it if it is threatened, and of re-discovering its conditions if they have changed'. He was haunted by the idea of man and society in disintegration. Here he appealed to the remedy of moral rules, defining and prescribing duties in all spheres of life, especially where men's anarchic and unstable desires had the greatest scope. This is a moral vision, for, as he said, 'the need for order, harmony and social solidarity is generally considered moral'.[21]

Where Marx valued a life in which in community with others 'the individual' has the means of 'cultivating his gifts in all directions', and where the relations between men are no longer defined by externally imposed categories and roles—by class and occupation—and men freely come together in freely-chosen activities and participate in controlling the conditions of their social life, Durkheim held that 'we must contract our horizon, choose a definite task and immerse ourselves in it completely, instead of trying to make ourselves a sort of creative masterpiece', and hoped to see men performing useful functions in a rationally organized society, in accordance with clearly defined roles, firmly attached to relevant groups and under the protective discipline of rules of conduct at home, at work and in politics. They both sought liberty, equality, democracy and community, but the content which they gave these notions was utterly different.

V

What is the relevance of these concepts today? This question needs to be subdivided into three more specific questions, which follow the lines of the preceding argument. First, how valid is the empirical hypothesis which each embodies? To what extent do they succeed in identifying and adequately explaining phenomena in modern industrial societies? Second, how plausible is the theory of human nature which each presupposes? What does the evidence from past and present societies, from sociology and psychology, suggest about the plausibility of their respective hypothetical predictions, and about the nature of the changes which men and institutions would have to undergo to attain

---

being . . .' (*Sixth letter*). For Schiller, and, I believe, for Marx it is 'the aesthetic formative impulse' which 'establishes . . . a joyous empire . . . wherein it releases man from all fetters of circumstance, and frees him, both physically and morally, from all that can be called constraint' (*ibid., Twenty-Seventh Letter*).

[21] *Division of Labour*, p. 63. Whereas Marx's model of disalienated work is artistic creation, Durkheim writes that 'art is a game. Morality, on the contrary, is life in earnest' and 'the distance separating art and morality' is 'the very distance that separates play from work' (*Moral Education*, New York, 1961, p. 273). This is the protestant ethic transposed into Kantian terms: 'the categorical imperative is assuming the following form: Make yourself usefully fulfil a determinate function' (*Division of Labour*, p. 43). As to self-realization, Durkheim writes, 'As for a simultaneous growth of all the faculties, it is only possible for a given being to a very limited degree' (*Division of Labour*, p. 237, amended translation, S. L.).

the conditions they predict and advocate? And third, how desirable is the ideal, how attractive is the vision to which each ultimately appeals? How today is one to evaluate these ideals: what degree of approximation to either, or both (or neither), are we to think desirable?

These questions are challenging and far-reaching. Here I shall raise them and offer tentative suggestions as to how one might begin to answer them.

One problem in answering the first question is to know at what level of generality it is being posed. How *specifically* is one to read Marx's account of alienation and Durkheim's of anomie? Marx and Durkheim identified certain features of their own societies and offered explanations of them. But they may also be seen to have identified features characteristic of a number of societies including their own; indeed, one may even see them, to some extent, as having identified features which may be said to characterize any conceivable society. Is it a specific type of technology, or form of organization, or structure of the economy, or is it the existence of classes or of private property, or the accumulation of capital, or the division of labour, or industrial society, or the human condition which is the crucial determinant of alienation? Is it the lack of a specific type of industrial organization (technical or administrative?), or the absence of appropriate occupational groups, or an economy geared to the pursuit of profit, or the cultural imperatives of a 'success ethic', or the fact of social mobility, or the erosion of a traditionally stable framework of authority, or social change, or industrial society, or the human condition, that is the major factor leading to anomie? Alienation and anomie are phenomena which have particular aspects, unique to particular forms of society or institutions, other aspects which are more general and still others which are universal. We may attempt to identify new forms of these phenomena, using these concepts and the hypotheses they embody in the attempt to describe and explain them. They are in this sense concepts of 'the middle range'. They allow for specific new hypotheses to account for particular new forms, or they may account for them by means of the existing, more general hypotheses. In general, the contemporary forms of alienation and anomie are best approached on the understanding that their causes are multiple and to be sought at different levels of abstraction. A systematic investigation of alienation and anomie would range from the most particular to the most universal in the search for causes.

Marx and Durkheim attributed, as we have seen, certain types of mental condition (specified positively, in terms of what occurs, and negatively, in terms of what is precluded) to certain types of social condition. Marx pointed to meaninglessness of work and a sense of powerlessness to affect the conditions of one's life, dissociation from the products of one's labour, the sense of playing a role in an impersonal system which one does not understand or control, the seeing of oneself and others within socially-imposed and artificial categories, the denial of human possibilities for a fully creative, spontaneous, egalitarian and reciprocal communal life. He attributed these, in particular, to the form taken by the division of labour under capitalism and, more generally, to the fact of class society. Durkheim pointed to greed, competitiveness, status-seeking, the sense of having rights without duties, the concentration on consumption and pleasure, the lack of a sense of community with others, of a feeling of limits to one's desires and aspirations, and of the experience of fulfilling a useful function and serving a purpose higher than one's own self-interest, and the denial of human possibilities for an ordered and balanced life, where everyone knows his station and its duties. He attributed these, in particular, to the industrial revolution and the failure of society to provide appropriate groups to adjust to it, and, more generally, to social disorganization.

We are familiar with countless examples of these phenomena, though in many cases not all the features isolated by the concepts are necessarily present. Let me give just two examples.

Alienation is found today in perhaps its most acute form among workers in assembly-line industries, such as the motor-car industry, where, as Blauner writes in his sensitive study of workers' alienation, 'the combination of technological, organizational and economic factors has resulted in the simultaneous intensification of all the dimensions of alienation'. Here, in the extreme situation, 'a depersonalized worker, estranged from himself and larger collectives, goes through the motions of work in the regimented milieu of the conveyor-belt for the sole purpose of earning his bread', 'his work has become almost completely compartmentalized from other areas of his life, so that there is little meaning left in it beyond the instrumental purpose', and it is 'unfree and unfulfilling and exemplifies the bureaucratic combination of the highly rational organization and the restricted specialist. In relation to the two giant bureaucracies which dominate his life, he is relatively powerless, atomized, depersonalized, and anonymous'.[22]

Likewise, anomie is noticeably evident and acute among 'the Unattached', well described by Mary Morse, especially those in 'Seagate'—the drifting, purposeless and unstable teenagers, who felt no connection with or obligation to family, work, school or youth organization, the children of *nouveau riche* parents, suffering from 'a sense of boredom, failure and restlessness' and refusing 'to accept limitations, whether their own or external'. Often there was 'a failure to achieve unrealistic or unattainable goals they had set for themselves or had had set for them'; also there was 'a general inability to postpone immediate pleasure for the sake of future gain', there was 'a craving for adventure', and 'leisure-time interests were short-spanned, constantly changing and interspersed liberally with periods of boredom and apathy'. Finally, they showed 'pronounced hostility towards adults', adult discipline was quite ineffective and, in general, 'all adults in authority were classed as "them"—those who were opposed to and against "us" '.[23]

---

[22] R. Blauner, *Alienation and Freedom: The Factory Worker and his Industry* (Chicago and London, 1964), pp. 182 and 122.

[23] M. Morse, *The Unattached* (Penguin Books, London, 1965), pp. 75–76 and 28–29.

These are merely two instances, but they illustrate the general point made above. The causes of alienation and anomie must be sought at different levels of abstraction. At the most specific level, all sorts of special factors may be of primary importance. In a case of alienation, it may be the technical or organizational character of an industry or the structure of a bureaucracy; in a case of anomie, it may be a combination of personal affluence and a breakdown, rejection or conflict of norms of authority at home, at school and at work. But clearly, too, the nature of the wider society is of crucial importance. The extent and nature of social stratification, the structure of the economy, the character of the political system, the pace of industrialization, the degree of pluralism, the nature of the predominant social values—all these will affect the nature and distribution of alienation and anomie. Again, one can plausibly argue that *some* degree of alienation and of anomie is inseparable from life in an industrial society, characterized as it is, on the one hand, by the ramifying growth of organization and bureaucracy in all spheres of life, by economic centralization and by the increasing remoteness and technical character of politics; and, on the other, by built-in and permanent social changes, by the impermanence of existing status hierarchies and the increasing role given to personal ambition and career mobility. And at the most general level, they may each be seen to relate to the most universal features of social structure and social change. In this sense, some alienation must exist wherever there are reified social relations, socially-given roles and norms; while some anomie must exist wherever hierarchies disintegrate and social control is weakened.

What about the plausibility of Marx's and Durkheim's theories of human nature? They each had definite views about men's needs, which they believed to be historically generated and empirically ascertainable. How plausible today is the picture of mutually co-operative individuals, each realizing a wide range of creative potentialities, in the absence of specific role-expectations, lasting distinctions between whole categories of men and externally imposed discipline, in conditions of inner and social harmony, where all participate in planning and controlling their environment? What, on the other hand, is the plausibility of the view of human happiness, in which men are socialized into specific roles, regulated, and to some extent repressed, by systems of rules and group norms (albeit based on justice, equality of opportunity and respect for the individual), serving the purposes of society by fulfilling organized functions —all of which they accept and respect as constituting a stable framework for their lives?

These questions confront all those who hold versions of these ideals today. One cannot begin to appraise either, or compare them with one another, until one has come to some view about the likelihood of either being realized. What evidence is there that if the social conditions are constituted in the way Marx and Durkheim wanted, men would experience and would value highly the satisfactions of which they speak? Here one would, for example, need to examine all the accumulated evidence throughout history of experiments in community-living and in workers' control, of communes, collective farms and kibbutzim, on the one hand; and of experience in 'human relations' and personnel management, of professionalism and of life in organizations, on the other. There is a vast amount of such evidence available, but it has never been systematically reviewed in this light.

Let us look at two examples in this connection. In the opinion of Friedmann the Israeli kibbutz represents 'an original and successful application, on a limited scale, of communist principles', nearer to 'the ethical ideal defined by the philosophy of Marx and Engels (for instance, with regard to the role of money, the distinction between manual and intellectual labour, family life)' than life in Moscow or on a kolkhoz. 'The kibbutz movement,' he writes, 'despite its limitations and its difficulties, constitutes the fullest and most successful "utopian" revolutionary experiment, the one which approximates most closely to the forms of life which communism has assigned itself as an aim. It is in the kibbutzim that I have met men of ample culture, and even creators, artists, writers, technicians, among whom the contradiction between intellectual and manual work, denounced by Marx, is truly eliminated in their daily life.' Friedmann goes on, of course, to qualify and elaborate this: in particular, he outlines the perpetual confrontation between the kibbutzim and the wider society, devoted to economic growth and 'imbued with models of abundance, where, with the development of the private sector, there is proclaimed a sort of material and moral New Economic Plan'.[24] He examines the attempts of the kibbutzim to reduce to a minimum the tensions and frustrations of community life and asks the crucial questions: whether the kibbutz will be able to adapt to the economic and technical demands of an industrial society, while retaining its essential values; and whether the wider society will evolve in a direction that is compatible or incompatible with these values.

Let us take a second example, which relates to the plausibility of Durkheim's ideal, the overcoming of anomie. Perhaps the best instance is the evidence accumulated and interpreted by the theorists of modern managerialism, concerned to remedy 'the acquisitiveness of a sick society' [25] and treating the factory, the corporation and the large organization as 'a social system'. Particularly relevant are the writings of the 'organicists', whose aim is to promote 'the values of social stability, cohesion and integration' [26] and to achieve, within the 'formal organization' (the 'explicitly stated system of control introduced by the company') the 'creation and distribution of satisfactions' among the members of the system.[27] Selznick, who typifies the attempt to explore communal values within large corporations and administrative organizations, argues that the organization requires 'stability' in its lines of authority, subtle

---

[24] G. Friedmann, *Fin du Peuple Juif?* (Paris, Gallimard, 1965), pp. 95, 99, 96.

[25] E. Mayo, *The Human Problems of an Industrial Civilisation* (New York, Macmillan, 1933), pp. 152–153.

[26] I am particularly indebted in the discussion of this example to the pages on this subject in S. S. Wolin, *Politics and Vision* (London, Allen and Unwin, 1961), pp. 407–414.

[27] F. J. Roethlisberger and W. J. Dickson, *Management and the Worker* (Cambridge, Mass., Harvard University Press, 1939), p. 551.

patterns of informal relationships, 'continuity' in its policies and 'homogeneity' in its outlook.[28] Another writer describes its reification and normative significance for those who participate in it in the following terms—terms of which Durkheim might well have approved: 'One might almost say that the organization has a character, an individuality, which makes the name real. The scientist will not accept any such reification or personalizing of an organization. But participants in these organizations are subject to no such scientific scruples, and generations of men have felt and thought about the organizations they belonged to as something real in themselves.' [29] For Selznick, social order and individual satisfaction are reconciled when 'the aspirations of individuals are so stimulated and controlled, and so ordered in their mutual relations, as to produce the desired balance of forces'.[30]

I have merely suggested two areas in which one might look for evidence that is relevant to the plausibility of the hypothetical predictions which partially constitute Marx's and Durkheim's theories of human nature. Clearly there is much else that is relevant in, for instance, the work of industrial sociologists, social psychologists, in community studies and the writings of organization theorists. It is also important to look at what evidence there is about the prevalence of existing tendencies in modern societies which favour or hinder the sorts of changes which would be necessary in order to approach these ideals. Here it would be necessary to look, for example, at the changes in the nature of occupations brought about by automation—the replacement of the detail worker by the more educated and responsible technician; at the effects of economic planning on small-scale decision-making; at the effects of the growth of organizations on status aspirations; at contemporary trends in consumption patterns. All this, and much else, is relevant to an assessment of the costs of approaching either ideal in our societies. Without these detailed inquiries, it is hardly possible to state firm conclusions, but it would appear that Durkheim's ideal is much nearer to and easier of realization in the industrial societies of both West and East than is that of Marx.

Finally, how is one to evaluate these ideas? To do so involves a commitment to values and an assessment of costs. Either may be seen to conflict with other values or may not be considered to be worth the cost of its realization. Both sociological evidence and conceptual inquiry are relevant in the attempt to decide these matters, but in the end what is required is an ultimate and personal commitment (for which good, or bad, reasons may, none the less, be advanced). One may, of course, hold, as both Marx and Durkheim in different ways did, that one's values are, as it were, embedded in the facts, but this is itself a committed position (for which, again, good, or bad, reasons may be advanced).

This is no place to argue about these matters at the length they require.

---

[28] Wolin, *op. cit.*, p. 412.

[29] E. W. Bakke, *Bonds of Organization*, quoted in Wolin, *op. cit.*, p. 506.

[30] P. Selznick, *Leadership in Administration*, quoted in Wolin, p. 413.

Let it be sufficient to say that these two quite opposite and incompatible ideals represent in a clear-cut form two major currents of critical and normative thinking about society, to be found throughout the whole tradition of political and social theory in the West and still very much in evidence.

It is becoming increasingly common for that tradition to be attacked, by the advocates of a 'scientific' social and political theory, as being rudimentary and speculative, and lacking in scientific detachment. It is all rather like Sir James Frazer's view of primitive religion as 'bastard science'. What is required, it is argued, is the abandonment of concepts which are internally related to theories of the good life and the good society. Evaluation of this sort should be kept strictly apart from the process of scientific inquiry.

Yet the desire for scientific rigour is not in itself incompatible with the sort of inquiry which is concerned precisely to put to the task of empirical analysis concepts which have the type of relation I have outlined to theories of human nature and thereby to prior evaluative perspectives. This type of inquiry is exactly what has primarily characterized social and political theory in the past (under which heading I include the writings of the classical and many modern sociologists). The case for eliminating it necessarily involves advocating the abandonment of the application of models of alternative and preferred forms of life to the critical analysis of actual forms. That case has yet to be made convincing.

Part Three

Practical Applications

7

Violence and Pacifism

Readings: Newton Garver, "What Violence Is"
Howard Zinn, "The Force of Nonviolence"
Christopher Caudwell, "Pacifism and
Violence: A Study in Bourgeois Ethics"

In this chapter we begin our consideration of practical moral and social issues of contemporary importance. In the readings that follow in this and later chapters, the reader will see (it is hoped) the practical implications of theories of the kind he has studied in the first two parts of the book. It is also hoped that these theories will help clarify and organize his thinking on these practical issues. The practical issues selected have obvious social, political, and legal implications in addition to their obvious moral importance. Moral issues that are essentially private (for example, How can one attain purity of heart?) have been omitted in favor of issues of a public character.

What makes a problem practical? Basically a problem is practical if it urgently calls for a *decision on how to act* in a particular context. Some obvious examples: Should one vote in support of a war that involves the killing of innocent civilians? Should one obey the law and accept a call from Selective Service, or should one be civilly disobedient? What response should one make to the trend of growing permissiveness with regard to abortion in America—should one support the legalization of such services or make use of them if they are legal? These and other problems of practical urgency will be discussed in the following chapters, and an attempt has been made to ensure that a wide variety of views are represented—utilitarians, Kantians, classical liberals, Marxists, and even a contemporary Hobbist.

This chapter explores the problem of violence and pacifism and attempts to come to terms with a question that has surely bothered many people in recent years: Is it ever right to employ violence in pursuit of important moral and political objectives? Those who answer no to this question are called *pacifists,* and it is important to assess the correctness of that position. Most people are inclined to have a confused view about pacifism—they tend to think it is not correct or that they could not act in that way (they might mumble something about its being too "ideal" or "utopian"), and yet they also tend to admire and respect those who are pacifists. Robert Paul Wolff has suggested that this muddled attitude is totally objectionable:

> Pacifists and others who refuse, under any circumstances, to employ techniques of physical coercion, are not saintly, or pure, or dedicated to a higher ethic. They are merely immoral. They permit ends to exist which they could eliminate by less evil means.[1]

Is Wolff correct? After reading the selections in this chapter, the reader will hopefully be in a better position to answer this question. Newton Garver attempts to analyze and clarify the concept of violence, and Howard Zinn presents a qualified defense of nonviolence. Christopher Caudwell, a Marxist, mounts strenuous arguments against pacifism.

Suggestions for Further Reading

Jeffrie G. Murphy, ed., *Civil Disobedience and Violence* (Belmont, Calif.: Wadsworth, 1971).

Jerome Shaffer, ed., *Violence* (New York: David McKay, 1971).

Mulford Q. Sibley, ed., *The Quiet Battle* (Boston: Beacon Press, 1969).

---

[1] Robert Paul Wolff, "Is Coercion 'Ethically Neutral'?", in *Coercion,* ed. J. Roland Pennock and John W. Chapman (New York: Atherton Press, 1972).

What Violence Is
Newton Garver

Most people deplore violence, some people embrace violence (perhaps reluctantly), and a few people renounce violence. But through all these

---

From *The Nation,* June 24, 1968. Reprinted by permission of the publisher. Newton Garver is a professor of philosophy at the State University of New York at Buffalo.

postures there runs a certain obscurity: it is never entirely clear just what violence is. Those who deplore violence loudest and most publicly are usually pillars of the status quo—school principals, businessmen, politicians, ministers. What they inveigh against most often is overt attack on property or against the "good order of society." They rarely see violence in defense of the status quo in the same light as violence directed against it. At the time of the Watts riots in 1965 Mr. Johnson urged Negroes to realize that nothing of value can be won through violent means—a proposition which may be true but which the President did not apply to the escalation in Vietnam he was just then embarked upon, and which it would never have occurred to him to apply to the actions of the Los Angeles police department. Since the President is not the only leader who deplores violence while at the same time perpetrating it, a little more clarity about what exactly we deplore might help all around.

Violence often involves physical force, and the association of force with violence is very close: in many contexts the words become synonyms. An obvious instance is the reference to a violent storm, a storm of great force. But in human affairs violence and force cannot be equated. Force without violence is often used on a person's body. If a man is in the throes of drowning, the standard Red Cross life-saving techniques specify force which is certainly not violence. To equate an act of rescue with an act of violence would be to lose sight entirely of the significance of the concept. Similarly, surgeons and dentists use force without doing violence.

Violence in human affairs is much more closely connected with the idea of violation than with the idea of force. What is fundamental about violence is that a person is violated. And if one immediately senses the truth of that statement, it must be because a person has certain rights which are undeniably, indissolubly, connected with his being a person. One of these is a right to his body, to determine what his body does and what is done to his body—inalienable because without his body he would cease to be a person. Apart from a body, what is essential to one's being a person is dignity. The dignity of a person does not consist in his remaining dignified, but rather in his ability to make his own decisions. In this respect what is fundamental about a person is radically different from what is fundamental about a dog. The way I treat my dog, which seems to be a good way to treat a dog, is to train him to respond in a more or less mechanical way to certain commands. However, to treat a human being in that way is an affront to his dignity, because a minimum of autonomy is essential to a human being.

The right to one's body and the right to autonomy are undoubtedly the most fundamental natural rights of persons. A subsidiary one stems from the right to autonomy. It is characteristic of human action to be purposive and to have results and consequences; freedom therefore is normally conceived as involving not only the right to decide what to do but also the right to dispose of or cope with the consequences of one's action. One aspect of this is the right to the product of one's labor, which has played an important role in the theory of both capitalism and communism. If this line of thought is extended to the point of considering one's property an extension of his person, the scope of the concept of violence becomes greatly enlarged—perhaps in harmony with popular thought on the subject, at least on the part of propertied persons (however, one should always bear in mind that even a propertied person can reconcile himself much more readily to loss of possessions than he can to loss of life). The right to cope with one's own problems and to face the consequences of one's acts (which I do not accord my dog) is typically abrogated by paternalism.

So violence in human affairs amounts to violating persons. It occurs in several markedly different forms, and can usually be classified into four different kinds, based on two criteria: whether the violence is personal or institutionalized, and whether the violence is overt or covert and quiet.

Overt physical assault of one person on the body of another is the most obvious form of violence. Mugging, rape and murder are the flagrant "crimes of violence," and when people speak of violence in the streets it is usually those acts that cross their minds. I share the general concern over the rising rate of these crimes, but deplore the tendency to limit the image of violence to just these three assaults. These are cases where an attack on a human body is also both clearly an attack on a person and clearly illegal. But even here we must not tie these characteristics in too tight a package, for some acts of violence are intended as a defense of law or a benefit to the person whose body is beaten—e.g., ordinary police activity (not "police brutality") and the corporal punishment of children by parents and teachers. The fact that policemen, parents and teachers invoke socially defined roles when they resort to violence indicates that these cases have institutional aspects that overshadow the purely personal ones; but that fact cannot erase the violence done. Of course not all cases are so clear (I leave to the reader to ponder just how, in sex acts, we distinguish on practical grounds between those that are violent and those that are not). But whenever you employ force on another person's body without his consent, you are attacking not just a physical entity but a person— and that is personal overt violence.

In war, what one army tries to inflict on another is what happens to individuals in cases of mugging and murder. The soldiers are responsible for acts of violence against "the enemy," at least in the logical sense that the violence would not have occurred if the soldiers had refused to act. The Nuremberg trials attempted to establish that individual soldiers are responsible morally and legally too, but this overlooked the extent to which the institutionalization of violence makes ambiguous its moral dimension. On the one hand, an individual soldier is not acting on his own initiative and responsibility; on the other, a group does not have a soul and cannot act except through the agency of individual men. Thus there is a real difficulty in assigning responsibility for such institutional violence. The other side of the violence, its object, is equally ambiguous, for "the enemy" is being attacked as an organized political force, and yet the bodies of individual men (and women and children) receive the blows. Warfare, therefore, because it is an institutionalized form of violence, differs from murder in certain fundamental respects.

Riots are another form of institutionalized violence, although their war-like character was not widely recognized until the publication of the report of the President's National Advisory Commission on Civil Disorders. Some persons maintain that a riot is basically a massive crime wave, but it also can take on a warlike character. One of the characteristics of the Watts riot, as readers of Robert Conot's *Rivers of Blood, Years of Darkness* know, was that the people who were supposed to be controlling the situation, the Los Angeles police and their various reinforcements, simply did not possess basic facts about the community. In particular, they did not know what persons could exercise a sort of leadership if the group were left alone.

So the Los Angeles police force and its various allies conducted what amounted to a war campaign. They acted like an army that seizes foreign territory, and their actions had the effect of breaking down whatever social structure there might have been—which in turn had the effect of releasing more overt violence. The military flavor of urban disturbances has increased over the years, and in 1967 the authorities of Newark and Detroit employed not only machine guns and automatic rifles but also tanks and armored personnel carriers, in what the Kerner Commission characterized as "indiscriminate and excessive use of force." For that reason the urban disorders of recent summers are quite different from criminal situations in which police act against individual miscreants.

The overt forms of violence are, on the whole, easier to recognize than quiet or covert violence, which does not necessarily involve direct physical assault on anybody's person or property. There are both personal and institutional forms of quiet violence. Consider first a case of what we might call psychological violence, involving individuals. The following item appeared in *The New York Times*:

> PHOENIX, Ariz., Feb. 6 (AP)—Linda Marie Ault killed herself, policemen said today, rather than make her dog Beauty pay for her night with a married man.
>
> The police quoted her parents, Mr. and Mrs. Joseph Ault, as giving this account:
>
> Linda failed to return home from a dance in Tempe Friday night. On Saturday she admitted she had spent the night with an Air Force lieutenant.
>
> The Aults decided on a punishment that would "wake Linda up." They ordered her to shoot the dog she had owned about two years.
>
> On Sunday, the Aults and Linda took the dog into the desert near their home. They had the girl dig a shallow grave. Then Mrs. Ault grasped the dog between her hands, and Mr. Ault gave his daughter a .22-caliber pistol and told her to shoot the dog.
>
> Instead, the girl put the pistol to her right temple and shot herself.

The police said there were no charges that could be filed against the parents except possible cruelty to animals.

The reason there can be no charges is that the parents did no physical damage to Linda. But that they did terrible violence to the girl the father himself recognized when he said to a detective, "I killed her; I killed her. It's just like I killed her myself." If we fail to recognize that a real psychological violence can be perpetrated on people, a violation of their autonomy, their dignity, their right to determine things for themselves, to be men rather than dogs, then we fail to realize the full dimension of what it is to do violence.

One of the obvious transition cases between overt personal violence and quiet personal violence is the threat. A person who does something under threat of being shot is degraded by losing his autonomy. We recognize that in law and morals: if a person so threatened takes money out of a safe and hands it to a robber, we say that that person acted under compulsion, and the responsibility for what is done lies only with the robber.

Of course, the person coerced with the threat of injury or death needn't surrender his autonomy; he *could* just refuse to hand over the loot. There can be a great deal of dignity in such a refusal, and one of the messages of Sartre's moral philosophy is that whenever one acts other than with full responsibility for his own actions, he is acting in bad faith. That very demanding philosophy puts great emphasis upon autonomy and dignity, and is not to be lightly dismissed. Nevertheless one cannot expect that people will act with such uncompromising strength and dignity. To recognize that they can be broken down by threats and other psychological pressures as well as by physical attack, and that to have acted under threat or duress is as good an excuse before the law as physical restraint, establishes for the community the concept of psychological violence.

Another insidious form of psychological violence is what might be called the "Freudian rebuff." It works like this: A person makes a comment on the Vietnamese war or on civil rights or on some other current topic. The person he is talking to then says: "Well, you're just saying that because of your relations with your father." The original speaker naturally objects: "Of course I had a father, but look at the facts." And he starts bringing out the journals and newspapers and presents facts and statistics from them. "You must have a terrible Oedipus complex; you're getting so excited about this." And the person then says: "Look, I've had some fights with my father, but I've read the paper and I have an independent interest in the civil rights question. It has nothing to do with my father." To which the response is: "Well, your denial just proves how deep your Oedipus complex is."

This type of Freudian rebuff has the effect of what John Henry Newman called "poisoning the wells." It gives its victim no ground to stand on. If he tries to advance facts and statistics, they are discounted and his involvement is attributed to Freudian factors. If he attempts to prove himself free of the aberration in question, his very protest is used as evidence against him. To structure a situation against a person in such a manner does violence to him by depriving him of his dignity: no matter what he does there is no way at all, so long as he accepts the problem in the terms in which it is presented, for him to make a response that will allow him to emerge with honor.

Although this sort of cocktail-party Freudianism is not very serious in casual conversations, there are many forms of this ploy where the whole life and character of a person may be involved. A classic literary and religious version is the dispute between Charles Kingsley and John Henry Newman in the nineteenth century, in which Kingsley challenged Newman's integrity and ended up losing his stature as a Protestant spokesman, and which is written up in fascinating detail in Newman's *Apologia*. A political variation is the Marxian rebuff where, of course, it is because of your class standing that you have such and such a view, and if you deny that the class standing is influencing you in that way, your very denial shows how deeply you are imbued with the obfuscating ideology. Between parent and child, as between husband and wife, there are variations which turn upon the identification (by one insistent party) of love with some particular action, so that the other party must either surrender his autonomy or acknowledge his faithlessness.

This sort of psychological violence is most damaging when the person structuring the situation is in some position of special authority, e.g., in schools. An imaginative child does something out of the ordinary, and the teacher's response is that he is a discipline problem. It now becomes impossible for the child to get out of being a problem. If he tries to do something creative, he will be stepping out of line again and thereby "confirming" that he is a discipline problem. If he stays in line, he will become a scholastic problem, thereby "confirming" that he did not have potential for anything but mischief. The result is a kind of stunted person typical of schools operating in large urban areas.

This last variation of the psychological rebuff leads to the fourth general category of violence, institutionalized quiet violence. The schools are an institution, and teachers are hired not so much to act on their own as to fulfill a predetermined classroom role. Violence done by the teacher may therefore not be personal but institutional: perpetrated while acting as a faithful agent of the educational system.

The idea of such institutional violence is very important. A clearer example may be a well-established system of slavery or colonial oppression, or the life in contemporary American ghettos. Once established, such a system may require relatively little overt violence to maintain it. It is legendary that Southerners used to boast, "We understand our nigras; they are happy here and wouldn't want any other kind of life"—and there is no reason to doubt that many a Southerner, raised in the system and sheltered, from the recurrent lynchings, believed it. In that setup it is possible for an institution to go along placidly, with no overt disturbances, and yet to be terribly brutal.

There is more violence in the black ghettos than anywhere else in America—even when the ghettos are quiet. At the time of the Harlem riots in

1964 the Negro psychologist Kenneth Clark said that there was more day-to-day violence in the life of the ghettos than there was in any day of those disturbances. I'm not sure exactly what he meant. There is a good deal of overt personal violence in the black ghettos, for reasons Fanon has explained in *The Wretched of the Earth*. But we must also recognize the quiet violence in the very operation of the system. Bernard Lafayette of SCLC speaks angrily of the violence of the status quo: "The real issue is that part of the 'good order of society' is the routine oppression and racism committed against millions of Americans every day. That is where the real violence is." A black ghetto in most American cities operates very like any system of slavery. Relatively little overt violence is needed to keep the institution going, and yet the institution violates the human beings involved because they are systematically denied the options which are open to the vast majority in the society. A systematic denial of options is one way to deprive men of autonomy.

Perhaps denying options would not do violence to people if each individual person were an island unto himself and individuality were the full truth about human life. But it is not. We are social beings; our whole sense of what we are is dependent on the fact that we live in society, and have open to us socially determined options. What access we have to the socially defined options is much more important than what language or what system of property rights we inherit at birth. The institutional form of quiet violence operates when people are deprived of choices in a systematic way by the very manner in which transactions normally take place. It is as real, and as wicked, as the thief with a knife.

The Force of Nonviolence
Howard Zinn

Four instances of violence come to my mind. One I read about in the newspapers; another I witnessed; in a third I was on the receiving end; in the fourth, the most brutal of them all, I was a perpetrator.

The first took place an hour's drive from my home in Atlanta, Georgia, when a mob in Athens, screaming epithets and hurling rocks, attacked the dormitory occupied by the first Negro girl to enter the University of Georgia.

The second I saw years ago as I walked through a slum area of the Lower East Side of New York: a little old Jew with a beard, pulling his pushcart, was arguing with a Negro who was demanding payment for his

From *The Nation*, March 17, 1972. Reprinted by permission of the publisher. Howard Zinn is a professor of government at Boston University.

work. The bearded man said he didn't have the money and the Negro said he needed it and the argument grew, and the Negro picked up a stick of wood and hit the old man on the side of the head. The old man continued pushing the cart down the street, blood running down his face, and the Negro walked away.

In the third instance, I took my wife and two-year-old daughter to a concert given in an outdoor area near the town of Peekskill, New York. The concert artist was Paul Robeson. As he sang under the open sky to an audience of thousands, a shouting, angry crowd gathered around the field. When the concert was over and we drove off the grounds, the cars moving in a long slow line, we saw the sides of the road filled with cursing, jeering men and women. Then the rocks began to fly. My wife was pregnant at the time. She ducked and pushed our daughter down near the floor of our car. All four side windows and the rear window were smashed by rocks. Sitting in the back seat was a young woman, a stranger, to whom we had given a lift. A flying rock fractured her skull. There were dozens of casualties that day.

The fourth incident occurred in World War II when I was a bombardier with the Eighth Air Force in Europe. The war was almost over. German territory was shrinking, and the Air Force was running out of targets. In France, long since reoccupied by our troops, there was still a tiny pocket of Nazi soldiers in a protected encampment near the city of Bordeaux. Someone in the higher echelons decided, though the end of the war was obviously weeks away, that this area should be bombed. Hundreds of Flying Fortresses went. In each bomb bay there were twenty-four one-hundred-pound fire-bombs, containing a new type of jellied gasoline. We set the whole area aflame and obliterated the encampment. Nearby was the ancient town of Royan; that, too, was almost totally destroyed. The Norden bombsight was not that accurate.

These four instances of violence possess something in common. None of them could have been committed by any animal other than man. The reason for this does not lie alone in man's superior ability to manipulate his environment. It lies in his ability to conceptualize his hatreds. A beast commits violence against specific things for immediate and visible purposes. It needs to eat. It needs a mate. It needs to defend its life. Man has these biological needs plus many more which are culturally created. Man will do violence not only against a specific something which gets in the way of one of his needs; he will do violence against a symbol which stands for, or which he believes stands for, that which prevents him from satisfying his needs. (Guilt by association is high-level thinking.)

With symbolic violence, the object of attack is deprived of its particularity. Only in this way can man overcome what I believe is his natural spontaneous feeling of oneness with other human beings. He must, by the substitution of symbol for reality, destroy in his consciousness the humanness of that being. To the angry crowds outside the dormitory in Athens, Georgia, their target was not Charlayne Hunter, an extremely attractive and intelligent young woman, sitting, brave and afraid, in her room. She was a "dirty nigger"—a symbol abstracted from life. To the Negro who committed violence on the streets of New York, this was not a pathetic old Jewish immigrant, forced in the last years of his life to peddle vegetables from a pushcart, but a dehumanized symbol of the historic white exploiter who used the Negro's labor and refused to pay him a just wage. To the screaming rock-throwers of Peekskill who fractured the skull of a young woman returning from a concert, the people in the car they attacked were not a family on an outing; in this car were people who had gone to hear a black-skinned communistic singer and who therefore were all congealed into a symbol representing nigger-loving communism. And as I set my intervalometer and toggled off my bombs over the city of Royan, I was not setting fire to people's homes, crushing and burning individual men, women and newborn babies. We were at war, we always dropped bombs on the enemy, and down there was the enemy.

The human ability to abstract, to create symbols standing for reality, has enabled man to compound his material possessions, to split the atom and orbit the earth. It also enables him to compound his hatreds, and expands his capacity for violence. But while there is no incentive to distort in the scientific process which changes reality to symbol for purposes of manipulation, and back to reality for purposes of realization, there *is* incentive, in social relations, for distorting the symbols of communication. With man's use of symbols, the potentiality for hatred and therefore for violence is enormously, logarithmically, magnified. And with word-symbols the possibility for distortion is infinite. In fact, distortion is inherent here, for while particles of light are sufficiently similar so that we can express the speed of all of them in a useful mathematical equation, human beings are so complex and particular, and their relationships so varied, that no generalized word can do justice to reality.

War is symbolic violence, with all people who happen to reside within the geographical boundaries of a nation-state constituting "the enemy." Race persecution is symbolic violence directed against all individuals, regardless of their specific characteristics, who can be identified with an abstracted physical type. In the execution chamber, the state puts to death anyone, regardless of individual circumstance, who fits the legal symbol: murderer. The law forcibly deprives of freedom everyone who falls within the symbolic definition of a criminal; sentences are sometimes meted out to individuals, but mostly to dehumanized lawbreakers whose acts match an abstract list of punishments.

There is symbolism also in the use of violence to effectuate desirable social change, whether through revolution, labor struggle, "just" wars or desegregation. This creates the probability that there will be only a partial correspondence between the specific obstacle to progress and the generalized, symbolized object of violence (the head of Marie Antoinette, the fifty-dollar-a-week scab, the civilian population of Dresden, the poor white in Mississippi). It may hurt the revolutionary reformer to think so, but the fact of symbolization in human violence creates a common problem for *all* users of violence, regardless of their ends. And it may displease the pacifist to say so, but these different ends do matter in deciding how much violence we should countenance in the rearrangement of the social structure.

Symbolism, with its inevitable distortions, complicates an already tough problem: developing an approach to nonviolence that is both realistic and moral. We need a rational approach that avoids both the blurred thinking shown by some advocates of nonviolence and the easy paths to brutality constructed by the "realists." I infinitely prefer the absolute pacifist to the sharp, cool *realpolitik* character who is found so often these days in academia, journalism and the government, but the same absolutism sometimes infects the nonviolence people, who emerged only recently out of the American desegregation battles and whose theories are less developed than their actions. The nonviolence people in America have been saved the consequences of a muddy theory by the favorable circumstances attending Southern desegregation, and because their technique has not been tested on more difficult problems.

The absolutism of some nonviolence spokesmen weakens their position, I believe, because people know, deep inside, even if they can't articulate the reasons, that there are times when violence is justifiable. For nonviolence seen as absolute pacifism is only one of a pair of linked values which humanitarian people share—peace and social justice. The desirability of the one must constantly be weighed against the need for the other. Also, the problem is subject to internal contradiction: sometimes the failure to use a measure of violence may make inevitable a far greater violence. Would it have been wrong to assassinate Hitler at that moment in the war when this might have brought a halt to general hostilities and the extermination of the Jews?

It is not true, as some say, that bad means always corrupt the ends. If the amount of evil embodied in the means is tiny and the amount of good created by the end is huge, then the end is not corrupted—either objectively in the result or subjectively in the conscience of the doer. This matter of conscience is often pointed to by the absolutist pacifist. Certainly, if a man sees a neighbor stealing his son's bicycle and knocks him unconscious with a baseball bat, the wielder of the bat may recover from his anger and say, "What a terrible thing I have done to save a bicycle!" But if he should see his neighbor—whom he knows to have a violent temper—pointing a shotgun at his wife and children, and does the same thing, will his conscience bother him then? Is the end corrupted by the means?

The Freedom Riders behaved nonviolently. But their action did bring violence against themselves, and against others. Nonviolence theorists will insist that the responsibility for the violence rests with those who committed it. But this dodges the question; the fact is that there was more violence in the world *after* the Freedom Riders began their rides than *before*. And for this there is only one justification: that the amount of violence was insignificant compared to the amount of justice won.

In a world of great injustice, we need social change. Social change requires action. Action may result, either by design or by accident, in violence. The fact must be faced. And violence is an evil, along with injustice. The only way, then, to decide upon a course of action is to weigh the damage of violence against the damage of social injustice. The nonviolent absolutist, in all logic, may have to forego social change, putting himself in the contradictory position of maintaining a status quo that tolerates violence like capital punishment and police brutality against Negroes. On the other hand, people who are prepared to pursue any course of action leading to social change may find themselves in the contradictory position of using such violent and uncontrollable means that there is no society left to enjoy the benefits of the changes they seek. Our values are multiple; they sometimes clash; and we need to weigh, weigh, weigh.

Yet, I must admit that there is a powerful and humane motive impelling the absolutist position: that once you give nervous, hostile and ill-informed people a theoretical justification for using violence in certain cases, it is like a tiny hole in the dike: the rationales rush through in a torrent, and violence becomes the normal, acceptable solution for a problem.

This happened in the area of free speech. When Justice Holmes, perceptively noting that free speech is not an absolute right, came up with his famous example—should a man be allowed to shout "Fire!" in a crowded theater?—the gates were down, and the witch-hunters rushed through. The "clear and present danger" doctrine became a "fairly clear and one-of-these-days danger" doctrine. We began to persecute Communists even though their ineffectualness indicated that they were stammerers shouting fire in a foreign language to a deaf audience. Now that the absolute and unequivocal dictum of the First Amendment has been pushed aside, anything goes. This is why Justice Black insists on an absolute defense of free speech. And this may be why pacifists insist on an unequivocal rejection of violence.

I think, however, that it is in the nature of speech that the exceptions to an absolute defense of its freedom would be very few, whereas in the complex sphere of social action, there may be many situations requiring some measure of force or of pressure that produces counterforce. Moreover, in the area of free speech, most situations allow polar solutions; you either permit the speech or deny it. In the tactics of social change, however, there are countless intermediate positions between total passivity and total violence. Still, it is terribly important to understand that our starting point should be pacifism, that the burden of proof should be placed on the arguer for violence. Just as a man should be considered innocent until proved guilty, a policy should be automatically nonviolent until the weight of reason, undistorted by symbolism, argues otherwise. And even here we need a court of appeals, because a cardinal fact about violence is that, once initiated, it tends to get out of hand. Its limits are not predictable.

The actual process of weighing violence versus injustice differs in each specific case. Symbols distort the weighing, but the amount of distortion depends on how far the symbol is from the reality. Sometimes people can refer fairly easily to the specific human situation, as was the case in the 1930's, when the epithets of "socialism" directed at the New Deal could not fool people in the presence of hunger. Such is the situation in the desegregation campaigns today, where visible and appealing Negroes push through the old stereotypes to confront white America. Desegregation is a self-propelling process, because as it proceeds it brings more and more whites into contact with human beings instead of racist symbols.

The most notable contribution of the desegregation movement to other worthy causes is as a showcase for nonviolence under conditions where the technique is shown in the best light. It indicates the possibility, heretofore not clearly enunciated by either pacifists or revolutionists, of using minimum force to achieve maximum justice. Here is nonviolence at its best—a golden mean between passivity and violence. Such techniques have been used countless times in the history of reform—in labor struggles, farmers' movements, etc.— but never yet accompanied by a theory which enables transfer to other social problems.

The weighing is easy, too, in another aspect of American life, but has here been ignored. This is in the area of legal violence against criminals and suspected criminals: capital punishment, police brutality, the murder of burglary suspects. Here, symbolism is still unassaulted by reason and humanity. Last month, in Atlanta, an eighteen-year-old boy was shot and killed while running away from the scene of a vending-machine robbery that had netted him $3.84. The policeman who shot him was not firing at a human being, but at a symbol: a thief, an enemy of society. The policeman was defending another symbol: private property. As symbols, abstracted from flesh and blood, the solution is simple: private property must be protected. As reality, it looks different: the life of an eighteen-year-old boy against the loss of $3.84.

In capital punishment, too, we are not weighing how much justice will be accomplished by the act of judicial murder. If we did, the answer would be obvious: execution of a human being—no matter how foul his deed—cannot bring more happiness, more justice, into the world. But the figure in the electric chair is not a human being, and the act is not weighed in terms of human values. He is a part of a mathematical equation in our law books which says simply that a person who has violated a certain kind of law must be murdered. Our law is symbolic, not human, so abstracted from life that it is capable of the most horrible injustice.

With regard to revolution as a means of changing the social order, the weighing of violence against injustice is more difficult, and the complexity of the problem varies from case to case. Though the American Revolution took seven years and tens of thousands of lives, we are so infatuated with the results that we don't dare question its desirability. Is it possible that methods short of all-out war might have eased Britain off the backs of the colonists? Probably not, except over a long period of time and with constant nonviolent harassment. My point here is not to pass judgment on what is a most complicated revolutionary situation, but to argue that the use of violence as a corrective is so ingrained in the human psychology that we don't even question it. The French, Russian and, more recently, the Cuban revolutions, involving shorter bursts of violence against more uncompromising and backward regimes, are easier to justify; and the fact that each brought on its own brand of Bonapartism does not vitiate the fact of long-term social transformation in a positive direction. Yet these revolutions may have shed more blood than was necessary to achieve their results. You are grateful even for an inept surgeon who removes a festering appendix, but will look next time for someone who will accomplish surgery with less damage.

It is in large-scale, international wars that the pacifist can hardly go wrong, for here the violence is so massive, so symbolic, so unfocused on specific targets, that even a tremendous turn for the better in the conditions of millions of people does not make easy a judgment for war. World War I, which caused twenty million deaths, is a classic example of mass murder for dubious gain; it was probably the most stupid war in history.

World War II assaults our emotions as we begin to weigh the results in terms of social justice against the degree of violence employed. The reality of Nazism was as close to the symbol of total evil as any phenomenon in human history. In no other war have the issues seemed as clear-cut. Because of this we were able to pass lightly over massive immorality on the part of the Allies—the killing of hundreds of thousands in indiscriminate bombing raids on cities, climaxed by the horrible deeds at Hiroshima and Nagasaki. Altogether, forty million persons' lives were wiped out. Could we have defeated Hitler at a lesser cost? With so many lives at stake, could we not have exploited every alternative, sane or wild? Could we not have used nonviolence in a thousand different ways? Perhaps we might have let Hitler take territory after territory, allowed his empire to become bloated and sick, meanwhile organizing an underground against him everywhere. I am not at all sure of this, but what I want to do is to challenge the automatic acceptance of the traditional response to evil. Not only conservatives, but liberals and social revolutionaries as well, are paralyzed by habit.

There are clearly many cases where the weighing of nonviolence against social justice is difficult. Ironically, however, in the situation today, involving rocket-propelled missiles and hundred-megaton warheads, the decision should be obvious and easy—and the peoples of the world have not made it. A fundamental reason is that it is always harder to check up on the reality behind the verbal symbol in international affairs than it is in domestic issues. And the passions of the cold war have created symbolic distortions on an unprecedented scale. This is seen in both elements of the slogan that sums up much of American thinking: that we must "fight" to save the "free world."

It should be apparent to anyone who coldly surveys the effects of multimegaton weapons—the fireball, the explosion, the fallout, the mass cremation —that the word "fight" is a monstrous euphemism, and that no possible combination of evils in the world today can balance on the scales the mammoth, irretrievable evil of a nuclear war. But we do not have an electronic mechanism to conjure up the right pictures as soon as the word "fight" is heard. Thus, whenever some political issue arises which is subject to inflammation, whether it is Berlin or Formosa or Cuba, we begin to talk of "fighting" or "making our stand here." Americans hearing the word "fight" think, perhaps, of the last war, never of annihilation, never of agony beyond the imagination. We need somehow to push aside these verbal symbols and let people confront with open eyes what Giraudoux in *Tiger at the Gates* has Hecuba describe as the face of war: the backside of a baboon, hairy and red with a fungus growth. The Russians and Chinese, their memories of death more pervading, may have less trouble than we do with symbolic obstacles. Yet Marxist terms like "struggle," which they use constantly, are loose enough to becloud a variety of dangerous actions. In every country of the world, it needs to be stated flatly now and through all present crises and possible crises: there is no piece of territory in the world, no city, no nation, no social system, whose preservation is worth a thermonuclear war.

We find ourselves at a point in history full of paradoxes: H-bombs have, by their test explosions alone, obliterated the traditional revolutionary idea of a "just war" and suggest caution to advocates of social upheaval. Yet social injustice is everywhere in the world, crying for correction. At this very moment the technique of nonviolence is brought to our attention by the sit-ins of the American South, by the sailors of the *Golden Rule,* by the demonstrators in Trafalgar Square. It is no one method, but an arsenal of methods, all of which start beyond passivity and stop short of war. It recognizes honestly that once passivity is renounced, some degree of force may enter the situation, but it is determined to keep this to a minimum, and starts always from the assumption of zero violence. Nonviolent activists win over the onlookers of the world and make things more difficult for the perpetrators of violence and injustice. They know the value of words as the tools of symbolic distortion which prevent people from perceiving reality; but they are especially concerned with human contact—interracial and international—as a way of directly smashing through the walls of symbol. While violence is blunt and undiscriminating, nonviolence is sharp, particularized, focused, flexible.

The Negro in the South has given the cue, but the nation has not taken it. That beautiful balance embodied by the sit-ins and Freedom Rides is cautiously condoned, but not emulated, by the government. And yet it is especially in the United States that the technique of nonviolence is demanded, at a time when domestic injustice and stupidity in foreign policy require assault. Ironically, our government is missing the golden mean of nonviolence on both counts, for it is passive in domestic affairs which it *can* control, and violent abroad in situations it *can't* control.

The truth is that our entire political system is geared toward a strange inversion. The antiquated structure of Congress—its committee system operating by seniority, the gerrymandered state legislatures—is only the manifestation of a basic political malaise that operates to make our legislative bodies representative of the most backward elements of the population. Our cumbersome lawmaking machinery, its controls supervised by Southern reactionaries, is not geared to the swift pace and zooming expectations of the twentieth century. This is shown in instance after instance where the President cannot get the mildest pieces of social-welfare legislation through Congress, or secure a petty amount of cash to support the United Nations. In foreign policy, on the other hand, he has a free hand. The result is that he is quicker to assault Cuba than to assault Congress.

George Kennan and others have argued convincingly that the most effective thing we can do in foreign affairs is to create a magnificent social system at home. The plain fact is that despite our superfluity of autos and television sets, we cannot really come before the world and say: here is your ideal social system, where the wealth of the nation is distributed in such a way as to eliminate poverty and insecurity, where the aged are taken care of and the sick are cured regardless of their finances, where all who want education can get it, where artists, poets, musicians and writers can achieve as much economic security as the man who designs a new Yo-Yo.

It was the feeble ineptitude of the strongest government on earth that brought on the sit-in movement. That seven hundred Negroes in Albany, Georgia, had to demonstrate in the streets to put into effect an Interstate Commerce Commission ruling that had not been enforced by the government is embarrassingly representative of the years since 1954.

What the Southern Negro has done for desegregation can also work for freedom of speech and assembly, for medical care, against capital punishment. Nonviolent techniques—the kind already used and many kinds still germinating in our imaginations—seem the only sensible answer to a world sitting in a minefield and yet needing to move. They can be effective in the swamp of representative government and within the stone walls of Communist bureaucracy. They employ humor, kindness, pressures, flexibility, attack and retreat—guerrilla warfare in time of peace. Today, when force is absolute, we may have to live, and advance, by our wits.

Man, separated from his fellow man by symbolic distortion, has been violent for most of his history. But he has also shown the ability to break through symbols, to make direct contact with other human beings and to renounce violence. He is not determined inexorably in either direction, the social psychologists and cultural anthropologists tell us. Perhaps here is our chief hope. Man is open to suggestion. And nonviolence uses neither compulsion nor silence. Calmly, powerfully, it suggests.

Pacifism and Violence:
A Study in Bourgeois Ethics
Christopher Caudwell

There is not much left of importance in bourgeois ethics. Chastity, sobriety, salvation and cleanliness have ceased to be topics on which the bourgeois feels very deeply. There is, in fact, only one issue on which the bourgeois conscience is to-day warmed into activity. Pacifism, always latent in the bourgeois creed, has now crystallised out as almost the only emotionally-charged belief left in Protestant Christianity or in its analogue, bourgeois 'idealism'.

I call it a distinctively bourgeois doctrine, because I mean by pacifism, not the love of peace as a good to be secured by a definite form of action, but the belief that any form of social constraint of others or any violent action is in itself wrong, and that violence such as War must be *passively* resisted because to use violence to end violence would be logically self-contradictory. I oppose pacifism in this sense to the Communist belief that the only way to secure peace is by a revolutionary change in the social system, and that ruling classes resist revolution violently and must therefore be overthrown by force.

But modern war is also distinctively bourgeois. Struggles such as the last war arise from the unequal Imperialist development of the bourgeois powers, and earlier wars of bourgeois culture were also fought for aims characteristic of bourgeois economy or, like the wars of the infant Dutch republic, represented the struggles of the growing bourgeois class against feudal forces. In its last stage of Fascism, when capitalism, throwing off the democratic forms which no longer serve its purpose, rules with open violence, bourgeois culture is also seen as aggressively militant. Are we Marxists then simply using labels indiscriminately when we class as characteristically bourgeois, both militancy *and* pacifism, meekness *and* violence?

No, we are not doing so, if we can show that we call bourgeois not all war and not all pacifism but only certain types of violence, and only certain types of non-violence; and if, further, we can show how the one fundamental bourgeois position generates both these apparently opposed viewpoints. We did the same thing when we showed that two philosophies which are apparently completely opposed—mechanical materialism and idealism—were both characteristically bourgeois, and both generated by the one bourgeois assumption.

Bourgeois pacifism is distinctive and should not be confused, for example,

From *Studies and Further Studies in a Dying Culture*. Copyright © 1971 by Monthly Review Press. Reprinted by permission of Monthly Review Press. Christopher Caudwell (Christopher St. John Sprigg, 1907–1937) was a British Communist writer. He was killed in action while fighting for the International Brigade in Spain.

with Eastern pacifism, any more than modern European warfare should be confused with feudal warfare. It is not merely that the social manifestations of it are different—this would necessarily arise from the different social organs of the two cultures. But the content also is different. Anyone who supposes that bourgeois pacifism will, for example, take the form of a University Anti-War Group lying down on the rails in front of a departing troop train like an Indian pacifist group, is to be ignorant of the nature of bourgeois pacifism and of whence it took its colour. The historic example of bourgeois pacifism is not Gandhi but Fox. The Society of Friends expresses the spirit of bourgeois pacifism. It is individual resistance.

To understand how bourgeois pacifism arises, we must understand how bourgeois violence arises. It arises, just as does feudal or despotic violence, from the characteristic economy of the system. As was first explained by Marx, the characteristics of bourgeois economy are that the bourgeois, held down and crippled productively by the feudal system, comes to see freedom and productive growth in lack of social organisation, in every man's administering his own affairs for his own benefit to the best of his ability and desire, and this is expressed in the absolute character of bourgeois property together with its complete alienability. His struggle to achieve this right did secure his greater freedom and productive power as compared with his position in the feudal system. The circumstances of the struggle and its outcome gave rise to the bourgeois dream—freedom as the absolute elimination of social relations.

But such a programme, if carried into effect, would mean the end of society and the break-down of economic production. Each man would struggle for himself, and if he saw another man with something he wanted, he would seize it, for by assumption no such social relations as co-operation exist. The saving and foresight which makes economic production possible would cease to exist. Man would become a brute.

But in fact the bourgeois had no desire for such a world. He lived by merchandising and banking, by *capital* as opposed to the land which was the basis of feudal exploitation. Therefore he meant by the 'absence of social restraints', the absence of any restraint on his ownership, alienation, or acquisition at will of the capital by which he lived. Private property is a social 'restraint', for others not owning it are 'restrained' from helping themselves to it by force or cunning, as they could in a 'state of nature'; but the bourgeois never included the ownership of capital as one of the social restraints that should be abolished, for the simple reason that it was not to him a restraint at all. It never therefore entered his head to regard it as such, and he saw nothing inconsistent in calling for the abolition of privilege, monopoly, and so forth, while hanging on to his capital.

Moreover, he had a cogent argument which, when he became more self-conscious, he could use. A social restraint is a social relation, that is, a relation between men. The relation between master and slave is a social relation and therefore a restraint on the liberty of one man by the other. In the same

way the relation between lord and serf is a relation between men and a restraint on human liberty; but the relation between a man and his property
is a relation between man and a thing, and is therefore no restraint on the
liberty of other men.

This argument was of course fallacious, for there can be no universal
relations of this kind as the fabric of society, there can only be relations
between men disguised as relations between things. The bourgeois defence of
private property only applies if I go out into the woods and pick up a stick
to walk with, or fashion an ornamental object for my adornment; it applies
to the possession of socially unimportant trifles or things for immediate consumption. As soon as bourgeois possession extends to the capital of the
community, consisting of the products of the community set aside to produce
goods in the future (in early bourgeois civilisation, grain, clothes, seed and
raw materials to supply the labourers of to-morrow, and in addition machinery
and plant for the same purpose to-day), this relation to a thing becomes a
relation among men, for it is now the labour of the community which the
bourgeois controls. The bourgeois right of private property leads to this, that
on the one hand the world and all that society has created in it belongs to
the bourgeois, and on the other hand stands the naked labourer, who is
forced by the needs of his body to sell his labour-power to the bourgeois in
order to feed himself and his master. The bourgeois will only buy his labour-
power, if he makes a profit from it. This social relation is only made possible
by—it *depends on*—the bourgeois ownership of capital. Thus, just as in slave-
owning or serf-owning civilisation there is a relation between men which is a
relation between a dominating and a dominated class, or between exploiters
and exploited; so there is in bourgeois culture, but whereas in earlier civilisations this relation between men is conscious and clear, in bourgeois culture
it is disguised as a system free from obligatory dominating relations between
men and containing only innocent relations between men and a thing.

Therefore, in throwing off all social restraint, the bourgeois seemed to
himself justified in retaining this one restraint of private property, for it did
not seem to him a restraint at all, but an inalienable right of man, the
fundamental natural right. Unfortunately for this theory, there are no natural
rights, only situations found in nature, and private property protected for
one man by others is not one of them. Bourgeois private property could only
be protected by coercion—the *have-nots* had to be coerced by the *haves* after
all, just as in feudal society. Thus a dominating relation as violent as in slave-
owning civilisations came into being, expressed in the police, the laws, the
standing army, and the legal apparatus of the bourgeois State. The whole
bourgeois State revolves round the coercive protection of private property,
alienable and acquirable by trading for private profit, and regarded as a
natural right, but a right which, strangely enough, can only be protected by
coercion, because it involves of its essence a right to dispose of and extract
profit from the labour-power of others, and so administer their lives.

Thus, after all, the bourgeois dream of liberty cannot be realised. Social restraints must come into being to protect this one thing that makes him a bourgeois. This 'freedom' to own private property seems to him inexplicably to involve more and more social restraints, laws, tariffs, and factory acts; and this 'society' in which only relations to a thing are permitted becomes more and more a society in which relations between men are elaborate and cruel. The more he aims for bourgeois freedom, the more he gets bourgeois restraint, for bourgeois freedom is an illusion.

Thus, just as much as in slave-owning society, bourgeois society turns out to be a society built on violent coercion of men by men, the more violent in that while the master must feed and protect his slave, whether he works or not, the bourgeois employer owns no obligation to the free labourer, not even to find him work. The whole bourgeois dream explodes in practice, and the bourgeois state becomes a theatre of the violent and coercive subjection of man to man for the purposes of economic production.

Unlike the violence of the footpad, the violence of the bourgeois though similar in motive plays a social rôle. It is the relation whereby social production is secured in bourgeois society, just as the master-to-slave relation secures production in a slave-owning civilisation. It is for its epoch the best method of securing production, and it is better to be a slave than a beast of the jungle, better to be an exploited labourer than a slave, not because the bourgeois employer is 'nicer' than the slave-owner (he is often a good deal crueller), but because the wealth of society as a whole is more with the former relation than the latter.

But no system of relations is static, it develops and changes. Slave-owning relations develop into Empires and then reveal their internal contradictions. They collapse. The story of the collapse of the Roman Empire is the story of the constant decline of the taxable wealth of the Empire between Augustus and Justinian as a result of increasing exploitation until, a poverty-stricken shell, it crumbled before the assaults of the barbarian, up till then easily repelled. In the same way, feudal civilisation, exhausted in England by the anarchy of the Wars of the Roses, collapsed. But not this time, before an external enemy; it fell before an internal enemy, the rising bourgeois class.

Bourgeois relations, too, developed. In the famous bourgeois booms and slumps, they show the potential decay of the system. This decay was retarded by Imperialism, that is, by forcibly imposing on other countries the 'natural rights' of the bourgeois. In these backward countries the bourgeois right to trade profitably and to alienate and acquire any property was forcibly imposed. Here too the bourgeois, out of his dominating relation to a thing, secretly imposed his dominating relation over men, which can yet be disguised as democracy, for does not democracy declare that all men are equal and none may enslave the other? Does it not exclude all relations of domination—despotism, slave-owning, feudal privilege—except the 'innocent' domination of capitalist over 'free' labourer?

But in this imperialising, a new situation arose—*external* war instead of *internal* violence and coercion. For now, in exploiting backward countries, or, it was called, 'civilising' them, one bourgeois State found itself competing with another, just as inside the State bourgeois competes with bourgeois.

But inside the State bourgeois competes with bourgeois peacefully, because it is the law—and this law was established for their own protection against the exploited. The laws forbidding one bourgeois to seize another's property by force arose as the result of the need to prevent the have-nots seizing property by force. It is an internal law, the law of the coercive State. If it had not been necessary for the existence of the whole bourgeois class for them to be protected against the seizing of their property by the exploited, the law against the forcible seizure of private property, coercively enforced and taught to the exploited as a 'necessary' law of society, would never have come into existence. For the individualistic, competitive nature of bourgeois trade (each 'getting the better' of the other) is such that no bourgeois sees anything wrong in impoverishing another bourgeois. If he is 'bust' or 'hammered'—well, it's the luck of the game. But all unite as a class against the exploited, for the existence of the class depends on this. If it is a case of a battle royal *inside* the bourgeois class, each bourgeois believes by nature and education that, given an equal chance, he will get the better of the other. This eternal optimism of the bourgeois is seen in the historic bourgeois appeals for 'fair-play', 'fair field and no favour', and all the other allied bourgeois slogans which express the ethics of the 'sporting' English gentleman.

It is quite different when the bourgeois States, through their coercive organisations, find themselves competing in the world arena for the backward lands. There is now no numerous exploited class menacing the existence of the class of bourgeois States *as a whole*. *Inside* the coercive State, if it came to a 'show-down', with street-fighting, bare hands, and man against man— the exploited would win. But in the Imperialistic arena the bourgeois States appear as highly developed organisms, for, thanks to the unification of the coercive State, they now dispose of all the resources of an advanced society, including the services, in the army, of the exploited class itself. The backward nations still play inside the world arena the role of the exploited class inside the State, but they are not a danger to the class of bourgeois States as a whole, as is the exploited class to the class of bourgeois as a whole inside the State. They are just inanimate things, almost defenceless, so much dead undeveloped territory.

There is then no world danger threatening the class of bourgeois States as a whole, as, in a State, revolution threatens the class of bourgeois as a whole. There is only individual competition among bourgeois States, and, as we have seen, the bourgeois never minds this. All he asks for is 'fair field and no favour' and he is certain that he will come out on top. He feels no need for a law to restrain competition among bourgeois. Hence the sovereign bourgeois State comes into being and battles bloodily with other bourgeois States for the booty of the backward territory. This is the age of Imperialism, culminating in the Great War.

Needless to say, the bourgeois finds the bourgeois dream—'a fair field and no favour'—when realised for the first time, far bloodier and more violent than he dreamed. War presently comes to seem to him 'unfair competition'. Like a price-cutting war, it alarms him and he feels someone from outside ought to stop it. He calls for aid; but there is no one 'outside'. For to whom, on heaven or earth, can he call, as a member of the class of independent *sovereign* States?

Still he has a dream. If the class of bourgeois in *one* country can have a State and police force enforcing order and non-violent competition, why not a State of States, a world-State, in which world peace is enforced?

This bourgeois hope perpetually recurs in the chaos of war, and the League of Nations is one form of it. But the one factor which secures internal law in the bourgeois State—the existence of a dangerous exploited class—does not exist in the *world* arena. No danger confronts the class of bourgeois States *as a whole,* and thus they can never unite to accept a coercive regulating law superior to their own wills. The danger only exists as among themselves and each, like a good bourgeois, believes that, by appropriate 'combination', treaty-making, and manoeuvring, he can best the others. The bourgeois dream of a peaceful Imperialism is unrealisable for want of a danger common to all bourgeois States to unite them. After a bitter experience of the unpleasantness of price-cutting, they can unite in a voluntary cartel, the League of Nations, but like a cartel it lacks the cohesion and coercive power of the bourgeois State and therefore lacks also its efficiency in mediating between bourgeois. It is like a price agreement to which all voluntarily adhere for their own individual benefit. Since, in bourgeois production in general, and Imperialist exploitation in particular, an agreement cannot work always for the good of all, it is only a matter of time before the cartel is denounced by some and we see the *have-not* bourgeois States (Germany and Italy) are outside the cartel, and arrayed against the *haves* (France and England), while that bourgeois State (America) whose interests do not lie in the same sphere of Imperialist exploitation, has never joined the cartel. Thus in spite of the bitterest lessons possible to a nation, proving the inefficiency of war as a palliative of slump, it is not possible for States whose forms coercively express bourgeois interests to acknowledge a superior co-ordinating force, which would produce in the international sphere legal machinery like that securing internal order in the State, for this internal machinery is directed against the dangerous exploited class, and in the international sphere there is no dangerous exploited class. Thus the peaceful World Federation of States, the League, becomes part of the bourgeois illusion, and the nations arm themselves still more heavily.

Could not Russia, as a proletarian State, furnish the equivalent in the international sphere of the exploited class, and force the independent bourgeois States to unite and crush her? This was the Trotsky nightmare, from which it followed that Socialism could not be established anywhere without a world revolution. But this theory overlooked the fact that Soviet Russia is not an exploited State. An exploited class, in a bourgeois State, is a class held up to ransom by the bourgeois, who hold the means of production in their hands. It is a case of: 'Work for us or die.' Such a situation can only be maintained by moral and physical coercion and therefore bourgeois 'rights' have to be maintained in this way perpetually; otherwise men would not naturally tolerate a situation where their very means of livelihood were in another's hands and could be only secured if they generated profit for that other. But in Russia this class has expropriated their expropriators. It is not a case of working for other bourgeois States or dying; the Russian workers are their own masters. Moreover, unlike other bourgeois States, there are no internal contradictions in their economy (accumulation of capital) forcing them to seek new fields of exploitation.

Russia appears, therefore, in the world arena, to the bourgeois States, not as an exploited class inherently dangerous but as an ordinary internally ordered coercive State—'one of themselves'. She competes with them in open world markets but, for reasons that do not concern them, does not seek backward countries on which to impose Imperialist exploitation. She can therefore join their cartel. In this cartel her duty is to join the bourgeois game—playing one alliance off against another—not to gain Imperialistic advantage but in order to secure peace for herself and for the unfortunate proletariat of the bourgeois States.

It is true that Russia is a danger to all bourgeois States in that her success is an inspiration to a proletarian revolution in every State. But the world proletarian revolution means the end of bourgeois economy, and this, to the bourgeois, is at first simply ludicrous. On the one hand he tells himself that Bolshevism is only a 'passing phase', and, on the other hand, that in modern Soviet Russia there is simply 'planned capitalism'. Moreover, the proletarian revolution will not come from Russia, it will come from inside, and it would therefore be pointless to attempt to stop, say, the British proletariat from rising by attacking Russia. On the contrary, such a move would hasten the very event that is dreaded. Thus, although the bourgeois States denounce Russia, they cannot be united in one common attack on her, but instead are ready to enter into pacts with her, to use her against each other.

That is not to say Russia is not in danger. On the contrary, all bourgeois States are in danger from each other in so far as they represent possible fields of Imperialistic exploitation. In this respect Russia is in as much danger from Germany as Britain from Germany. It is therefore necessary for her to arm herself as heavily as her bourgeois neighbours and try to strengthen herself by pacts, the international equivalent of cartels and trade agreements.

Only when the bourgeois begins to see the inevitability of Communism does he begin to regard Russia as a greater danger than any other bourgeois State. But this realisation is just what causes the capitalist class to resort to Fascism and therefore the Fascist States constitute the main danger to Russia to-day.

This, then, is the analysis of bourgeois violence. It is not like something that descends from heaven for a time to madden the human race. It is implicit in the bourgeois illusion.

The whole bourgeois economy is built on the violent domination of men by men through the private possession of social capital. It is always there, waiting ready at any moment to flame out in a Peterlee or an Amritsar within the bourgeois State, or a Boer War or Great War outside it.

As long as the bourgeois economy remains a positive constructive force, that violence is hidden. Society does not contain a powerful internal pressure until productive forces have outgrown the system of productive relations. Until this revolutionary pressure develops, it is therefore unnecessary for coercion to show itself bloodily or on a wide scale.

But when bourgeois economy is riven by its own contradictions, when private profit is seen to be public harm, when poverty and unemployment grow in the midst of the means of plenty, bourgeois violence becomes more open. These contradictions drive the bourgeois States to Imperialistic wars, in which violence reigns without a qualifying factor. Internally violence instead of 'reason' alone suffices to maintain the bourgeois system. Since the capitalistic system is openly proving its inefficiency, people are no longer content with a form of government, parliamentary democracy, in which economic production is run by the bourgeois class, leaving the people as a whole only the power to settle, within narrow limits, through Parliament, the apportionment of a merely administrative budget. They see this to be a sham, and see no reason to tolerate the sham. There is a growing demand for socialism, and the capitalist class where this grows pressing, resort to open violence. They use the revolt against ineffectual democracy to establish a dictatorship, and this dictatorship, which seizes power with the cry 'Down with Capitalism', in fact establishes capitalism still more violently, as in Fascist Italy and Germany. The brutal oppression and cynical violence of Fascism is the summit of bourgeois decline. The violence at the heart of the bourgeois illusion emerges inside as well as outside the State.

The justification of bourgeois violence is an important part of bourgeois ethics. The coercive control of social labour by a limited class is justified as a relation to a thing. Even as late as Hegel, this justification is given quite naïvely and simply. Just as I go out and break off a stick of wood from the primitive jungle and convert it to my purpose, so the bourgeois is supposed to convert the thing 'capital' to his use. Domination over men is wicked; domination over things is legitimate.

The nature of bourgeois economy made it possible for Hegel to believe this seriously. But when the true nature of bourgeois economy had been analysed by Marx, as a dominating relation over men through ownership of the means of social labour and individual livelihood, how could this naïve bourgeois attitude persist? Only by vilifying Marx, by always attacking him violently without explaining his views, and by continuing to teach, preach and practise the old bourgeois theory. It was then that the bourgeois illusion became the bourgeois lie, a conscious deception festering at the heart of bourgeois culture.

Bourgeois ethics include the more difficult task of justification of the violence of bourgeois war. The Christian-bourgeois ethic has been equal even to this. Consonant to the bourgeois illusion, all interference with the liberty of another is wicked and immoral. If one is attacked in one's liberty, one is therefore compelled to defend outraged morality and attack in turn. All bourgeois wars are therefore justified by both parties as wars of defence. Bourgeois liberty includes the right to exercise all bourgeois occupations— alienating, trading, and acquiring for profit—and since these involve establishing dominating relations over others, it is not surprising that the bourgeois often finds himself attacked in his liberty. It is impossible for the bourgeois to exercise his full liberty without infringing the liberty of another. It is impossible therefore to be thoroughly bourgeois and not give occasion for 'just' wars.

Meanwhile bourgeois discomforts generate an opposition to bourgeois violence. At each stage of bourgeois development men could be found who were impregnated with the bourgeois illusion, that man is free and happy only when without social restraints, and who yet found in bourgeois economy multiplying coercions and restraints. We saw why these exist; the bourgeois economy requires coercion and restraint for its very life. The big bourgeois dominates the *petit bourgeois,* just as both dominate the proletariat. But these early bourgeois rebels could not see this. They demanded a return to the bourgeois dream—'equal rights for all', 'freedom from social restraints', the 'natural rights' of men. They thought that this would free them from the big bourgeoisie, and give them equal competition once again.

Thus originated the cleavage between conservatives and liberals, between the big bourgeois in possession and the little bourgeois wishing to be in possession. The one sees that his position depends on maintaining things as they are; the other sees his as depending on more bourgeois freedom, more votes for all, more freedom for private property to be alienated, acquired, and owned, more free competition, less privilege.

The liberal is the active force. But so far from being revolutionary, as he thinks, he is evolutionary. In striving for bourgeois freedom and fair competition he produces by this very action an increase in the social restraints he hates. He builds up the big bourgeoisie in trying to support the little, although he may make himself a big bourgeois in the process. He increases unfairness by trying to secure fairness. Free trade gives birth to tariffs, Imperialism and monopoly, because it is hastening the development of bourgeois economy, and these things are the necessary end of bourgeois development. He calls into being the things he loathes because, as long as he is in the grip of the bourgeois illusion that freedom consists in absence of social planning, he must put himself, by loosening social ties, more powerfully in the grip of coercive social forces.

This 'revolutionary' liberal, this hater of coercion and violence, this lover of free competition, this friend of liberty and human rights, is therefore the very man damned by history not merely to be powerless to stop these things, but to be forced by his own efforts to produce coercion and violence and unfair competition and slavery. He does not merely refrain from opposing bourgeois violence, he generates it, by helping on the development of bourgeois economy.

To-day, as the bourgeois pacifist, he helps to generate the violence, war, and Fascist and Imperialist brutality he hates. In so far as he is a genuine pacifist and not merely a completely muddled man hesitating between the paths of revolution and non-co-operation, his thesis is this, 'I hate violence and war and social oppression, and all these things are due to social relations. I must therefore abstain from social relations. Belligerent and revolutionary alike are hateful to me.'

But to abstain from social relations, is to abstain from life. As long as he draws or earns an income, he participates in bourgeois economy, and upholds the violence which sustains it. He is in sleeping partnership with the big bourgeoisie, and that is the essence of bourgeois economy. If two other countries are at war, he is powerless to intervene and stop them, for that means social co-operation—social co-operation issuing in coercion, like a man separating quarrelling friends, and that action is by his definition barred to him. If the big bourgeoisie of his own country decide to go to war and mobilise the coercive forces, physical and moral, of the State, he can do nothing real, for the only real answer is co-operation with the proletariat to resist the coercive action of the big bourgeoisie and oust them from power. If Fascism develops, he cannot suppress it in the bud before it has built up an army to intimidate the proletariat, for he believes in 'free speech'. He can only watch the workers being bludgeoned and beheaded by the forces he allowed to develop.

His position rests firmly on the bourgeois fallacy. He thinks that man as an individual has power. He does not see that even in the unlikely event of everyone's taking his viewpoint and saying, 'I will passively resist,' his purpose will still not be achieved. For men cannot in fact cease to co-operate, because society's work must be carried on—grain must be reaped, clothes spun, electricity generated or man will perish from the earth. Only his position as a member of a parasitic class could have given him any other illusion. A worker sees that his very life depends on economic co-operation and that this co-operation of itself imposes social relations which in bourgeois economy must be bourgeois, that is, must in greater or less measure give into the hands of the big bourgeoisie the violent issues of life and death. Passive resistance is not a real programme, but an apology for supporting the old programme. A man either participates in bourgeois economy, or he revolts and tries to establish another economy. Another apparent road is to break up society and return to the jungle, the solution of *anarchy*. But that is no solution at all. The only real alternative to bourgeois economy is proletarian economy, i.e., socialism, and therefore one either participates in bourgeois economy or is a proletarian revolutionary. The fact that one participates passively in bourgeois economy, that one does not oneself wield the bludgeon or fire the cannon, so far from being a defence really makes one's position more disgusting, just as a fence is more unpleasant than a burglar, and a pimp than a prostitute. One lets others do the dirty work, and merely participates in the benefit. The bourgeois pacifist occupies perhaps the most ignoble place of a man in any civilisation. He is the Christian Protestant whose ethics have been made ridiculous by the development of the culture that evolved them; but this does not prevent his deriving complacency from observing them. He sits on the head of the worker and, while the big bourgeois kicks him, advises him to lie quiet. When (as did some pacifists during the general strike) he 'maintains essential services' during the 'violent' struggles of the proletariat for freedom, he becomes a portent.

Pacifism, for all its spacious moral aspect, is, like Protestant Christianity, the creed of ultra-individualism and selfishness, just as Roman Catholicism is the creed of monopoly and privileged domination. This selfishness is seen in all the defences the bourgeois pacifist makes of his creed.

The first defence is that it is wrong. It is a 'sin' to slay or resort to violence. Christ forbids it. The pacifist who resorts to violence imbrues his soul with heinous guilt. In this conception nothing appears as important but the pacifist's own soul. It is this precious soul of his that he is worrying about, like the good bourgeoise about her honour which is such an important social asset. Society can go to the devil if his soul is intact. So imbued is he with bourgeois notions of sin, that it never occurs to him that a preoccupation with one's own soul and one's own salvation is selfish. It may be that a man is right to save his own skin before all; that the pacifist above all must prevent the contamination of his precious soul by the mortal sin of violence. But what is this but the translation into spiritual terms of the good old bourgeois rule of *laissez-faire* and bourgeoisdom—May the devil take the hindmost? It is a spiritual *laissez-faire*. It is a belief that the interests of society—*God's* purpose—are best served by not performing any action, however beneficial to others, if it would imperil one's own 'soul'. This is crystallised in the maxim, 'One may not do ill that good may come of it.'

Primitives have a more social conception of sin. Sin is reprehensible because it involves the whole tribe in danger. The sinner flees from the tribe because he has involved it in evil, not in order to save himself; he is damned by his sin. Going into the desert, he slays himself or is slain, thus lifting from the tribe, after it has performed appropriate purifications, the evil in which he has involved it. Both conceptions are bound in error, but this savage conception is nobler and more altruistic than the bourgeois conception in which each man is responsible solely for his own sins, and purifies them by a private resort to the blood of Christ. The pacifist has remembered the saying of Cain: 'Am I my brother's keeper?'

This tribal conception of salvation was partly retained in feudal society by the Church, which kept clearly in mind the unity of the Church Militant, the Church Suffering, and the Church Triumphant, each of which, by its prayers, could communicate with or help the others. The feudal Christian prayed for the Holy Souls suffering in Purgatory, expected those living to pray for him when dead, and continually called on the departed members of the tribe, the Triumphant Souls of the Saints in heaven, to help him, to such an extent that, in this strong social grouping, God was almost forgotten. The social unity alone emerges, and individual sin becomes pardoned by the mere act of socialisation, in the confessional.

Thus Catholicism symbolised the social nature of feudalism; the 'tribe' was all Christendom. Its typical act was the Crusade, the violent assault of Christendom on paganism.

Protestantism, the religion of the bourgeoisie, necessarily revolted against tribal Catholicism. As a religion, it 'reformed' all the social elements in Catholicism. It became Catholicism minus the social elements and plus individualism. Authority was abandoned; the priest, the repository of the magic and conscience of the tribe was shorn of his power; the prayers for the dead and to the saints were unindividualistic, therefore purgatory did not exist and the saints were helpless. Each man was to be his own judge, bear his own sin, and work out his own salvation. The notion of individual guilt, as in Bunyan and the Puritans, reached a pitch it had never achieved in Catholic countries. Hence too the new phenomenon of 'conversion', in which this intolerable self-induced burden of guilt is thrown into the bosom of Christ. For man cannot in fact live alone. This conversion was evidence of it; that the individualism of bourgeoisdom is only a façade, and that at the very moment he proclaims it, the individual needs some fictitious entity or Divine Scapegoat on whom he can fling, in a final act of selfishness, the responsibility he never completely bore.

Thus pacifism as a method of avoiding the moral guilt of violence, is selfish. The pacifist claims, as a primary duty, the right of saving his *own* skin. We are not concerned with whether it is ethically right for man to consider himself first. To the bourgeois philosophy, properly expressed, it is so. To another system of social relations it cannot be right. To a third— communism, it is neither right nor wrong, it is impossible, for all individual actions affect others in society. This fact makes the bourgeois inconsistent, and at one moment want to give his life for others and at the next to sacrifice their lives to preserve his soul.

Some pacifists, however, make a different defence. They are not concerned with their own souls. They are only thinking of others. Pacifism is the only way to stop violence and oppression. Violence breeds violence; oppression breeds oppression. How far is this argument well grounded, and not merely a rationalisation of the bourgeois illusion?

No pacifist has yet explained the causal chain by which non-resistance ends violence. It is true that it does so in this obvious way, that if no resistance is made to violent commands, no violence is necessary to enforce them. Thus if *A* does everything *B* asks him, it will not be necessary for *B* to use violence. But a dominating relation of this kind is in essence violent, although violence is not overtly shown. Subjection is subjection, and rapacity rapacity, even if the weakness of the victim, or the fear inspired by the victor, makes the process non-forcible. Non-resistance will not prevent it, any more than the lack of claws on the part of prey prevents carnivores battening on them. On the contrary, the carnivore selects as his victim animals of the kind. The remedy is the elimination of carnivores, that is, the extinction of classes that live by preying on others.

Another assumption is that man, being what he is, the sight of his defenceless victims will arouse his pity. Now this assumption is not in itself ridiculous, but it needs examination. Is it a historical fact that the defencelessness of his victims has ever aroused man's pity? History records millions of opposite cases, of Tamburlaine and his atrocities, Attila and his Huns (checked only by violence), Mohammedan incursions, primitive slayings, the Danes and their monastic massacres. Can anyone in good faith advance the proposition that non-resistance defeats violence? How could slave-owning states exist, if peaceful submission touched the hearts of the conquerors? How could man bear to slaughter perpetually the dumb unresisting races of sheep, swine, and oxen?

Moreover, the argument makes the usual bourgeois error of eternalising its categories, the belief that there is a kind of abstract Robinson Crusoe man of whose actions definite predictions can be made. But how can one seriously subsume under one category Tamburlaine, Socrates, a Chinese mandarin, a modern Londoner, an Aztec priest, a Paleolithic hunter, and a Roman galley-slave? There is no abstract man, but men in different networks of social relations, with similar heredities but moulded into different proclivities by education and the constant pressure of social being.

To-day, it is man in bourgeois social relations with whom we are concerned. Of what effect would it be if we no longer resisted violence, if England, for example, at the beginning of the Great War, had passively permitted Germany to occupy Belgium, and accept without resistance all that Germany wished to do?

There is this much truth in the pacifist argument: that a country in a state of bourgeois social relations cannot act like a nomad horde. Bourgeoisdom has discovered that Tamburlaine exploitation does not pay so well as bourgeois exploitation. It is of no use to a bourgeois to sweep over a country, to lift all the wine and fair women and gold thereof and sweep out again. The fair women grow old and ugly, the wine is drunk, and the gold avails for nothing but ornaments. That would be Dead Sea fruit in the mouth of bourgeois culture, which lives on an endless diet of profit and a perpetual domination.

Bourgeois culture has discovered that what pays is bourgeois violence. This is more subtle and less overt than Tamburlaine violence. Roman violence, which consisted in bringing home not only fair women and gold, but slaves also, and making them work in the household, farms, and mines, occupied a mid-position. Bourgeois culture has discovered that those social relations are most profitable to the bourgeois which do not include rapine and personal slavery, but on the contrary forbid it. Therefore the bourgeois, wherever he has conquered non-bourgeois territory, such as Australia, America, Africa, or India, has imposed bourgeois, not Tamburlaine, social relations. In the name of liberty, self-determination, and democracy, or sometimes without these names, they enforce the bourgeois essence, private property, and the owner-ship of the means of production for profit, and its necessary prerequisite, the free labourer forced to dispose of his labour, for a wage, in the market. This priceless bourgeois discovery has produced material wealth beyond the dreams of a Tamburlaine or a Crœsus.

Consequently England need have no fear that a victorious Germany would have raped all Englishwomen and beheaded all Englishmen and transported the Elgin marbles to Berlin. Bourgeois States do not do such things. It would have confined itself to taking England's Imperial possessions and completing the profitable task of converting them to full bourgeois social relations. It would also have attempted to cripple England as a trade competitor by a heavy indemnity. In other words, resist or not, it would, if victorious, have done to England what victorious England did to Germany.

Thus, even if the pacifist dream was realised, bourgeois violence would go on. But in fact it would not be realised. How could a bourgeois coercive State submit to having its source of profits violently taken away by another bourgeois State, and not use all the sources of violence at its disposal to stop it? Would it not rather disrupt the whole internal fabric of its State than permit such a thing? Is bourgeoisdom not now disrupting violently the whole fabric of society, rather than forgo its private profits and give up the system of economy on which it is based? Fascism and Nazism, bloodily treading the road to bankruptcy, are evidence of this. Bourgeois economy, because it is unplanned, will cut its own throat rather than reform, and pacifism is only the expression of this last-ditch stand of bourgeois culture, which will at the best rather do nothing than do the thing that will end the social relations on which it is based.

Have we the courage to realise forcibly our views? What guarantee have we of their truth? The only real guarantee *is* action. We have the courage to enforce our beliefs upon physical matter, to build up the material substratum of society in houses, roads, bridges, and ships, despite the risk to human life, because our theories, generated by action, are tested in action. Let the bridge fall, the ship sink, the house collapse if we are wrong. We have investigated the causality of nature; let it be proved upon ourselves if we are wrong.

Exactly the same applies to social relations. Bridges have collapsed be-fore now, cultures have mouldered in decay, vast civilisations have foundered, but they did not decay uselessly. From each mistake we have learned some-thing, and the Tamburlaine society, the slave-owning society, the feudal soci-ety, proved upon the test of action have failed. Yet it has only been partial failure; with each we learned a little more, just as the most recent bridge embodies lessons learned from the collapse of the first. Always the lesson was the same, it was the violence, the dominating relation between master and slave, lord and serf, bourgeois and proletarian, which was the weakness in the bridge.

But the pacifist, like all bourgeois theoreticians, is obsessed with the lazy lust of the absolute. 'Give me,' they all cry, 'absolute truth, absolute justice, some rule-of-thumb standard by which I can evade the strenuous task of finding the features of reality by intimate contact with it in action. Give me some logical talisman, some philosopher's stone, by which I can test all acts in theory and say, this is right. Give me some principle such as, *Violence is wrong,* so that I can simply refrain from all violent action and know that I am right.' But the only absolute they find is the standard of bourgeois economy. 'Abstain from social action.' Standards are made, not found.

Man cannot live without acting. Even to cease to act, to let things go their own way, is a form of acting, as when I drop a stone that perhaps starts an avalanche. And since man is always acting, he is always exerting force, always altering or maintaining the position of things, always revolutionary or conservative. Existence is the exercise of force on the physical environment and on other men. The web of physical and social relations that binds men into one universe ensures that nothing we do is without its effect on others, whether we vote or cease to vote, whether we help the police or let them go their way, whether we let two combatants fight or separate them forcibly or assist one against the other, whether we let a man starve to death or move heaven and earth to assist him. Man can never rest on the absolute; all acts involve consequences, and it is man's task to find out these consequences, and act accordingly. He can never choose between action and inaction, he can only choose between life and death. He can never absolve himself with the ancient plea, 'My intentions were good', or 'I meant it for the best', or 'I have broken no commandment'. Even savages have a more vital conception than this, with whom an act is judged by its consequences, even as a bridge is judged by its stability. Therefore it is man's task to find out the consequences of acts: which means discovering the laws of social relations, the impulses, causes and effects of history.

Thus it is beside the point to ask the pacifist whether he would have defended Greece from the Persian or his sister from a would-be ravisher. Modern society imposes a different and more concrete issue. Under which banner of violence will he impose himself? The violence of bourgeois relations, or the violence not only to resist them but to end them? Bourgeois social relations are revealing, more and more insistently, the violence of exploitation and dispossession on which they are founded; more and more they harrow man with brutality and oppression. By abstaining from action the pacifist enrolls himself under this banner, the banner of things as they are and getting worse, the banner of the increasing violence and coercion exerted by the *haves* on the *have-nots*. He calls increasingly into being the violences of poverty, deprivation, artificial slumps, artistic and scientific decay, fascism, and war.

Or he can enroll himself under the revolutionary banner, of things as they will be. In doing so he accepts the stern necessity that he who is to replace a truth or an institution or a system of social relations, must substitute a better, that he who is to pull down a bridge, however inefficient, must put instead a better bridge. Bourgeois social relations were better perhaps than slave-owning, what can the revolutionary find better than them? And, having found them, how is he to bring them about? For one must not only plan the bridge, one must see how it is to be built, by violence, by force, by blasting the living rock and tugging and sweating at the stones that make it.

Thus, for the negativism of pacifism, which shores up the decaying world and tolerates man's increasing misery, the revolutionary must substitute the positivism of communism. He must forge a new economy adequate to take over bourgeois social relations and purge them of the coercive violence at their heart. But this violence grew from a class relation, the domination of an exploited by an exploiting class. To end this violence means building the classless State. Hating the violence of the bourgeois State, either in peace or war, the revolutionary must produce a society which needs neither violence in peace nor in war. Since it is material reality with which he is dealing, he must see the only path by which bourgeois social relations of violence can be turned into peaceful communist social relations. It is the path of revolution and the dictatorship of the proletariat, followed by the withering away of the State. If he does not clearly see—as an architect sees the building of foundations, and the transportation of material—this mode of transformation of bourgeois violence into communist peace, his socialism remains an empty dream, he is still at heart a pacifist, a partisan of things as they are, you will still find him in fact, for all his theoretical protestations, enrolled beneath the banner of bourgeois violence, strike-breaking or giving fascism 'free speech'.

To expropriate the expropriators, to oppose their coercion by that of the workers, to destroy all the instruments of class coercion and exploitation crystallised in the bourgeois State, is the first task. Who can lead the struggle but the exploited, and not only all the exploited but those whose very exploitation has organised them, massed them together, and made them co-operate socially, the proletariat. Since a dispossessed class will fight to the last ditch, while there is hope, how can the transition be affected other than violently, substituting the dictatorship of the proletariat and its necessary forms for the former dictatorship of the bourgeoisie and its characteristic forms?

But whereas the dictatorship of the bourgeois minority perpetuated itself, because the dispossessed class was also the exploited class, the dictatorship of the proletarian majority does not perpetuate itself, for it does not exploit the dispossessed class, but is itself both owner and worker of the means of production. Thus, as the dispossessed class disappears, the dictatorship of the proletariat in all its forms withers away. The pacifist's dream is realised. Violence departs from the world of men. Man at last becomes free.

8

Abortion, War, and the Killing of the Innocent

Readings: Jonathan Bennett, "Whatever the Consequences" Philippa Foot, "Abortion and the Doctrine of the Double Effect"

Suppose that one is not a pacifist and thus believes that there may be circumstances in which war could be justified. For such a person, there still remains the problem of determining what *means* are morally permissible to employ in the prosecution of a war that one believes is justified. Even a pacifist should worry about this question of means; for even if he believes that war is always wrong, he should at least consider the possibility that there are degrees of wrongness—that is, the possibility that wars fought with some means are even worse than wars fought with other means. For example: Is it ever morally permissible to attempt to bring the enemy to his knees by such tactics as the terror bombing of civilian population centers, a tactic that involves the massive killing of women, children, and the elderly? This practice was employed as a tactic by both the Nazis and the Allies in World War II and has been used in Vietnam. Is war a situation in which anything goes, or does even such a barbarous context require moral limitations on the means employed? If it does, to what extent should these limitations be institutionalized into international law?

Consider another kind of case. A woman discovers she is pregnant and that she does not want to have the child. Is it ever morally permissible for her to seek and obtain an abortion? Some possible reasons she might desire an abortion are the following: poor physical health, psychiatric problems, reaction to having been raped, poverty, the danger of having a deformed child, and mere convenience. Is an abortion morally permissible in any of these circumstances? Is it morally permissible in all of them? In those circumstances (if any) where it is not morally permissible, should it be legally permissible?

Although these cases seem different, and are different in many respects, they do raise in common one important moral problem: Is it ever morally permissible, in order to obtain a good result, to kill an innocent person? There is a problem, of course, as to whether a fetus should be regarded as a person, but its status is not too different perhaps from that of a small child killed by a bomb in time of war—a case which almost everyone would describe as the killing of an innocent person. (One of the important philosophical concerns here, of course, is to attempt to clarify concepts like "innocence" and "person" in these contexts.) The issue of killing the innocent provides a good focus for the conflict between teleologists in ethics (for example, utilitarians) and deontologists (for example, Kantians). The former will be inclined to say that if the consequences of killing an innocent person would be better on the whole than the consequences of not so killing (for example, the defeat of Nazism or saving the life of a mother) then the killing, although regrettable, is justified. The latter will not be happy about going this route; for they, particularly if their deontological commitment is to justice, will be extremely skeptical about the moral permissibility of sacrificing an innocent person, without his consent, for the good of others.

The two readings in this section take abortion as the specific problem for discussion, but it would be an interesting exercise for the student to determine the extent to which the same arguments have application to the problem of killing the innocent in time of war. He is likely to discover that the overlap is great indeed. One position having clear application to both issues is the doctrine, drawn from Catholic moral theology, of the "double effect." According to this doctrine it is always wrong to deliberately kill an innocent person—that is, to kill an innocent person as one's final purpose or end or as a means to one's final purpose or end. It is not always wrong, however, to engage in a course of action one knows will, as a matter of fact, result in the death of an innocent person so long as that is not one's final end or a means to it. Thus: It is wrong to crush the skull of a fetus to save the life of the mother, for that would be to directly intend its death as a means to the end of saving the mother's life. If one does not operate, the mother may indeed die. But this, being but a known or highly probable consequence of not operating and not one's intention or purpose in not operating, is permissible. Or consider a war case: It is wrong to bomb civilians for the purpose of demoralizing the enemy, for this would be to intend their killing as a means to one's purpose of winning the war. It is not wrong, however, to bomb a military in-stallation with the knowledge that a few bombs may unintentionally go off target and result in the deaths of some innocent persons in the vicinity. For this killing is inadvertent and not intended.

Jonathan Bennett, in his article, regards the doctrine of the double effect and the distinctions it involves as fundamentally confused. He concludes that only a fanatic would accept a principle of the form "Never do X (for ex-ample, kill the innocent) whatever the consequences." He thus illustrates a fundamentally teleological commitment in morality. Philippa Foot, agreeing that the doctrine of the double effect as traditionally formulated is confused, believes that it can be replaced with a related, but not identical, distinction (between harmony and failing to aid) which does exhibit an important moral insight of a deontological nature.

Suggestions for Further Reading

Richard B. Brandt, "Utilitarianism and the Rules of War," *Philosophy and Public Affairs,* Winter 1972.

Jeffrie G. Murphy, "The Killing of the Innocent," *The Monist,* October 1973.

Thomas Nagel, "War and Massacre," *Philosophy and Public Affairs,* Winter 1972.

Judith Jarvis Thomson, "A Defense of Abortion," *Philosophy and Public Affairs,* Fall 1971.

Richard Wasserstrom, ed., *War and Morality* (Belmont, Calif.: Wadsworth, 1970).

Whatever the Consequences
Jonathan Bennett

The following kind of thing can occur.[1] A woman in labour will certainly die unless an operation is performed in which the head of her unborn child is crushed or dissected; while if it is not performed the child can be delivered, alive, by post-mortem Caesarian section. This presents a straight choice be-tween the woman's life and the child's.

In a particular instance of this kind, some people would argue for se-curing the woman's survival on the basis of the special facts of the case: the

From *Analysis* 26 (1966). Reprinted by permission of the author. Jonathan Bennett is a professor of philosophy at the University of British Columbia.

[1] J. K. Feeney and A. P. Barry in *Journal of Obstetrics and Gynaecology of the British Empire* (1954), p. 61; R. L. Cecil and H. F. Conn (eds.), *The Specialties in General Practice* (Philadelphia, 1957), p. 410.

woman's terror, or her place in an established network of affections and de-
pendences, or the child's physical defects, and so on. For them, the argument
could go the other way in another instance, even if only in a very special one
—e.g., where the child is well formed and the woman has cancer which will
kill her within a month anyway.

Others would favour the woman's survival in any instance of the kind
presented in my opening paragraph, on the grounds that women are human
while unborn children are not. This dubious argument does not need to be
attacked here, and I shall ignore it.

Others again would say, just on the facts as stated in my first paragraph,
that the *child* must be allowed to survive. Their objection to any operation
in which an unborn child's head is crushed, whatever the special features of
the case, goes like this:

> To do the operation would be to kill the child, while to refrain from
> doing it would not be to kill the woman but merely to conduct oneself
> in such a way that—as a foreseen but unwanted consequence—the
> woman died. The question we should ask is not: "The woman's life or
> the child's?," but rather: "To kill, or not to kill, an innocent human?"
> The answer to *that* is that it is always absolutely wrong to kill an inno-
> cent human, even in such dismal circumstances as these.

This line of thought needs to be attacked. Some able people find it acceptable; it is presupposed by the Principle of Double Effect[2] which permeates
Roman Catholic writing on morals; and I cannot find any published statement
of the extremely strong philosophical case for its rejection.

I shall state that case as best I can. My presentation of it owes much to
certain allies and opponents who have commented on earlier drafts. I grate-
fully acknowledge my debt to Miss G. E. M. Anscombe, A. G. N. Flew,
A. Kenny and T. J. Smiley; and especially to the late Douglas F. Wallace.

The Plan of Attack

There is no way of disproving the principle: "It would always be wrong
to kill an innocent human, whatever the consequences of not doing so." The
principle is consistent and reasonably clear; it can be fed into moral syllo-
gisms to yield practical conclusions; and although its application to borderline
cases may raise disturbing problems, this is true of any moral principle. Someone who thinks that the principle is laid down by a moral authority whose
deliverances are to be accepted without question, without *any* testing against
the dictates of the individual conscience, is vulnerable only to arguments

---

[2] See G. Kelly, *Medico-Moral Problems* (Dublin, 1955), p. 20; C. J. McFadden, *Medical
Ethics* (London, 1962), pp. 27–33; T. J. O'Donnell, *Morals in Medicine* (London, 1959), pp.
39–44; N. St. John-Stevas, *The Right to Life* (London, 1963), p. 71.

about the credentials of his alleged authority; and these are not my present concern. So I have no reply to make to anyone who is prepared to say: "I shall obey God's command never to kill an innocent human. I shall make no independent moral assessment of this command—whether to test the reasonableness of obeying it, or to test my belief that it *is* God's command, or for any other purpose." My concern is solely with those who accept the principle: "It would always be wrong to kill an innocent human, whatever the consequences of not doing so," not just because it occurs in some received list of moral principles but also because they think that it can in some degree be recommended to the normal conscience. Against this, I shall argue that a normal person who accepts the principle must either have failed to see what it involves or be passively and unquestioningly obedient to an authority.

I do not equate "the normal conscience" with "the 'liberal' conscience." Of course, the principle *is* rejected by the "liberal" majority; but I shall argue for the stronger and less obvious thesis that the principle is in the last resort on a par with "It would always be wrong to shout, whatever the consequences of not doing so," or "It would always be wrong to leave a bucket in a hallway, whatever, etc." It is sometimes said that we "should not understand" someone who claimed to accept such wild eccentricities as these as fundamental moral truths—that he would be making a logical mistake, perhaps about what it is for something to be a "moral" principle. I need not claim so much. It is enough to say that such a person, if he was sincere and in his right mind, could safely be assumed to have delivered himself over to a moral authority and to have opted out of moral thinking altogether. The same could be said of anyone who accepted *and really understood* the principle: "It would always be wrong to kill an innocent human, whatever the consequences of not doing so." This principle is accepted by reasonable people who, though many of them give weight to some moral authority, have not abdicated from independent moral thinking. Clearly, they regard the principle as one which others might be led to accept, or at least to take seriously, on grounds other than subservience to an authority. From this fact, together with the thesis for which I shall argue, it follows that those who accept the principle (like others who at least treat it with respect) have not thought it through, have not seen what it comes to in concrete cases where it yields a different practical conclusion from that yielded by "It is wrong to kill an innocent human unless there are very powerful reasons for doing so." I aim to show what the principle comes to in these cases, and so to expose it for what it is.

My arguments will tell equally against any principle of the form "It would always be wrong to . . . , whatever the consequences of not doing so"; but I shall concentrate on the one principle about killing, and indeed on its application to the kind of obstetrical situation described in my opening paragraph.

I need a label for someone who accepts principles of the form: "It would always be wrong to . . . , whatever the consequences of not doing so."

"Roman Catholic" is at once too wide, and too narrow; "intrinsicalist" is nasty; "absolutist" is misleading; "deontologist" means too many other things as well. Reluctantly, I settle for "conservative." This use has precedents, but I offer it as a stipulative definition—an expository convenience and not a claim about "conservatism" in any ordinary sense.

Well then: When the conservative condemns the operation described in my opening paragraph, he does so *partly* because the operation involves the death of an innocent human. So does its non-performance; but for the conservative the dilemma is asymmetrical because the two alternatives involve human deaths in different ways: in one case the death is part of a killing, in the other there is no killing and a death occurs only as a consequence of what is done. From the premiss that operating would be killing an innocent human, together with the principle: "It would always be wrong to kill an innocent human, whatever, etc.," it does follow that it would be wrong to operate. But the usual conservative—the one I plan to attack—thinks that his principle has *some* measure of acceptability on grounds other than unquestioning obedience to an authority. He must therefore think that the premiss: "In this case, operating would be killing an innocent human while not-operating would involve the death of an innocent human only as a consequence" gives *some* reason for the conclusion: "In this case, operating would be wrong." I shall argue that it gives no reason at all: once the muddles have been cleared away, it is just not humanly possible to see the premiss as supporting the conclusion, however weakly, except by accepting the principle "It would always be wrong, etc." as an unquestionable *donnée*.

The Action / Consequence Distinction

When James killed Henry, what happened was this: James contracted his fingers round the handle of a knife, and moved his hand in such a way that the knife penetrated Henry's body and severed an artery; blood escaped from the wound, the rate of oxygen-transfer to Henry's body-cells fell drastically, and Henry died. In general, someone's performing a physical action includes his moving some part or parts of his body. (The difference between "He moved his hand" and "His hand moved" is not in question here: I am referring to movements which he *makes*.) He does this in a physical environment, and other things happen in consequence. A description of what he *did* will ordinarily entail something not only about his movements but also, *inter alia*, about some of their upshots. Other upshots will not ordinarily be covered by any description of "what he did," but will be counted amongst "the consequences of what he did." There are various criteria for drawing the line between what someone did and the consequences of what he did; and there can be several proper ways of drawing it in a given case.

This last point notwithstanding, there are wrong ways of dividing a set of happenings into action and consequences. Even where it is not positively wrong to give a very parsimonious account of "what he did," it may be preferable to be more inclusive. If in my chosen example the obstetrician does the operation, it is true that he crushes the child's head with the consequence that the child dies, but a better account, perhaps, would say that he *kills* the child by crushing its head. There can certainly be outright wrongness at the other end of the scale: we cannot be as inclusive as we like in our account of "what he did." If at the last time when the operation could save the woman's life the obstetrician is resignedly writing up his notes, it is just not true that, as he sits at his desk, he is killing the woman; nor, indeed, is he killing her at any other time.

The use of the action/consequence distinction in the conservative premiss is, therefore, perfectly correct. Operating *is* killing; not-operating is not. What are we saying when we say this? By what criteria is the action/consequence distinction drawn in the present case? I shall try, by answering this, to show that in this case one cannot attach moral significance to the fact that the line drawn by the distinction falls where it does. Briefly, the criteria for the action/consequence distinction fall into two groups: those which could support a moral conclusion but which do not apply to every instance of the obstetrical example; and those which do apply to the example but which it would be wildly eccentric to think relevant to the moral assessment of courses of action. There is no overlap between the two groups.

Aspects of the Distinction: First Group

Some differences which tend to go with the action/consequence distinction, and are perhaps to be counted amongst the criteria for it, clearly do have moral significance. None of them, however, is generally present in the obstetrical example.

Given a question about whether some particular upshot of a movement I made is to be covered by the description of what I *did:*

(a) The answer may depend in part upon whether in making the movement I was entirely confident that that upshot would ensue; and this could reasonably be thought relevant to the moral assessment of my conduct. This aspect of the action/consequence distinction, however, is absent from most instances of the obstetrical example. The classification of not-operating as something other than killing does not imply that the obstetrician rates the woman's chance of survival (if the operation is not performed) higher than the child's chance of survival (if it is performed). If it did imply this then, by contraposition, not-operating would in many such cases have to be classified as killing after all.

(b) The answer may depend in part upon how certain or inevitable it was that that upshot would ensue from my movement, or upon how confidently I ought to have expected it to ensue; and that too may have a strong bearing on the moral assessment of my conduct. But it gets no grip on the obstetrical example, for in many cases of that kind there is moral certainty on both sides of the dilemma. If the conservative says that the action/consequence distinction, when correctly drawn, is always associated with morally significant differences in the inevitability of upshots of movements, then he is vulnerable to an argument by contraposition like the one in (a). He is vulnerable in other ways as well, which I shall discuss in my next section.

(c) The answer may depend in part upon whether I made the movement partly or wholly for the sake of achieving that upshot; and this is a morally significant matter. But the obstetrical example is symmetrical in that respect also: if the obstetrician crushes the child's head he does so not because this will lead to the child's death or because it constitutes killing the child, but because that is his only way of removing the child's body from the woman's.

To summarize: moral conclusions may be supported by facts (a) about what is expected, but in the example each upshot is confidently expected; (b) about what is inevitable, but in the example each upshot is inevitable; or (c) about what is ultimately aimed at, but in the example neither upshot is aimed at.

I have suggested that a conservative might say: "The action/consequence distinction is always associated with a morally significant difference in the degree to which upshots are certain or inevitable." This is false; but let us grant it in order to see whether it can help the conservative on the obstetrical example. I concede, for purposes of argument, that if the operation is not performed the woman will pretty certainly die, while if it is performed the child will even more certainly die.

What use can the conservative make of this concession? Will he say that the practical decision is to be based on a weighing of the comparative desirability of upshots against the comparative certainty of their achievement? If so, then he must allow that there *could* be a case in which it was right to kill the child—perhaps a case where a healthy young widow with four children is bearing a hydrocephalic child, and where her chance of survival if the operation is not performed is *nearly* as bad as the child's chance of survival if it is performed. If a professed "conservative" allows that there could, however improbably, be such a case, then he is not a conservative but a consequentialist; he does after all base his final judgment on the special features of the case; and he has misrepresented his position by using the language of action and consequence to express his implausible views about the comparative inevitability of upshots. On the other hand, if the conservative still absolutely rules out the killing of the child, whatever the details of the particular case, then what could be his point in claiming that there is a difference in degree of inevitability? The moral significance of this supposed difference would, at best, have to be conceded to be an obscure one which threw no light on why anyone should adopt the conservative view.

A certain conservative tactic is at issue here. Miss G. E. M. Anscombe has said:

> If someone really thinks, *in advance,* that it is open to question whether such an action as procuring the judicial execution of the innocent should be quite excluded from consideration—I do not want to argue with him; he shows a corrupt mind.[3]

The phrase "quite excluded from consideration" clearly places Miss Anscombe as what I am calling a "conservative." (The phrase "a corrupt mind," incidentally, tends to confirm my view that conservatives think their position can stand the light of day, i.e., that they do not see it as tenable only by those who passively obey some moral authority.) Now, in the course of a footnote to this passage Miss Anscombe remarks:

> In discussion when this paper was read, as was perhaps to be expected, this case was produced: a government is required to have an innocent man tried, sentenced and executed under threat of a "hydrogen bomb war." It would seem strange to me to have much hope of averting a war threatened by such men as made this demand. But the most important thing about the way in which cases like this are invented in discussions, is the assumption that only two courses are open: here, compliance and open defiance. No one can say in advance of such a situation what the possibilities are going to be—e.g., that there is none of stalling by a feigned willingness to comply, accompanied by a skilfully arranged "escape" of the victim.

This makes two points about the case as described: there might be nothing we could do which would have a good chance of averting a war; and if there were one such thing we could do there might be several. The consequentialist might meet this by trying yet again to describe a case in which judicially executing an innocent man *is* the only thing we could do which would have a good chance of averting a war. When he had added the details which block off the other alternatives, his invented case may well be far removed from present political likelihood; it may even be quite fantastic. Still, what does the conservative say about it?

Here is Miss Anscombe, at her most gamesome, on the subject of "fantastic" examples:

> A point of method I would recommend to the corrupter of the youth would be this: concentrate on examples which are either banal: you have promised to return a book, but . . . and so on, or fantastic: what

[3] G. E. M. Anscombe, "Modern Moral Philosophy," *Philosophy,* vol. 33 (1958), p. 17.

you ought to do if you have to move forward, and stepping with your right foot meant killing twenty-five young men, while stepping with your left foot would kill fifty drooling old ones. (Obviously the right thing to do would be to jump and polish off the lot.) [4]

The cards are now well stacked; but this is a game in which a conservative should not be taking a hand at all. Someone may say (i): "In no situation could it be right to procure the judicial execution of the innocent: political probability aside, the judicial execution of the innocent is absolutely impermissible in any possible circumstances." Or some may say (ii): "It is never right to procure the judicial execution of the innocent: a situation in which this would be right has never arisen, isn't going to arise, and cannot even be described without entering into the realm of political fantasy." These are different. The former is conservatism, according to which "the judicial execution of the innocent should be quite excluded from consideration." The latter is not conservatism: according to it, the judicial execution of the innocent is taken into consideration, assessed in the light of the political probabilities of the world we live in, and excluded on that basis. The former is Miss Anscombe's large type; the latter, apparently, is her footnote. The difference between (i) "In no situation could it be right . . ." and (ii) "No situation is even remotely likely to occur in which it would be right . . ." can be masked by dismissing what is relevant but unlikely as "fantastic" and therefore negligible. But the difference between the two positions is crucial even if in the first instance it can be brought out only by considering "fantastic" possibilities. The two may yield the same real-life practical conclusions, but (ii) can be understood and argued with in a way in which (i) cannot. If someone accepts (ii), and is not afraid to discuss a "fantastic" but possible situation in which he would approve the judicial execution of an innocent man, he can be challenged to square this with his contrary judgment in regard to some less fantastic situation. Whether he could meet the challenge would depend on the details of his moral position and of the situations in question. The point is that we should know where we stood with him: for example, we should know that it was *relevant* to adduce evidence about how good the chances would be of averting war in this way in this situation, or in that way in that. It is just this sort of thing which the unwavering conservative must regard as irrelevant; and that is what is wrong with his position. Miss Anscombe says: "No one can say in advance of such a situation what the possibilities are going to be"; but the central objection to conservatism is, precisely, that it says in advance that for the judging of the proposed course of action *it does not matter* what the possibilities are going to be. Why,

---

[4] G. E. M. Anscombe, "Does Oxford Moral Philosophy Corrupt the Youth?," *The Listener*, February 14, 1957, p. 267. See also the correspondence in ensuing numbers, and Michael Tanner, "Examples in Moral Philosophy," *Proceedings of the Aristotelian Society*, vol. 65 (1964–65).

then, go on about them—if not to disguise conservatism as something else when the going gets tough?

I have based this paper on the obstetrical example in the hope that, without being jeered at for having "invented" an example which is "fantastic," I could present a kind of case in which a conservative principle would yield a practical conclusion different from any likely to be arrived at by consequentialist arguments. The claim that in these cases there would always be a morally significant difference between the woman's chance of survival and the child's could only be another attempt to get the spotlight off conservatism altogether—to get the consequentialist to accept the conservative's conclusion and forget about his principle. In the obstetrical example, the attempt is pretty desperate (though, with the aid of judiciously selected statistics, it is made often enough); with other kinds of examples, used to examine this or other conservative principles, it might be easier for the conservative to make a show of insisting on the addition of details which render the examples "fantastic." But this does not mean that the case against conservatism is stronger here than elsewhere. It means only that the obstetrical example gives less scope than most for the "there-might-be-another-way-out" move, or protective-coloration gambit, which some conservatives sometimes use when they shelter their position by giving the impression that it does not really exist.

A conservative might invoke inevitability, without comparing degrees of it in the consequentialist manner, by saying that if the operation is not performed the woman still has *some* chance of survival while if it is performed the child has *none*. Barring miracles, this is wrong about the woman; not barring miracles, it is wrong about the child. It could seem plausible only to someone who did not bar miracles but took a peculiar view of how they operate. Some people do attach importance in this regard to the fact that if the operation is not performed the woman may take some time to die: they seem to think—perhaps encouraged by an eccentric view of God as powerful but *slow*—that the longer an upshot is delayed the more room there is for a miraculous intervention. This belief, whatever the assumptions which underlie it, gives no help to the conservative position. For suppose the obstetrician decides to try, after operating and delivering the child, to repair its head by microsurgery. The woman's supposed "some chance" of survival if the child's head is not crushed is of the same kind as the obstetrician's "some chance" of saving the child after crushing its head: in each case there is what the well-informed plain man would call "no chance," but in each case it will take a little time for the matter to be finally settled by the events themselves—for the woman to die or the obstetrician to admit failure. Would the conservative say that the obstetrician's intention to try to save the child in this way, though hopeless, completely alters the shape of the problem and perhaps makes it all right for the obstetrician to crush the child's head? If so, then what we have here is a morality of gestures and poses.

Aspects of the Distinction: Second Group

I return to the main thread of my argument. Of the remaining three aspects of the action/consequence distinction, it was not quite true to say that all are present in (every instance of) the obstetrical example; for the first of them has not even that merit. The main point, however, is that even if it were always present it would not help the conservative—though it might help us to diagnose his trouble.

(d) Someone's decision whether an upshot of a movement of mine is to be covered by his description of what I *did* may depend partly on his moral assessment of my role in the total situation. Your condemnation of me, or perhaps your approval, may be reflected in your putting on the "action" side of the line an upshot which an indifferent onlooker would count as merely a "consequence." This aspect of the action/consequence distinction—if indeed it is one independently of those already discussed—cannot help the conservative who believes that a premiss using the distinction tends to *support* a moral conclusion. That belief demands a relevance relation which slopes the other way.

There seem to be just two remaining aspects to the action/consequence distinction. Certainly, there are only two which do appear in all instances of the obstetrical example. These two must be the sole justification for saying that operating would be killing while not-operating would not be killing; and so they must bear the whole weight of any conservative but non-authoritarian case against killing the child.

(e) Operating is killing-the-child because if the obstetrician operates there is a high degree of *immediacy* between what he does with his hands and the child's dying. This immediacy consists in the brevity or absence of time-lag, spatial nearness, simplicity of causal connexions, and paucity of intervening physical objects. The relations amongst these are complex; but they are severally relevant to the action/consequence distinction, and in the obstetrical example they all pull together, creating an overwhelming case for calling the performance of the operation the *killing* of the child.

(f) Not-operating is not killing-the-woman because it is not *doing* anything at all but is merely *refraining* from doing something.

Since (e) and (f) are so central to the action/consequence distinction generally, it is appropriate that they should sometimes bear its whole weight, as they do in the conservative's (correct) application of the distinction to the obstetrical example. But if (e) and (f) are all there is to the premiss: "In this case, operating would be killing an innocent human while not-operating would involve the death of an innocent human only as a consequence," then this premiss offers no support at all to the conclusion: "In this case, operating would be wrong."

The matters which I group under "immediacy" in (e) may borrow moral significance from their loose association with facts about whether and in what degree upshots are (a) expected, (b) inevitable or (c) aimed at. In none of these respects, however, is there a relevant asymmetry in the obstetrical example. The question is: why should a difference in degree of immediacy, unaccompanied by other relevant differences, be taken to support a moral discrimination? I cannot think of a remotely plausible answer which does not consist solely in an appeal to an authority.[5]

Suggestions come to mind about "not getting one's hands dirty"; and the notion of what I call "immediacy" does help to show how the literal and the metaphorical are mingled in some uses of that phrase. In so doing, however, it exposes the desire to "keep one's hands clean," in cases like the obstetrical example, as a symptom of muddle or primness or, worst of all, a moral egoism like Pilate's. (To be fair: I do not think that many conservatives would answer in this way. If they used similar words it would probably not be to express the nasty sentiment I have mentioned but rather to say something like: "I must obey God's law; and the rest is up to God." Because this suggests a purely authoritarian basis, and because it certainly has nothing to do with immediacy, it lies beyond my present scope.)

Similarly with the acting/refraining distinction in (f). I shall argue in my next section that our criteria for this distinction do not invest it with any moral significance whatever—except when the distinction is drawn on the basis of independently formed moral judgments, and then it cannot help the conservative case for the reason given in (d). And if neither (e) immediacy nor (f) acting/refraining separately has moral significance, then clearly they cannot acquire any by being taken together.

Acting and Refraining

Suppose the obstetrician does not operate, and the woman dies. He does not kill her, but he *lets her die*. The approach suggested by these words is just an unavoidable nuisance, and I shall not argue from it. When I say "he lets her die," I mean only that he knowingly refrains from preventing her death which he alone could prevent, and he cannot say that her survival is in a general way "none of my business" or "not [even *prima facie*] my concern." If my arguments so far are correct, then this one fact—the fact that the non-operating obstetrician *lets the woman die* but does not *kill her*—is the only remaining feature of the situation which the conservative can hope

---

[5] Conservatives use words like "direct" to cover a jumble of factors of which immediacy is the most prominent. Pius XII has said that a pain-killing, life-shortening drug may be used "if there exists no direct causal link, either through the will of interested parties or by the nature of things, between the induced consciousness [*sic*] and the shortening of life . . ." (Quoted in St. John-Stevas, *op. cit.*, p. 61.)

to adduce as supporting his judgment about what ought to be done in every instance of the obstetrical example.[6] Let us examine the difference between "*X* killed *Y*" and "*X* let *Y* die."

Some cases of letting-die are also cases of killing. If on a dark night *X* knows that *Y*'s next step will take him over the edge of a high cliff, and he refrains from uttering a simple word of warning because he doesn't care or because he wants *Y* dead, then it is natural to say not only that *X* lets *Y* die but also that he kills him—even if it was not *X* who suggested the route, removed the fence from the cliff-top, etc. Cases like this, where a failure-to-prevent is described as a doing partly *because* it is judged to be wicked or indefensible, are beside my present point; for I want to see what difference there is between killing and letting-die which might be a *basis for* a moral judgment. Anyway, the letting-die which is also killing must involve malice or wanton indifference, and there is nothing like that in the obstetrical example. In short, to count these cases as relevant to the obstetrical example would be to suggest that not-operating would after all be killing the woman—a plainly false suggestion which I have disavowed. I wish to criticise the conservative's argument, not to deny his premiss. So from now on I shall ignore cases of letting-die which are also cases of killing; and it will make for brevity to pretend that they do not exist. For example, I shall say that killing involves moving one's body—which is false of some of these cases, but true of all others.

One more preliminary point: the purposes of the present enquiry do not demand that a full analysis be given either of "*X* killed *Y*" or of "*X* let *Y* die." We can ignore any implications either may have about what *X* (a) expected, (b) should have expected, or (c) was aiming at; for the obstetrical example is symmetrical in all those respects. We can also ignore the fact that "*X* killed *Y*" loosely implies something about (e) immediacy which is not implied by "*X* let *Y* die," for immediacy in itself has no moral significance.

Consider the statement that *Joe killed the calf*. A certain aspect of the analysis of this will help us to see how it relates to *Joe let the calf die*. To say that Joe killed the calf is to say that

(1) Joe moved his body

and

(2) the calf died;

but it is also to say something about how Joe's moving was connected with the calf's dying—something to the effect that

---

[6] In a case where the child cannot survive anyway: "It is a question of the *direct taking* of one innocent life or merely *permitting* two deaths. In other words, there is question of one *murder* against two deaths . . ." Kelly, *op. cit.*, p. 181.

(3) if Joe had not moved as he did, the calf would not have died.

How is (3) to be interpreted? We might take it, rather strictly, as saying

(3′) If Joe had moved in *any* other way, the calf would not have died.

This, however, is too strong to be a necessary condition of Joe's having killed the calf. Joe may have killed the calf even if he could have moved in other ways which would equally have involved the calf's dying. Suppose that Joe cut the calf's throat, but could have shot it instead: in that case he clearly killed it; but (3′) denies that he killed it, because the calf might still have died even if Joe had moved in just the way he did.

We might adopt a weaker reading of (3), namely as saying

(3″) Joe could have moved in *some* other way without the calf's dying.

But where (3′) was too strong to be necessary, (3″) is too weak to express a sufficient connexion between Joe's moving and the calf's dying. It counts Joe as having killed the calf not only in cases where we should ordinarily say that he killed it but also in cases where the most we should say is that he let it die.

The truth lies somewhere between (3′), which is appropriate to "Joe killed the calf in the only way open to him," and (3″), which is appropriate to "Joe killed the calf or let it die." Specifically, the connexion between Joe's moving and the calf's dying which is appropriate to "Joe killed the calf" but not to "Joe let the calf die" is expressed by

(3‴) Of all the other ways in which Joe might have moved, *relatively* few satisfy the condition: if Joe had moved like that, the calf would have died.

And the connexion which is appropriate to "Joe let the calf die" but not to "Joe killed the calf" is expressed by

(4) Of all the other ways in which Joe might have moved, *almost all* satisfy the condition: if Joe had moved like that, the calf would have died.

This brings me to the main thesis of the present section: apart from the factors I have excluded as already dealt with, the difference between "*X* killed

Y" and "X let Y die" *is* the difference between (3‴) and (4). When the killing/letting-die distinction is stripped of its implications regarding immediacy, intention, etc.—which lack moral significance or don't apply to the example—all that remains is a distinction having to do with where a set of movements lies on the scale which has "the only set of movements which would have produced that upshot" at one end and "movements other than the only set which would have produced that upshot" at the other.

This, then, is the conservative's residual basis for a moral discrimination between operating and not-operating. Operating would be killing: if the obstetrician makes movements which constitute operating, then the child will die; and there are very few other movements he could make which would also involve the child's dying. Not-operating would only be letting-die: if throughout the time when he could be operating the obstetrician makes movements which constitute not-operating, then the woman will die; but a vast majority of alternative movements he could make during that time would equally involve the woman's dying. I do not see how anyone doing his own moral thinking about the matter could find the least shred of moral significance in *this* difference between operating and not-operating.

Suppose you are told that X killed Y in the only way possible in the circumstances; and this, perhaps together with certain other details of the case, leads you to judge X's conduct adversely. Then you are told: "You have been misled: there is another way in which X could have killed Y." Then a third informant says: "That is wrong too: there are two other ways . . . , etc." Then a fourth: "No: there are three other ways . . . , etc." Clearly, these successive corrections put no pressure at all on your original judgment: you will not think it relevant to your judgment on X's killing of Y that it could have been carried out in any one of n different ways. But the move from "X killed Y in the only possible way" to "X killed Y in one of the only five possible ways" is of the same *kind* as the move from "X killed Y" to "X let Y die" (except for the latter's implications about immediacy); and the moral insignificance of the former move is evidence for the moral insignificance of the latter move also.

The difference between "X killed Y" and "X let Y die" is the sum-total of a vast number of differences such as that between "X killed Y in one of the only n possible ways" and "X killed Y in one of the only $n + 1$ possible ways." If the difference between ". . . n . . ." and ". . . $n + 1$ . . ." were morally insignificant only because it was *too small* for any moral discrimination to be based upon it, then the sum-total of millions of such differences might still have moral significance. But in fact the differences in question, whatever their size, are of the *wrong kind* for any moral discrimination to be based upon them. Suppose you have judged X adversely, on the basis of the misinformation: "X killed Y in the only way possible in the circumstances"; and this is then replaced, in one swoop, by the true report: "X did not kill Y at all, though he did knowingly let Y die." Other things being equal, would this give you the slightest reason to retract your adverse judgment? Not a bit of it! It would be perfectly reasonable for you to reply: "The fact remains that X chose to conduct himself in a way which he knew would involve Y's death. At first I thought his choice could encompass Y's death only by being the choice of some rather specific course of conduct; whereas the revised report shows me that X's choice could have encompassed Y's death while committing X to very little. At first I thought it had to be a choice to act; I now realize that it could have been a choice to refrain. What of it?"

There are several things a conservative is likely to say at this point—all equivalent. "When we know that the crucial choice could have been a choice to refrain from something, we can begin to allow for the possibility that it may have been a choice to refrain from doing something wrong, such as killing an innocent human." Or: "You say 'other things being equal,' but in the obstetrical example they aren't equal. By representing letting-die as a kind of wide-optioned killing you suppress the fact that the alternative to letting the woman die is killing the child."

Replies like these are available to the conservative only if he does not need them and can break through at some other point; for they assume the very point which is at issue, namely that in every instance of the obstetrical example it would be wrong to kill the child. I think that in some cases it would indeed be wrong—(I do not press for a blanket judgment on all instances of the example—quite the contrary); and in such a case the obstetrician, if he rightly let the woman die, could defend his doing so on the basis of the details of the particular case. Furthermore, he might wish to begin his defence by explaining: "I let the woman die, but I did not kill her"; for letting-die is in general likely to be more defensible than killing. My analysis incidentally shows one reason why: the alternatives to killing are always very numerous, and the odds are that at least one of them provides an acceptable way out of the impasse; whereas the alternative to letting-die is always some fairly specific course of conduct, and if there are conclusive objections to *that* then there's an end of the matter. All this, though, is a matter of likelihoods. It is no help in the rare case where the alternatives to killing, numerous as they are, arguably do *not* include an acceptable way out of the impasse because they all involve something of the same order of gravity as a killing, namely a letting-die. The conservative may say: "Where innocent humans are in question, letting-die is not of the same order of gravity as killing: for one of them is not, and the other is, absolutely wrong in all possible circumstances." But this, like the rejoinders out of which this paragraph grew, assumes the very point which is at issue. All these conservative moves come down to just one thing: "At this point your argument fails; for the wrongness of killing the child, in any instance of the obstetrical example, *can* be defended on the basis of your own analysis of the acting/refraining distinction—plus the extra premiss that it would always be wrong to kill the child."

The Stress on the Specific

My argument is finished; but its strategy might be thought to be open to a certain criticism which I want to discuss.

The obstetrical example is a *kind* of situation, on every instance of which the conservative makes a certain judgment. I have argued that this judgment, as applied to many instances of the example, cannot be defended except by the unquestioning invocation of authority. This would have been damaging to the conservative position even if I had appealed only to "fantastic" kinds of instances such as seldom or never occur; but in fact my claims have been true of many real-life instances of the obstetrical example. Still, a conservative might resist my drive towards the relatively specific, my insistence upon asking: "What is there about *this* kind of instance which justifies your judgment upon it?" He might claim that even my opening paragraph presents so special a kind of situation that he cannot fairly be asked to find in *it* something which supports his judgment other than by a blanket appeal to his general principle that it would always be wrong to kill an innocent human. There are two ways in which he might defend this stand: they look alike, but their fatal defects are very different.

The first is by the use of a sub-Wittgensteinian argument from the nature of language. Although I have never encountered it, it is a possible and plausible objection to my strategy of argument. The conservative might say: "Granted that facts about (a) expectation, (b) inevitability and (c) intention are irrelevant to the way the action/consequence distinction applies to the obstetrical example; it does not follow that when we apply the distinction to the example *all* we are doing—apart from (d) reflecting our already-formed moral judgments—is to report facts about (e) immediacy and (f) acting/refraining. Language and thought don't work like this. When we say: 'Operating would be killing; not-operating would not be killing though it would have death as a consequence,' we are not *just* talking about immediacy and specificity of options. We are using words which, *qua* words in the language, are laden with associations having to do with (a)–(d); and these associations of the words cannot simply be ignored or forgotten in a particular case. Language is not atomic in that way, and it would be at best a clumsy instrument if it were."

I agree that we often do, and perhaps must sometimes, decide our conduct in one situation partly through verbal carry-overs from others in which similar conduct could be justified more directly. But I think that everyone will agree that the more serious a practical problem is, the greater is our obligation to resist such verbal carry-overs and scrutinize the particular problem in order to see what there is about *it* which would justify this or that solution to it. A practical problem in which human lives are at stake is a deeply serious one, and it would be an abdication from all moral seriousness to settle it by verbal carry-overs. I am not saying: "Take pity on the poor woman, and never mind what the correct description of the situation is." I am opposing someone who says: "This is the correct description of the situation—never mind what its force is in this particular case."

The second objection to my stress on the particular case, or the specific kind of case, is one which conservatives do sometimes use; and it connects with a muddle which is not special to conservatives. It goes like this: "We must have rules. If every practical problem had to be solved on the spot, on the basis of the fine details of the particular case, the results would be disastrous. Take a situation which falls under some rule which I know to be justified in most situations. There may not be time or means for me to learn much more about the present situation than just that it does fall under the rule; the details of the case, even if I can discover them, may be too complex for me to handle; my handling of them, even if intellectually efficient, may without my knowing it be self-interested or corrupt; by deciding, however uncorruptly, not to follow the rule on this occasion, I may weaken its hold on me in other situations where it clearly ought to be followed; and even if I could be sure that I was in no such danger, I might help others into it by publicly breaking the rule." [7]

This is all true, but it does not help the conservative. Notice first that it tells against undue attention to individual cases rather than against undue attention to limited kinds of cases: its target is not the specific but the particular. Still, it could be developed into an attack on over-stressing very specifically detailed kinds of cases: its opening words would then have to be replaced by: "We must have rather general rules." This is true too, but it is still no help to the conservative.

This argument for our bringing practical problems under rather general rules is based on the consequences of our not doing so: it points to the dangers attendant on suspending a general rule and considering whether one's practical problem might be better resolved by applying a less general one. But sometimes these dangers will be far too slight to justify doing what a given general rule enjoins in a particular situation. If the thesis under discussion is to have any practical upshot which is not ludicrous ("Never break any general rule which would enjoin the right action in more cases than not"), or vague to the point of vacuity ("Always apply some fairly general rule"), or merely question-begging ("Never break a rule forbidding an action which really is absolutely impermissible"), then it must allow us to raise questions of the form: "Need we be deterred by the dangers attendant on suspending *this* rule in favour of *this* more specific rule in *this* kind of situation?" The answer will depend upon what the challenged general rule is, what the proposed substitute for it is, the intelligence and character of the agent, and the likelihood that his breaking the rule (if it comes to that) would become generally known and, if known, demoralizing to others. These matters need not be so complex as to defeat finite intelligence, or so primrose-strewn that fallen man dare not

---

[7] For a gesture in this direction, see St. John-Stevas, *op. cit.,* pp. 14–16. See also McFadden, *op. cit.,* p. 133.

venture among them. Furthermore, they can themselves be embodied in rules carefully formulated in advance—meta-rules about the kinds of situations in which this or that ground-level general rule may be suspended in favour of this or that more specific one.

Here is a possible case. A certain obstetrician accepts the rule, "Do not kill innocent humans," as applicable in every kind of situation he has thought of except the kind described in my opening paragraph. He wants a rule for this kind too, as a shield against the confusions, temptations and pressures of the concrete situation; and after reflection he adopts the following: "If the child is not hydrocephalic it is not to be killed. If it is hydrocephalic it is to be killed unless either (a) the woman is bound to die within a month anyway, or (b) the woman has no other children under eighteen and she is known to be a chronic acute depressive. If (a) or (b) or both are true, the child is not to be killed."

By preferring this rule to the more general one for instances of the obstetrical example, the obstetrician is not rendering it likely that in some situations he will flounder around not knowing what rule about killing to apply. For he has a clear enough meta-rule: "If the only way to save a woman's life is to kill the child she is bearing, apply this rule: . . . ; otherwise apply the rule: Do not kill innocent humans."

The obstetrician is not satisfied with his ground-level rule for instances of the obstetrical example, and he hopes to be able to improve it. Still, he is resigned to his rule's ignoring various matters which, though they are relevant to what the ideally right action would be, would involve him in the dangers of over-specificity mentioned above. "Is the woman a potential murderess or the child a mongol?"—the answers are probably unobtainable. "In what ways would the woman's death represent a real loss to others?"—the answer, even if discoverable, could be so complex as to elude any manageable rule. "Would either course of action bring the medical profession into undeserved but seriously damaging disrepute?"—it would be too easy for that to be unconsciously conflated with the question of which course would best further the obstetrician's own career. "Would the child, if delivered alive, be especially helpful to students of hydrocephalus?"—asking that could be the first step on a downward path: by allowing one woman to die partly because her child will be medically interesting if alive, even an uncorrupt man may ease the way towards allowing some other woman to die partly because *she* will be medically interesting when dead.

Although he pays heed—neurotically pays far too much heed—to the conservative's warnings against over-specificity, this obstetrician arrives at a conclusion quite different from the conservative's. That is the crux. The conservative who warns against the dangers of overspecifying is trying to find a consequentialist basis for his whole position. Unlike the "protective-coloration gambit" discussed earlier, this is legitimate enough in itself; but it simply does not yield the conservative position on the matter under discussion. For it to do so, the conservative would have to show that our obstetrician's more specific rule is *too* dangerous in the ways mentioned above; and he would have to do this without applying danger-inflating standards which would commit him also to condemning as too dangerous the suspension of the general rule: "Never leave a bucket in a hall-way." He may object: "Buckets in hall-ways are not important enough to provide a fair analogy. Where something as grave as killing is in question, we should be especially sensitive to the dangers of suspending a general rule." But then when something as grave as letting someone die is involved in applying the rule, we should be especially reluctant to accept, without good empirical evidence, popular clichés about the dangers of suspending general rules. The two points cancel out.

Of course, there are these dangers, and we should guard against them. To assess them at all precisely, though, would require more than we know of sociology, psychology and the philosophy of mind; and so our guarding against them can consist only in our keeping the urge towards specificity under some restraint, our remembering that in this matter it is not always true that the sky is the limit. The conservative who hopes to secure his position by pointing out these dangers must claim that he *can* assess them, and can discover in them a simple, sweeping pattern which picks out a certain list of general rules as the ones which ought never to be suspended by anyone in any circumstances. No one would explicitly make so preposterous a claim.

"So you do at any rate retreat from act- to rule-utilitarianism?" No. Rule-utilitarianism can be presented (1) as a quasi-mystical doctrine about the importance of rule following "per se," or (2) as a doctrine about the importance of rule-following because of what rule-following empirically *is,* because of what happens when people follow rules and what happens when they don't. In version (1), rule-utilitarianism is a distinct doctrine which has nothing to recommend it. In version (2), it is just part of a thorough act-utilitarianism. (In most actual presentations, there is a cloudy attempt to combine (2)'s reasonableness with (1)'s rejection of act-utilitarianism.) In this section I have been discussing what the consequences might be, for myself or others, of my suspending or breaking a given general rule. These are among, not additional to, the consequential factors whose relevance I have been urging all through the paper. There has been no retreat.

Conclusion

Principles of the form: "It would always be wrong to . . . , whatever the consequences of not doing so" seem defensible because the action/consequence distinction does often have a certain kind of moral significance. But in proportion as a situation gives real work to the rider ". . . whatever the consequences of not doing so," in proportion as it puts pressure on this rider, in proportion as the "consequences of not doing so" give some moral reason for "doing so"—to that extent the action/consequence distinction lacks moral significance in that situation. The obstetrical example is just an extreme case: there the rider serves to dismiss the entire moral case against applying the principle; and, proportionately, the action/consequence distinction carries no moral weight at all.

The phenomenon of conservatism, then, can be explained as follows. The conservative naturally thinks that the action/consequence distinction has great moral significance because of its frequent connexion with differences concerning (a) expectation, (b) inevitability, (c) intention and (d) independently formed moral judgments. He then encounters cases like the obstetrical example, where (a)–(d) are irrelevant but where the distinction can still be applied because of facts about (e) immediacy and (f) acting/refraining. Failing to see that in these cases the distinction has lost absolutely all its moral bite, and perhaps encouraged by a mistake about "rule-following per se," he still applies his principle in the usual way. Those who do not follow him in this he finds lax or opportunist or corrupt; and many of them half agree, by conceding to his position a certain hard and unfeeling uprightness. Both are wrong. Conservatism, when it is not mere obedience, is mere muddle.

Abortion and the Doctrine of the Double Effect
Philippa Foot

One of the reasons why most of us feel puzzled about the problem of abortion is that we want, and do not want, to allow to the unborn child the rights that belong to adults and children. When we think of a baby about to be born it seems absurd to think that the next few minutes or even hours could make so radical a difference to its status; yet as we go back in the life of the foetus we are more and more reluctant to say that this is a human being and must be treated as such. No doubt this is the deepest source of our dilemma, but it is not the only one. For we are also confused about the general question of what we may and may not do where the interests of human beings conflict. We have strong intuitions about certain cases; saying, for instance, that it is all right to raise the level of education in our country, though statistics allow us to predict that a rise in the suicide rate will follow, while it is not all right to kill the feeble-minded to aid cancer research. It is not easy, however, to see the principles involved, and one way of throwing light on the abortion

From *The Oxford Review* 5 (1967). Reprinted by permission of the author. Philippa Foot is a senior research fellow at Sommerville College, Oxford.

issue will be by setting up parallels involving adults or children once born. So we will be able to isolate the "equal rights" issue, and should be able to make some advance.

I shall not, of course, discuss all the principles that may be used in deciding what to do where the interest or rights of human beings conflict. What I want to do is to look at one particular theory, known as the "doctrine of the double effect" which is invoked by Catholics in support of their views on abortion but supposed by them to apply elsewhere. As used in the abortion argument this doctrine has often seemed to non-Catholics to be a piece of complete sophistry. In the last number of the *Oxford Review* it was given short shrift by Professor Hart.[1] And yet this principle has seemed to some non-Catholics as well as to Catholics to stand as the only defence against decisions on other issues that are quite unacceptable. It will help us in our difficulty about abortion if this conflict can be resolved.

The doctrine of the double effect is based on a distinction between what a man foresees as a result of his voluntary action and what, in the strict sense, he intends. He intends in the strictest sense both those things that he aims at as ends and those that he aims at as means to his ends. The latter may be regretted in themselves but nevertheless desired for the sake of the end, as we may intend to keep dangerous lunatics confined for the sake of our safety. By contrast a man is said not strictly, or directly, to intend the foreseen consequences of his voluntary actions where these are neither the end at which he is aiming nor the means to this end. Whether the word "intention" should be applied in both cases is not of course what matters: Bentham spoke of "oblique intention," contrasting it with the "direct intention" of ends and means, and we may as well follow his terminology. Everyone must recognize that some such distinction can be made, though it may be made in a number of different ways, and it is the distinction that is crucial to the doctrine of the double effect. The words "double effect" refer to the two effects that an action may produce: the one aimed at, and the one foreseen but in no way desired. By "the doctrine of the double effect" I mean the thesis that it is sometimes permissible to bring about by oblique intention what one may not directly intend. Thus the distinction is held to be relevant to moral decision in certain difficult cases. It is said for instance that the operation of hysterectomy involves the death of the foetus as the foreseen but not strictly or directly intended consequence of the surgeon's act, while other operations kill the child and count as the direct intention of taking an innocent life, a distinction that has evoked particularly bitter reactions on the part of non-Catholics. If you are permitted to bring about the death of the child, what does it matter how it is done? The doctrine of the double effect is also used to show why in another case, where a woman in labour will die unless a craniotomy operation is performed, the intervention is not to be condoned. There, it is said, we may not operate but must let the mother die. We foresee her death but do not directly

---

[1] H. L. A. Hart, "Intention and Punishment," *Oxford Review,* Number 4, Hilary 1967.

intend it, whereas to crush the skull of the child would count as direct intention of its death.[2]

This last application of the doctrine has been queried by Professor Hart on the ground that the child's death is not strictly a means to saving the mother's life and should logically be treated as an unwanted but foreseen consequence by those who make use of the distinction between direct and oblique intention. To interpret the doctrine in this way is perfectly reasonable given the language that has been used; it would, however, make nonsense of it from the beginning. A certain event may be desired under one of its descriptions, unwanted under another, but we cannot treat these as two different events, one of which is aimed at and the other not. And even if it be argued that there are here two different events—the crushing of the child's skull and its death—the two are obviously much too close for an application of the doctrine of the double effect. To see how odd it would be to apply the principle like this we may consider the story, well known to philosophers, of the fat man stuck in the mouth of the cave. A party of potholers have imprudently allowed the fat man to lead them as they make their way out of the cave, and he gets stuck, trapping the others behind him. Obviously the right thing to do is to sit down and wait until the fat man grows thin; but philosophers have arranged that flood waters should be rising within the cave. Luckily (luckily?) the trapped party have with them a stick of dynamite with which they can blast the fat man out of the mouth of the cave. Either they use the dynamite or they drown. In one version the fat man, whose head is *in* the cave, will drown with them; in the other he will be rescued in due course.[3] Problem: may they use the dynamite or not? Later we will find parallels to this example. Here it is introduced for light relief and because it will serve to show how ridiculous one version of the doctrine of the double effect would be. For suppose that the trapped explorers were to argue that the death of the fat man might be taken as a merely foreseen consequence of the act of blowing him up. ("We didn't want to kill him . . . only to blow him into small pieces" or even ". . . only to blast him out of the mouth of the cave.") I believe that those who use the doctrine of the double effect would rightly reject such a suggestion, though they will, of course, have considerable difficulty in explaining where the line is to be drawn. What is to be the criterion of "closeness" if we say that anything very close to what we are literally aiming at counts as if part of our aim?

Let us leave this difficulty aside and return to the arguments for and against the doctrine, supposing it to be formulated in the way considered most effective by its supporters, and ourselves bypassing the trouble by taking what must on any reasonable definition be clear cases of "direct" or "oblique" intention.

---

[2] For discussions of the Catholic doctrine on abortion see Glanville Williams, *The Sanctity of Life and the Criminal Law* (New York, 1957); also N. St. John-Stevas, *The Right to Life* (London, 1963).

[3] It was Professor Hart who drew my attention to this distinction.

The first point that should be made clear, in fairness to the theory, is that no one is suggesting that it does not matter what you bring about as long as you merely foresee and do not strictly intend the evil that follows. We might think, for instance, of the (actual) case of wicked merchants selling, for cooking, oil they knew to be poisonous and thereby killing a number of innocent people, comparing and contrasting it with that of some unemployed gravediggers, desperate for custom, who got hold of this same oil and sold it (or perhaps *they* secretly gave it away) in order to create orders for graves. They strictly (directly) intend the deaths they cause, while the merchants could say that it was not part of their *plan* that anyone should die. In morality, as in law, the merchants, like the gravediggers, would be considered as murderers; nor are the supporters of the doctrine of the double effect bound to say that there is the least difference between them in respect of moral turpitude. What they are committed to is the thesis that *sometimes* it makes a difference to the permissibility of an action involving harm to others that this harm, although foreseen, is not part of the agent's direct intention. An end such as earning one's living is clearly not such as to justify *either* the direct or oblique intention of the death of innocent people, but in certain cases one is justified in bringing about knowingly what one could not directly intend.

It is now time to say why this doctrine should be taken seriously in spite of the fact that it sounds rather odd, that there are difficulties about the distinction on which it depends, and that it seemed to yield one sophistical conclusion when applied to the problem of abortion. The reason for its appeal is that its opponents have often *seemed* to be committed to quite indefensible views. Thus the controversy has raged around examples such as the following. Suppose that a judge or magistrate is faced with rioters demanding that a culprit be found for a certain crime and threatening otherwise to take their own bloody revenge on a particular section of the community. The real culprit being unknown, the judge sees himself as able to prevent the bloodshed only by framing some innocent person and having him executed. Beside this example is placed another in which a pilot whose aeroplane is about to crash is deciding whether to steer from a more to a less inhabited area. To make the parallel as close as possible it may rather be supposed that he is the driver of a runaway tram which he can only steer from one narrow track on to another; five men are working on one track and one man on the other; anyone on the track he enters is bound to be killed. In the case of the riots the mob have five hostages, so that in both the exchange is supposed to be one man's life for the lives of five. The question is why we should say, without hesitation, that the driver should steer for the less occupied track, while most of us would be appalled at the idea that the innocent man could be framed. It may be suggested that the special feature of the latter case is that it involves the corruption of justice, and this is, of course, very important indeed. But if we remove that special feature, supposing that some private individual is to kill an innocent person and pass him off as the criminal we still find ourselves horrified by the idea. The doctrine of the double effect offers us a way out of the difficulty, insisting that it is one thing to steer towards someone foreseeing that you will kill him and another to aim at his death as part of your plan. Moreover there is one very important element of good in what is here insisted. In real life it would hardly ever be certain that the man on the narrow track would be killed. Perhaps he might find a foothold on the side of the tunnel and cling on as the vehicle hurtled by. The driver of the tram does *not* then leap off and brain him with a crowbar. The judge, however, needs the death of the innocent man for his (good) purposes. If the victim proves hard to hang he must see to it that he dies another way. To choose to execute him is to choose that this evil *shall come about,* and this must therefore count as a *certainty* in weighing up the good and evil involved. The distinction between direct and oblique intention is crucial here, and is of great importance in an uncertain world. Nevertheless this is no way to defend the doctrine of the double effect. For the question is whether the difference between aiming at something and obliquely intending it is *in itself* relevant to moral decisions; not whether it is important when correlated with a difference of certainty in the balance of good and evil. Moreover we are particularly interested in the application of the doctrine of the double effect to the question of abortion, and no one can deny that in medicine there are sometimes certainties so complete that it would be a mere quibble to speak of the "probable outcome" of this course of action or that. It is not, therefore, with a merely philosophical interest that we should put aside the uncertainty and scrutinize the examples to test the doctrine of the double effect. Why can we not argue from the case of the steering driver to that of the judge?

Another pair of examples poses a similar problem. We are about to give to a patient who needs it to save his life a massive dose of a certain drug in short supply. There arrive, however, five other patients each of whom could be saved by one-fifth of that dose. We say with regret that we cannot spare our whole supply of the drug for a single patient, just as we should say that we could not spare the whole resources of a ward for one dangerously ill individual when ambulances arrive bringing in the victims of a multiple crash. We feel bound to let one man die rather than many if that is our only choice. Why then do we not feel justified in killing people in the interests of cancer research or to obtain, let us say, spare parts for grafting on to those who need them? We can suppose, similarly, that several dangerously ill people can be saved only if we kill a certain individual and make a serum from his dead body. (These examples are not over fanciful considering present controversies about prolonging the life of mortally ill patients whose eyes or kidneys are to be used for others.) Why cannot we argue from the case of the scarce drug to that of the body needed for medical purposes? Once again the doctrine of the double effect comes up with an explanation. In one kind of case but not the other we aim at the death of the innocent man.

A further argument suggests that if the doctrine of the double effect is rejected this has the consequence of putting us hopelessly in the power of bad men. Suppose for example that some tyrant should threaten to torture five men if we ourselves would not torture one. Would it be our duty to do so, supposing we believed him, because this would be no different from choosing to rescue five men from his tortures rather than one? If so anyone who wants us to do something we think wrong has only to threaten that otherwise he himself will do something we think worse. A mad murderer, known to keep his promises, could thus make it our duty to kill some innocent citizen to prevent him from killing two. From this conclusion we are again rescued by the doctrine of the double effect. If we refuse, we foresee that the greater number will be killed but we do not intend it: it is he who intends (that is strictly or directly intends) the death of innocent persons; we do not.

At one time I thought that these arguments in favour of the doctrine of the double effect were conclusive, but I now believe that the conflict should be solved in another way. The clue that we should follow is that the strength of the doctrine seems to lie in the distinction it makes between what we *do* (equated with direct intention) and what we allow (thought of as obliquely intended). Indeed it is interesting that the disputants tend to argue about whether we are to be held responsible for what we allow as we are for what we do.[4] Yet it is not obvious that this is what they should be discussing, since the distinction between what one does and what one allows to happen is not the same as that between direct and oblique intention. To see this one has only to consider that it is possible *deliberately* to allow something to happen, aiming at it either for its own sake or as part of one's plan for obtaining something else. So one person might want another person dead, and deliberately allow him to die. And again one may be said to *do* things that one does not aim at, as the steering driver would kill the man on the track. Moreover there is a large class of things said to be brought about rather than either done or allowed, and either kind of intention is possible. So it is possible to *bring about* a man's death by getting him to go to sea in a leaky boat, and the intention of his death may be either direct or oblique.

Whatever it may, or may not, have to do with the doctrine of the double effect, the idea of *allowing* is worth looking into in this context. I shall leave aside the special case of giving permission, which involves the idea of authority, and consider the two main divisions into which cases of allowing seem to fall. There is firstly the allowing which is forbearing to prevent. For this we need a sequence thought of as somehow already in train, and something that the agent could do to intervene. (The agent must be able to intervene, but does not do so.) So, for instance, he could warn someone, but *allows* him to walk into a trap. He could feed an animal but *allows* it to die for lack of food. He could stop a leaking tap but *allows* the water to go on flowing. This is the case of allowing with which we shall be concerned, but the other should be

---

[4] See, e.g., J. Bennett, "Whatever the Consequences," *Analysis*, January 1966, and G. E. M. Anscombe's reply in *Analysis*, June 1966. See also Miss Anscombe's "Modern Moral Philosophy" in *Philosophy*, January 1958.

mentioned. It is the kind of allowing which is roughly equivalent to *enabling;* the root idea being the removal of some obstacle which is, as it were, holding back a train of events. So someone may remove a plug and *allow* water to flow; open a door and *allow* an animal to get out; or give someone money and *allow* him to get back on his feet.

The first kind of allowing requires an omission, but there is no other general correlation between omission and allowing, commission and bringing about or doing. An actor who fails to turn up for a performance will generally spoil it rather than allow it to be spoiled. I mention the distinction between omission and commission only to set it aside.

Thinking of the first kind of allowing (forebearing to prevent), we should ask whether there is any difference, from the moral point of view, between what one does or causes and what one merely allows. It seems clear that on occasions one is just as bad as the other, as is recognized in both morality and law. A man may murder his child or his aged relatives, by allowing them to die of starvation as well as by giving poison; he may also be convicted of murder on either account. In another case we would, however, make a distinction. Most of us allow people to die of starvation in India and Africa, and there is surely something wrong with us that we do; it would be nonsense, however, to pretend that it is only in law that we make a distinction between allowing people in the underdeveloped countries to die of starvation and sending them poisoned food. There is worked into our moral system a distinction between what we owe people in the form of aid and what we owe them in the way of non-interference. Salmond, in his *Jurisprudence,* expressed as follows the distinction between the two.

> A positive right corresponds to a positive duty, and is a right that he on whom the duty lies shall do some positive act on behalf of the person entitled. A negative right corresponds to a negative duty, and is a right that the person bound shall refrain from some act which would operate to the prejudice of the person entitled. The former is a right to be positively benefited; the latter is merely a right not to be harmed.[5]

As a general account of rights and duties this is defective, since not all are so closely connected with benefit and harm. Nevertheless for our purposes it will do well. Let us speak of negative duties when thinking of the obligation to refrain from such things as killing or robbing, and of the positive duty, e.g., to look after children or aged parents. It will be useful, however, to extend the notion of positive duty beyond the range of things that are strictly called duties, bringing acts of charity under this heading. These are owed only in a rather loose sense, and some acts of charity could hardly be said to be *owed* at all, so I am not following ordinary usage at this point.

---

[5] J. Salmond, *Jurisprudence,* 11th edition, p. 283.

Let us now see whether the distinction of negative and positive duties explains why we see differently the action of the steering driver and that of the judge, of the doctors who withhold the scarce drug and those who obtain a body for medical purposes, of those who choose to rescue the five men rather than one man from torture and those who are ready to torture the one man themselves in order to save five. In each case we have a conflict of duties, but what kind of duties are they? Are we, in each case, weighing positive duties against positive, negative against negative, or one against the other? Is the duty to refrain from injury, or rather to bring aid?

The steering driver faces a conflict of negative duties, since it is his duty to avoid injuring five men and also his duty to avoid injuring one. In the circumstances he is not able to avoid both, and it seems clear that he should do the least injury he can. The judge, however, is weighing the duty of not inflicting injury against the duty of bringing aid. He wants to rescue the innocent people threatened with death but can do so only by inflicting injury himself. Since one does not *in general* have the same duty to help people as to refrain from injuring them, it is not possible to argue to a conclusion about what he should do from the steering driver case. It is interesting that, even where the strictest duty of positive aid exists, this still does not weigh as if a negative duty were involved. It is not, for instance, permissible to commit a murder to bring one's starving children food. If the choice is between inflicting injury on one or many there seems only one rational course of action; if the choice is between aid to some at the cost of injury to others, and refusing to inflict the injury to bring the aid, the whole matter is open to dispute. So it is not inconsistent of us to think that the driver must steer for the road on which only one man stands while the judge (or his equivalent) may not kill the innocent person in order to stop the riots. Let us now consider the second pair of examples, which concern the scarce drug on the one hand and on the other the body needed to save lives. Once again we find a difference based on the distinction between the duty to avoid injury and the duty to provide aid. Where one man needs a massive dose of the drug and we withhold it from him in order to save five men, we are weighing aid against aid. But if we consider killing a man in order to use his body to save others, we are thinking of doing him injury to bring others aid. In an interesting variant of the model, we may suppose that instead of killing someone we deliberately let him die. (Perhaps he is a beggar to whom we are thinking of giving food, but then we say "No, they need bodies for medical research.") Here it does seem relevant that in allowing him to die we are aiming at his death, but presumably we are inclined to see this as a violation of negative rather than positive duty. If this is right, we see why we are unable in either case to argue to a conclusion from the case of the scarce drug.

In the examples involving the torturing of one man or five men, the principle seems to be the same as for the last pair. If we are bringing aid (rescuing people about to be tortured by the tyrant), we must obviously rescue the larger rather than the smaller group. It does not follow, however, that we would be justified in inflicting the injury, or getting a third person to do so, in order to save the five. We may therefore refuse to be forced into acting by the threats of bad men. To refrain from inflicting injury ourselves is a stricter duty than to prevent other people from inflicting injury, which is not to say that the other is not a very strict duty indeed.

So far the conclusions are the same as those at which we might arrive following the doctrine of the double effect, but in others they will be different, and the advantage seems to be all on the side of the alternative. Suppose, for instance, that there are five patients in a hospital whose lives could be saved by the manufacture of a certain gas, but that this inevitably releases lethal fumes into the room of another patient whom for some reason we are unable to move. His death, being of no use to us, is clearly a side effect, and not directly intended. Why then is the case different from that of the scarce drug, if the point about that is that we foresaw but did not strictly intend the death of the single patient? Yet it surely is different. The relatives of the gassed patient would presumably be successful if they sued the hospital and the whole story came out. We may find it particularly revolting that someone should be *used* as in the case where he is killed or allowed to die in the interest of medical research, and the fact of *using* may even determine what we would decide to do in some cases, but the principle seems unimportant compared with our reluctance to bring such injury for the sake of giving aid.

My conclusion is that the distinction between direct and oblique intention plays only a quite subsidiary role in determining what we say in these cases, while the distinction between avoiding injury and bringing aid is very important indeed. I have not, of course, argued that there are no other principles. For instance it clearly makes a difference whether our positive duty is a strict duty or rather an act of charity: feeding our own children or feeding those in far away countries. It may also make a difference whether the person about to suffer is one thought of as uninvolved in the threatened disaster, and whether it is his presence that constitutes the threat to the others. In many cases we find it very hard to know what to say, and I have not been arguing for any general conclusion such as that we may never, whatever the balance of good and evil, bring injury to one for the sake of aid to others, even when this injury amounts to death. I have only tried to show that even if we reject the doctrine of the double effect we are not forced to the conclusion that the size of the evil must always be our guide.

Let us now return to the problem of abortion, carrying out our plan of finding parallels involving adults or children rather than the unborn. We must say something about the different cases in which abortion might be considered on medical grounds.

First of all there is the situation in which nothing that can be done will save the life of child and mother, but where the life of the mother can be saved by killing the child. This is parallel to the case of the fat man in the mouth of the cave who is bound to be drowned with the others if nothing is done. Given the certainty of the outcome, as it was postulated, there is no serious conflict of interests here, since the fat man will perish in either case, and it is reasonable that the action that will save someone should be done. It is a great objection to those who argue that the direct intention of the death of an innocent person is never justifiable that the edict will apply even in this case. The Catholic doctrine on abortion must here conflict with that of most reasonable men. Moreover we would be justified in performing the operation whatever the method used, and it is neither a necessary nor a good justification of the special case of hysterectomy that the child's death is not directly intended, being rather a foreseen consequence of what is done. What difference could it make as to how the death is brought about?

Secondly we have the case in which it is possible to perform an operation which will save the mother and kill the child or kill the mother and save the child. This is parallel to the famous case of the shipwrecked mariners who believed that they must throw someone overboard if their boat was not to founder in a storm, and to the other famous case of the two sailors, Dudley and Stephens, who killed and ate the cabin boy when adrift on the sea without food. Here again there is no conflict of interests so far as the decision to act is concerned; only in deciding whom to save. Once again it would be reasonable to act, though one would respect someone who held back from the appalling action either because he preferred to perish rather than do such a thing or because he held on past the limits of reasonable hope. In real life the certainties postulated by philosophers hardly ever exist, and Dudley and Stephens were rescued not long after their ghastly meal. Nevertheless if the certainty were absolute, as it might be in the abortion case, it would seem better to save one than none. Probably we should decide in favour of the mother when weighing her life against that of the unborn child, but it is interesting that, a few years later, we might easily decide it the other way.

The worst dilemma comes in the third kind of example where to save the mother we must kill the child, say by crushing its skull, while if nothing is done the mother will perish but the child can be safely delivered after her death. Here the doctrine of the double effect has been invoked to show that we may not intervene, since the child's death would be directly intended while the mother's would not. On a strict parallel with cases not involving the unborn we might find the conclusion correct though the reason given was wrong. Suppose, for instance, that in later life the presence of a child was certain to bring death to the mother. We would surely not think ourselves justified in ridding her of it by a process that involved its death. For in general we do not think that we can kill one innocent person to rescue another, quite apart from the special care that we feel is due to children once they have prudently got themselves born. What we would be prepared to do when a great many people were involved is another matter, and this is probably the key to one quite common view of abortion on the part of those who take quite seriously the rights of the unborn child. They probably feel that if *enough* people are involved one must be sacrificed, and they think of the mother's life against the unborn child's life as if it were many against one. But of course many people do not view it like this at all, having no inclination to accord to the foetus or unborn child anything like ordinary human status in the matter of rights. I have not been arguing for or against these points of view but only trying to discern some of the currents that are pulling us back and forth. The levity of the examples is not meant to offend.

9

Punishment
and Rehabilitation

Reading: Stanley I. Benn, "Punishment"

No decent man could approve of the present practices of criminal punishment in America. As recent prison riots have brought to light, most American prisons are inhuman pestholes that breed crime rather than reduce it. Only an extremely shortsighted person could advocate more of the same as a solution to the growing problem of crime in our society; but alas, as usual, there is no poverty of shortsighted people in positions of influence and power.

For this reason, such books as Dr. Karl Menninger's widely acclaimed *The Crime of Punishment* are in many ways a welcome contribution to the "law and order" debate in American society. Menninger, an eminent psychiatrist, dramatically points out the failures and the inhumanities within our present penal practices and persuasively advocates drastic reform. And for this much all reasonable and decent men should surely be grateful to him. However, he goes beyond such negative criticism and advocates an alternative method of handling the crime problem; and his alternative method is, to say the least, highly controversial.

Like many psychiatrists, Menninger tends to regard criminal behavior as symptomatic of personality disorder. Thus, he proposes that we drop our present practice of punishing people in prisons and indeed that we drop the whole complex business of the criminal law and criminal procedure. In his view, this practice wastes time and money, is inhuman, and fails to perform the important task of eliminating crime; for punishment, he claims, neither deters nor reforms men. Retribution, the only other possible justification left, can be rejected since it rests, according to Menninger, on an outdated and unscientific conception of personal responsibility or free will.

Since criminal behavior is really a kind of sickness, then, the response to such behavior should be therapeutic. Criminal behavior should be cured, not punished. Menninger proposes that instead of perpetuating the inhuman practice of confining people in prisons, we should treat and rehabilitate them in hospitals. When necessary, for their good and ours, we may even employ preventive and indefinite detention. Since this confinement will be for therapy, and not for punishment, it will not be objectionable but will rather be a benefit to all concerned.

Menninger's suggestions sound wonderful, but they may be too good to be true. We should certainly humanize our present penal institutions and increase opportunities for at least voluntary therapy. But should we abandon the criminal process entirely? Would we really benefit even the criminal if we did so? At least in the criminal law a prisoner has some procedural protections contained in our Bill of Rights. But there is no therapeutic bill of rights—no developed concept of "cruel and unusual *therapy*," which might be used to block such things as electric shocks, lobotomies, and certain drugs. Defective as the criminal process is, would it be obviously better to move toward what Nicholas Kittrie has called the "therapeutic state" in which psychiatrists have increased political power and discretionary control over the lives of citizens? (This has happened in Soviet Russia, and the increasing number of political dissidents there classified as "mentally ill" is disquieting.) There are surely grounds for skepticism with respect to a move toward therapy as a comprehensive response to crime. Attica was a disgrace to America, certainly, but it would have been no less a disgrace had it been called a hospital rather than a prison.

What is the explanation of crime? Does it flow, as many traditionalists would say, from the free and responsible decisions of wicked men? Is it, as many psychiatrists would say, a kind of mental illness? Or is it perhaps, as many Marxist and non-Marxist sociologists would say, a product of defective socioeconomic institutions, institutions which are themselves so "criminal" that those who have power in them lack the moral right to demand either therapy or punishment for those who act against the rules? Perhaps the correct answer is some combination of all the above. And this possibility alone should make us wary of any simple and neat solution to the problem of how we should deal with criminal behavior. Simple solutions on this question are almost certain to be simpleminded.

The following selection by Stanley I. Benn should provide a solid groundwork on which to generate reasonable discussion of punishment and criminal rehabilitation. His essay is an attempt to present a fair and balanced presentation and appraisal of certain classic theories of punishment. He closes with a brief consideration of the pros and cons of a therapeutic response to criminality.

Suggestions for Further Reading

H. B. Acton, ed., *The Philosophy of Punishment* (New York: St. Martin's Press, 1969).

Nicholas N. Kittrie, *The Right to be Different: Deviance and Enforced Therapy* (Baltimore: Johns Hopkins Press, 1971).

Karl Menninger, *The Crime of Punishment* (New York: Viking Press, 1968).

Herbert Morris, "Persons and Punishment," *The Monist,* October, 1968.

Jeffrie G. Murphy, "Criminal Punishment and Psychiatric Fallacies," *Law and Society Review,* August 1969.

Jeffrie G. Murphy, ed., *Punishment and the Rehabilitative Ideal* (Belmont, Calif.: Wadsworth, forthcoming).

Thomas S. Szasz, *Law, Liberty, and Psychiatry* (New York: Macmillan, 1963).

Barbara Wootton, *Crime and the Criminal Law* (London: Stevens, 1963).

Punishment
Stanley I. Benn

The word "punishment" is used in varying contexts. The punishment meted out by the state to a criminal or by a parent to his children is not the same as the punishment boxers give or receive. The latter, however, is punishment only in a metaphorical sense, for it lacks several of the features necessary to a standard case of punishment. Characteristically, punishment is unpleasant. It is inflicted on an offender because of an offense he has committed; it is deliberately imposed, not just the natural consequence of a person's action (like a hang-over), and the unpleasantness is essential to it, not an accidental accompaniment to some other treatment (like the pain of the dentist's drill). It is imposed by an agent authorized by the system of rules against which an offense has been committed; a lynching is not a standard

Reprinted with permission of the publisher from *The Encyclopedia of Philosophy,* Paul Edwards, Editor-in-Chief, Volume 7, pp. 29–35. Copyright © 1967 by Crowell Collier and Macmillan, Inc. Stanley I. Benn, until recently a lecturer in government at the University of Southampton, is now at the Australian National University, Canberra.

case of punishment. Philosophers who have written on punishment have usually had in mind punishment in the standard sense rather than in any extended or metaphorical sense.

The philosopher's interest in punishment is mainly connected with questions of justification. It is, prima facie, wrong to deliberately inflict suffering or deprivation on another person, yet punishment consists in doing precisely this. What conditions, the philosopher asks, would justify it? Or, more generally, what kind of consideration would count toward a justification? For instance, if a person had already committed a crime, that would clearly be relevant to the question of whether he ought to be punished (although it might not be conclusive). What if he were only expected to commit a crime in the future? Or, again, is it relevant to the question of whether this man should be punished to say that punishing him would deter others? And assuming that criminals ought to be punished, how should we set about deciding appropriate penalties?

It is not, of course, the business of the moral or social philosopher to provide a justification for any particular act or system of punishment or even of the institution of punishment in general. Philosophers are not necessarily apologists for their society and age. They are interested in the procedures and modes of argument that we are committed to by our fundamental conceptions of morality and in criteria of criticism and justification rather than in inquiries into whether actual institutions satisfy them.

Philosophers, it is true, have not always made this distinction, they have often worked on the understanding that a philosophical argument could be seriously shaken by showing that it leads to conclusions inconsistent with some widely approved institution or moral rule. Moreover, for many philosophers, if such a rule or institution seemed to imply a principle inconsistent with other moral principles accepted by the society, there must necessarily be some broader principle, which a philosopher could discover and by which the conflict could be resolved. Applied to the case of punishment, this would mean that a philosopher must reconcile the apparently conflicting principles that wrongdoers should be punished and that it is wrong to deliberately make another man suffer. But this is surely a misconception of the nature of philosophy. There is no point, after all, in asking whether and how punishment can be justified if one assumed in advance that it can. For justification a number of contingent facts are required that the philosopher as such is not qualified to provide. His task is to analyze what is being asked for and so to point out what kinds of facts and arguments are admissible to the discussion.

Justification of Punishment

The question of justification arises at two levels. One can take for granted the principle that wrongdoers should be punished and ask whether a particular case of punishment was justified. At this level the philosopher is concerned

with the criteria in a general system which any particular act of p...
must satisfy. One can, however, question the very idea of punishment
institution which involves deliberately inflicting pain or deprivation. Than
the philosophical question of how one justifies a set of rules or an inst...
like a penal system. Corresponding to these two levels of justification are
broadly opposed approaches to punishment, the retributivist and the utilitar...
Each, in fact, has been taken to offer an answer to the problems at both leve...
but the persuasive force of retributivism is mainly in its answers to problem...
of the first type, and of utilitarianism to questions of the second type. Characteristically, the retributivist stresses guilt and desert, looking back to the
crime to justify punishment and denying that the consequences of punishment,
beneficial or otherwise, have any relevance to justification. The utilitarian, on
the other hand, insists that punishment can be justified only if it has beneficent
consequences that outweigh the intrinsic evil of inflicting suffering on human
beings.

Retributivist Theories

The most thoroughgoing retributivists, exemplified by Kant, maintain
that the punishment of crime is right in itself, that it is fitting that the guilty
should suffer, and that justice, or the moral order, requires the institution of
punishment. This, however, is not to justify punishment but, rather, to deny
that it needs any justification. To say that something is right or good in itself
means that it does not need to be justified in terms of the value or rightness of
anything else. Its intrinsic value is appreciated immediately or intuitively. But
since at least some people do doubt that punishment is right, an appeal to intuition is necessarily unsatisfactory. Again, to say "it is fitting" or "justice demands" that the guilty should suffer is only to reaffirm that punishment is right,
not to give grounds for thinking so.

Some retributivists, while admitting that punishment is, prima facie, evil,
maintain that it is nevertheless better that the wicked should be punished than
that they should prosper more than the virtuous and, perhaps, at their expense. In this view, the function of criminal law is to punish wickedness or immorality in order to maintain a kind of cosmic distributive justice. However,
it is not self-evident that wickedness should be punished any more than it is
self-evident that legal guilt should be. Archbishop Temple, himself a retributivist, declared that he had no "intuition that it is good that the wicked should
suffer." Nor is it clear that virtue must be rewarded or that universal justice
requires the kind of human rectification that this sort of retributivism en-
visages. Of course, in a universe in which the wicked prospered, there might
be no incentive to virtue, but this is essentially a utilitarian mode of argument.
Again, evil motives and a bad character are necessary conditions of wickedness but not of legal guilt and criminal liability. The state's function is to
punish breaches of those rules which in the public interest ought to be up-

It is a matter of indifference in law (but not in morals) that some men observe the rules do so from the unworthy motive of fear and others break them laudable motives of principle. Conversely, it is at least doubtful that the criminal law should provide penalties for offenses against morality where the public interest is at stake—e.g., whether it should extend to of lying other than, say, false pretenses and perjury.

Though immorality is neither a necessary nor a sufficient condition for punishment, the relation between law and morals is nevertheless a close one, and what punishment is to the one, blame is to the other. Both regulate social intercourse, and in any given society the aims and ideals upheld by the law will usually correspond, more or less, with those upheld by the dominant morality. Moreover, in the family and the school punishment is often used to reinforce moral condemnation as part of the process of moral education. Some writers who regard punishment as moral retribution couple this idea with the argument that the point of punishment is to be found in what Lord Justice Denning has called "the emphatic denunciation by the community of a crime." In this view, punishment reinforces the community's respect for its legal and moral standards, which criminal acts would tend to undermine if they were not solemnly denounced. There is, however, no intrinsic reason why denunciation should take precisely the form of inflicting suffering on criminals, unless, perhaps, one accepts Ewing's view that punishment has the advantage of impressing both on the criminal and on everyone else that a breach of law and morals is so serious that society must do something to prevent it. That, however, is surely to justify punishment by its utility in maintaining respect for the law. Rashdall refers to "the enormous importance of the criminal law in promoting the moral education of the public mind," but Rashdall was a utilitarian who justified punishment by reference to "the production of good effects on conscious beings."

For Hegel punishment is necessary to annul the wrong done by the criminal. By this he means something more than restitution or compensation, neither of which is, strictly speaking, punishment. It is, rather, that the criminal has upset the balance of the moral order, which can be restored only by his being made to suffer. Or, in terms of the dialectic, crime is a negation of right and as such a nullity; punishment negates the negation, thus reaffirming the right. But in what sense can punishment be said to restore the balance or annul the wrong, unless it is taken for granted that criminals deserve to be punished? This is precisely the point in question.

Utilitarian Theories

The utilitarian position is exemplified in Bentham's remark that "all punishment is a mischief. . . . If it ought at all to be admitted, it ought only to be admitted in as far as it promises to exclude some greater evil." By re forming the criminal, by deterring him or others from similar offenses in the future, or by directly preventing further offenses by imprisonment, deportation, or execution, the good that comes out of punishment may outweigh (so the utilitarian argues) the intrinsic evil of suffering deliberately inflicted. Without such effects, or if the suffering inflicted exceeded the suffering avoided, the institution would be unjustified.

The critics of utilitarianism claim that if people generally could be persuaded that an innocent man was guilty, utilitarianism would justify punishing him since as a warning to others he would be just as useful as a genuine offender. Again, offenders might be deterred by threatening to punish their wives and children, particularly, if as is so often the case with political terrorists and resistance fighters, it were difficult to catch the offenders themselves. Or, again, if punishment could be justified as a way of reforming criminals, it would seem better to punish them before, rather than after, they committed their crimes. Retributivists claim that utilitarians are in danger of losing sight of two conditions which are necessary to the very idea of punishment—namely, that an offense should have been committed and that punishment shall be of the offender himself, who alone can be said to deserve it. "Punishment is punishment," wrote F. H. Bradley, "only when it is deserved"; punishment for any other reason is "a crying injustice."

The dilemma of utilitarianism, then, at least in its crude form, is that it justifies punishing innocent people provided that such punishment causes less suffering than might otherwise be caused by the would-be criminals it deters. Some utilitarians argue that in the end the deception would break down, that it could not be used systematically, or that the long-term consequences would be bad for society. But these answers are unsatisfactory because they depend on assumptions of purely contingent consequences. Our revulsion against punishing innocent men seems to go deeper than that. In any case, these answers will not meet the case for punishing hostages, which can certainly be done systematically and requires no deception or secrecy.

Punishment and Principles of Justice

To meet the above criticisms, a crude utilitarianism would have to be supplemented by other moral principles—namely, that differences in treatment must be justified by relevant differences in circumstance or condition, where "relevance" is defined in the light of general rules, and that every human being should be treated with at least a minimum of respect as a source of claims and not as a mere instrument for the promotion of the interests of others. It can be argued that punishment of the innocent or of hostages is an abuse not because it necessarily makes for more unhappiness than it prevents but because it treats innocent men in a way that is appropriate only for the guilty and makes an arbitrary difference in treatment between them and other innocent men. Moreover, a legal system is designed to guide conduct by laying down rules and attaching penalties to those who choose to break them. It is acceptable, in the words of J. D. Mabbott, only because "the criminal makes the essential choice; he 'brings it on himself.' " Otherwise, punishment would not be consistent with the principle of respect for persons. The hostage, on the other hand, has no chance to settle his own fate; he is used as a mere lever for manipulating other people's conduct, and his own interest is subordinate to that of the other members of society. Punishment of the innocent ignores, in short, fundamental procedural rules of justice and morality without which utilitarianism would make little sense, for unless everyone is worthy of equal consideration as a source of claims, whose interest is to count in assessing the utility of a course of action? Whom are we entitled to treat as simply a tool for advancing other men's interests—as Aristotle's "slave by nature"—and what would count as a reason for considering other men before him?

This has bearing, too, on the reasons for accepting as excuses such defenses as duress, unavoidable accident, or ignorance of fact—conditions under which an offender can claim that he could not help doing what he did. Bentham argued that to punish anyone under such conditions would be pointless and, therefore, mischievous, because the threat of penalties could not possibly deter anyone in the future who was similarly placed. Now, it is true that nothing would be lost if such people escaped punishment, provided they could be distinguished from cheats trying to take advantage of such excuses and provided enough offenders without such excuses could be detected to furnish examples for others. The principle of "strict liability," which exists in some legal systems for certain offenses, has been defended on the utilitarian ground that it is impossible to tell a genuine excuse from a pretense. It is questionable, however, whether a person who would otherwise be treated as innocent ought to be treated as guilty because someone else might otherwise escape a merited penalty. Punishing the man who commits an offense through ignorance or accident, because it is too difficult to tell whether he really did it on purpose or because we have to make an example of *someone,* is very like punishing the innocent as a warning to the guilty. The utilitarian case for these excuses is unsatisfactory inasmuch as it makes them subject to such qualifications.

A better ground for such excuses is that punishment is morally acceptable only if it is the consequence of an act freely chosen by the criminal, which it would not be under these conditions. A man acting in ignorance or by accident cannot be said to bring his punishment on himself. Punishment, seen as a way of influencing conduct, cannot be justified if there has been no real possibility of choice. Moreover, the punishment of involuntary offenses introduces into men's lives the possibility of disasters which they can neither foresee nor avert.

Utilitarianism, then, must be supplemented by principles of justice if it is not to clash with other moral principles that are usually considered fundamental. It has, however, the merit, as an approach to the justification of punishment, that it provides a clear procedure for determining whether the institution is acceptable in general terms. This the retributivist approach cannot do because it denies the relevance of weighing advantages and disadvantages, which is what we ultimately must do in moral criticism of rules and institutions. Consequently, a retributivist justification of punishment as an institution usually turns out to be a denial of the necessity for justification, a veiled reference to the beneficial results of punishment (a utilitarianism in disguise), or an appeal to religious authority.

When it is a question of justifying a particular case of punishment, however, the retributivist is in a far stronger position. There would be no point in having a general rule if on every occasion that it had to be applied one had to consider whether the advantages in this particular case warranted acting in accordance with it. Moreover, the point of punishment as deterrent would be quite lost were there no general expectation, based on the general operation of the rule, that guilty men would be punished. Assuming, then, that a penal system can be justified in utilitarian terms, any offense is at least prima facie an occasion for a penalty. Equally, without an offense there is no question of a penalty. The retributivist contention that punishment is justified if, and only if, it is deserved is really applicable, therefore, to the justification of particular instances of punishment, the institution as such being taken for granted.

Severity of Punishment

The clash between the utilitarian and retributivist approaches to punishment also arises in considering the criteria by which appropriate punishments are assessed. The retributivist insists that the punishment must fit the crime; the utilitarian relates the penalty to the general aims of the system, to the prevention of further crime, and, perhaps, to the reform of the criminal.

The most extreme form of retributivism is the law of retaliation: "an eye for an eye." This alone, Kant claimed, could provide a just measure of the penalty, since it was the crime itself and nothing else that settled it. However, to try to apply it literally might be monstrously cruel, or, as Kant recognized, it might be absurd. Thieves can be deprived of their property and murderers hanged, but what penalty is appropriate to the dope-peddler, the blackmailer, and the smuggler?

There is not much sense, either, in trying to construct a table of equivalents so that the amount of suffering inflicted by the criminal could be meted out to him in some other form. How can such a table be drawn up? How many years must a blackmailer spend in jail to experience suffering equal to his victim's? Is it possible, in any case, to make comparisons of suffering between persons? Of course, we do assess the gravity of an offense and try to ensure that the punishment for a trivial offense is less severe than for a serious one. But this is possible only because we take for granted an existing scale of penalties and grade new offenses accordingly. Such grading does not imply an intrinsic relation between the crime and the penalty apart from that established by the scale. Some retributivists admit this but claim nevertheless that the penalties prescribed by the law ought to reflect the moral heinousness of the offense. The most serious offenses against morals deserve the most severe penalties. This, however, only shifts the question a step back, for what makes one moral offense more serious than another?

Utilitarians have tended to concentrate on deterrence, turning away from the actual criminal act except as one of a class of actions that might be prevented by punishing the particular instance severely enough (but only just enough) to make the action unattractive to the offender and to possible future offenders. Unfortunately, there are always people who cannot be deterred or reformed. Beyond a certain point the additional suffering one would have to inflict on all offenders to reduce their number might be so great as to exceed the amount of suffering thereby averted. The aim of the utilitarian, then, would presumably be to select the penalty at which the aggregate of suffering caused by crimes actually committed and punishments actually inflicted would be the smallest possible.

The utilitarian approach has often been criticized as justifying severe penalties for trivial offenses and vice versa. To eliminate parking offenses might need heavier penalties than to eliminate blackmail, which would be monstrous. But this criticism misses the point of the utilitarian case. There would, indeed, be no objection to threatening the severest penalty for any offense providing the threat never had to be carried out. Punishment is only an unfortunate consequence of the fact that the threats, which are the true operative elements in the system, are partially ineffective and would be wholly ineffective if they were not carried out when they failed to deter. In fixing penalties, the utilitarian's problem is not, therefore, to minimize the number of offenses, irrespective of the punishment inflicted, but to minimize the total amount of suffering from both sources. If we call parking offenses trivial, we mean that each one causes relatively little suffering; therefore, we are prepared to put up with a large number of them rather than incur the cost of making offenders suffer heavy penalties. Blackmail, on the other hand, causes so much suffering that if heavier penalties would yield even a small reduction in the number of offenses, there might be a net gain even though offenders would suffer more than they did before. In this way a utilitarian might agree with the retributivist that severe penalties ought to be restricted to serious offenses, but he would argue that we call an offense serious precisely because it causes a great deal of suffering. For the retributivist only serious crimes *deserve* severe penalties; for the utilitarian only serious crimes are worth averting at the cost of severe penalties.

The utilitarian approach to this matter does not supply a procedure for sentencing particular criminals (any more than a justification for punishment as an institution would be a case for any particular application of it). Arguing from expected consequences, one might establish a kind of standard penalty for each class of offense. Officials drafting new rules might consider whether a proposed maximum penalty would keep offenses down to manageable proportions, or people concerned about road accidents might argue that heavier penalties for motoring offenses would make drivers more careful. Deciding the sentence in a particular case, however, is clearly a different matter. The maximum penalty is a limiting factor, but questions like the degree of responsibility, provocation, and the offender's previous record are all relevant. However, one might reasonably ask why, as a matter of principle, they should be relevant.

Punishment and Responsibility

The problem of responsibility arises in relation to punishment as it does in relation to blame in moral theory. The principle, discussed already, that a man ought not to be punished for doing what he cannot help creates difficulties when extended to actions which a man could not help doing because of his own state of mind instead of external or contingent factors, like duress or ignorance of fact. An insane man, as defined, say, by the M'Naghten rules (that is, one who did not know what he was doing or did not know that what he was doing was wrong), cannot be said to choose his act because he cannot know it for what it is. But sometimes a man may know that what he is doing is wrong yet still be unable to stop himself from doing it. He may be subject, for instance, to an irresistible temptation or provocation. But how is that to be understood? A temptation is not irresistible merely because a particular man has yielded to it or even because he might have been expected to yield to it. However, a temptation may be so strong that we might expect any ordinary person to yield to it (even though a few people may in fact resist it), or, as one might say, it might be "more than human nature can stand." In that sense it may be "irresistible."

Some people, of course, find it much more difficult than others to resist temptation. Some, like kleptomaniacs, are "impelled" to act in the sense that deliberation neither plays, nor could play, any part in what they do. Such people might be distinguished from plain wrongdoers by the fact that nothing —not blame, punishment, praise, or rational argument—seems to affect their disposition to break the rules. Or, again, their actions may lack any point, or if they can be said to have any point, it is only in relation to a set of aims and standards of achievement so distorted and eccentric that they are intelligible only to a psychiatrist. The kleptomaniac who steals nylon stockings for which he has no possible use (according to ordinary standards of utility) might properly be said to be unable to help stealing them. Far more difficult is the case of the psychopath, who seems to have no wish to resist temptation or, rather, who knows that some of the things he wants to do are wrong in the sense that other people disapprove of them but on whom this knowledge enforces no internal restraint beyond prompting a degree of caution. Criminals of this type would once have been described as "wicked" but are now often described as incapable of self-control. To say, however, that they are not responsible for their acts creates the odd situation that anyone is liable to punishment who usually resists temptation but sometimes fails, whereas the man who never resists is not liable at all.

The determinist has a short way with these difficulties. Since everyone's actions are the response of his character to a given set of circumstances, how can anyone ever be held responsible for his actions? We do what we must, given what we are, and what we are is the end of a causal chain going back to before we were born. If one knew a person well enough, one might predict that under given conditions he would commit a crime. Is this compatible with saying that he can choose whether to do so, or is his belief in his freedom to choose simply an illusion? Can the result of a genuine choice be predicted?

To say that something is predictable is not, however, the same as saying it is unavoidable. We can forecast a man's actions just because we know the kind of choices that he regularly makes. The more we know of his dispositions and his preferences, the more likely we are to be right. But that does not mean that he never acts voluntarily or that he never makes a real choice but only thinks he does. If all choices are illusions, what would a real choice be like? A man's behavior may be predictable because he can be relied upon to do what is reasonable, but to act with good reason is the very reverse of being subject to an inner compulsion. An essential difference between voluntary and involuntary action is that it makes sense to speak of the motives, aims, and reasons for the former but only of the causes of the latter. It is only when a person's behavior seems pointless or when explanations in terms of aims do not seem sufficient that we look for the kind of cause which would justify saying that he could not help himself. Of course, a complete account of voluntary and rational behavior must refer to causes as necessary conditions for action, but such causes would not constitute a sufficient explanation. An account of the electronic activity in the brain would not provide a sufficient explanation of a move in a game of chess unless the move was so completely and absurdly irrelevant that it had to be accounted for simply as the result of a nervous twitch. In that case, however, it would not really be a move in the game at all, not an action, indeed, but something that happens to the player. The weakness of the determinist position, insofar as it purports to undermine the notion of responsibility, is that it treats such abnormalities as the explanatory model for the normal.

It is arguable, in any case, that the concept of responsibility *requires* that human behavior be causally accountable rather than the reverse. As Hume pointed out in *An Enquiry Concerning Human Understanding,*

> [Where actions] . . . proceed not from some *cause in the character* and disposition of the person who performed them, they can neither redound to his honour, if good; nor infamy, if evil. . . . The person is not answerable for them; and as they proceeded from nothing in him that is durable and constant, and leave nothing of that nature behind them, it is impossible [that] he can, upon their account, become the object of punishment or vengeance.

In Hume's view universal causality is consistent with the concept of choice and is a necessary condition for responsibility and, therefore, for blame and punishment.

Strictly speaking, all that is necessary for a theory of punishment is that human conduct should be capable of being modified by threats. For some people—for instance, compulsive lawbreakers like kleptomaniacs—that is not the case. Others, however, commit crimes believing they can escape punishment; still others, in a spirit of rebellion, indifference, or, more rarely, of martyrdom, prefer to do what they want and risk the consequences rather than conform. Why they prefer it—what conditions account for their being the men they are—is irrelevant. To say "they prefer it" is to say they might have chosen to do otherwise but did not, and that is all that is necessary for the concept "responsibility." To ask whether they were free to prefer otherwise, being what they were, is to ask whether they could choose to choose, and it is not clear that this really means anything. The experience of punishment may provide a reason for choosing differently next time, but to have a reason for choosing is not to be without a choice and, therefore, without responsibility.

Extenuation

Though a criminal may be held responsible for his actions, there may nevertheless be circumstances which, so it is said, diminish responsibility or extenuate guilt. Temptation or provocation, though not irresistible, may have been very great. The offender may have had a good character, and there may be no reason to expect any future lapse.

In some cases mitigation of sentence on such grounds can be readily justified in utilitarian terms. Little is to be gained by punishing the obviously exceptional lapse; a very small penalty might be enough to dissuade other respectable people who might otherwise be tempted to imitate it and for whom the shame of being treated as a criminal, whatever the penalty, is usually deterrent enough.

However, it is not easy to show, at least in utilitarian terms, that mitigation is reasonable in all the instances in which it is commonly thought appropriate. Nor does everyone agree on what are extenuating circumstances. It is not self-evident that whoever is sorely (but not irresistibly) tempted should be treated more leniently than people who have done the same thing but under less temptation. A strong temptation might be withstood if there were sufficient counterinducement. Leniency might weaken the resolve of others in the future. Some people treat crimes of passion leniently; others would say that the temptation is so commonly felt that if people were not discouraged from taking the law into their own hands by treating offenses of this kind severely, such offenses would rapidly multiply. Again, some people would accept a plea of drunkenness as an extenuation of an offense, whereas others would consider it an aggravation.

It is doubtful whether our ideas on this aspect of punishment depend on utilitarian considerations. Nor is there any reason to suppose that any system of utilitarian argument could show them to be consistent and rational. It was suggested earlier that though the criteria of morality and law, of blame and punishment, are not identical, they influence one another. If we blame people less for yielding to strong temptation, we also feel they deserve a less severe punishment. But this only shifts the question a step back. Why should temptation mitigate blame?

A possible answer might be that at least some temptations can be pleaded as partial justifications. Thus, a man who pleads that he killed someone to shorten his sufferings or a woman who kills her deformed baby is appealing to another moral principle to excuse the act. Similarly, a man who kills his wife's lover might claim that his victim was violating his rights. These are not complete justifications, as a plea of self-defense would be, but they are excuses which count, as it were, against the initial presumption of guilt and so incline us to look at the offense more sympathetically and more leniently, whatever the advantages of severity in terms of deterrence, prevention, or reform. There is nothing irrational in striking a balance of desert.

But differences of opinion about a criminal's deserts often turn not on the way such a balance is struck but on the extent to which his judges (or their critics) are able to comprehend his action. Anyone who could imagine himself tempted in similar circumstances would probably be more sympathetic than someone who could not and who would therefore see no reason for being indulgent. On the other hand, anyone who suspected that he himself might yield to such a temptation and who flinched from the possibility might react to it with very great severity indeed.

Punishment and Reform

There is no reason to suppose, then, that the sentencing practice of the courts will display rational and consistent principles; furthermore, any attempt to set up criteria of rational judgment on strictly utilitarian principles is likely to cut across deeply rooted moral convictions. Accordingly, some criminologists and psychiatrists, like Eliot Slater and Bernard Glueck, and some penal reformers, like Barbara Wootton, have swung away from the general conceptions of punishment and desert. Instead of asking what penalty is warranted by the crime, whether the agent was fully responsible for his action, whether circumstances exonerate him wholly or in part, they prefer to ask what kind of treatment is most likely to rehabilitate him, subject, of course, to the example it might set for others.

This comes very close to repudiating altogether the concept of punishment as a deliberate infliction of suffering, which the criminal deserves, consequent to a voluntary breach of the law. First, the treatment most likely to rehabilitate him need not be unpleasant (though if it is to instill a measure of discipline, it very well may be). And, second, avoiding the question of moral responsibility, the reformer also avoids the question of what the criminal deserves, because the reformer's prime concern is with the treatment he needs. Criminals would no more deserve punishment than the sick deserve medicine. Indeed, for such writers as Samuel Butler and the American lawyer Clarence Darrow, criminality is a kind of sickness to be treated rather than a wrong to be punished.

Attractive as this approach may seem on humanitarian grounds, it has at least one serious consequence. The concepts of responsibility and desert cannot be discarded without some loss. For it is not a necessary condition of medical treatment that a patient must have shown symptoms of a disease; those exposed to smallpox are vaccinated before they develop a fever. Without the principle that punishment must be deserved, there would be no obstacle to subjecting people likely to become criminals to corresponding forms of penal prophylaxis. Moreover, if we substitute for punishment the idea of rehabilitative treatment, there is nothing against sentencing a person of bad character to a severe course of treatment for the most trivial offense if his character would be better for it in the end. This would clearly be incompatible with the usually accepted principle that trivial offenses should not carry severe penalties.

Reformism of this kind is open to attack from another quarter. The point has been made by Hegel and Bosanquet, among others, that retributive punishment is a kind of tribute to the moral personality of the criminal. It is precisely as a morally responsible agent, recognized as capable of making reasoned choices and accepting the consequences, that the criminal is punishable. Bosanquet goes so far as to say that punishment is "his right, of which he must not be defrauded." It is to be distinguished, argued Bradley, from the discipline or correction appropriately administered to animals and children. Punishment "is inflicted because of wrong-doing, as desert, the latter is applied as means of improvement." Since rational adults are neither animals nor children, no one has the right to treat them as if they were. It might be similarly argued that lunatics are under tutelage because they are incapable of looking after their own interests and cannot be expected to respect those of other people. The sane criminal, on the contrary, can be made to pay for his antisocial choices in order to demonstrate to him and, through him, to others that crime does not pay, but it diminishes his stature as a rational adult to deny that he is responsible for ordering his own life and to impose upon him ends of another person's choosing.

Nevertheless, retributivists have often been much concerned with moral reformation. They have insisted, however, that this was something the criminal must do for himself. Because it was associated with shame and rejection, punishment could bring the criminal up short and force him to reconsider his life in the light of society's condemnation of his actions. But the remorse which was a necessary condition for self-reformation was entirely dependent on the criminal's recognition that his punishment was deserved. Without that there could be no inward reformation, no reassertion of moral standards, but only a sense of resentment and injustice. Accordingly, punishment can yield the benefits of reform only if it is thought of, above everything else, as retributive —as the appropriate desert of a responsible guilty agent. It is this which distinguishes the retributive approach to moral reformation from the kind of utilitarianism which turns its back on desert and responsibility and is concerned only with the needs of rehabilitation.

It is, of course, an open question whether punishment ever does produce the kind of self-reformation the Hegelians had in mind or whether it does so more often than it produces a moral decay. Indeed, our knowledge of the facts of criminal behavior is probably far too scanty and uncertain for us to know how relevant much of the philosophical discussion of punishment really is. We cannot say for sure that a penal system is justified because it tends to reform criminals. Nor do we know, for that matter, whether the deterrent view of punishment is applicable to all kinds of crime. Many people commit offenses without seeming to take any account of consequences before they act, and they repeat the same offenses again and again in spite of punishment. Perhaps those who do not, would not repeat them even without punishment. Perhaps there would be no more cases of certain classes of crime than there are already; perhaps the only people to commit them are those who also do not take account of consequences before they act. It seems likely that some potential offenders are deterred from evading taxes or from smuggling by the threat of punishment, but is there any certain evidence that the threat of punishment deters anyone who would otherwise commit rape or arson? Utilitarians tend to assume that punishment as an institution can be justified by its beneficial consequences, but the argument depends on certain a priori assumptions about criminal (or would-be criminal) behavior that may be greatly overintellectualized. However, even though research should prove the usual utilitarian justifications for punishment groundless, that does not mean that some other, non-utilitarian justification is better. The proper procedure may well be to ask, with the utilitarian, whether the consequences are by and large beneficial; it is equally possible that punishment as an institution might fail that test. A theory of punishment that led to the conclusion that all punishment was wrong need be no more necessarily mistaken than a theory that led to a similar conclusion as regards, say, slavery, which, after all, was accepted as uncritically in Aristotle's day as punishment is today.

10

Liberty, Coercion, and the Values of Democracy

Readings: John Stuart Mill, Selections from On Liberty *and* Considerations on Representative Government *Herbert Marcuse, "The New Forms of Control"*

What form of government would a moral man choose for himself and others? The position of *liberalism* generally holds (1) that freedom or liberty is the most important human value and (2) that democratic forms of government are most likely to maximize this value. According to this position, freedom or liberty is to be understood as the ability, without hindrance from others, to gain satisfaction for one's wants and desires, insofar as this is compatible with a like liberty for others.

John Stuart Mill is generally regarded as the most persuasive spokesman for this kind of liberalism. And one of his great strengths is that he perceives some of the pathologies to which democracy is susceptible. One of these pathologies, which Mill calls the "tyranny of the majority," results from the power that a majority has in a democracy to coerce an unpopular minority. To cure this pathology, Mill suggests that democracies should subscribe (in a legal constitution perhaps) to the following principle: society is justified in coercing any one of its members only to prevent harm to others. Only if the democratic principle of majority rule is limited in this way can the tyranny of the majority be avoided.

Herbert Marcuse, a contemporary Marxist, believes that even a democracy so limited will still have grave defects. Modern technological societies, even those calling themselves democracies, have subtle and terribly dangerous ways of repressing their citizens. This kind of repression is dangerous just because it does not *seem* repressive at all, since a substantial number of people in the population have most of their needs and desires satisfied. Suppose, however, that these needs and desires are *artificial*—that is, manufactured and satisfied by the power elite in a society to ensure that citizens remain pliant and cooperative. This supposition forms the basis for Marcuse's disquieting commentary on contemporary Western democracies. To use the language of Marx, the evil of these societies is that, despite the wants they satisfy, they have failed to reduce alienation. Indeed they rest on it.[1]

Suggestions for Further Reading

Arnold S. Kaufman, "Wants, Needs and Liberalism," *Inquiry,* Summer 1971.

Alasdair MacIntyre, *Herbert Marcuse: An Exposition and a Polemic* (New York: The Viking Press, 1970). (Reviewed by Jeffrie G. Murphy, *U.C.L.A. Law Review,* May 1971.)

C. B. Macpherson, "The Maximization of Democracy," in *Philosophy, Politics and Society, Third Series,* ed. Peter Laslett and W. G. Runciman (Oxford: Basil Blackwell, 1967).

Peter Radcliff, ed., *Limits of Liberty* (Belmont, Calif.: Wadsworth, 1966).

David Spitz, *Patterns of Anti-Democratic Thought* (New York: The Free Press, 1965).

Richard Wasserstrom, ed., *Morality and the Law* (Belmont, Calif.: Wadsworth, 1971).

Robert Paul Wolff, *In Defense of Anarchism* (New York: Harper Torchbooks, 1970).

---

[1] As the essay "The Subjection of Women" in Chapter 11 clearly shows, Mill was by no means totally insensitive to this point. Note also that Mill sometimes uses the concept of *interest* instead of need, want, or desire.

From On Liberty (*1859*)
John Stuart Mill

The subject of this Essay is not the so-called Liberty of the Will, so unfortunately opposed to the misnamed doctrine of Philosophical Necessity; but Civil, or Social Liberty: the nature and limits of the power which can be legitimately exercised by society over the individual. A question seldom stated, and hardly ever discussed, in general terms, but which profoundly influences the practical controversies of the age by its latent presence, and is likely soon to make itself recognized as the vital question of the future. It is so far from being new, that, in a certain sense, it has divided mankind, almost from the remotest ages; but in the stage of progress into which the more civilized portions of the species have now entered, it presents itself under new conditions, and requires a different and more fundamental treatment.

The struggle between Liberty and Authority is the most conspicuous feature in the portions of history with which we are earliest familiar, particularly in that of Greece, Rome, and England. But in old times this contest was between subjects, or some classes of subjects, and the Government. By liberty, was meant protection against the tyranny of the political rulers. The rulers were conceived (except in some of the popular governments of Greece) as in a necessarily antagonistic position to the people whom they ruled. They consisted of a governing One, or a governing tribe or caste, who derived their authority from inheritance or conquest, who, at all events, did not hold it at the pleasure of the governed, and whose supremacy men did not venture, perhaps did not desire, to contest, whatever precautions might be taken against its oppressive exercise. Their power was regarded as necessary, but also as highly dangerous; as a weapon which they would attempt to use against their subjects, no less than against external enemies. To prevent the weaker members of the community from being preyed upon by innumerable vultures, it was needful that there should be an animal of prey stronger than the rest, commissioned to keep them down. But as the king of the vultures would be no less bent upon preying on the flock than any of the minor harpies, it was indispensable to be in a perpetual attitude of defense against his beak and claws. The aim, therefore, of patriots was to set limits to the power which the ruler should be suffered to exercise over the community; and this limitation was what they meant by liberty. . . .

A time, however, came, in the progress of human affairs, when men ceased to think it a necessity of nature that their governors should be an independent power, opposed in interest to themselves. It appeared to them much better that the various magistrates of the State should be their tenants or delegates, revocable at their pleasure. In that way alone, it seemed, could they have complete security that the powers of government would never be abused to their disadvantage. By degrees this new demand for elective and temporary rulers became the prominent object of the exertions of the popular party, wherever any such party existed; and superseded, to a considerable extent, the previous efforts to limit the power of rulers. As the struggle proceeded for making the ruling powers emanate from the periodical choice of the ruled, some persons began to think that too much importance had been attached to the limitation of the power itself. *That* (it might seem) was a resource against rulers whose interests were habitually opposed to those of the people. What was now wanted was, that the rulers should be identified with the people; that their interest and will should be the interest and will of the nation. The nation did not need to be protected against its own will. There was no fear of its tyrannizing over itself. Let the rulers be effectually responsible to it, promptly removable by it, and it could afford to trust them with power of which it could itself dictate the use to be made. Their power was but the nation's own power, concentrated, and in a form convenient for exercise. . . .

But, in political and philosophical theories, as well as in persons, success discloses faults and infirmities which failure might have concealed from observation. The notion, that the people have no need to limit their power over themselves, might seem axiomatic, when popular government was a thing only dreamed about, or read of as having existed at some distant period of the past. . . .

In time, however, a democratic republic came to occupy a large portion of the earth's surface, and made itself felt as one of the most powerful members of the community of nations; and elective and responsible government became subject to the observations and criticisms which wait upon a great existing fact. It was now perceived that such phrases as "self-government," and "the power of the people over themselves," do not express the true state of the case. The "people" who exercise the power are not always the same people with those over whom it is exercised; and the "self-government" spoken of is not the government of each by himself, but of each by all the rest. The will of the people, moreover, practically means the will of the most numerous or the most active *part* of the people; the majority, or those who succeed in making themselves accepted as the majority; the people, consequently, *may* desire to oppress a part of their number; and precautions are as much needed against this as against any other abuse of power. The limitation, therefore, of the power of government over individuals loses none of its importance when the holders of power are regularly accountable to the community, that is, to the strongest party therein. This view of things, recommending itself equally to the intelligence of thinkers and to the inclination of those important classes in European society to whose real or supposed interests democracy is adverse, has had no difficulty in establishing itself; and in political speculations "the tyranny of the majority" is now generally included among the evils against which society requires to be on its guard.

Like other tyrannies, the tyranny of the majority was at first, and is still vulgarly, held in dread, chiefly as operating through the acts of the public authorities. But reflecting persons perceived that when society is itself the tyrant—society collectively, over the separate individuals who compose it—its means of tyrannizing are not restricted to the acts which it may do by the hands of its political functionaries. Society can and does execute its own mandates: and if it issues wrong mandates instead of right, or any mandates at all in things with which it ought not to meddle, it practices a social tyranny more formidable than many kinds of political oppression, since, though not usually upheld by such extreme penalties, it leaves fewer means of escape, penetrating much more deeply into the details of life, and enslaving the soul itself. Protection, therefore, against the tyranny of the magistrate is not enough: there needs protection also against the tyranny of the prevailing opinion and feeling; against the tendency of society to impose, by other means than civil penalties, its own ideas and practices as rules of conduct on those who dissent from them; to fetter the development, and, if possible, prevent the formation, of any individuality not in harmony with its ways, and compel all characters to fashion themselves upon the model of its own. There is a limit to the legitimate interference of collective opinion with individual independence: and to find that limit, and maintain it against encroachment, is as indispensable to a good condition of human affairs, as protection against political despotism. . . .

The object of this Essay is to assert one very simple principle, as entitled to govern absolutely the dealings of society with the individual in the way of compulsion and control, whether the means used be physical force in the form of legal penalties, or the moral coercion of public opinion. That principle is, that the sole end for which mankind are warranted, individually or collectively, in interfering with the liberty of action of any of their number is self-protection. That the only purpose for which power can be rightfully exercised over any member of a civilized community, against his will, is to prevent harm to others. His own good, either physical or moral, is not a sufficient warrant. He cannot rightfully be compelled to do or forbear because it will be better for him to do so, because it will make him happier, because, in the opinions of others, to do so would be wise, or even right. These are good reasons for remonstrating with him, or reasoning with him, or persuading him, or entreating him, but not for compelling him, or visiting him with any evil in case he do otherwise. To justify that, the conduct from which it is desired to deter him, must be calculated to produce evil to someone else. The only part of the conduct of anyone, for which he is amenable to society, is that which concerns others. In the part which merely concerns himself, his independence is, of right, absolute. Over himself, over his own body and mind, the individual is sovereign. . . .

It is proper to state that I forgo any advantage which could be derived to my argument from the idea of abstract right, as a thing independent of utility. I regard utility as the ultimate appeal on all ethical questions; but it must be utility in the largest sense, grounded on the permanent interests of man as a progressive being. Those interests, I contend, authorize the subjection of individual spontaneity to external control, only in respect to those actions of each, which concern the interest of other people. . . .

But there is a sphere of action in which society, as distinguished from the individual, has, if any, only an indirect interest; comprehending all that portion of a person's life and conduct which affects only himself, or if it also affects others, only with their free, voluntary, and undeceived consent and participation. When I say only himself, I mean directly, and in the first instance: for whatever affects himself, may affect others through himself; and the objection which may be grounded on this contingency will receive consideration in the sequel. This, then, is the appropriate region of human liberty. It comprises, first, the inward domain of consciousness; demanding liberty of conscience, in the most comprehensive sense; liberty of thought and feeling; absolute freedom of opinion and sentiment on all subjects, practical or speculative, scientific, moral, or theological. The liberty of expressing and publishing opinions may seem to fall under a different principle, since it belongs to that part of the conduct of an individual which concerns other people; but, being almost of as much importance as the liberty of thought itself, and resting in great part on the same reasons, is practically inseparable from it. Secondly, the principle requires liberty of tastes and pursuits; of framing the plan of our life to suit our own character; of doing as we like, subject to such consequences as may follow: without impediment from our fellow creatures, so long as what we do does not harm them, even though they should think our conduct foolish, perverse, or wrong. Thirdly, from this liberty of each individual, follows the liberty, within the same limits, of combination among individuals; freedom to unite, for any purpose not involving harm to others: the persons combining being supposed to be of full age, and not forced or deceived.

No society in which these liberties are not, on the whole, respected, is free, whatever may be its form of government; and none is completely free in which they do not exist absolute and unqualified. The only freedom which deserves the name, is that of pursuing our own good in our own way, so long as we do not attempt to deprive others of theirs, or impede their efforts to obtain it. Each is the proper guardian of his own health, whether bodily, or mental and spiritual. Mankind are greater gainers by suffering each other to live as seems good to themselves, than by compelling each to live as seems good to the rest. . . .

Apart from the peculiar tenets of individual thinkers, there is also in the world at large an increasing inclination to stretch unduly the powers of society over the individual, both by the force of opinion and even by that of legislation: and as the tendency of all the changes taking place in the world is to strengthen society, and diminish the power of the individual, this encroachment is not one of the evils which tend spontaneously to disappear, but, on the contrary, to grow more and more formidable. The disposition of mankind, whether as rulers or as fellow citizens, to impose their own opinions and inclinations as a rule of conduct on others, is so energetically supported by some of the best and by some of the worst feelings incident to human nature, that it is hardly ever kept under restraint by anything but want of power; and as the power is not declining, but growing, unless a strong barrier of moral conviction can be raised against the mischief, we must expect, in the present circumstances of the world, to see it increase.

It will be convenient for the argument, if, instead of at once entering upon the general thesis, we confine ourselves in the first instance to a single branch of it, on which the principle here stated is, if not fully, yet to a certain point, recognized by the current opinions. This one branch is the Liberty of Thought: from which it is impossible to separate the cognate liberty of speaking and of writing. Although these liberties, to some considerable amount, form part of the political morality of all countries which profess religious toleration and free institutions, the grounds, both philosophical and practical, on which they rest, are perhaps not so familiar to the general mind, nor so thoroughly appreciated by many even of the leaders of opinion, as might have been expected. Those grounds, when rightly understood, are of much wider application than to only one division of the subject, and a thorough consideration of this part of the question will be found the best introduction to the remainder. . . .

The time, it is to be hoped, is gone by, when any defense would be necessary of the "liberty of the press" as one of the securities against corrupt or tyrannical government. No argument, we may suppose, can now be needed, against permitting a legislature or an executive, not identified in interest with the people, to prescribe opinions to them, and determine what doctrines or what arguments they shall be allowed to hear. This aspect of the question, besides, has been so often and so triumphantly enforced by preceding writers, that it needs not be specially insisted on in this place. . . . Let us suppose, therefore, that the government is entirely at one with the people, and never thinks of exerting any power of coercion unless in agreement with what it conceives to be their voice. But I deny the right of the people to exercise such coercion, either by themselves or by their government. The power itself is illegitimate. The best government has no more title to it than the worst. It is as noxious, or more noxious, when exerted in accordance with public opinion, than when in opposition to it. If all mankind minus one, were of one opinion, and only one person were of the contrary opinion, mankind would be no more justified in silencing that one person, than he, if he had the power, would be justified in silencing mankind. Were an opinion a personal possession of no value except to the owner; if to be obstructed in the enjoyment of it were simply a private injury, it would make some difference whether the injury was inflicted only on a few persons or on many. But the peculiar evil of silencing the expression of an opinion is, that it is robbing the human race; posterity as well as the existing generation; those who dissent from the opinion, still more than those who hold it. If the opinion is right, they are deprived of the opportunity of exchanging error for truth: if wrong, they lose, what is almost as great a benefit, the clearer perception and livelier impression of truth, produced by its collision with error.

It is necessary to consider separately these two hypotheses, each of which has a distinct branch of the argument corresponding to it. We can never be sure that the opinion we are endeavoring to stifle is a false opinion; and if we were sure, stifling it would be an evil still.

First: the opinion which it is attempted to suppress by authority may possibly be true. Those who desire to suppress it, of course deny its truth; but they are not infallible. They have no authority to decide the question for all mankind, and exclude every other person from the means of judging. To refuse a hearing to an opinion, because they are sure that it is false, is to assume that *their* certainty is the same thing as *absolute* certainty. All silencing of discussion is an assumption of infallibility. Its condemnation may be allowed to rest on this common argument, not the worse for being common.

Unfortunately for the good sense of mankind, the fact of their fallibility is far from carrying the weight in their practical judgment, which is always allowed to it in theory; for while everyone well knows himself to be fallible, few think it necessary to take any precautions against their own fallibility, or admit the supposition that any opinion, of which they feel very certain, may be one of the examples of the error to which they acknowledge themselves to be liable. Absolute princes, or others who are accustomed to unlimited deference, usually feel this complete confidence in their own opinions on nearly all subjects. People more happily situated, who sometimes hear their opinions disputed, and are not wholly unused to be set right when they are wrong, place the same unbounded reliance only on such of their opinions as are shared by all who surround them, or to whom they habitually defer: for in proportion to a man's want of confidence in his own solitary judgment, does he usually repose, with implicit trust, on the infallibility of "the world" in general. And the world, to each individual, means the part of it with which he comes in contact; his party, his sect, his church, his class of society: the man may be called, by comparison, almost liberal and large-minded to whom it means anything so comprehensive as his own country or his own age. Nor is his faith in this collective authority at all shaken by his being aware that other ages, countries, sects, churches, classes, and parties have thought, and even now think, the exact reverse. He devolves upon his own world the responsibility of being in the right against the dissentient worlds of other people; and it never troubles him that mere accident has decided which of these numerous worlds is the object of his reliance, and that the same causes which make him a Churchman in London, would have made him a Buddhist or a Confucian in Peking. Yet it is as evident in itself, as any amount of argument can make it, that ages are no more infallible than individuals; every age having held many opinions which subsequent ages have deemed not only false but absurd; and it is as certain that many opinions, now general, will be rejected by future ages, as it is that many, once general, are rejected by the present.

The objection likely to be made to this argument would probably take some such form as the following. There is no greater assumption of infallibility in forbidding the propagation of error, than in any other thing which is done by public authority on its own judgment and responsibility. Judgment is given to men that they may use it. Because it may be used erroneously, are men to be told that they ought not to use it at all? To prohibit what they think pernicious, is not claiming exemption from error, but fulfilling the duty incumbent on them, although fallible, of acting on their conscientious conviction. If we were never to act on our opinions, because those opinions may be wrong, we should leave all our interests uncared for, and all our duties unperformed. An objection which applies to all conduct, can be no valid objection to any conduct, in particular. It is the duty of governments, and of individuals, to form the truest opinions they can; to form them carefully, and never impose them upon others unless they are quite sure of being right. But when they are sure (such reasoners may say), it is not conscientiousness but cowardice to shrink from acting on their opinions, and allow doctrines which they honestly think dangerous to the welfare of mankind, either in this life or in another, to be scattered abroad without restraint, because other people, in less enlightened times, have persecuted opinions now believed to be true. Let us take care, it may be said, not to make the same mistake: but governments and nations have made mistakes in other things, which are not denied to be fit subjects for the exercise of authority: they have laid on bad taxes, made unjust wars. Ought we therefore to lay on no taxes, and, under whatever provocation, make no wars? Men, and governments, must act to the best of their ability. There is no such thing as absolute certainty, but there is assurance sufficient for the purposes of human life. We may, and must, assume our opinion to be true for the guidance of our own conduct: and it is assuming no more when we forbid bad men to pervert society by the propagation of opinions which we regard as false and pernicious.

I answer, that it is assuming very much more. There is the greatest difference between presuming an opinion to be true, because, with every opportunity for contesting it, it has not been refuted, and assuming its truth for the purpose of not permitting its refutation. Complete liberty of contradicting and disproving our opinion, is the very condition which justifies us in assuming its truth for purposes of action; and on no other terms can a being with human faculties have any rational assurance of being right.

When we consider either the history of opinion, or the ordinary conduct of human life, to what is it to be ascribed that the one and the other are no worse than they are? Not certainly to the inherent force of the human understanding; for, on any matter not self-evident, there are ninety-nine persons totally incapable of judging of it, for one who is capable; and the capacity of the hundredth person is only comparative; for the majority of the eminent men of every past generation held many opinions now known to be erroneous, and did or approved numerous things which no one will now justify. Why is it, then, that there is on the whole a preponderance among mankind of rational opinions and rational conduct? If there really is this preponderance—which there must be unless human affairs are, and have always been, in an almost desperate state—it is owing to a quality of the human mind, the source of everything respectable in man either as an intellectual or as a moral being, namely, that his errors are corrigible. He is capable of rectifying his mistakes, by discussion and experience. Not by experience alone. There must be discussion, to show how experience is to be interpreted. Wrong opinions and practices gradually yield to fact and argument: but facts and arguments, to produce any effect on the mind, must be brought before it. Very few facts are able to tell their own story, without comments to bring out their meaning. The whole strength and value, then, of human judgment, depending on the one property, that it can be set right when it is wrong, reliance can be placed on it only when the means of setting it right are kept constantly at hand. In the case of any person whose judgment is really deserving of confidence, how has it become so? Because he has kept his mind open to criticism of his opinions and conduct. Because it has been his practice to listen to all that could be said against him; to profit by as much of it as was just, and expound to himself, and upon occasion to others, the fallacy of what was fallacious. Because he has felt, that the only way in which a human being can make some approach to knowing the whole of a subject, is by hearing what can be said about it by persons of every variety of opinion, and studying all modes in which it can be looked at by every character of mind. No wise man ever acquired his wisdom in any mode but this; nor is it in the nature of human intellect to become wise in any other manner. The steady habit of correcting and completing his own opinion by collating it with those of others, so far from causing doubt and hesitation in carrying it into practice, is the only stable foundation for a just reliance on it: for, being cognizant of all that can, at least obviously, be said against him, and having taken up his position against all gainsayers—knowing that he has sought for objections and difficulties, instead of avoiding them, and has shut out no light which can be thrown upon the subject from any quarter— he has a right to think his judgment better than that of any person, or any multitude, who have not gone through a similar process.

It is not too much to require that what the wisest of mankind, those who are best entitled to trust their own judgment, find necessary to warrant their relying on it, should be submitted to by that miscellaneous collection of a few wise and many foolish individuals, called the public. The most intolerant of churches, the Roman Catholic Church, even at the canonization of a saint, admits, and listens patiently to, a "devil's advocate." The holiest of men, it appears, cannot be admitted to posthumous honors, until all that the devil could say against him is known and weighed. If even the Newtonian philosophy were not permitted to be questioned, mankind could not feel as complete assurance of its truth as they now do. The beliefs which we have most warrant for, have no safeguard to rest on, but a standing invitation to the whole world to prove them unfounded. If the challenge is not accepted, or is accepted and the attempt fails, we are far enough from certainty still; but we have done the best that the existing state of human reason admits of; we have neglected nothing that could give the truth a chance of reaching us: if the lists are kept open, we may hope that if there be a better truth, it will be found when the human mind is capable of receiving it; and in the meantime we may rely on having attained such approach to truth, as is possible in our own day. This is the amount of certainty attainable by a fallible being, and this the sole way of attaining it.

Strange it is, that men should admit the validity of the arguments for free discussion, but object to their being "pushed to an extreme"; not seeing that unless the reasons are good for an extreme case, they are not good for any case. Strange that they should imagine that they are not assuming infallibility, when they acknowledge that there should be free discussion on all subjects which can possibly be *doubtful,* but think that some particular principle or doctrine should be forbidden to be questioned because it is so *certain,* that is, because *they are certain* that it is certain. To call any proposition certain, while there is any one who would deny its certainty if permitted, but who is not permitted, is to assume that we ourselves, and those who agree with us, are the judges of certainty, and judges without hearing the other side.

In the present age—which has been described as "destitute of faith, but terrified at scepticism"—in which people feel sure, not so much that their opinions are true, as that they should not know what to do without them—the claims of an opinion to be protected from public attack are rested not so much on its truth, as on its importance to society. There are, it is alleged, certain beliefs, so useful, not to say indispensable to well-being, that it is as much the duty of governments to uphold those beliefs, as to protect any other of the interests of society. In a case of such necessity, and so directly in the line of their duty, something less than infallibility may, it is maintained, warrant, and even bind, governments, to act on their own opinion, confirmed by the general opinion of mankind. It is also often argued, and still oftener thought, that none but bad men would desire to weaken these salutary beliefs; and there can be nothing wrong, it is thought, in restraining bad men, and prohibiting what only such men would wish to practice. This mode of thinking makes the justification of restraints on discussion not a question of the truth of doctrines, but of their usefulness; and flatters itself by that means to escape the responsibility of claiming to be an infallible judge of opinions. But those who thus satisfy themselves, do not perceive that the assumption of infallibility is merely shifted from one point to another. The usefulness of an opinion is itself matter of opinion: as disputable, as open to discussion, and requiring discussion as much, as the opinion itself. There is the same need of an infallible judge of opinions to decide an opinion to be noxious, as to decide it to be false, unless the opinion condemned has full opportunity of defending itself. And it will not do to say that the heretic may be allowed to maintain the utility or harmlessness of his opinion, though forbidden to maintain its truth. The truth of an opinion is part of its utility. If we would know whether or not it is desirable that a proposition should be believed, is it possible to exclude the consideration of whether or not it is true? In the opinion, not of bad men, but of the best men, no belief which is contrary to truth can be really useful: and can you prevent such men from urging that plea, when they are charged with culpability for denying some doctrine which they are told is useful, but which they believe to be false? Those who are on the side of received opinions, never fail to take all possible advantage of this plea; you do not find *them* handling the question of utility as if it could be completely abstracted from that of truth: on the contrary, it is, above all, because their doctrine is the "truth," that the knowledge or the belief of it is held to be so indispensable. There can be no fair discussion of the question of usefulness, when an argument so vital may be employed on one side, but not on the other. And in point of fact, when law or public feeling do not permit the truth of an opinion to be disputed, they are just as little tolerant of a denial of its usefulness. The utmost they allow is an extenuation of its absolute necessity, or of the positive guilt of rejecting it.

In order more fully to illustrate the mischief of denying a hearing to opinions because we, in our own judgment, have condemned them, it will be desirable to fix down the discussion to a concrete case; and I choose, by preference, the cases which are least favorable to me—in which the argument against freedom of opinion, both on the score of truth and on that of utility, is considered the strongest. Let the opinions impugned be the belief in a God and in a future state, or any of the commonly received doctrines of morality. To fight the battle on such ground, gives a great advantage to an unfair antagonist; since he will be sure to say (and many who have no desire to be unfair will say it internally), Are these the doctrines which you do not deem sufficiently certain to be taken under the protection of law? Is the belief in a God one of the opinions, to feel sure of which, you hold to be assuming infallibility? But I must be permitted to observe, that it is not the feeling sure of a doctrine (be it what it may) which I call an assumption of infallibility. It is the undertaking to decide that question *for others,* without allowing them to hear what can be said on the contrary side. And I denounce and reprobate this pretension not the less, if put forth on the side of my most solemn convictions. However positive anyone's persuasion may be, not only of the falsity but of the pernicious consequences—not only of the pernicious consequences, but (to adopt expressions which I altogether condemn) the immorality and impiety of an opinion; yet if, in pursuance of that private judgment, though backed by the public judgment of his country or his contemporaries, he prevents the opinion from being heard in its defense, he assumes infallibility. And so far from the assumption being less objectionable or less dangerous because the opinion is called immoral or impious, this is the case of all others in which it is most fatal. These are exactly the occasions on which the men of one generation commit those dreadful mistakes, which excite the astonishment and horror of posterity. It is among such that we find the instances memorable in history, when the arm of the law has been employed to root out the best men and the noblest doctrines; with deplorable success as to the men, though some of the doctrines have survived to be (as if in mockery) invoked, in defense of similar conduct towards those who dissent from *them,* or from their received interpretation.

Mankind can hardly be too often reminded, that there was once a man named Socrates, between whom and the legal authorities and public opinion of his time, there took place a memorable collision. Born in an age and country abounding in individual greatness, this man has been handed down to us by those who best knew both him and the age, as the most virtuous man in it; while *we* know him as the head and prototype of all subsequent teachers of virtue, the source equally of the lofty inspiration of Plato and the judicious utilitarianism of Aristotle, *"i maëstri di color che sanno,"* the two headsprings of ethical as of all other philosophy. This acknowledged master of all the eminent thinkers who have since lived—whose fame, still growing after more than two thousand years, all but outweighs the whole remainder of the names which make his native city illustrious—was put to death by his countrymen, after a judicial conviction, for impiety and immorality. Impiety, in denying the gods recognized by the State; indeed his accuser asserted (see the *Apologia*) that he believed in no gods at all. Immorality, in being, by his doctrines and instructions, a "corruptor of youth." Of these charges the tribunal, there is every ground for believing, honestly found him guilty, and condemned the man who probably of all then born had deserved best of mankind, to be put to death as a criminal.

To pass from this to the only other instance of judicial iniquity, the mention of which, after the condemnation of Socrates, would not be an anti-climax: the event which took place on Calvary rather more than eighteen hundred years ago. The man who left on the memory of those who witnessed his life and conversation, such an impression of his moral grandeur, that eighteen subsequent centuries have done homage to him as the Almighty in person, was ignominiously put to death, as what? As a blasphemer. Men did not merely mistake their benefactor; they mistook him for the exact contrary of what he was, and treated him as that prodigy of impiety, which they themselves are now held to be, for their treatment of him. The feelings with which mankind now regard these lamentable transactions, especially the later of the two, render them extremely unjust in their judgment of the unhappy actors. These were, to all appearance, not bad men—not worse than men commonly are, but rather the contrary; men who possessed in a full, or somewhat more than a full measure, the religious, moral, and patriotic feelings of their time and people: the very kind of men who, in all times, our own included, have every chance of passing through life blameless and respected. The high-priest who rent his garments when the words were pronounced, which, according to all the ideas of his country, constituted the blackest guilt, was in all probability quite as sincere in his horror and indignation, as the generality of respectable and pious men now are in the religious and moral sentiments they profess; and most of those who now shudder at his conduct, if they had lived in his time, and been born Jews, would have acted precisely as he did. Orthodox Christians who are tempted to think that those who stoned to death the first martyrs must have been worse men than they themselves are, ought to remember that one of those persecutors was Saint Paul.

Let us add one more example, the most striking of all, if the impressiveness of an error is measured by the wisdom and virtue of him who falls into it. If ever anyone, possessed of power, had grounds for thinking himself the best and most enlightened among his contemporaries, it was the Emperor

Marcus Aurelius. Absolute monarch of the whole civilized world, he preserved through life not only the most unblemished justice, but what was less to be expected from his Stoical breeding, the tenderest heart. The few failings which are attributed to him, were all on the side of indulgence: while his writings, the highest ethical product of the ancient mind, differ scarcely perceptibly, if they differ at all, from the most characteristic teachings of Christ. This man, a better Christian in all but the dogmatic sense of the word, than almost any of the ostensibly Christian sovereigns who have since reigned, persecuted Christianity. Placed at the summit of all the previous attainments of humanity, with an open, unfettered intellect, and a character which led him of himself to embody in his moral writings the Christian ideal, he yet failed to see that Christianity was to be a good and not an evil to the world, with his duties to which he was so deeply penetrated. Existing society he knew to be in a deplorable state. But such as it was, he saw, or thought he saw, that it was held together, and prevented from being worse, by belief and reverence of the received divinities. As a ruler of mankind, he deemed it his duty not to suffer society to fall in pieces; and saw not how, if its existing ties were removed, any others could be formed which could again knit it together. The new religion openly aimed at dissolving these ties: unless, therefore, it was his duty to adopt that religion, it seemed to be his duty to put it down. Inasmuch then as the theology of Christianity did not appear to him true or of divine origin; inasmuch as this strange history of a crucified God was not credible to him, and a system which purported to rest entirely upon a foundation to him so wholly unbelievable, could not be foreseen by him to be that renovating agency which, after all abatements, it has in fact proved to be; the gentlest and most amiable of philosophers and rulers, under a solemn sense of duty, authorized the persecution of Christianity. To my mind this is one of the most tragical facts in all history. It is a bitter thought, how different a thing the Christianity of the world might have been, if the Christian faith had been adopted as the religion of the empire under the auspices of Marcus Aurelius instead of those of Constantine. But it would be equally unjust to him and false to truth, to deny, that no one plea which can be urged for punishing anti-Christian teaching, was wanting to Marcus Aurelius for punishing, as he did, the propagation of Christianity. No Christian more firmly believes that Atheism is false, and tends to the dissolution of society, than Marcus Aurelius believed the same things of Christianity; he who, of all men then living, might have been thought the most capable of appreciating it. Unless anyone who approves of punishment for the promulgation of opinions, flatters himself that he is a wiser and better man than Marcus Aurelius —more deeply versed in the wisdom of his time, more elevated in his intellect above it—more earnest in his search for truth, or more singleminded in his devotion to it when found—let him abstain from that assumption of the joint infallibility of himself and the multitude, which the great Antoninus made with so unfortunate a result. . . .

But, indeed, the dictum that truth always triumphs over persecution, is one of those pleasant falsehoods which men repeat after one another till they pass into commonplaces, but which all experience refutes. History teems with instances of truth put down by persecution. If not suppressed forever, it may be thrown back for centuries. To speak only of religious opinions: the Reformation broke out at least twenty times before Luther, and was put down. Arnold of Brescia was put down. Fra Dolcino was put down. Savonarola was put down. The Albigeois were put down. The Vaudois were put down. The Lollards were put down. The Hussites were put down. Even after the era of Luther, wherever persecution was persisted in, it was successful. In Spain, Italy, Flanders, the Austrian empire, Protestantism was rooted out; and, most likely, would have been so in England, had Queen Mary lived, or Queen Elizabeth died. Persecution has always succeeded, save where the heretics were too strong a party to be effectually persecuted. No reasonable person can doubt that Christianity might have been extirpated in the Roman Empire. It spread, and became predominant, because the persecutions were only occasional, lasting but a short time, and separated by long intervals of almost undisturbed propagandism. It is a piece of idle sentimentality that truth, merely truth, has any inherent power denied to error, of prevailing against the dungeon and the stake. Men are not more zealous for truth than they often are for error, and a sufficient application of legal or even of social penalties will generally succeed in stopping the propagation of either. The real advantage which truth has, consists in this, that when an opinion is true, it may be extinguished once, twice, or many times, but in the course of ages there will generally be found persons to rediscover it, until some one of its reappearances falls on a time when from favorable circumstances it escapes persecution until it has made such head as to withstand all subsequent attempts to suppress it.

It will be said, that we do not now put to death the introducers of new opinions: we are not like our fathers who slew the prophets, we even build sepulchers to them. It is true we no longer put heretics to death; and the amount of penal infliction which modern feeling would probably tolerate, even against the most obnoxious opinions, is not sufficient to extirpate them. But let us not flatter ourselves that we are yet free from the stain even of legal persecution. Penalties for opinion, or at least for its expression, still exist by law; and their enforcement is not, even in these times, so unexampled as to make it at all incredible that they may some day be revived in full force. In the year 1857, at the summer assizes of the county of Cornwall, an unfortunate man,[1] said to be of unexceptionable conduct in all relations of life, was sentenced to twenty-one months' imprisonment, for uttering, and writing on a gate, some offensive words concerning Christianity. Within a month of the same time, at the Old Bailey, two persons, on two separate occasions,[2] were rejected as jurymen, and one of them grossly insulted by

---

[1] Thomas Pooley, Bodmin Assizes, July 31, 1857. In December following, he received a free pardon from the Crown.

[2] George Jacob Holyoake, August 17, 1857; Edward Truelove, July, 1857.

the judge and by one of the counsel, because they honestly declared that they had no theological belief; and a third, a foreigner,[3] for the same reason, was denied justice against a thief. This refusal of redress took place in virtue of the legal doctrine, that no person can be allowed to give evidence in a court of justice, who does not profess belief in a God (any god is sufficient) and in a future state; which is equivalent to declaring such persons to be outlaws, excluded from the protection of the tribunals; who may not only be robbed or assaulted with impunity, if no one but themselves, or persons of similar opinions, be present, but anyone else may be robbed or assaulted with impunity, if the proof of the fact depends on their evidence. The assumption on which this is grounded is that the oath is worthless, of a person who does not believe in a future state; a proposition which betokens much ignorance of history in those who assent to it (since it is historically true that a large proportion of infidels in all ages have been persons of distinguished integrity and honor); and would be maintained by no one who had the smallest conception how many of the persons in greatest repute with the world, both for virtues and for attainments, are well known, at least to their intimates, to be unbelievers. The rule, besides, is suicidal, and cuts away its own foundation. Under pretense that atheists must be liars, it admits the testimony of all atheists who are willing to lie, and rejects only those who brave the obloquy of publicly confessing a detested creed rather than affirm a falsehood. A rule thus self-convicted of absurdity so far as regards its professed purpose, can be kept in force only as a badge of hatred, a relic of persecution; a persecution, too, having the peculiarity, that the qualification for undergoing it, is the being clearly proved not to deserve it. The rule, and the theory it implies, are hardly less insulting to believers than to infidels. For if he who does not believe in a future state, necessarily lies, it follows that they who do believe are only prevented from lying, if prevented they are, by the fear of hell. We will not do the authors and abettors of the rule the injury of supposing, that the conception which they have formed of Christian virtue is drawn from their own consciousness.

These, indeed, are but rags and remnants of persecution, and may be thought to be not so much an indication of the wish to persecute, as an example of that very frequent infirmity of English minds, which makes them take a preposterous pleasure in the assertion of a bad principle, when they are no longer bad enough to desire to carry it really into practice. But unhappily there is no security in the state of the public mind, that the suspension of worse forms of legal persecution, which has lasted for about the space of a generation, will continue. In this age the quiet surface of routine is as often ruffled by attempts to resuscitate past evils, as to introduce new benefits. What is boasted of at the present time as the revival of religion, is always, in narrow and uncultivated minds, at least as much the revival of bigotry; and where there is the strong permanent leaven of intolerance in the feelings of a people,

---

[3] Baron de Gleichen, Marlborough-street Police Court, August 4, 1857.

which at all times abides in the middle classes of this country, it needs but little to provoke them into actively persecuting those whom they have never ceased to think proper objects of persecution. For it is this—it is the opinions men entertain, and the feelings they cherish, respecting those who disown the beliefs they deem important, which makes this country not a place of mental freedom. For a long time past, the chief mischief of the legal penalties is that they strengthen the social stigma. It is that stigma which is really effective, and so effective is it, that the profession of opinions which are under the ban of society is much less common in England, than is, in many other countries, the avowal of those which incur risk of judicial punishment. . . . Our merely social intolerance kills no one, roots out no opinions, but induces men to disguise them, or to abstain from any active effort for their diffusion. With us, heretical opinions do not perceptibly gain, or even lose, ground in each decade or generation; they never blaze out far and wide, but continue to smolder in the narrow circles of thinking and studious persons among whom they originate, without ever lighting up the general affairs of mankind with either a true or a deceptive light. And thus is kept up a state of things very satisfactory to some minds, because, without the unpleasant process of fining or imprisoning anybody, it maintains all prevailing opinions outwardly undisturbed, while it does not absolutely interdict the exercise of reason by dissentients afflicted with the malady of thought. A convenient plan for having peace in the intellectual world, and keeping all things going on therein very much as they do already. But the price paid for this sort of intellectual pacification, is the sacrifice of the entire moral courage of the human mind. A state of things in which a large portion of the most active and inquiring intellects find it advisable to keep the general principles and grounds of their convictions within their own breasts, and attempt, in what they address to the public, to fit as much as they can of their own conclusions to premises which they have internally renounced, cannot send forth the open, fearless characters, and logical, consistent intellects who once adorned the thinking world. The sort of men who can be looked for under it, are either mere conformers to commonplace, or time-servers for truth, whose arguments on all great subjects are meant for their hearers, and are not those which have convinced themselves. Those who avoid this alternative, do so by narrowing their thoughts and interest to things which can be spoken of without venturing within the region of principles, that is, to small practical matters, which would come right of themselves, if but the minds of mankind were strengthened and enlarged, and which will never be made effectually right until then: while that which would strengthen and enlarge men's minds, free and daring speculation on the highest subjects, is abandoned.

Those in whose eyes this reticence on the part of heretics is no evil, should consider in the first place, that in consequence of it there is never any fair and thorough discussion of heretical opinions; and that such of them as could not stand such a discussion, though they may be prevented from spreading, do not disappear. But it is not the minds of heretics that are deteriorated most, by the ban placed on all inquiry which does not end in the orthodox conclusions. The greatest harm done is to those who are not heretics, and whose whole mental development is cramped, and their reason cowed, by the fear of heresy. Who can compute what the world loses in the multitude of promising intellects combined with timid characters, who dare not follow out any bold, vigorous, independent train of thought, lest it should land them in something which would admit of being considered irreligious or immoral? Among them we may occasionally see some man of deep conscientiousness, and subtle and refined understanding, who spends a life in sophisticating with an intellect which he cannot silence, and exhausts the resources of ingenuity in attempting to reconcile the promptings of his conscience and reason with orthodoxy, which yet he does not, perhaps, to the end succeed in doing. No one can be a great thinker who does not recognize, that as a thinker it is his first duty to follow his intellect to whatever conclusions it may lead. Truth gains more even by the errors of one who, with due study and preparation, thinks for himself, than by the true opinions of those who only hold them because they do not suffer themselves to think. Not that it is solely, or chiefly, to form great thinkers, that freedom of thinking is required. On the contrary, it is as much and even more indispensable, to enable average human beings to attain the mental stature which they are capable of. There have been, and may again be, great individual thinkers, in a general atmosphere of mental slavery. But there never has been, nor ever will be, in that atmosphere, an intellectually active people. When any people has made a temporary approach to such a character, it has been because the dread of heterodox speculation was for a time suspended. Where there is a tacit convention that principles are not to be disputed; where the discussion of the greatest questions which can occupy humanity is considered to be closed, we cannot hope to find that generally high scale of mental activity which has made some periods of history so remarkable. . . .

Let us now pass to the second division of the argument, and dismissing the supposition that any of the received opinions may be false, let us assume them to be true, and examine into the worth of the manner in which they are likely to be held, when their truth is not freely and openly canvassed. However unwillingly a person who has a strong opinion may admit the possibility that his opinion may be false, he ought to be moved by the consideration that however true it may be, if it is not fully, frequently, and fearlessly discussed, it will be held as a dead dogma, not a living truth.

There is a class of persons (happily not quite so numerous as formerly) who think it enough if a person assents undoubtingly to what they think true, though he has no knowledge whatever of the grounds of the opinion, and could not make a tenable defense of it against the most superficial objections. Such persons, if they can once get their creed taught from authority, naturally think that no good, and some harm, comes of its being allowed to be questioned. Where their influence prevails, they make it nearly impossible for the received opinion to be rejected wisely and considerately, though it may still be rejected rashly and ignorantly; for to shut out discussion entirely is seldom possible, and when it once gets in, beliefs not grounded on conviction are apt to give way before the slightest semblance of an argument. Waiving, however, this possibility—assuming that the true opinion abides in the mind, but abides as a prejudice, a belief independent of, and proof against, argument—this is not the way in which truth ought to be held by a rational being. This is not knowing the truth. Truth, thus held, is but one superstition the more accidentally clinging to the words which enunciate a truth.

If the intellect and judgment of mankind ought to be cultivated, a thing which Protestants at least do not deny, on what can these faculties be more appropriately exercised by anyone, than on the things which concern him so much that it is considered necessary for him to hold opinions on them? If the cultivation of the understanding consists in one thing more than in another, it is surely in learning the grounds of one's own opinions. Whatever people believe, on subjects on which it is of the first importance to believe rightly, they ought to be able to defend against at least the common objections. But, some one may say, "Let them be *taught* the grounds of their opinions. It does not follow that opinions must be merely parroted because they are never heard controverted. Persons who learn geometry do not simply commit the theorems to memory, but understand and learn likewise the demonstrations; and it would be absurd to say that they remain ignorant of the grounds of geometrical truths, because they never hear anyone deny, and attempt to disprove them." Undoubtedly: and such teaching suffices on a subject like mathematics, where there is nothing at all to be said on the wrong side of the question. The peculiarity of the evidence of mathematical truths is, that all the argument is on one side. There are no objections, and no answers to objections. But on every subject on which difference of opinion is possible, the truth depends on a balance to be struck between two sets of conflicting reasons. Even in natural philosophy, there is always some other explanation possible of the same facts; some geocentric theory instead of heliocentric, some phlogiston instead of oxygen; and it has to be shown why that other theory cannot be the true one: and until this is shown, and until we know how it is shown, we do not understand the grounds of our opinion. But when we turn to subjects infinitely more complicated, to morals, religion, politics, social relations, and the business of life, three-fourths of the arguments for every disputed opinion consist in dispelling the appearances which favor some opinion different from it. The greatest orator, save one, of antiquity, has left it on record that he always studied his adversary's case with as great, if not with still greater, intensity than even his own. What Cicero practiced as the means of forensic success, requires to be imitated by all who study any subject in order to arrive at the truth. He who knows only his own side of the case, knows little of that. His reasons may be good, and no one may have been able to refute them. But if he is equally unable to refute the reasons on the opposite side; if he does not so much as know what they are, he has no ground for preferring either opinion. The rational position for him would be suspension of judgment, and unless he contents himself with that, he is either led by authority, or adopts, like the generality of the world, the side to which he feels most inclination. Nor is it enough that he should hear the arguments of adversaries from his own teachers, presented as they state them, and accompanied by what they offer as refutations. That is not the way to do justice to the arguments, or bring them into real contact with his own mind. He must be able to hear them from persons who actually believe them; who defend them in earnest, and do their very utmost for them. He must know them in their most plausible and persuasive form; he must feel the whole force of the difficulty which the true view of the subject has to encounter and dispose of; else he will never really possess himself of the portion of truth which meets and removes that difficulty. Ninety-nine in a hundred of what are called educated men are in this condition; even of those who can argue fluently for their opinions. Their conclusion may be true, but it might be false for anything they know: they have never thrown themselves into the mental position of those who think differently from them, and considered what such persons may have to say; and consequently they do not, in any proper sense of the word, know the doctrine which they themselves profess. They do not know those parts of it which explain and justify the remainder; the considerations which show that a fact which seemingly conflicts with another is reconcilable with it, or that, of two apparently strong reasons, one and not the other ought to be preferred. All that part of the truth which turns the scale, and decides the judgment of a completely informed mind, they are strangers to; nor is it ever really known, but to those who have attended equally and impartially to both sides, and endeavored to see the reasons of both in the strongest light. So essential is this discipline to a real understanding of moral and human subjects, that if opponents of all important truths do not exist, it is indispensable to imagine them, and supply them with the strongest arguments which the most skillful devil's advocate can conjure up.

To abate the force of these considerations, an enemy of free discussion may be supposed to say, that there is no necessity for mankind in general to know and understand all that can be said against or for their opinions by philosophers and theologians. That it is not needful for common men to be able to expose all the misstatements or fallacies of an ingenious opponent. That it is enough if there is always somebody capable of answering them, so that nothing likely to mislead uninstructed persons remains unrefuted. That simple minds, having been taught the obvious grounds of the truths inculcated in them, may trust to authority for the rest, and being aware that they have neither knowledge nor talent to resolve every difficulty which can be raised, may repose in the assurance that all those which have been raised have been or can be answered, by those who are specially trained to the task.

Conceding to this view of the subject the utmost that can be claimed for it by those most easily satisfied with the amount of understanding of truth which ought to accompany the belief of it; even so, the argument for free discussion is in no way weakened. For even this doctrine acknowledges that mankind ought to have a rational assurance that all objections have been satisfactorily answered; and how are they to be answered if that which requires to be answered is not spoken? or how can the answer be known to be satisfactory, if the objectors have no opportunity of showing that it is unsatisfactory? If not the public, at least the philosophers and theologians who are to resolve the difficulties, must make themselves familiar with those difficulties in their most puzzling form; and this cannot be accomplished unless they are freely stated, and placed in the most advantageous light which they admit of. The Catholic Church has its own way of dealing with this embarrassing problem. It makes a broad separation between those who can be permitted to receive its doctrines on conviction, and those who must accept them on trust. Neither, indeed, are allowed any choice as to what they will accept; but the clergy, such at least as can be fully confided in, may admissibly and meritoriously make themselves acquainted with the arguments of opponents, in order to answer them, and may, therefore, read heretical books; the laity, not unless by special permission, hard to be obtained. This discipline recognizes a knowledge of the enemy's case as beneficial to the teachers, but finds means, consistent with this, of denying it to the rest of the world: thus giving to the *élite* more mental culture, though not more mental freedom, than it allows to the mass. By this device it succeeds in obtaining the kind of mental superiority which its purposes require; for though culture without freedom never made a large and liberal mind, it can make a clever *nisi prius* advocate of a cause. But in countries professing Protestantism, this resource is denied; since Protestants hold, at least in theory, that the responsibility for the choice of a religion must be borne by each for himself, and cannot be thrown off upon teachers. Besides, in the present state of the world, it is practically impossible that writings which are read by the instructed can be kept from the uninstructed. If the teachers of mankind are to be cognizant of all that they ought to know, everything must be free to be written and published without restraint.

If, however, the mischievous operation of the absence of free discussion, when the received opinions are true, were confined to leaving men ignorant of the grounds of those opinions, it might be thought that this, if an intellectual, is no moral evil, and does not affect the worth of the opinions, regarded in their influence on the character. The fact, however, is, that not only the grounds of the opinion are forgotten in the absence of discussion, but too often the meaning of the opinion itself. The words which convey it, cease to suggest ideas, or suggest only a small portion of those they were originally employed to communicate. Instead of a vivid conception and a living belief, there remain only a few phrases retained by rote; or, if any part, the shell and husk only of the meaning is retained, the finer essence being lost. The great chapter in human history which this fact occupies and fills, cannot be too earnestly studied and meditated on.

It is illustrated in the experience of almost all ethical doctrines and religious creeds. They are all full of meaning and vitality to those who originate them, and to the direct disciples of the originators. Their meaning continues to be felt in undiminished strength, and is perhaps brought out into even fuller consciousness, so long as the struggle lasts to give the doctrine or creed an ascendancy over other creeds. At last it either prevails, and becomes the general opinion, or its progress stops; it keeps possession of the ground it has gained, but ceases to spread further. When either of these results has become apparent, controversy on the subject flags, and gradually dies away. The doctrine has taken its place, if not as a received opinion, as one of the admitted sects or divisions of opinion: those who hold it have generally inherited, not adopted it; and conversion from one of these doctrines to another, being now an exceptional fact, occupies little place in the thoughts of their professors. Instead of being, as at first, constantly on the alert either to defend themselves against the world, or to bring the world over to them, they have subsided into acquiescence, and neither listen, when they can help it, to arguments against their creed, nor trouble dissentients (if there be such) with arguments in its favor. From this time may usually be dated the decline in the living power of the doctrine. We often hear the teachers of all creeds lamenting the difficulty of keeping up in the minds of believers a lively apprehension of the truth which they nominally recognize, so that it may penetrate the feelings, and acquire a real mastery over the conduct. No such difficulty is complained of while the creed is still fighting for its existence: even the weaker combatants then know and feel what they are fighting for, and the difference between it and other doctrines; and in that period of every creed's existence, not a few persons may be found, who have realized its fundamental principles in all the forms of thought, have weighed and considered them in all their important bearings, and have experienced the full effect on the character, which belief in that creed ought to produce in a mind thoroughly imbued with it. But when it has come to be an hereditary creed, and to be received passively, not actively—when the mind is no longer compelled, in the same degree as at first, to exercise its vital powers on the questions which its belief presents to it, there is a progressive tendency to forget all of the belief except the formularies, or to give it a dull and torpid assent, as if accepting it on trust dispensed with the necessity of realizing it in consciousness, or testing it by personal experience; until it almost ceases to connect itself at all with the inner life of the human being. Then are seen the cases, so frequent in this age of the world as almost to form the majority, in which the creed remains as it were outside the mind, encrusting and petrifying it against all other influences addressed to the higher parts of our nature; manifesting its power by not suffering any fresh and living conviction to get in, but itself doing nothing for the mind or heart, except standing sentinel over them to keep them vacant.

To what an extent doctrines intrinsically fitted to make the deepest impression upon the mind may remain in it as dead beliefs, without being ever realized in the imagination, the feelings, or the understanding, is exemplified by the manner in which the majority of believers hold the doctrines of Christianity. By Christianity I here mean what is accounted such by all churches and sects—the maxims and precepts contained in the New Testament. These are considered sacred, and accepted as laws, by all professing Christians. Yet it is scarcely too much to say that not one Christian in a thousand guides or tests his individual conduct by reference to those laws. The standard to which he does refer it, is the custom of his nation, his class, or his religious profession. He has thus, on the one hand, a collection of ethical maxims, which he believes to have been vouchsafed to him by infallible wisdom as rules for his government; and on the other, a set of everyday judgments and practices, which go a certain length with some of those maxims, not so great a length with others, stand in direct opposition to some, and are, on the whole, a compromise between the Christian creed and the interests and suggestions of worldly life. To the first of these standards he gives his homage; to the other his real allegiance. All Christians believe that the blessed are the poor and humble, and those who are ill-used by the world; that it is easier for a camel to pass through the eye of a needle than for a rich man to enter the kingdom of heaven; that they should judge not, lest they be judged; that they should swear not at all; that they should love their neighbor as themselves; that if one take their cloak, they should give him their coat also; that they should take no thought for the morrow; that if they would be perfect, they should sell all that they have and give it to the poor. They are not insincere when they say that they believe these things. They do believe them, as people believe what they have always heard lauded and never discussed. But in the sense of that living belief which regulates conduct, they believe these doctrines just up to the point to which it is usual to act upon them. The doctrines in their integrity are serviceable to pelt adversaries with; and it is understood that they are to put forward (when possible) as the reasons for whatever people do that they think laudable. But anyone who reminded them that the maxims require an infinity of things which they never even think of doing, would gain nothing but to be classed among those very unpopular characters who affect to be better than other people. The doctrines have no hold on ordinary believers—are not a power in their minds. They have an habitual respect for the sound of them, but no feeling which spreads from the words to the things signified, and forces the mind to take *them* in, and make them conform to the formula. Whenever conduct is concerned, they look round for Mr. *A* and *B* to direct them how far to go in obeying Christ.

Now we may be well assured that the case was not thus, but far otherwise, with the early Christians. Had it been thus, Christianity never would have expanded from an obscure sect of the despised Hebrews into the religion of the Roman empire. When their enemies said, "See how these Christians love one another" (a remark not likely to be made by anybody now), they assuredly had a much livelier feeling of the meaning of their creed than they have ever had since. And to this cause, probably, it is chiefly owing that Christianity now makes so little progress in extending its domain, and after eighteen centuries, is still nearly confined to Europeans and the descendants of Europeans. Even with the strictly religious, who are much in earnest about their doctrines, and attach a greater amount of meaning to many of them than people in general, it commonly happens that the part which is thus comparatively active in their minds is that which was made by Calvin, or Knox, or some such person much nearer in character to themselves. The sayings of Christ co-exist passively in their minds, producing hardly any effect beyond what is caused by mere listening to words so amiable and bland. There are many reasons, doubtless, why doctrines which are the badge of a sect retain more of their vitality than those common to all recognized sects, and why more pains are taken by teachers to keep their meaning alive; but one reason certainly is, that the peculiar doctrines are more questioned, and have to be oftener defended against open gainsayers. Both teachers and learners go to sleep at their post, as soon as there is no enemy in the field.

The same thing holds true, generally speaking, of all traditional doctrines —those of prudence and knowledge of life, as well as morals or religion. All languages and literatures are full of general observations on life, both as to what it is, and how to conduct oneself in it; observations which everybody knows, which everybody repeats, or hears with acquiescence, which are received as truisms, yet of which most people first truly learn the meaning, when experience, generally of a painful kind, has made it a reality to them. How often, when smarting under some unforeseen misfortune or disappointment, does a person call to mind some proverb or common saying, familiar to him all his life, the meaning of which, if he had ever before felt it as he does now, would have saved him from the calamity. There are indeed reasons for this, other than the absence of discussion: there are many truths of which the full meaning *cannot* be realized, until personal experience has brought it home. But much more of the meaning even of these would have been understood, and what was understood would have been far more deeply impressed on the mind, if the man had been accustomed to hear it argued *pro* and *con* by people who did understand it. The fatal tendency of mankind to leave off thinking about a thing when it is no longer doubtful, is the cause of half their errors. A contemporary author has well spoken of "the deep slumber of a decided opinion."

But what! (it may be asked) Is the absence of unanimity an indispensable condition of true knowledge? Is it necessary that some part of mankind should persist in error, to enable any to realize the truth? Does a belief cease to be real and vital as soon as it is generally received—and is a proposition never thoroughly understood and felt unless some doubt of it remains? As soon as mankind have unanimously accepted a truth, does the truth perish within them? The highest aim and best result of improved intelligence, it has hitherto been thought, is to unite mankind more and more in the acknowledgment of all important truths: and does the intelligence only last as long as it has not achieved its object? Do the fruits of conquest perish by the very completeness of the victory?

I affirm no such thing. As mankind improve, the number of doctrines which are no longer disputed or doubted will be constantly on the increase: and the well-being of mankind may almost be measured by the number and gravity of the truths which have reached the point of being uncontested. The cessation, on one question after another, of serious controversy, is one of the necessary incidents of the consolidation of opinion; a consolidation as salutary in the case of true opinions, as it is dangerous and noxious when the opinions are erroneous. But though this gradual narrowing of the bounds of diversity of opinion is necessary in both senses of the term, being at once inevitable and indispensable, we are not therefore obliged to conclude that all its consequences must be beneficial. The loss of so important an aid to the intelligent and living apprehension of a truth, as is afforded by the necessity of explaining it to, or defending it against, opponents, though not sufficient to outweigh, is no trifling drawback from, the benefit of its universal recognition. Where this advantage can no longer be had, I confess I should like to see the teachers of mankind endeavoring to provide a substitute for it; some contrivance for making the difficulties of the question as present to the learner's consciousness, as if they were pressed upon him by a dissentient champion, eager for his conversion.

But instead of seeking contrivances for this purpose, they have lost those they formerly had. The Socratic dialectics, so magnificently exemplified in the dialogues of Plato, were a contrivance of this description. They were essentially a negative discussion of the great questions of philosophy and life, directed with consummate skill to the purpose of convincing anyone who had merely adopted the commonplaces of received opinion, that he did not understand the subject—that he as yet attached no definite meaning to the doctrines he professed; in order that, becoming aware of his ignorance, he might be put in the way to attain a stable belief, resting on a clear apprehension both of the meaning of doctrines and of their evidence. The school disputations of the middle ages had a somewhat similar object. They were intended to make sure that the pupil understood his own opinion, and (by necessary correlation) the opinion opposed to it, and could enforce the grounds of the one and confute those of the other. These last-mentioned contests had indeed the incurable defect, that the premises appealed to were taken from authority, not from reason; and, as a discipline to the mind, they were in every respect inferior to the powerful dialectics which formed the intellects of the *"Socratici viri":* but the modern mind owes far more to both than it is generally willing to admit, and the present modes of education contain nothing which in the smallest degree supplies the place either of the one or of the other. A person who derives all his instruction from teachers or books, even if he escape the besetting temptation of contenting himself with cram, is under no compulsion to hear both sides; accordingly it is far from a frequent accomplishment, even among thinkers, to know both sides; and the weakest part of what everybody says in defense of his opinion, is what he intends as a reply to antagonists. It is the fashion of the present time to disparage negative logic—that which points out weaknesses in theory or errors in practice, without establishing positive truths. Such negative criticism would indeed be poor enough as an ultimate result; but as a means to attaining any positive knowledge or conviction worthy the name, it cannot be valued too highly; and until people are again systematically trained to it, there will be few great thinkers, and a low general average of intellect, in any but the mathematical and physical departments of speculation. On any other subject no one's opinions deserve the name of knowledge, except so far as he has either had forced upon him by others, or gone through of himself, the same mental process which would have been required of him in carrying on an active controversy with opponents. That, therefore, which when absent, it is so indispensable, but so difficult, to create, how worse than absurd it is to forego, when spontaneously offering itself! If there are any persons who contest a received opinion, or who will do so if law or opinion will let them, let us thank them for it, open our minds to listen to them, and rejoice that there is someone to do for us what we otherwise ought, if we have any regard for either the certainty or the vitality of our convictions, to do with much greater labor for ourselves.

It still remains to speak of one of the principal causes which make diversity of opinion advantageous, and will continue to do so until mankind shall have entered a stage of intellectual advancement which at present seems at an incalculable distance. We have hitherto considered only two possibilities: that the received opinion may be false, and some other opinion, consequently, true; or that, the received opinion being true, a conflict with the opposite error is essential to a clear apprehension and deep feeling of its truth. But there is a commoner case than either of these; when the conflicting doctrines, instead of being one true and the other false, share the truth between them; and the nonconforming opinion is needed to supply the remainder of the truth, of which the received doctrine embodies only a part. Popular opinions, on subjects not palpable to sense, are often true, but seldom or never the whole truth. They are a part of the truth; sometimes a greater, sometimes a smaller part, but exaggerated, distorted, and disjoined from the truths by which they ought to be accompanied and limited. Heretical opinions, on the other hand, are generally some of these suppressed and neglected truths, bursting the bonds which kept them down, and either seeking reconciliation with the truth contained in the common opinion, or fronting it as enemies, and setting themselves up, with similar exclusiveness, as the whole truth. The latter case is hitherto the most frequent, as, in the human mind, one-sidedness has always been the rule, and many-sidedness the exception. Hence, even in revolutions of opinion, one part of the truth usually sets while another rises. Even progress, which ought to superadd, for the most part only substitutes, one partial and incomplete truth for another; improvement consisting chiefly in this, that the new fragment of truth is more wanted, more adapted to the needs of the time, than that which it displaces. Such being the partial character of prevailing opinions, even when resting on a true foundation, every opinion which embodies somewhat of the portion of truth which the common opinion omits, ought to be considered precious, with whatever amount of error and confusion that truth may be blended. No sober judge of human affairs will feel bound to be indignant because those who force on our notice truths which we should otherwise have overlooked, overlook some of those which we see. Rather, he will think that so long as popular truth is one-sided, it is more desirable than otherwise that unpopular truth should have one-sided asserters too; such being usually the most energetic, and the most likely to compel reluctant attention to the fragment of wisdom which they proclaim as if it were the whole. . . .

In politics, again, it is almost a commonplace, that a party of order or stability, and a party of progress or reform, are both necessary elements of a healthy state of political life; until the one or the other shall have so enlarged its mental grasp as to be a party equally of order and of progress, knowing and distinguishing what is fit to be preserved from what ought to be swept away. Each of these modes of thinking derives its utility from the deficiencies of the other; but it is in a great measure the opposition of the other that keeps each within the limits of reason and sanity. Unless opinions favorable to democracy and to aristocracy, to property and to equality, to cooperation and to competition, to luxury and to abstinence, to sociality and individuality, to liberty and discipline, and all the other standing antagonisms of practical life, are expressed with equal freedom, and enforced and defended with equal talent and energy, there is no chance of both elements obtaining their due; one scale is sure to go up, and the other down. Truth, in the great practical concerns of life, is so much a question of the reconciling and combining of opposites, that very few have minds sufficiently capacious and impartial to make the adjustment with an approach to correctness, and it has to be made by the rough process of a struggle between combatants fighting under hostile banners. On any of the great open questions just enumerated, if either of the two opinions has a better claim than the other, not merely to be tolerated, but to be encouraged and countenanced, it is the one which happens at the particular time and place to be in a minority. That is the opinion which, for the time being, represents the neglected interests, the side of human well-being which is in danger of obtaining less than its share. I am aware that there is not, in this country, any intolerance of differences of opinion on most of these topics. They are adduced to show, by admitted and multiplied examples, the universality of the fact, that only through diversity of opinion is there, in the existing state of human intellect, a chance of fair play to all sides of the truth. When there are persons to be found, who form an exception to the apparent unanimity of the world on any subject, even if the world is in the right, it is always probable that dissentients have something worth hearing to say for themselves, and that truth would lose something by their silence. . . .

I do not pretend that the most unlimited use of the freedom of enunciating all possible opinions would put an end to the evils of religious or philosophical sectarianism. Every truth which men of narrow capacity are in earnest about, is sure to be asserted, inculcated, and in many ways even acted on, as if no other truth existed in the world, or at all events none that could limit or qualify the first. I acknowledge that the tendency of all opinions to become sectarian is not cured by the freest discussion, but is often heightened and exacerbated thereby; the truth which ought to have been, but was not, seen, being rejected all the more violently because proclaimed by persons regarded as opponents. But it is not on the impassioned partisan, it is on the calmer and more disinterested bystander, that this collision of opinions works its salutary effect. Not the violent conflict between parts of the truth, but the quiet suppression of half of it, is the formidable evil; there is always hope when people are forced to listen to both sides; it is when they attend only to one that errors harden into prejudices, and truth itself ceases to have the effect of truth, by being exaggerated into falsehood. And since there are few mental attributes more rare than that judicial faculty which can sit in intelligent judgment between two sides of a question, of which only one is represented by an advocate before it, truth has no chance but in proportion as every side of it, every opinion which embodies any fraction of the truth, not only finds advocates, but is so advocated as to be listened to.

We have now recognized the necessity to the mental well-being of mankind (on which all their other well-being depends) of freedom of opinion, and freedom of the expression of opinion, on four distinct grounds; which we will now briefly recapitulate.

First, if any opinion is compelled to silence, that opinion may, for aught we can certainly know, be true. To deny this is to assume our own infallibility.

Secondly, though the silenced opinion be an error, it may, and very commonly does, contain a portion of truth; and since the general or prevailing opinion of any subject is rarely or never the whole truth, it is only by the collision of adverse opinions that the remainder of the truth has any chance of being supplied.

Thirdly, even if the received opinion be not only true, but the whole truth; unless it is suffered to be, and actually is, vigorously and earnestly contested, it will, by most of those who receive it, be held in the manner of a prejudice, with little comprehension or feeling of its rational grounds. And not only this, but, fourthly, the meaning of the doctrine itself will be in danger of being lost, or enfeebled, and deprived of its vital effect on the character and conduct: the dogma becoming a mere formal profession, inefficacious for good, but cumbering the ground, and preventing the growth of any real and heartfelt conviction, from reason or personal experience.

Before quitting the subject of freedom of opinion, it is fit to take some notice of those who say, that the free expression of all opinions should be permitted, on condition that the manner be temperate, and do not pass the bounds of fair discussion. Much might be said on the impossibility of fixing where these supposed bounds are to be placed; for if the test be offense to those whose opinion is attacked, I think experience testifies that this offense is given whenever the attack is telling and powerful, and that every opponent who pushes them hard, and whom they find it difficult to answer, appears to them, if he shows any strong feeling on the subject, an intemperate opponent. But this, though an important consideration in a practical point of view, merges in a more fundamental objection. Undoubtedly the manner of asserting an opinion, even though it be a true one, may be very objectionable, and may justly incur severe censure. But the principal offenses of the kind are such as it is mostly impossible, unless by accidental self-betrayal, to bring home to conviction. The gravest of them is, to argue sophistically, to suppress facts or arguments, to misstate the elements of the case, or misrepresent the opposite opinion. But all this, even to the most aggravated degree, is so continually done in perfect good faith, by persons who are not considered, and in many other respects may not deserve to be considered, ignorant or incompetent, that it is rarely possible on adequate grounds conscientiously to stamp the misrepresentation as morally culpable; and still less could law presume to interfere with this kind of controversial misconduct. With regard to what is commonly meant by intemperate discussion, namely invective, sarcasm, personality, and the like, the denunciation of these weapons would deserve more sympathy if it were ever proposed to interdict them equally to both sides; but it is only desired to restrain the employment of them against the prevailing opinion: against the unprevailing they may not only be used without general disapproval, but will be likely to obtain for him who uses them the praise of honest zeal and righteous indignation. Yet whatever mischief arises from their use, is greatest when they are employed against the comparatively defenseless; and whatever unfair advantage can be derived by any opinion from this mode of asserting it, accrues almost exclusively to received opinions. The worst offense of this kind which can be committed by a polemic, is to stigmatize those who hold the contrary opinion as bad and immoral men. To calumny of this sort, those who hold any unpopular opinion are peculiarly exposed, because they are in general few and uninfluential, and nobody but themselves feels much interested in seeing justice done them; but this weapon is, from the nature of the case, denied to those who attack a prevailing opinion: they can neither use it with safety to themselves, nor, if they could, would it do anything but recoil on their own cause. In general, opinions contrary to those commonly received can only obtain a hearing by studied moderation of language, and the most cautious avoidance of unnecessary offense, from which they hardly ever deviate even in a slight degree without losing ground: while unmeasured vituperation employed on the side of the prevailing opinion, really does deter people from professing contrary opinions, and from listening to those who profess them. For the interest, therefore, of truth and justice, it is far more important to restrain this employment of vituperative language than the other; and, for example, if it were necessary to choose, there would be much more need to discourage offensive attacks on infidelity, than on religion. It is, however, obvious that law and authority have no business with restraining either, while opinion ought, in every instance, to determine its verdict by the circumstances of the individual case; condemning everyone, on whichever side of the argument he places himself, in whose mode of advocacy either want of candor, or malignity, bigotry, or intolerance of feeling manifest themselves; but not inferring these vices from the side which a person takes, though it be the contrary side of the question to our own: and giving merited honor to everyone, whatever opinion he may hold, who has calmness to see and honesty to state what his opponents and their opinions really are, exaggerating nothing to their discredit, keeping nothing back which tells, or can be supposed to tell, in their favor. This is the real morality of public discussion: and if often violated, I am happy to think that there are many controversialists who to a great extent observe it, and a still greater number who conscientiously strive towards it. . . .

. . . Such being the reasons which make it imperative that human beings should be free to form opinions, and to express their opinions without reserve; and such the baneful consequences to the intellectual, and through that to the moral nature of man, unless this liberty is either conceded, or asserted in spite of prohibition; let us next examine whether the same reasons do not require that men should be free to act upon their opinions—to carry these out in their lives, without hindrance, either physical or moral, from their fellow-men, so long as it is at their own risk and peril. This last proviso is of course indispensable. No one pretends that actions should be as free as opinions. On the contrary, even opinions lose their immunity when the circumstances in which they are expressed are such as to constitute their expression a positive instigation to some mischievous act. An opinion that corn-dealers are starvers of the poor, or that private property is robbery, ought to be unmolested when simply circulated through the press, but may justly incur punishment when delivered orally to an excited mob assembled before the house of a corn-dealer, or when handed about among the same mob in the form of a placard. Acts, of whatever kind, which without justifiable cause do harm to others, may be, and in the more important cases absolutely require to be, controlled by the unfavorable sentiments, and, when needful, by the active interference of mankind. The liberty of the individual must be thus far limited; he must not make himself a nuisance to other people. But if he refrains from molesting others in what concerns them, and merely acts according to his own inclination and judgment in things which concern himself, the same reasons which show that opinion should be free, prove also that he should be allowed, without molestation, to carry his opinions into practice at his own cost. That mankind are not infallible; that their truths, for the most part, are only half-truths; that unity of opinion, unless resulting from the fullest and freest comparison of opposite opinions, is not desirable, and diversity not an evil, but a good, until mankind are much more capable than at present of recognizing all sides of the truth, are principles applicable to men's modes of action, not less than to their opinions. As it is useful that while mankind are imperfect there should be different opinions, so it is that there should be different experiments of living; that free scope should be given to varieties of character, short of injury to others; and that the worth of different modes of life should be proved practically, when anyone thinks fit to try them. It is desirable, in short, that in things which do not primarily concern others, individuality should assert itself. Where not the person's own character, but the traditions or customs of other people are the rule of conduct, there is wanting one of the principal ingredients of human happiness, and quite the chief ingredient of individual and social progress. . . .

. . . A person whose desires and impulses are his own—are the expression of his own nature, as it has been developed and modified by his own culture—is said to have a character. One whose desires and impulses are not his own, has no character, no more than a steam-engine has a character. If, in addition to being his own, his impulses are strong, and are under the government of a strong will, he has an energetic character. Whoever thinks that individuality of desires and impulses should not be encouraged to unfold itself, must maintain that society has no need of strong natures—is not the better for containing many persons who have much character—and that a high general average of energy is not desirable. . . .

. . . Society has now fairly got the better of individuality; and the danger which threatens human nature is not the excess, but the deficiency, of personal impulses and preferences. . . .

. . . It is not by wearing down into uniformity all that is individual in themselves, but by cultivating it, and calling it forth, within the limits imposed by the rights and interests of others, that human beings become a noble and beautiful object of contemplation; and as the works partake the character of those who do them, by the same process human life also becomes rich, diversified, and animating, furnishing more abundant aliment to high thoughts and elevating feelings, and strengthening the tie which binds every individual to the race, by making the race infinitely better worth belonging to. In proportion to the development of his individuality, each person becomes more valuable to himself, and is therefore capable of being more valuable to others. There is a greater fullness of life about his own existence, and when there is more life in the units there is more in the mass which is composed of them. As much compression as is necessary to prevent the stronger specimens of human nature from encroaching on the rights of others cannot be dispensed with; but for this there is ample compensation even in the point of view of human development. The means of development which the individual loses by being prevented from gratifying his inclinations to the injury of others, are chiefly obtained at the expense of the development of other people. And even to himself there is a full equivalent in the better development of the social part of his nature, rendered possible by the restraint put upon the selfish part. To be held to rigid rules of justice for the sake of others, develops the feelings and capacities which have the good of others for their object. But to be restrained in things not affecting their good, by their mere displeasure, develops nothing valuable, except such force of character as may unfold itself in resisting the restraint. If acquiesced in, it dulls and blunts the whole nature. To give any fair play to the nature of each, it is essential that different persons should be allowed to lead different lives. In proportion as this latitude has been exercised in any age, has that age been noteworthy to posterity. Even despotism does not produce its worst effects, so long as individuality exists under it; and whatever crushes individuality is despotism, by whatever name it may be called, and whether it professes to be enforcing the will of God or the injunctions of men.

Having said that the individuality is the same thing with development, and that it is only the cultivation of individuality which produces, or can produce, well-developed human beings, I might here close the argument: for what more or better can be said of any condition of human affairs than that it brings human beings themselves nearer to the best thing they can be? or what worse can be said of any obstruction to good than that it prevents this? Doubtless, however, these considerations will not suffice to convince those who most need convincing; and it is necessary further to show that these developed human beings are of some use to the undeveloped—to point out to those who do not desire liberty, and would not avail themselves of it, that they may be in some intelligible manner rewarded for allowing other people to make use of it without hindrance.

In the first place, then, I would suggest that they might possibly learn something from them. . . .

. . . It is important to give the freest scope possible to uncustomary things, in order that it may in time appear which of these are fit to be converted into customs. But independence of action, and disregard of custom, are not solely deserving of encouragement for the chance they afford that better modes of action, and customs more worthy of general adoption, may be struck out; nor is it only persons of decided mental superiority who have a just claim to carry on their lives in their own way. There is no reason that all human existence should be constructed on some one or some small number of patterns. If a person possesses any tolerable amount of common sense and experience, his own mode of laying out his existence is the best, not because it is the best in itself, but because it is his own mode. . . .

[Custom and popular prejudice] form so great a mass of influences hostile to individuality, that it is not easy to see how it can stand its ground. It will do so with increasing difficulty, unless the intelligent part of the public can be made to feel its value—to see that it is good there should be differences, even though not for the better, even though, as it may appear to them, some should be for the worse. If the claims of individuality are ever to be asserted, the time is now, while much is still wanting to complete the enforced assimilation. It is only in the earlier stages that any stand can be successfully made against the encroachment. The demand that all other people shall resemble ourselves grows by what it feeds on. If resistance waits till life is reduced *nearly* to one uniform type, all deviations from that type will come to be considered impious, immoral, even monstrous and contrary to nature. Mankind speedily become unable to conceive diversity, when they have been for some time unaccustomed to see it. . . .

From Considerations on Representative Government (*1861*)
John Stuart Mill

There is no difficulty in showing that the ideally best form of government is that in which the sovereignty, or supreme controlling power in the last resort, is vested in the entire aggregate of the community, every citizen not only having a voice in the exercise of the ultimate sovereignty, but being, at least occasionally, called on to take an actual part in the government by the personal discharge of some public function, local or general.

To test this proposition, it has to be examined in reference to the two branches into which, as pointed out in the last chapter, the inquiry into the goodness of a government conveniently divides itself, namely, how far it promotes the good management of the affairs of society by means of the existing faculties, moral, intellectual, and active, of its various members, and what is its effect in improving or deteriorating those faculties.

The ideally best form of government, it is scarcely necessary to say, does not mean one which is practicable or eligible in all states of civilization, but the one which, in the circumstances in which it is practicable and eligible, is attended with the greatest amount of beneficial consequences, immediate and prospective. A completely popular government is the only polity which can make out any claim to this character. It is pre-eminent in both the departments between which the excellence of a political Constitution is divided. It is both more favorable to present good government, and promotes a better and higher form of national character than any other polity whatsoever.

Its superiority in reference to present well-being rests upon two principles, of as universal truth and applicability as any general propositions which can be laid down respecting human affairs. The first is that the rights and interests of every or any person are only secure from being disregarded when the person interested is himself able, and habitually disposed, to stand up for them. The second is, that the general prosperity attains a greater height, and is more widely diffused, in proportion to the amount and variety of the personal energies enlisted in promoting it.

Putting these two propositions into a shape more special to their present application—human beings are only secure from evil at the hands of others in proportion as they have the power of being, and are, self-*protecting;* and they only achieve a high degree of success in their struggle with Nature in proportion as they are self-*dependent,* relying on what they themselves can do, either separately or in concert, rather than on what others do for them.

The former proposition—that each is the only safe guardian of his own rights and interests—is one of those elementary maxims of prudence which every person capable of conducting his own affairs implicitly acts upon wherever he himself is interested. Many, indeed, have a great dislike to it as a political doctrine, and are fond of holding it up to obloquy as a doctrine of universal selfishness. To which we may answer, that whenever it ceases to be true that mankind, as a rule, prefer themselves to others, and those nearest to them to those more remote, from that moment Communism is not only practicable, but the only defensible form of society, and will, when that time arrives, be assuredly carried into effect. For my own part, not believing in universal selfishness, I have no difficulty in admitting that Communism would even now be practicable among the *élite* of mankind, and may become so among the rest. But as this opinion is anything but popular with those defenders of existing institutions who find fault with the doctrine of the general predominance of self-interest, I am inclined to think they do in reality believe that most men consider themselves before other people. It is not, however, necessary to affirm even this much in order to support the claim of all to participate in the sovereign power. We need not suppose that when power resides in an exclusive class, that class will knowingly and deliberately sacrifice the other classes to themselves: it suffices that, in the absence of its natural defenders, the interest of the excluded is always in danger of being overlooked; and, when looked at, is seen with very different eyes from those of the persons whom it directly concerns. In this country, for example, what are called the working classes may be considered as excluded from all direct participation in the government. I do not believe that the classes who do participate in it have in general any intention of sacrificing the working classes to themselves. They once had that intention; witness the persevering attempts so long made to keep down wages by law. But in the present day their ordinary disposition is the very opposite: they willingly make considerable sacrifices, especially of their pecuniary interest, for the benefit of the working classes, and err rather by too lavish and indiscriminating beneficence; nor do I believe that any rulers in history have been actuated by a more sincere desire to do their duty toward the poorer portion of their countrymen. Yet does Parliament, or almost any of the members composing it, ever for an instant look at any question with the eyes of a working man? When a subject arises in which the laborers as such have an interest, is it regarded from any point of view but that of the employers of labor? I do not say that the working men's view of these questions is in general nearer to the truth than the other, but it is sometimes quite as near; and in any case it ought to be respectfully listened to, instead of being, as it is, not merely turned away from, but ignored. On the question of strikes, for instance, it is doubtful if there is so much as one among the leading members of either House who is not firmly convinced that the reason of the matter is unqualifiedly on the side of the masters, and that the men's view of it is simply absurd. Those who have studied the question know well how far this is from being the case, and in how different, and how infinitely less superficial a manner the point would have to be argued if the classes who strike were able to make themselves heard in Parliament.

It is an inherent condition of human affairs that no intention, however sincere, of protecting the interests of others can make it safe or salutary to tie up their own hands. Still more obviously true is it that by their own hands only can any positive and durable improvement of their circumstances in life be worked out. Through the joint influence of these two principles, all free communities have both been more exempt from social injustice and crime, and have attained more brilliant prosperity than any others, or than they themselves after they lost their freedom. Contrast the free states of the world, while their freedom lasted, with the contemporary subjects of monarchical or oligarchical despotism: the Greek cities with the Persian satrapies, the Italian republics, and the free towns of Flanders and Germany, with the feudal monarchies of Europe; Switzerland, Holland, and England with Austria or ante-revolutionary France. Their superior prosperity was too obvious ever to have been gainsaid; while their superiority in good government and social relations is proved by the prosperity, and is manifest besides in every page of history. If we compare, not one age with another, but the different governments which coexisted in the same age, no amount of disorder which exaggeration itself can pretend to have existed amidst the publicity of the free states can be compared for a moment with the contemptuous trampling upon the mass of the people which pervaded the whole life of the monarchical countries, or the disgusting individual tyranny which was of more than daily occurrence under the systems of plunder which they called fiscal arrangements, and in the secrecy of their frightful courts of justice.

It must be acknowledged that the benefits of freedom, so far as they have hitherto been enjoyed, were obtained by the extension of its privileges to a part only of the community, and that a government in which they are extended impartially to all is a desideratum still unrealized. But, though every approach to this has an independent value, and in many cases more than an approach could not, in the existing state of general improvement, be made, the participation of all in these benefits is the ideally perfect conception of free government. In proportion as any, no matter who, are excluded from it, the interests of the excluded are left without the guaranty accorded to the rest, and they themselves have less scope and encouragement than they might otherwise have to that exertion of their energies for the good of themselves and of the community, to which the general prosperity is always proportioned.

Thus stands the case as regards present well-being—the good management of the affairs of the existing generation. If we now pass to the influence of the form of government upon character, we shall find the superiority of popular government over every other to be, if possible, still more decided and indisputable.

This question really depends upon a still more fundamental one, viz., which of two common types of character, for the general good of humanity, it is most desirable should predominate—the active or the passive type; that which struggles against evils or that which endures them; that which bends to circumstances, or that which endeavors to make circumstances bend to itself.

The commonplaces of moralists and the general sympathies of mankind, are in favor of the passive type. Energetic characters may be admired, but the acquiescent and submissive are those which most men personally prefer. The passiveness of our neighbors increases our own sense of security, and plays into the hands of our willfulness. Passive characters, if we do not happen to need their activity, seem an obstruction the less in our own path. A contented character is not a dangerous rival. Yet nothing is more certain than that improvement in human affairs is wholly the work of the uncontented characters; and, moreover, that it is much easier for an active mind to acquire the virtues of patience, than for a passive one to assume those of energy. . . .

The striving, go-ahead character of England and the United States is only a fit subject of disapproving criticism on account of the very secondary objects on which it commonly expends its strength. In itself it is the foundation of the best hopes for the general improvement of mankind. It has been acutely remarked, that whenever anything goes amiss, the habitual impulse of French people is to say, "Il faut de la patience"; and of English people, "What a shame." The people who think it a shame when anything goes wrong—who rush to the conclusion that the evil could and ought to have been prevented, are those who, in the long run, do most to make the world better. If the desires are low placed, if they extend to little beyond physical comfort, and the show of riches, the immediate results of the energy will not be much more than the continual extension of man's power over material objects; but even this makes room, and prepares the mechanical appliances for the greatest intellectual and social achievements; and while the energy is there, some persons will apply it, and it will be applied more and more, to the perfecting not of outward circumstances alone, but of man's inward nature. Inactivity, unaspiringness, absence of desire, is a more fatal hindrance to improvement than any misdirection of energy, and is that through which alone, when existing in the mass, any very formidable misdirection by an energetic few becomes possible. It is this, mainly, which retains in a savage or semi-savage state the great majority of the human race.

Now there can be no kind of doubt that the passive type of character is favored by the government of one or a few, and the active self-helping type by that of the many. Irresponsible rulers need the quiescence of the ruled more than they need any activity but that which they can compel. Submissiveness to the prescriptions of men as necessities of nature is the lesson inculcated by all governments upon those who are wholly without participation in them.

The will of superiors, and the law as the will of superiors, must be passively yielded to. But no men are mere instruments or materials in the hands of their rulers who have will, or spirit, or a spring of internal activity in the rest of their proceedings, and any manifestation of these qualities, instead of receiving encouragement from despots, has to get itself forgiven by them. Even when irresponsible rulers are not sufficiently conscious of danger from the mental activity of their subjects to be desirous of repressing it, the position itself is a repression. Endeavor is even more effectually restrained by the certainty of its impotence than by any positive discouragement. Between subjection to the will of others and the virtues of self-help and self-government, there is a natural incompatibility. This is more or less complete, according as the bondage is strained or relaxed. Rulers differ very much in the length to which they carry the control of the free agency of their subjects, or the suppression of it by managing their business for them. But the difference is in degree, not in principle; and the best despots often go the greatest lengths in chaining up the free agency of their subjects. A bad despot, when his own personal indulgences have been provided for, may sometimes be willing to let the people alone; but a good despot insists on doing them good by making them do their own business in a better way than they themselves know of. . . .

Very different is the state of the human faculties where a human being feels himself under no other external restraint than the necessities of nature, or mandates of society which he has his share in imposing, and which it is open to him, if he thinks them wrong, publicly to dissent from, and exert himself actively to get altered. No doubt, under a government partially popular, this freedom may be exercised even by those who are not partakers in the full privileges of citizenship; but it is a great additional stimulus to anyone's self-help and self-reliance when he starts from even ground, and has not to feel that his success depends on the impression he can make upon the sentiments and dispositions of a body of whom he is not one. It is a great discouragement to an individual, and a still greater one to a class, to be left out of the constitution; to be reduced to plead from outside the door to the arbiters of their destiny, not taken into consultation within. The maximum of the invigorating effect of freedom upon the character is only obtained when the person acted on either is, or is looking forward to become a citizen as fully privileged as any other. What is still more important than even this matter of feeling is the practical discipline which the character obtains from the occasional demand made upon the citizens to exercise, for a time and in their turn, some social function. It is not sufficiently considered how little there is in most men's ordinary life to give any largeness either to their conceptions or to their sentiments. Their work is a routine; not a labor of love, but of self-interest in the most elementary form, the satisfaction of daily wants; neither the thing done, nor the process of doing it, introduces the mind to thoughts or feelings extending beyond individuals; if instructive books are within their reach, there is no stimulus to read them; and, in most cases, the individual has no access to any person of cultivation much superior to his own. Giving him something to do for the public supplies, in a measure, all these deficiencies. If circumstances allow the amount of public duty assigned him to be considerable, it makes him an educated man. Notwithstanding the defects of the social system and moral ideas of antiquity, the practice of the dicastery and the ecclesia raised the intellectual standard of an average Athenian citizen far beyond anything of which there is yet an example in any other mass of men, ancient or modern. The proofs of this are apparent in every page of our great historian of Greece; but we need scarcely look further than to the high quality of the addresses which their great orators deemed best calculated to act with effect on their understanding and will. A benefit of the same kind, though far less in degree, is produced on Englishmen of the lower middle class by their liability to be placed on juries and to serve parish offices, which, though it does not occur to so many, nor is so continuous, nor introduces them to so great a variety of elevated considerations as to admit of comparison with the public education which every citizen of Athens obtained from her democratic institutions, makes them nevertheless very different beings, in range of ideas and development of faculties, from those who have done nothing in their lives but drive a quill, or sell goods over a counter. Still more salutary is the moral part of the instruction afforded by the participation of the private citizen, if even rarely, in public functions. He is called upon, while so engaged, to weigh interests not his own; to be guided, in case of conflicting claims, by another rule than his private partialities; to apply, at every turn, principles and maxims which have for their reason of existence the general good; and he usually finds associated with him in the same work minds more familiarized than his own with these ideas and operations, whose study it will be to supply reason to his understanding, and stimulation to his feeling for the general good. He is made to feel himself one of the public, and whatever is their interest to be his interest. Where this school of public spirit does not exist, scarcely any sense is entertained that private persons, in no eminent social situation, owe any duties to society except to obey the laws and submit to the government. There is no unselfish sentiment of identification with the public. Every thought or feeling, either of interest or of duty, is absorbed in the individual and in the family. The man never thinks of any collective interest, of any objects to be pursued jointly with others, but only in competition with them, and in some measure at their expense. A neighbor, not being an ally or an associate, since he is never engaged in any common undertaking for joint benefit, is therefore only a rival. Thus even private morality suffers, while public is actually extinct. Were this the universal and only possible state of things, the utmost aspirations of the lawgiver or the moralist could only stretch to make the bulk of the community a flock of sheep innocently nibbling the grass side by side.

From these accumulated considerations, it is evident that the only government which can fully satisfy all the exigencies of the social state is one in which the whole people participate; that any participation, even in the smallest public function, is useful; that the participation should everywhere be as great as the general degree of improvement of the community will allow; and that nothing less can be ultimately desirable than the admission of all to a share in the sovereign power of the state. But since all cannot, in a community exceeding a single small town, participate personally in any but some very minor portions of the public business, it follows that the ideal type of a perfect government must be representative.

The New Forms of Control
Herbert Marcuse

A comfortable, smooth, reasonable, democratic unfreedom prevails in advanced industrial civilization, a token of technical progress. Indeed, what could be more rational than the suppression of individuality in the mechanization of socially necessary but painful performances; the concentration of individual enterprises in more effective, more productive corporations; the regulation of free competition among unequally equipped economic subjects; the curtailment of prerogatives and national sovereignties which impede the international organization of resources. That this technological order also involves a political and intellectual coordination may be a regrettable and yet promising development.

The rights and liberties which were such vital factors in the origins and earlier stages of industrial society yield to a higher stage of this society: they are losing their traditional rationale and content. Freedom of thought, speech, and conscience were—just as free enterprise, which they served to promote and protect—essentially *critical* ideas, designed to replace an obsolescent material and intellectual culture by a more productive and rational one. Once institutionalized, these rights and liberties shared the fate of the society of which they had become an integral part. The achievement cancels the premises.

To the degree to which freedom from want, the concrete substance of all freedom, is becoming a real possibility, the liberties which pertain to a state of lower productivity are losing their former content. Independence of thought, autonomy, and the right to political opposition are being deprived of their basic critical function in a society which seems increasingly capable of satisfying the needs of the individuals through the way in which it is organized. Such a society may justly demand acceptance of its principles and institutions,

From *One Dimensional Man.* Copyright © 1964 by Herbert Marcuse. Reprinted by permission of Beacon Press. Herbert Marcuse is an extremely influential writer on social and political philosophy. In his work, he has attempted to draw together important insights from Marx, Hegel and Freud. His other books include *Reason and Revolution* (1941), *Eros and Civilization* (1955), and *An Essay on Liberation* (1969). For a sharply critical study of Marcuse's thought, see *Herbert Marcuse: An Exposition and a Polemic* by Alasdair MacIntyre (New York: Viking Press, 1970), and the review of his book in *U.C.L.A. Law Review,* May 1971.

and reduce the opposition to the discussion and promotion of alternative policies *within* the status quo. In this respect, it seems to make little difference whether the increasing satisfaction of needs is accomplished by an authoritarian or a non-authoritarian system. Under the conditions of a rising standard of living, non-conformity with the system itself appears to be socially useless, and the more so when it entails tangible economic and political disadvantages and threatens the smooth operation of the whole. Indeed, at least in so far as the necessities of life are involved, there seems to be no reason why the production and distribution of goods and services should proceed through the competitive concurrence of individual liberties.

Freedom of enterprise was from the beginning not altogether a blessing. As the liberty to work or to starve, it spelled toil, insecurity, and fear for the vast majority of the population. If the individual were no longer compelled to prove himself on the market, as a free economic subject, the disappearance of this kind of freedom would be one of the greatest achievements of civilization. The technological processes of mechanization and standardization might release individual energy into a yet uncharted realm of freedom beyond necessity. The very structure of human existence would be altered; the individual would be liberated from the work world's imposing upon him alien needs and alien possibilities. The individual would be free to exert autonomy over a life that would be his own. If the productive apparatus could be organized and directed toward the satisfaction of the vital needs, its control might well be centralized; such control would not prevent individual autonomy, but render it possible.

This is a goal within the capabilities of advanced industrial civilization, the "end" of technological rationality. In actual fact, however, the contrary trend operates: the apparatus imposes its economic and political requirements for defense and expansion on labor time and free time, on the material and intellectual culture. By virtue of the way it has organized its technological base, contemporary industrial society tends to be totalitarian. For "totalitarian" is not only a terroristic political coordination of society, but also a non-terroristic economic-technical coordination which operates through the manipulation of needs by vested interests. It thus precludes the emergence of an effective opposition against the whole. Not only a specific form of government or party rule makes for totalitarianism, but also a specific system of production and distribution which may well be compatible with a "pluralism" of parties, newspapers, "countervailing powers," etc.

Today political power asserts itself through its power over the machine process and over the technological organization of the apparatus. The government of advanced and advancing industrial societies can maintain and secure itself only when it succeeds in mobilizing, organizing, and exploiting the technical, scientific, and mechanical productivity available to industrial civilization. And this productivity mobilizes society as a whole, above and beyond any particular individual or group interests. The brute fact that the machine's physical (only physical?) power surpasses that of the individual, and of any particular group of individuals, makes the machine the most effective political instrument in any society whose basic organization is that of the machine process. But the political trend may be reversed; essentially the power of the machine is only the stored-up and projected power of man. To the extent to which the work world is conceived of as a machine and mechanized accordingly, it becomes the *potential* basis of a new freedom for man.

Contemporary industrial civilization demonstrates that it has reached the stage at which "the free society" can no longer be adequately defined in the traditional terms of economic, political, and intellectual liberties, not because these liberties have become insignificant, but because they are too significant to be combined within the traditional forms. New modes of realization are needed, corresponding to the new capabilities of society.

Such new modes can be indicated only in negative terms because they would amount to the negation of the prevailing modes. Thus economic freedom would mean freedom *from* the economy—from being controlled by economic forces and relationships; freedom from the daily struggle for existence, from earning a living. Political freedom would mean liberation of the individuals *from* politics over which they have no effective control. Similarly, intellectual freedom would mean the restoration of individual thought now absorbed by mass communication and indoctrination, abolition of "public opinion" together with its makers. The unrealistic sound of these propositions is indicative, not of their utopian character, but of the strength of the forces which prevent their realization. The most effective and enduring form of warfare against liberation is the implanting of material and intellectual needs that perpetuate obsolete forms of the struggle for existence.

The intensity, the satisfaction and even the character of human needs, beyond the biological level, have always been preconditioned. Whether or not the possibility of doing or leaving, enjoying or destroying, possessing or rejecting something is seized as a *need* depends on whether or not it can be seen as desirable and necessary for the prevailing societal institutions and interests. In this sense, human needs are historical needs and, to the extent to which the society demands the repressive development of the individual, his needs themselves and their claim for satisfaction are subject to overriding critical standards.

We may distinguish both true and false needs. "False" are those which are superimposed upon the individual by particular social interests in his repression: the needs which perpetuate toil, aggressiveness, misery, and injustice. Their satisfaction might be most gratifying to the individual, but this happiness is not a condition which has to be maintained and protected if it serves to arrest the development of the ability (his own and others) to recognize the disease of the whole and grasp the chances of curing the disease. The result then is euphoria in unhappiness. Most of the prevailing needs to relax, to have fun, to behave and consume in accordance with the advertisements, to love and hate what others love and hate, belong to this category of false needs.

Such needs have a societal content and function which are determined by external powers over which the individual has no control; the development and satisfaction of these needs is heteronomous. No matter how much such needs may have become the individual's own, reproduced and fortified by the conditions of his existence; no matter how much he identifies himself with them and finds himself in their satisfaction, they continue to be what they were from the beginning—products of a society whose dominant interest demands repression.

The prevalence of repressive needs is an accomplished fact, accepted in ignorance and defeat, but a fact that must be undone in the interest of the happy individual as well as all those whose misery is the price of his satisfaction. The only needs that have an unqualified claim for satisfaction are the vital ones—nourishment, clothing, lodging at the attainable level of culture. The satisfaction of all these needs is the prerequisite for the realization of *all* needs, of the unsublimated as well as the sublimated ones.

For any consciousness and conscience, for any experience which does not accept the prevailing societal interest as the supreme law of thought and behavior, the established universe of needs and satisfactions is a fact to be questioned—questioned in terms of truth and falsehood. These terms are historical throughout, and their objectivity is historical. The judgment of needs and their satisfaction, under the given conditions, involves standards of *priority*— standards which refer to the optimal development of the individual, of all individuals, under the optimal utilization of the material and intellectual resources available to man. The resources are calculable. "Truth" and "falsehood" of needs designate objective conditions to the extent to which the universal satisfaction of vital needs and, beyond it, the progressive alleviation of toil and poverty, are universally valid standards. But as historical standards, they do not only vary according to area and stage of development, they also can be defined only in (greater or lesser) *contradiction* to the prevailing ones. What tribunal can possibly claim the authority of decision?

In the last analysis, the question of what are true and false needs must be answered by the individuals themselves, but only in the last analysis; that is, if and when they are free to give their own answer. As long as they are kept incapable of being autonomous, as long as they are indoctrinated and manipulated (down to their very instincts), their answer to this question cannot be taken as their own. By the same token, however, no tribunal can justly arrogate to itself the right to decide which needs should be developed and satisfied. Any such tribunal is reprehensible, although our revulsion does not do away with the question: how can the people who have been the object of effective and productive domination by themselves create the conditions of freedom?

The more rational, productive, technical, and total the repressive administration of society becomes, the more unimaginable the means and ways by which the administered individuals might break their servitude and seize their own liberation. To be sure, to impose Reason upon an entire society is a paradoxical and scandalous idea—although one might dispute the righteousness of a society which ridicules this idea while making its own population into objects of total administration. All liberation depends on the consciousness of servitude, and the emergence of this consciousness is always hampered by the predominance of needs and satisfactions which, to a great extent, have become the individual's own. The process always replaces one system of preconditioning by another; the optimal goal is the replacement of false needs by true ones, the abandonment of repressive satisfaction.

The distinguishing feature of advanced industrial society is its effective suffocation of those needs which demand liberation—liberation also from that which is tolerable and rewarding and comfortable—while it sustains and absolves the destructive power and repressive function of the affluent society. Here, the social controls exact the overwhelming need for the production and consumption of waste; the need for stupefying work where it is no longer a real necessity; the need for modes of relaxation which soothe and prolong this stupefaction; the need for maintaining such deceptive liberties as free competition at administered prices, a free press which censors itself, free choice between brands and gadgets.

Under the rule of a repressive whole, liberty can be made into a powerful instrument of domination. The range of choice open to an individual is not the decisive factor in determining the degree of human freedom, but *what* can be chosen and what *is* chosen by the individual. The criterion for free choice can never be an absolute one, but neither is it entirely relative. Free election of masters does not abolish the masters or the slaves. Free choice among a wide variety of goods and services does not signify freedom if these goods and services sustain social controls over a life of toil and fear—that is, if they sustain alienation. And the spontaneous reproduction of superimposed needs by the individual does not establish autonomy; it only testifies to the efficacy of the controls.

Our insistence on the depth and efficacy of these controls is open to the objection that we overrate greatly the indoctrinating power of the "media," and that by themselves the people would feel and satisfy the needs which are now imposed upon them. The objection misses the point. The preconditioning does not start with the mass production of radio and television and with the centralization of their control. The people enter this stage as preconditioned receptacles of long standing: the decisive difference is in the flattening out of the contrast (or conflict) between the given and the possible, between the satisfied and the unsatisfied needs. Here, the so-called equalization of class distinctions reveals its ideological function. If the worker and his boss enjoy the same television program and visit the same resort places, if the typist is as attractively made up as the daughter of her employer, if the Negro owns a Cadillac, if they all read the same newspaper, then this assimilation indicates not the disappearance of classes, but the extent to which the needs and satis-factions that serve the preservation of the Establishment are shared by the underlying population.

Indeed, in the most highly developed areas of contemporary society, the transplantation of social into individual needs is so effective that the difference between them seems to be purely theoretical. Can one really distinguish be-tween the mass media as instruments of information and entertainment, and as agents of manipulation and indoctrination? Between the automobile as nuisance and as convenience? Between the horrors and the comforts of functional archi-tecture? Between the work for national defense and the work for corporate gain? Between the private pleasure and the commercial and political utility involved in increasing the birth rate?

We are again confronted with one of the most vexing aspects of advanced industrial civilization: the rational character of its irrationality. Its productivity and efficiency, its capacity to increase and spread comforts, to turn waste into need, and destruction into construction, the extent to which this civilization transforms the object world into an extension of man's mind and body makes the very notion of alienation questionable. The people recognize themselves in their commodities; they find their soul in their automobile, hi-fi set, split-level home, kitchen equipment. The very mechanism which ties the individual to his society has changed, and social control is anchored in the new needs which it has produced.

The prevailing forms of social control are technological in a new sense. To be sure, the technical structure and efficacy of the productive and destruc-tive apparatus has been a major instrumentality for subjecting the population to the established social division of labor throughout the modern period. More-over, such integration has always been accompanied by more obvious forms of compulsion: loss of livelihood, the administration of justice, the police, the armed forces. It still is. But in the contemporary period, the technological con-trols appear to be the very embodiment of Reason for the benefit of all social groups and interests—to such an extent that all contradiction seems irrational and all counteraction impossible.

No wonder then that, in the most advanced areas of this civilization, the social controls have been introjected to the point where even the individual protest is affected at its roots. The intellectual and emotional refusal "to go along" appears neurotic and impotent. This is the socio-psychological aspect of the political event that marks the contemporary period: the passing of the historical forces which, at the preceding stage of industrial society, seemed to represent the possibility of new forms of existence.

But the term "introjection" perhaps no longer describes the way in which the individual by himself reproduces and perpetuates the external controls ex-ercised by his society. Introjection suggests a variety of relatively spontaneous processes by which a Self (Ego) transposes the "outer" into the "inner." Thus introjection implies the existence of an inner dimension distinguished from and even antagonistic to the external exigencies—an individual consciousness and an individual unconscious *apart from* public opinion and behavior.[1] The idea of "inner freedom" here has its reality: it designates the private space in which man may become and remain "himself."

Today this private space has been invaded and whittled down by technological reality. Mass production and mass distribution claim the *entire* individual, and industrial psychology has long since ceased to be confined to the factory. The manifold processes of introjection seem to be ossified in almost mechanical reactions. The result is, not adjustment but *mimesis:* an immediate identification of the individual with *his* society and, through it, with the society as a whole.

This immediate, automatic identification (which may have been characteristic of primitive forms of association) reappears in high industrial civilization; its new "immediacy," however, is the product of a sophisticated, scientific management and organization. In this process, the "inner" dimension of the mind in which opposition to the status quo can take root is whittled down. The loss of this dimension, in which the power of negative thinking—the critical power of Reason—is at home, is the ideological counterpart to the very material process in which advanced industrial society silences and reconciles the opposition. The impact of progress turns Reason into submission to the facts of life, and to the dynamic capability of producing more and bigger facts of the same sort of life. The efficiency of the system blunts the individuals' recognition that it contains no facts which do not communicate the repressive power of the whole. If the individuals find themselves in the things which shape their life, they do so, not by giving, but by accepting the law of things— not the law of physics but the law of their society.

I have just suggested that the concept of alienation seems to become questionable when the individuals identify themselves with the existence which is imposed upon them and have in it their own development and satisfaction. This identification is not illusion but reality. However, the reality constitutes a more progressive stage of alienation. The latter has become entirely objective; the subject which is alienated is swallowed up by its alienated existence. There is only one dimension, and it is everywhere and in all forms. The achievements of progress defy ideological indictment as well as justification; before their tribunal, the "false consciousness" of their rationality becomes the true consciousness.

This absorption of ideology into reality does not, however, signify the "end of ideology." On the contrary, in a specific sense advanced industrial culture is *more* ideological than its predecessor, inasmuch as today the ideology is in the process of production itself. In a provocative form, this proposition reveals the political aspects of the prevailing technological rationality. The productive apparatus and the goods and services which it produces "sell" or im-

---

[1] The change in the function of the family here plays a decisive role: its "socializing" functions are increasingly taken over by outside groups and media. See my *Eros and Civilization* (Boston: Beacon Press, 1955), pp. 96 ff.

pose the social system as a whole. The means of mass transportation and communication, the commodities of lodging, food, and clothing, the irresistible output of the entertainment and information industry carry with them prescribed attitudes and habits, certain intellectual and emotional reactions which bind the consumers more or less pleasantly to the producers and, through the latter, to the whole. The products indoctrinate and manipulate; they promote a false consciousness which is immune against its falsehood. And as these beneficial products become available to more individuals in more social classes, the indoctrination they carry ceases to be publicity; it becomes a way of life. It is a good way of life—much better than before—and as a good way of life, it militates against qualitative change. Thus emerges a pattern of *one-dimensional thought and behavior* in which ideas, aspirations, and objectives that, by their content, transcend the established universe of discourse and action are either repelled or reduced to terms of this universe. They are redefined by the rationality of the given system and of its quantitative extension.

The trend may be related to a development in scientific method: operationalism in the physical, behaviorism in the social sciences. The common feature is a total empiricism in the treatment of concepts; their meaning is restricted to the representation of particular operations and behavior. The operational point of view is well illustrated by P. W. Bridgman's analysis of the concept of length.

> We evidently know what we mean by length if we can tell what the length of any and every object is, and for the physicist nothing more is required. To find the length of an object, we have to perform certain physical operations. The concept of length is therefore fixed when the operations by which length is measured are fixed: that is, the concept of length involves as much and nothing more than the set of operations by which length is determined. In general, we mean by any concept nothing more than a set of operations; *the concept is synonymous with the corresponding set of operations.*[2]

Bridgman has seen the wide implications of this mode of thought for the society at large:

> To adopt the operational point of view involves much more than a mere restriction of the sense in which we understand "concept," but means a far-reaching change in all our habits of thought, in that we

---

[2] P. W. Bridgman, *The Logic of Modern Physics* (New York: Macmillan, 1928), p. 5. The operational doctrine has since been refined and qualified. Bridgman himself has extended the concept of "operation" to include the "paper-and-pencil" operations of the theorist (in Philipp J. Frank, *The Validation of Scientific Theories* [Boston: Beacon Press, 1954], Chap. II). The main impetus remains the same: it is "desirable" that the paper-and-pencil operations "be capable of eventual contact, although perhaps indirectly, with instrumental operations."

shall no longer permit ourselves to use as tools in our thinking concepts of which we cannot give an adequate account in terms of operations.[3]

Bridgman's prediction has come true. The new mode of thought is today the predominant tendency in philosophy, psychology, sociology, and other fields. Many of the most seriously troublesome concepts are being "eliminated" by showing that no adequate account of them in terms of operations or behavior can be given. The radical empiricist onslaught . . . thus provides the methodological justification for the debunking of the mind by the intellectuals —a positivism which, in its denial of the transcending elements of Reason, forms the academic counterpart of the socially required behavior.

Outside the academic establishment, the "far-reaching change in all our habits of thought" is more serious. It serves to coordinate ideas and goals with those exacted by the prevailing system, to enclose them in the system, and to repel those which are irreconcilable with the system. The reign of such a one-dimensional reality does not mean that materialism rules, and that the spiritual, metaphysical, and bohemian occupations are petering out. On the contrary, there is a great deal of "Worship together this week," "Why not try God," Zen, existentialism, and beat ways of life, etc. But such modes of protest and transcendence are no longer contradictory to the status quo and no longer negative. They are rather the ceremonial part of practical behaviorism, its harmless negation, and are quickly digested by the status quo as part of its healthy diet.

One-dimensional thought is systematically promoted by the makers of politics and their purveyors of mass information. Their universe of discourse is populated by self-validating hypotheses which, incessantly and monopolistically repeated, become hypnotic definitions or dictations. For example, "free" are the institutions which operate (and are operated on) in the countries of the Free World; other transcending modes of freedom are by definition either anarchism, communism, or propaganda. "Socialistic" are all encroachments on private enterprises not undertaken by private enterprise itself (or by government contracts), such as universal and comprehensive health insurance, or the protection of nature from all too sweeping commercialization, or the establishment of public services which may hurt private profit. This totalitarian logic of accomplished facts has its Eastern counterpart. There, freedom is the way of life instituted by a communist regime, and all other transcending modes of freedom are either capitalistic, or revisionist, or leftist sectarianism. In both camps, ideas are non-behavioral and subversive. The movement of thought is stopped at barriers which appear as the limits of Reason itself.

Such limitation of thought is certainly not new. Ascending modern rationalism, in its speculative as well as empirical form, shows a striking contrast between extreme critical radicalism in scientific and philosophic method on the

---

[3] P. W. Bridgman, *The Logic of Modern Physics,* p. 31.

one hand, and an uncritical quietism in the attitude toward established and functioning social institutions. Thus Descartes' *ego cogitans* was to leave the "great public bodies" untouched, and Hobbes held that "the present ought always to be preferred, maintained, and accounted best." Kant agreed with Locke in justifying revolution *if and when* it has succeeded in organizing the whole and in preventing subversion.

However, these accommodating concepts of Reason were always contradicted by the evident misery and injustice of the "great public bodies" and the effective, more or less conscious rebellion against them. Societal conditions existed which provoked and permitted real dissociation from the established state of affairs; a private as well as political dimension was present in which dissociation could develop into effective opposition, testing its strength and the validity of its objectives.

With the gradual closing of this dimension by the society, the self-limitation of thought assumes a larger significance. The interrelation between scientific-philosophical and societal processes, between theoretical and practical Reason, asserts itself "behind the back" of the scientists and philosophers. The society bars a whole type of oppositional operations and behavior; consequently, the concepts pertaining to them are rendered illusory or meaningless. Historical transcendence appears as metaphysical transcendence, not acceptable to science and scientific thought. The operational and behavioral point of view, practiced as a "habit of thought" at large, becomes the view of the established universe of discourse and action, needs and aspirations. The "cunning of Reason" works, as it so often did, in the interest of the powers that be. The insistence on operational and behavioral concepts turns against the efforts to free thought and behavior *from* the given reality and *for* the suppressed alternatives. Theoretical and practical Reason, academic and social behaviorism meet on common ground: that of an advanced society which makes scientific and technical progress into an instrument of domination.

"Progress" is not a neutral term; it moves toward specific ends, and these ends are defined by the possibilities of ameliorating the human condition. Advanced industrial society is approaching the stage where continued progress would demand the radical subversion of the prevailing direction and organization of progress. This stage would be reached when material production (including the necessary services) becomes automated to the extent that all vital needs can be satisfied while necessary labor time is reduced to marginal time. From this point on, technical progress would transcend the realm of necessity, where it served as the instrument of domination and exploitation which thereby limited its rationality; technology would become subject to the free play of faculties in the struggle for the pacification of nature and of society.

Such a state is envisioned in Marx's notion of the "abolition of labor." The term "pacification of existence" seems better suited to designate the historical alternative of a world which—through an international conflict which transforms and suspends the contradictions within the established societies—advances on the brink of a global war. "Pacification of existence" means the development of man's struggle with man and with nature, under conditions where the competing needs, desires, and aspirations are no longer organized by vested interests in domination and scarcity—an organization which perpetuates the destructive forms of this struggle.

Today's fight against this historical alternative finds a firm mass basis in the underlying population, and finds its ideology in the rigid orientation of thought and behavior to the given universe of facts. Validated by the accomplishments of science and technology, justified by its growing productivity, the status quo defies all transcendence. Faced with the possibility of pacification on the grounds of its technical and intellectual achievements, the mature industrial society closes itself against this alternative. Operationalism, in theory and practice, becomes the theory and practice of *containment*. Underneath its obvious dynamics, this society is a thoroughly static system of life: self-propelling in its oppressive productivity and in its beneficial coordination. Containment of technical progress goes hand in hand with its growth in the established direction. In spite of the political fetters imposed by the status quo, the more technology appears capable of creating the conditions for pacification, the more are the minds and bodies of man organized against this alternative.

The most advanced areas of industrial society exhibit throughout these two features: a trend toward consummation of technological rationality, and intensive efforts to contain this trend within the established institutions. Here is the internal contradiction of this civilization: the irrational element in its rationality. It is the token of its achievements. The industrial society which makes technology and science its own is organized for the ever-more-effective domination of man and nature, for the ever-more-effective utilization of its resources. It becomes irrational when the success of these efforts opens new dimensions of human realization. Organization for peace is different from organization for war; the institutions which served the struggle for existence cannot serve the pacification of existence. Life as an end is qualitatively different from life as a means.

Such a qualitatively new mode of existence can never be envisaged as the mere by-product of economic and political changes, as the more or less spontaneous effect of the new institutions which constitute the necessary prerequisite. Qualitative change also involves a change in the *technical* basis on which this society rests—one which sustains the economic and political institutions through which the "second nature" of man as an aggressive object of administration is stabilized. The techniques of industrialization are political techniques; as such, they prejudge the possibilities of Reason and Freedom.

To be sure, labor must precede the reduction of labor, and industrialization must precede the development of human needs and satisfactions. But as all freedom depends on the conquest of alien necessity, the realization of freedom depends on the *techniques* of this conquest. The highest productivity of labor can be used for the perpetuation of labor, and the most efficient industrialization can serve the restriction and manipulation of needs.

When this point is reached, domination—in the guise of affluence and liberty—extends to all spheres of private and public existence, integrates all authentic opposition, absorbs all alternatives. Technological rationality reveals its political character as it becomes the great vehicle of better domination, creating a truly totalitarian universe in which society and nature, mind and body are kept in a state of permanent mobilization for the defense of this universe.

11

The Liberation
of Women

Reading: John Stuart Mill,
"The Subjection of Women" (abridged)

From Father's hands I passed into yours. You arranged everything according to your tastes, and I acquired the same tastes, or I pretended to —I'm not sure which—a little of both, perhaps. Looking back on it all, it seems to me I've lived here like a beggar, from hand to mouth. I've lived by performing tricks for you, Torvald. But that's the way you wanted it. You and Father have done me a great wrong. You've prevented me from becoming a real person. . . . I believe that before all else I am a human being, just as you are—or at least that I should try and become one. . . . I can no longer be satisfied with what most people say—or what they write in books. I must think things out for myself —get clear about them.[1]

Nora's words as she leaves her husband in Henrik Ibsen's play *A Doll's House* strike a responsive chord in the consciousness of many women today. For many women are coming to see themselves as members of an oppressed class —legally oppressed in such matters as employment opportunity and salary

---

[1] From *Six Plays by Henrik Ibsen,* translated by Eva Le Gallienne (New York: Random House, copyright 1951, 53, 55, and 57). Passage used with permission of Random House.

and socially oppressed in a wide and complex variety of ways involving, among other things, a failure of society to take them seriously except as sexual objects and a corruption of their capacities to be autonomous persons by the social roles they are required to adopt for social survival.

Now these are complex and controversial claims, and there is no better foundation on which to build a discussion of them than John Stuart Mill's classic essay "The Subjection of Women." This essay is quite remarkable in the extent to which it anticipates much that is current in discussions of the topic today. As one would expect, Mill addresses himself to the "liberal" issue of equal legal and political rights for women. Here he argues largely as a utilitarian, claiming that the denial of such rights to women harms everyone in the long run. Women are harmed in an obvious way; society at large is harmed by not being able to profit from the kinds of contribution that emancipated women could make to science, culture, and politics. The basic argument, however, is simple: women, as mature adults affected in important ways by social policies, have as much right as anyone else to participate in the formation of those policies. One who denies this assumes a burden of proof which cannot, in Mill's judgment, be borne.

Mill also addresses himself to more "radical" issues than issues of civil rights. The basic problem facing women, he argues, is that they find it difficult to attain a position of personal autonomy—that is, to form an accurate picture of their own nature and desires and choices. (Marx would say they are *alienated* from themselves.) Their social role tends to corrupt their consciousness, making them think of themselves as inferior beings, as playthings or "dolls" for man's enjoyment, as fit for no tasks other than childraising and housework. Their problem, in the language of Marcuse, is that they have been led to develop a set of *artificial* needs which cut them off from their true natures. As Marx puts it: "It is not the consciousness of men that determines their social being but is rather their social being that determines their consciousness." In the case of women, Mill would argue, their social being has corrupted their consciousness. And thus their ultimate liberation will not be obtained until this corruption of consciousness has been overcome. We may well be living now through times when, at least for many women, this corrupt consciousness is being overcome. If so, these are times that Mill would welcome.

Mill, then, provides a start for a discussion of the liberation of women. It is only a start, of course, because there are many issues he does not raise—issues which perhaps, as a man, he could not even see. As one might expect of a nineteenth century Englishman, for example, he cannot quite bring himself to discuss directly the problems of *physical* sexuality. One gets the feeling that he rather disapproves of the whole business and wishes it would quietly go away. Important issues such as the detailed nature of the family structure and childraising in a society of liberated women are left generally unexplored. He is confident, however, that much that is now good and decent in relations of love and marriage between men and women will not disappear with the liberation of women. Indeed, he argues, these relations will radically be improved when the two partners have the courage to relate as equals.

Some people may object, on ideological grounds, to the inclusion of an essay on this topic written by a *man*. To this objection, three observations are relevant. First, Mill's being a man *may* have made him miss or misinterpret some aspects of women's oppression, but this is surely not *necessarily* so. His arguments can be and should be evaluated objectively, by both men and women, in terms of their soundness or lack of it and not in terms of their sexual genesis. Second, it is frequently the case that the intellectual leaders of any revolution will be drawn from the privileged and not from the oppressed class. Having profited from their position of privilege, they often have an intellectual perspective and luxury to think and write which is denied to the oppressed. Marx, remember, was not an industrial proletariat. Third, and finally, it is worth quoting a remark made by Elizabeth Cady Stanton, a woman well-known in the history of the women's movement in America, on reading Mill's essay in 1869:

> I lay the book down with a peace and joy I never felt before, for it is the first response from any man to show he is capable of seeing and feeling all the nice shades and degrees of woman's wrongs and the central point of her weakness and degradation.

Suggestions for Further Reading

Simone de Beauvoir, *The Second Sex* (New York: Bantam Books, 1961).

Shulamith Firestone, *The Dialectic of Sex* (New York: Bantam Books, 1971).

Juliet Mitchell, *Woman's Estate* (New York: Pantheon Books, 1971).

Robin Morgan, ed., *Sisterhood Is Powerful* (New York: Vintage Books, 1970).

The Subjection of Women (abridged)
John Stuart Mill

The object of this Essay is to explain as clearly as I am able, the grounds of an opinion which I have held from the very earliest period when I had formed any opinions at all on social or political matters, and which, instead of being weakened or modified, has been constantly growing stronger by the progress of reflection and the experience of life: That the principle which regulates the existing social relations between the two sexes—the legal sub-

This essay was first published in 1869.

ordination of one sex to the other—is wrong in itself, and now one of the chief hindrances to human improvement; and that it ought to be replaced by a principle of perfect equality, admitting no power or privilege on the one side, nor disability on the other.

The very words necessary to express the task I have undertaken, show how arduous it is. But it would be a mistake to suppose that the difficulty of the case must lie in the insufficiency or obscurity of the grounds of reason on which my conviction rests. The difficulty is that which exists in all cases in which there is a mass of feeling to be contended against. So long as an opinion is strongly rooted in the feelings, it gains rather than loses in stability by having a preponderating weight of argument against it. For if it were accepted as a result of argument, the refutation of the argument might shake the solidity of the conviction; but when it rests solely on feeling, the worse it fares in argumentative contest, the more persuaded its adherents are that their feeling must have some deeper ground, which the arguments do not reach; and while the feeling remains, it is always throwing up fresh intrenchments of argument to repair any breach made in the old. And there are so many causes tending to make the feelings connected with this subject the most intense and most deeply-rooted of all those which gather round and protect old institutions and customs, that we need not wonder to find them as yet less undermined and loosened than any of the rest by the progress of the great modern spiritual and social transition; nor suppose that the barbarisms to which men cling longest must be less barbarisms than those which they earlier shake off. . . .

The generality of a practice is in some cases a strong presumption that it is, or at all events once was, conducive to laudable ends. This is the case, when the practice was first adopted, or afterwards kept up, as a means to such ends, and was grounded on experience of the mode in which they could be most effectually attained. If the authority of men over women, when first established, had been the result of a conscientious comparison between different modes of constituting the government of society; if, after trying various other modes of social organization—the government of women over men, equality between the two, and such mixed and divided modes of government as might be invented—it had been decided, on the testimony of experience, that the mode in which women are wholly under the rule of men, having no share at all in public concerns, and each in private being under the legal obligation of obedience to the man with whom she has associated her destiny, was the arrangement most conducive to the happiness and well being of both; its general adoption might then be fairly thought to be some evidence that, at the time when it was adopted, it was the best: though even then the considerations which recommended it may, like so many other primeval social facts of the greatest importance, have subsequently, in the course of ages, ceased to exist. But the state of the case is in every respect the reverse of this. In the first place, the opinion in favour of the present system, which entirely subordinates the weaker sex to the stronger, rests upon theory only; for there never has been trial made of any other: so that experience, in the sense in which it is vulgarly opposed to theory, cannot be pretended to have pronounced any verdict. And in the second place, the adoption of this system of inequality never was the result of deliberation, or forethought, or any social ideas, or any notion whatever of what conduced to the benefit of humanity or the good order of society. It arose simply from the fact that from the very earliest twilight of human society, every woman (owing to the value attached to her by men, combined with her inferiority in muscular strength) was found in a state of bondage to some man. Laws and systems of polity always begin by recognising the relations they find already existing between individuals. They convert what was a mere physical fact into a legal right, give it the sanction of society, and principally aim at the substitution of public and organized means of asserting and protecting these rights, instead of the irregular and lawless conflict of physical strength. Those who had already been compelled to obedience became in this manner legally bound to it. Slavery, from being a mere affair of force between the master and the slave, became regularized and a matter of compact among the masters, who, binding themselves to one another for common protection, guaranteed by their collective strength the private possessions of each, including his slaves. In early times, the great majority of the male sex were slaves, as well as the whole of the female. And many ages elapsed, some of them ages of high cultivation, before any thinker was bold enough to question the rightfulness, and the absolute social necessity, either of the one slavery or of the other. By degrees such thinkers did arise: and (the general progress of society assisting) the slavery of the male sex has, in all the countries of Christian Europe at least (though, in one of them, only within the last few years) been at length abolished, and that of the female sex has been gradually changed into a milder form of dependence. But this dependence, as it exists at present, is not an original institution, taking a fresh start from considerations of justice and social expediency—it is the primitive state of slavery lasting on, through successive mitigations and modifications occasioned by the same causes which have softened the general manners, and brought all human relations more under the control of justice and the influence of humanity. It has not lost the taint of its brutal origin.[1] No presumption in its favour, therefore, can be drawn from the fact of its existence. The only such presumption which it could be supposed to have, must be grounded on

---

[1] I am far from pretending that wives are in general no better treated than slaves; but no slave is a slave to the same lengths, and in so full a sense of the word, as a wife is. Hardly any slave, except one immediately attached to the master's person, is a slave at all hours and all minutes; in general he has, like a soldier, his fixed task, and when it is done, or when he is off duty, he disposes, within certain limits, of his own time, and has a family life into which the master rarely intrudes. "Uncle Tom" under his first master had his own life in his "cabin," almost as much as any man whose work takes him away from home, is able to have in his own family. But it cannot be so with the wife. Above all, a female slave has (in Christian countries) an admitted right, and is considered under a moral obligation, to refuse to her master the last familiarity. Not so the wife: however brutal a tyrant she may unfortunately be chained to—though she may know that he hates her, though it may be his daily pleasure to torture her, and though she may feel it impossible not to loathe him—he can claim from her and enforce the lowest degradation of a human being, that of being made the instrument of an animal function contrary to her inclinations.

its having lasted till now, when so many other things which came down from the same odious source have been done away with. And this, indeed, is what makes it strange to ordinary ears, to hear it asserted that the inequality of rights between men and women has no other source than the law of the strongest.

That this statement should have the effect of a paradox, is in some respects creditable to the progress of civilization, and the improvement of the moral sentiments of mankind. We now live—that is to say, one or two of the most advanced nations of the world now live—in a state in which the law of the strongest seems to be entirely abandoned as the regulating principle of the world's affairs: nobody professes it, and, as regards most of the relations between human beings, nobody is permitted to practise it. When any one succeeds in doing so, it is under cover of some pretext which gives him the semblance of having some general social interest on his side. This being the ostensible state of things, people flatter themselves that the rule of mere force is ended; that the law of the strongest cannot be the reason of existence of anything which has remained in full operation down to the present time. However any of our present institutions may have begun, it can only, they think, have been preserved to this period of advanced civilization by a well-grounded feeling of its adaptation to human nature, and conduciveness to the general good. They do not understand the great vitality and durability of institutions which place right on the side of might; how intensely they are clung to; how the good as well as the bad propensities and sentiments of those who have power in their hands, become identified with retaining it; how slowly these bad institutions give way, one at a time, the weakest first, beginning with those which are least interwoven with the daily habits of life; and how very rarely those who have obtained legal power because they first had physical, have ever lost their hold of it until the physical power had passed over to the other side. Such shifting of the physical force not having taken place in the case of women; this fact, combined with all the peculiar and characteristic features of the particular case, made it certain from the first that this branch of the system of right founded on might, though softened in its most atrocious features at an earlier period than several of the others, would be the very last to disappear. It was inevitable that this one case of a social relation grounded on force, would survive through generations of institutions grounded on equal justice, an almost solitary exception to the general character of their laws and customs; but which, so long as it does not proclaim its own origin, and as discussion has not brought out its true character, is not felt to jar with modern civilization, any more than domestic slavery among the Greeks jarred with their notion of themselves as a free people. . . .

If people are mostly so little aware how completely, during the greater part of the duration of our species, the law of force was the avowed rule of general conduct, any other being only a special and exceptional consequence of peculiar ties—and from how very recent a date it is that the affairs of society in general have been even pretended to be regulated according to any moral law; as little do people remember or consider, how institutions and customs which never had any ground but the law of force, last on into ages and states of general opinion which never would have permitted their first establishment. Less than forty years ago, Englishmen might still by law hold human beings in bondage as saleable property: within the present century they might kidnap them and carry them off, and work them literally to death. This absolutely extreme case of the law of force, condemned by those who can tolerate almost every other form of arbitrary power, and which, of all others, presents features the most revolting to the feelings of all who look at it from an impartial position, was the law of civilized and Christian England within the memory of persons now living: and in one half of Anglo-Saxon America three or four years ago, not only did slavery exist, but the slave trade, and the breeding of slaves expressly for it, was a general practice between slave states. Yet not only was there a greater strength of sentiment against it, but, in England at least, a less amount either of feeling or of interest in favour of it, than of any other of the customary abuses of force: for its motive was the love of gain, unmixed and undisguised; and those who profited by it were a very small numerical fraction of the country, while the natural feeling of all who were not personally interested in it, was unmitigated abhorrence. So extreme an instance makes it almost superfluous to refer to any other: but consider the long duration of absolute monarchy. In England at present it is the almost universal conviction that military despotism is a case of the law of force, having no other origin or justification. Yet in all the great nations of Europe except England it either still exists, or has only just ceased to exist, and has even now a strong party favourable to it in all ranks of the people, especially among persons of station and consequence. Such is the power of an established system, even when far from universal; when not only in almost every period of history there have been great and well-known examples of the contrary system, but these have almost invariably been afforded by the most illustrious and most prosperous communities. In this case, too, the possessor of the undue power, the person directly interested in it, is only one person, while those who are subject to it and suffer from it are literally all the rest. The yoke is naturally and necessarily humiliating to all persons, except the one who is on the throne, together with, at most, the one who expects to succeed to it. How different are these cases from that of the power of men over women! I am not now prejudging the question of its justifiableness. I am showing how vastly more permanent it could not but be, even if not justifiable, than these other dominations which have nevertheless lasted down to our own time. Whatever gratification of pride there is in the possession of power, and whatever personal interest in its exercise, is in this case not confined to a limited class, but common to the whole male sex. Instead of being, to most of its supporters, a thing desirable chiefly in the abstract, or, like the political ends usually contended for by factions, of little private importance to any but the leaders; it comes home to the person and hearth of every male head of a family, and of every one who looks forward to being so. The clodhopper exercises, or is to exercise, his share of the power equally with the highest nobleman. And the case is that in which the desire of power is the strongest: for every one who desires power, desires it most over those who are nearest to him, with whom his life is passed, with whom he has most concerns in common, and in whom any independence of his authority is oftenest likely to interfere with his individual preferences. If, in the other cases specified, power manifestly grounded only on force, and having so much less to support them, are so slowly and with so much difficulty got rid of, much more must it be so with this, even if it rests on no better foundation than those. We must consider, too, that the possessors of the power have facilities in this case, greater than in any other, to prevent any uprising against it. Every one of the subjects lives under the very eye, and almost, it may be said, in the hands, of one of the masters—in closer intimacy with him than with any of her fellow-subjects; with no means of combining against him, no power of even locally overmastering him, and, on the other hand, with the strongest motives for seeking his favour and avoiding to give him offence. In struggles for political emancipation, everybody knows how often its champions are bought off by bribes, or daunted by terrors. In the case of women, each individual of the subject-class is in a chronic state of bribery and intimidation combined. In setting up the standard of resistance, a large number of the leaders, and still more of the followers, must make an almost complete sacrifice of the pleasures or the alleviations of their own individual lot. If ever any system of privilege and enforced subjection had its yoke tightly riveted on the necks of those who are kept down by it, this has. I have not yet shown that it is a wrong system: but every one who is capable of thinking on the subject must see that even if it is, it was certain to outlast all other forms of unjust authority. And when some of the grossest of the other forms still exist in many civilized countries, and have only recently been got rid of in others, it would be strange if that which is so much the deepest-rooted had yet been perceptibly shaken anywhere. There is more reason to wonder that the protests and testimonies against it should have been so numerous and so weighty as they are.

Some will object, that a comparison cannot fairly be made between the government of the male sex and the forms of unjust power which I have adduced in illustration of it, since these are arbitrary, and the effect of mere usurpation, while it on the contrary is natural. But was there ever any domination which did not appear natural to those who possessed it? There was a time when the division of mankind into two classes, a small one of masters and a numerous one of slaves, appeared, even to the most cultivated minds, to be a natural, and the only natural, condition of the human race. No less an intellect, and one which contributed no less to the progress of human thought, than Aristotle, held this opinion without doubt or misgiving; and rested it on the same premises on which the same assertion in regard to the dominion of men over women is usually based, namely that there are different natures among mankind, free natures, and slave natures; that the Greeks were of a free nature, the barbarian races of Thracians and Asiatics of a slave nature. But why need I go back to Aristotle? Did not the slaveowners of the Southern United States maintain the same doctrine, with all the fanaticism with which men cling to the theories that justify their passions and legitimate their personal interests? Did they not call heaven and earth to witness that the dominion of the white man over the black is natural, that the black race is by nature incapable of freedom, and marked out for slavery? some even going so far as to say that the freedom of manual labourers is an unnatural order of things anywhere. Again, the theorists of absolute monarchy have always affirmed it to be the only natural form of government; issuing from the patriarchal, which was the primitive and spontaneous form of society, framed on the model of the paternal, which is anterior to society itself, and, as they contend, the most natural authority of all. Nay, for that matter, the law of force itself, to those who could not plead any other, has always seemed the most natural of all grounds for the exercise of authority. Conquering races hold it to be Nature's own dictate that the conquered should obey the conquerors, or, as they euphoniously paraphrase it, that the feebler and more unwarlike races should submit to the braver and manlier. The smallest acquaintance with human life in the middle ages, shows how supremely natural the dominion of the feudal nobility over men of low condition appeared to the nobility themselves, and how unnatural the conception seemed, of a person of the inferior class claiming equality with them, or exercising authority over them. It hardly seemed less so to the class held in subjection. The emancipated serfs and burgesses, even in their most vigorous struggles, never made any pretension to a share of authority; they only demanded more or less of limitation to the power of tyrannizing over them. So true is it that unnatural generally means only uncustomary, and that everything which is usual appears natural. The subjection of women to men being a universal custom, any departure from it quite naturally appears unnatural. But how entirely, even in this case, the feeling is dependent on custom, appears by ample experience. Nothing so much astonishes the people of distant parts of the world, when they first learn anything about England, as to be told that it is under a queen: the thing seems to them so unnatural as to be almost incredible. To Englishmen this does not seem in the least degree unnatural, because they are used to it; but they do feel it unnatural that women should be soldiers or members of parliament. In the feudal ages, on the contrary, war and politics were not thought unnatural to women, because not unusual; it seemed natural that women of the privileged classes should be of manly character, inferior in nothing but bodily strength to their husbands and fathers. The independence of women seemed rather less unnatural to the Greeks than to other ancients, on account of the fabulous Amazons (whom they believed to be historical), and the partial example afforded by the Spartan women; who, though no less subordinate by law than in other Greek states, were more free in fact, and being trained to bodily exercises in the same manner with men, gave ample proof that they were not naturally disqualified for them. There can be little doubt that Spartan experience suggested to Plato, among many other of his doctrines, that of the social and political equality of the two sexes.

But, it will be said, the rule of men over women differs from all these others in not being a rule of force: it is accepted voluntarily; women make no complaint, and are consenting parties to it. In the first place, a great number of women do not accept it. Ever since there have been women able to make their sentiments known by their writings (the only mode of publicity which society permits to them), an increasing number of them have recorded protests against their present social condition: and recently many thousands of them, headed by the most eminent women known to the public, have petitioned Parliament for their admission to the Parliamentary Suffrage. The claim of women to be educated as solidly, and in the same branches of knowledge, as men, is urged with growing intensity, and with a great prospect of success; while the demand for their admission into professions and occupations hitherto closed against them, becomes every year more urgent. Though there are not in this country, as there are in the United States, periodical Conventions and an organized party to agitate for the Rights of Women, there is a numerous and active Society organized and managed by women, for the more limited object of obtaining the political franchise. Nor is it only in our own country and in America that women are beginning to protest, more or less collectively, against the disabilities under which they labour. France, and Italy, and Switzerland, and Russia now afford examples of the same thing. How many more women there are who silently cherish similar aspirations, no one can possibly know; but there are abundant tokens how many *would* cherish them, were they not so strenuously taught to repress them as contrary to the proprieties of their sex. It must be remembered, also, that no enslaved class ever asked for complete liberty at once. When Simon de Montfort called the deputies of the commons to sit for the first time in Parliament, did any of them dream of demanding that an assembly, elected by their constituents, should make and destroy ministries, and dictate to the king in affairs of state? No such thought entered into the imagination of the most ambitious of them. The nobility had already these pretensions; the commons pretended to nothing but to be exempt from arbitrary taxation, and from the gross individual oppression of the king's officers. It is a political law of nature that those who are under any power of ancient origin, never begin by complaining of the power itself, but only of its oppressive exercise. There is never any want of women who complain of ill usage by their husbands. There would be infinitely more, if complaint were not the greatest of all provocatives to a repetition and increase of the ill usage. It is this which frustrates all attempts to maintain the power but protect the woman against its abuses. In no other case (except that of a child) is the person who has been proved judicially to have suffered an injury, replaced under the physical power of the culprit who inflicted it. Accordingly wives, even in the most extreme and protracted cases of bodily ill usage, hardly ever dare avail themselves of the laws made for their protection: and if, in a moment of irrepressible indignation, or by the interference of neighbours, they are induced to do so, their whole effort afterwards is to disclose as little as they can, and to beg off their tyrant from his merited chastisement.

All causes, social and natural, combine to make it unlikely that women should be collectively rebellious to the power of men. They are so far in a position different from all other subject classes, that their masters require something more from them than actual service. Men do not want solely the obedience of women, they want their sentiments. All men, except the most brutish, desire to have, in the woman most nearly connected with them, not a forced slave but a willing one, not a slave merely, but a favourite. They have therefore put everything in practice to enslave their minds. The masters of all other slaves rely, for maintaining obedience, on fear; either fear of themselves, or religious fears. The masters of women wanted more than simple obedience, and they turned the whole force of education to effect their purpose. All women are brought up from the very earliest years in the belief that their ideal of character is the very opposite to that of men; not self-will, and government by self-control, but submission, and yielding to the control of others. All the moralities tell them that it is the duty of women, and all the current sentimentalities that it is their nature, to live for others; to make complete abnegation of themselves, and to have no life but in their affections. And by their affections are meant the only ones they are allowed to have— those to the men with whom they are connected, or to the children who constitute an additional and indefeasible tie between them and a man. When we put together three things—first, the natural attraction between opposite sexes; secondly, the wife's entire dependence on the husband, every privilege or pleasure she has being either his gift, or depending entirely on his will; and lastly, that the principal object of human pursuit, consideration, and all objects of social ambition, can in general be sought or obtained by her only through him, it would be a miracle if the object of being attractive to men had not become the polar star of feminine education and formation of character. And, this great means of influence over the minds of women having been acquired, an instinct of selfishness made men avail themselves of it to the utmost as a means of holding women in subjection, by representing to them meekness, submissiveness, and resignation of all individual will into the hands of a man, as an essential part of sexual attractiveness. Can it be doubted that any of the other yokes which mankind have succeeded in breaking, would have subsisted till now if the same means had existed, and had been as sedulously used, to bow down their minds to it? If it had been made the object of the life of every young plebeian to find personal favour in the eyes of some patrician, of every young serf with some seigneur; if domestication with him, and a share of his personal affections, had been held out as the prize which they all should look out for, the most gifted and aspiring being able to reckon on the most desirable prizes; and if, when this prize had been obtained, they had been shut out by a wall of brass from all interests not centering in him, all feelings and desires but those which he shared or inculcated; would not serfs and seigneurs, plebeians and patricians, have been as broadly distinguished at this day as men and women are? and would not all but a thinker here and there, have believed the distinction to be a fundamental and unalterable fact in human nature?

The preceding considerations are amply sufficient to show that custom, however universal it may be, affords in this case no presumption, and ought not to create any prejudice, in favour of the arrangements which place women in social and political subjection to men. But I may go farther, and maintain that the course of history, and the tendencies of progressive human society, afford not only no presumption in favour of this system of inequality of rights, but a strong one against it; and that, so far as the whole course of human improvement up to this time, the whole stream of modern tendencies, warrants any inference on the subject, it is, that this relic of the past is discordant with the future, and must necessarily disappear. . . .

At present, in the more improved countries, the disabilities of women are the only case, save one, in which laws and institutions take persons at their birth, and ordain that they shall never in all their lives be allowed to compete for certain things. The one exception is that of royalty. Persons still are born to the throne; no one, not of the reigning family, can ever occupy it, and no one even of that family can, by any means but the course of hereditary succession, attain it. All other dignities and social advantages are open to the whole male sex: many indeed are only attainable by wealth, but wealth may be striven for by any one, and is actually obtained by many men of the very humblest origin. The difficulties, to the majority, are indeed insuperable without the aid of fortunate accidents; but no male human being is under any legal ban: neither law nor opinion superadd artificial obstacles to the natural ones. Royalty, as I have said, is excepted: but in this case every one feels it to be an exception—an anomaly in the modern world, in marked opposition to its customs and principles, and to be justified only by extraordinary special expediencies, which, though individuals and nations differ in estimating their weight, unquestionably do in fact exist. But in this exceptional case, in which a high social function is, for important reasons, bestowed on birth instead of being put up to competition, all free nations contrive to adhere in substance to the principle from which they nominally derogate; for they circumscribe this high function by conditions avowedly intended to prevent the person to whom it ostensibly belongs from really performing it; while the person by whom it is performed, the responsible minister, does obtain the post by a competition from which no full-grown citizen of the male sex is legally excluded. The disabilities, therefore, to which women are subject from the mere fact of their birth, are the solitary examples of the kind in modern legislation. In no instance except this, which comprehends half the human race, are the higher social functions closed against any one by a fatality of birth which no exertions, and no change of circumstances, can overcome; for even religious disabilities (besides that in England and in Europe they have practically almost ceased to exist) do not close any career to the disqualified person in case of conversion.

The social subordination of women thus stands out an isolated fact in modern social institutions; a solitary breach of what has become their fundamental law; a single relic of an old world of thought and practice exploded in everything else, but retained in the one thing of most universal interest; as if a gigantic dolmen, or a vast temple of Jupiter Olympus, occupied the site of St. Paul's and received daily worship, while the surrounding Christian churches were only resorted to on fasts and festivals. This entire discrepancy between one social fact and all those which accompany it, and the radical opposition between its nature and the progressive movement which is the boast of the modern world, and which has successively swept away everything else of an analogous character, surely affords, to a conscientious observer of human tendencies, serious matter for reflection. It raises a prima facie presumption on the unfavourable side, far outweighing any which custom and usage could in such circumstances create on the favourable; and should at least suffice to make this, like the choice between republicanism and royalty, a balanced question.

The least that can be demanded is, that the question should not be considered as prejudged by existing fact and existing opinion, but open to discussion on its merits, as a question of justice and expediency: the decision on this, as on any of the other social arrangements of mankind, depending on what an enlightened estimate of tendencies and consequences may show to be most advantageous to humanity in general, without distinction of sex. And the discussion must be a real discussion, descending to foundations, and not resting satisfied with vague and general assertions. It will not do, for instance, to assert in general terms, that the experience of mankind has pronounced in favour of the existing system. Experience cannot possibly have decided between two courses, so long as there has only been experience of one. If it be said that the doctrine of the equality of the sexes rests only on theory, it must be remembered that the contrary doctrine also has only theory to rest upon. All that is proved in its favour by direct experience, is that mankind have been able to exist under it, and to attain the degree of improvement and prosperity which we now see; but whether that prosperity has been attained sooner, or is now greater, than it would have been under the other system, experience does not say. On the other hand, experience does say, that every step in improvement has been so invariably accompanied by a step made in raising the social position of women, that historians and philosophers have been led to adopt their elevation or debasement as on the whole the surest test and most correct measure of the civilization of a people or an age. Through all the progressive period of human history, the condition of women has been approaching nearer to equality with men. This does not of itself prove that the assimilation must go on to complete equality; but it assuredly affords some presumption that such is the case.

Neither does it avail anything to say that the *nature* of the two sexes adapts them to their present functions and position, and renders these appropriate to them. Standing on the ground of common sense and the constitution of the human mind, I deny that any one knows, or can know, the nature of the two sexes, as long as they have only been seen in their present relation to one another. If men had ever been found in society without women, or women without men, or if there had been a society of men and women in which the women were not under the control of the men, something might have been positively known about the mental and moral differences which may be inherent in the nature of each. What is now called the nature of women is an eminently artificial thing—the result of forced repression in some directions, unnatural stimulation in others. It may be asserted without scruple, that no other class of dependents have had their character so entirely distorted from its natural proportions by their relation with their masters; for, if conquered and slave races have been, in some respects, more forcibly repressed, whatever in them has not been crushed down by an iron heel has generally been let alone, and if left with any liberty of development, it has developed itself according to its own laws; but in the case of women, a hot-house and stove cultivation has always been carried on of some of the capabilities of their nature, for the benefit and pleasure of their masters. Then, because certain products of the general vital force sprout luxuriantly and reach a great development in this heated atmosphere and under this active nurture and watering, while other shoots from the same root, which are left outside in the wintry air, with ice purposely heaped all round them, have a stunted growth, and some are burnt off with fire and disappear; men, with that inability to recognise their own work which distinguishes the unanalytic mind, indolently believe that the tree grows of itself in the way they have made it grow, and that it would die if one half of it were not kept in a vapour bath and the other half in the snow.

Of all difficulties which impede the progress of thought, and the formation of well-grounded opinions on life and social arrangements, the greatest is now the unspeakable ignorance and inattention of mankind in respect to the influences which form human character. Whatever any portion of the human species now are, or seem to be, such, it is supposed, they have a natural tendency to be: even when the most elementary knowledge of the circumstances in which they have been placed, clearly points out the causes that made them what they are. Because a cottier deeply in arrears to his landlord is not industrious, there are people who think that the Irish are naturally idle. Because constitutions can be overthrown when the authorities appointed to execute them turn their arms against them, there are people who think the French incapable of free government. Because the Greeks cheated the Turks, and the Turks only plundered the Greeks, there are persons who think that the Turks are naturally more sincere: and because women, as is often said, care nothing about politics except their personalities, it is supposed that the general good is naturally less interesting to women than to men. History, which is now so much better understood than formerly, teaches another lesson: if only by showing the extraordinary susceptibility of human nature to external influences, and the extreme variableness of those of its manifestations which are supposed to be most universal and uniform. But in history, as in travelling, men usually see only what they already had in their own minds; and few learn much from history, who do not bring much with them to its study.

Hence, in regard to that most difficult question, what are the natural differences between the two sexes—a subject on which it is impossible in the present state of society to obtain complete and correct knowledge—while almost everybody dogmatizes upon it, almost all neglect and make light of the only means by which any partial insight can be obtained into it. This is an analytic study of the most important department of psychology, the laws of the influence of circumstances on character. For, however great and apparently ineradicable the moral and intellectual differences between men and women might be, the evidence of their being natural differences could only be negative. Those only could be inferred to be natural which could not possibly be artificial—the residuum, after deducting every characteristic of either sex which can admit of being explained from education or external circumstances. The profoundest knowledge of the laws of the formation of character is indispensable to entitle any one to affirm even that there is any difference, much more what the difference is, between the two sexes considered as moral and rational beings; and since no one, as yet, has that knowledge (for there is hardly any subject which, in proportion to its importance, has been so little studied), no one is thus far entitled to any positive opinion on the subject. Conjectures are all that can at present be made; conjectures more or less probable, according as more or less authorized by such knowledge as we yet have of the laws of psychology, as applied to the formation of character. . . .

I have dwelt so much on the difficulties which at present obstruct any real knowledge by men of the true nature of women, because in this as in so many other things "opinio copiæ inter maximas causas inopiæ est"; and there is little chance of reasonable thinking on the matter, while people flatter themselves that they perfectly understand a subject of which most men know absolutely nothing, and of which it is at present impossible that any man, or all men taken together, should have knowledge which can qualify them to lay down the law to women as to what is, or is not, their vocation. Happily, no such knowledge is necessary for any practical purpose connected with the position of women in relation to society and life. For, according to all the principles involved in modern society, the question rests with women themselves—to be decided by their own experience, and by the use of their own faculties. There are no means of finding what either one person or many can do, but by trying—and no means by which any one else can discover for them what it is for their happiness to do or leave undone.

One thing we may be certain of—that what is contrary to women's nature to do, they never will be made to do by simply giving their nature free play. The anxiety of mankind to interfere in behalf of nature, for fear lest nature should not succeed in effecting its purpose, is an altogether unnecessary solicitude. What women by nature cannot do, it is quite superfluous to forbid them from doing. What they can do, but not so well as the men who are their competitors, competition suffices to exclude them from; since nobody asks for protective duties and bounties in favour of women; it is only asked that the present bounties and protective duties in favour of men should be recalled. If women have a greater natural inclination for some things than for others, there is no need of laws or social inculcation to make the majority of them do the former in preference to the latter. Whatever women's services are most wanted for, the free play of competition will hold out the strongest induce-ments to them to undertake. And, as the words imply, they are most wanted for the things for which they are most fit; by the apportionment of which to them, they of his hire, impressment is no longer advocated. Those who attempt to force women into marriage by closing all other doors against them, lay themselves open to a similar retort. If they mean what they say, their opinion must evidently be, that men do not render the married condition so desirable to women, as to induce them to accept it for its own recommendations. It is not a sign of one's thinking the boon one offers very attractive, when one allows only Hobson's choice, "that or none." And here, I believe, is the clue to the feelings of those men, who have a real antipathy to the equal freedom of women. I believe they are afraid, not lest women should be unwilling to marry, for I do not think that any one in reality has that apprehension; but lest they should insist that marriage should be on equal conditions; lest all women of spirit and capacity should prefer doing almost anything else, not in their own eyes degrading, rather than marry, when marrying is giving them-selves a master, and a master too of all their earthly possessions. And truly, if this consequence were necessarily incident to marriage, I think that the ap-prehension would be very well founded. I agree in thinking it probable that few women, capable of anything else, would, unless under an irresistible *entrainement,* rendering them for the time insensible to anything but itself, choose such a lot, when any other means were open to them of filling a con-ventionally honourable place in life: and if men are determined that the law of marriage shall be a law of despotism, they are quite right, in point of mere policy, in leaving to women only Hobson's choice. But, in that case, all that has been done in the modern world to relax the chain on the minds of women, has been a mistake. They never should have been allowed to receive a literary education. Women who read, much more women who write, are, in the existing constitution of things, a contradiction and a disturbing element: and it was wrong to bring women up with any acquirements but those of an odalisque, or of a domestic servant. . . .

But how, it will be asked, can any society exist without government? In a family, as in a state, some one person must be the ultimate ruler. Who shall decide when married people differ in opinion? Both cannot have their way, yet a decision one way or the other must be come to.

It is not true that in all voluntary association between two people, one of them must be absolute master: still less that the law must determine which of them it shall be. The most frequent case of voluntary association, next to marriage, is partnership in business: and it is not found or thought necessary to enact that in every partnership, one partner shall have entire control over the concern, and the others shall be bound to obey his orders. No one would enter into partnership on terms which would subject him to the responsibilities of a principal, with only the powers and privileges of a clerk or agent. If the law dealt with other contracts as it does with marriage, it would ordain that one partner should administer the common business as if it was his private concern; that the others should have only delegated powers; and that this one should be designated by some general presumption of law, for example as being the eldest. The law never does this: nor does experience show it to be necessary that any theoretical inequality of power should exist between the partners, or that the partnership should have any other conditions than what they may themselves appoint by their articles of agreement. Yet it might seem that the exclusive power might be conceded with less danger to the rights and interests of the inferior, in the case of partnership than in that of marriage, since he is free to cancel the power by withdrawing from the connexion. The wife has no such power, and even if she had, it is almost always desirable that she should try all measures before resorting to it.

It is quite true that things which have to be decided every day, and cannot adjust themselves gradually, or wait for a compromise, ought to depend on one will: one person must have their sole control. But it does not follow that this should always be the same person. The natural arrangement is a division of powers between the two; each being absolute in the executive branch of their own department, and any change of system and principle requiring the consent of both. The division neither can nor should be pre-established by the law, since it must depend on individual capacities and suitabilities. If the two persons chose, they might pre-appoint it by the marriage contract, as pecuniary arrangements are now often pre-appointed. There would seldom be any difficulty in deciding such things by mutual consent, unless the marriage was one of those unhappy ones in which all other things as well as this, become subjects of bickering and dispute. The division of rights would naturally follow the division of duties and functions; and that is already made by consent, or at all events not by law, but by general custom, modified and modifiable at the pleasure of the persons concerned.

The real practical decision of affairs, to whichever may be given the legal authority, will greatly depend, as it even now does, upon comparative qualifications. The mere fact that he is usually the eldest, will in most cases give the preponderance to the man; at least until they both attain a time of life at which the difference in their years is of no importance. There will naturally also be a more potential voice on the side, whichever it is, that brings the means of support. Inequality from this source does not depend on the law of marriage, but on the general conditions of human society, as now constituted. The influence of mental superiority, either general or special, and of superior decision of character, will necessarily tell for much. It always does so at present.

And this fact shows how little foundation there is for the apprehension that the powers and responsibilities of partners in life (as of partners in business), cannot be satisfactorily apportioned by agreement between themselves. They always are so apportioned, except in cases in which the marriage institution is a failure. Things never come to an issue of downright power on one side, and obedience on the other, except where the connexion altogether has been a mistake, and it would be a blessing to both parties to be relieved from it. Some may say that the very thing by which an amicable settlement of differences becomes possible, is the power of legal compulsion known to be in reserve; as people submit to an arbitration because there is a court of law in the background, which they know that they can be forced to obey. But to make the cases parallel, we must suppose that the rule of the court of law was, not to try the cause, but to give judgment always for the same side, suppose the defendant. If so, the amenability to it would be a motive with the plaintiff to agree to almost any arbitration, but it would be just the reverse with the defendant. The despotic power which the law gives to the husband may be a reason to make the wife assent to any compromise by which power is practically shared between the two, but it cannot be the reason why the husband does. That there is always among decently conducted people a practical compromise, though one of them at least is under no physical or moral necessity of making it, shows that the natural motives which lead to a voluntary adjustment of the united life of two persons in a manner acceptable to both, do on the whole, except in unfavourable cases, prevail. The matter is certainly not improved by laying down as an ordinance of law, that the superstructure of free government shall be raised upon a legal basis of despotism on one side and subjection on the other, and that every concession which the despot makes may, at his mere pleasure, and without any warning, be recalled. Besides that no freedom is worth much when held on so precarious a tenure, its conditions are not likely to be the most equitable when the law throws so prodigious a weight into one scale; when the adjustment rests between two persons one of whom is declared to be entitled to everything, the other not only entitled to nothing except during the good pleasure of the first, but under the strongest moral and religious obligation not to rebel under any excess of oppression.

A pertinacious adversary, pushed to extremities, may say, that husbands indeed are willing to be reasonable, and to make fair concessions to their partners without being compelled to it, but that wives are not: that if allowed any rights of their own, they will acknowledge no rights at all in any one else, and never will yield in anything, unless they can be compelled, by the man's mere authority, to yield in everything. This would have been said by many persons some generations ago, when satires on women were in vogue, and men thought it a clever thing to insult women for being what men made them. But it will be said by no one now who is worth replying to. It is not the doctrine of the present day that women are less susceptible of good feeling, and consideration for those with whom they are united by the strongest ties, than men are. On the contrary, we are perpetually told that women are better than men, by those who are totally opposed to treating them as if they were as good; so that the saying has passed into a piece of tiresome cant, intended to put a complimentary face upon an injury, and resembling those celebrations of royal clemency which, according to Gulliver, the king of Lilliput always prefixed to his most sanguinary decrees. If women are better than men in anything, it surely is in individual self-sacrifice for those of their own family. But I lay little stress on this, so long as they are universally taught that they are born and created for self-sacrifice. I believe that equality of rights would abate the exaggerated self-abnegation which is the present artificial ideal of feminine character, and that a good woman would not be more self-sacrificing than the best man: but on the other hand, men would be much more unselfish and self-sacrificing than at present, because they would no longer be taught to worship their own will as such a grand thing that it is actually the law for another rational being. There is nothing which men so easily learn as this self-worship: all privileged persons, and all privileged classes, have had it. The more we descend in the scale of humanity, the intenser it is; and most of all in those who are not, and can never expect to be, raised above any one except an unfortunate wife and children. The honourable exceptions are proportionally fewer than in the case of almost any other human infirmity. Philosophy and religion, instead of keeping it in check, are generally suborned to defend it; and nothing controls it but that practical feeling of the equality of human beings, which is the theory of Christianity, but which Christianity will never practically teach, while it sanctions institutions grounded on an arbitrary preference of one human being over another. . . .

After what has been said respecting the obligation of obedience, it is almost superfluous to say anything concerning the more special point included in the general one—a woman's right to her own property; for I need not hope that this treatise can make any impression upon those who need anything to convince them that a woman's inheritance or gains ought to be as much her own after marriage as before. The rule is simple: whatever would be the husband's or wife's if they were not married, should be under their exclusive control during marriage; which need not interfere with the power to tie up property by settlement, in order to preserve it for children. Some people are sentimentally shocked at the idea of a separate interest in money matters, as inconsistent with the ideal fusion of two lives into one. For my own part, I am one of the strongest supporters of community of goods, when resulting from an entire unity of feeling in the owners, which makes all things common between them. But I have no relish for a community of goods resting on the doctrine, that what is mine is yours but what is yours is not mine; and I should prefer to decline entering into such a compact with any one, though I were myself the person to profit by it. . . .

The *power* of earning is essential to the dignity of a woman, if she has not independent property. But if marriage were an equal contract, not implying the obligation of obedience; if the connexion were no longer enforced to the oppression of those to whom it is purely a mischief, but a separation, on just terms (I do not now speak of a divorce), could be obtained by any woman who was morally entitled to it; and if she would then find all honourable employments as freely open to her as to men; it would not be necessary for her protection, that during marriage she should make this particular use of her faculties. Like a man when he chooses a profession, so, when a woman marries, it may in general be understood that she makes choice of the management of a household, and the bringing up of a family, as the first call upon her exertions, during as many years of her life as may be required for the purpose; and that she renounces, not all other objects and occupations, but all which are not consistent with the requirements of this. The actual exercise, in a habitual or systematic manner, of outdoor occupations, or such as cannot be carried on at home, would by this principle be practically interdicted to the greater number of married women. But the utmost latitude ought to exist for the adaptation of general rules to individual suitabilities; and there ought to be nothing to prevent faculties exceptionally adapted to any other pursuit, from obeying their vocation notwithstanding marriage: due provision being made for supplying otherwise any falling-short which might become inevitable, in her full performance of the ordinary functions of mistress of a family. These things, if once opinion were rightly directed on the subject, might with perfect safety be left to be regulated by opinion, without any interference of law. . . .

On the other point which is involved in the just equality of women, their admissibility to all the functions and occupations hitherto retained as the monopoly of the stronger sex, I should anticipate no difficulty in convincing any one who has gone with me on the subject of the equality of women in the family. I believe that their disabilities elsewhere are only clung to in order to maintain their subordination in domestic life; because the generality of the male sex cannot yet tolerate the idea of living with an equal. Were it not for that, I think that almost every one, in the existing state of opinion in politics and political economy, would admit the injustice of excluding half the human race from the greater number of lucrative occupations, and from almost all high social functions; ordaining from their birth either that they are not, and cannot by any possibility become, fit for employments which are legally open to the stupidest and basest of the other sex, or else that however fit they may be, those employments shall be interdicted to them, in order to be preserved for the exclusive benefit of males. In the last two centuries, when (which was seldom the case) any reason beyond the mere existence of the fact was thought to be required to justify the disabilities of women, people seldom assigned as a reason their inferior mental capacity; which, in times when there was a real trial of personal faculties (from which all women were not excluded) in the struggles of public life, no one really believed in. The reason given in those days was not women's unfitness, but the interest of society, by which was meant the interest of men: just as the *raison d'état,* meaning the convenience of the government, and the support of existing authority, was deemed a sufficient explanation and excuse for the most flagitious crimes. In the present day, power holds a smoother language, and whomsoever it oppresses, always pretends to do so for their own good: accordingly, when anything is forbidden to women, it is thought necessary to say, and desirable to believe, that they are incapable of doing it, and that they depart from their real path of success and happiness when they aspire to it. But to make this reason plausible (I do not say valid), those by whom it is urged must be prepared to carry it to a much greater length than any one ventures to do in the face of present experience. It is not sufficient to maintain that women on the average are less gifted than men on the average, with certain of the higher mental faculties, or that a smaller number of women than of men are fit for occupations and functions of the highest intellectual character. It is necessary to maintain that no women at all are fit for them, and that the most eminent women are inferior in mental faculties to the most mediocre of the men on whom those functions at present devolve. For if the performance of the function is decided either by competition, or by any mode of choice which secures regard to the public interest, there needs to be no apprehension that any important employments will fall into the hands of women inferior to average men, or to the average of their male competitors. The only result would be that there would be fewer women than men in such employments; a result certain to happen in any case, if only from the preference always likely to be felt by the majority of women for the one vocation in which there is nobody to compete with them. Now, the most determined depreciator of women will not venture to deny, that when we add the experience of recent times to that of ages past, women, and not a few merely, but many women, have proved themselves capable of everything, perhaps without a single exception, which is done by men, and of doing it successfully and creditably. The utmost that can be said is, that there are many things which none of them have succeeded in doing as well as they have been done by some men—many in which they have not reached the very highest rank. But there are extremely few, dependent only on mental faculties, in which they have not attained the rank next to the highest. Is not this enough, and much more than enough, to make it a tyranny to them, and a detriment to society, that they should not be allowed to compete with men for the exercise of these functions? Is it not a mere truism to say, that such functions are often filled by men far less fit for them than numbers of women, and who would be beaten by women in any fair field of competition? What difference does it make that there may be men somewhere, fully employed about other things, who may be still better qualified for the things in question than these women? Does not this take place in all competitions? Is there so great a superfluity of men fit for high duties, that society can afford to reject the service of any competent person? Are we so certain of always finding a man made to our hands for any duty or function of social importance which falls vacant, that we lose nothing by putting a ban upon one-half of mankind, and refusing beforehand to make their faculties available, however distinguished they may be? And even if we could do without them, would it be consistent with justice to refuse to them their fair share of honour and distinction, or to deny to them the equal moral right of all human beings to choose their occupation (short of injury to others) according to their own preferences, at their own risk? Nor is the injustice confined to them: it is shared by those who are in a position to benefit by their services. To ordain that any kind of persons shall not be physicians, or shall not be advocates, or shall not be members of parliament, is to injure not them only, but all who employ physicians or advocates, or elect members of parliament, and who are deprived of the stimulating effect of greater competition on the exertions of the competitors, as well as restricted to a narrower range of individual choice.

It will perhaps be sufficient if I confine myself, in the details of my argument, to functions of a public nature: since, if I am successful as to those, it probably will be readily granted that women should be admissible to all other occupations to which it is at all material whether they are admitted or not. And here let me begin by marking out one function, broadly distinguished from all others, their right to which is entirely independent of any question which can be raised concerning their faculties. I mean the suffrage, both parliamentary and municipal. The right to share in the choice of those who are to exercise a public trust, is altogether a distinct thing from that of competing for the trust itself. If no one could vote for a member of parliament who was not fit to be a candidate, the government would be a narrow oligarchy indeed. To have a voice in choosing those by whom one is to be governed, is a means of self-protection due to every one, though he were to remain for ever excluded from the function of governing: and that women are considered fit to have such a choice, may be presumed from the fact, that the law already gives it to women in the most important of all cases to themselves: for the choice of the man who is to govern a woman to the end of life, is always supposed to be voluntarily made by herself. In the case of election to public trusts, it is the business of constitutional law to surround the right of suffrage with all needful securities and limitations; but whatever securities are sufficient in the case of the male sex, no others need be required in the case of women. Under whatever conditions, and within whatever limits, men are admitted to the suffrage, there is not a shadow of justification for not admitting women under the same. The majority of the women of any class are not likely to differ in political opinion from the majority of the men of the same class, unless the question be one in which the interests of women, as such, are in some way involved; and if they are so, women require the suffrage, as their guarantee of just and equal consideration. This ought to be obvious even to those who coincide in no other of the doctrines for which I contend. Even if every woman were a wife, and if every wife ought to be a slave, all the more would these slaves stand in need of legal protection: and we know what legal protection the slaves have, where the laws are made by their masters.

With regard to the fitness of women, not only to participate in elections, but themselves to hold offices or practise professions involving important public responsibilities; I have already observed that this consideration is not essential to the practical question in dispute: since any woman, who succeeds in an open profession, proves by that very fact that she is qualified for it. And in the case of public offices, if the political system of the country is such as to exclude unfit men, it will equally exclude unfit women: while if it is not, there is no additional evil in the fact that the unfit persons whom it admits may be either women or men. As long therefore as it is acknowledged that even a few women may be fit for these duties, the laws which shut the door on those exceptions cannot be justified by any opinion which can be held respecting the capacities of women in general. But, though this last consideration is not essential, it is far from being irrelevant. An unprejudiced view of it gives additional strength to the arguments against the disabilities of women, and reinforces them by high considerations of practical utility.

Let us at first make entire abstraction of all psychological considerations tending to show, that any of the mental differences supposed to exist between women and men are but the natural effect of the differences in their education and circumstances, and indicate no radical difference, far less radical inferiority, of nature. Let us consider women only as they already are, or as they are known to have been; and the capacities which they have already practically shown. What they have done, that at least, if nothing else, it is proved that they can do. When we consider how sedulously they are all trained away from, instead of being trained towards, any of the occupations or objects reserved for men, it is evident that I am taking a very humble ground for them, when I rest their case on what they have actually achieved. For, in this case, negative evidence is worth little, while any positive evidence is conclusive. It cannot be inferred to be impossible that a woman should be a Homer, or an Aristotle, or a Michael Angelo, or a Beethoven, because no woman has yet actually produced works comparable to theirs in any of those lines of excellence. This negative fact at most leaves the question uncertain, and open to psychological discussion. But it is quite certain that a woman can be a Queen Elizabeth, or a Deborah, or a Joan of Arc, since this is not inference, but fact. Now it is a curious consideration, that the only things which the existing law excludes women from doing, are the things which they have proved that they are able to do. There is no law to prevent a woman from having written all the plays of Shakespeare, or composed all the operas of Mozart. But Queen Elizabeth or Queen Victoria, had they not inherited the throne, could not have been intrusted with the smallest of the political duties, of which the former showed herself equal to the greatest. . . .

This fact is in accordance with the best general conclusions which the world's imperfect experience seems as yet to suggest, concerning the peculiar tendencies and aptitudes characteristic of women, as women have hitherto been. I do not say, as they will continue to be; for, as I have already said more than once, I consider it presumption in any one to pretend to decide what women are or are not, can or cannot be, by natural constitution. They have always hitherto been kept, as far as regards spontaneous development, in so unnatural a state, that their nature cannot but have been greatly distorted and disguised; and no one can safely pronounce that if women's nature were left to choose its direction as freely as men's, and if no artificial bent were attempted to be given to it except that required by the conditions of human society, and given to both sexes alike, there would be any material difference, or perhaps any difference at all, in the character and capacities which would unfold themselves. I shall presently show, that even the least contestable of the differences which now exist, are such as may very well have been produced merely by circumstances, without any difference of natural capacity. But, looking at women as they are known in experience, it may be said of them, with more truth than belongs to most other generalizations on the subject, that the general bent of their talents is towards the practical. This statement is conformable to all the public history of women, in the present and the past. It is no less borne out by common and daily experience. . . .

The concessions of the privileged to the unprivileged are so seldom brought about by any better motive than the power of the unprivileged to extort them, that any arguments against the prerogative of sex are likely to be little attended to by the generality, as long as they are able to say to themselves that women do not complain of it. That fact certainly enables men to retain the unjust privilege some time longer; but does not render it less unjust. Exactly the same thing may be said of the women in the harem of an Oriental: they do not complain of not being allowed the freedom of European women. They think our women insufferably bold and unfeminine. How rarely it is that even men complain of the general order of society; and how much rarer still would such complaint be, if they did not know of any different order existing anywhere else. Women do not complain of the general lot of women; or rather they do, for plaintive elegies on it are very common in the writings of women, and were still more so as long as the lamentations could not be suspected of having any practical object. Their complaints are like the complaints which men make of the general unsatisfactoriness of human life; they are not meant to imply blame, or to plead for any change. But though women do not complain of the power of husbands, each complains of her own husband, or of the husbands of her friends. It is the same in all other cases of servitude, at least in the commencement of the emancipatory movement. The serfs did not at first complain of the power of their lords, but only of their tyranny. The Commons began by claiming a few municipal privileges; they next asked an exemption for themselves from being taxed without their own consent; but they would at that time have thought it a great presumption to claim any share in the king's sovereign authority. The case of women is now the only case in which to rebel against established rules is still looked upon with the same eyes as was formerly a subject's claim to the right of rebelling against his king. A woman who joins in any movement which her husband disapproves, makes herself a martyr, without even being able to be an apostle, for the husband can legally put a stop to her apostleship. Women cannot be expected to devote themselves to the emancipation of women, until men in considerable number are prepared to join with them in the undertaking.

There remains a question, not of less importance than those already discussed, and which will be asked the most importunately by those opponents whose conviction is somewhat shaken on the main point. What good are we to expect from the changes proposed in our customs and institutions? Would mankind be at all better off if women were free? If not, why disturb their minds, and attempt to make a social revolution in the name of an abstract right?

It is hardly to be expected that this question will be asked in respect to the change proposed in the condition of women in marriage. The sufferings, immoralities, evils of all sorts, produced in innumerable cases by the subjection of individual women to individual men, are far too terrible to be overlooked. Unthinking or uncandid persons, counting those cases alone which are extreme, or which attain publicity, may say that the evils are exceptional; but no one can be blind to their existence, nor, in many cases, to their intensity. And it is perfectly obvious that the abuse of the power cannot be very much checked while the power remains. It is a power given, or offered, not to good men, or to decently respectable men, but to all men; the most brutal, and the most criminal. There is no check but that of opinion, and such men are in general within the reach of no opinion but that of men like themselves. If such men did not brutally tyrannize over the one human being whom the law compels to bear everything from them, society must already have reached a paradisiacal state. There could be no need any longer to curb men's vicious propensities. Astræa must not only have returned to earth, but the heart of the worst man must have become her temple. The law of servitude in marriage is a monstrous contradiction to all the principles of the modern world, and to all the experience through which those principles have been slowly and painfully worked out. It is the sole case, now that negro slavery has been abolished, in which a human being in the plenitude of every faculty is delivered up to the tender mercies of another human being, in the hope forsooth that this other will use the power solely for the good of the person subjected to it. Marriage is the only actual bondage known to our law. There remain no legal slaves, except the mistress of every house.

It is not, therefore, on this part of the subject, that the question is likely to be asked, *Cui bono?* We may be told that the evil would outweigh the good, but the reality of the good admits of no dispute. In regard, however, to the larger question, the removal of women's disabilities—their recognition as the equals of men in all that belongs to citizenship—the opening to them of all honourable employments, and of the training and education which qualifies for those employments—there are many persons for whom it is not enough that the inequality has no just or legitimate defence; they require to be told what express advantage would be obtained by abolishing it.

To which let me first answer, the advantage of having the most universal and pervading of all human relations regulated by justice instead of injustice. The vast amount of this gain to human nature, it is hardly possible, by any explanation or illustration, to place in a stronger light than it is placed by the bare statement, to any one who attaches a moral meaning to words. All the selfish propensities, the self-worship, the unjust self-preference, which exist among mankind, have their source and root in, and derive their principal nourishment from, the present constitution of the relation between men and women. Think what it is to a boy, to grow up to manhood in the belief that without any merit or any exertion of his own, though he may be the most frivolous and empty or the most ignorant and stolid of mankind, by the mere fact of being born a male he is by right the superior of all and every one of an entire half of the human race: including probably some whose real superiority to himself he has daily or hourly occasion to feel; but even if in his whole conduct he habitually follows a woman's guidance, still, if he is a fool, she thinks that of course she is not, and cannot be, equal in ability and judgment to himself; and if he is not a fool, he does worse—he sees that she is superior to him, and believes that, notwithstanding her superiority, he is entitled to command and she is bound to obey. What must be the effect on his character, of this lesson? And men of the cultivated classes are often not aware how deeply it sinks into the immense majority of male minds. For, among right-feeling and well-bred people, the inequality is kept as much as possible out of sight; above all, out of sight of the children. As much obedience is required from boys to their mother as to their father: they are not permitted to domineer over their sisters, nor are they accustomed to see these postponed to them, but the contrary; the compensations of the chivalrous feeling being made prominent, while the servitude which requires them is kept in the background. Well brought-up youths in the higher classes thus often escape the bad influences of the situation in their early years, and only experience them when, arrived at manhood, they fall under the dominion of facts as they really exist. Such people are little aware, when a boy is differently brought up, how early the notion of his inherent superiority to a girl arises in his mind; how it grows with his growth and strengthens with his strength; how it is inoculated by one schoolboy upon another; how early the youth thinks himself superior to his mother, owing her perhaps forbearance, but no real respect; and how sublime and sultan-like a sense of superiority he feels, above all, over the woman whom he honours by admitting her to a partnership of his life. Is it imagined that all this does not pervert the whole manner of existence of the man, both as an individual and as a social being? It is an exact parallel to the feeling of a hereditary king that he is excellent above others by being born a king, or a noble by being born a noble. The relation between husband and wife is very like that between lord and vassal, except that the wife is held to more unlimited obedience than the vassal was. However the vassal's character may have been affected, for better and for worse, by his subordination, who can help seeing that the lord's was affected greatly for the worse? whether he was led to believe that his vassals were really superior to himself, or to feel that he was placed in command over people as good as himself, for no merits or labours of his own, but merely for having, as Figaro says, taken the trouble to be born. The self-worship of the monarch, or of the feudal superior, is matched by the self-worship of the male. Human beings do not grow up from childhood in the possession of unearned distinctions, without pluming themselves upon them. Those whom privileges not acquired by their merit, and which they feel to be disproportioned to it, inspire with additional humility, are always the few, and the best few. The rest are only inspired with pride, and the worst sort of pride, that which values itself upon accidental advantages, not of its own achieving. Above all, when the feeling of being raised above the whole of the other sex is combined with personal authority over one individual among them; the situation, if a school of conscientious and affectionate forbearance to those whose strongest points of character are conscience and affection, is to men of another quality a regularly constituted Academy or Gymnasium for training them in arrogance and overbearingness; which vices, if curbed by the certainty of resistance in their intercourse with other men, their equals, break out towards all who are in a position to be obliged to tolerate them, and often revenge themselves upon the unfortunate wife for the involuntary restraint which they are obliged to submit to elsewhere.

The example afforded, and the education given to the sentiments, by laying the foundation of domestic existence upon a relation contradictory to the first principles of social justice, must, from the very nature of man, have a perverting influence of such magnitude, that it is hardly possible with our present experience to raise our imaginations to the conception of so great a change for the better as would be made by its removal. All that education and civilization are doing to efface the influences on character of the law of force, and replace them by those of justice, remains merely on the surface, as long as the citadel of the enemy is not attacked. The principle of the modern movement in morals and politics, is that conduct, and conduct alone, entitles to respect: that not what men are, but what they do, constitutes their claim to deference; that, above all, merit, and not birth, is the only rightful claim to power and authority. If no authority, not in its nature temporary, were allowed to one human being over another, society would not be employed in building up propensities with one hand which it has to curb with the other. The child would really, for the first time in man's existence on earth, be trained in the way he should go, and when he was old there would be a chance that he would not depart from it. But so long as the right of the strong to power over the weak rules in the very heart of society, the attempt to make the equal right of the weak the principle of its outward actions will always be an uphill struggle; for the law of justice, which is also that of Christianity, will never get possession of men's inmost sentiments; they will be working against it, even when bending to it.

The second benefit to be expected from giving to women the free use of their faculties, by leaving them the free choice of their employments, and opening to them the same field of occupation and the same prizes and encouragements as to other human beings, would be that of doubling the mass of mental faculties available for the higher service of humanity. Where there is now one person qualified to benefit mankind and promote the general improvement, as a public teacher, or an administrator of some branch of public or social affairs, there would then be a chance of two. Mental superiority of any kind is at present everywhere so much below the demand; there is such a deficiency of persons competent to do excellently anything which it requires any considerable amount of ability to do; that the loss to the world, by refusing to make use of one-half of the whole quantity of talent it possesses, is extremely serious. It is true that this amount of mental power is not totally lost. Much of it is employed, and would in any case be employed, in domestic management, and in the few other occupations open to women and from the remainder indirect benefit is in many individual cases obtained, through the personal influence of individual women over individual men. But these benefits are partial; their range is extremely circumscribed; and if they must be admitted, on the one hand, as a deduction from the amount of fresh social power that would be acquired by giving freedom to one-half of the whole sum of human intellect, there must be added, on the other, the benefit of the stimulus that would be given to the intellect of men by the competition; or (to use a more true expression) by the necessity that would be imposed on them of deserving precedency before they could expect to obtain it.

This great accession to the intellectual power of the species, and to the amount of intellect available for the good management of its affairs, would be obtained, partly, through the better and more complete intellectual education of women, which would then improve *pari passu* with that of men. Women in general would be brought up equally capable of understanding business, public affairs, and the higher matters of speculation, with men in the same class of society; and the select few of the one as well as of the other sex, who were qualified not only to comprehend what is done or thought by others, but to think or do something considerable themselves, would meet with the same facilities for improving and training their capacities in the one sex as in the other. In this way, the widening of the sphere of action for women would operate for good, by raising their education to the level of that of men, and making the one participate in all improvements made in the other. But independently of this, the mere breaking down of the barrier would of itself have an educational virtue of the highest worth. The mere getting rid of the idea that all the wider subjects of thought and action, all the things which are of general and not solely of private interest, are men's business, from which women are to be warned off—positively interdicted from most of it, coldly tolerated in the little which is allowed them—the mere consciousness a woman would then have of being a human being like any other, entitled to choose her pursuits, urged or invited by the same inducements as any one else to interest herself in whatever is interesting to human beings, entitled to exert the share of influence on all human concerns which belongs to an individual opinion, whether she attempted actual participation in them or not—this alone would effect an immense expansion of the faculties of women, as well as enlargement of the range of their moral sentiments. . . .

What marriage may be in the case of two persons of cultivated faculties, identical in opinions and purposes, between whom there exists that best kind of equality, similarity of powers and capacities with reciprocal superiority in them—so that each can enjoy the luxury of looking up to the other, and can have alternately the pleasure of leading and of being led in the path of development—I will not attempt to describe. To those who can conceive it, there is no need; to those who cannot, it would appear the dream of an enthusiast. But I maintain, with the profoundest conviction, that this, and this only, is the ideal of marriage; and that all opinions, customs, and institutions which favour any other notion of it, or turn the conceptions and aspirations connected with it into any other direction, by whatever pretences they may be coloured, are relics of primitive barbarism. The moral regeneration of mankind will only really commence, when the most fundamental of the social relations is placed under the rule of equal justice, and when human beings learn to cultivate their strongest sympathy with an equal in rights and in cultivation.

Thus far, the benefits which it has appeared that the world would gain by ceasing to make sex a disqualification for privileges and a badge of subjection, are social rather than individual; consisting in an increase of the general fund of thinking and acting power, and an improvement in the general conditions of the association of men with women. But it would be a grievous understatement of the case to omit the most direct benefit of all, the unspeakable gain in private happiness to the liberated half of the species; the difference to them between a life of subjection to the will of others, and a life of rational freedom. After the primary necessities of food and raiment, freedom is the first and strongest want of human nature. While mankind are lawless, their desire is for lawless freedom. When they have learnt to understand the meaning of duty and the value of reason, they incline more and more to be guided and restrained by these in the exercise of their freedom; but they do not therefore desire freedom less; they do not become disposed to accept the will of other people as the representative and interpreter of those guiding principles. On the contrary, the communities in which the reason has been most cultivated, and in which the idea of social duty has been most powerful, are those which have most strongly asserted the freedom of action of the individual— the liberty of each to govern his conduct by his own feelings of duty, and by such laws and social restraints as his own conscience can subscribe to. . . .

When we consider the positive evil caused to the disqualified half of the human race by their disqualification—first in the loss of the most inspiriting and elevating kind of personal enjoyment, and next in the weariness, disappointment, and profound dissatisfaction with life, which are so often the substitute for it; one feels that among all the lessons which men require for carrying on the struggle against the inevitable imperfections of their lot on earth, there is no lesson which they more need, than not to add to the evils which nature inflicts, by their jealous and prejudiced restrictions on one another. Their vain fears only substitute other and worse evils for those which they are idly apprehensive of: while every restraint on the freedom of conduct of any of their human fellow creatures (otherwise than by making them responsible for any evil actually caused by it), dries up *pro tanto* the principal fountain of human happiness, and leaves the species less rich, to an inappreciable degree, in all that makes life valuable to the individual human being.

12

Civil
Disobedience

*Readings: John Dickinson, "A Working
Theory of Sovereignty" (abridged)
John Rawls, "The Justification
of Civil Disobedience"*

We have now come full circle, and we return to the problems with which
we began in our consideration of Plato's *Crito*—the problems of fidelity to law
and civil disobedience. Socrates, you will recall, articulated certain principles
(never return injury for injury, respect the state as you would a parent, and
honor your contracts), which, in his judgment, made it morally obligatory on
him to accept his legal punishment despite his belief in the *injustice* of that
punishment. Thus, at the very least, Socrates seems committed to the view
that the injustice of a law or verdict is not in itself a sufficient reason for disobedience or escape.

Of course, Socrates, being a pioneer in moral philosophy, had vague views
about the nature and importance of utility (for example, the extent to which
one should worry about harm that may come to one's friends) and presented
only sketchy accounts of justice, law, and social obligation. And, of course,
he fails to raise at all the issues that a Marxist would regard as central to his
predicament (for example, the question of the extent to which the legal system
under which he lived was an instrument of class oppression and exploitation).
Despite this, however, Socrates did manage to get some of the major issues out
in the open; and this was itself a considerable achievement. Since the reader

is at this point familiar with much of the important moral and social writing that has taken place since Socrates' death, it should be possible to develop a sophisticated assessment of Socrates' position and to place that position within the context of moral and social theory.

In the first selection in this chapter, John Dickinson (who may be regarded as a contemporary Hobbist) presents a strong case against the permissibility of civil disobedience. Thus it is likely that he would approve of the ultimate outcome of the *Crito*. In the second selection, John Rawls applies in practice many of the theoretical ideas that you have seen him develop in other parts of this book. He outlines circumstances in which he believes civil disobedience would be justified. As one would expect, his account is based on principles of justice rather than of utility. At the very least, he would probably believe that Socrates did not appreciate the full moral complexity of the situation described in the *Crito*. Although rightly (in Rawls' judgment) rejecting all utilitarian considerations, Socrates did not seem to consider the possibility that considerations of justice could, in certain circumstances, dictate a disobedience to law.

Suggestions for Further Reading

Hugo Adam Bedau, ed., *Civil Disobedience: Theory and Practice* (New York: Pegasus Books, 1969).

Jeffrie G. Murphy, ed., *Civil Disobedience and Violence* (Belmont, Calif.: Wadsworth, 1971).

Robert Paul Wolff, *In Defense of Anarchism* (New York: Harper Torchbooks, 1970).

A Working Theory
of Sovereignty (abridged)
John Dickinson

The current assaults on the doctrine of sovereignty perform worthwhile service if they show realistically that sovereignty is not something inherent in the nature of things,—that it is not something, as Austin is wrongly supposed to have thought,[1] which exists and must exist at all times and places. It is

---

From *Political Science Quarterly* 43, No. 1 (March 1928), 32–59. Reprinted by permission. Footnotes have been renumbered. This is the concluding installment of Dickinson's article. Part I was published in the December 1927 issue of the *Political Science Quarterly*. John Dickinson was a professor of political science at Princeton University.

[1] This is not fair to Austin: see *The Province of Jurisprudence Determined,* 2d ed. (London, 1861), pp. 179–180. "Austin fully recognizes the existence of communities, or aggregates of men, in which no dissection could disclose a person or group answering to his definition of a sovereign."—Maine, *Early History of Institutions,* 4th ed. (London, 1885), p. 377.

not. It is simply a key-element in a pattern of possible organization to which actual practice may or may not conform, but which remains the only type of organization capable of sustaining what we mean by a régime of law. It is true that even an organization built on the lines of the pattern may not always function perfectly as it is supposed to do. It is also true that in a world where positive law is not organized on a world-wide scale, but where a number of independent systems of such law have grown up to jostle one another, an enormous gap is left for lawless violence to operate between them. It may be that in the present state of differences between national ideals and cultures this yawning void in the operation of positive law is inevitable and even de-sirable as a guarantee of freedom for beneficial adjustments. In any event, however, it would seem clear that a régime of law in the positive sense, in so far as it is realized at all, prevails only within the limits of each nation-state, and does so only because, and only in so far as, such a state is organ-ized on the principle of sovereignty. At times internal disturbances may occur, and one law and sovereignty be violently or clandestinely displaced or sup-planted by another; at other times, as is apparently now happening within the British Empire, the bonds of positive law may quietly wear thin and dissolve into a flimsy web of mere voluntary cooperation before the parts break com-pletely loose into separate sovereignties; but the typical civilized nation-state, as we are accustomed to it, is normally organized under sovereignty, and normally exhibits internally the working of a single unified system of positive law.

Now there can be no doubt that a régime of positive law, where it is strictly realized, has its disadvantages as well as its advantages. It emphasizes order and stability and uniformity, sometimes at the expense of what may be thought to be justice, but almost always at the expense, to some degree, of adaptability and progress. Its mode of operation is to set human conduct into theoretically rigid grooves for the sake of certainty and predictability, and to that extent to put barriers in the way of an experimental quest by private individuals and groups for new and more satisfactory adjustments. Hence arises the familiar and age-old conflict between the claims of order on the one side and of liberty on the other,—a conflict which becomes pro-gressively acute when extensive changes in the setting of human life and in the technique of satisfying human wants crowd upon the world and make new adjustments imperative. We are living in the welter of such a period of change today.

At such a time either of two courses seems open to the protagonists of progress. On the one hand they may direct their efforts toward bringing posi-tive law as near as may be into step with the march of the new demands by attempting to so constitute the sovereign organ as to make it more and more delicately responsive to the new impulses within the community. Along this path, and along this path alone, will seriously emerge the challenge to improve the machinery of government, as well as the sole hope and chance of effecting such improvements; for the improvement of government means precisely the difficult task of so altering its machinery as to increase its responsiveness to the needs of the community without impairing its value as an instrument of certainty and order. If we adopt this line of approach, there will be no occasion to question the validity of sovereignty in the sense in which I have sought to describe it; on the contrary, the ultimate responsibility will and must be centered on the sovereign as an indispensable instrumentality of beneficial change, and attention must therefore be all the more insistently narrowed to the practical question of how the sovereign organ is to be constituted, and what forces are to be allowed to play most powerfully upon it. We must accept jural sovereignty as an essential lever of progress; we set it up that we may have a focal point from which to go forward and take up the deeper and distinct, if yet intimately related, questions of practical politics,—the questions how best to mobilize for desirable political ends the actual power, social, economic, moral, which always lies behind the jural sovereign and sets it in motion for good ends or bad.

But of course another method of approach is open. We may take a short cut, and directly challenge sovereignty itself; which, whether we realize it or not, means questioning the value of a régime of positive law as an instrument for the achievement by a community of its internal adjustments. We may be so distrustful lest the sovereign organ fall under the influence of forces which we regard as malign and mischievous that we will refuse to vest any agency with final authority to pronounce what is law, and what is not, as between contending individuals or groups or interests. As Will Rogers recently said in reference to a dispute between the United States and Mexico, we may be so sure of our case that we are unwilling to trust any judge to decide in our favor. We may, in other words, be so anxious that our favorite among the contenders shall win, that we will be unwilling to subject his chance of winning to the possibly adverse decision of an organ which can conceivably be convinced by the other side. If we take this position, we really deny the advantages of a politically organized society; we fall back on a preference for voluntary cooperation backed by the ever-present threat of an appeal to force, in case of disagreement, over a state of affairs where the force of the community is constantly mobilized behind a central law-declaring agency. We express a preference for the condition of free adjustments which at present prevails in international politics, with their voluntary treaties and diplomatic negotiations interspersed by occasional passages at arms, over the condition existing within highly organized nation-states, where sinister influences, by gaining control of the government, can conceivably clothe their selfish purposes with the authority of law.

The importance of the controversy over sovereignty in its current form hinges precisely on the fact that consciously or unconsciously it is a challenge to choose between these two different attitudes of approach to the disputed issues of political and social reform. Shall we admit that because of the limitations and dangers of positive law, freedom to break through it at the will of the individual who thinks himself right must be erected into a normal working-part of the system of government, available at all times, rather than kept in reserve in the form of an extra-legal power of revolution for use only as an abnormal safety-valve and last resort in exceptional cases of great oppression? This admission is in substance what is demanded by writers who are attacking the concept of sovereignty; they seem to be seeking primarily for a way to regularize and legalize disobedience to existing positive law. Of course this is really to make a régime of positive law impossible; for a law which can be legally broken at the will of the law-breaker can never be positive law in any intelligible sense. The basic question at stake in the controversy over sovereignty is therefore what our attitude shall be toward breaches of positive law, and so how we shall approach the age-old question of obedience,—the question of the *Antigone* and the *Crito*. Shall we regard disobedience as properly a normal, i.e., a *legal* thing, or as only the abnormal, and therefore illegal, though perhaps at times morally justifiable, thing? What concessions to sovereignty are inevitable if we would have the advantages of a legally ordered society?

The bluntness of this antithesis, and the quality of the choice to which it is a challenge, appear to be generally obscured and confused in the arguments of those who attack the concept of sovereignty. They would apparently have their cake of legal order and eat it, too; and they elude the difficult but essentially commonplace major issue, by almost always straddling it. On the one hand they insist, as Professor McIlwain points out,[2] on taking sovereignty in an altogether too pretentious and inflated sense, and then quite properly rejecting it; on the other, they refuse to perceive the value or importance of the concept in its properly limited juristic application. They insist on confusing rather than connecting legal considerations with the political and factual considerations which lie under and around law, and yet are outside of it.[3] Of course law and the forces which play upon it must always be studied together and not abstractly dissociated; but they can only be fruitfully connected if their elements of distinctness are duly recognized. Thus the question of whether a law is a "good" law,—i.e., one which we regard as beneficial to the community,—is and must always be recognized as separate and quite distinct from the question of whether it is a law at all. Again, the question of whether a law is enforceable must be kept distinct from the question of whether it is a law. Questions of whether a law is good, or whether it is en-

---

[2] *Economica* (November, 1926), p. 259.

[3] The fact that law may be the product of certain forces operating upon and through a particular type of law-making machinery hardly justifies our saying that law *is*, or is identical with, those forces. The result requires that the forces should operate on a particular point, the sovereign, and in a way adapted to produce influence at that point, and this necessity conditions their success or failure in realizing their objectives. "When we talk about law, we think not of the influencing or pressure as a process, but of the status of the activities, the pressures being assumed to have worked themselves through to a conclusion or balance."—Arthur F. Bentley, *The Process of Government* (Chicago, 1908), p. 272. But this balance is never reached in the sense of producing law until the sovereign has spoken, and registered the point at which the balance is struck; therefore it seems an incomplete statement to say, as Mr. Bentley does, that "law is merely a manner of statement of interest-group facts," *ibid.*, p. 274.

forceable, are eminently proper for consideration prior to its enactment, or as arguments for its repeal; but if, because of its badness or non-enforceability, it can really never be law at all, enactment and repeal become matters of no great consequence. We must therefore determine where to draw the line between what is and what is not law separately from, and not as a part of, the question of getting good laws and keeping clear of bad ones, if our discussion is to be fruitful and lead to practical results. If we talk of both things as if they were the same thing, we can never be sure of what it is that we are talking about.

The capital indictments which so-called political pluralists, as represented by Mr. G. D. H. Cole and Mr. Laski in his earlier books, have brought against the concept of sovereignty seem to be all based on this fundamental confusion between legal considerations on the one hand and moral, social, and factual considerations on the other hand. Thus Mr. Laski[4] has pointed out insistently that the "will" of the so-called sovereign can never be an absolute "will,"—that it is almost certain to be controlled by some group, some interest, or combination of interests and forces within or without the community; and that the identity, the nature, of this controlling influence is of major practical consequence. So indeed it is, in connection with all questions of the goodness and badness of laws and forms of government, and with the reform of constitutional machinery; but hardly in connection with the question of the positive legality of a governmental act or pronouncement. Mr. Laski, however, goes on to argue that in the normal situation the sovereign is not really sovereign. "In sober fact, government is exerted in the interest of those who control its exercise. . . . The conclusion is forced upon us that the state permits a sinister manipulation of its power. . . . If authority is thus subject to exploitation it must be subject to limitation also. . . . Its policy is only sovereign where it is serving the sovereign purpose"— i.e., "the unique realization of the common good." [5]

In these sentences the writer seems deflected from the major issue in two directions. In the first place, in saying that the sovereign is only sovereign when serving the common good, he seems to be taking altogether too high and mystical a view of the nature of sovereignty, and of the positive law which proceeds from it. He apparently vests positive law,—i.e., a valid pronouncement of the sovereign—with a sanctity so elevated that he is unwilling to admit to it anything that is not in accordance with his own conception of the ultimate philosophical purposes of the state. This is a recurrence of the ancient unwillingness among men to admit that there can ever be discrepancy between law and justice; the unwillingness to vest with the

---

[4] What is here said is not intended, and should not be understood, as a critique of Mr. Laski's political theories in general. I have merely chosen certain of his statements to illustrate the particular attitude toward sovereignty which I am discussing because they are such clear and definite expressions of that theory. These statements are often corrected, or balanced by other statements of a contrary tendency, elsewhere in Mr. Laski's writings.

[5] Laski, *Authority in the Modern State* (New Haven, 1919), pp. 40, 41.

character of law any rule which is not thought to be objectively the one and only best rule for application to the particular circumstances of the case in hand. Now of course positive law ought so far as is humanly possible to conform to the highest ideal standards of justice conceivable at the time and place; if it does not so conform, it is doubtless the civic duty of all members of the community to do their best to bring about such conformity; and if the machinery of government does not readily permit progressive improvement in this direction, it should be overhauled in order that it may do so. But even so, we cannot be purists and insist that until the necessary improvements are brought about, the bad old rule with which we are dissatisfied is not entitled to be considered as law in even the positive sense.[6] Positive law is and must always be a thing of rough and ready adjustments; much of convenience, policy, compromise, doubtful experiment, inevitably enter into its make-up. All the members of the community will by no means be able to agree on

---

[6] "Power is held not for evil but for good, and deflection from the path of right purpose ought to involve the withdrawal of authority for its exercise."—Laski, *Authority in the Modern State*, p. 46. Both Grotius and Kant grappled with this problem and reached the opposite conclusion. The passages from Grotius are as follows: "There are some who assert that the people should obey the king when he governs rightly, but that when the king rules ill he is subject to the people. Now if those who reason thus were to say that things which are manifestly iniquitous ought not to be done though commanded by the king, they would say what is true. . . . But this does not carry with it any right of legal command or compulsion on the part of the people." (*De Jure Belli ac Pacis*), bk. I, chap. iii, § 9. "In most governments the good of the governed is the object. . . . But it does not follow that therefore the people are legally superior to the king; for guardianship is instituted for the good of the ward and yet the guardian has legal authority over the ward. Of course, in the case of guardianship, the guardian, if he neglects his duty to his ward, may be superseded; but this is no argument that kings may be legally removed, because there is this important difference, that the guardian has a legal superior [i.e., the state], but in political government, because we cannot have an infinite gradation of superiors, we must stop at some person or body whose transgressions, having no superior legal judge, are the province of God alone" [i.e., as we should now say, of morality].—*Ibid.*, bk. I, chap. iii, § 8. "If the people intended to have a share in the government along with the king, such limits ought to be assigned to the power of each as may easily be recognized by a proper legal distinction of persons, places and matters. But the goodness or badness of an act, which are often matters of great doubt especially in political affairs, are not a fit ground of distinction to supply the basis for such a distribution of authority. The most extreme confusion will follow if the king and people both claim jurisdiction of the same matter on the basis of a charge of good or evil conduct."—*Ibid.*, bk. I, chap. iii, § 9. In other words, the question of whether legal authority exists in the legal sovereign cannot be made to depend upon a judgment as to the goodness or badness of his acts by a person or persons who otherwise do not constitute a part of the sovereign organization. The same point is made by Kant, who says that under a constitution where the people do not form a part of the sovereign body, "they do not have the right to determine by their judgment how it is to be administered, for suppose they had such a right, and that it was directly opposed to the judgment of the actual sovereign, who would there be to decide with which of them the right lay? . . . There would therefore have to be another sovereign above the sovereign to decide between it and the people; but this is a contradistinction."—"Principles of Politics," trans. by Hastie, in *Eternal Peace and Other Essays* (Boston, World Peace Foundation, 1914), p. 44. But of course a legal right of resistance through the exercise of electoral machinery may be reserved to the people under constitutional law: "A political constitution under which the people by their representatives in Parliament can legally resist the executive power and its representative ministers is called a limited constitution."—Kant, *Philosophy of Law*, trans. by Hastie (Edinburgh, 1887), p. 180. Of course both Grotius and Kant were dealing not with the question of individual resistance, but with that of organized revolt by the people under a constitution whereby they were not legally entitled to a voice in the government. But the central point at issue in both cases is substantially the same— i.e., whether or not the fact that the legal sovereign fails to rule in accordance with the common good gives a *legal* right of disobedience to persons otherwise not entitled to participate in the exercise of sovereignty.

what justice in the highest sense is, or on what particular demands it makes in any given situation; meanwhile if they are not to fight out their differences, there must be some rule to settle them by. We can never proceed toward getting the best rule until we first consent that there shall at least be a rule, and we will never consent that there shall be a rule if we insist on having what we privately regard as the best rule, or else on having no rule at all.[7] We must therefore be willing to allow the character of positive law to much that we might well wish were otherwise; and this involves no disrespect to the nature of law properly conceived. It is too late to regard law as a Heaven-born goddess, or as other than a matter of human convenience. Unless we are sheer anarchists, a rule sanctioned by the highest authority in the state is ordinarily preferable to no rule at all, until we can get a better one; and if we feel that because of exceptional circumstances this is not so in a particular case, then we must frankly face in that special case the moral or social issue of revolution, and not hide our heads in the sand by pretending that we are only upholding law when we are resisting the ordinances of the authorized law-declaring organ of the community.

In the second place, the language quoted from Mr. Laski seems to show a certain confusion in refusing to regard as law a rule proclaimed by the sovereign organ whenever such a rule can be thought to result from selfish pressure brought to bear upon the sovereign by contending interests. We get off the track if we proceed to say that such a rule is in reality nothing more than an expression of the "private" will of the strongest special interest, on the ground that the interest exerting the decisive force is really the sovereign. Factually, it may indeed be called the cause of the sovereign's action, but still it must act through the sovereign; and if there were no sovereign through which it had to act, its action might well be quite different. The helm controls the ship no less because some one must give direction to the helm; and the sovereign controls the law no less because some one may give direction to the sovereign.[8] The fact that forces will exert pressure is not the important thing; of course they will; the important thing is the way they must go about exerting it. Now in a community politically organized under sovereignty, they must exert it through the sovereign; in the absence of sovereignty there is no legal obstacle to prevent them from exerting it directly against their opponents to the point of actual intimidation and violence. The difference is not unimportant; it may be only a difference of degree, but still it produces vital differences in both methods and results. It is never quite enough to see in the politically organized community only a pressure of competing interests, as

---

[7] "It does not matter whether the common good is recognized by an existing state. My duty is to act as though it ought to be recognized. My citizenship implies conduct on my part which attempts the enforcement of that recognition where it is denied. I may, of course, in such action encounter the hostile forces of the state."—Laski, *A Grammar of Politics* (New Haven, 1925), p. 96.

[8] See Woodrow Wilson, *An Old Master and Other Essays* (New York, 1893): "It is none the less sovereign because it must be observant of the preferences of those whom it governs," p. 88.

the pluralists so often do. The competition and the pressure undeniably exist, but there exists also a structure of legal processes which set limits to their action, and often deflect its direction. The kind of competition which goes on between opposing interests within a nation-state is certainly a different kind of competition in enough important particulars from that which goes on between "independent" nation-states to warrant recognizing the differences. Within the nation-state, organized under sovereignty, the competing interests must adapt their competitive methods to the fact that there is a central authority which must transmute their purposes into its own before they can claim legal validity. Now if they succeed in bringing this result to pass, it may well be that by adding the authority of the sovereign to their own strength they will thereby become immeasurably stronger than they would be in a free field with nothing but their own resources to rely upon; on the other hand, in a government that is at all well organized, they will hardly succeed in thus translating their purposes into law for any considerable period of time without constantly consenting to modify those purposes very materially so as to bring them into at least some measure of harmony with those of other important groups in the community. Fundamentally, of course, it comes down to whether the mechanism of government is, or is not, well planned. If it is so planned and organized as to prevent its falling completely under the control of a dominant group against the will of other groups, then practically all its acts, although they may often or indeed generally seem to favor one group at the expense of others, are almost certain to be the results of adjustments and compromises in which the favored group is compelled to give some *quid pro quo*. Government, if it performs its function, is simply a great central coordinating agency from which these adjustments ultimately emerge; and Mr. Laski deserves credit for the fact that no one has stated this more tellingly than he himself has done.[9] But even if government is not well organized, and performs its functions ill, still it sometimes accomplishes one important purpose; even if it habitually favors one group in the community at the expense of others, and advances the interests of the former to the utter disregard of the latter, it may yet afford the advantages, whatever we hold them worth, of peace and order. It at least enables men to know the rules they must live under and the authority to which they must submit if they would be law-abiding. Now there are times, no doubt, when this is not a good thing; there is a peace which is the "bitterest bitterness" and worse than any war; and at such times the anarchy of resistance and civil war may be the only thinkable portal to a fairer and better world. But ad-

---

[9] *A Grammar of Politics*, pp. 66–70. Mr. Cole would deny the supreme coordinating function to the "State", by which he apparently understands, however, nothing more than a state having a government as at present usually constituted; but he recognizes the need for some agency to exercise that function "in order to prevent the sort of 'cat-and-dog' fight which went on between Church and State in the Middle Ages," *Social Theory* (New York, 1920), p. 138, and this agency he would establish in the form of a "Joint Council or Congress of the supreme bodies representing each of the main functions in Society," *ibid.*, pp. 134–135. But what is this but government with a particular form of organization and under some other name?

mitting all this, there is still a truth in the old commonplace that one tyrant is preferable to many; and the age of Augustus, the age of the Medici and of the Tudors, bear witness that as a general rule men appear to find the peace and order even of a despotism a more satisfactory environment wherein to work out their purposes than a continual conflict of authorities, though the latter be shot through with the purest passion for civil or religious liberty of a Brutus or a Becket.

Of course if government is to perform effectively its function of a co-ordinating agency for adjusting the contrary aims and interests of competing individuals and groups, it must be possessed of a certain independent strength of its own to prevent it from becoming only an instrument in the hands of one or more of the competitors. A feeble government is of no use in effecting adjustments, for the reason that on the one hand it inevitably degenerates into a mere tool of one group without ability to compel that group to yield consideration to other groups; and because, on the other hand, it cannot lend enough reenforcement to the strength of the favored group to preserve the peace of the community against the discontented outbreaks of rival groups. A strong government, on the contrary, even if it happens to be so organized as to fall under the domination of a special group, may indeed fail to effect adjustments in the sense of securing to other groups the fair measure of their claims and interests; but, none the less, it may still, if wisely and shrewdly administered, as was the old Venetian Republic, successfully preserve the advantages of peace and order. It must be wisely and shrewdly administered, however, because there are things which even the strongest government cannot venture to do without endangering or destroying its effectiveness and even its existence. This is a point which sceptics on the subject of sovereignty have delighted to labor. The classic example to enforce their argument has been the hypothetical case of a constitutionally absolute despot who should promulgate a law outraging some deep-seated religious prejudice of his subjects.[10] Obviously such a law would not be obeyed, and could not be successfully enforced. More than likely it would initiate a rebellion which would result in the overthrow of the despot. This situation has been urged as a conclusive argument against the validity of the doctrine of sovereignty. If, it is said, the sovereign is thus absolutely limited in the nature of the laws which he can make, how can he be considered as a truly sovereign law-maker at all?

Such a question is but one more manifestation of the tendency to take sovereignty in the unwarrantably broad sense which we have already discarded; it proceeds from again confusing legal with factual considerations. Legally a sovereign may well promulgate laws which actually he is unable to enforce; if he does so habitually, then we must predict as a matter of future

---

[10] "Everyone knows that to regard the King in Parliament as a sovereign body in the Austinian sense is absurd. No Parliament would dare to disfranchise the Roman Catholics or to prohibit the existence of trade unions. If it made the attempt, it would cease to be a Parliament."—Laski, *A Grammar of Politics*, p. 52.

historical fact either that sovereignty will go into abeyance, as it did during the Middle Ages, or else that the sovereign will be supplanted by a shrewder or a stronger one. These, however, are purely factual results which until they eventuate can have nothing to do with the question of whether for the time being we are to regard the sovereign's acts as vested or not with legal character or validity; all that they indicate is that legal sovereignty is, as I have said, no necessary and inherent part of the order of nature, existing inexorably everywhere, but rather something which can come into existence, be transferred, or disappear as a result of the ineptitude of the sovereign or of social or cultural changes within the community or of other historical circumstances of many different kinds. Of these circumstances the most immediate and urgent are of course those which bear upon the question of whether or not the supposed sovereign is generally obeyed. If he is habitually disobeyed, as were the Holy Roman Emperors in a great part of the dominions to which they laid claim, then we can only say that in a community where such a situation prevails, sovereignty has really ceased to exist; its laws and promulgations are but blank cartridges, mere *bruta fulmina*. It is sometimes hard to tell in a given case whether this point has yet been reached; but whether it has been reached or not is a practical question of fact which has no direct bearing on the question of what for the time being is or is not the law; there is no legal way of determining whether habitual disobedience of the sovereign's laws and judgments has gotten to the point where he can no longer be properly said to be sovereign. The factual nature of the question and the practical solution which has to be applied to it are illustrated by the method of international law in distinguishing between so-called sovereigns *de jure* and sovereigns *de facto*.

It is by no means to be inferred from what has just been said that sovereignty is purely a matter of the possession of supreme physical force. That would be a misconception. It may be that the sovereign's laws will be respected only or chiefly because he has the actual power to compel acquiescence; but altogether apart from the matter of physical power, they may under other circumstances be as completely respected because no one ever thinks seriously of questioning them. It is not at all essential that physical sanctions should be the sole or principal factor producing obedience; the important thing is only that the obedience should in fact exist. It may exist either because of the strength of habit or custom, or because of the prevalent fear of religious sanctions, or for some other reason of similar nature; under such circumstances a sovereign almost entirely without physical power may long receive a full and effective obedience. At other times the possession or exertion of physical power may be required to bring about this result; and under still other circumstances, even physical power itself may be utterly ineffective to produce it. The causes of obedience are complicated and obscure, and raise fundamental and highly interesting political questions; but they are not the same questions as the question of the nature of sovereignty and its relation to law. They are connected with it to the extent, and only to the extent, of our having to say that sovereignty cannot function except in an atmosphere where obedience, i.e., acquiescence in the sovereign's determinations, however it may be produced, is the normal and habitual condition, disobedience the abnormal and temporary.

Just as it is not necessary to say that sovereignty is founded on force, neither is it necessary to insist that laws must be regarded as primarily the sovereign's *commands*.[11] It is sufficient to regard them as his pronouncements, or as dependent for their legal character upon his determinations. The idea of a command seems too frequently to have carried with it to the minds of many thinkers the notion that a law must somehow be an arbitrary expression of the sovereign's unmotivated or purely selfish "will" or caprice,— that it must be evolved in his inner consciousness out of nothing, and without any regard for the customary or ideal notions of right and wrong which men ordinarily consult in determining their conduct. If this is the implication of the word "command" as used in the orthodox Austinian expositions of sovereignty, then the word should certainly be abandoned, and some other and less misleading word substituted. The function of the sovereign is not to create laws arbitrarily *ex nihilo,* but to be the source or mouthpiece of final and authoritative pronouncements of the rules of conduct which are to be called laws. There is no logical reason why these pronouncements should not be, there is every moral reason why they should be, culled from and based upon the most carefully reasoned prevailing opinions of right and wrong.[12] That they should always exactly coincide with the dictates of abstract right is too much either to expect or demand, for the very reason which makes sovereignty indispensable to a régime of legal order: namely, that questions of right and wrong are not matters of absolute mathematical demonstration, but lie so frequently within the twilight zone of rational differences of opinion, and that there is therefore need for the exercise by some recognized organ of what Mr. Justice Holmes has aptly termed the "sovereign prerogative of choice."[13] It is precisely the making of this choice which is the characteristic act of sovereignty; it may be well made or ill, it may be made from good motives but ignorantly, or from bad motives and in willful disregard of the considerations upon which it should properly be based. The sovereign makes laws, but makes them always out of existing materials,— ideas, interests, demands; he may make them because he thinks them right, or because he believes they will advance his material interests, or only because he is compelled by circumstances to do so; the important thing is that it is his act which entitles them to be called laws, which puts on them the

---

[11] Laski, *A Grammar of Politics,* p. 51.

[12] That the sovereign person or group actually wields the stored-up force of society by an uncontrolled exercise of will is certainly never in accordance with fact. A despot with a disturbed brain is the sole conceivable example of such sovereignty. The vast mass of influences, which we call for shortness moral, perpetually shapes, limits or forbids the actual direction of the forces of society by its sovereign."—Maine, *op. cit.,* p. 359.

[13] *Collected Legal Papers* (New York, 1920), p. 239.

stamp and genuine hall-mark of law, although some men or many men may have insisted all along that they should be law and have even called them law. On the other hand, his act denies the character of law to all contrary and inconsistent rules, despite the fact that many other men may have insisted with equal strength of conviction that it was these latter which were entitled to genuine legal validity. The sovereign is thus not so much a creative influence as an organ of final choice; the practical effectiveness of his choice in the form of the maintenance of legal order depends on the practical and factual question of whether his choice is or is not generally acquiesced in and accepted and obeyed. A sovereign making choices and promulgating laws which are habitually disregarded is not for practical political purposes a sovereign,—is not a sovereign *de facto*—although in the absence of a competing claimant for sovereignty who is habitually obeyed, he may continue to be called legally a sovereign *de jure*. But a sovereign *de jure* who is not also sovereign *de facto* is to all political intents no sovereign at all; the price that is paid for such a state of things is simply the abeyance of legal order and so of sovereignty in the true sense, and the existence of what in its practical effect amounts to a condition of anarchy.

Does it not therefore seem to follow that after all it is the factual aspects of sovereignty which are the most important? In one sense, yes; but only in one sense,—i.e., only if we mean by "important" the question whether sovereignty is effective in doing what it can valuably do,—and only if we limit the admission to the single factual consideration of whether or not sovereignty,—i.e., a régime of legal order,—exists. Such matters as what causes enable it to exist, and what are the forces which influence its acts when it does exist, and which set limits to the scope of its effective power, are altogether different and collateral questions, equally important though they of course are as independent subjects of political investigation. The only factual consideration which is pertinent in considering the nature and meaning of juristic sovereignty is whether or not in a given community the thing exists; and this is a question which can be approached only after we have first determined what we intend to signify by the word sovereignty. A theoretical discussion of the nature of legal order and of its connection with the concept of sovereignty such as was contained in the first part of this paper is thus an indispensable prerequisite to any consideration of the factual question of the existence of sovereignty. We must have the pattern in our minds before we can test the conformity of the facts to it; we must know what it is we are looking for before we can look for it.

It is from this angle that the real importance of the doctrine of legal or juristic sovereignty emerges. That doctrine is essential for enabling us to understand what legal order consists in; and we must understand what legal order consists in before we can go on to consider the practical questions of the advantages and disadvantages of legal order and the best devices for increasing the one and diminishing the other. Thus, although the doctrine of legal sovereignty may be in a direct sense unimportant, as Mr. Laski suggests it is,[14] for answering questions as to the true location and proper use of political power, indirectly it is of vast importance in paving the way for a consideration of precisely these practical political questions against a proper back-ground and a proper setting; because it states with the baldness and sharpness of a ground-plan sketch the requirements of legal order and the nature of the price which men must pay for it. Having determined this question, and only after having determined it, can we go on to ask how the price can be lowered to an irreducible minimum of inconvenience.

The question of the meaning of sovereignty and legal order in this sense takes on special importance in periods where an existing sovereignty begins to be threatened on a significant scale with disobedience to its laws and decrees. At such a time we are faced with the possibility, if not as yet with the certainty, of the break-down and disappearance of sovereignty through increasing disobedience; and only a firm grasp of the significance of sovereignty for legal order will enable us intelligently to balance the cost of resistance against the cost of obedience.

Suppose, for example, that we do not accept the doctrine of sovereignty. We will then insist that laws do not derive their validity from the stamp of the sovereign, but that a rule may be validly a law which is directly contrary to the rule which the sovereign is seeking to enforce. But if this is the case, and if we must look not to the sovereign but to some other source to assure us what is the law, where else are we to look? Mr. Laski has suggested the only possible answer,—we must look within, each man to his own individual conscience.[15] If we use this method of approach we have no choice but to say that the validity of all law is derived from the conscience of the individual. The question of obedience or resistance then becomes a simple one. All that is involved is for each individual to set side by side and compare the law as promulgated by the sovereign with what his own conscience tells him is the law, and if there is a discrepancy between the two precepts, then he is not merely morally justified, he is legally authorized, to disobey. There are but two factors to be taken in account in solving the problem,— the sovereign's pronouncement on the one hand and the individual's own conception of the law,—i.e., of what is right,—on the other. His career as a member of civil society becomes a continuous process of such comparisons, and he stands at every moment on the brink of disobedience and resistance. "The only ground upon which the individual can give or be asked his support for the state is from the conviction that what it is aiming at is, in each particular action, good. . . . It deserves his allegiance, it should receive

---

[14] "What we desire to know is not what has the legal right to prevail but what does in actual fact prevail, and the reasons that explain its dominance. Here, it is clear enough, the legal theory of sovereignty is worthless."—Laski, *Authority in the Modern State,* p. 41. See also Bentley, *The Process of Government,* p. 264.

[15] "The individual is ultimately the supreme arbiter of his behaviour; and he most fully realizes the purpose of the state when he offers to it the substance, whatever that may be, of his judgment."—*A Grammar of Politics,* p. 63. "The state is for [the individual] sovereign only where his conscience is not stirred against its performance."—*Authority in the Modern State,* p. 43.

it, only where it commands his conscience. . . . Its purpose is at each stage subject to examination." [16] The individual is thus invited to assume habitually what Mr. Laski has elsewhere called the "Athanasius attitude." [17]

The doubt which suggests itself in connection with this attitude is that possibly it may be too naïve,—that possibly it may not be sophisticated enough to comprehend the full challenge of civil society. It is the primitive attitude of Antigone,[18] rather than the mature comprehension of Socrates. Its capital defect is that it leaves fundamentally out of account the chief and most difficult factor in the whole problem—the question, namely, of the advantage, not merely to all individuals but to each individual, of having a legally ordered society to live in, and of the price which he must perforce pay to get it. This factor is the thing which really causes all the difficulty; and it is the major factor. If there were no question but of a conflict between two opposing wills, the will of the citizen as one individual and the will of the sovereign as another, the problem would be quite easy; the individual could not fairly be expected to surrender his will until convinced intellectually and morally that he was wrong. But so to state the problem is to simplify it out of all recognition. It is not a question of a bare conflict between the individual and the sovereign; the conflict must be regarded as rather between the individual and all that the sovereign stands for. The individual may be convinced and reasonably convinced that the sovereign is wrong, unfairly, brutally wrong; but the deeper question must at once arise of what is involved in disobeying the sovereign.

For sovereignty, as we have seen, is a prerequisite of legal order; a prerequisite, that is, of a condition of affairs where the disputes which will honestly and inevitably arise between man and man, and which will as often be due to a real and involuntary difference in intellectual outlook as to a clash between purely selfish purposes, are settled peaceably by a publicly authorized arbiter, and, so far as possible, by impartial rules, rather than by the rough arbitrament of force and chance. The very essence and meaning of civil society is precisely the fact that the former method rather than

---

[16] *Ibid.,* p. 46. A more extreme statement is that of Thoreau, "Civil Disobedience," *Writings* (Boston, 1906): "Must the citizen, even for a moment or in the least degree, resign his conscience to the legislator? Why has every man a conscience then? I think we should be men first and subjects afterwards." Vol. IV, p. 358. "There will never be a really free and enlightened state until the state comes to recognize the individual as a higher and independent power from which all its own power and authority are derived and treats him accordingly." *Ibid.,* p. 387.

[17] I would urge against this position the criticism that it reverses the proper order of the burden of proof, that it shifts improperly the presumption of validity. The presumption must be in favor of state action; the burden of proof on the refractory individual. The state must not continually be justifying itself to the individual; the individual must justify himself morally in the exceptional cases when he feels morally compelled to resist the state.

[18] Antigone submits to her punishment, not like Socrates under a sense that it is something owed to civil society, but merely because she must bow to superior force; and she insists on the justice of her position, and protests against the injustice of her punishment, to the bitter end: "What rule of divine justice have I transgressed? . . . It is my piety which wins me the name of impious. But if my death be, as it might seem, the pleasure of the gods, I will suffer death ere I confess that I have sinned; and if, on the other hand, the gods do not approve of my death, and these men are the guilty ones, may they suffer no more woes than they have unjustly done to me."—Sophocles, *Antigone,* lines 921–928.

the latter is the one which habitually prevails; and this essential method of civil society is just the thing which we strike at whenever we disobey or resist the sovereign. The question of obedience thus raises far more than the mere question of the agreement or disagreement in a particular case between the sovereign's law applying to the case in hand, and what the individual's private conscience tells him the law ought to be; properly approached, it brings dominantly into the foreground the large issue of the desirability of preserving public authority and civil society itself. This is the great truth so clearly put by Socrates, when in answer to Crito's plea for disobedience he represents the City as standing before him and saying, "Tell us, Socrates, what is it you mean to do? Nothing more nor less than to overthrow us by this attempt of yours,—to overthrow the laws and the whole commonwealth so far as in you lies. For do you imagine that a city can stand and not be overthrown, when the decisions of the judges have no power, when they are made of no effect and destroyed by private persons?" [19] In other words, something of vastly superior consequence is involved than the essential rightness or wrongness in the given case of any particular exercise of sovereign power; what is involved, fundamentally, is the value and validity of civil society in contrast with the freedom, the flexibility, the experimentalism, of anarchy, whether the latter take the form of benevolent cooperation or of forceful competition. Civil society cannot stand when the decisions of the judges are made of no effect by private persons; and the Athanasius attitude, to be defensible, must balance not particular differences of opinion between the individual conscience and the sovereign will, but

---

[19] *Crito*, Everyman's ed, chap. xi, p. 359. The point made by Socrates seems to be grasped, although but dimly, by Mr. Cole, but his statement is valuable if only for his apparent concession that the right of disobedience has no more than a subjective personal basis. He says: "In most forms of social theory . . . the state is assumed to be an altogether superior kind of association or superassociation, quite different from all the other associations to which a man may belong. . . . And whereas no man in his senses would believe that it is my real will to carry out all the decisions of my cricket-club without questioning, men can be brought to think of the state so as to say, 'Theirs not to reason why, theirs but to do and die.' . . . We may be prepared to stretch more points in favor of accepting a decision of the state than of the cricket-club because we regard the maintenance of the State as more important; but, if we reason at all, we must apply our reason to the decrees of the state as well as to those of other associations. A difference of degree may remain; but the difference in kind has disappeared. . . . A man owes not one absolute social loyalty and other subordinate loyalties which must always in case of need be overridden by it, but a number of relative and limited loyalties of varying importance and intensity, but not essentially differing in kind. If this is so, and if the association to which we owe our ultimate loyalty is not externally determined for us by the character of the association itself, it follows that the choice of ultimate loyalty, in a case where loyalties conflict, necessarily resides in the individual himself. It is true that the functional Society which we envisage includes in its structure forms of co-ordination, and, in the last resort, co-ercion. Thus, in making his choice of loyalties, the individual cannot choose without incurring a risk of penalty, and does not escape altogether from the possibility of being co-erced. That, however, is not the immediate point which I have in mind. . . . The immediate point is that of the moral and not of the physical, or co-ercive, obligation upon the individual, and a great moral victory is won for individual liberty by the successful assertion of the individual's ultimate and unassailable moral right to choose for himself among conflicting social loyalties. Even if Society punishes him for choosing in a manner contrary to that prescribed by its co-ordinating organization, it has no right to blame him, or call him 'traitor', merely because his choice is contrary to the social precept. It is his business how he chooses, even if the consequences are still a sphere for social definition." (*Social Theory*, pp. 188–190.)

the value of the end which conscience has at stake as against the value of civil society.[20]

For there are of course ends which from time to time do validly out-weigh the maintenance for the time being of the orderly processes of civil society. Revolution, like war, is no doubt entitled to a place as one of the indispensable ingredients of progress in the existing, and perhaps in any, state of human nature. The only point I am insisting on is that revolution should always be recognized for what it is,—a lapse into anarchy. Only so, in any specific case, can the wisdom of taking the plunge be fairly assessed; only so can the full meaning of the alternative between obedience and re-sistance be grasped in all its awful implications.[21] The chief defect in the doctrine of the denial of sovereignty is that it glosses over with thin sugar-coating this fundamental alternative. The doctrine that there exists some-where a law above, and independent of, the law of the sovereign, and capable of being discovered for himself by each private individual so as to justify disobedience to the positive law,[22] carries with it the implication that

---

[20] This point is often made by Mr. Laski himself, e.g.: "A right to disobedience . . . is . . . reasonably to be exercised only at the margins of political conduct. No community could hope to fulfil its purpose if rebellion became a settled habit of the population."—*A Grammar of Politics*, p. 62. "The real obligation of obedience is to the total interest of our fellow-men."—*Ibid.*, p. 64. "The point at which resistance becomes an expedient factor is not a matter for definition or prophecy; it will vary with the circumstances of each age. All we can say is that at times in the history of a state there may well come a point where the maintenance of order seems to some group of men worthless as an end compared to achieving, by other than con-stitutional means, some good deemed greater than peace."—*Authority in the Modern State*, pp. 53–54.

[21] This was recognized, for example, by Benjamin Constant: "Obedience to law is a duty, but, like all duties, it is not absolute, it is relative; it rests on the supposition that the law emanates from a legitimate source and is confined within just limits. This duty does not cease when the law departs from this rule only in certain respects. We ought to sacrifice a great deal for the sake of the public peace; we should render ourselves guilty in the eyes of morality if, by too inflexible attachment to our rights we should disturb the peace as soon as it seemed to us that they were being infringed upon in the name of law." If we "say that we obey laws only in so far as they are just, we shall find ourselves authorizing resistance to law in the most sense-less and culpable instances, and anarchy will reign." On the other hand, only a subjective moral validity can be allowed to the test which Constant seeks to establish for rightful disobedience: "No duty would bind us to obey laws which not only restrain our legitimate liberties and limit actions with which they had no right to interfere, but which would also command us to act contrary to the eternal principles of justice and piety. . . . As long as a law, even though bad, does not tend to deprave us, as long as authority demands of us only such sacrifices as render us neither vile nor cruel, we can submit to it." These quotations from his *Cours de Politique Constitutionelle* (additions et notes: "Des Droits Individus") are given in Elizabeth W. Schermer-horn, *Benjamin Constant* (Boston and New York, 1924), p. 381. For an excellent statement of the issues involved in disobedience, see T. H. Green, *Lectures on the Principles of Political Obligation*, §§ 143–147, in *Works*, edited by Nettleship (London, 1906), vol. II, pp. 454–459.

[22] This view possesses a perennial appeal for extreme reformers, e.g., the abolitionists before the American Civil War. Thus one of their platforms declares that since slavery is contrary to the natural rights of man, and since "the moral laws of the Creator are paramount to all human laws . . . therefore, Resolved, that we . . . owe it to the Sovereign Ruler of the Universe, as a proof of our allegiance to him, in all our civil relations and offices, whether as private citizens or as public functionaries sworn to support the Constitution of the United States, to regard and to treat the third clause of the second section of the fourth article of that instrument, whenever applied to the case of a fugitive slave, as utterly null and void, and consequently as forming no part of the Constitution of the United States whenever we are called upon or sworn to support it."—*Emancipator Extra*, Tract No. 1, reprinted in K. H. Porter, *National Party Platforms* (New York, 1924), pp. 13–14. So William Hosmer, in his *Higher Law in its Relation to Civil Government* (Auburn, 1852), p. 79, maintains that the individual is the judge of what the

civil society itself exists, and can exist, apart from and independently of obedience to the sovereign; and that therefore resistance by the individual to the sovereign is not necessarily anything like so serious and ultimate a thing as an assault on civil society is readily seen to be. The essential meaning of resistance is obscured, the price which it entails belittled. And at the same time the price that we must pay for civil society itself is belittled. For the demand which civil society makes that private individual will and purpose be always subordinated to the will of the authorized public representative of the society, on no other and no better ground than merely that the one is private and the other public, is by implication denied, if we accept the doctrine that civil society does not depend for its existence and functioning on obedience to its constituted representative. A view of civil society is thus produced which evades the necessity for political organization, —which tolerates the claim of separate and discrete groups within the state to be independent of the jurisdiction of, and immune from interference by, the state, and which in pursuance of the same conviction is capable of seeing in an unorganized "society of nations" a substantial substitute for an organized League. The theory seeks to have its cake of order without having to pay the price of organization.

This was the theory that dominated the thought of the Western world throughout the medieval centuries.[23] It is a theory the defectiveness of which

---

"higher law" commands, and of when the positive law is in keeping with it, and if it is not, he should then refuse obedience. For these references I am indebted to an unpublished thesis on *Natural Law in American Political Theory* by my friend Dr. Benjamin F. Wright, Jr., of Harvard University. The theory that the isolated private individual is entitled to judge for himself as to what the "higher law" commands has inevitable anarchistic implications; and an effort to avoid these sometimes takes the form of holding that such authority belongs not to private judgment, but to some organized agency independent of the state organization, e.g., the church. This view has naturally been favored by Roman Catholic writers as in accord with the historic position of that body. Thus Orestes A. Brownson, an American Roman Catholic, denied the right of revolution except when the Church "as the representative of the highest authority on earth, determines when resistance is proper and prescribes its forms and extent." *Works,* ed. by Henry F. Brownson (Detroit, 1884), vol. XV, pp. 397–398. Any act against civil government is forbidden by God's law unless the infallible Church, as the interpreter of that law on earth, declares otherwise. But the people must beware of doing this for themselves, for individualistic interpretation of this higher law is the complete negation of all government.—*Ibid.,* vol. XVII, p. 12. For these references I am also indebted to Dr. Wright's thesis, *supra.* What is substantially the same doctrine is advanced by Father Cathrein in his hand-book in even stronger form, since he allows to the Church an actual veto on governmental action in all matters which touch spiritual concerns, as well as the right to decide conclusively what matters belong to this class. Thus he says: "It is for the Church to judge whether any law or ordinance concerning a temporal matter is sinful, or in any other way harmful to the spiritual welfare of the subjects, and in consequence the Church is vested with legal authority to require the civil power to repeal or amend such a law, and in case of necessity the Church has even the legal authority to render such a law null and void." This position is reached on the ground that the "mere co-existence, side by side, of Church and State in complete equality would give rise to perpetual dissensions without any means of settling them with juristic finality. Nor would a merely directive power of one over the other be sufficient, without the power of imposing a legal obligation and enforcing it with penalties; for this would lack the necessary effectiveness. There remains therefore only the indirect power of jurisdiction either of the State over the Church, or of the Church over the State. But the indirect power of the State over the Church must be rejected . . . for the primacy must be given to that association which is the more pre-eminent and noble, and the Church is more pre-eminent than the State." *Philosophia Moralis,* 7th ed. (Freiburg-in-B., 1911), p. 438, § 646. The translation is my own.

[23] See my *Statesman's Book of John of Salisbury* (New York, 1927), introd., pp. xxvii–xl.

is in large part cured if we are able to accept a presupposition which to the mind of the Middle Ages was a commonplace,—the presupposition, namely, that there not merely exists a body of law above and independent of human choice, but that the precepts of that law are fixed, definite and capable of being as clearly perceived in identical form by every human intelligence as are the elementary truths of mathematics.[24] Men obviously need no sovereign to exercise a prerogative of choice in order to tell them whether twice two is five or four. If the laws which distinguish right from wrong are equally well defined by "nature," we need no sovereign to tell us whether the issue of watered stock by a corporation is illegal, or whether or not relief by injunction is a lawful remedy to apply in a labor dispute. Men thought, not so long ago, that the one right answer to every such question could be reached by mathematical demonstration. If this were so, there would be no need for a sovereign law-declaring agency. But during the past few centuries there has been growing doubt as to whether it is really so; and the conflict between the faith and the doubt is quaintly reflected in the inconsistency of a central passage of Locke's *Second Treatise of Civil Government:* "In the state of Nature there are many things wanting. Firstly, there wants an established, settled, known law. . . . For though the law of Nature be plain and intelligible to all rational creatures, yet men, being biased by their interest, as well as ignorant for want of study of it, are not apt to allow of it as a law binding to them in the application of it to their particular cases." [25] In other words, the law of nature is there, but we need an authoritative human organ to tell us what it is.[26] "Those who are united into one body and have a common established law and judicature to appeal to . . . are in civil society with one another, but those who have no such common appeal are in the state of nature."

Even, then, if we grant the existence of a "law" that is not of men's making, but recognize that room remains for possible differences of opinion as to its specific precepts, we shall still have to admit the need for political organization, the need for a sovereign to "declare" that law authoritatively; and we shall then be driven forward to face the important practical problems incidental to devising a mechanism of organization best adapted to cause the precepts of the sovereign to conform to the precepts of the "higher" law. But this is a task which the doctrine of resistance minimizes and discourages. If each individual is entitled to search in his own conscience for the precept of the higher law applicable to the case in hand, and then to

---

[24] See my *Administrative Justice and the Supremacy of Law* (Cambridge, 1927), pp. 115 *et seq.* Cf. Bynkershoek, "If men were reasonable, they would know the law accurately without more."—*De Foro Legatorum,* chap. iii. *Opera Minora,* ed. secunda (Leyden, 1744).

[25] *Second Treatise of Civil Government,* chap. ix, § 124.

[26] The same criticism is applicable to the theory of the "sovereignty of reason" put forward by Constant, Cousin, Guizot, and other French liberals of the first half of the nineteenth century. See C. E. Merriam, *History of Sovereignty Since Rousseau* (New York, 1900), chap. v. "Reason" requires an authoritative interpretation, and so an authoritative interpreter, unless anarchy is to result.

disobey the sovereign should his inquiry lead to a different conclusion from that which that sovereign has reached, the importance of having a sovereign who will reach the right conclusion in the first place is vastly decreased; for if no law made by the sovereign need be obeyed unless it is a good law, the question of whether the sovereign makes bad laws becomes of relatively secondary consequence. From this point of view, therefore, the real guaranty of good government is the "right" of resistance, not the perfecting of the governmental machinery adapted to produce the best results under given circumstances. In answer to this theory it should be sufficient to point out that the whole history of progress in the art of government has consisted in the gradual substitution of the latter for the former of these guaranties. Revolution was during long ages the only effective way by which the ordinary acts of government could be corrected; the efforts of many centuries have been spent on devising less wasteful and more orderly methods of control. These efforts have proceeded on the assumption that it is not compatible with the existence of civil society to leave to each individual the protection of his own rights; that so long as the normal conditions of civil order prevail, the sovereign, as the organ of the community, must be entitled to the obedience of the individual precisely because, and for no other reason than because, the sovereign *is* the organ of the community; and that therefore the protection of the individual under normal circumstances must be found not in the "right" of resistance, but in the manner and plan whereby sovereign power is organized and constituted.

The fact that in civil society the individual is thus not entitled to set his own idea of the "higher" precepts which the government should follow against the sovereign's version of them, does not mean that there are no such precepts.[27] Whether they constitute a body of "higher law" or not, is of course a wholly different question; but nothing that has been said implies that there are no canons of morality and justice which the sovereign ought to embody in his positive laws. On the contrary, the institution of sovereignty exists primarily because of the need of an organ to focus and formulate these fundamental, but more or less vague and disputed, canons into precise and uniform rules which on the one hand have the fixity and generality necessary for a rule of law, and which on the other hand represent the moral conceptions that command acceptance among the most influential members of the community rather than views which are held merely by isolated private thinkers. In a realm of ideas where there is so much room for differences of opinion as in connection with the precepts of morality, it is absolutely necessary to have such an authoritative declaration of the rule before there can properly be any thought of enforcing it as a rule of com-

---

[27] This seems to be the heart of Mr. Laski's misunderstanding: "Within the sphere of law, there is therefore . . . no such thing as an unjust command."—*Grammar of Politics*, p. 50. There is no such thing as an illegal law, and "within the sphere of law" no question arises as to whether a law, otherwise proved to be a law, is just; but this emphatically does not mean that there is no such thing as an unjust law.

munity action. It may, and doubtless often will, result that the rule selected by the sovereign for enforcement, precisely because it will be a rule reflecting the morality of the crowd or the morality of the wealthy or military class, will offend the consciences of the individuals who constitute the most enlightened and morally advanced element of the community. Under such circumstances is not the right of this class to resist essential in order to secure moral progress? As a last resort and in extraordinary situations where the stake is sufficiently high, the answer must certainly be, yes; but always with full recognition of the fact that such resistance constitutes rebellion, and entails for the time being a dissolution of the conditions of civil order. Under a properly adjusted constitution, the necessity should seldom occur, because such a constitution would, on the one hand, provide adequate channels for the views of this class to exert an influence upon the sovereign as far as is compatible with the obvious fact that laws must be made to fit the average rather than the exceptional man; and because, on the other hand, under such a constitution the sovereign would doubtless be wise enough to limit to the narrowest point his interference with those kinds of individual action from which moral improvement can properly be expected to occur.

With such a guaranty, however, resting as it does on no more secure foundation than the intelligent discretion of the sovereign, the partisans of progress, no less than the partisans of property, are not wont to be content. If they have not always gone so far as to champion the right of private resistance, they have none the less generally fallen back on what is substantially but a variant of the same doctrine, and have insisted that the discretion of the sovereign must be subjected to, and limited by, law. Their appeal has been the traditional one from a "government by men" to a "government by law." This demand obviously assumes the possibility of the existence of a body of law which is not merely independent of the sovereign's creation, but which can in some way be enforced against the sovereign to limit the scope of his authority. The idea is not quite the same, however, as the one we have been considering, of a "higher" body of natural law, self-evident to the human reason, and hence capable of enforcement against the government by the independent resistance of private individuals; it contemplates ordinarily a set of more positive rules of a definitely juristic nature, embodied in precedents and fundamental documents, and enforceable through some sort of judicial procedure. In this form the theory is widely prevalent, particularly in the United States, and connotes what is commonly meant when we speak of "government of law." But, on analysis, it is a theory which presents very serious difficulties in both its branches,—i.e., both as respects the source, and also the method of enforcement, of the law which is to control the sovereign.

As respects enforcement, if this is not to be left to the unregulated private action of individuals and groups, it must be put in the hands of some definite agency or organ, analogous to the Supreme Court of the United

States. But when we have erected an organ of this kind with a power of control over the supposedly sovereign organ, it is obvious that we have in effect either simply transferred sovereignty from the latter to the former, or else we have only geared the two together into a compound sovereign system like the American, where one organ within the system checks another. In either event, however, we have completely failed to establish over the sovereign an agency of control from without. It is the old difficulty of attempting to set a guard over the guardians. But if the law of infinite series makes it for this reason impossible for law to control the sovereign through a law-enforcement agency, cannot law still control even without such an agency? We have seen above that physical compulsion is not a necessary sanction of law if obedience be paid to it for some other reason; is it not conceivable that the sovereign might respect the precepts of a "higher" law though there can be no way of enforcing these against it? But here we run against an even more deep-seated difficulty: who is to pronounce this higher law which the sovereign is supposed to be ready and willing to obey? To be sure, it is embodied in custom and precedent and fundamental instruments; but still it lies scattered far and wide among them, and the rule applicable to any given case will almost invariably have to be pieced together out of different materials and from different sources with a powerful amalgam of inference and policy. The task, in other words, is not like a problem in mathematics: it demands the exercise of choice and discretion. Who is to perform this task if there can be no independent agency outside the sovereign to apply and enforce the law against it? Obviously only the sovereign itself, or some organ within the sovereign system; and in this event can we say that the sovereign is really controlled by law, where it must rest with the sovereign itself to formulate and declare the law which is supposed to control it?

Certainly it should at least be clear that the sovereign can not be controlled by law in the same sense as are the individuals who live under sovereignty; and it is therefore misleading to speak of controlling the sovereign by law, if we have in mind the concept of positive law.[28] On the contrary, the situation is quite similar to that considered in the first part of this

---

[28]This does not mean that there may not be rules of positive constitutional law, i.e., rules enforceable by the courts against other organs which for the time being form elements of the system of sovereignty. Such rules exist even in England. See Dicey, *Law of the Constitution,* 8th ed., pp. 23–25. But in England Parliament could at any time change these rules and so release itself from any inhibitory effect that they may have on its freedom of action. *Ibid.,* pp. 441 *et seq.* In the same way there is no inconsistency between the doctrine of sovereignty and the suability of the state by private individuals. In other words, the sovereign system of organs may be so constituted that specific organs which form a part of the sovereign system may be subjected to law made by the whole system and enforced against them on the motion of individuals by some other part of the system. But there are necessarily limits to such accountability. Thus it seems obvious that there can be no suit for damages caused by an adverse judicial decision—even Duguit admits this, *Law in the Modern State,* trans. by Laski (New York, 1919), p. 220—or for loss accruing from the passage of a general law, E. Duthoit, *Aux Confins de la Morale et du Droit Public* (Paris, 1919), p. 103, since the very object of such laws is often to shift burdens from one part of the community to another. So in the case of certain executive acts,—e.g., regulations which are legislative in character, or diplomatic acts, *ibid.,* p. 113.

article in discussing the nature of international law. There exists, that is, a body of materials of a properly juristic character from which there can be formulated a rule, or various possible rules, capable of being applied to a proposed act of the sovereign; but apart from the sovereign itself, there is, and can be, no organ to make an authoritative pronouncement of the rule. Constitutional experts, like other private individuals may and generally do, differ with one another, and with the sovereign as well, as to what the rule really is; but it is only the sovereign's opinion that counts in the final analysis. Such control is not control in the usual sense of the term; all that can validly be said is that the sovereign in deciding upon its course of action where a constitutional issue is involved does or ought to take into account a body of juristic materials from which one or another constitutional rule can be deduced by processes of so-called legal reasoning. For this task some governments are better equipped than others. Thus, in the Supreme Court, there is fitted into the American system of sovereign organs one which is peculiarly well adapted to exercise this juristic control over other parts of the system. But we must never delude ourselves into believing either that the Supreme Court is not a part of the governmental system, or that the constitutional law which it administers comes into being by spontaneous generation without the active intervention of the Court. The acts of the Court are controlled by law, but only by law as the Court declares it.

The judicial character of the American Supreme Court serves none the less to conceal to some extent the real nature of the way in which law is limited in its effectiveness to act as a check on the sovereign. This is much better illustrated in the English Constitution by the relation of Parliament to the so-called "law" of the Constitution. Here it is obvious that the sovereign organ is bound by that law only in the sense of being expected to take certain juristic materials into consideration as one of the controlling or limiting factors in connection with any proposed action. In other words it is expected to arrive at its determination in part by the use of legal reasoning upon legal materials. But it is of course free to perform the sovereign act of interpreting those materials in its own way and of determining how much or how little weight to give to them. It is bound by them only because, and only in so far as, it is willing to be; its obedience to the Constitution is a matter of custom, of morality if you will, rather than a strictly legal obedience. And so, although less obviously, is the obedience of the American Supreme Court to the Constitution in the ultimate analysis. The fact that it is a court requires, to be sure, that its actions are always taken, or at least always appear to be taken, on exclusively legal grounds—there are other organs charged with making the decisions of policy; but, even so, the law which binds the Court is what the Court itself makes it—under its potent alchemy the same constitutional provision has at different times been made to yield exactly contrary results, and frequently to yield results at variance with what constitutional experts have deemed right; and should the practice of rendering decisions without opinions ever come into vogue, it might become difficult to tell how or to what extent legal considerations could be made responsible in any given case for the Court's decision.

It therefore seems necessary to revise our idea of a "government of laws" as contrasted with a "government of men." It cannot mean a government where disembodied rules inexorably control by their automatic operation the determinations of the human sovereign; for laws require to be formulated and interpreted and administered by human agencies, and the agencies charged with these tasks have the laws in their power to bend or mold or break them. It can only mean a government where the sovereign is imbued with what we may describe as habits of constitutional morality and of self-imposed respect for self-imposed rules. Only in this sense and subject to these limitations is the idea freed from misleading and mischievous implications.

From the point of view of political science, the doctrine of sovereignty therefore means in the last place as in the first that law is and must ever be at the mercy of human agencies; that good government cannot rest on the futile attempt to set up automatic barriers of abstract law to limit the action of the human sovereign, but that it requires a careful attention to the organization of governmental agencies into a system responsive to those forces whose influence in the community it is desirable and practicable to promote; and that its effective functioning will always depend not merely on machinery but on the existence within the organs of government as well as within the community at large of certain habits and states of mind which will make for restraint on the part of the one, and for obedience on the part of the other.

The Justification of Civil Disobedience
John Rawls

Introduction

I should like to discuss briefly, and in an informal way, the grounds of civil disobedience in a constitutional democracy. Thus, I shall limit my remarks to the conditions under which we may, by civil disobedience, prop-

Originally presented at the meetings of the American Political Science Association, September 1966. Some revisions have been made and two paragraphs have been added to the last section. Copyright 1968 by John Rawls. Reprinted by permission of the author.

erly oppose legally established democratic authority; I am not concerned with the situation under other kinds of government nor, except incidentally, with other forms of resistance. My thought is that in a reasonably just (though of course not perfectly just) democratic regime, civil disobedience, when it is justified, is normally to be understood as a political action which addresses the sense of justice of the majority in order to urge reconsideration of the measures protested and to warn that in the firm opinion of the dissenters the conditions of social cooperation are not being honored. This characterization of civil disobedience is intended to apply to dissent on fundamental questions of internal policy, a limitation which I shall follow to simplify our questions.

The Social Contract Doctrine

It is obvious that the justification of civil disobedience depends upon the theory of political obligation in general, and so we may appropriately begin with a few comments on this question. The two chief virtues of social institutions are justice and efficiency, where by the efficiency of institutions I understand their effectiveness for certain social conditions and ends the fulfillment of which is to everyone's advantage. We should comply with and do our part in just and efficient social arrangements for at least two reasons: first of all, we have a natural duty not to oppose the establishment of just and efficient institutions (when they do not yet exist) and to uphold and comply with them (when they do exist); and second, assuming that we have knowingly accepted the benefits of these institutions and plan to continue to do so, and that we have encouraged and expected others to do their part, we also have an obligation to do our share when, as the arrangement requires, it comes our turn. Thus, we often have both a natural duty as well as an obligation to support just and efficient institutions, the obligation arising from our voluntary acts while the duty does not.

Now all this is perhaps obvious enough, but it does not take us very far. Any more particular conclusions depend upon the conception of justice which is the basis of a theory of political obligation. I believe that the appropriate conception, at least for an account of political obligation in a constitutional democracy, is that of the social contract theory from which so much of our political thought derives. If we are careful to interpret it in a suitably general way, I hold that this doctrine provides a satisfactory basis for political theory, indeed even for ethical theory itself, but this is beyond our present concern.[1] The interpretation I suggest is the following: that the

---

[1] By the social contract theory I have in mind the doctrine found in Locke, Rousseau, and Kant. I have attempted to give an interpretation of this view in: "Justice as Fairness," *Philosophical Review* (April, 1958); "Justice and Constitutional Liberty," *Nomos*, VI (1963); "The Sense of Justice," *Philosophical Review* (July 1963).

principles to which social arrangements must conform, and in particular the principles of justice, are those which free and rational men would agree to in an original position of equal liberty; and similarly, the principles which govern men's relations to institutions and define their natural duties and obligations are the principles to which they would consent when so situated. It should be noted straightway that in this interpretation of the contract theory the principles of justice are understood as the outcome of a hypothetical agreement. They are principles which would be agreed to if the situation of the original position were to arise. There is no mention of an actual agreement nor need such an agreement ever be made. Social arrangements are just or unjust according to whether they accord with the principles for assigning and securing fundamental rights and liberties which would be chosen in the original position. This position is, to be sure, the analytic analogue of the traditional notion of the state of nature, but it must not be mistaken for a historical occasion. Rather it is a hypothetical situation which embodies the basic ideas of the contract doctrine; the description of this situation enables us to work out which principles would be adopted. I must now say something about these matters.

The contract doctrine has always supposed that the persons in the original position have equal powers and rights, that is, that they are symmetrically situated with respect to any arrangements for reaching agreement, and that coalitions and the like are excluded. But it is an essential element (which has not been sufficiently observed although it is implicit in Kant's version of the theory) that there are very strong restrictions on what the contracting parties are presumed to know. In particular, I interpret the theory to hold that the parties do not know their position in society, past, present, or future; nor do they know which institutions exist. Again, they do not know their own place in the distribution of natural talents and abilities, whether they are intelligent or strong, man or woman, and so on. Finally, they do not know their own particular interests and preferences or the system of ends which they wish to advance: they do not know their conception of the good. In all these respects the parties are confronted with a veil of ignorance which prevents any one from being able to take advantage of his good fortune or particular interests or from being disadvantaged by them. What the parties do know (or assume) is that Hume's circumstances of justice obtain: namely, that the bounty of nature is not so generous as to render cooperative schemes superfluous nor so harsh as to make them impossible. Moreover, they assume that the extent of their altruism is limited and that, in general, they do not take an interest in one another's interests. Thus, given the special features of the original position, each man tries to do the best he can for himself by insisting on principles calculated to protect and advance his system of ends whatever it turns out to be.

I believe that as a consequence of the peculiar nature of the original position there would be an agreement on the following two principles for assigning rights and duties and for regulating distributive shares as these are determined by the fundamental institutions of society: first, each person is to have an equal right to the most extensive liberty compatible with a like liberty for all; second, social and economic inequalities (as defined by the institutional structure or fostered by it) are to be arranged so that they are both to everyone's advantage and attached to positions and offices open to all. In view of the content of these two principles and their application to the main institutions of society, and therefore to the social system as a whole, we may regard them as the two principles of justice. Basic social arrangements are just insofar as they conform to these principles, and we can, if we like, discuss questions of justice directly by reference to them. But a deeper understanding of the justification of civil disobedience requires, I think, an account of the derivation of these principles provided by the doctrine of the social contract. Part of our task is to show why this is so.

The Grounds of
Compliance with an Unjust Law

If we assume that in the original position men would agree both to the principle of doing their part when they have accepted and plan to continue to accept the benefits of just institutions (the principle of fairness), and also to the principle of not preventing the establishment of just institutions and of upholding and complying with them when they do exist, then the contract doctrine easily accounts for our having to conform to just institutions. But how does it account for the fact that we are normally required to comply with unjust laws as well? The injustice of a law is not a sufficient ground for not complying with it any more than the legal validity of legislation is always sufficient to require obedience to it. Sometimes one hears these extremes asserted, but I think that we need not take them seriously.

An answer to our question can be given by elaborating the social contract theory in the following way. I interpret it to hold that one is to envisage a series of agreements as follows: first, men are to agree upon the principles of justice in the original position. Then they are to move to a constitutional convention in which they choose a constitution that satisfies the principles of justice already chosen. Finally they assume the role of a legislative body and guided by the principles of justice enact laws subject to the constraints and procedures of the just constitution. The decisions reached in any stage are binding in all subsequent stages. Now whereas in the original position the contracting parties have no knowledge of their society or of their own position in it, in both a constitutional convention and a legislature, they do know certain general facts about their institutions, for example, the statistics regarding employment and output required for fiscal and economic policy. But no one knows particular facts about his own social class or his place in the distribution of natural assets. On each occasion the contracting parties have the knowledge required to make their agreement rational from the appropriate point of view, but not so much as to make them prejudiced. They are unable to tailor principles and legislation to take advantage of their social or natural position; a veil of ignorance prevents their knowing what this position is. With this series of agreements in mind, we can characterize just laws and policies as those which would be enacted were this whole process correctly carried out.

In choosing a constitution the aim is to find among the just constitutions the one which is most likely, given the general facts about the society in question, to lead to just and effective legislation. The principles of justice provide a criterion for the laws desired; the problem is to find a set of political procedures that will give this outcome. I shall assume that, at least under the normal conditions of a modern state, the best constitution is some form of democratic regime affirming equal political liberty and using some sort of majority (or other plurality) rule. Thus it follows that on the contract theory a constitutional democracy of some sort is required by the principles of justice. At the same time it is essential to observe that the constitutional process is always a case of what we may call imperfect procedural justice: that is, there is no feasible political procedure which guarantees that the enacted legislation is just even though we have (let us suppose) a standard for just legislation. In simple cases, such as games of fair division, there are procedures which always lead to the right outcome (assume that equal shares is fair and let the man who cuts the cake take the last piece). These situations are those of perfect procedural justice. In other cases it does not matter what the outcome is as long as the fair procedure is followed: fairness of the process is transferred to the result (fair gambling is an instance of this). These situations are those of pure procedural justice. The constitutional process, like a criminal trial, resembles neither of these; the result matters and we have a standard for it. The difficulty is that we cannot frame a procedure which guarantees that only just and effective legislation is enacted. Thus even under a just constitution unjust laws may be passed and unjust policies enforced. Some form of the majority principle is necessary but the majority may be mistaken, more or less willfully, in what it legislates. In agreeing to a democratic constitution (as an instance of imperfect procedural justice) one accepts at the same time the principle of majority rule. Assuming that the constitution is just and that we have accepted and plan to continue to accept its benefits, we then have both an obligation and a natural duty (and in any case the duty) to comply with what the majority enacts even though it may be unjust. In this way we become bound to follow unjust laws, not always, of course, but provided the injustice does not exceed certain limits. We recognize that we must run the risk of suffering from the defects of one another's sense of justice; this burden we are prepared to carry as long as it is more or less evenly distributed or does not weigh too heavily. Justice binds us to a just constitution and to the unjust laws which may be enacted under it in precisely the same way that it binds us to any other social arrangement. Once we take the sequence of stages into account, there is nothing unusual in our being required to comply with unjust laws.

It should be observed that the majority principle has a secondary place as a rule of procedure which is perhaps the most efficient one under usual circumstances for working a democratic constitution. The basis for it rests essentially upon the principles of justice and therefore we may, when conditions allow, appeal to these principles against unjust legislation. The justice of the constitution does not insure the justice of laws enacted under it; and while we often have both an obligation and a duty to comply with what the majority legislates (as long as it does not exceed certain limits), there is, of course, no corresponding obligation or duty to regard what the majority enacts as itself just. The right to make law does not guarantee that the decision is rightly made; and while the citizen submits in his conduct to the judgment of democratic authority, he does not submit his judgment to it.[2] And if in his judgment the enactments of the majority exceed certain bounds of injustice, the citizen may consider civil disobedience. For we are not required to accept the majority's acts unconditionally and to acquiesce in the denial of our and others' liberties; rather we submit our conduct to democratic authority to the extent necessary to share the burden of working a constitutional regime, distorted as it must inevitably be by men's lack of wisdom and the defects of their sense of justice.

The Place of Civil Disobedience in a Constitutional Democracy

We are now in a position to say a few things about civil disobedience. I shall understand it to be a public, nonviolent, and conscientious act contrary to law usually done with the intent to bring about a change in the policies or laws of the government.[3] Civil disobedience is a political act in the sense that it is an act justified by moral principles which define a conception of civil society and the public good. It rests, then, on political conviction as opposed to a search for self or group interest; and in the case of a constitutional democracy, we may assume that this conviction involves the conception of justice (say that expressed by the contract doctrine) which underlies the constitution itself. That is, in a viable democratic regime there is a common conception of justice by reference to which its citizens regulate their political

---

[2] On this point see A. E. Murphy's review of Yves Simon's *The Philosophy of Democratic Government* (1951) in the *Philosophical Review* (April, 1952).

[3] Here I follow H. A. Bedau's definition of civil disobedience. See his "On Civil Disobedience," *Journal of Philosophy* (October, 1961).

affairs and interpret the constitution. Civil disobedience is a public act which the dissenter believes to be justified by this conception of justice and for this reason it may be understood as addressing the sense of justice of the majority in order to urge reconsideration of the measures protested and to warn that, in the sincere opinion of the dissenters, the conditions of social cooperation are not being honored. For the principles of justice express precisely such conditions, and their persistent and deliberate violation in regard to basic liberties over any extended period of time cuts the ties of community and invites either submission or forceful resistance. By engaging in civil disobedience a minority leads the majority to consider whether it wants to have its acts taken in this way, or whether, in view of the common sense of justice, it wishes to acknowledge the claims of the minority.

Civil disobedience is also civil in another sense. Not only is it the outcome of a sincere conviction based on principles which regulate civic life, but it is public and nonviolent, that is, it is done in a situation where arrest and punishment are expected and accepted without resistance. In this way it manifests a respect for legal procedures. Civil disobedience expresses disobedience to law within the limits of fidelity to law, and this feature of it helps to establish in the eyes of the majority that it is indeed conscientious and sincere, that it really is meant to address their sense of justice.[4] Being completely open about one's acts and being willing to accept the legal consequences of one's conduct is a bond given to make good one's sincerity, for that one's deeds are conscientious is not easy to demonstrate to another or even before oneself. No doubt it is possible to imagine a legal system in which conscientious belief that the law is unjust is accepted as a defense for noncompliance, and men of great honesty who are confident in one another might make such a system work. But as things are such a scheme would be unstable; we must pay a price in order to establish that we believe our actions have a moral basis in the convictions of the community.

The nonviolent nature of civil disobedience refers to the fact that it is intended to address the sense of justice of the majority and as such it is a form of speech, an expression of conviction. To engage in violent acts likely to injure and to hurt is incompatible with civil disobedience as a mode of address. Indeed, an interference with the basic rights of others tends to obscure the civilly disobedient quality of one's act. Civil disobedience is nonviolent in the further sense that the legal penalty for one's action is accepted and that resistance is not (at least for the moment) contemplated. Nonviolence in this sense is to be distinguished from nonviolence as a religious or pacifist principle. While those engaging in civil disobedience have often held some such principle, there is no necessary connection between it and civil disobedience. For on the interpretation suggested, civil disobedience in a democratic society is best understood as an appeal to the principles of

---

[4] For a fuller discussion of this point to which I am indebted, see Charles Fried, "Moral Causation," *Harvard Law Review* (1964).

justice, the fundamental conditions of willing social cooperation among free men, which in the view of the community as a whole are expressed in the constitution and guide its interpretation. Being an appeal to the moral basis of public life, civil disobedience is a political and not primarily a religious act. It addresses itself to the common principles of justice which men can require one another to follow and not to the aspirations of love which they cannot. Moreover by taking part in civilly disobedient acts one does not foreswear indefinitely the idea of forceful resistance; for if the appeal against injustice is repeatedly denied, then the majority has declared its intention to invite submission or resistance and the latter may conceivably be justified even in a democratic regime. We are not required to acquiesce in the crushing of fundamental liberties by democratic majorities which have shown themselves blind to the principles of justice upon which justification of the constitution depends.

The Justification of Civil Disobedience

So far we have said nothing about the justification of civil disobedience, that is, the conditions under which civil disobedience may be engaged in consistent with the principles of justice that support a democratic regime. Our task is to see how the characterization of civil disobedience as addressed to the sense of justice of the majority (or to the citizens as a body) determines when such action is justified.

First of all, we may suppose that the normal political appeals to the majority have already been made in good faith and have been rejected, and that the standard means of redress have been tried. Thus, for example, existing political parties are indifferent to the claims of the minority and attempts to repeal the laws protested have been met with further repression since legal institutions are in the control of the majority. While civil disobedience should be recognized, I think, as a form of political action within the limits of fidelity to the rule of law, at the same time it is a rather desperate act just within these limits, and therefore it should, in general, be undertaken as a last resort when standard democratic processes have failed. In this sense it is not a normal political action. When it is justified there has been a serious breakdown; not only is there grave injustice in the law but a refusal more or less deliberate to correct it.

Second, since civil disobedience is a political act addressed to the sense of justice of the majority, it should usually be limited to substantial and clear violations of justice and preferably to those which, if rectified, will establish a basis for doing away with remaining injustices. For this reason there is a presumption in favor of restricting civil disobedience to violations of the first principle of justice, the principle of equal liberty, and to barriers which contravene the second principle, the principle of open offices which protects equality of opportunity. It is not, of course, always easy to tell whether these principles are satisfied. But if we think of them as guaranteeing the fundamental equal political and civil liberties (including freedom of conscience and liberty of thought) and equality of opportunity, then it is often relatively clear whether their principles are being honored. After all, the equal liberties are defined by the visible structure of social institutions; they are to be incorporated into the recognized practice, if not the letter, of social arrangements. When minorities are denied the right to vote or to hold certain political offices, when certain religious groups are repressed and others denied equality of opportunity in the economy, this is often obvious and there is no doubt that justice is not being given. However, the first part of the second principle which requires that inequalities be to everyone's advantage is a much more imprecise and controversial matter. Not only is there a problem of assigning it a determinate and precise sense, but even if we do so and agree on what it should be, there is often a wide variety of reasonable opinion as to whether the principle is satisfied. The reason for this is that the principle applies primarily to fundamental economic and social policies. The choice of these depends upon theoretical and speculative beliefs as well as upon a wealth of concrete information, and all of this mixed with judgment and plain hunch, not to mention in actual cases prejudice and self-interest. Thus unless the laws of taxation are clearly designed to attack a basic equal liberty, they should not be protested by civil disobedience; the appeal to justice is not sufficiently clear and its resolution is best left to the political process. But violations of the equal liberties that define the common status of citizenship are another matter. The deliberate denial of these more or less over any extended period of time in the face of normal political protest is, in general, an appropriate object of civil disobedience. We may think of the social system as divided roughly into two parts, one which incorporates the fundamental equal liberties (including equality of opportunity) and another which embodies social and economic policies properly aimed at promoting the advantage of everyone. As a rule civil disobedience is best limited to the former where the appeal to justice is not only more definite and precise, but where, if it is effective, it tends to correct the injustices in the latter.

Third, civil disobedience should be restricted to those cases where the dissenter is willing to affirm that everyone else similarly subjected to the same degree of injustice has the right to protest in a similar way. That is, we must be prepared to authorize others to dissent in similar situations and in the same way, and to accept the consequences of their doing so. Thus, we may hold, for example, that the widespread disposition to disobey civilly clear violations of fundamental liberties more or less deliberate over an extended period of time would raise the degree of justice throughout society and would insure men's self-esteem as well as their respect for one another. Indeed, I believe this to be true, though certainly it is partly a matter of conjecture.

As the contract doctrine emphasizes, since the principles of justice are principles which we would agree to in an original position of equality when we do not know our social position and the like, the refusal to grant justice is either the denial of the other as an equal (as one in regard to whom we are prepared to constrain our actions by principles which we would consent to) or the manifestation of a willingness to take advantage of natural contingencies and social fortune at his expense. In either case, injustice invites submission or resistance; but submission arouses the contempt of the oppressor and confirms him in his intention. If straightway, after a decent period of time to make reasonable political appeals in the normal way, men were in general to dissent by civil disobedience from infractions of the fundamental equal liberties, these liberties would, I believe, be more rather than less secure. Legitimate civil disobedience properly exercised is a stabilizing device in a constitutional regime, tending to make it more firmly just.

Sometimes, however, there may be a complication in connection with this third condition. It is possible, although perhaps unlikely, that there are so many persons or groups with a sound case for resorting to civil disobedience (as judged by the foregoing criteria) that disorder would follow if they all did so. There might be serious injury to the just constitution. Or again, a group might be so large that some extra precaution is necessary in the extent to which its members organize and engage in civil disobedience. Theoretically the case is one in which a number of persons or groups are equally entitled to and all want to resort to civil disobedience, yet if they all do this, grave consequences for everyone may result. The question, then, is who among them may exercise their right, and it falls under the general problem of fairness. I cannot discuss the complexities of the matter here. Often a lottery or a rationing system can be set up to handle the case; but unfortunately the circumstances of civil disobedience rule out this solution. It suffices to note that a problem of fairness may arise and that those who contemplate civil disobedience should take into account. They may have to reach an understanding as to who can exercise their right in the immediate situation and to recognize the need for special constraint.

The final condition, of a different nature, is the following. We have been considering when one has a right to engage in civil disobedience, and our conclusion is that one has this right should three conditions hold: when one is subject to injustice more or less deliberate over an extended period of time in the face of normal political protests; where the injustice is a clear violation of the liberties of equal citizenship; and provided that the general disposition to protest similarly in similar cases would have acceptable consequences. These conditions are not, I think, exhaustive but they seem to cover the more obvious points; yet even when they are satisfied and one has the right to engage in civil disobedience, there is still the different question of whether one should exercise this right, that is, whether by doing so one is likely to further one's ends. Having established one's right to protest one is then free to consider these tactical questions. We may be acting within our

rights but still foolishly if our action only serves to provoke the harsh retaliation of the majority; and it is likely to do so if the majority lacks a sense of
justice, or if the action is poorly timed or not well designed to make the appeal to the sense of justice effective. It is easy to think of instances of this
sort, and in each case these practical questions have to be faced. From the
standpoint of the theory of political obligation we can only say that the
exercise of the right should be rational and reasonably designed to advance
the protester's aims, and that weighing tactical questions presupposes that one
has already established one's right, since tactical advantages in themselves
do not support it.

Conclusion:
Several Objections Considered

In a reasonably affluent democratic society justice becomes the first virtue
of institutions. Social arrangements irrespective of their efficiency must be
reformed if they are significantly unjust. No increase in efficiency in the form
of greater advantages for many justifies the loss of liberty of a few. That we
believe this is shown by the fact that in a democracy the fundamental liberties
of citizenship are not understood as the outcome of political bargaining nor
are they subject to the calculus of social interests. Rather these liberties are
fixed points which serve to limit political transactions and which determine
the scope of calculations of social advantage. It is this fundamental place of
the equal liberties which makes their systematic violation over any extended
period of time a proper object of civil disobedience. For to deny men these
rights is to infringe the conditions of social cooperation among free and rational persons, a fact which is evident to the citizens of a constitutional regime
since it follows from the principles of justice which underlie their institutions. The justification of civil disobedience rests on the priority of justice
and the equal liberties which it guarantees.

It is natural to object to this view of civil disobedience that it relies too
heavily upon the existence of a sense of justice. Some may hold that the
feeling for justice is not a vital political force, and that what moves men are
various other interests, the desire for wealth, power, prestige, and so on.
Now this is a large question the answer to which is highly conjectural and
each tends to have his own opinion. But there are two remarks which may
clarify what I have said: first, I have assumed that there is in a constitutional
regime a common sense of justice the principles of which are recognized to
support the constitution and to guide its interpretation. In any given situation
particular men may be tempted to violate these principles, but the collective
force in their behalf is usually effective since they are seen as the necessary
terms of cooperation among free men; and presumably the citizens of a

democracy (or sufficiently many of them) want to see justice done. Where these assumptions fail, the justifying conditions for civil disobedience (the first three) are not affected, but the rationality of engaging in it certainly is. In this case, unless the costs of repressing civil dissent injures the economic self-interest (or whatever) of the majority, protest may simply make the position of the minority worse. No doubt as a tactical matter civil disobedience is more effective when its appeal coincides with other interests, but a constitutional regime is not viable in the long run without an attachment to the principles of justice of the sort which we have assumed.

Then, further, there may be a misapprehension about the manner in which a sense of justice manifests itself. There is a tendency to think that it is shown by professions of the relevant principles together with action of an altruistic nature requiring a considerable degree of self-sacrifice. But these conditions are obviously too strong, for the majority's sense of justice may show itself simply in its being unable to undertake the measures required to suppress the minority and to punish as the law requires the various acts of civil disobedience. The sense of justice undermines the will to uphold unjust institutions and so a majority despite its superior power may give way. It is unprepared to force the minority to be subject to injustice. Thus, although the majority's action is reluctant and grudging, the role of the sense of justice is nevertheless essential, for without it the majority would have been willing to enforce the law and to defend its position. Once we see the sense of justice as working in this negative way to make established injustices indefensible, then it is recognized as a central element of democratic politics.

Finally, it may be objected against this account that it does not settle the question of who is to say when the situation is such as to justify civil disobedience. And because it does not answer this question, it invites anarchy by encouraging every man to decide the matter for himself. Now the reply to this is that each man must indeed settle this question for himself, although he may, of course, decide wrongly. This is true on any theory of political duty and obligation, at least on any theory compatible with the principles of a democratic constitution. The citizen is responsible for what he does. If we usually think that we should comply with the law, this is because our political principles normally lead to this conclusion. There is a presumption in favor of compliance in the absence of good reasons to the contrary. But because each man is responsible and must decide for himself as best he can whether the circumstances justify civil disobedience, it does not follow that he may decide as he pleases. It is not by looking to our personal interests or to political allegiances narrowly construed, that we should make up our mind. The citizen must decide on the basis of the principles of justice that underlie and guide the interpretation of the constitution and in the light of his sincere conviction as to how these principles should be applied in the circumstances. If he concludes that conditions obtain which justify civil disobedience and conducts himself accordingly, he has acted conscientiously and perhaps mistakenly, but not in any case at his convenience.

In a democratic society each man must act as he thinks the principles of political right require him to. We are to follow our understanding of these principles, and we cannot do otherwise. There can be no morally binding legal interpretation of these principles, not even by a supreme court or legislature. Nor is there any infallible procedure for determining what or who is right. In our system the Supreme Court, Congress, and the President often put forward rival interpretations of the Constitution. Although the Court has the final say in settling any particular case, it is not immune from powerful political influence that may change its reading of the law of the land. The Court presents its point of view by reason and argument; its conception of the Constitution must, if it is to endure, persuade men of its soundness. The final court of appeal is not the Court, or Congress, or the President, but the electorate as a whole.[5] The civilly disobedient appeal in effect to this body. There is no danger of anarchy as long as there is a sufficient working agreement in men's conceptions of political justice and what it requires. That men can achieve such an understanding when the essential political liberties are maintained is the assumption implicit in democratic institutions. There is no way to avoid entirely the risk of devisive strife. But if legitimate civil disobedience seems to threaten civil peace, the responsibility falls not so much on those who protest as upon those whose abuse of authority and power justifies such opposition.

---

[5] For a presentation of this view to which I am indebted, see A. M. Bickel, *The Least Dangerous Branch* (Indianapolis, 1962), especially Chapters 5 and 6.